CONTINUED ON THE BACK INSIDE COVER

Music
An Appreciation

Also by the Author

Music: An Appreciation—Brief Edition

TENTH EDITION

Music
An Appreciation

Roger Kamien

Zubin Mehta Chair in Musicology, Emeritus

The Hebrew University of Jerusalem

with Anita Kamien

Connect
Learn
Succeed™

MUSIC: AN APPRECIATION

2 3 4 5 6 7 8 9 0 DOW/DOW 9 8 7 6 5 4 3 2 1 0

ISBN: 978-0-07-802508-2
MHID: 0-07-802508-7

Vice President and Editor-in-Chief: *Michael J. Ryan*
Publisher: *Christopher Freitag*
Director of Development: *Rhona Robbin*
Development Editor: *Emily Pecora*
Editorial Coordinator: *Sarah Remington*
Marketing Manager: *Stacy Ruel*
Senior Managing Editor: *Christina Gimlin*
Senior Production Editor: *Mel Valentín*
Art Editor: *Ayelet Arbel*
Interior Designer: *Lisa Buckley*
Cover Designer: *Ashley Bedell / Preston Thomas*
Cover Images: *Joshua Kamien (violin); Scott Dunlap/Getty Images (computer)*
Photo Research Coordinator: *Nora Agbayani*
Photo Researcher: *Susan Friedman*
Media Project Manager: *Thomas Brierly*
Buyer II: *Tandra Jorgensen*
Composition: *10/12 Minion Pro by Thompson Type*
Printing: *45# New Era Matte Plus, RR Donnelley*
Credits: The credits section for this book begins on page 560 and is considered an extension of the copyright page.

Library of Congress Cataloging-in-Publication Data

Kamien, Roger.
　　Music : an appreciation / Roger Kamien. — 10th ed.
　　　　p. cm.
　　Includes bibliographical references.
　　ISBN-13: 978-0-07-802508-2 (alk. paper)
　　ISBN-10: 0-07-802508-7 (alk. paper)
　　1. Music appreciation.　I. Title.
　MT90.K34 2010
　780—dc22

　　　　　　　　　　　　　　2010019136

About the Author

ROGER KAMIEN was born in Paris in 1934 and was brought to the United States at the age of six months. He received his B.A. in music from Columbia College in New York, and his M.A. and Ph.D in musicology from Princeton University. He studied piano with Nadia Reisenberg and Claudio Arrau. During 1957–1959, he returned to Paris as a Fulbright scholar, for research on eighteenth-century music.

Professor Kamien taught music history, theory, and literature for two years at Hunter College and then for twenty years at Queens College of the City University of New York, where he was coordinator of the music appreciation courses. During this time he was also active as a pianist, appearing both in the United States and in Europe. In 1983, he was appointed to the Zubin Mehta Chair of Musicology at the Hebrew University of Jerusalem.

In addition to *Music: An Appreciation,* Dr. Kamien was the editor of The Norton Scores and one of the coauthors of *A New Approach to Keyboard Harmony* and a contributor to *The Cambridge Companion to Beethoven.* He has also written articles and reviews for journals including *Music Forum, Beethoven Forum, Musical Quarterly, Journal of Music Theory, Music Theory Spectrum, Journal of Musicology,* and *Journal of the American Musicological Society.*

In recent years, he has appeared as a piano soloist in thirty countries on five continents. He frequently performs together with his wife, the conductor-pianist Anita Kamien, who has also contributed in many ways to *Music: An Appreciation.* The Kamiens have three children and seven grandchildren.

For Anita, David, Joshua, and Adina

Contents

PART

II

PART THREE
The Renaissance   93

PART
III

PART
IV

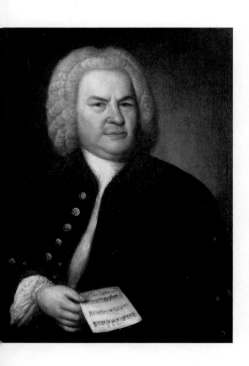

PART SEVEN
The Twentieth Century and Beyond   357

PART
VII

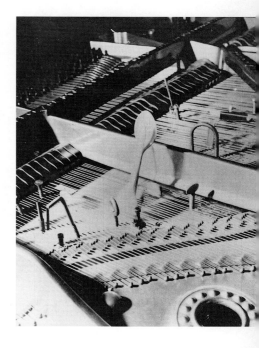

PART NINE
Music for Stage and Screen   493
Music for Stage and Screen   494

PART
X

PART
XI

Appendices   548

Listening Outlines and Vocal Music Guides Listed by Composer

Music Connects

Music connects people, whether across the front of a stage, over time and space, or even via the Internet. When we listen to music we see through the lens of another creative spirit to experience some part of the world in a different way. In *Music: An Appreciation,* Roger Kamien draws on a life lived as performer, teacher, and scholar to connect students to the beauties and complexities of music.

Connection is a theme that runs through this revision of *Music: An Appreciation.* To begin with, almost every new feature is the result of what we learned by connecting with students and teachers in new ways. McGraw-Hill's extensive program of student-centered research led to design changes and the new Part Summary feature. Three national symposia connected us with music appreciation faculty from across the country and gave us new insights into course objectives and challenges. This led to perhaps the most exciting feature of the new edition—*Connect Kamien.*

Connect Kamien creates an integrated program around *Music: An Appreciation* that connects students to music, and instructors to students, in powerful ways. Providing new ways of reading the text, listening to the music, and demonstrating their understanding, Connect Kamien creates a richer experience for students and teachers alike. Connect Kamien offers:

- a new web-based assignment and assessment platform
- interactive listening outlines with streaming audio for all selections
- listening quizzes and assignments for every selection
- video opera and film excerpts
- an audio glossary
- and much more.

For more information, samples, and demonstrations go to www.connectkamien.com.

Music Connects to Knowledge

Music: An Appreciation encourages mastery of the language of music and the language used to talk about music.

A Strong foundation—Part I of the book examines the elements of music both in general terms and with reference to illustrative pieces that are attractive, brief, and representative of a variety of periods. Mastery of the wide number of terms introduced in this Part is reinforced through Connect Kamien and the Interactive Glossary and Example Locator.

Flexible organization—The text takes a chronological approach but can be adapted easily to individual teaching methods. Each Part is divided into short, relatively independent sections that can be studied in any order; some could even be omitted. Likewise, student reading is broken down into smaller chunks, aiding student learning.

Beat

Beats can be shown as a succession of marks on a time line.

When you clap your hands or tap your foot to music, you are responding to its beat. *Beat* is a regular, recurrent pulsation that divides music into equal units of time. Beats can be represented by marks on a time line:

Beats

Time

In music, beats occur as often as every ¼ second or as seldom as every 1½ seconds. Sometimes the beat is powerful and easy to feel, as in marches or rock music; but sometimes it may be barely noticeable, suggesting feelings like floating or aimlessness.

The pulse of music is communicated in different ways. Sometimes the beat is explicitly pounded out—by a bass drum in a marching band, for instance. At other times the beat is sensed rather than actually heard.

Sing the beginning of *America* up to the words *Land where my fathers died:*

My coun- try 'tis of thee, Sweet land of lib- er- ty,
Of thee I sing. Land (etc.)

Each of the marks represents a beat. Did you notice that you automatically held *sing* for 3 beats? You *sensed* the beat because you were aware of it and expected it to continue.

Beats form the background against which the composer places notes of varying lengths. Beats are basic units of time by which all notes are measured. A note may last

NEW! Interactive Glossary and Example Locator—The Glossary in the text is now supported by an online Example Locator fully loaded with clickable listening samples for the forms, styles, and instruments listed in the glossary. Users can combine a review of musical terms with instant access to clear musical examples of these terms.

New and updated content—New and updated content pertaining to music's foundations includes:

- A full video performance of Britten's Young Person's Guide to the Orchestra, newly recorded for McGraw-Hill by the Philadelphia Orchestra conducted by Charles Dutoit (Part I, Chapter 2)
- New, clearer explanation of Two-Part (Binary) Form (Part I, Chapter 9)
- Updated discussion on the ways people access and listen to music (Part VII)
- Expanded coverage of film music features a listening outline and film clip (accessible online) of the "tower scene" from Alfred Hitchcock's *Vertigo*. (Part IX, Chapter 2)

PART
IV

Music Connects to Culture

Music: An Appreciation presents music as a lens through which we can understand the human experience.

Cultural context—Each of the stylistic parts (Parts II through VII, examining music from the Middle Ages to the present; and Parts VIII to IX, dealing with jazz, music for stage and screen, rock, and nonwestern music) begins with a richly illustrated chapter opener that discusses the main stylistic, cultural, and historical trends of the period. These part openers include time lines that place musical events within their cultural and historical content.

New! Part Summaries—Part summaries at the end of each part aid student learning by providing summaries of key terms, principal forms, main composers, and style features. These summaries tie the chapters of each part together, encouraging students to think again of the larger cultural context surrounding individual pieces and aiding in student review and retention.

The Baroque Period Summary

IMPORTANT TERMS

- Affections, p. 122
- Terraced dynamics, p. 123
- Clavichord, p. 123
- Basso continuo, p. 124
- Figured bass, p. 124
- Movement, p. 125
- Tutti, p. 128
- Ritornello form, p. 128
- Ritornello, p. 128
- Subject, p. 131
- Answer, p. 132
- Countersubject, p. 132
- Episode, p. 132
- Stretto, p. 132
- Pedal point, p. 132
- Inversion, p. 132
- Retrograde, p. 132
- Augmentation, p. 132
- Diminution, p. 132
- Prelude, p. 132
- Libretto, p. 136
- Librettist, p. 136
- Voice categories of opera, p. 136
- Aria, p. 136
- Recitative, p. 136
- Ensemble, p. 137

Music in Society

- Music was composed to order for specific events.
- The primary areas of employment for musicians were in aristocratic courts, the church, and the opera house. Composers working in aristocratic courts were considered servants.
- Some aristocrats became accomplished musicians.
- Large towns employed musicians for a variety of functions.

Important Style Features

Mood and Emotional Expression
- In instrumental music, a section or entire movement will express one basic mood throughout ("unity of mood").
- In vocal music, changes of mood in the text are often accompanied by changes in the music.

Rhythm
- Rhythmic patterns heard at the beginning of a piece are often repeated throughout.
- The rhythmic pulse is regular, consistent, and strong, typically featuring a constantly moving bass line, even when the music is in a slow tempo.
- The unity of rhythm provides compelling drive and energy that are characteristic of baroque music.

Dynamics
- Terraced dynamics change suddenly rather than gradually and are a major feature of baroque music.

Engaging biographies—Discussions of composers' lives, individual styles, and representative works stimulate curiosity and enthusiasm about the process of composition, and meaningfully place individual composers and performers within specific cultural contexts.

New and updated content—New and revised content relating to music's cultural connections includes:

- New discussion of the Renaissance Lute Song (Part III, Chapter 3)
- New discussion of the Argentinian composer Alberto Ginastera and his exciting nationalistic piece *Malambo* (Part VII, Chapter 18)
- New translation for and background information on Ompeh, a song from the central region of Ghana (Part XI, Chapter 2)

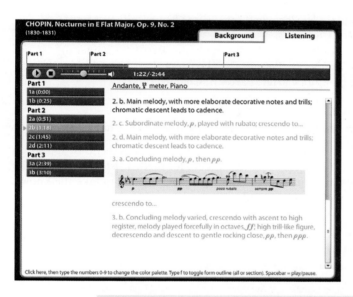

Music Connects to Experience

Music: An Appreciation **aims to enhance the experience of listening to music, both within and beyond the classroom.**

Listening Outlines—Listening Outlines, to be followed while musical pieces are heard, focus attention on musical events as they unfold. New online versions of the outlines are animated to guide the student through the outline while the music plays. In-text versions are easy to follow because they describe what students can readily hear. Listening Outlines develop students' listening skills and reinforce their understanding of musical forms and elements.

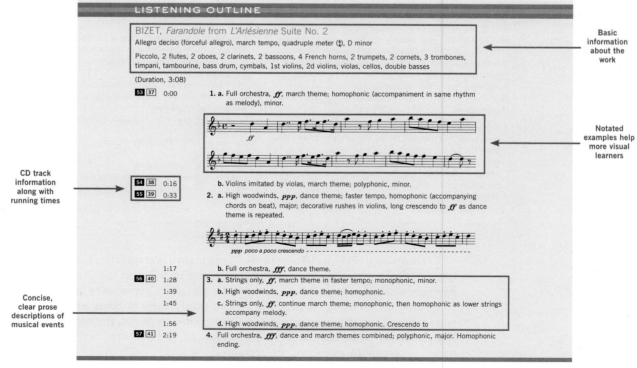

Vocal Music Guides—The study of music with vocal texts—such as songs, choruses, and operas—is enhanced by Vocal Music Guides, in which the sung text appears with marginal notes indicating the relationships between words and music. These guides help the listener to follow the thought, story, or drama in a vocal selection. New animated versions of these guides are also available online.

Listening Program—The listening program is produced by Sony and features high quality recordings of leading performers and ensembles. Two different CD sets (a 9 CD Basic set and a 5 CD Brief set) are available. In addition, all selections are included in Connect Kamien in streaming format, accompanied by animated Listening Outlines.

Pieces and performance new to the 10th edition include:

- Bourrée from Suite in E Minor for Lute by Johann Sebastian Bach (Part I Chapter 9)
- *Flow My Tears* by John Dowland (Part III, Chapter 3)
- Passsamezzo and Galliard by Caroubel—new, more historically informed performances (Part III, Chapter 3)
- Romance in E Flat Minor by Clara Wieck Schumann (Part VI, Chapter 6)
- "Malambo" from the *Estancia* ballet suite by Ginastera (Part VII, Chapter 18)
- *Shard* for solo guitar by Elliot Carter (Part VII, Chapter 19)
- *Koko* by Charlie Parker (Part VIII, Chapter 6)
- *America,* from *West Side Story* (Part IX, Chapter 2)
- Music from the "tower scene" in Hitchcock's *Vertigo* (Part IX, Chapter 3)

New! Beyond the Classroom sections—Beyond the Classroom sections, appearing at the end of each Part Summary, prepare the student for further listening outside the classroom. Listening tips and guiding questions prompt students to take the knowledge offered by *Music: An Appreciation* and use it outside of class, making it their own.

Beyond the Classroom: Attending an Opera

Opera was one of the most important genres invented during the baroque era. Thousands of operas have been composed since then, and they remain one of the most popular forms of entertainment today. When you attend a live opera performance or listen to a recording, you will notice that certain aspects do not change regardless of when the music was composed, whereas other features vary considerably. Pay attention to these similarities and differences. Newer productions now may incorporate computer-generated projections to the set and scenery, demonstrating opera's great ability to adapt to the times. To more fully enjoy an opera performance, ask yourself the following questions:

- What features of the music might indicate when it was composed? For example, if you are listening to an opera from the baroque period, do you notice recitatives accompanied by a basso continuo? Do any of the arias repeat the opening section, as in a da capo aria, and if so, is the repeated music ornamented by the singer?
- What are the voice types of the lead singers and any secondary characters?

- Is there a chorus, and if so, what role does the chorus play in the drama?
- Are there any duets, trios, or larger ensembles of singers?
- What number and kinds of instruments are used in the orchestra?
- Does the opera feature dancing at any point?
- Are the scenery and costumes characteristic of the period and locale, or do they represent another time and place?
- Are computer-generated projections used to create scenery? Do you notice any other digital enhancements added to the projection?
- Is the opera sung in its original language or in English translation?
- If there are supertitles above the stage, are they helpful or distracting?
- Did you notice a prompter?
- Did the performance appear to go as rehearsed, or did you notice anything unusual or notable about it?

Performance Perspective essays—Performance Perspective essays, highlighting musicians whose recorded performances are included in the listening program, heighten readers' awareness of the vital role played by performers in making music come alive. Often using the performers' own words, these discussions shed light on a wide range of issues, including the emotions evoked by music, the nature of interpretive decisions, historically accurate performances, and the ways in which recordings have heightened the impact of performances.

New and updated performance perspective boxes include:

- New Performance Perspective box in Paul Hillier (Part II, Chapter 5)
- Updated Performance Perspective box on Luciano Pavarotti (Part VI, Chapter 18)
- New Performance Perspective box on Gustavo Dudamel (Part VII, Chapter 18)
- Updated Performance Perspective box on Ravi Shankar (Part XI, Chapter 3)

Supplements

Support for Students

Two different CD sets are available for purchase. A Basic Set of 9 audio CDs [0077377621] contains all of the selections discussed in Listening Outlines and Vocal Music Guides as well as other works covered in the text. A Brief Set of 5 audio CDs [0077377729] contains a smaller selection of works covered in the text. Complete listings for both CD sets are found on the endpapers of the book.

The text-specific **Online Learning Center** (www.mhhe.com/kamien10e) provides a link to listening software that works in conjunction with the audio CD set to bring the listening guides from the text to life, along with a wealth of additional teaching and learning resources. Student material includes activities and demonstrations, quizzes, outlines, and more.

A **Student Study Guide** is available for purchase through Create, our online custom content provider. The Student Study Guide provides study materials and listening activities. Contact your local McGraw-Hill sales representative or go to www.mhhe.com/create for more details.

With the **CourseSmart eTextbook** version of this title, students can save up to 50% off the cost of a print book, reduce their impact on the environment, and access powerful web tools for learning. For maximum portability, eTextbooks can be viewed on an iPhone or iPod Touch, and they can be printed

Support for Instructors

Instructor resources on the **Online Learning Center** (www.mhhe.com/kamien10e) include an instructor's manual, test bank, computerized test bank, book-specific CPS questions, and PowerPoint Presentations. All online material can be integrated with leading course management systems.

Acknowledgments

Over the course of seventeen editions of the brief and basic versions of *Music: An Appreciation,* many wonderful reviewers, colleagues, and friends have contributed immeasurably to the growth and improvement of the text. By now, they are too numerous to thank by name. However, I want to express my particular gratitude to those instructors around the country whose valuable suggestions were incorporated in the most recent editions.

Rob Alley, Arkansas State University
Sergio Bezard, Miami-Dade College
Len Bobo, East Central Community College
Michael Boyle, Oklahoma City Community College
Molly M. Breckling, Austin Peay State University
Antonio Briseno, University of Texas, Brownsville
Carol Britt, Nicholls State University
Lester Brothers, University of Central Missouri
Valerie Calhoun, Gordon College
Sylvia H. Carver, Austin Peay State University

Daniel Copher, Florida Atlantic University
Patricia Cox, Harding University
Emily Hanna Crane, Austin Peay State University
Jack DeBoer, Grand Valley State University
Willis Delony, Louisiana State University
Daniel Fairchild, University of Wisconsin, Platteville
William Fitzhugh, Volunteer State Community College
Eric Fried, Texas Tech University
Gary Gackstatter, St. Louis Community College
Lisa Gelfand, Broward Community College
Peter E. Gerschefski, University of Tennessee, Chattanooga
Kay Guiles, Jones County Junior College
Erin Haupt, St. Charles Community College
Deborah Hicks, Walters State Community College
Celeste Johnson, Oklahoma State University
Bryan King, Auburn University
Andrew Kosciesza, Montgomery County Community College
Sheree Gardner Lence, Itawamba Community College
Susan Lindahl, Central Michigan University
James C. Loos, Des Moines Area Community College
Peggy Lupton, Cape Fear Community College
Holly Maurer, Central Piedmont Community College
Greg McLean, Georgia Perimeter College
Alison Nikitopoulos, Louisiana State University
Roy Nitzberg, Queens College
James Orlick, South Carolina State University
Michael J. Pecherek, Illinois Valley Community College
Gary Pritchard, Cerritos College
Catherine Roche-Wallace, University of Louisiana, Lafayette
Henry Runkles, University of Arkansas, Fayetteville
Andrew Santander, Gainesville State College
Anthony Scelba, Kean University
Jack Schmidt, Lock Haven University
Michael Scott, Southwest Tennessee Community College
Kenneth Sipley, Northwest Mississippi Community College
Michael Turpin, Kilgore College
Lise Uhl, McLennan Community College
Kathryn White, University of North Carolina, Pembroke
Mary Wolinski, Western Kentucky University
Elizabeth Wollman, Baruch College

Additionally, I would like to thank all of the instructors who took the time to respond to a survey that was of vital importance in guiding me through the difficult process of making changes in the music selections.

McGraw-Hill's faculty development symposia in music have been a valuable source of feedback and information to me. I'd especially like to thank the attendees at the spring 2010 Philadelphia event for their contributions to the design of Connect Kamien: Joshua Barrett (Mercy College), Marcelo Bussiki (Blinn College), Jonathan Chenoweth (University of Northern Iowa), John Cloer (University of North Carolina), Gregory Dewhirst (Tarrant County College), Kimberly Harris (Collin County College), Andrew Krikun (Bergen County College), Barry McVinney (Pulaski Technical College), Daniel Pittman (Georgia Southern University), Carolyn Quin (Riverside Community College), Mattson Topper (Brookhaven College), Mary Wolinksi (Western Kentucky University).

My deep thanks go to James Hurd, *El Camino College,* Catherine Coppola, *Hunter College,* and Susan Helfter, *University of Southern California* for taking the time to meet with me and discuss their classroom experiences and their experiences using this text. I would also like to thank Dr. Aviva Stanislawski for her assistance in choosing repertoire, and Prof. Kwasi Ampene for his translation of the *Ompeh* text.

A very special thank you goes to Steven Kreinberg at Temple University for helping me create the new Part Summary and Beyond the Classroom features and for many valuable suggestions offered during the revision process.

I want to express my thanks for the expert assistance of my publisher at McGraw-Hill, Chris Freitag, the development editor, Emily Pecora, and the editorial coordinator, Sarah Remington. I am grateful for the superb work of Sue Gamer, the copyeditor, Mel Valentín, production editor, Ashley Bedell, the designer, and Nora Agbayani, the photo research coordinator. I'd like to thank Tom Laskey at Sony Music Special Products for providing an outstanding package of CD recordings.

My wife, the conductor-pianist Anita Kamien, has contributed to every aspect of this book. She clarified ideas, helped choose representative pieces, and worked tirelessly to improve the Listening Outlines. Her advice and encouragement were essential to the completion of *Music: An Appreciation, Tenth Edition.*

Roger Kamien

Elements

Rhythm and harmony find their way into
the inward places of the soul . . .

— *Plato*

All musical elements come together when people play or sing.

Music plays a vital role in human society. It provides entertainment and emotional release, and it accompanies activities ranging from dances to religious ceremonies. Music is heard everywhere: in auditoriums, homes, elevators, sports arenas, and places of worship, and on the street.

Recorded performance is a sensational innovation of the twentieth century. Today, the Internet gives access to a practically unlimited variety of recorded sounds and images. Portable audio and media players permit us to hear and watch what we want, wherever we want.

Live performances provide special excitement. In a live performance, artists put themselves on the line; training and magnetism must overcome technical difficulties to involve the listener's emotions. What is performed, how it sounds, how the artist feels about it that evening—all this exists for a fleeting moment and can never be repeated. An audience responds to

Informal music making is a source of pleasure for players and listeners.

the excitement of such a moment, and feelings are exchanged between stage and hall.

Our response to a musical performance or an artist is subjective and rooted in deep feeling. Even professional critics can differ strongly in their evaluations of a performance. There is no one "truth" about what

we hear and feel. Does the performer project a concept, an overall idea, or an emotion? Do some sections of a piece, but not others, communicate something to you? Can you figure out why? It's up to us as listeners to evaluate performances of music. Alert and repeated listening will enhance our ability to compare performances and judge music so that we can fully enjoy it.

People listen to music in many different ways. Music can be a barely perceived background or a totally absorbing experience. Part I of this book, "Elements," introduces concepts that can contribute to your enjoyment of a wide range of musical styles. For example, awareness of tone color—the quality that distinguishes one instrument from another—can heighten your pleasure when a melody passes from a clarinet to a trumpet. Perceptive, aware listening makes any musical experience more intense and satisfying.

The audience at an outdoor concert in Atlanta, Georgia. Whether in a public park or a concert hall, live performances have a special electricity.

Elvis Presley: The exchange between singer and audience contains something magical, direct, and spellbinding.

Music making transcends boundaries of many kinds. Pictured here are musicians playing in a gamelan, an ensemble found in Indonesia.

The use of computers and electronics has revolutionized the way we create, play, and listen to music.

1 Sound: Pitch, Dynamics, and Tone Color

Sounds bombard our ears every day—the squeaks and honks of traffic, a child's laugh, the bark of a dog, the patter of rain. Through them we learn what's going on; we need them to communicate. By listening to speech, cries, and laughter, we learn what others think and how they feel. But silence, an absence of sound, also communicates. When we hear no sound in the street, we assume no cars are passing. When someone doesn't answer a question or breaks off in the middle of a sentence, we quickly notice, and we draw conclusions from the silence.

Sounds may be perceived as pleasant or unpleasant. Fortunately, we can direct our attention to specific sounds, shutting out those that don't interest us. At a party, for instance, we can choose to ignore the people near us and focus instead on a conversation across the room. Actually, we shut out most sounds, paying attention only to those of interest. The composer John Cage (1912–1992) may have meant to show this with his "composition" entitled *4'33"*, in which a musician sits at a piano for 4 minutes and 33 seconds—and does nothing. The silence forces the people in the audience to direct their attention to whatever noises, or sounds, they themselves are making. In a sense, the audience "composes" this piece. To get the effect, listen to the sounds that fill the silence around you right now.

What are these sounds that we hear? What is "sound"? What causes it, and how do we hear it?

Sound begins with the vibration of an object, such as a table that is pounded or a string that is plucked. The vibrations are transmitted to our ears by a *medium,* which is usually air. As a result of the vibrations, our eardrums start vibrating too, and *impulses,* or signals, are transmitted to the brain. There the impulses are selected, organized, and interpreted.

Music is part of this world of sound, an art based on the organization of sounds in time. We distinguish music from other sounds by recognizing the four main properties of musical sounds: *pitch, dynamics* (loudness or softness), *tone color,* and *duration*. We'll look now at the first three of these properties of musical sound. Duration—the length of time a musical sound lasts—is discussed in Section 3, "Rhythm."

Pitch: Highness or Lowness of Sound

Pitch is the relative highness or lowness that we hear in a sound. No doubt you've noticed that most men speak and sing in a lower range of pitches than women or children do. And when you sing the beginning of *The Star-Spangled Banner,* the pitch on *see* is higher than the one on *say:*

<pre>
                                              see,

Oh,   you

                    can

     say!
</pre>

4

Without differences of pitch, speech would be boring, and—worse—there would be no music as we know it.

The pitch of a sound is determined by the frequency of its vibrations. The faster the vibrations, the higher the pitch; the slower the vibrations, the lower the pitch. Vibration frequency is measured in cycles per second. On a piano the highest-frequency tone is 4,186 cycles per second, and the lowest is about 27 cycles per second.

In general, the smaller the vibrating object, the faster its vibrations and the higher its pitch. All other things being equal, plucking a short string produces a higher pitch than plucking a long string. The relatively short strings of a violin produce higher pitches than do the longer strings of a double bass.

In music, a sound that has a definite pitch is called a **tone.** It has a specific frequency, such as 440 cycles per second. The vibrations of a tone are regular and reach the ear at equal time intervals. On the other hand, noiselike sounds (squeaking brakes or clashing cymbals) have an indefinite pitch because they are produced by irregular vibrations.

Two tones will sound different when they have different pitches. The "distance" in pitch between any two tones is called an **interval.** When tones are separated by the interval called an **octave,** they sound very much alike. Sing the opening of *The Star-Spangled Banner* again. Notice that the tone you produce on *see* sounds like your tone on *say,* even though it's higher. (Sing the *say* and *see* tones several times.) An octave lies between them. The vibration frequency of the *say* tone is exactly half that of the *see* tone. If the *say* tone was 440 cycles per second, the *see* tone—an octave higher—would be 880 cycles per second. A tone an octave lower than the *say* tone would be half of 440, or 220 cycles per second. When sounded at the same time, two tones an octave apart blend so well that they almost seem to merge into one tone.

The interval of an octave is important in music. It is the interval between the first and last tones of the familiar scale. Sing this scale slowly:

```
                                        do
                                    ti
                                la
                            sol
                        fa
                    mi
                re
            do
```

You will notice that you fill the octave with seven different pitches before arriving at the high *do,* which "duplicates" the low *do* you start on. You do not slide up as a siren does; you fill the octave with a specific number of pitches. If you start from the higher *do* and continue the scale upward, each of your original seven tones will be "duplicated" an octave higher. This group of seven tones was the basis of music in western civilization for centuries. The seven tones are produced by the white keys of the piano keyboard, as shown in the illustration at the left.

As time passed, five pitches were added to the original seven. These five are produced by the black keys of the keyboard. All twelve tones, like the original seven, are "duplicated" in higher and lower octaves. Every tone has "close relatives" 1, 2, 3, or more octaves away. (In nonwestern music, the octave may be divided into a different number of tones—say, seventeen or twenty-two.)

The distance between the lowest and highest tones that a voice or instrument can produce is called its **pitch range,** or simply its **range.** The range of the average untrained voice is between 1 and 2 octaves; a piano's range is over 7 octaves. When men and women sing the same melody, they usually sing it an octave apart.

Organization of pitch is a composer's first resource. In Sections 5 and 6, where melody and harmony are explored, we will look at how pitch is organized. For now, we'll simply observe that composers can create a special mood by using very low or

Seven different tones are produced by the white keys of the piano.

very high pitches. For example, low pitches can intensify the sadness of a funeral march; high pitches can make a dance sound lighter. And a steady rise in pitch often increases musical tension.

Though most music we know is based on definite pitches, indefinite pitches—such as those made by a bass drum or by cymbals—are important as well. Some percussion instruments, such as gongs, cowbells, and woodblocks, come in different sizes and therefore produce higher or lower indefinite pitches. Contrasts between higher and lower indefinite pitches play a vital role in contemporary western music and in musical cultures around the world.

Dynamics

Degrees of loudness or softness in music are called *dynamics*—our second property of sound. Loudness is related to the amplitude of the vibration that produces the sound. The harder a guitar string is plucked (the farther it moves from the fingerboard), the louder its sound. When instruments are played more loudly or more softly, or when there is a change in how many instruments are heard, a dynamic change results; such a change may be made either suddenly or gradually. A gradual increase in loudness often creates excitement, particularly when the pitch rises, too. On the other hand, a gradual decrease in loudness can convey a sense of calm.

A performer can emphasize a tone by playing it more loudly than the tones around it. We call an emphasis of this kind an *accent.* Skillful, subtle changes of dynamics add spirit and mood to performances. Sometimes these changes are written in the music; often, though, they are not written but are inspired by the performer's feelings about the music.

When notating music, composers have traditionally used Italian words, and their abbreviations, to indicate dynamics. The most common terms are

Term	Abbreviation	Meaning
pianissimo	*pp*	*very soft*
piano	*p*	*soft*
mezzo piano	*mp*	*moderately soft*
mezzo forte	*mf*	*moderately loud*
forte	*f*	*loud*
fortissimo	*ff*	*very loud*

For extremes of softness and loudness, composers use *ppp* or *pppp* and *fff* or *ffff*. The following notations indicate gradual changes in dynamics:

Symbol	Term	Meaning
	decrescendo (decresc.) *or* *diminuendo* (dim.)	gradually softer
	crescendo (cresc.)	gradually louder

Like many elements of music, a dynamic indication is not absolutely precise. A tone has a dynamic level—is soft or loud—in relation to other tones around it. The loudest sound of a single violin is tiny compared with the loudest sound of an entire orchestra, and even tinier compared with an amplified rock group. But it can be considered fortissimo (very loud) within its own context.

Tone Color

We can tell a trumpet from a flute even when each of them is playing the same tone at the same dynamic level. The quality that distinguishes them—our third property of musical sound—is called ***tone color,*** or ***timbre*** (pronounced *tam'-ber*). Tone color is described by words such as *bright, dark, brilliant, mellow,* and *rich.*[*]

Like changes in dynamics, changes in tone color create variety and contrast. When the same melody is played by one instrument and then by another, it takes on different expressive effects because of each instrument's tone color. On the other hand, a contrast in tone color may be used to highlight a new melody: after violins play a melody, an oboe may present a contrasting one.

Tone colors also build a sense of continuity; it is easier to recognize the return of a melody when the same instruments play it each time. Specific instruments can reinforce a melody's emotional impact: the brilliant sound of a trumpet is suited to heroic or military tunes; the soothing tone color of a flute fits the mood of a calm melody. In fact, composers often create a melody with a particular instrument's tone color in mind.

A practically unlimited variety of tone colors is available to composers. Combining different instruments—violin, clarinet, and trombone, for example—results in new colors that the instruments cannot produce by themselves. And tone color can be changed by varying the number of instruments or voices that perform a melody. Finally, electronic techniques developed in recent years allow composers to create colors completely unlike those of traditional instruments.

Listening Outlines, Vocal Music Guides, and the Properties of Sound

Reading about pitch, dynamics, and tone color without hearing music is too abstract. To understand and recognize the properties of sound, we must *listen for them.* In this book, listening outlines (for instrumental music) and vocal music guides (for music with vocal texts) will help focus your attention on musical events as they unfold. These outlines and guides must be read *as you listen to the music;* otherwise, their value to you is limited.

In a *listening outline,* each item describes some musical sound. It may point out dynamics, instruments, pitch level, or mood. (Remember, though, that indications of mood in music are subjective. What one person calls "triumphant," for instance, someone else may call "determined.")

In a *vocal music guide,* the vocal text appears with brief marginal notes that indicate the relationship between words and music and help the listener follow the thought, story, or drama.

The outlines and guides are preceded by descriptions of the music's main features. Within the guide or outline, timings and compact disc (CD) track numbers appear at the left (**boldface** for the Basic Set, lightface for the Brief Set). In addition, the outlines include instrumentation, notes about our recordings (where important), and the duration of selections in our recordings.

Before you listen to a piece of music, you will find it helpful to glance over the entire listening outline or vocal music guide. Then, while hearing one passage, look ahead to learn what's next. For example, in the listening outline for the Prelude to Act III of Richard Wagner's opera *Lohengrin,* the first item (1*a*) is "Full orchestra, very loud (***ff***),

---

[*]An explanation of the physical basis of tone color appears in Appendix 2.

main melody in violins, cymbal crashes." While listening to the music described by item 1*a*, glance at item 1*b*: "Brass melody, pulsating accompaniment in strings."

Sometimes, not all the instruments playing are listed; instead, only those that are prominent at a given moment are shown. For example, item 2 in the listening outline for *Lohengrin* reads "Soft (*p*), contrasting oboe melody. Melody repeated by flute. Clarinet and violins continue." Although other instruments can be heard, this description focuses attention on the instruments that play the melody.

Following are our first four listening outlines.

Lohengrin, Prelude to Act III (1848), by Richard Wagner

Basic Set:

CD 1 ▮**1**

In the Prelude to Act III of his opera *Lohengrin*, Richard Wagner (1813–1883) makes wide and brilliant use of dynamic contrasts to set the scene for the wedding of the hero and heroine. The prelude opens with a feeling of exultation—great energy is conveyed by the massive sound of the full orchestra. Later, the music suddenly becomes calm and gentle as we hear fewer instruments, playing softly. This is followed by another sudden contrast when Wagner again employs the full orchestra.

LISTENING OUTLINE

WAGNER, *Lohengrin,* Prelude to Act III

3 flutes, 3 oboes, 3 clarinets, 3 bassoons, 4 French horns, 3 trumpets, 3 trombones, bass tuba, timpani, triangle, cymbals, tambourine, 1st violins, 2d violins, violas, cellos, double basses

(Duration,)

▮**1**	0:00	**1.** **a.**	Full orchestra, very loud (*ff*), main melody in violins, cymbal crashes.
▮**2**	0:26	**b.**	Brass melody, pulsating accompaniment in strings.
	1:13	**c.**	Full orchestra, main melody in violins, cymbal crashes.
▮**3**	1:25	**2.**	Soft (*p*), contrasting oboe melody. Melody repeated by flute. Clarinet and violins continue.
▮**4**	2:16	**3.** **a.**	Full orchestra, very loud (*ff*), main melody in violins, cymbal crashes.
	2:27	**b.**	Brass melody, pulsating accompaniment in strings.
	2:52	**c.**	Cymbals, very loud orchestral close.

Prelude in C Minor for Piano, Op. 28,* No. 20 (1839), by Frédéric Chopin

Basic Set:

CD 1 ▮**5**

In Prelude in C Minor, Op. 28, No. 20, by Frédéric Chopin (1810–1849), dynamic change is produced by a single instrument, the piano. A decrease in volume from very loud (*ff*) to soft (*p*), and then to very soft (*pp*), contributes to a feeling of emotional progression within this miniature lasting only 1½ minutes; it's as though a majestic funeral march becomes increasingly personal.

---

*The abbreviation *op.* stands for *opus,* Latin for *work.* An opus number is a way of identifying a piece or set of pieces. Usually, within a composer's output, the higher the opus number of a composition, the later it was written.

LISTENING OUTLINE

CHOPIN, Prelude in C Minor for Piano

Piano

(Duration, 1:34)

5 0:00	**1.**	Heavy chords, very loud (*ff*).
6 0:26	**2.**	New section, soft (*p*).
7 0:53	**3.**	Very soft (*pp*) repeat of preceding section. Loud chord at end.

Basic Set:
CD 1 **8**

Brief Set:
CD 1 **1**

The Firebird, Scene 2 (1910), by Igor Stravinsky

In the second—and final—scene of the ballet *The Firebird,* Igor Stravinsky (1882–1971) repeats one melody over and over, creating variety and contrast through changes of dynamics, tone color, and rhythm. During this scene, the hero triumphs and becomes engaged to a beautiful princess.

The second scene begins softly but becomes increasingly grand as the music gradually grows louder (crescendo), more instruments play, and the melody is repeated at higher pitches. After this slow buildup to a climax, there's a sudden quiet as all the instruments but the strings stop playing. A quick crescendo then leads to a brilliant concluding section.

LISTENING OUTLINE

STRAVINSKY, *The Firebird,* Scene 2

Piccolo, 3 flutes, 3 oboes, English horn, 3 clarinets, bass clarinet, 3 bassoons, contrabassoon, 4 French horns, 6 trumpets, tuba, timpani, triangle, cymbals, bass drum, 3 harps, 1st violins, 2d violins, violas, cellos, double basses

(Duration, 3:06)

8 **1**	0:00	**1. a.**	Slow melody in French horn, soft (*p*), quivering string accompaniment.
	0:29	**b.**	Violins, soft, melody an octave higher. Flutes join.
	0:43	**c.**	Grows louder (crescendo) as more instruments enter.
	1:03	**d.**	Violins and flutes, loud (*f*), melody at even higher octave, crescendo to
	1:17	**e.**	Full orchestra, melody very loud (*ff*), timpani (kettledrums).
	1:34	**f.**	Suddenly very soft (*pp*), strings, quick crescendo to
9 **2**	1:41	**2. a.**	Brasses, very loud (*ff*), melody in quick detached notes, timpani.
	2:04	**b.**	Melody in slower, accented notes, brasses, *ff*, timpani, music gradually slows.
	2:35	**c.**	High held tone, *ff*, brass chords, extremely loud (*fff*), lead to sudden *pp* and crescendo to extremely loud close.

Basic Set:
CD 1 **10**

Brief Set:
CD 1 **3**

C-Jam Blues (1942), by Duke Ellington and His Famous Orchestra

A succession of different tone colors contributes to the variety within *C-Jam Blues* (1942), as performed by Duke Ellington and His Famous Orchestra. A repeated-note melody is played first by the piano and then by saxophones. Then we hear solos by the violin, cornet, tenor saxophone, trombone, and clarinet. These solos are improvised by the players. Each instrument is first heard alone and then heard with accompaniment. The cornet and trombones are played with mutes, devices inserted into the instrument to alter its sound. *C-Jam Blues* ends climactically when the full band is heard for the first time.

LISTENING OUTLINE

ELLINGTON, *C-Jam Blues*

Piano (Duke Ellington), violin (Ray Nance), 2 trumpets (Wallace Jones, Ray Nance), cornet (Rex Stewart), 2 trombones (Joe "Tricky Sam" Nanton, Lawrence Brown), valve trombone (Juan Tizol), clarinet (Barney Bigard), 2 alto saxophones (Johnny Hodges, Otto Hardwick), 2 tenor saxophones (Barney Bigard, Ben Webster), baritone saxophone (Harry Carney), guitar (Fred Guy), bass (Junior Raglin), percussion (Sonny Greer)

10 3	0:00	**1.**	Piano, repeated-note melody, accompanied by bass, guitar, drums.
11 4	0:17	**2.**	Saxophones, repeated-note melody, accompanied by rhythm section (piano, bass, guitar, percussion).
12 5	0:33	**3.**	Violin alone, then accompanied by rhythm section.
13 6	0:54	**4.**	Muted cornet alone, then accompanied by rhythm section.
14 7	1:15	**5.**	Tenor saxophone alone, then accompanied by rhythm section.
15 8	1:37	**6.**	Muted trombone alone, then accompanied by rhythm section.
16 9	1:59	**7.**	Clarinet alone, then accompanied by band.
17 10	2:20	**8.**	Full band.

2 Performing Media: Voices and Instruments

Voices

Throughout history, singing has been the most widespread and familiar way of making music. Ancient Greek drama included a chanting chorus, and the Bible records that Moses, Miriam, and the Israelites sang to glorify the Lord. Singers seem always to have had a magnetic appeal, and even today adoring audiences imitate the looks and lifestyles of their favorites.

The exchange between singer and audience contains a bit of magic, something direct and spellbinding. Probably because the singer becomes an instrument, we identify with him or her especially—a human body like our own expressing emotions through sounds and words.

The voice has a unique ability to fuse a word with a musical tone, and for this reason poetry and singing have been inseparable in many cultures. Singing can make words easier to remember and can heighten their emotional effect.

For many reasons, it is difficult to sing well. In singing we use wider ranges of pitch and volume than in speaking, and we hold vowel sounds longer. Singing demands a greater supply and control of breath. Air from the lungs is controlled by the lower abdominal muscles and the diaphragm. The air makes the vocal cords vibrate, and the singer's lungs, throat, mouth, and nose come into play to produce the desired sound.

Throughout history, singing has been the most widespread way of making music. Shown here are the Westminster Choir and the New Jersey Symphony Orchestra, conducted by Bernard Labadie.

The pitch of the tone varies with the tension of the vocal cords; the tighter they are, the higher the pitch.

The range of a singer's voice depends both on training and on physical makeup. Professional singers can command 2 octaves or even more, whereas an untrained voice is usually limited to about 1½ octaves. Men's vocal cords are longer and thicker than women's, and this difference produces a lower range of pitches. The classification of voice ranges for women and men follows, arranged from highest to lowest. (The four basic ranges are soprano, alto, tenor, and bass.)

Women	Men
soprano	*tenor*
mezzo-soprano	*baritone*
alto (or contralto)	*bass*

Because of differences in taste, methods of singing vary widely from culture to culture. Asian singing, for example, is more nasal than that of the west. While classical singers in our culture stand erect, singers in west Africa stand bending forward; and singers in India sit on the floor. In fact, there are differences in performing styles in the west alone: classical, popular, jazz, folk, and rock music are all sung differently. Classical singers, for example, normally don't rely on microphones, but rock gets its point across partly by amplification.

Until the late 1600s, most music of western culture was vocal. But by the end of the seventeenth century, instrumental music rivaled vocal music in importance. Since then, composers have continued to write solo and choral vocal works, with and without instrumental accompaniment. There are compositions for male chorus; for female chorus; and for mixed chorus, which usually combines sopranos, altos, tenors, and basses. The accompaniment to vocal works ranges from a single instrument such as a guitar or piano to an entire orchestra.

Musical Instruments

People around the world use musical instruments that vary greatly in construction and tone color. An *instrument* may be defined as any mechanism—other than the voice—that produces musical sounds. Western musicians usually classify instruments in six broad categories: **string** (such as guitar and violin); **woodwind** (flute, clarinet); **brass** (trumpet, trombone); **percussion** (bass drum, cymbals); **keyboard** (organ, piano); and **electronic** (synthesizer).*

An instrument is often made in different sizes that produce different ranges. For instance, the saxophone family includes sopranino, soprano, alto, tenor, baritone, and bass saxophones.

An instrument's tone color may vary with the **register** (part of the total range) in which it is played. A clarinet sounds dark and rich in its low register, but its high register is brilliant and piercing.

Instrumental performers try to match the beautiful, flexible tone of a singer's voice. Yet most instruments have a wider range of pitches than the voice does. While a trained singer's range is about 2 octaves, many instruments command 3 or 4 octaves, and some have 6 or 7. Also, instruments usually produce tones more rapidly than the voice. When writing music for a specific instrument, composers have to consider its range of pitches and dynamics and how fast it can produce tones.

Instruments provide entertainment and accompany singing, dancing, religious rites, and drama. But they have served other functions, too. In some cultures, instruments are thought to have magical powers. Bells are worn to guard against harm, and rattles are used by traditional healers. In parts of Africa, drums are so sacred that religious rites are not performed without them, and special ceremonies and sacrifices are sometimes enacted when the drums are being made.

Instruments have been used for communication as well. Detailed messages have been sent by drumbeats; hunters have blown horns for signals; and musicians have announced the time by sounding brass instruments from towers. Trumpets have been used for military signals and to bolster soldiers' courage in battle. For centuries, trumpets and kettledrums announced kings and queens.

Musical instruments have even been status symbols. During the nineteenth century and the early twentieth century, the piano was a fixture in any home that aspired to be middle-class. "Proper" young ladies were expected to learn the piano as one of many "accomplishments." Such ideas lost their currency when women began to move more freely in the world (around the time of World War I), and when the radio and phonograph began to replace the piano as a source of home entertainment. Still, even today there are status implications in the type of audio equipment someone owns. Though a stereo is not a musical instrument, a connection can be made between the parlor piano of 1900 and today's elaborate "home entertainment centers."

Instruments' popularity rises and falls with changing musical tastes and requirements. Today only a fraction of all known instruments are used. However, interest in music of earlier times has led to the resurrection of instruments such as the harpsichord, an ancestor of the piano; and the recorder, a relative of the flute. Modern replicas of ancient instruments are being built and played. In fact, modern musicians are flexible and far-ranging in their choice of instruments. Rock composers have used nonwestern instruments such as the Indian sitar (a plucked string instrument). Jazz musicians are turning to classical instruments such as the flute, while classical composers are using instruments associated with jazz, such as the vibraphone.

Compositions may be written for solo instruments, for small groups, and for orchestras with over 100 musicians. Whatever the group, it may include instruments from only one category (say, strings) or from several categories. Modern symphony

*The scientific classification of instruments, based on the way sound is made, has five categories: chordophones (a stretched string is the sound generator—our "string" category); aerophones (a column of air is the sound generator—our "woodwind" and "brass" categories); idiophones (instruments whose own material is the sound generator, such as cymbals, gongs, and bells—part of our "percussion" category); membranophones (instruments with a stretched skin or some other membrane for the sound generator, such as drums—part of our "percussion" category); and electrophones (instruments generating their sounds by means of electricity—our "electronic" category).

A marching band performing in the Tournament of Roses Parade in Pasadena, California.

A symphony orchestra.

orchestras contain string, woodwind, brass, and percussion instruments. (The illustration on the next page shows a typical seating plan for a large orchestra.) Keyboard instruments also find their way into the modern orchestra as needed. Bands consist mainly of brass, woodwind, and percussion instruments.

Instruments commonly used for western music are described in this chapter, by categories. Nonwestern instruments are discussed in Part XI.

String Instruments The *violin, viola, cello* (*violoncello*), and *double bass* (sometimes called simply a *bass*) form the symphony orchestra's string section. They vary

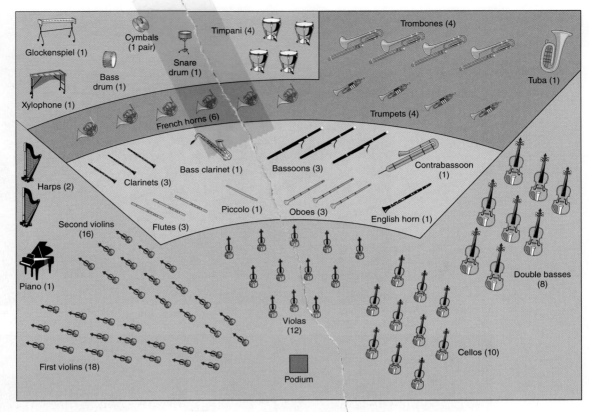

Typical seating plan for a large orchestra (about 100 instrumentalists), showing the distribution of instruments.

in tone color as well as in size and range: the violin is the smallest and has the highest range; the double bass is the largest and has the lowest range. For symphonic music the strings are usually played with a **bow,** a slightly curved stick strung tightly with horsehair (see the illustration below). Symphonic strings also may be plucked with the finger.

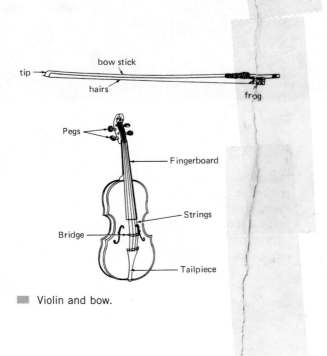

Violin and bow.

Strings

The violin is often used as a solo instrument. In the orchestra, the violins are divided into first and second violins, with the first violins frequently playing the main melody. The violinist shown here is Gil Shaham.

The body of the viola is about two inches longer than that of the violin, and thus the viola's range is somewhat lower. Its tone color is darker, thicker, and a little less brilliant than the violin's. The violist here is Tabea Zimmermann.

Although eighteenth-century composers generally used the cello in its bass and baritone registers, later composers exploited its upper registers as well. The cellist shown here is Yo-Yo Ma.

The double bass (or bass) has a very heavy tone and is less agile than other string instruments. It is generally played with a bow in symphonic music; but in jazz and popular music it is commonly played by plucking the strings as shown here. The bassist is Tarus Mateen.

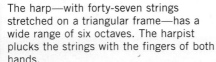

The harp—with forty-seven strings stretched on a triangular frame—has a wide range of six octaves. The harpist plucks the strings with the fingers of both hands.

The guitar has six strings, which are plucked with the fingers or strummed with a plectrum, or pick. The frets on the fingerboard mark the places where the strings must be pressed with the fingers of the other hand. John Williams is the guitarist shown here.

Of all the instrumental groups, the strings have the greatest versatility and expressive range. They produce many tone colors and have wide ranges of pitch and dynamics. String players can produce tones that are brilliant and rapid or slow and throbbing; they can control tone as subtly as a singer. Orchestral works tend to rely more on the strings than on any other group. Even with their differing tone colors, the four string instruments blend beautifully. Here it will be helpful to consider the construction and tone production of the string instruments; the violin can represent the entire family.

The hollow wooden body of the violin supports four strings made of gut or wire. The strings stretch, under tension, from a *tailpiece* on one end over a wooden *bridge* to the other end, where they are fastened around wooden *pegs*. The bridge holds the strings away from the *fingerboard* so that they can vibrate freely; the bridge also transmits the strings' vibrations to the *body*, which amplifies and colors the tone. Each string is tuned to a different pitch by tightening or loosening the pegs. (The greater the tension, the higher the pitch.)

The musician makes a string vibrate by drawing the bow across it with the right hand. The speed and pressure of the bow stroke control the dynamics and tone color of the sound produced. Pitch is controlled by the musician's left hand. By pressing a string against the fingerboard, the player varies the length of its vibrating portion and so changes its pitch. This is called *stopping* a string (because the vibrations are stopped at a certain point along the string's length). Thus, a range of pitches can be drawn from each of the four strings.

Basically the viola, cello, and double bass are made in the same manner and produce sound by similar means. How the string instruments are played—what string performance techniques are used—determines which of many musical effects they will produce. The most frequently used techniques are listed here:

Pizzicato (plucked string): The musician plucks the string, usually with a finger of the right hand. In jazz, the double bass is played mainly as a plucked instrument, rather than being bowed.

Double stop (two notes at once): By drawing the bow across two strings, a string player can sound two notes at once. And by rotating the bow rapidly across three strings (*triple stop*) or four strings (*quadruple stop*), three or four notes can be sounded almost—but not quite—together.

Vibrato: The string player can produce a throbbing, expressive tone by rocking the left hand while pressing the string down. This causes small pitch fluctuations that make the tone warmer.

Mute: The musician can veil or muffle the tone by fitting a clamp (mute) onto the bridge.

Tremolo: The musician rapidly repeats tones by quick up-and-down strokes of the bow. This can create a sense of tension, when loud; or a shimmering sound, when soft.

Harmonics: Very high-pitched tones, like a whistle's, are produced when the musician lightly touches certain points on a string. (See Appendix 2.)

Though the violin, viola, cello, and double bass are similar, they, like members of any family, have their differences. The photographs in this section show why each adds something distinctive to the orchestra's total sound.

Some string instruments are not played with a bow but are plucked instead, with the fingers or with a *plectrum* (plural, *plectra*). The most important of these are the *harp* and the *guitar.* The harp is the only plucked string instrument that has gained wide acceptance in the symphony orchestra.

Woodwind Instruments The woodwind instruments are so named because they produce vibrations of air within a tube that traditionally was made of wood. During the twentieth century, however, piccolos and flutes came to be made of metal. All the woodwinds have little holes along their length that are opened and closed by the fingers or by pads controlled by a key mechanism. By opening and closing these holes, the woodwind player changes the length of the vibrating air column and so varies the pitch.

The main woodwind instruments of the symphony orchestra are as follows, arranged in four families, in approximate order of range from highest (piccolo) to lowest (contrabassoon). (Only the two most frequently used instruments of each family are listed.)

Flute Family	**Clarinet Family**	**Oboe Family**	**Bassoon Family**
piccolo			
flute	*clarinet*	*oboe*	
		English horn	
	bass clarinet		
			bassoon
			contrabassoon

Woodwind instruments are great individualists and are much less alike in tone color than the various strings. The flute, with its silvery tone, differs more from the nasal-sounding oboe than the violin does from the viola. The woodwinds' unique tone colors result largely from the different ways in which vibrations are produced. Flute and piccolo players blow across the edge of a mouth hole much as one makes sounds by blowing across the top of an empty bottle. (Players of the *recorder,* a relative of the flute, blow through a "whistle" mouthpiece.) The rest of the woodwind instruments rely on a vibrating reed. A *reed* is a very thin piece of cane, about 2½ inches long, that is set into vibration by a stream of air. There are single- and double-reed woodwinds. In *single-reed woodwinds* the reed is fastened over a hole in the mouthpiece and vibrates when the player blows into the instrument. The clarinet and bass clarinet are single-reed woodwinds. The *saxophone,* too, an instrument used mainly in bands, has a single reed.

In *double-reed woodwinds* two narrow pieces of cane are held between the musician's lips. The oboe, English horn, bassoon, and contrabassoon are double-reed woodwinds.

Woodwinds

The piccolo—whose name is short for *flauto piccolo,* or small flute—is half the size of the flute and plays an octave higher. The piccolo's high register is shrill and whistlelike.

The flute has a high range and is extremely agile, capable of producing a rapid succession of tones. Its tone is full and velvety in the low register and bright and sparkling at the top. Shown here is the flutist James Galway.

The oboe has a nasal, intense, expressive tone. Because the oboe's pitch is difficult to adjust, the entire orchestra is tuned to its A.

The English horn is neither English nor a horn, but simply a low, or alto, oboe.

The clarinet can produce tones very rapidly and has a wide range of dynamics and tone color. Pictured here is Benny Goodman.

The recorder, like the flute and piccolo, has no reed. The recorder's tone resembles a flute's but is softer and gentler. It is commonly found in five sizes: sopranino, soprano, alto, tenor, and bass.

The tone of the bassoon is deeply nasal.

The contrabassoon can produce the lowest pitch in the orchestra.

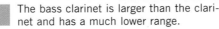 The bass clarinet is larger than the clarinet and has a much lower range.

The saxophone has a single-reed mouthpiece like a clarinet, but its tube is made of brass. Its tone is rich, husky, and speechlike. Shown here is the jazz saxophonist Sonny Rollins.

Heard by itself, a reed produces only a squawklike sound. Although the tone color of reed woodwinds is mainly determined by the bore of the instrument's tube, the reed does affect the tone color somewhat. Professional woodwind players spend much time soaking and shaping their supply of reeds to ensure the best possible tone.

Tone colors also differ greatly among the various registers of each woodwind instrument. In general, low registers tend to be breathy and thick, and top registers are more penetrating. Unlike the strings, which can be double-stopped, the woodwinds can produce only a single note at a time. In symphonic music they are frequently given melodic solos. Woodwind instruments are well suited for outdoors (shepherds have played simple woodwinds for thousands of years). Therefore, they are often featured in music that evokes a rustic mood.

Brass Instruments From high register to low, the main instruments of the symphony orchestra's brass section are the *trumpet, French horn* (sometimes called simply a *horn*), *trombone,* and *tuba.* Trumpets and trombones are often used in jazz and rock groups.

The vibrations of brass instruments come from the musician's lips as he or she blows into a cup- or funnel-shaped *mouthpiece.* The vibrations are amplified and colored in a tube that is coiled (to make it easy to carry and play). The tube is flared at the end to form a *bell.* Modern brass instruments are actually made of brass, but their earlier counterparts were made of hollow animal horns, elephant tusks, wood, and even glass.

Some brass instruments, such as the cornet, baritone horn, and euphonium, are used mainly in concert and marching bands. The *cornet* is similar in shape to the trumpet, but its tone is more mellow. The *baritone horn* looks like a tuba and has the same range as the trombone. The *euphonium* is the tenor instrument of the tuba family.

The pitch of brass instruments is regulated both by varying lip tension and by using *slides* and *valves* to change the length of the tube through which the air vibrates.

Brass

The French horn has a tone that is less brassy, more mellow, and more rounded than the trumpet's.

The thick, heavy tone of the tuba is used to add weight to the lowest register of an orchestra or band.

The trumpet sounds brilliant, brassy, and penetrating. The trumpeter shown here is Wynton Marsalis.

The trombone has a tone that combines the brilliance of a trumpet with the mellowness of a French horn.

The trombone uses a slide, a U-shaped tube that fits into two parallel straight tubes. By pulling the slide in or pushing it out, the player changes the length of tubing and makes it possible to play different pitches. The trumpet, French horn, and tuba use three or four valves to divert air through various lengths of tubing. The longer the length of tubing through which air is diverted, the lower the possible pitch. Valves came into common use around 1850. Before then, French horn and trumpet players would insert additional curves of tubing (called *crooks*) into their instruments to change the range of available pitches. When valves came into use, these instruments could produce many more tones and became much more flexible.

Brass players can alter the tone color of their instruments by inserting a **mute** into the bell. Mutes for brass instruments come in different shapes and are made of wood, plastic, or metal. They are most common in jazz, where they create a variety of effects, including a buzzing sound, a mellowing of the tone, and the comical "wah-wah."

Brasses are powerful instruments, often used at climaxes and for bold, heroic statements. Since the late nineteenth century, they are frequently given rapid solo passages as well. Today, brass instruments are very popular, owing to ensembles such as the Canadian Brass and soloists like the trumpeter Wynton Marsalis.

Percussion Instruments Most percussion instruments of the orchestra are struck by hand, with sticks, or with hammers. Some are shaken or rubbed. Percussion instruments are subdivided into instruments of definite and indefinite pitch, depending on whether they produce a tone or a noiselike sound.

Definite Pitch	Indefinite Pitch
timpani (kettledrums)	*snare drum (side drum)*
glockenspiel	*bass drum*
xylophone	*tambourine*
celesta	*triangle*
chimes	*cymbals*
	gong (tam-tam)

The vibrations of percussion instruments are set up by stretched membranes, like the calfskin of the kettledrum, or by plates or bars made of metal, wood, or other sonorous materials. Extremely loud sounds may be drawn from percussion instruments like the bass drum or cymbals. In a symphony orchestra, one percussionist may play several different instruments during a composition.

Percussion instruments have long been used to emphasize rhythm and to heighten climaxes. But until the twentieth century, they played a far less important role in western music than strings, woodwinds, or brasses. Since 1900, composers have been more willing to exploit the special colors of the percussion group and have occasionally written entire pieces to show it off, such as *Ionisation* (1931) by Edgard Varèse. Jazz and rock musicians, of course, have made good use of percussion instruments. Yet, for all these recent explorations, western musicians barely approach the incredibly varied use of percussion found in Africa and Asia, where subtle changes of rhythm, tone color, and dynamics are used with great imagination.

Percussion

The timpani (kettledrums) are the only orchestral drums of definite pitch. A calfskin head is stretched over a hemispherical copper shell. Varying the tension of the head using adjustable screws around the head or a pedal changes the pitch of the timpani. One percussionist generally plays two to four timpani, each tuned to a different pitch.

The xylophone consists of a set of wooden bars that are struck with two hard hammers to produce a dry, wooden tone.

The metal bars of the glockenspiel (orchestral bells) are struck with two hammers to produce a tone that is bright and silvery.

The bass drum—the largest of the orchestral drums—is almost three feet in diameter.

The celesta looks like a small upright piano, but its sounding mechanism is like a glockenspiel's. Metal bars are struck by hammers that are controlled by a keyboard. The celesta's tone is tinkling and graceful.

Chimes are a set of metal tubes hung from a frame. They are struck with a hammer and sound like church bells.

The triangle is struck with a metal beater and makes a tinkling, bell-like sound.

The dry rattling sound of the snare drum (or side drum) is produced by the vibration of snares—strings that are tightly stretched against the bottom head. The snare drum is often used in marches.

When struck by a beater, the gong (or tam-tam) produces long-lasting sounds that can seem solemn, mysterious, or frightening.

The tambourine is often used to create a Spanish or Italian effect. The player shakes it or strikes it with the knuckles.

Cymbals are round brass plates. They usually are struck together with a sliding motion, and their sound penetrates like a sharp crash.

Keyboard Instruments The piano, harpsichord, organ, and accordion are the best-known keyboard instruments. A keyboard permits the performer to play several tones at the same time easily and rapidly. This capacity justifies grouping instruments that are otherwise quite different: the piano and harpsichord produce sounds through vibrating strings; the organ uses vibrating air columns. The piano and, to a lesser extent, the organ are sometimes used in modern symphony orchestras for coloristic effects. All keyboard instruments are played solo as well.

During the last two centuries, more great music has been written for the *piano* than for any other solo instrument. The piano is exceptionally versatile. A pianist can play many notes at once, including both a melody and its accompaniment. The piano commands a wide range of pitches. Its eighty-eight keys span more than seven octaves. The dynamic range is broad, from a faint whisper to a powerful fortissimo. Because of its dynamic flexibility, the Italians named it the *pianoforte* (meaning *soft-loud*).

When a pianist's finger strikes a key, a felt-covered hammer swings up against a string. The greater the force on the key, the more powerful the hammer's blow on the string, and the louder the tone produced. When the pianist releases the key, a felt *damper* comes down on the string to stop the vibrations and end the tone. The steel strings are held under tension by an iron frame. Below the strings is a wooden sounding board, which amplifies and colors the strings' vibrations.

There are usually three pedals on a piano. Most important is the *damper pedal,* on the right, which allows a pianist to sustain tones even after the keys are released. The *una corda* pedal, on the left, commonly known as the *soft pedal,* veils the sound. The *sostenuto* pedal, in the middle, is rarely used (and in fact is often missing from upright pianos); it allows the pianist to sustain some tones without sustaining others.

Keyboard

The piano is exceptionally versatile. Shown here is the pianist Lang Lang.

The harpsichord has plucked strings controlled by one or two keyboards.

The piano was invented around 1700, came into fairly wide use in the 1780s, and was mechanically perfected by the 1850s. Today it is among the most popular instruments and is used for solos, for accompaniments, and in combination with one other instrument or many other instruments.

The **harpsichord** has strings that are plucked by a set of *plectra* (little wedges of plastic, leather, or quill). These are controlled by one or two keyboards. The harpsichord was the main stringed keyboard instrument from about 1500 to 1775, when it was gradually replaced by the piano. Although largely forgotten during the nineteenth century, the harpsichord was revived during the twentieth century for the

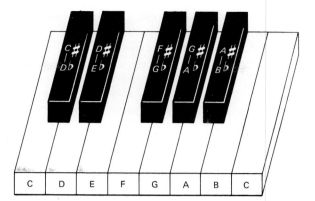

The twelve pitches of the octave and their positions on the piano keyboard.

those played by a pianist's right hand), and the **bass clef,** used for relatively low ranges (played by the pianist's left hand):

Treble Clef

Bass Clef

Keyboard music calls for a wide range of pitches to be played by both hands; for such music, the **grand staff**—a combination of the treble and bass staves—is used. The following illustration shows how the notes on the grand staff are related to the piano keyboard. Note that the C nearest to the middle of the keyboard is called **middle C.**

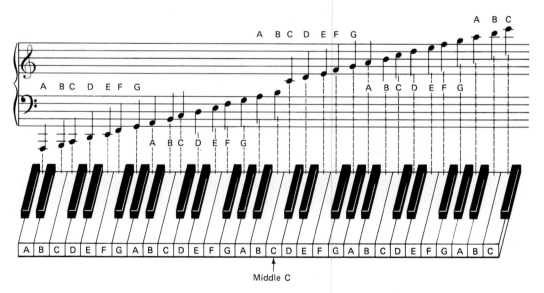

Notes on the grand staff and their positions on the piano keyboard.

Notating Rhythm

Music notation does not indicate the exact duration of tones; instead, it shows how long one tone lasts in relation to others in the same piece. A single note on the staff lasts longer or shorter depending on how it looks—on whether it is white or black and has a **stem** or **flags.**

A pipe organ has many sets of pipes controlled from several keyboards and pedals. The organist varies the sound by selecting different combinations of the pipes.

performance of music composed before 1750. It was also put to new use in works by twentieth-century composers.

A *pipe organ* has many sets of pipes controlled from several keyboards, including a pedal keyboard played by the organist's feet. The keys control valves from which air is blown across or through openings in the pipes. Various sets of pipes are brought into play by pulling knobs called *stops*. Each set of pipes has a particular tone color that the organist uses alone or with others. The larger the organ, the more tone colors are available. Organists, unlike pianists, cannot make subtle changes of dynamics by varying finger pressure. Instead, dynamic change is produced by adding to or reducing the number of pipes being played, by moving from one keyboard to another, or by opening and closing the shutters (much like Venetian blinds) that surround some groups of pipes. The organ has a greater range of pitch, volume, and tone color than any other traditional instrument. Its tones last for as long as a finger or a foot is held on a key or pedal.

The greatest period of organ music and organ building was from 1600 to 1750, when the organ became known as the "king of instruments." Although mostly connected with religious services, today the organ is found in many auditoriums and is used in concerts.

The **accordion** has free steel reeds that are controlled by a treble keyboard with piano keys, played by the right hand; and a bass keyboard with buttons, played by the left hand. The reeds are caused to vibrate by air pressure from a bellows.

Electronic Instruments Electronic instruments produce or amplify sound through electronic means; they were invented as early as 1904 but have had a significant impact on music only since 1950. Today, electronic and computer technologies are developing rapidly, changing continually, and increasingly blending together. Electronic instruments for performing and composing music include amplified instruments, such as the electric piano, organ, and guitar; tape studios; synthesizers; computers; and various "hybrid" technologies.

The *tape studio* was the main tool of composers of electronic music during the 1950s. (In Part VII, we'll study Edgard Varèse's *Poème électronique,* which was created in a tape studio.) The raw material in tape studios consisted of recorded sounds of definite and indefinite pitch that might be electronic or from "real life"—flutes, birdcalls,

Today's electronic music studios create a wide range of sounds with the use of computers, synthesizers, digital recorders, and a variety of electronic effects and filters.

and so forth. The composer manipulated these in various ways: by speeding them up or slowing them down, altering their pitch and duration, giving them echoes, filtering them to change tone color, mixing them, and editing the tape (as by cutting and splicing) to play them in any desired order. Rhythm could be fully controlled, because the duration of a sound depended only on the length of a tape segment. However, tape splicing and rerecording were difficult, inaccurate, and time-consuming processes, and many composers of the 1960s turned to synthesizers, which appeared around 1955.

Synthesizers are systems of electronic components that generate, modify, and control sound. They can generate a huge variety of musical sounds and noises, and the composer has complete control over pitch, tone color, loudness, and duration. Most synthesizers can be "played" by means of a keyboard—an addition to the mechanisms of the tape studio.

Synthesizers vary in size and capacity. The mid-1950s saw the invention of the RCA Mark II synthesizer, an enormous (and unique) vacuum-tube synthesizer occupying an entire wall of the Columbia-Princeton Electronic Music Center in New York City. During the 1960s and 1970s, smaller, less expensive transistorized synthesizers such as the Moog and Buchla were developed; these were installed in electronic music studios at universities and advertising agencies, played in live rock concerts and concerts of electronic music, and used to create film and television scores. Highly sophisticated synthesizers using computer capabilities have now been developed, and several different technologies are in use.

Analog synthesis—the earliest of the synthesizer technologies, which predominated until about 1980—uses a mixture of complex sounds that are shaped by filtering. Like all analog technology, it is based on representing data in terms of measurable physical quantities, in this case sound waves.

Digital frequency modulation (FM) synthesis, invented by John Chowning, was patented by Yamaha and has been associated with Yamaha instruments. Like all digital technology, it is based on representing physical quantities—here, points on sound waves—as numbers.

Effects devices, which include reverberators, echo devices, and stereo splitters, are often integrated into synthesizers and the synthesis process. They are used in almost all recorded music (especially popular music) and in some live music.

Sampling is considered a synthesizer technology, since it involves placing brief digital recordings of live sounds under the control of a synthesizer keyboard; but although the sounds can be modified during playback, no actual synthesis is present. Sampling can be seen as an advanced form of composing by tape splicing: it allows the composer to record short segments of sounds (these are the "samples") digitally and then manipulate them. Sampling has been integrated into relatively inexpensive computer-linked keyboards and is one of the most important aspects of today's electronic music making.

A significant development in synthesizing technology is known as *musical instrument digital interface (MIDI):* this is a standard adopted by manufacturers for interfacing synthesizer equipment. MIDI has allowed the device actually played on to be separated from tone generation; thus there are now keyboards that look, feel, and play like a piano; wind controllers played like a woodwind instrument; and string controllers played like a violin or cello. Also, control signals can be fed to and from a MIDI instrument into and out of a personal computer, and users can store and edit music and convert to and from musical notation.

Historically, **computers** were the third means of producing sounds on audiotape; they were developed for this purpose after the tape studio and synthesizers. Computers are used both as control devices to drive MIDI equipment and for direct digital synthesis.

The 1970s and 1980s saw the development of small computers with which composers could instantly hear the music they programmed; since then, computers have become even more sophisticated. Computers are used for music synthesis (mainly to produce sounds not otherwise obtainable), to help composers write scores (following rules selected by the composer), to store samples of audio signals, to control synthesizing mechanisms, and so on. In **computer music,** some or all of the sounds are generated and manipulated by computer.

Obviously, it is not entirely possible (or particularly useful) to consider modern electronic music devices and processes separately: the distinction between synthesizer technology and computer technology is not clear-cut. To increase the variety of sound and the composer's control over it, today's electronic music studios contain and integrate a wide variety of equipment, including tape recorders, synthesizers, computers, and devices for mixing and filtering sound.

All this equipment enables the composer to exploit the entire spectrum of sound as never before. But the quality of the music produced still depends on the imagination and organizing power of the human mind.

The Young Person's Guide to the Orchestra, Op. 34 (1946), by Benjamin Britten

connect
A complete video performance of this work by the Philadelphia Orchestra is available in *Connect Kamien.*

Basic Set:
CD 1 [18]

Brief Set:
CD 1 [11]

Benjamin Britten (1913–1976), an English composer, wrote the attractive *Young Person's Guide to the Orchestra* in 1946 as an introduction to the instruments of the orchestra. He used a theme by Henry Purcell, a great English composer of the seventeenth century. (A *theme* is a melody used as the basis for a musical composition.) The majestic theme is presented first by the full orchestra, and then by each section of the orchestra in turn: woodwinds, brasses, strings, and percussion. Thirteen *variations,* or varied repetitions of the theme, are then heard. Each highlights a different instrument. The variations differ in dynamics, speed, and tone color, as well as mood. They follow each other without pause and last from about 30 seconds to 1 minute each. (Variation 13, however, which features many percussion instruments, lasts almost 2 minutes.) Woodwind, string, and brass instruments are generally presented from highest to lowest in range.

Variation 13 is followed immediately by a concluding section beginning with a lively new tune played by an unaccompanied piccolo. Then other instruments enter, each playing the same tune. After woodwind, string, brass, and percussion instruments have had their turn, the brasses bring back the main theme and provide an exciting ending.

LISTENING OUTLINE

BRITTEN, *The Young Person's Guide to the Orchestra*

Piccolo, 2 flutes, 2 oboes, 2 clarinets, 2 bassoons, 4 horns, 2 trumpets, 3 trombones, tuba, timpani, bass drum, snare drum, cymbals, tambourine, triangle, Chinese block, xylophone, castanets, gong, whip, 1st violins, 2d violins, violas, cellos, double basses

(Duration, 17:23)

Theme

18 11	0:00	**a.**	Full orchestra
19 12	0:41	**b.**	Woodwind section
20 13	1:11	**c.**	Brass section
21 14	1:42	**d.**	String section
22 15	2:07	**e.**	Percussion section
23 16	2:26	**f.**	Full orchestra

Woodwinds

24 17	3:00	**Variation 1:**	Flutes and piccolo
25 18	3:30	**Variation 2:**	Oboes
26 19	4:33	**Variation 3:**	Clarinets
27 20	5:16	**Variation 4:**	Bassoons

Strings

28 21	6:13	**Variation 5:**	Violins
29 22	6:58	**Variation 6:**	Violas
30 23	7:38	**Variation 7:**	Cellos
31 24	8:34	**Variation 8:**	Double basses
32 25	9:32	**Variation 9:**	Harp

Brasses

33 26	10:23	**Variation 10:**	French horns
34 27	11:03	**Variation 11:**	Trumpets
35 28	11:38	**Variation 12:**	Trombones and tuba

Percussion

36 29	12:39	**Variation 13: a.**	Timpani (kettledrums); bass drum and cymbals
37 30	13:06	**b.**	Tambourine and triangle; snare drum (side drum) and Chinese block (a hollow wooden block that is struck with a drumstick)
38 31	13:28	**c.**	Xylophone
39 32	13:40	**d.**	Castanets and gong
40 33	13:49	**e.**	Whip (two hinged pieces of wood that are slapped against each other)
41 34	13:54	**f.**	Entire percussion section; xylophone and triangle

Concluding Section

42 35	14:32	**a.**	Unaccompanied piccolo, lively new tune, tune played in turn by flutes, oboes, clarinets, and bassoons, crescendo.
	15:42	**b.**	Lively tune played in turn by 1st violins, *p*; 2d violins, violas, cellos, double basses, woodwinds accompany, crescendo; quick decrescendo introduces
	16:11	**c.**	Harp, lively tune, crescendo in strings and woodwinds.
	16:22	**d.**	Lively tune played in turn by French horns, *ff*, trumpets, trombones and tuba, orchestra accompanies.
	16:41		
	16:50	**e.**	Percussion, *f*, accompanied by orchestra, *p*, crescendo to
		f.	Main theme in brasses, *ff*, together with lively tune in high woodwinds and strings. Full orchestra, percussion, long-held closing chord, *fff*.

The Stars and Stripes Forever (1897), by John Philip Sousa

Basic Set:
CD 1 **43**

One of the most popular of all band marches, *The Stars and Stripes Forever* (1897), was written by the American composer and conductor John Philip Sousa (1854–1932), who was nicknamed the "march king." *The Stars and Stripes Forever* displays the power and vitality of band music. The march begins with a short introduction, followed by two different melodies that are predominantly loud. We then hear the flowing main melody, which is played softly. After a transitional passage, there is a return of the main melody, this time combined with a new piccolo tune. *The Stars and Stripes Forever* builds to a climactic concluding section in which the main melody—it is now played loudly—and the piccolo tune are accompanied by a new trombone melody.

LISTENING OUTLINE

SOUSA, *The Stars and Stripes Forever*

Piccolo, 2 flutes, 2 oboes, 1st clarinets, 2d clarinets, 3d clarinets, alto clarinet, bass clarinet, 2 bassoons, 2 alto saxophones, tenor saxophone, baritone saxophone, bass saxophone, 3 cornets, 2 trumpets, 4 French horns, baritone horn, euphonium, 3 trombones, 2 basses, double bass, timpani, bass drum, snare drum, cymbals

(Duration, 3:09)

43 0:00	**1. a.**	Band, *ff*, introduces
0:03	**b.**	First melody, *ff*, in quick detached notes, cymbal crashes, soft, suddenly loud, soft. First melody repeated.
44 0:30	**2.**	Brasses, *ff*, second melody in longer notes, cymbal crashes. Second melody repeated.
45 0:58	**3.**	Soft and flowing main melody, saxophones, clarinets.
1:25	**4.**	Brasses, *ff*, low tones alternating with high tones, rise to climax, cymbal crashes, snare drum. Becomes softer (decrescendo).
46 1:47	**5.**	High piccolo tune combined with soft main melody.
2:14	**6.**	Brasses, *ff*, low tones alternating with high tones, rise to climax, cymbal crashes, snare drum.
2:36	**7.**	High piccolo tune and loud main melody accompanied by new trombone melody. Full band, *fff*, at end.

3 Rhythm

Rhythm is basic to life. We see it in the cycle of night and day, the four seasons, the rise and fall of tides. More personally, we feel rhythm as we breathe. We find it in our heartbeats and our walking.

The essence of rhythm is a recurring pattern of tension and release, of expectation and fulfillment. This rhythmic alternation seems to pervade the flow of time. Time, as we live it, has fantastic diversity; each hour has sixty minutes, but how different one hour may seem from another!

Rhythm forms the lifeblood of music, too. In its widest sense, **rhythm** is the flow of music through time. Musical time is like lived time in its endless variety. It also seems to pass at varying speeds and intensities. Yet there is an essential difference between music and life. In music, a composer can control the passage of time. In life, such

Dancing is closely linked to the rhythms of music. The ballet dancer Mikhail Baryshnikov is shown here in a performance of Tchaikovsky's *The Nutcracker.*

order eludes us. We delight in surrendering to a world of musical time that is ordered yet somehow related to our feelings and moods. We also enjoy letting the rhythm of music stimulate movement in our bodies, as when we dance.

Rhythm has several interrelated aspects, which we'll consider in turn: beat, meter, accent and syncopation, and tempo.

Beat

When you clap your hands or tap your foot to music, you are responding to its beat. *Beat* is a regular, recurrent pulsation that divides music into equal units of time. Beats can be represented by marks on a time line:

Beats can be shown as a succession of marks on a time line.

Beats
|
└─┴┴┴┴┴┴┴┴┴┴┴┴┴┴┴┴┴┴┴┴┴┴┴┴┴┴┴┴┴┴─────────────►
                    Time

In music, beats occur as often as every ¼ second or as seldom as every 1½ seconds. Sometimes the beat is powerful and easy to feel, as in marches or rock music; but sometimes it may be barely noticeable, suggesting feelings like floating or aimlessness.

The pulse of music is communicated in different ways. Sometimes the beat is explicitly pounded out—by a bass drum in a marching band, for instance. At other times the beat is sensed rather than actually heard.

Sing the beginning of *America* up to the words *Land where my fathers died:*

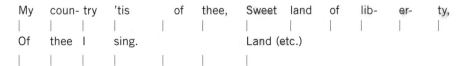

My	coun-	try	'tis		of	thee,	Sweet	land	of	lib-	er-	ty,
|	|	|	|		|	|	|	|	|	|	|	|
Of	thee	I	sing.				Land (etc.)					
|	|	|	|	|	|	|						

Each of the marks represents a beat. Did you notice that you automatically held *sing* for 3 beats? You *sensed* the beat because you were aware of it and expected it to continue.

Beats form the background against which the composer places notes of varying lengths. Beats are basic units of time by which all notes are measured. A note may last a fraction of a beat, an entire beat, or more than a beat. In the excerpt from *America,* for example, each of the three syllables in the words *My country* lasts 1 beat; *'tis* lasts 1½ beats; and *of* lasts only ½ beat. It was already noted that *sing* is held for 3 beats. Thus, in this portion of the song, we have notes ranging in length from ½ beat to 3 beats.

When we talk about the combination of different note lengths in *America,* we are considering its rhythm. Earlier, rhythm was broadly defined as the flow of music through time. More specifically, **rhythm** can be de fined as the particular arrangement of note lengths in a piece of music. The rhythm of a melody is an essential feature of its personality. Indeed, we might recognize *America* merely by clapping out its rhythm without actually singing the tones. The *beat* of *America* is an even, regular pulsation. But its *rhythm* flows freely, sometimes matching the beat, sometimes not.

Meter

When we sing *America,* some beats feel stronger or more stressed than others. The stress comes regularly on the first of every 3 beats:

My	coun-	try,	'tis		of	thee,
beat	beat	beat	**beat**	beat		beat

Therefore we count the beats of *America* as **1**–2–3, **1**–2–3:

My	coun-	try,	'tis		of	thee,
1	2	3	**1**	2		3
Sweet	land	of	lib-		er-	ty,
1	2	3	**1**	2		3
Of	thee	I	sing.			
1	2	3	**1**	2		3

In music we find a repeated pattern of a strong beat plus one or more weaker beats. The organization of beats into regular groups is called **meter.** A group containing a fixed number of beats is called a **measure.** There are several types of meter, which are based on the number of beats in a measure.

When a measure has 2 beats, it is in **duple meter;** we count **1**–2, **1**–2, and so on:

Ma- ry	had	a	lit- tle	lamb,	lit- tle	lamb,	lit- tle	lamb,
1	2	|**1**	2	|**1**	2	|**1**	2	

The vertical lines mark the beginning or end of the measure. The first, or stressed, beat of the measure is known as the **downbeat.**

A pattern of 3 beats to the measure is known as **triple meter.** As we have seen in *America,* we count **1**–2–3, **1**–2–3, and so on. All waltzes are in triple meter.

Another basic metrical pattern is **quadruple meter,** which has 4 beats to the measure. As usual, the downbeat is strongest; but there is another stress on the third beat, which is stronger than the second and fourth beats and weaker than the first: **1**–2–*3*–4, **1**–2–*3*–4. In the following example of quadruple meter, the first word is on the **upbeat,** an unaccented pulse preceding the downbeat:

Mine eyes	have	seen the	glo- ry	of the	com- ing of	the Lord;	He is
|**1**	2		*3*	4	|**1**	2	*3*	4	|

Jazz and rock are usually in quadruple meter. Both duple and quadruple meter reflect the left-right, left-right pattern of walking or marching.

Sextuple meter contains six rather quick beats to the measure. The downbeat is strongest, and the fourth beat also receives a stress: **1**–2–3–*4*–5–6. For example:

Oh, give	me	a	home		where the buf-		fa- lo	roam,		where the
|1	2	3	4	5	6	|1	2 3	4	5 6	|

Note that the measure is subdivided into two groups of 3 beats each: 1–2–3/4–5–6. Thus, sextuple meter is a combination of duple and triple meter. Melodies in sextuple meter often create a feeling of smooth flow, as in *Silent Night.*

Quintuple meter, with 5 beats to the measure, and *septuple meter,* with 7 beats to the measure, occur frequently in twentieth-century music and in today's music and are found occasionally in earlier music. Each of these meters combines duple and triple meter. In quintuple meter, for example, the measure is subdivided into groups of 2 and 3 beats: 1–2–3/4–5 or 1–2/3–4–5.

Accent and Syncopation

An important aspect of rhythm is the way individual notes are stressed—how they get special emphasis. A note is emphasized most obviously by being played louder than the notes around it, that is, by receiving a dynamic **accent.** A note is sometimes especially accented when it is held longer or is higher in pitch than those notes near it. In *The Star-Spangled Banner, see* is naturally accented by being longer and higher in pitch than *Oh, say can you.* In speech as well, we stress individual words through loudness, length, and pitch.

When an accented note comes where we normally would *not* expect one, the effect is known as **syncopation.** There is a syncopation when an "offbeat" note is accented— that is, when the stress comes *between* two beats. In the following example, syncopation occurs on the accented *my,* which comes between beats 1 and 2:

Give **my**	re-	gards	to	Broad-		way		
1	2	3	4	|1	2	3	4	|

A syncopation also occurs when a weak beat is accented, as in 1–**2**–3–4 or 1–2–3–**4.** Such contradictions of the meter surprise the listener and create rhythmic excitement. Syncopation is a characteristic feature of jazz.

Tempo

We've seen that the speed of the beat may be fast or slow. The speed of the beat is known as **tempo,** the basic pace of the music. A fast tempo is associated with a feeling of energy, drive, and excitement. A slow tempo often contributes to a solemn, lyrical, or calm mood. Such associations are rooted in the way we feel and act. When we're excited, our hearts beat more rapidly than when we're calm; we tend to move and speak more quickly.

A **tempo indication** is usually given at the beginning of a piece. As with dynamics, the terms that show tempo (at the left) are in Italian.

largo	very slow, broad
grave	very slow, solemn
adagio	slow
andante	moderately slow, a walking pace
moderato	moderate
allegretto	moderately fast
allegro	fast
vivace	lively
presto	very fast
prestissimo	as fast as possible

Qualifying words are sometimes added to tempo indications to make them more specific. The two most commonly used are *molto* (*much*) and *non troppo* (*not too much*). We thus get phrases like *allegro molto* (*very fast*) and *allegro non troppo* (*not too fast*).

As with dynamics, all these terms indicate only approximate tempos; they are relative. A piece marked *andante,* for example, might be played faster by one musician than by another. With the markings as a guide, each performer chooses the tempo that seems appropriate for a piece. But there is no one "right" tempo. A piece can sound equally convincing at slightly different speeds.

The same tempo is not always used throughout a piece. A gradual quickening of tempo may be indicated by writing **accelerando** (*becoming faster*), and a gradual slowing down of tempo by **ritardando** (*becoming slower*). An accelerando, especially when combined with a rise in pitch and volume, increases excitement, and a ritardando is associated with less tension and a feeling of conclusion.

Since about 1816, composers have been able to indicate their preferred tempos by means of a **metronome,** an apparatus that produces ticking sounds or flashes of light at any desired musical speed. The metronome setting indicates the exact number of beats per minute. For example, andante might be represented by the metronome number 60 and allegro by the number 116.

I Got Rhythm (1930), by George Gershwin

Basic Set:
CD 1 `47`

Pervasive syncopations give a jazzy feeling to the song *I Got Rhythm,* which was written by George Gershwin (1898–1937) for the musical comedy *Girl Crazy.* The song is in duple meter, with two quick beats to the measure. In our recording, it is performed by a soprano, with orchestral accompaniment.

In the opening rhythmic pattern to the words *I got rhy-thm,* a syncopation occurs when the accented tone *I* comes on the "offbeat," *between* beats 1 and 2.

I		got	rhy-	thm		**I**		got	mu-	sic	
1		2		1	2		1	2		1	2	

The next emphasized tone *rhy-(thm)* falls *on* the first beat and therefore is *not* syncopated.

This opening rhythmic pattern is repeated for *I got music* and for later parts of the melody.

Old	Man	Troub-	le			**I**		don't	mind	him	
1	2		1	2		1	2		1	2	

The recurrence of the rhythmic pattern on different pitches helps give *I Got Rhythm* its wonderful sense of unity and drive.

Unsquare Dance (1961), by Dave Brubeck

Basic Set:
CD 1 `48`

Unsquare Dance is in septuple meter, with 7 quick beats to the measure. The composer, Dave Brubeck (b. 1920), writes that this unusual meter makes *Unsquare Dance* "a challenge to the foot-tappers, finger-snappers, and hand-clappers. Deceitfully simple, it refuses to be squared." The piece is performed by a small jazz group consisting of piano, double bass, and percussion. It begins with only a pattern of beats and then becomes more active rhythmically and melodically. The meter is established by pizzicato bass tones on beats 1, 3, and 5, and by hand claps on beats 2, 4, 6, and 7:

	Clap		Clap		Clap	Clap
1	2	3	4	5	6	7
Bass		Bass		Bass		

(This septuple meter combines duple and triple meter. Each measure is subdivided into groups of 2 and 3 beats: 1–2, 3–4, 5–6–7.) Exciting syncopations occur when weak beats 2 and 4 are accented by hand claps.

After the opening 6 measures, the piano enters with an introductory musical idea that begins on the upbeat and emphasizes the first beat of each measure. Soon the piano part becomes more tuneful and rhythmically intricate. After the piano solo, the bass and hand claps are joined by percussive sounds in a rhythm that is faster than the beat. The final piano solo rounds off *Unsquare Dance* on a comic note.

4 Music Notation

We use written words to express our thoughts and communicate with others when we can't be with them. In music, ideas are also written down, or *notated,* so that performers can play pieces unknown to them.

Notation is a system of writing music so that specific pitches and rhythms can be communicated. It is explained here—very briefly—primarily to help you recognize rising and falling melodic lines and long and short notes so that you can follow the music examples in this book. (You will find it helpful to review the material on pitch and rhythm in Sections 1 and 3.)

Notating Pitch

With music notation, we can indicate exact pitches by the upward or downward placement of symbols—called *notes*—on a *staff.* A **note** is an oval. (Its duration is indicated by whether it is black or white or has a *stem* and *flags,* as will be explained later, under "Notating Rhythm.") A **staff** (plural, *staves*) is a set of five horizontal lines. Notes are positioned either on the lines of the staff or between them, in the spaces; the higher a note is placed on the staff, the higher its pitch:

If a pitch falls above or below the range indicated by the staff, short, horizontal **ledger lines** are used:

Seven of the twelve pitches (tones) that fill the octave in western music are named after the first seven letters of the alphabet: A, B, C, D, E, F, G. This sequence is repeated over and over to represent the "same" tones in higher and lower octaves, and it corresponds to the white keys of the piano. The other five tones of the octave correspond to the black keys of the piano and are indicated by one of the same seven letters plus a **sharp sign** (♯) or a **flat sign** (♭) (see the illustration on the next page). Thus, the pitch between C and D may be called C sharp (C♯; higher than C) or D flat (D♭; lower than D). A **natural sign** (♮) is used to cancel a previous sharp or flat sign.

A **clef** is placed at the beginning of the staff to show the pitch of each line and space. The two most common clefs are the **treble clef,** used for relatively high ranges (such as

Following is a chart that shows the relationships of the duration symbols:

One whole note lasts as long as 2 half notes or 4 quarter notes, and so on. As shown, the flags of several eighth notes or sixteenth notes in succession are usually joined by a horizontal **beam.**

To lengthen the duration of a tone (and add rhythmic variety), we can make it a **dotted note;** adding a dot (·) to the right of a note increases its duration by half. Thus, 1 quarter note ordinarily equals 2 eighth notes, but 1 dotted quarter note equals 3 eighth notes:

Frequently, a dotted note is followed by one that is much shorter; this long-short pattern, called **dotted rhythm,** strongly emphasizes the beat (and is therefore often used in marches).

A **tie** (⌢) is another way to lengthen the duration of a note. When two notes in a row are the same pitch and are connected by a tie, the first note is lengthened by the duration of the second. In the following example, the note on *dell* lasts as long as 1 dotted quarter note plus 1 quarter note; the two tied notes become one continuous sound:

The farm - er in the dell, ___ The farm - er in the dell, ___

We also can add rhythmic variety by shortening the duration of a note. One method is the **triplet,** three notes of equal duration notated as a group within a curved line and the number 3. Such a group lasts only as long as if it were two notes of equal value:

Notating Silence (Rests)

Duration of silence is notated by using a symbol called a **rest.** Rests are pauses; their durations correspond to those of notes:

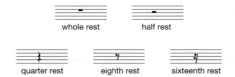

whole rest   half rest

quarter rest   eighth rest   sixteenth rest

Notating Meter

A *time signature* (or *meter signature*) shows the meter of a piece. It appears at the beginning of the staff at the start of a piece (and again later if the meter changes) and consists of two numbers, one on top of the other. The upper number tells how many beats fall in a measure; the lower number tells what kind of note gets the beat (2 = half note, for instance, and 4 = quarter note). Thus the time signature $\frac{2}{4}$ shows that there are 2 beats to the measure (duple meter) and a quarter note gets 1 beat. Duple meter may also be shown as $\frac{2}{2}$ (or by its symbol, ¢); quadruple meter is usually $\frac{4}{4}$ (or ℂ). The most common triple meter is $\frac{3}{4}$.

The Score

A *score* shows the music for each instrumental or vocal category in a performing group; often, an orchestral score will show more than fifteen different staves of notation (see the illustration on the next page).

A page from the orchestra score of Tchaikovsky's *Romeo and Juliet.*

5 Melody

For many of us, music means melody. We've sung in schools, cars, camps, and the shower. After hearing a piece of music, we usually remember its melody best. Familiar melodies have the power to recall past emotions and experiences. Words and instruments aren't required; we don't need singers and large orchestras—just a few notes.

Melody is easier to recognize than to define. It must have something special, since melody is common to the music of all times and all peoples, but probably the elusive "something" that evokes so much feeling will never be captured by a dictionary definition. We do know that a **melody** is a series of single tones that add up to a recognizable whole. A melody begins, moves, and ends; it has direction, shape, and continuity. The up-and-down movement of its pitches conveys tension and release, expectation and arrival. This is the melodic *curve,* or *line.*

A melody moves by small intervals called **steps** or by larger ones called **leaps.** A step is the interval between two adjacent tones in the *do-re-mi* scale (from *do* to *re, re* to *mi,* etc.). Any interval larger than a step is a leap (*do* to *mi,* for example). Besides moving up or down by step or leap, a melody may simply repeat the same note. A melody's *range* is the distance between its lowest and highest tones. Range may be wide or narrow. *Mary Had a Little Lamb* moves mostly by step within a narrow range; *Rock-a-Bye Baby* has a wider range and many leaps as well as steps. Melodies written for instruments tend to have a wider range than those for voices, and they often contain wide leaps and rapid notes that would be difficult to sing.

The specific order of the long and short notes in a melody is important. A well-known melody can be almost unrecognizable if it is not sung in proper rhythm. Note durations, as well as pitches, contribute to the distinctive character of a melody. For example, the smooth, even rhythm of *Twinkle, Twinkle, Little Star* is calm, but the snappy, dotted (long-short) rhythm of *The Battle Hymn of the Republic* is exciting. Try reversing these rhythms: the first melody will lose its calmness, and the second will lack excitement.

How the tones of a melody are performed can vary its effect, too. Sometimes they are sung or played in a smooth, connected style called **legato.** Or they may be performed in a short, detached manner called **staccato.**

Many melodies are made up of shorter parts called **phrases.** These short units may have similar pitch and rhythm patterns that help unify the melody. On the other hand, contrasting phrases can furnish variety. Phrases often appear in balanced pairs; a first phrase of rising pitches may be followed by a second phrase of falling pitches. The second phrase may partly repeat the first but have a more conclusive ending, a point of arrival. Such a resting place at the end of a phrase is called a **cadence.**

As you get deeper into the music explored in this book, you'll find a wealth of melodies: vocal and instrumental, long and short, simple and complex. To help sort them out, let's see how some basic melodic principles apply to four familiar tunes. These are short melodies, easy to sing and easy to remember.

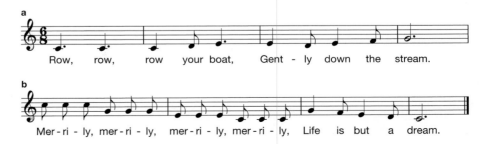

Row, Row, Row Your Boat is first. Sing the tune only up to the word *stream*. Notice that on *stream* the melody comes to a point of arrival, a resting place. This ends the first phrase of the melody. But the melody seems incomplete, as though it had posed a question. Now sing the rest of the melody, the second phrase, beginning on *merrily*. It ends conclusively and seems to answer the question. Each phrase has a point of arrival, a cadence. The first phrase ends with an **incomplete cadence,** which sets up expectations; the second phrase ends with a **complete cadence,** which gives an answer, a sense of finality.

Each phrase of *Row, Row, Row Your Boat* is the same length, a formula typical of many melodies called *tunes*. The two phrases create a feeling of symmetry and balance. The first begins with repeated notes (C–C–C—*Row, row, row*) and then moves upward by step (D–E–F–G—*your boat, Gently down the stream*); the second moves downward by leap (C–G–E–C—*Merrily, merrily, merrily, merrily*) and finally by step (G–F–E–D–C—*Life is but a dream*). Often the highest tone of a melody will be the **climax,** the emotional focal point. In this song the climax comes on the first *merrily,* at the beginning of the second phrase. The leaps create a carefree quality in the quick notes on the repeated *merrily.*

The two contrasting phrases of the song can be symbolized by the letters a and b. In discussing music it's helpful to let letters represent various sections of a piece. Lowercase letters (a, b, etc.) are used for phrases and relatively short sections, while capital letters (A, B, etc.) are used for longer sections. When the phrases or sections of the music differ significantly, as in this song, we use different letters: a b. When one section exactly repeats another, the letter is repeated: a a. When a section is a varied repetition of a previous one, the previous letter is repeated but with a prime mark: a a′.

Now sing the entire nursery tune *Mary Had a Little Lamb:*

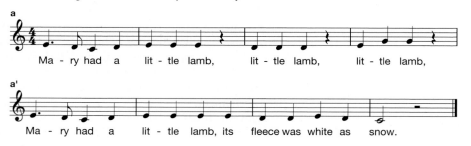

Like *Row, Row, Row Your Boat,* this melody has two balancing phrases, the first ending up in the air with an incomplete cadence, and the second ending conclusively with a complete cadence. However, the two songs also differ from each other. In *Mary Had a Little Lamb* the second phrase begins exactly like the first. The melody starts over again but proceeds to a different, more conclusive ending. This partial repetition serves to unify the melody. The phrases in *Mary Had a Little Lamb* may be symbolized as a a′. As we'll see, melodic repetition, both exact and varied, plays an important unifying role in all kinds of music.

Both repeated and contrasting phrases can be heard in the cowboy song *Home on the Range:*

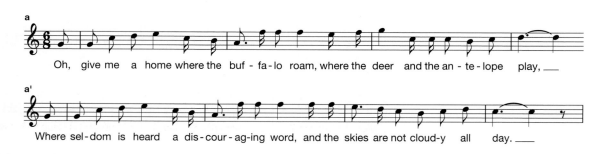

A yearning quality is projected here through a longer and more complex form than that of the two other tunes. There are four phrases, and, as in *Mary Had a Little Lamb,* the second phrase is a repetition of the first but has a more conclusive ending. (Sing the first two phrases a few times, comparing the note on *play* with the note on *day*.) The first two phrases may be outlined a a′ (to show repetition with variation). Contrast is introduced in the third phrase of the melody, the climactic refrain *Home, home on the range.* This phrase begins in a new way—on the highest pitch of the melody—and may be labeled b. The concluding fourth phrase (*Where seldom is heard*) is a repetition of the beginning but with a final ending. The song as a whole is outlined a a′ b a′. The principle of *statement* (a a′), *departure* or *contrast* (b), and *return* (a′) that governs *Home on the Range* is essential to musical form.

Our final example, *America,* differs from the other songs in that its phrases are not of equal length:

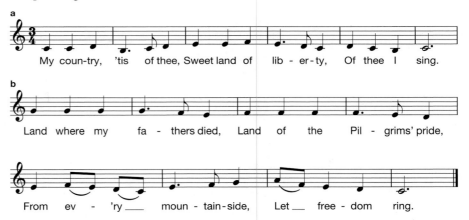

The second phrase (starting from *Land*) is longer than the first and creates a feeling of continuation rather than balance or symmetry. An interesting aspect of *America* is that a repeated rhythmic pattern is used to unify the melody. The rhythmic pattern for *My country 'tis of thee* is repeated for *Sweet land of liberty, Land where my fathers died,* and *Land of the Pilgrims' pride.*

Notice that the melody for *Land of the Pilgrims' pride* is simply a repetition a little lower of the preceding *Land where my fathers died.* Such a repetition of a melodic pattern on a higher or lower pitch is called a **sequence.** This is an impelling device of varied repetition that gives a melody a strong sense of direction.

We've considered tunes that are complete in themselves. Frequently, a melody will serve as the starting point for a more extended piece of music and, in stretching out, will go through all kinds of changes. This kind of melody is called a theme.

The concepts and vocabulary introduced in this chapter can be used to study melodies of any style. Try using them to examine your favorite songs. You may pinpoint parts that you like and, consequently, enjoy the melodies a bit more because you know what makes them tick.

Basic Set:
CD 1 **49**

Main melody (A)
49 0:00
Contrasting melody (B)
50 0:45
Return of main melody (A)
51 1:13

Over the Rainbow (1938), by Harold Arlen

A beautiful legato melody creates a feeling of wonderment in *Over the Rainbow*, by Harold Arlen (1905–1986). This song is from the movie *The Wizard of Oz* (1939), starring the young Judy Garland. Like many popular songs, *Over the Rainbow* has a main melody (A) and a contrasting one (B). The song can be outlined as A A B A, followed by a closing part. The main melody (A: *Somewhere over the rainbow way up high . . .*) is presented and then repeated with different words (A: *Somewhere over the rainbow skies are blue . . .*). Then we hear the contrasting melody (B: *Someday I'll wish upon a star . . .*), and then a return of the main melody (A: *Somewhere over the rainbow bluebirds fly . . .*). The closing part of the song (*If happy little bluebirds fly . . .*) is a varied and abridged return of the contrasting melody.

The main melody (A) grows out of the opening upward leap of an octave that beautifully expresses the word *somewhere.*

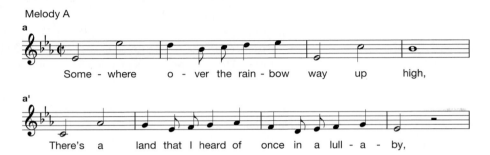

A large upward leap followed by a downward step appears three times, with changes of pitch, giving the melody a sense of unity and direction.

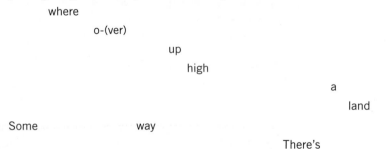

The second upward leap, which is slightly smaller than the first, is appropriate for the words *way up.* In all, the melody features upward leaps from low tones to higher tones that gradually descend.

Melody A is made up of two related phrases that can be symbolized as a (*Somewhere over the rainbow . . .*) and a′ (*There's a land . . .*). The second phrase (a′) begins somewhat like the first; but it starts on a lower pitch, and its upward leap is smaller. Whereas the first phrase (a) ends up in the air with an incomplete cadence (on *high*), the second phrase (a′) ends definitively with a complete cadence (on *lullaby*). The feeling given by A of motion to a conclusion is heightened by a sequence: the melodic pattern for *land that I heard of* is repeated on a lower pitch for *once in a lulla(by).*

Melody B is more speechlike in character.

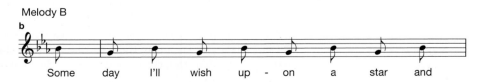

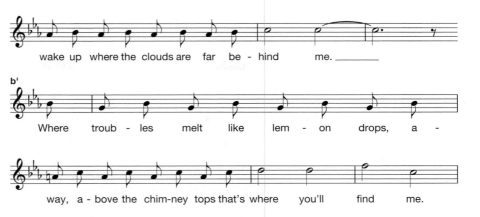

wake up where the clouds are far be - hind me. _____

b'

Where troub - les melt like lem - on drops, a -

way, a - bove the chim-ney tops that's where you'll find me.

It moves in a narrower range, uses quicker rhythms, and repeats two-note patterns. Like the main tune, melody B contains two phrases: b (*Someday I'll wish . . .*) and b´ (*Where troubles melt . . .*). It rises to a climax on its next-to-last tone (*find*). Together, melodies A and B produce a satisfying feeling of balance in this enchanting song.

6 Harmony

When folksingers accompany themselves on a guitar, they add support, depth, and richness to the melody. We call this *harmonizing*. Most music in western culture is a blend of melody and harmony.

Harmony refers to the way chords are constructed and how they follow each other. A *chord* is a combination of three or more tones sounded at once. Essentially, a chord is a group of simultaneous tones, and a melody is a series of individual tones heard one after another. As a melody unfolds, it provides clues for harmonizing—some of the tones of the melody are usually included in the chords of the accompaniment. But a melody does not always dictate a specific series, or *progression,* of chords. The same melody may be harmonized in several musically convincing ways. A musician such as a folksinger will experiment and choose the chords that best fit a melody's mood. Chord progressions will enrich a melody by adding emphasis, surprise, suspense, or finality. In today's popular music, a songwriter often composes the melody while an arranger supplies the accompanying chords. Composers of classical music create both the melody and the harmony, often at the same time.

There is a tendency to think that a melody is composed first and that the chords are added later. Actually, it's often the other way around. For centuries, repeated chord progressions have given rise to improvised melodies. In jazz, for example, a pianist may play the same basic progression of chords over and over again while a trumpet player invents a continually changing melody to fit the piano's pattern. When several jazz musicians improvise different melodies at once, their music is held together by the organized chordal background—by the harmony.

Taylor Swift blends melody and harmony by accompanying herself on the guitar.

As different as Bach, Beethoven, jazz, folk, and rock may seem, some of the same chord progressions can be heard in all. Although new chords and new progressions continually enter the language of music, the basic chordal vocabulary has remained fairly constant. We'll look now at a few principles of harmony that have proved so useful for so long.

Consonance and Dissonance

Some chords have been considered stable and restful, others unstable and tense. A tone combination that is stable is called a **consonance.** Consonances are points of arrival, rest, and resolution. (Whoever coined the phrase *living in harmony with others* had consonance in mind.) A tone combination that is unstable is called a **dissonance.** Its tension demands an onward motion to a stable chord. A dissonance has its **resolution** when it moves to a consonance. When this resolution is delayed or accomplished in unexpected ways, a feeling of drama, suspense, or surprise is created. In this way a composer plays with the listener's sense of expectation. Dissonant chords are active and move music forward. Traditionally they have been considered harsh and have been used in music that expresses pain, grief, and conflict.

Now that consonance and dissonance have been defined, be aware that they can exist in varying degrees. Some consonant chords are more stable than others, and some dissonant chords are more tense than others. Dissonant chords have been used with increasing freedom over the centuries, so that often a chord considered intolerably harsh in one period has later come to seem rather mild.

The Triad

A great variety of chords have been used in music. Some chords consist of three different tones; others have four, five, or even more. Depending on their makeup, chords sound simple or complex, calm or tense, bright or dark.

The simplest, most basic chord is the **triad** (pronounced *try'-ad*), which consists of three tones. To indicate that a triad's three tones are played at one time, it is notated as follows:

A triad is made up of alternate tones of the scale, such as the first tone (*do*), the third (*mi*), and the fifth (*sol*). The bottom tone is called the *root;* the others are a third and a fifth above the root. (From *do* to *mi* in the scale is the interval of a third; from *do* to *sol* is the interval of a fifth.)

A triad built on the first, or tonic, note of the scale (*do*) is called the **tonic chord** (*do-mi-sol*); it is the main chord of a piece, the most stable and conclusive. Traditionally, the tonic chord would usually begin a composition and almost always end it.

The triad built on the fifth note of the scale (*sol*) is next in importance to the tonic. It is called the **dominant chord** (*sol-ti-re*). The dominant chord is strongly pulled toward the tonic chord. This attraction has great importance in music. A dominant chord sets up tension that is resolved by the tonic chord. The progression from dominant to tonic gives a strong sense of conclusion, and that's why it is used so often at the end of a phrase, a melody, or an entire piece. In *America,* for example, the next-to-last syllable is harmonized by a dominant chord, and the last word by the tonic chord:

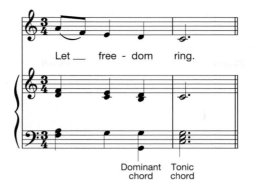

Dominant chord   Tonic chord

A progression from dominant chord to tonic chord is called a **cadence.** The word *cadence* means both the resting point at the end of a melodic phrase (as was noted above, in Section 5) and a chord progression that gives a sense of conclusion.

Broken Chords (Arpeggios)

A chord has just been described as a group of tones played together, as a block of sound. But the tones of a chord also may be presented in other ways. When the individual tones of a chord are sounded one after another, it is called a **broken chord,** or an **arpeggio.** Arpeggios may appear in the melody or in the accompaniment. *The Star-Spangled Banner* is a melody that begins with such a broken chord, or arpeggio. The notes of the tonic chord are heard one after another instead of together:

Broken chord (arpeggio)   Chord

As you go on with your study of music in this book, the importance of harmony will become more and more apparent. You'll see that chord progressions can produce powerful emotional effects and can be more than simply a background for melody. Sometimes the expressiveness of a melody depends on the accompanying harmony, as in Chopin's Prelude in E Minor, which will be examined next.

Harmony helps give music variety and movement. There's a relaxation of tension when a dissonant chord resolves to a consonant chord; and there's a sense of conclusion when the dominant chord moves to the tonic. The effects of harmony are endless, varying with the style of a particular era and the desires of individual composers.

Prelude in E Minor for Piano, Op. 28, No. 4 (1839), by Frédéric Chopin

Basic Set:
CD 1 52

Brief Set:
CD 1 36

Chopin's harmony makes a vital contribution to the brooding quality of this miniature lasting around 2 minutes. Without the pulsating chords of its accompaniment, the melody might seem aimless and monotonous. It hardly moves, alternating obsessively between a long note and a shorter one right above it. But the returning long note seems to change in color, because each time there is a different dissonant chord below it. The dissonant chords underscore the melancholy of this prelude, which is meant to be played *espressivo* (*expressively*).

In the middle of the prelude, a return of the opening melody leads to a brief but passionate climax with a crescendo, faster rhythm, and an acceleration of tempo (accelerando). The agitation rapidly subsides as we again hear returning long notes in the melody. Toward the end of the piece, a mildly dissonant chord is followed by a brief pause. This silence is filled with expectancy, as we wait for the dissonance to resolve. Finally the tension is released in the three solemn chords of the closing cadence.

LISTENING OUTLINE

CHOPIN, Prelude in E Minor for Piano

Largo, Duple meter ($\frac{2}{2}$), E minor

Piano

(Duration, 2:16)

`52` `36` 0:00   **1.** Sad melody with obsessively returning long notes, accompanied by pulsating dissonant chords, ***p***,

accompaniment stops, melody rises to

1:00   **2. a.** Return of sad melody; tempo acceleration and crescendo to ***f*** climax, decrescendo.

1:25   **b.** Obsessive long notes in melody, ***p***, soft dissonant chord, brief pause.

1:56   **c.** Final cadence of three low chords.

Roger Kamien, Pianist, Playing Chopin's Prelude in E Minor

A performer conveys to the listener the sound and emotional message of music. Like an actor playing a role, a performer breathes life into symbols on a page. Both actors and musicians move their audiences through changes of pace and emphasis.

Since indications of tempo, dynamics, legato, and staccato are not absolutely precise, much is left to the interpretation of the performer. A composition marked allegro (fast), for example, might be played more rapidly by one performer than another. Fine singers or instrumentalists put a personal stamp on the music they perform, so the same piece can sound quite different when interpreted by different artists.

To illustrate the role of the performer, I would like to share with you some of the decisions involved in my performance of Chopin's Prelude in E Minor, Op. 28,

No. 4, included in the recording set (see the discussion and listening outline on pages 47–48). For me, the Prelude in E Minor is an emotional journey from the profound grief of the beginning, through a climactic outburst of despair, to a final acceptance of death. My tempo is very slow (largo), as Chopin indicates, but not excessively so. To emphasize the changes in color of the long notes in the melody, which return obsessively, I play each one at a slightly different dynamic level. In the pulsating accompanying chords, I stress the dissonant tones, either by subtly lengthening them, or by playing them a little louder than the consonant tones. To intensify the climax that grows out of the return of the opening melody, I momentarily quicken the tempo, as Chopin indicates. Toward the end of the Prelude, I give extra time to the pause following the questioning dissonant chord, thus heightening expectancy before the final low cadence.

You may find it interesting to compare my recorded performance of Chopin's Prelude in E Minor with performances by two other pianists. How do the three performances differ in expression, tempo, dynamic range, and relationship between melody and accompaniment? All three pianists have played the same notes, and yet they have made three different statements. That is what molding an interpretation means.

7 Key

Practically all familiar melodies are built around a central tone. The other tones of the melody gravitate toward this central one. Since the central tone is especially stable and restful, a melody usually ends on it. To feel the gravitational pull of a central tone, sing *America* and stop after the next-to-last word, *freedom;* then, after a few seconds, sing the ending tone of *ring.*

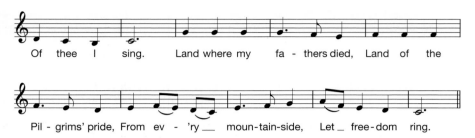

Of thee I sing. Land where my fa - thers died, Land of the

Pil - grims' pride, From ev - 'ry ⌣ moun-tain-side, Let ⌣ free-dom ring.

You probably felt uneasy until you supplied the last tone. This central tone is the **key-note,** or **tonic,** of the melody. The keynote can be E, or A, or any of the twelve tones that fill the octave in western music. When a piece is in the key of C, for example, C is the keynote, or tonic.

Key involves not only a central tone but also a central scale and chord. A piece in the key of C has a basic scale, *do-re-mi-fa-sol-la-ti-do,* with C as its *do,* or tonic. And the basic chord of a piece in C is a tonic triad with C as its root, or bottom tone. As was noted in Section 6, the tonic triad is made up of *do-mi-sol*—the first, third, and fifth tones of the basic scale. Just as familiar melodies generally end on the keynote, compositions traditionally end with the restful tonic chord. *Key,* then, refers to the presence of a central note, scale, and chord within a piece. Another term for key is **tonality.**

After 1900, some composers abandoned the traditional system, but even today much of the music we hear is built around a central tone, chord, and scale.

The Major Scale

So far, we've referred to the *do-re-mi-fa-sol-la-ti-do* scale as a main element of key, but we have not actually defined what a scale is. A **scale** is made up of the basic pitches of a piece of music arranged in order from low to high or from high to low. Many different scales have been used in various eras and cultures. The basic scales of western music from the late 1600s to 1900 were the *major* and *minor.* These scales continued to be widely used during the twentieth century.

Let's first consider the **major scale,** the familiar *do-re-mi-fa-sol-la-ti-do.* Sing this scale and note that you produce seven different pitches and then arrive at the high *do*—the eighth tone—which is really a duplication of the first tone an octave higher. As was pointed out in Section 1, the octave is the distance or interval between the first and eighth tones of the major scale. The major scale has a specific pattern of intervals between its successive tones.

Two kinds of intervals are found in the major scale: *half steps* and *whole steps.* The **half step** is the smallest interval traditionally used in western music. The **whole step** is twice as large as the half step. Here is the pattern of whole and half steps making up the major scale:

Pattern of whole and half steps making up the major scale.

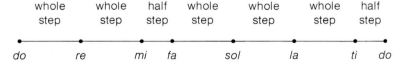

whole step	whole step	half step	whole step	whole step	whole step	half step
do	re	mi	fa	sol	la	ti do

There is an especially strong pull from *ti* to *do,* because the interval is a small one, a half step. You'll feel this pull when you sing the scale and stop on *ti.*

The illustration on the next page shows a major scale with C as the beginning tone. The C major scale uses only the white keys of the piano. There are half steps between the tones E and F, and between B and C; these pairs of tones are not separated by black keys. *America* as notated near the beginning of this section is based on the C major scale; it is in the key of C major.

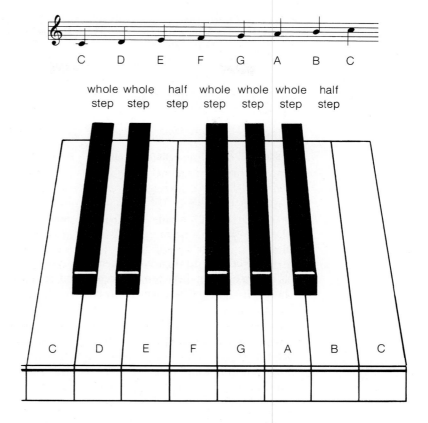

Major scale beginning on C.

We can construct similar major scales by starting on any one of the twelve tones that fill an octave. The same pattern of intervals can begin on any of these tones, and so there are twelve possible major scales. To understand this better, imagine the major scale as a ruler on which eight marks are spaced irregularly (as shown in the previous *do-re-mi* diagram). The pattern of marks stays the same no matter where the "ruler" is placed. Similarly, the pattern of whole and half steps making up a major scale will sound the same even when the scales start on different keynotes.

For us, the important point is not the technicality of half and whole steps but the idea of a scale as a pattern of intervals. Also important is the idea of the keynote (or beginning, or tonic) of the major scale; it is the scale's central tone toward which all others seem to pull. The conclusive quality we hear in the keynote is not a result of any law of nature—it's rooted in cultural conditioning.

The Minor Scale

Along with the major scale, the minor scale is fundamental to western music. *Joshua Fought the Battle of Jericho* is a tune based on a minor scale:

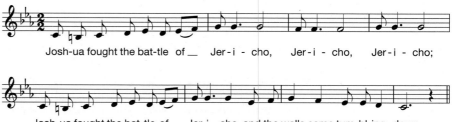

The *minor scale*—like the major—consists of seven different tones and an eighth tone that duplicates the first an octave higher; but it differs from the major scale in its pattern of intervals. The pattern of the minor scale also can begin on any of the twelve tones in an octave, and so there are twelve possible minor scales. As just noted, *Joshua Fought the Battle of Jericho* is based on a minor scale beginning on C; it is in the key of C minor. Here is a comparison between a major and a minor scale both starting on C:*

C major scale	whole step		whole step		half step		whole step		whole step		whole step		half step	
		C		D		E		F		G		A		B	C

C minor scale	whole step		half step		whole step		whole step		half step		whole step		whole step	
		C		D		E♭		F		G		A♭		B♭	C

The crucial difference between major and minor is that in the minor scale there is only a half step between the second and third tones. A major scale has a whole step here. This small difference greatly changes the sound of a scale and the mood of music using that scale. Music based on minor scales tends to sound serious or melancholy. Almost all funeral marches, for example, are in minor keys. Also, the tonic triad built from a minor scale is a minor chord, but a triad built from a major scale is a major chord. Minor chords sound darker than major chords. Composers use the differences between minor and major to create contrasts of mood. A serious or agitated melody in C minor may be followed by a brighter tune in C major. We learn to tell the difference between minor and major as we learn to distinguish one color from another, by repeated exposure.

The Key Signature

When a piece of music is based on a major scale, we say it is in a *major key;* when it is based on a minor scale, it is said to be in a *minor key.* For instance, a piece based on a major scale with D as its keynote is in the key of D major. Similarly, if a composition is based on a minor scale with the keynote F, the composition is in the key of F minor. Each major or minor scale has a specific number of sharps or flats ranging from none to seven. To indicate the key of a piece of music, the composer uses a *key signature,* consisting of sharp or flat signs immediately following the clef sign at the beginning of the staff.

To illustrate, here is the key signature for D major, which contains two sharps:

By using a key signature, a composer avoids having to write a sharp or a flat sign before every sharped or flatted note in a piece. (The seven sharps in the key of C sharp major and the seven flats in the key of C flat major would otherwise make notation very complicated!)

---

*The minor scale shown in the example above is the *natural minor,* one of the three minor scales. The other two kinds are the *harmonic minor* and the *melodic minor* scales. The three types of minor scales have slight variations in their patterns of intervals, but all can begin on any tone of the octave, and all will produce a sound that contrasts with the major scale as described here.

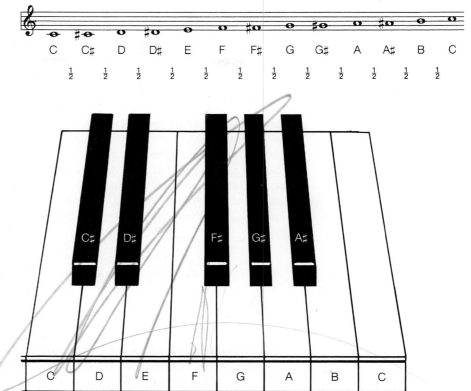

The chromatic scale consists of all twelve tones of the octave—all the white keys and black keys in one octave on the piano.

The Chromatic Scale

The twelve tones of the octave—*all* the white and black keys in one octave on the piano—form the ***chromatic scale.*** Unlike those of the major or minor scales, tones of the chromatic scale are all the same distance apart. As the illustration above shows, each tone is a half step away from the next one.

The word *chromatic* comes from the Greek word *chroma, color.* Its derivation provides a clue to the traditional function of the chromatic scale, which is to color or embellish the tones of the major and minor scales. The chromatic scale is not like the major or minor: it does not define a key. Its tones contribute a sense of motion and tension. Composers throughout history have used it to evoke strong feelings of grief, loss, and sorrow. We'll see that since 1900 it has become independent of major and minor scales and has been used as the basis for entire compositions.

Modulation: Change of Key

Most short melodies we know remain in a single key from beginning to end. However, in longer pieces of music, variety and contrast are created by using more than one key. A composition may begin in the key of C major, for example, and then proceed to G major. Shifting from one key to another within the same piece is called ***modulation.***

A modulation is like a temporary shift in the center of gravity. When the music starts out in the key of C major, for instance, C is the central tone, and the C major scale and chord predominate. With a modulation to G major, G temporarily becomes the central tone, and the G major scale and chord are now the main ones. Though modulations are sometimes subtle and difficult to spot, they produce subconscious effects that increase our enjoyment of the music.

Tonic Key

No matter how often a piece changes key, there is usually one main key, called the *tonic* or *home key.* The tonic key is the central key around which the whole piece is organized. Traditionally, a piece would usually begin in the home key and practically always end in it. A composition in the key of C major, for example, would begin in the home key, modulate to several other keys—say, G major and A minor—and finally conclude in the home key of C major. The other keys are subordinate to the tonic.

Modulating away from the tonic key is like visiting: we may enjoy ourselves during the visit, but after a while we're glad to go home. In music, modulations set up tensions that are resolved by returning to the home key. For centuries, the idea of a central key was a basic principle of music. But after 1900, some composers wrote music that ignored the traditional system. The results of this revolutionary step are explored in Part VII, "The Twentieth Century and Beyond."

8 | Musical Texture

At a particular moment within a piece, we may hear one unaccompanied melody, several simultaneous melodies, or a melody with supporting chords. To describe these various possibilities, we use the term *musical texture;* it refers to how many different layers of sound are heard at once, to what kind of layers they are (melody or harmony), and to how they are related to each other.

Like fabric, musical texture is described as transparent, dense, thin, thick, heavy, or light. Composers can vary the textures within their music to create contrast and drama. We'll look now at the three basic musical textures—*monophonic, polyphonic,* and *homophonic.*

Monophonic Texture

The texture of a single melodic line without accompaniment is *monophonic,* meaning literally *having one sound.* If you sing alone, you make monophonic music. Performance of a single melodic line at the same pitch by more than one instrument or voice is playing or singing in *unison* and results in a fuller, richer-sounding monophonic texture. Examples of unison, with men and women singing the same notes in different octaves, appear in the *Hallelujah* chorus by George Frideric Handel, analyzed on pages 177–178.

Polyphonic Texture

Simultaneous performance of two or more melodic lines of relatively equal interest produces the texture called *polyphonic,* meaning *having many sounds.* In polyphony several melodic lines compete for attention. (When several jazz musicians improvise different melodies at once, they produce polyphony.) Polyphony adds a dimension that has been compared to perspective in painting: each line enriches and heightens the expression of the others.

This mutual enhancement points up a difference between music and speech. If many people are saying different things at one time, the result can be confusing. But when several different melodies are sung together, highly expressive sounds may be created. This technique of combining several melodic lines into a meaningful whole is called **counterpoint.** (The term *contrapuntal texture* is sometimes used in place of *polyphonic texture.*)

To fully enjoy the simultaneous flow of several melodic lines, you may have to hear a piece of music a few times. Repeated hearings lead to a satisfying awareness of how the whole is woven from the parts. It's often helpful to listen first for the top line, then for the bottom line, and then for the middle lines. Such selective listening increases our appreciation of contrasting rhythms and melodic shapes and gives us a chance to hear how different lines are emphasized at any given moment.

Polyphonic music often contains **imitation,** which occurs when a melodic idea is presented by one voice or instrument and is then restated immediately by another voice or instrument. It's as though different lines of texture play follow the leader. Imitation is familiar to anyone who has sung *Row, Row, Row Your Boat:*

This familiar tune is a *round,* a song in which several people sing the same melody but each singer starts at a different time. By the time the first singer has reached *Merrily, merrily,* the second singer is only at *Gently down the stream* and the third is just beginning *Row, row, row your boat.* At any one time, all the voices are singing different parts of the same tune.

A round like *Row, Row, Row Your Boat* is an example of strict imitation; the different voices play follow the leader with exactly the same melody. But imitation is usually freer—the imitating line begins like the first line but then goes off on its own. A delightful feeling of give-and-take results when a short melodic idea is quickly passed from one voice or instrument to another. This happens often in polyphonic texture.

Homophonic Texture

When we hear one main melody accompanied by chords, the texture is **homophonic.** Attention is focused on the melody, which is supported and colored by sounds of subordinate interest. Homophonic texture is familiar to anyone who has heard a folksinger accompany himself or herself on a guitar. Though the accompaniment may be distinctive, it is there mainly to help carry the sound and meaning of the melody.

Row, Row, Row Your Boat, when harmonized by chords, is an example of homophonic texture:

A hymn sung by a choir can be another example of homophony. The melody of the hymn is sung by the voice on top, while other voices have lower lines that harmonize, or blend, with the melody but are less individual. Generally, these lower voices sing notes that are different from the main tune but move in the same rhythm. All the voices moving together produce a progression of chords, one for each syllable of the text.

Accompaniments in homophonic music vary widely in character and importance. They range from subdued background chords to surging sounds that almost hide the main melody. An expressive quality in the melody can be strengthened by the rhythm or harmony that accompanies it. Sometimes a subordinate line may assert its individuality briefly and compete for the listener's attention. At such times the texture is probably best described as being between homophonic and polyphonic.

Changes of Texture

A composer can create variety and contrast by changing textures within a composition. He or she might begin with a melody and a simple accompaniment and later weave the melody into a polyphonic web, or create drama by contrasting a single voice with massive chords sung by a chorus. A good example of textural variety is Georges Bizet's *Farandole.*

Farandole from *L'Arlésienne* Suite No. 2 (1879), by Georges Bizet[*]

Basic Set:
CD 1 53

Brief Set:
CD 1 37

The *Farandole* comes from music by Georges Bizet (1838–1875) for the play *L'Arlésienne* (*The Woman of Arles*), set in southern France. Two contrasting themes are heard in this exciting orchestral piece. The first, in minor, is a march theme adapted from a southern French folksong. The lively second theme, in major, has the character of the *farandole,* a southern French dance.

---

[*]*L'Arlésienne* Suites No. 1 and No. 2 are sets of pieces from the theater music composed by Bizet. Suite No. 2 was arranged by Bizet's friend Ernest Guiraud in 1879, after the composer's death.

Many changes of texture contribute to the *Farandole*'s exciting mood. The piece contains two kinds of homophonic texture: in one, the accompaniment and melody have the same rhythm; in the other, the rhythm of the accompaniment differs from that of the melody. The *Farandole* opens with the march theme and its accompaniment in the same rhythm. But when the lively dance theme is first presented, its accompanying chords do not duplicate the rhythm of the melody; instead, they simply mark the beat.

The *Farandole* also includes two kinds of polyphony: with and without imitation. Soon after the opening, the march theme is presented by the violins and then is imitated by the violas. At the end of the piece, polyphony results when the march and dance themes—previously heard in alternation—are presented simultaneously. In this concluding section, both themes are in major.

The *Farandole* also contains monophonic texture, which sets off the homophony and polyphony. Monophony is heard when the march theme is played by the strings in unison.

LISTENING OUTLINE

BIZET, *Farandole* from *L'Arlésienne* Suite No. 2

Allegro deciso (forceful allegro), march tempo, quadruple meter ($\frac{4}{4}$), D minor

Piccolo, 2 flutes, 2 oboes, 2 clarinets, 2 bassoons, 4 French horns, 2 trumpets, 2 cornets, 3 trombones, timpani, tambourine, bass drum, cymbals, 1st violins, 2d violins, violas, cellos, double basses

(Duration, 3:08)

53 **37** 0:00 **1. a.** Full orchestra, *ff*, march theme; homophonic (accompaniment in same rhythm as melody), minor.

54 **38** 0:16 **b.** Violins imitated by violas, march theme; polyphonic, minor.

55 **39** 0:33 **2. a.** High woodwinds, ***ppp***, dance theme; faster tempo, homophonic (accompanying chords on beat), major; decorative rushes in violins, long crescendo to *ff* as dance theme is repeated.

1:17 **b.** Full orchestra, ***fff***, dance theme.

56 **40** 1:28 **3. a.** Strings only, *ff*, march theme in faster tempo; monophonic, minor.

1:39 **b.** High woodwinds, ***ppp***, dance theme; homophonic.

1:45 **c.** Strings only, *ff*, continue march theme; monophonic, then homophonic as lower strings accompany melody.

1:56 **d.** High woodwinds, ***ppp***, dance theme; homophonic. Crescendo to

57 **41** 2:19 **4.** Full orchestra, ***fff***, dance and march themes combined; polyphonic, major. Homophonic ending.

9 | Musical Form

The word *form* is associated with shape, structure, organization, and coherence. Form calls to mind the human body or a balanced arrangement of figures in a painting. **Form** in music is the organization of musical elements in time. In a musical composition, pitch, tone color, dynamics, rhythm, melody, and texture interact to produce a sense of shape and structure. All parts of the composition are interrelated. Our memory lets us perceive the overall form by recalling the various parts and how they relate to each other. The form becomes clearer as we develop awareness and recall these parts through repeated listening. As listeners, we can respond more fully to the emotional power and meaning of a musical composition when we appreciate its form.

Techniques That Create Musical Form

Form has already been explored in connection with simple tunes like *Mary Had a Little Lamb* and *Home on the Range* (see Section 5). These tunes have phrases that are repeated—exactly or with variation—and phrases that are contrasted. Repetition, contrast, and variation are essential techniques in short tunes as well as in compositions lasting much longer. **Repetition** creates a sense of unity; **contrast** provides variety; and **variation,** in keeping some elements of a musical thought while changing others, gives a work unity and variety at the same time.

Repetition Musical repetition appeals to the pleasure we get in recognizing and remembering something. In a play, a scene or act is rarely repeated, but in music the repetition of melodies or extended sections is a technique widely used for binding a composition together. Through repetition, a melody is engraved in the memory.

The passage of time in music, as in life, influences the way we react to events. When a musical idea returns during a piece, the effect produced is not duplication but balance and symmetry.

Contrast Forward motion, conflict, and change of mood all come from contrast. Opposition—of loud and soft, strings and woodwinds, fast and slow, major and minor—propels and develops musical ideas. Sometimes the opposing ideas will have a common element that establishes a sense of continuity. At other times the contrast will be complete. (The contrast between black and white is different from the contrast between black and gray.) The separate identities of contrasting ideas are heightened if they are placed near each other. A composer can emphasize the power and excitement of one musical idea by contrasting it with another idea that is calm and lyrical, much as a photographer can show the height of a building by including a human figure in the photograph.

Variation In the variation of a musical idea, some of its features will be retained while others are changed. For example, the melody might be restated with a different accompaniment. Or the pitches of a melody might stay the same while its rhythmic pattern is changed. A whole composition can be created from a series of variations on a single musical idea.

Types of Musical Form

When *form* was defined at the beginning of this section, it was explained that a composition is made up of interrelated ideas. We looked at the basic techniques for combining these ideas into a coherent whole; repetition, contrast, and variation are used constantly in music of different styles and times. In Section 5 you studied several such patterns. (Remember that lowercase letters represented phrases or relatively short sections and capital letters represented longer sections.) *Home on the Range,* for example, was outlined as a a′ b a′. Other songs could be outlined by the same pattern of letters. (Think of *Oh, Susanna* or *Deck the Halls with Boughs of Holly.*) These songs are said to have the same form, or to be of the same formal type. It's important to note, however, that two compositions having the same form may be different in every other respect. Composers have used certain forms or patterns to organize their musical ideas. As listeners, we can respond more fully to music when we appreciate its form. We'll look now at two basic types of musical form: three-part, or ternary; and two-part, or binary.

Three-Part (Ternary) Form: A B A   During the last few centuries **three-part form (A B A)** has probably been used most frequently. This form can be represented as *statement* (A), *contrast* or departure (B), *return* (A). When the return of A is varied, the form is outlined A B A′. (Wagner's Prelude to Act III of *Lohengrin,* analyzed in Section 1, is in A B A′ form.) The contrast between A and B can be of any kind; A and B can be of equal or unequal length; and the way A returns after B differs from piece to piece— A may come back unexpectedly, or it may be clearly signaled (if B comes to a definite end with a cadence and a pause), or there may be a transition smoothly linking the two.

The sections of an A B A composition can be subdivided, for example, as follows:

A	B	A
a b a	c d c	a b a

In some pieces, a listener might mistake subsection b within the first A for the arrival of B; but as the music progresses, the greater contrast one hears with B will make it clear that b is a subsection. (For example, in Tchaikovsky's *Dance of the Reed Pipes,* studied below, the English horn melody in item 1c in the listening outline introduces a brief contrast within the A section, whereas the trumpet melody in item 2a brings a greater contrast and initiates the B section.)

Dance of the Reed Pipes from *Nutcracker* Suite (1892), by Peter Ilyich Tchaikovsky

Basic Set:
CD 1 58

Brief Set:
CD 1 42

The *Nutcracker* Suite is a set of dances from the fairy-tale ballet *The Nutcracker* by Peter Ilyich Tchaikovsky (1840–1893). *Dance of the Reed Pipes* is a particularly clear example of A B A′ form. Section A features three flutes playing a staccato melody which conveys a light, airy feeling and is repeated several times. The B section contrasts in tone color, melody, and key—it features a trumpet melody accompanied by brasses and cymbals. This melody moves by step within a narrow range, in contrast to the opening flute melody, which has a wide range and many leaps as well as steps. The F sharp minor key of the middle section contrasts with the D major key of the opening section. The concluding A′ section, in D major, is a shortened version of the opening A section.

LISTENING OUTLINE

TCHAIKOVSKY, *Dance of the Reed Pipes* from *Nutcracker* Suite

Three-part (ternary) form: A B A′

Moderato assai (very moderate), duple meter ($\frac{2}{4}$), D major

3 flutes, 2 oboes, English horn, 2 clarinets, bass clarinet, 2 bassoons, 4 French horns, 2 trumpets, 3 trombones, tuba, timpani, cymbals, 1st violins, 2d violins, violas, cellos, double basses

(Duration, 2:05)

A

 0:00   **1. a.** Low pizzicato strings, *p*, introduce

0:03   **b.** 3 flutes, staccato melody in major, pizzicato strings accompany. Melody repeated.

0:29   **c.** English horn melody, legato, flutes accompany, staccato.

0:41   **d.** 3 flutes, staccato melody, pizzicato strings accompany. Melody repeated. Cadence.

B

59 43   1:06   **2. a.** Trumpet melody in minor, brasses and cymbals accompany.

1:19   **b.** Strings repeat trumpet melody. Flutes lead back to

A′

60 44   1:37   **3.** 3 flutes, staccato melody in major, strings accompany. Melody repeated. Cadence.

Two-Part (Binary) Form: A B A composition made up of two sections is in *two-part form (A B).* Two-part form, frequently called *binary form,* gives a sense of *statement* (A) and *counterstatement* (B). Usually, compositions in two-part form repeat both parts: A A B B. Like the sections in three-part form, parts A and B in two-part form are often divided into subsections.

The two sections of a composition in binary form are often similar in rhythm, melody, and texture. However, the conclusion of each section is usually signaled by a cadence, held tones, or a brief pause. Part A begins in the tonic (home) key and ends either in the tonic or in a new key. Part B ends in the home key and brings a feeling of completion.

Bourrée from Suite in E Minor for Lute (probably around 1710), by Johann Sebastian Bach

This lighthearted bourrée—a type of dance-inspired piece in duple meter—comes from the Suite in E minor for lute, by Johann Sebastian Bach (1685–1750). The *lute* is a plucked string instrument popular during the sixteenth and seventeenth centuries. In

Basic Set:
CD 1 [61]

Brief Set:
CD 1 [45]

our recording, Julian Bream performs this bourrée—a favorite of classical guitarists—on an acoustic guitar.

Lasting about 1½ minutes, this bourrée is in two-part (binary) form, and is outlined A A B B, because each section is repeated. Throughout the bourrée, a lilting three-note rhythm, short-short-long, pervades the dancelike melody, which is supported by a steadily moving bass line. Within each section, rhythmic motion is almost continuous except for long, held tones which close parts A and B. These longer notes help define the conclusion of each section.

Part A, about 15 seconds in duration, is made up of two brief balancing phrases (a a′). The melody of these phrases gradually descends, almost entirely by step. The first phrase (a), in minor, closes with a quick downward scale pattern in the melody. The second phrase (a′) begins exactly like the first but proceeds to a different ending on a held major chord. In our recording, the guitarist chooses to repeat part A more loudly. (There are no indications of dynamics in Bach's score of the bourrée.)

Part B, about 30 seconds in length, is twice as long as A. The melody of B is more playful because it moves by leap as well as by step. It contains four brief phrases, each ending with a held note in the melody. The fourth phrase of B differs from the previous phrases because it quickly descends, repeating a three-note melodic pattern at increasingly lower pitches. (This is a downward *sequence*.) Part B ends in minor with a low, held octave. In our recording, the guitarist plays part B at a fairly soft dynamic level and concludes the repetition of B with a slight slowing of tempo to heighten the feeling of finality.

LISTENING OUTLINE

BACH, Bourrée from Suite in E Minor for Lute

Two-part (binary) form: A A B B

Duple meter ($\frac{2}{2}$), E minor

Acoustic guitar

(Duration 1:32)

A

61 | 45 | 0:00

1. Dancelike melody (a) in minor, short-short-long rhythm, moves downward mostly by step. Melody repeats (a′), descends to long, low, major chord. Soft dynamic level.

A   0:14   Part A repeated more loudly.

B

62 | 46 | 0:26

2. Three soft phrases with skips and steps, short-short-long rhythm continues; each brief phrase ends with long note in melody.

Fourth phrase quickly descends in sequential repetition of short-short-long pattern; minor key, long low octave ends B.

Downward sequence

B   0:57   Part B repeated.

Listening for Form

The musical patterns covered in this section fall into clearly defined units. However, music is continuous in its flow and sometimes can't be subdivided quite so easily. Some music seems to fit none of the frequently used patterns. But such music is not formless— it has a unique form that can be discovered through repeated hearings.

Again, it's important to lean on memory when you listen to music. Spotting musical ideas when they occur is fine, but it's only the beginning. The goal is to put the related ideas together by recognizing and remembering them and by finding the relationships between them. Through alert, repeated listening their overall shape will be made clear, and your response to music will be more satisfying.

10 Performance

Without a performer, music would remain soundless on a page. Unlike books and paintings, music speaks to us through a re-creator, a musician who makes the printed music sound. A composition, even a familiar one, can be a new experience each time it's performed.

It is the job of the ***performer*** to bring life to the printed symbols laid out by a composer. Just how loud is a chord marked ***f***? How fast is a section labeled *allegro?* No matter how many specific indications of rhythm, dynamics, or accent appear on a page, much is left to the performer. Like that of an actor, his or her interpretation is full of subtle timings and inflections. Performers project to an audience a mixture of their own feelings and the composer's intentions. Critics sometimes say about a particularly convincing interpretation that a performer is "identified" with a work and its composer. That's how close the relationship can be.

Music created at the same time it's performed is called ***improvisation.*** Bach at the organ and Beethoven at the piano were brilliant improvisers; their musical ideas flowed instantly from brain to fingers. Improvisation today is a vital aspect of jazz and nonwestern music.

Before the nineteenth century, performers were expected to add certain *ornaments,* or embellishing notes, not indicated in the printed music. Such ***embellishments*** offered variety and a sense of the performer's individuality. The many musicians today who perform music of the seventeenth and eighteenth centuries have made a point of

The virtuoso violinist Anne-Sophie Mutter, an artist of extraordinary technical mastery.

learning these devices from the past. With such knowledge they can play the music as the composer intended it to be played.

Music composed before 1600 presents the challenge of deciding what instruments to use. Often these were not specified by early composers; and to make things more difficult, some of the original instruments are not readily available today.

Like musical styles, performance styles change from generation to generation. A wide range of performance practices coexist during every historical period. Today, for example, some musicians play a composition as they think it was performed during the composer's lifetime. They will play on replicas of old instruments and use early performance techniques (as described in treatises of the period). The size of a vocal or instrumental group will be reduced to what was available in a church in 1360 or a castle in 1760. This quest for historical accuracy can be difficult, because concrete evidence about early performance practice is often sparse.

Other musicians today choose to use modern instruments when performing music of the eighteenth century and early nineteenth century. They believe that modern instruments can convey the composer's message more effectively than early instruments. Keyboard artists, for instance, will play Bach on a twentieth- or twenty-first-century concert grand piano rather than on a harpsichord, because their audiences are used to a much wider range of dynamics and are hearing the performances in larger halls. These musicians choose to use all our modern resources to make the composer's message come alive.

The Performer

Outstanding performers of music, nearly always, have been people with special talents that were recognized in childhood—a beautiful voice, unusual manual dexterity, an excellent ear for pitch, a keen memory. Like athletes, they have exceptional coordination, strength, and competitive drive. Most solo pianists and violinists play professionally before the age of fifteen. Singers and woodwind players wait longer for serious training, because their bodies need to mature.

Natural gifts are not enough. A developing performer studies for years with fine teachers, practices many hours a day, and cultivates musical taste and a sense of style. Out of all this may come a *virtuoso,* an artist of extraordinary technical mastery. The great solo performers are a breed apart. Above and beyond their natural gifts and training, they project a personal magnetism that can draw cheers from an audience. These rare few are constantly renewed by the challenge of performance and can make their hundredth playing of a work as exciting as their first. The discomforts of constant travel and the demands on their energy are minor matters—they thrive on communication through music.

What happens to the many fine instrumentalists who are not among the "rare few"? They teach, or play in orchestras, or both. Until fairly recently, wages for orchestral musicians were notoriously low. Musicians therefore formed orchestral committees and improved their lives through collective bargaining. But even with higher pay and increased benefits, players must often engage in additional freelance work. Many feel that they're subsidizing their art, but they're willing to do so. As a member of their audience, one does well to appreciate that performers today—however glamorous they may seem—do not have an easy life.

The Conductor

A *conductor,* the leader of a group of musicians, represents responsibility and authority. The conductor's "instruments" are the orchestra, band, and chorus. He or she holds performers together and makes them translate a piece into a meaningful whole. Many, though not all, conductors hold a thin stick called a *baton* in one hand to beat time and indicate pulse and tempo. With the other hand they control the balance among the instruments or voices so that the most important musical ideas will be brought out. Conducting styles vary greatly among these powerful individuals, but usually a conductor will use the left hand to indicate expression and to cue musicians.

Most of the conductor's work is done in rehearsal, where technical problems and expressive possibilities are worked over to his or her satisfaction. When a hundred instruments or voices sound at once, the conductor must be able to detect mistakes and performers who are out of tune. Conductors read the orchestral score and "hear" it in their minds. (An example of such a score—from Tchaikovsky's *Romeo and Juliet*—is shown on page 40.) Often conductors memorize the score so that they will be free to make eye contact with the musicians and thus control fine points of interpretation. In performance, different conductors seem flamboyant, reserved, graceful, or angular. But however they look, all conductors are trying to project an overall concept of a musical work.

The experience of most conductors includes mastery of at least one musical instrument and extended study of orchestration, music theory, and composition. Conductors are, as needed, diplomats, dictators, and teachers; their role traditionally has been thought of as the most glamorous in the music profession. In the early nineteenth century, composers began to write increasingly complex music that demanded more and more musicians. This trend fostered the rise of the virtuoso conductor—one who not only can hold all the forces together but also can draw sounds from them that make interpretive sense.

Before the nineteenth century, the beat was given either by the first violinist or by the keyboard player, or by both. From this early custom came a title still used today—*concertmaster.* In a modern symphony orchestra the *concertmaster* is the principal first violinist, who sits at the conductor's immediate left. Solo violin music that occurs in symphonic works is played by the concertmaster. He or she also assists the conductor by seeing that the string players' music contains appropriate bowing indications and supervising the tuning of the orchestra before the conductor appears.

Gustavo Dudamel conducting the Los Angeles Philharmonic Orchestra.

Recorded and Live Performance

Think of the music you have heard during the last few weeks. How much of it was live and how much was recorded? Today, most people's contact with music comes primarily through recordings. Before 1888—when the phonograph became commercially available—things were very different. To experience music, you had to listen to live performers, or play or sing yourself.

The decade from 1900 to 1910 witnessed several milestones in the history of recorded sound, including the first recordings of a complete opera and symphony, and opera arias sung by Enrico Caruso, the world-famous Italian tenor. Early recorded performances were relatively poor in sound quality and limited to about three minutes per side of a 78-rpm record. During the later twentieth century, such technological advances as long-playing records, audiotape, multichannel recording, and compact discs brought higher-fidelity sound reproduction and increased the potential playing time per recording.

Performances heard as recordings may never even have existed "live," played by the performer from beginning to end. Instead, they are often made up of segments combined from several different performances in the recording studio. (It's understandable that musicians want their recording to be note-perfect. However, too much intervention in the recording studio may result in a loss of vitality and spontaneity.)

Through *dubbing,* recordings have made available new listening experiences not possible in live performance. Beeps, clangs, whistles, never-ending gongs, and other effects can be added to music electronically at a composer's whim. Echo chambers and other equipment have given a new dimension to tone.

It's only in the last 250 years or so that concert-hall listening has developed. Before that, music was heard in a church or palace, on the street, or at home. Much music was intended for amateurs to enjoy around their fireplaces. In church, at dances, or on ceremonial occasions, the listener often was also a performer.

In a live performance, artists put themselves on the line; training and magnetism must overcome technical difficulties to involve the listeners' emotions. What is performed, how it sounds, how the artist feels about it that evening—all this exists for a fleeting moment and can never be repeated. An audience responds to the excitement of such a moment, and feelings are exchanged between stage and hall.

Despite the special electricity of a live performance, there are people who object to coughs and sneezes, the price of tickets, and the fact that seats in a concert hall don't recline. They prefer the living room, where they can choose in comfort from a staggering variety of music and performers on recordings. But in the living room, recorded music can become background sound. Carried to extremes, this can lessen our ability to concentrate. Total satisfaction from music requires that we focus attention as we would at a live performance.

Although recordings have wooed some people away from concert halls, it's also true that they have helped to build audiences for live performances. Enthusiasm for a recording has filled innumerable seats in concert halls. So even though it's an individual matter, most alert listeners will try to strike a happy balance between the voltages offered by the concert hall and by the wall socket.

Judging Performance

If you have ever listened to two music lovers arguing after a concert about the merits of what they have just heard, you know how much heat can be generated. Responses to a musical performance are highly subjective. One listener may be deeply moved by the performer's emotional involvement in the music, while the other may find the same performance excessively sentimental.

Does the performer draw you into the music? Is the artist's tone rich and vibrant, and does he or she sing or play in tune? Does the performance have enough variety and flexibility of dynamics and tempo? Subtle effects of phrasing dynamics, tone color, and tempo become more noticeable to someone who has listened to a number of performers. Try listening to the same work played by three different musicians—say, violinists. At first, you may like the second violinist best, but by the third hearing you may decide that it was the first violinist who made the most of what the composer tried to say. By listening to the same compositions played by different musicians, you can enhance your appreciation of the performer's art.

11 Musical Style

We use the word *style* in reference to everything from clothing to cooking, automobiles to paintings. In music, **style** refers to a characteristic way of using melody, rhythm, tone color, dynamics, harmony, texture, and form. The particular way these elements are combined can result in a total sound that's distinctive or unique.

When we hear an unfamiliar piece on the radio and identify it as jazz, Italian opera, or a symphony by Beethoven, we are responding to its style. We speak of the musical style of an individual composer, a group of composers, a country, or a particular period in history. Compositions created in the same geographical area or around the same time are often similar in style. Yet composers using the same musical vocabulary can create a personal manner of expression, just as people dressed in a similar style can have an individual look.

Like most other things, musical styles change from one era in history to the next. These changes are continuous, and so any boundary line between one stylistic period and the next can be only an approximation. Though sudden turning points do occur in the history of music, even the most revolutionary new styles are usually foreshadowed in earlier compositions. And few changes of style sweep away the past entirely. Even after a new style has become established, elements of the previous style are usually preserved in the musical language.

The history of western art music can be divided into the following stylistic periods:

Middle Ages (450–1450)
Renaissance (1450–1600)
Baroque (1600–1750)
Classical (1750–1820)
Romantic (1820–1900)
Twentieth century to 1945
1945 to the present

The chapters that follow will describe the general features of each period and show how that period differs from the preceding one. An awareness of the characteristics of a style helps you to know what to listen for in a composition written in a particular period. And by knowing the common practice of a period, you can better appreciate the innovative or unique features of a particular composition.

Music is not created in a vacuum. To fully understand the style of a composition, one has to be aware of its function in society. Is a piece meant to provide entertainment in an aristocrat's castle, a concert hall, or a middle-class home? Is it designed to accompany singing, dancing, religious rites, or drama? Musical style is shaped by political, economic, social, and intellectual developments as well. And often, similar features of style can be found in different arts of the same period.

The history of music is probably as old as the history of the human race itself. There is pictorial evidence of musical activity in Egypt as early as 3000 B.C. We know that music played an important role in the cultures of ancient Israel, Greece, and Rome. But hardly any notated music has survived from these ancient civilizations.

The first stylistic period to be considered in this book is the European Middle Ages, from which notated music *has* come down to us. Through the power of notation, music created over 1,000 years ago can come alive today.

Elements: Summary

IMPORTANT TERMS

- Sound, p. 4
- Pitch, p. 4
- Tone, p. 5
- Interval, p. 5
- Octave, p. 5
- Pitch range (range), p. 5
- Dynamics, p. 6
  - pianissimo
  - piano
  - mezzo piano
  - mezzo forte
  - forte
  - fortissimo
  - decrescendo (diminuendo)
  - crescendo
- Accent, p. 6
- Tone color (timbre), p. 7
- Voices, p. 11
  - Women
    - soprano
    - mezzo-soprano
    - alto (contralto)
  - Men
    - tenor
    - baritone
    - bass
- Musical instruments
  - string, p. 12
  - woodwind, p. 12
  - brass, p. 12
  - percussion, p. 12
  - keyboard, p. 12
  - electronic, p. 12
  - register, p. 12
- String instruments
  - violin, p. 13
  - viola, p. 13
  - cello, p. 13
  - double bass, p. 13
  - bow, p. 14
  - pizzicato, p. 16
  - stop (double, triple, quadruple), p. 17
  - vibrato, p. 17
  - mute, p. 17
  - tremolo, p. 17
  - harmonics, p. 17
  - plectrum, p. 17
  - harp, p. 17
  - guitar, p. 17
- Woodwind instruments
  - piccolo, p. 17
  - flute, p. 17
  - clarinet, p. 17
  - bass clarinet, p. 17

- oboe, p. 17
- English horn, p. 17
- bassoon, p. 17
- contrabassoon, p. 17
- recorder, p. 17
- reed, p. 17
- single-reed woodwinds, p. 17
- saxophone, p. 17
- double-reed woodwinds, p. 17
- Brass instruments
  - trumpet, p. 20
  - French horn, p. 20
  - trombone, p. 20
  - tuba, p. 20
  - cornet, p. 20
  - baritone horn, p. 20
  - euphonium, p. 20
  - mute, p. 22
- Percussion instruments
  - Definite pitch
    - timpani (kettledrums), p. 22
    - glockenspiel, p. 22
    - xylophone, p. 22
    - celesta, p. 22
    - chimes, p. 22
  - Indefinite pitch
    - snare drum (side drum), p. 22
    - bass drum, p. 22
    - tambourine, p. 22
    - triangle, p. 22
    - cymbals, p. 22
    - gong (tam-tam), p. 22
- Keyboard instruments
  - piano, p. 25
  - harpsichord, p. 26
  - pipe organ, p. 27
  - accordion, p. 27
- Electronic instruments
  - tape studio, p. 27
  - synthesizer, p. 28
  - computer, p. 29
  - computer music, p. 29
- Theme, p. 29
- Variation, p. 29
- Rhythm, p. 31
- Beat, p. 32
- Meter, p. 33
  - duple meter
  - triple meter
  - quadruple meter
  - quintuple meter
  - sextuple meter
  - septuple meter
- Measure, p. 33

- Downbeat, p. 33
- Upbeat, p. 33
- Accent, p. 34
- Syncopation, p. 34
- Tempo, p. 34
- Tempo indication, p. 34
  - largo
  - grave
  - adagio
  - andante
  - moderato
  - allegretto
  - allegro
  - vivace
  - presto
  - prestissimo
- Accelerando, p. 35
- Ritardando, p. 35
- Metronome, p. 35
- Notation, p. 36
- Note, p. 36
- Staff, p. 36
- Ledger lines, p. 36
- Sharp sign, p. 36
- Flat sign, p. 36
- Natural sign, p. 36
- Clef (treble and bass), p. 36
- Grand staff, p. 37
- Middle C, p. 37
- Stem, p. 37
- Flag, p. 37
- Beam, p. 38
- Dotted note, p. 38
- Dotted rhythm, p. 38
- Tie, p. 38
- Triplet, p. 38
- Rest, p. 38
- Time signature (meter signature), p. 39
- Score, p. 39
- Melody, p. 41
- Step, p. 41
- Leap, p. 41
- Legato, p. 41
- Staccato, p. 41
- Phrase, p. 41
- Cadence, p. 41
- Incomplete cadence, p. 42
- Complete cadence, p. 42
- Climax, p. 42
- Sequence, p. 43
- Harmony, p. 45
- Chord, p. 45
- Progression, p. 45
- Consonance, p. 46

FEATURED COMPOSERS

- Richard Wagner (1813–1883)
- Frédéric Chopin (1810–1849)
- Igor Stravinsky (1882–1971)
- Duke Ellington (1899–1974)
- Benjamin Britten (1913–1976)
- John Philip Sousa (1854–1932)
- George Gershwin (1898–1937)
- Dave Brubeck (b. 1920)
- Harold Arlen (1905–1986)
- Georges Bizet (1838–1875)
- Peter Ilyich Tchaikovsky (1840–1893)
- Johann Sebastian Bach (1685–1750)

Beyond the Classroom: What to Listen For in Music

We hear music all the time, but we don't always *listen* to music. Separating the various elements of music into their different component parts, then integrating them back together, is an exercise that benefits all students of music listening. Describing accurately what is happening in the music at any moment helps us enjoy music more deeply by understanding it more completely.

The American composer Aaron Copland (1900–1990), called by some the "dean of American music," frequently spoke and wrote about music listening. In his book *What to Listen For in Music* (1939), Copland describes three planes of music listening: the sensuous, the expressive, and the purely musical.

At the sensuous level, one bathes in the sound of music, enjoying music simply for the sheer pleasure and beauty of the sound. Copland explains that everyone listens to one degree or another on this plane; even seasoned music listeners do so, particularly when they seek consolation or an escape. Copland notes that the sensuous sound plane is an important aspect of understanding any composer's individual style.

At the expressive level, one considers the meaning behind the notes themselves. By *meaning*, Copland refers not to music describing a specific object or event, such as a storm or a battle, but rather to the uniquely personal aspect of what the music "says" to us. This plane is far easier to understand intuitively than it is to articulate. Copland explains that the meaning of a great musical work may change for us as we change over time.

At the purely musical level, the listener listens to music to understand the individual musical components, how they are used, and how they interact. Though this might seem like an academic exercise, the more one understands about music and how it functions, the greater one's listening pleasure can be.

Copland's three planes of listening are not mutually exclusive; we frequently shift between these planes as we listen to music. In particular, great works of music require repeated listening to fully comprehend all that is there to discover and enjoy.

When you attend a concert or listen to any musical selection, ask yourself the following questions:

- What individual musical elements do you hear? What words might you use to describe each one?
- Does the music use instruments, voices, or both? Which specific instruments or voices do you hear? How many of each do you notice?
- Do any elements change as the composition progresses? If so, which elements change and in what way do they change?
- If you listen to a song, how does the music express the words through its melody, harmony, rhythm, tempo, dynamics, and accompaniment?
- On which of Copland's music listening planes did you listen?

qui non abijt in confilio

The Middle Ages

Then I saw the lucent sky in which I heard different kinds of music. . . . I heard the praises of the joyous citizens of heaven, steadfastly persevering in the ways of truth.

— Hildegard of Bingen

Most medieval music was vocal, though musicians also performed on a wide variety of instruments. A page from the Peterborough Psalter.

TIME LINE
Middle Ages (450–1450)

	450–1000	1000–1300	1300–1450
Historical and Cultural Events	**455** Sack of Rome by Vandals **590–604** Reign of Pope Gregory I (the Great) **800** Charlemagne crowned Holy Roman Emperor	**1066** Norman Conquest **1096–99** First Crusade **1215** Magna Carta signed	**1337–1453** Hundred Years' War **1347–52** Black death **1431** Joan of Arc executed by the English
Arts and Letters	**c. 700** *Beowolf* **c. 800** *Book of Kells*	**1163** Beginning of Notre Dame Cathedral in Paris **1273** Thomas Aquinas, *Summa Theologica*	**1321** Dante, *The Divine Comedy* **1351** Boccaccio, *Decameron* **1387–1400** Chaucer, *The Canterbury Tales*
Music	**c. 900** Earliest notated Gregorian chant manuscripts	**c. 1100–1300** Troubadours and trouvères **c. 1150** Hildegard of Bingen, *O successores* **begun c. 1170** School of Notre Dame	**c. 1360** Guillaume de Machaut *Notre Dame* Mass 

A thousand years of European history are spanned by the phrase *Middle Ages.* Beginning around 450 with the disintegration of the Roman empire, the early Middle Ages was a time of migrations, upheavals, and wars. But the later Middle Ages (until about 1450) were a period of cultural growth: Romanesque churches and monasteries (1000–1150) and Gothic cathedrals (1150–1450) were constructed, towns grew, and universities were founded. The later Middle Ages also witnessed the crusades, a series of wars undertaken by European Christians—primarily between 1096 and 1291—to recover the holy city of Jerusalem from the Muslims.

During the Middle Ages a very sharp division existed among three main social classes: nobility, peasantry, and clergy. Nobles were sheltered within fortified castles surrounded by moats. During wars, noblemen engaged in combat as knights in armor, while noblewomen managed estates, ran households, and looked after the sick. In peacetime, the nobles amused themselves with hunting, feasting, and tournaments. Peasants—the vast majority of the population—lived miserably in one-room huts. Many were serfs, bound to the soil and subject to feudal overlords. All segments of society felt the powerful influence of the Roman Catholic church. In this age of faith, hell was very real, and heresy was the gravest crime. Monks in monasteries held a virtual monopoly on learning; most people—including the nobility—were illiterate.

In the fourteenth century, an age of disintegration, Europe suffered through the Hundred Years' War (1337–1453) and the black death—or bubonic plague (around 1350)—which killed one-fourth of its population. By this time, both the feudal system and the authority of the church had been weakened. From 1378 to 1417, two rival popes claimed authority; and at one time there were three. Even devout Christians were confused. Literature of the time, such as Chaucer's *Canterbury Tales* (1387–1400) and Boccaccio's *Decameron* (after 1348), stressed graphic realism and earthly sensuality rather than virtue and heavenly rewards.

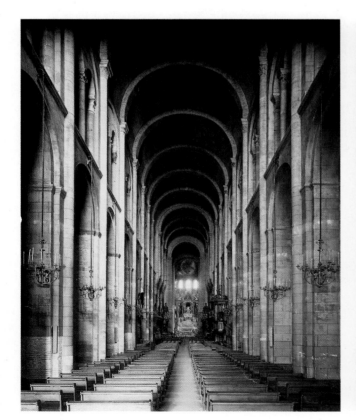 

Architecture changed during the Middle Ages from the Romanesque style, seen in the eleventh-century nave at left, to the Gothic style of the thirteenth-century Cathedral of Reims, at right.

Choir of Cathedral of Reims. During the Middle Ages, religious teachings were imparted, and beliefs were strengthened, by biblical scenes depicted in stained-glass windows.

During the Middle Ages, artists were more concerned with religious symbolism than with lifelike representation. *Madonna and Child Enthroned* by an anonymous Byzantine artist of the thirteenth century.

1 Music in the Middle Ages
(450–1450)

Just as the cathedral dominated the medieval landscape and mind, so was it the center of musical life. Most of the important musicians were priests and worked for the church. An important occupation in thousands of monasteries was liturgical singing. Boys received music education in schools associated with churches and cathedrals. Women were not allowed to sing in church but did make music in convents. Nuns learned to sing, and some—like Hildegard of Bingen (1098–1179), abbess of Rupertsberg—wrote music for their choirs. With this preeminence of the church, it is not surprising that for centuries only sacred music was notated.

Most medieval music was vocal, though musicians also performed on a wide variety of instruments. Church officials required monks to sing with proper pronunciation, concentration, and tone quality. For example, Saint Bernard, the twelfth-century mystic and head of the abbey at Clairvaux in France, ordered his monks to sing vigorously, "pronouncing the words of the Holy Spirit with becoming manliness and resonance and affection; and correctly, that while you chant you ponder on nothing but what you chant."

The church frowned on instruments because of their earlier role in pagan rites. After about 1000, however, organs and bells became increasingly common in cathedrals and monastic churches. For three centuries or so, organs were played mainly on feast days and other special occasions. Sometimes the clergy complained about noisy organs that distracted worshippers. "Whence hath the church so many Organs," complained St. Aethelred, a twelfth-century abbot. "To what purpose, I pray you, is that terrible blowing of bellows, expressing rather the cracks of thunder than the sweetness of a Voyce." Aethelred criticized people who watched the organ as if "in a theater not a place of worship."

Today, we know relatively little about how medieval music sounded. Few medieval instruments have survived; and music manuscripts of the time do not indicate tempo, dynamics, or names of instruments. In some kinds of medieval music, the notation indicates pitch, but not rhythm. Singers and instrumentalists often appear together in pictures and in literary descriptions, but it is not certain whether polyphonic music was performed with voices alone or with voices and instruments.

2 Gregorian Chant

For over 1,000 years, the official music of the Roman Catholic church has been *Gregorian chant,* which consists of melody set to sacred Latin texts and sung without accompaniment. (The chant is monophonic in texture.) The melodies of Gregorian chant were meant to enhance specific parts of religious services. They set the atmosphere for prayers and ritual actions. For centuries, composers have based original compositions on chant melodies. (Since the Second Vatican Council of 1962–1965, however, most Roman Catholic services have been celebrated in the native language of each country, and so today Gregorian chant is no longer common.)

Gregorian chant conveys a calm, otherworldly quality; it represents the voice of the church, rather than that of any single individual. Its rhythm is flexible, without meter, and has little sense of beat. The exact rhythm of chant melodies is uncertain, because precise time values were not notated. But its free-flowing rhythm gives Gregorian chant a floating, almost improvisational character. The melodies tend to move by step within a narrow range of pitches. Depending on the nature and importance of the text, they are simple or elaborate; some are little more than recitations on a single tone; others contain complex melodic curves.

Gregorian chant is named after Pope Gregory I (the Great), who reorganized the Catholic liturgy during his reign from 590 to 604. Although medieval legend credits Pope Gregory with the creation of Gregorian chant, we know that it evolved over many centuries. Some of its practices, such as the singing of psalms, came from the Jewish synagogues of the first centuries after Christ. Most of the several thousand melodies known today were created between A.D. 600 and 1300.

At first Gregorian melodies were passed along by oral tradition, but as the number of chants grew to the thousands, they were notated to ensure musical uniformity throughout the western church. (The illustration on page 77 shows an example of medieval chant notation.) The earliest surviving chant manuscripts date from about the ninth century. The composers of Gregorian chant—like the sculptors who decorated early medieval churches—remain almost completely unknown.

Medieval monks and nuns spent several hours of each day singing Gregorian chant in two types of services: the office and the mass. Each type included both sung and spoken texts in Latin. The office consisted of eight services, the first before sunrise and the last at sunset. The *mass,* the highlight of the liturgical day, was a ritual reenactment of the Last Supper. Some texts of the mass remained the same from day to day throughout most of the church year, whereas other texts were meant only for particular feasts, such as Christmas, Epiphany, or Easter.

The Church Modes

The "otherworldly" sound of Gregorian chant results partly from the unfamiliar scales used. These scales are called **church modes** (or sometimes simply *modes*). Like major and minor scales, church modes consist of seven different tones and an eighth tone that duplicates the first an octave higher. However, their patterns of whole and half steps are different. The church modes were the basic scales of western music during the Middle Ages and Renaissance and were used in secular as well as sacred music. Much western folk music follows the patterns of the church modes. For example, the sea chantey *What Shall We Do with the Drunken Sailor?* is in a mode called *Dorian.*

Alleluia: Vidimus stellam (We Have Seen His Star)

Basic Set:
CD 1 63

Brief Set:
CD 1 47

An elaborate and jubilant Gregorian chant is the Alleluia from the Mass for Epiphany. The word *alleluia* is a Latinized form of the Hebrew *hallelujah* (*praise ye the Lord*). In this chant (shown on page 78 in medieval notation), many notes are sung to single syllables of text. The long series of tones on *ia* is a wordless expression of joy and religious ecstasy. The monophonic texture of the chant is varied by an alternation between a soloist and a choir singing in unison. The chant is in A B A form; the opening *alleluia* melody is repeated after a middle section that is set to a biblical verse.

Manuscript page with a Gregorian chant in medieval notation. The illustration within the initial R depicts the resurrection of Christ.

VOCAL MUSIC GUIDE

Alleluia: Vidimus stellam

63 **47** 0:00

A

| Solo, opening phrase | *Alleluia.* | Hallelujah. |
| Choir, many tones on *ia* | *ia.* | jah. |

64 **48** 0:24

B

| Choir | *Vidimus stellam ejus in Oriente et venimus cum muneribus adorare Dominum.* | We have seen his star in the east and are come with gifts to worship the Lord. |

65 **49** 1:44

A

| Choir, opening phrase with many tones on *ia* | *Alleluia.* | Hallelujah. |

Medieval chant notation for
Alleluia: Vidimus stellam.

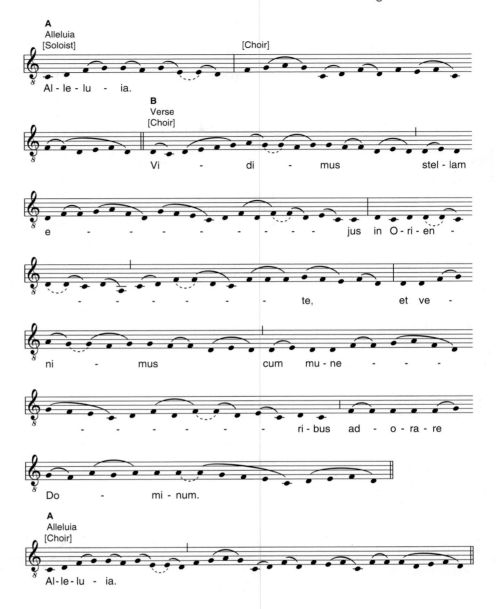

A
Alleluia
[Soloist]   [Choir]

Al - le - lu - ia.

B
Verse
[Choir]

Vi - di - mus stel - lam

e - - - - - - - - - jus in O - ri - en -

- te, et ve -

ni - mus cum mu - ne - - -

- - - - - - ri - bus ad - o - ra - re

Do - mi - num.

A
Alleluia
[Choir]

Al - le - lu - ia.

O successores (You successors), by Hildegard of Bingen

A late, highly expressive example of Gregorian chant is *O successores* (*You successors*) by the nun Hildegard of Bingen (1098–1179), abbess of Rupertsberg in Germany. Hildegard was one of the most creative and many-sided personalities of the Middle Ages. A visionary and mystic, she was active in religious and diplomatic affairs. She also wrote poetry and music; treatises on theology, science, and medicine; and a musical drama, *Ordo virtutum* (*Play of the Virtues*), which is the earliest known morality play. She was the first woman composer from whom a large number of works—monophonic sacred songs—have survived.

The chant *O successores* was composed to be sung by the nuns in Hildegard's convent. It is in praise of the holy confessors who are successors of Christ. (Christ is referred to as *lion* and *lamb* in the text.) Hildegard explained that the words came to her in a vision: "Then I saw the lucent sky, in which I heard different kinds of music. . . . I heard the praises of the joyous citizens of heaven, steadfastly persevering in the ways of truth."

Basic Set:
CD 1 66

Brief Set:
CD 1 50

The chant is notated in the manuscript as a single melodic line, without accompaniment. However, in our recording the performers have added a drone accompaniment. A **drone** consists of one or more long, sustained tones accompanying a melody. In *O successores,* two simultaneous sustained notes at the interval of a fifth are played on a fiddle, a medieval bowed string instrument. It may well be that such an accompaniment accords with medieval performance practice.

The melody is sung by a women's choir and is made up of several different phrases. This chant usually has one to four notes to each syllable; only at the end are many notes sung on the final syllable. The melody creates a sense of progression and growth as it moves gradually through a wide pitch range (an octave and a sixth). At first, the melody seems calm as it proceeds primarily by step within a low register. However, beginning with the word *sicut* there are several ascents to high notes and wide upward leaps of a fifth (on the words *et, vos, qui,* and *semper*). The climactic tone (on the important word *officio, service*) is reserved for the concluding phrase, which gently descends by step (on the word *agni, lamb*) to the original low register. *O successores* seems more speechlike than *Alleluia: Vidimus stellam,* where many tones are sung to single syllables of text. Hildegard's chant has a larger pitch range, more wide leaps, and a greater feeling of motion toward a climax near the end.

VOCAL MUSIC GUIDE

HILDEGARD OF BINGEN, *O successores*

| 66 | 50 |

Low register	*O successores fortissimi leonis* *inter templum et altare—* *dominantes in ministratione eius—*	You successors of the mightiest lion between the temple and the altar— you the masters in his household—
Melody rises and falls	*sicut angeli sonant in laudibus,* *et sicut adsunt populis in adiutorio,* *vos estis inter illos,* *qui haec faciunt,* *semper curam habentes*	as the angels sound forth praises and are here to help the nations, you are among those who accomplish this, forever showing your care
Climax on *officio,* long descent on *agni*	*in officio agni.*	in the service of the lamb.

3 Secular Music in the Middle Ages

Despite the predominance of Gregorian chant throughout the Middle Ages, there was also much music outside the church. The pleasures of secular music and dance were vividly evoked by the thirteenth-century theologian Henri de Malines, as he reminisced about his life as a young student in Paris. "This servant of God gladly heard music performed upon reed instruments, pipes, and every kind of musical instrument." Henri "knew how to play a fiddle, bringing together in harmonious fashion, a melodious touching of the strings and drawing of the bow. He was familiar with and willingly sang all kinds of monophonic songs in various languages." Henri created poems and melodies and was a "merry and amorous leader . . . of dances in wooded places, arranging parties and games, and interspersing the sport of dancing with others."

The first large body of secular songs surviving in decipherable notation were composed during the twelfth and thirteenth centuries by French nobles called *troubadours* and *trouvères*. Among the best-known of these poet-musicians were the troubadour Guillaume IX, duke of Aquitaine, from southern France; and the trouvère Chastelain de Couci, from northern France. During this age of chivalry, knights gained great reputations as musical poets, as they might have done earlier by fighting bravely. Many of their love songs have been preserved because nobles had clerics write them down. These songs were usually performed by court minstrels, and most of them deal with love; but there are also songs about the Crusades, dance songs, and spinning songs. In southern France, there were women troubadours—such as Beatriz de Dia—who addressed their songs to men.

Some 1,650 troubadour and trouvère melodies have been preserved. The notation does not indicate rhythm, but it's likely that many had a regular meter with a clearly defined beat. They thus differ from the free, nonmetrical rhythm of Gregorian chant.

During the Middle Ages, wandering minstrels (or *jongleurs*—*juggler* comes from this French word) performed music and acrobatics in castles, taverns, and town squares. Minstrels had no civil rights and were on the lowest social level, with prostitutes and slaves; only a lucky few found steady work in the service of the nobility. But they were an important source of information in a time when there were no newspapers. They usually sang songs written by others and played instrumental dances on harps, fiddles (ancestors of the violin), and lutes (plucked string instruments).

Many secular songs in the Middle Ages dealt with love. The illustration shows the German poet-composer Frauenlob (c. 1255–1318) with a group of musicians.

Dances in the Middle Ages were often accompanied by instrumental music.

Estampie (Thirteenth Century)

Basic Set:
CD 1 67

Brief Set:
CD 1 51

The *estampie,* a medieval dance, is one of the earliest surviving forms of instrumental music. In the manuscript for this **estampie,** a single melodic line is notated and, as usual, no instrument is specified. In our recording, the melody is played on a *rebec* (a bowed string instrument) and a *pipe* (a tubular wind instrument). Since medieval minstrels probably improvised modest accompaniments to dance tunes, the performers have added a drone—two simultaneous, repeated notes at the interval of a fifth, played on a *psaltery* (a plucked or struck string instrument). The estampie is in triple meter and has a strong, fast beat.

4 The Development of Polyphony: Organum

For centuries, western music was basically monophonic, having a single melodic line. But sometime between 700 and 900, the first steps were taken in a revolution that eventually transformed western music. Monks in monastery choirs began to add a second melodic line to Gregorian chant. In the beginning, this second line was improvised, not written down; it duplicated the chant melody at a different pitch. The two lines were in parallel motion, note against note, at the interval of a fourth or a fifth. (The interval from *do* to *fa* is a fourth; from *do* to *sol* is a fifth.)

Sit glo - ri - a Do - mi - ni in se - cu - la

Medieval music that consists of Gregorian chant and one or more additional melodic lines is called **organum.** Between 900 and 1200, organum became truly polyphonic, and the melody added to the chant became more independent. Instead of moving strictly parallel to the chant, it developed a melodic curve of its own. Sometimes this line was in contrary motion to the chant, moving up as the chant moved down. The second line became even more independent around 1100, when the chant and the added melody were no longer restricted to a note-against-note style. Now the two lines could differ rhythmically as well as melodically. The chant, on the bottom, was generally sung in very long notes while the added melody, on top, moved in shorter notes.

Medieval listeners must have been startled to hear religious music in which the added melody was more attractive than the chant. In fact, at times the chant tones were so slow and dronelike that the original melody was hardly recognizable. Nonetheless, the chant represented the authority of the church. And respect for the church was so great that for centuries most polyphonic music was created by placing new melodic lines against known chants.

School of Notre Dame: Measured Rhythm

After 1150, Paris—the intellectual and artistic capital of Europe—became the center of polyphonic music. The University of Paris attracted leading scholars, and the Cathedral of Notre Dame (begun in 1163) was the supreme monument of Gothic architecture. Two successive choirmasters of Notre Dame, Leonin and Perotin, are among the first notable composers known by name. They and their followers are referred to as the *school of Notre Dame.*

From about 1170 to 1200, the Notre Dame composers developed rhythmic innovations. Earlier polyphonic music was probably performed in the free, unmeasured rhythms of Gregorian chant. But the music of Leonin and Perotin used *measured rhythm,* with definite time values and clearly defined meter. For the first time in music history, notation indicated precise rhythms as well as pitches. At first the new notation was limited to only certain rhythmic patterns, and the beat had to be subdivided into threes, the symbol of the Trinity. Despite these limitations, much fine polyphonic music was composed during the late twelfth century and the thirteenth century.

The Cathedral of Notre Dame in Paris.

Modern listeners sometimes find medieval polyphony hollow and thin, probably because it has relatively few triads, which in later periods became the basic consonant chords. The triad contains two intervals of a third; medieval music theorists considered this interval a dissonance. (An interval of a third separates *do* and *mi,* and *mi* and *sol.*) But as the Middle Ages advanced, triads and thirds were used more often, and polyphonic music gradually became fuller and richer by our standards. As an example of Notre Dame polyphony, we'll listen to *Alleluia: Nativitas,* by Perotin.

Alleluia: Nativitas (The Birth; 1200?), by Perotin

Basic Set:
CD 1 `68`

Perotin (late twelfth to early thirteenth century) was the first known composer to write music with more than two voices. *Alleluia: Nativitas,* an organum in three voices, is based on a Gregorian alleluia melody—for the nativity of the Virgin Mary—that Perotin placed in the lowest voice part. In our recording, the three voice parts are sung by a group of male voices reinforced by instruments.

A chant that is used as the basis for polyphony is known as a **cantus firmus** (*fixed melody*). Above the cantus firmus, or preexisting melody, Perotin wrote two additional lines that move much more quickly. As many as sixty-six tones of the upper voices are sung against one long, sustained tone of the chant. But only three chant tones—the first, second, and last—are treated in this dronelike way. In the middle of the piece, the chant tones are speeded up so that only about three tones are sung above each chant tone. (This speeding up was a practical necessity, since a chant sung entirely in long notes seems endless, and church services were already long enough!)

The top voices of *Alleluia: Nativitas* have a clearly defined meter, which we would notate today as a fast $\frac{6}{8}$ (**1**–2–3–**4**–5–6). They relentlessly repeat rhythmic patterns: long-short-long, long-short-long. The rhythmic contrast between bottom and top voices is typical of medieval polyphony. The narrow range of the three voices is also characteristic; they are never more than an octave apart. When sung together, the tones of the different parts produce chords that have a hollow ring. As the three voices of *Alleluia: Nativitas* resounded under the vaulted ceilings of Notre Dame, they must have seemed like a cathedral of tones.

5 Fourteenth-Century Music: The "New Art" in Italy and France

As we have seen in the opening to Part II (page 73), the fourteenth century was an age of disintegration that witnessed the Hundred Years' War, the catastrophic plague known as the black death, and a weakening of the feudal system and the Catholic church. Literary works of the fourteenth century stressed sensuality more than virtue.

Given this atmosphere, it's not surprising that secular music became more important than sacred music in the fourteenth century. Composers wrote polyphonic music that was *not* based on Gregorian chant, including drinking songs and pieces in which birdcalls, dogs' barks, and hunters' shouts were imitated.

By the early fourteenth century, a new system of music notation had evolved, and a composer could specify almost any rhythmic pattern. Now beats could be subdivided into two as well as three. Syncopation—rarely used earlier—became an important rhythmic practice. Changes in musical style in the fourteenth century were so profound that music theorists referred to Italian and French music as the **new art** (**ars nova** in Latin).

As contrasting examples of fourteenth-century music, we'll study a song about spring by Francesco Landini and a love song and a mass by Guillaume de Machaut, respectively the leading Italian and French composers of the time.

Francesco Landini

Francesco Landini (?–1397), the most celebrated Italian composer of the fourteenth century, was born near Florence, where he worked much of his life; he was blind from childhood. Landini was a famous organist, a poet, a scholar, and the inventor of a new string instrument. The secular emphasis in fourteenth-century music is illustrated by Landini's works, which consist exclusively of Italian songs for two or three voices dealing with subjects ranging from nature and love to morality and politics.

Ecco la primavera
(*Spring has come;* Fourteenth Century)

Basic Set:

CD 1 69

Ecco la primavera is a carefree song for two voice parts about the joys of springtime. The song is in triple meter and has a strong, fast beat. Its rhythmic vitality comes from syncopation, a characteristic feature of fourteenth-century music.

Ecco la primavera is a **ballata,** an Italian poetic and musical form that originated as a song to accompany dancing. The text is sung to two musically similar units, A (longer) and B (shorter), arranged as follows: A BB AA.

Though notated for only two voices, *Ecco la primavera* may originally have been played by instruments as well. In our performance, the song is introduced by recorders playing units ABB. Then female and male singers perform units A BB AA, with period instruments reinforcing the vocal melodies and drums and bells providing rhythmic background. The joyousness of *Ecco la primavera* evokes the vanished world of fourteenth-century Florence.

VOCAL MUSIC GUIDE

LANDINI, *Ecco la primavera*

69   0:00
Recorder introduction
ABB

70   0:26

A   Ecco la primavera, / Che 'l cor fa rallegrare; / Temp'è d'annamorare / E star con lieta cera.

Spring has come. / It makes the heart joyful; / now is the time to fall in love / and be happy.

71   0:37

B   No' vegiam l'aria e 'l tempo / Che pur chiam' allegreçça.

We see the air and the fine weather / which also call us to be happy.

B   0:45   In questo vago tempo / Ogni cosa à vaghecça.

In this sweet time, / everything is beautiful.

A   0:52   L'erbe con gran freschecca / E fior' coprono i prati, / E gli albori adornati / Sono in simil manera.

Flowers and fresh green grass / cover the meadows, / and the trees too / are in blossom.

A   1:03   Ecco la primavera, / Che 'l cor fa rallegrare, / Temp'è d'annamorare / E star con lieta cera.

Spring has come. / It makes the heart joyful; / now is the time to fall in love / and be happy.

Guillaume de Machaut

Guillaume de Machaut (about 1300–1377), who was famous as both a musician and a poet, was born in the French province of Champagne. He studied theology and spent much of his life in the service of various royal families. Around 1323, he became secretary and chaplain to John, king of Bohemia, whom he accompanied on trips and military campaigns throughout Europe. In his later years he lived mainly in Reims, where he served as a church official.

Machaut traveled to many courts and presented beautifully decorated copies of his music and poetry to noble patrons. These copies make Machaut one of the first important composers whose works have survived. The decline of the church in the fourteenth century is reflected in Machaut's output, which consists mainly of courtly love songs for one to four performers. We'll consider, first, one of his love songs, and then the *Notre Dame* Mass, the best-known composition of the fourteenth century.

Puis qu'en oubli sui de vous (*Since I am forgotten by you;* around 1363)

Basic Set:
CD 1 72

Brief Set:
CD 1 52

When he was about sixty, Machaut fell in love with Peronne, a beautiful young noblewoman. For several years they exchanged poems and letters, but the difference in age eventually proved too great and their relationship ended in mutual disappointment. Machaut immortalized their love in his greatest narrative poem, *Le Livre Dou Voir Dit* (*The Book of the True Poem,* 1363–1365). Along with the narrative, the *Voir Dit* contains lyric poems and letters by Machaut and Peronne as well as nine musical compositions, including the song *Puis qu'en oubli sui de vous* (*Since I am forgotten by you*).

This melancholy work expresses Machaut's "farewell to joy," since he has been forgotten by his beloved. The song consists of a vocal melody and two accompanying parts in an exceptionally low pitch range. Since these lower parts have no texts in the medieval manuscript, it is not certain whether they are meant to be sung or to be played by instruments. In our recording, they are performed by two solo voices.

Puis qu'en oubli sui de vous is a **rondeau,** one of the main poetic and musical forms in fourteenth- and fifteenth-century France. The poem has eight lines, each ending with either the syllable *mis* or the syllable *mant* (see the French text in the Vocal Music Guide below). Lines 1–2 constitute the poetic refrain, which returns as lines 7–8; line 1 appears again as line 4.

The music consists of two phrases, a and b. (These phrases are indicated to the left of the French text in the Vocal Music Guide.) Phrase a is used for lines ending with *mis*. It begins with long notes, pauses in the middle, and ends with an incomplete cadence.

Phrase b is set to lines ending with *mant*. It begins with short notes, flows continuously, and ends with a complete cadence.

The endings of both phrases contain syncopation, a rhythmic feature of fourteenth-century music. *Puis qu'en oubli* is a heartfelt message of courtly love.

VOCAL MUSIC GUIDE

MACHAUT, *Puis qu'en oubli*

72	52			
		a	*Puis qu'en oubli sui de vous dous amis*	Since I am forgotten by you, sweet friend,
		b	*Vie amoureuse et joie a dieu commant*	I say farewell to joy and a life of love.
		a	*Mar vi le jour que m'amour en vous mis*	Ill-fated was the day I placed my love in you,
		a	*Puis qu'en oubli sui de vous dous amis*	Since I am forgotten by you, sweet friend.
		a	*Mais ce tenray que je vous ay promis*	But what I have promised you I will maintain,
		b	*C'est que jamais n'aray nul autre amant*	Which is that I shall never have any other lover.
		a	*Puis qu'en oubli sui de vous dous amis*	Since I am forgotten by you, sweet friend.
		b	*Via amoureuse et joie a dieu commant*	I say farewell to joy and a life of love.

Notre Dame Mass (Mid-Fourteenth Century)

Machaut's *Notre Dame* Mass, one of the finest compositions known from the Middle Ages, is also of great historical importance: it is the first polyphonic treatment of the mass ordinary by a known composer.

The **mass ordinary** consists of texts that remain the same from day to day throughout the church year. The five sung prayers of the ordinary are the Kyrie, Gloria, Credo, Sanctus, and Agnus Dei. Since the fourteenth century, these five texts have often been set to polyphonic music and have inspired some of the greatest choral works. (In the service, the Kyrie and Gloria were sung in succession, whereas the Credo, Sanctus, and Agnus Dei were separated by liturgical activity and by other texts sung as Gregorian chant.) In each age, composers have responded to the mass in their own particular style. This centuries-old tradition of the mass gives invaluable insight into the long span of music and its changing styles.

The *Notre Dame* Mass is written for four voice parts. How Machaut wanted his mass to be performed in unknown, but it is likely that four solo voices were employed. In our recording, the four voice parts are sung by a small group of male singers. The *Notre Dame* Mass was probably composed in the early 1360s for performance at the cathedral of Reims. We'll examine the Agnus Dei of the mass as an example of fourteenth-century polyphony.

Agnus Dei

Basic Set:
CD 1 [73]

Brief Set:
CD 1 [53]

Machaut's music for the Agnus Dei—a prayer for mercy and peace—is solemn and elaborate. It is in triple meter. Complex rhythmic patterns contribute to its intensity. The two upper parts are rhythmically active and contain syncopation, a characteristic of fourteenth-century music. The two lower parts move in longer notes and play a supporting role.

The Agnus Dei is based on a Gregorian chant, which Machaut furnished with new rhythmic patterns and placed in the tenor, one of the two lower parts. Since the chant, or cantus firmus, is rhythmically altered within a polyphonic web, it is more a musical framework than a tune to be recognized. The harmonies of the Agnus Dei include stark dissonances, hollow-sounding chords, and full triads.

Like the chant melody on which it is based, the Agnus Dei is in three sections. It may be outlined as follows:

Agnus Dei (I)	Agnus Dei (II)	Agnus Dei (III)
A	B	A

The same text appears in each section, except for a change from *miserere nobis (have mercy on us)* to *dona nobis pacem (grant us peace)* in the concluding Agnus Dei (III). A and B are similar in mood, rhythm, and texture and end with the same hollow-sounding chord. The division into three sections is thought to symbolize the Trinity. In Machaut's time, music was meant to appeal to the mind as much as to the ear.

VOCAL MUSIC GUIDE

MACHAUT, Agnus Dei from *Notre Dame* Mass

[73] [53] 0:00
A   *Agnus Dei, qui tollis peccata mundi: miserere nobis.*   Lamb of God, who taketh away the sins of the world, have mercy on us.

[74] [54] 1:01
B   *Agnus Dei, qui tollis peccata mundi: miserere nobis.*   Lamb of God, who taketh away the sins of the world, have mercy on us.

[75] [55] 2:15
A   *Agnus Dei, qui tollis peccata mundi: dona nobis pacem.*   Lamb of God, who taketh away the sins of the world, grant us peace.

Paul Hillier Conducting the Agnus Dei from Machaut's Notre Dame Mass

The distinguished choral conductor and singer Paul Hillier performs highly diverse vocal works ranging from Machaut's *Notre Dame* Mass (c. 1360) to *The Little Match Girl Passion* (2007) by the American composer David Lang. "I've always been equally interested in contemporary music as in early music," Hillier has said.

Hillier was born in 1949 in the English town of Dorchester, where he sang in the local church choir. In his early teens, he became a fan of Elvis Presley and won a dance competition doing the twist. He later studied singing and acting at the Guildhall School of Music and Drama in London, where he developed his interest in medieval and renaissance music. After graduating, Hillier became a singer at St. Paul's Cathedral and in 1973 founded the Hilliard Ensemble, an unaccompanied male vocal quartet specializing in early music. His many CDs with this and other choral ensembles have gained worldwide acclaim and he has won two Grammys, in 2007 and 2010. In addition to conducting and singing, he has been active as a writer and a music educator, including a decade spent teaching in California and Indiana.

The 1987 recording by the Hilliard Ensemble of Machaut's *Notre Dame* Mass uses six unaccompanied male voices (including Hillier himself). Hillier has written, "this Mass for four voices was almost certainly written to be sung by a small group of singers, and without any instruments." He believes that the work poses special challenges for the singer: "The music is fun to sing, but also quite difficult. It needs to be sung very much in tune, and not all singers can do that! . . . The rhythms too are not very easy, especially in the top two voices which dance around with endless syncopations and flourishes. And yet the music needs to sound graceful and easy!" Hillier finds it helpful in rehearsal to have the two lower voices sung separately, without the upper parts. "The lower two voices," he writes, "are supports, like pillars in architecture; yet these also need to be phrased gracefully. . . . This is one way I rehearse the music—and it helps me to find the right tempo, one at which the lower voices make sense, even though the top voices have to go quite fast." Hillier stresses the importance of maintaining musical direction and flow. "I also enjoy the moments when all four voices come to rest just for a moment in the middle of a phrase, before setting off again in a new direction." For Hillier, the *Notre Dame* Mass "still speaks strongly to us as music. It may sound 'medieval' (whatever that means), but I think it comes across as being both strange and yet inevitable—and as fresh as if it had been composed yesterday." His performance with the Hilliard Ensemble of the *Agnus Dei* from the Mass is included on our recording set.

The Middle Ages: Summary

Music in Society

- The Middle Ages in music extends from roughly 450 to 1450.
- During the Middle Ages, musicians worked for churches, courts, and towns.
- The most important musicians were priests and worked for the church.
- Vocal music was more important than instrumental music.
- Women were not permitted to sing in church, but they could make music in convents, where they also could receive musical training.
- Secular song and dance flourished.

Important Style Features

Mood and Emotional Expression
- Gregorian chant conveys a calm, otherworldly, spiritual quality.
- Medieval composers were relatively uninterested in expressing the emotions of a text.

Rhythm
- Gregorian chant rhythm is flexible, without meter, and has little sense of beat; as a result, the music has a floating quality.
- Troubadour and trouvère notation does not indicate rhythm, but much of this music most likely had a regular meter with a clearly defined beat.
- Dances have a regular, clearly defined beat.
- Notre Dame composers developed the first instances of western notation that indicated measured rhythms with definite time values.
- In ars nova, the beat could be subdivided into two as well as three, and syncopation became an important rhythmic practice.

Dynamics
- Dynamic indications do not appear in medieval scores.

Tone Color
- Indications of instruments do not appear in music manuscripts.
- Occasionally vocal or instrumental music will be accompanied by a drone.

Melody and Harmony
- For centuries, medieval composers based original compositions on chant melodies.
- Chant melodies of the Middle Ages often move by step within a narrow range.
- Medieval music theorists considered the interval of a third a dissonance; thus, the music occasionally can sound hollow to us. In the later Middle Ages, thirds and triads are used more often.
- Music is based on church modes rather than major and minor scales.

Texture
- For hundreds of years, western music was basically monophonic.
- Sometime between 700 and 900 C.E., a second line of music was added to Gregorian chant, creating organum.
- Starting around 1200, composers wrote polyphonic music in three and four voice parts.

Performance Practice

- We know very little about how medieval music sounded and how it was performed.
- Most music was vocal, though musicians also performed on a wide variety of instruments, particularly in secular settings. The church frowned on instruments, however, owing to their earlier role in pagan rites.
- Much music was passed down for generations through oral tradition and memorization, since music notation was either nonexistent or primitive.
- Jongleurs performed music and acrobatics in castles, taverns, and town squares. French troubadours and trouvères created the first large body of secular songs in the twelfth and thirteenth centuries.
- Medieval minstrels probably improvised modest accompaniments to dances.

Beyond the Classroom: Listening to Medieval Music

The Middle Ages span nearly 1,000 years, and consequently, the music of this era demonstrates a remarkable variety of styles and forms. This was the era that witnessed the creation and development of music notation, and polyphonic secular and sacred music in two or more voice parts.

Recent scholarship has provided some information regarding the music and instruments of this period, but we know relatively little about how the music from this era may have sounded. Today, concerts sometimes feature medieval music, enabling us to gain insight into how people worshipped in the church and entertained themselves during the Middle Ages.

Over the past several years, recorded performances of Gregorian chant and other music of medieval composers have attracted great interest throughout the world, posting record-breaking sales of CDs and Internet downloads. A variety of speculation exists over why this music would become so popular all of a sudden; however, one reason may be that the calm, spiritual quality of the music soothes the nerves of a world caught up by the frenetic pace of modern-day life.

When listening to music from the Middle Ages at a concert or on a recording, ask yourself these questions:

- Does the music seem to "float" rhythmically, as in Gregorian chant, or is there a regular beat?
- If there is a regular beat, do you hear beats subdivided only into regular groups of three, or do you hear a mixture of beats divisible into groups of two or three or combinations of both?
- In vocal music:
  - Is the texture of the music monophonic? If the texture is polyphonic, how many different vocal parts do you hear?
  - Is there an instrumental drone accompanying the singers?
  - In what language is the music being sung?
  - Is the text sacred or secular? If sacred, is the text from the mass ordinary?
- At a concert of live music, are dancers participating in the performance?

The Renaissance

The man that hath no music in himself,
Nor is not mov'd with concord of sweet sounds,
Is fit for treasons, strategems and spoils.

— William Shakespeare

During the Renaissance, music was an important leisure activity; every educated person was expected to play an instrument and read musical notation. *A Concert,* by the Italian painter Lorenzo Costa (1460–1535), shows a man playing a lute accompanying himself and two other singers.

Renaissance (1450–1600)

| 1450–1500 | 1500–1600 |

Historical and Cultural Events

1453 Fall of Constantinople

1456 Gutenberg Bible

1492 Columbus reaches America

1517 Martin Luther's ninety-five theses, start of the Reformation

1545–63 Council of Trent

1558–1603 Elizabeth I, queen of England

1588 Spanish Armada defeated

Arts and Letters

1482 Botticelli, *La Primavera*

c. 1503 Leonardo da Vinci, *Mona Lisa*

1504 Michelangelo, *David*

1505 Raphael, *School of Athens*

c. 1570 Titian, *Venus and the Lute Player*

1596 Shakespeare, *Romeo and Juliet*

Music

c. 1475 Josquin Desprez, *Ave Maria . . . Virgo Serena*

1563 Giovanni Pierluigi da Palestrina, *Pope Marcellus Mass*

c. 1600 John Dowland, *Flow My Tears*

1601 Thomas Weelkes, *As Vesta Was Descending*

The fifteenth and sixteenth centuries in Europe have come to be known as the Renaissance. People then spoke of a "rebirth," or *renaissance,* of human creativity. It was a period of exploration and adventure—consider the voyages of Christopher Columbus (1492), Vasco da Gama (1498), and Ferdinand Magellan (1519–1522). The Renaissance was an age of curiosity and individualism, too, as can be seen in the remarkable life of Leonardo da Vinci (1452–1519), who was a painter, sculptor, architect, engineer, and scientist—and a fine musician as well.

During the Renaissance, the dominant intellectual movement, which was called *humanism,* focused on human life and its accomplishments. Humanists were not concerned with an afterlife in heaven or hell. Though devout Christians, they were captivated by the cultures of ancient Greece and Rome. They became intoxicated with the beauty of ancient languages—Greek and Latin—and with the literature of antiquity. Humanism strongly influenced art throughout the Renaissance. Painters and sculptors were attracted to subjects drawn from classical literature and mythology. Once again they depicted the nude human body, which had been a favorite theme of antiquity but an object of shame and concealment during the Middle Ages. Medieval artists had been concerned more with religious symbolism than with lifelike representation. They had

During the Renaissance, the Virgin Mary was depicted as a beautiful, idealized young woman. Renaissance painters emphasized balance and used perspective to create an illusion of depth. *Madonna del Granduca* (c. 1505) by Raphael.

Renaissance sculptors and painters once again depicted the nude human body, which had been an object of shame and concealment during the Middle Ages. *David* (1504) by Michelangelo.

Classical mythology was an important source of inspiration for Renaissance art. *La Primavera* (*Spring;* c. 1482) by Sandro Botticelli depicts Venus (center); the Three Graces and Mercury (left); and Flora, Spring, and Zephyrus (right).

conceived of a picture as a flat, impenetrable surface on which persons or objects were shown. Renaissance painters like Raphael (1483–1520) and Leonardo da Vinci were more interested in realism and used linear perspective, a geometrical system for creating an illusion of space and depth. During the Renaissance, painters no longer treated the Virgin Mary as a childlike, unearthly creature; they showed her as a beautiful young woman.

The Catholic church was far less powerful during the Renaissance than it had been during the Middle Ages, for the unity of Christendom was exploded by the Protestant Reformation led by Martin Luther (1483–1546). No longer did the church monopolize learning. Aristocrats and the upper middle class now considered education a status symbol, and they hired scholars to teach their children. The invention of printing with movable type (around 1450) accelerated the spread of learning. Before 1450, books were rare and extremely expensive because they were copied entirely by hand. But by 1500, 15 million to 20 million copies of 40,000 editions had been printed in Europe.

Renaissance artists were strongly influenced by the cultures of ancient Greece and Rome. *The School of Athens* (1505) by Raphael, showing the Greek philosophers Aristotle and Plato (center). Plato is painted in the likeness of Leonardo da Vinci.

1 Music in the Renaissance
(1450–1600)

The Renaissance in music occurred between 1450 and 1600. (Some historians place the beginning of the Renaissance as early as 1400.) As in the other arts, the horizons of music were greatly expanded. The invention of printing widened the circulation of music, too, and the number of composers and performers increased.

In keeping with the Renaissance ideal of the "universal man," every educated person was expected to be trained in music. "I am not pleased with the courtier if he be not also a musician," Castiglione wrote in *The Book of the Courtier* (1528). Shakespeare's stage directions call for music more than 300 times, and his plays are full of beautiful tributes to music:

> The man that hath no music in himself,
> Nor is not mov'd with concord of sweet sounds,
> Is fit for treasons, stratagems and spoils.
> *(The Merchant of Venice)*

As in the past, musicians worked in churches, courts, and towns. Church choirs grew in size. (The papal choir in Rome increased from ten singers in 1442 to twenty-four in 1483.) Although polyphonic church music in the Middle Ages was usually sung by several soloists, during the Renaissance it was performed by an entire (male) choir. The church remained an important patron of music, but musical activity gradually shifted to the courts. Kings, princes, and dukes competed for the finest composers. A single court might have ten to sixty musicians, including singers as well as instrumentalists. Women functioned as virtuoso singers at several Italian courts during the late Renaissance. A court music director would compose secular pieces to entertain the nobility and sacred works for the court chapel. The nobility often brought their musicians along when traveling from one castle to another.

Renaissance town musicians played for civic processions, weddings, and religious services. In general, musicians enjoyed higher status and pay than ever before. Composers were no longer content to remain unknown; like other artists, they sought credit for their work.

Many leading Renaissance composers came from the Low Countries (Flanders), an area which now includes parts of the Netherlands, Belgium, and northern France. These Flemish composers were regarded highly and held important positions throughout Europe, but especially in Italy, which became the leading music center in the sixteenth century. Other countries with a vibrant musical life in the Renaissance were Germany, England, and Spain.

Characteristics of Renaissance Music

Words and Music In the Renaissance, as in the Middle Ages, vocal music was more important than instrumental music. The humanistic interest in language influenced vocal music, creating a close relationship between words and music. Renaissance composers wrote music to enhance the meaning and emotion of the text. "When one of the words expresses weeping, pain, heartbreak, sighs, tears and other similar things, let the harmony be full of sadness," wrote Zarlino, a music theorist of the sixteenth century. By contrast, medieval composers had been relatively uninterested in expressing the emotions of a text.

Renaissance composers often used **word painting,** musical representation of specific poetic images. For example, the words *descending from heaven* might be set to a descending melodic line, and *running* might be heard with a series of rapid notes. Yet despite this emphasis on capturing the emotion and imagery of a text, Renaissance music may seem calm and restrained to us. While there *is* a wide range of emotion in Renaissance music, it is usually expressed in a moderate, balanced way, with *no* extreme contrasts of dynamics, tone color, or rhythm.

Texture   The texture of Renaissance music is chiefly polyphonic. A typical choral piece has four, five, or six voice parts of nearly equal melodic interest. Imitation among the voices is common: each presents the same melodic idea in turn, as in a round. Homophonic texture, with successions of chords, is also used, especially in light music, like dances. The texture may vary within a piece to provide contrast and bring out aspects of the text as it develops.

Renaissance music sounds fuller than medieval music. The bass register was used for the first time, expanding the pitch range to more than four octaves. With this new emphasis on the bass line came richer harmony. Renaissance music sounds mild and relaxed, because stable, consonant chords are favored; triads occur often, while dissonances are played down.

Renaissance choral music did not need instrumental accompaniment. For this reason, the period is sometimes called the "golden age" of unaccompanied—*a cappella*—choral music. Even so, on special occasions instruments were combined with voices. Instruments might duplicate the vocal lines to reinforce the sound, or they might take the part of a missing singer. But parts written exclusively for instruments are rarely found in Renaissance choral music.

Rhythm and Melody   In Renaissance music, rhythm is more a gentle flow than a sharply defined beat. This is because each melodic line has great rhythmic independence: when one singer is at the beginning of his or her melodic phrase, the others may already be in the middle of theirs. This technique makes singing Renaissance music both a pleasure and a challenge, for each singer must maintain an individual rhythm. But pitch patterns in Renaissance melodies are easy to sing. The melody usually moves along a scale with few large leaps.

2 Sacred Music in the Renaissance

The two main forms of sacred Renaissance music are the motet and the mass. They are alike in style, but a mass is a longer composition. The Renaissance **motet** is a polyphonic choral work set to a sacred Latin text other than the ordinary of the mass. The Renaissance **mass** is a polyphonic choral composition made up of five sections: Kyrie, Gloria, Credo, Sanctus, and Agnus Dei.

Josquin Desprez and the Renaissance Motet

Josquin Desprez (about 1440–1521), a contemporary of Leonardo da Vinci and Christopher Columbus, was a master of Renaissance music. Like many Flemish composers, he had an international career. Josquin was born in the province of Hainaut—today part of Belgium—and spent much of his life in Italy, serving in dukes' private chapels and in the papal choir at Rome. In his later years, he worked for Louis XII of France and held several church posts in his native land.

Josquin's compositions, which include masses, motets, and secular vocal pieces, strongly influenced other composers and were praised enthusiastically by music lovers. Martin Luther, for example, remarked: "God has His Gospel preached also through the medium of music; this may be seen from the compositions of Josquin, all of whose works are cheerful, gentle, mild, and lovely; they flow and move along and are neither forced nor coerced and bound by rigid and stringent rules, but, on the contrary, are like the song of the finch."

Ave Maria . . . virgo serena (Hail, Mary . . . serene virgin; c. 1475)

Basic Set:
CD 1 76

Brief Set:
CD 1 56

Josquin's four-voice motet *Ave Maria . . . virgo serena* is an outstanding Renaissance choral work. This Latin prayer to the Virgin is set to delicate and serene music. The opening uses polyphonic imitation, a technique typical of the period.

The short melodic phrase on *Ave Maria* is presented by the soprano voice and then imitated in turn by the alto, tenor, and bass. The next two words, *gratia plena* (*full of grace*), have a different melody, which also is passed from voice to voice. Notice that each voice enters while the preceding one is in the middle of its melody. This overlapping creates a feeling of continuous flow. Josquin adapted the melody for the opening phrases from a Gregorian chant, but the rest of the motet was not based on a chant melody.

Josquin skillfully varies the texture of this motet; two, three, or four voices are heard at one time. In addition to the imitation among individual voices, there is imitation between pairs of voices: duets between the high voices are imitated by the two lower parts. Sometimes the texture almost becomes homophonic, as at the words *Ave, vera virginitas*. Here, also, is a change from duple to triple meter, and the tempo momentarily becomes more animated. But soon the music returns to duple meter and a more peaceful mood. *Ave Maria* ends with slow chords that express Josquin's personal plea to the Virgin: *O Mother of God, remember me. Amen.*

VOCAL MUSIC GUIDE

JOSQUIN, *Ave Maria . . . virgo serena*

76 **56** 0:00	Each soprano phrase imitated in turn by alto, tenor, and bass. Duple meter.	*Ave Maria gratia plena dominus tecum, virgo serena.*	Hail Mary, full of grace, the Lord is with thee, serene Virgin.
0:49	High duet imitated by three lower voices.	*Ave, cuius conceptio,*	Hail, whose conception,
	All four voices. Increased rhythmic animation reflects "new joy."	*solemni plena gaudio, coelestia terrestria nova replet laetitia.*	full of great jubilation, fills Heaven and Earth with new joy.
1:32	High duet imitated by low duet. Soprano phrase imitated by alto, tenor, and bass.	*Ave, cuius nativitas nostra fuit solemnitas, ut lucifer lux oriens verum solem praeveniens.*	Hail, whose birth brought us joy, as Lucifer, the morning star, went before the true sun.
2:17	High duet imitated by low duet. High duet. Low duet.	*Ave, pia humilitas, sine viro fecunditas, cuius annuntiatio nostra fuit salvatio.*	Hail, pious humility, fruitful without a man, whose Annunciation brought us salvation.
77 **57** 2:50	Triple meter.	*Ave, vera virginitas, immaculata castitas, cuius purificatio nostra fuit purgatio.*	Hail, true virginity, immaculate chastity, whose purification brought our cleansing.
78 **58** 3:16	Duple meter, high duets imitated by lower voices.	*Ave praeclara omnibus angelicis virtutibus, cuius assumptio nostra glorificatio.*	Hail, glorious one in all angelic virtues, whose Assumption was our glorification.
	Brief pause. Sustained chords.	*O mater Dei, memento mei. Amen.*	O Mother of God, remember me. Amen.

Palestrina and the Renaissance Mass

During the sixteenth century, Italian composers attained the excellence of such earlier Flemish musicians as Josquin Desprez. Among the most important Italian Renaissance composers was Giovanni Pierluigi da Palestrina (about 1525–1594), who devoted himself to music for the Catholic church. His career was thus centered in Rome, where he held important church positions, including that of music director for St. Peter's.

Palestrina's music includes 104 masses and some 450 other sacred works; it is best understood against the background of the Counter-Reformation. During the early 1500s, the Catholic church was challenged and questioned by the Protestants and,

A miniature showing a mass at the court of Philip the Good in Burgundy.

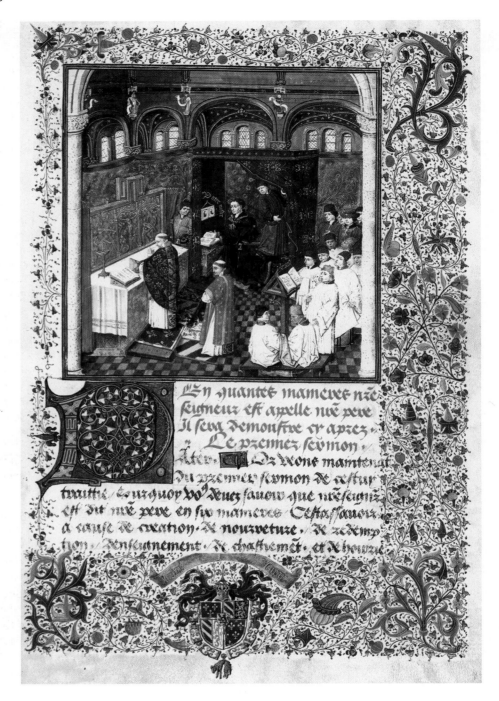

as a result, sought to correct abuses and malpractices within its structure, as well as to counter the move toward Protestantism. This need to strengthen the church led to the founding of the Jesuit order (1540) and the convening of the Council of Trent (1545–1563), which considered questions of dogma and organization.

During its deliberations, the council discussed church music, which many felt had lost its purity. Years before, the scholar Desiderius Erasmus (about 1466–1536) had complained: "We have introduced an artificial and theatrical music into the church, a bawling and agitation of various voices, such as I believe had never been heard in the theaters of the Greeks and Romans. . . . Amorous and lascivious melodies are heard such as elsewhere accompany only the dances of courtesans and clowns." At the council sessions, church music was attacked because it used secular tunes, noisy instruments, and theatrical singing. Some complained that complex polyphony made it impossible to understand the sacred texts; they wanted only monophonic music—Gregorian chant—for the mass. The council finally decreed that church music should be composed not "to give empty pleasure to the ear," but to inspire religious contemplation.

The restraint and serenity of Palestrina's works reflect this emphasis on a more spiritual music. For centuries, church authorities have regarded his masses as models of church music because of their calmness and otherworldly quality. Even today, the technical perfection of his style is a model for students of counterpoint.

Pope Marcellus Mass (1562–1563)

Palestrina's *Pope Marcellus* Mass, his most famous mass, was long thought to have convinced the Council of Trent that polyphonic masses should be kept in Catholic worship. While we now know that this work did *not* play that role, it does reflect the council's desire for a clear projection of the sacred text. It is dedicated to Pope Marcellus II, who reigned briefly in 1555 while Palestrina was a singer in the papal choir.

The *Pope Marcellus* Mass is written for an a cappella choir of six voice parts: soprano, alto, two tenors, and two basses. We'll focus on the first section of the mass, the Kyrie.

Kyrie

Basic Set:

CD 1 79

Brief Set:

CD 1 59

The Kyrie has a rich polyphonic texture. Its six voice parts constantly imitate each other, yet blend beautifully. This music sounds fuller than Josquin's *Ave Maria*, in part because six voices are used rather than four. The elegantly curved melodies summon the spirit of Gregorian chant. They flow smoothly and can be sung easily. Upward leaps are balanced at once by downward steps, as in the opening melody:

The Kyrie of the *Pope Marcellus* Mass is written in three different sections:

1. *Kyrie eleison.*   Lord, have mercy.
2. *Christe eleison.*   Christ, have mercy.
3. *Kyrie eleison.*   Lord, have mercy.

This text is short, and words are repeated with different melodic lines to express calm supplication. The rhythm flows continuously to the end of each section, when all voices come together on sustained chords. Each of the three sections begins in a thin texture with only some of the voices sounding; but as the other voices enter, the music becomes increasingly full and rich. In our recording, the third section sounds climactic because it is performed in a somewhat faster tempo and at a louder dynamic level than the first two sections.

VOCAL MUSIC GUIDE

PALESTRINA, *Kyrie* from *Pope Marcellus* Mass

79 59 0:00	Tenor quickly imitated in turn by three other voice parts; remaining two voice parts join. Voices imitate each other and repeat words. Sustained chord, pause end section.	1. *Kyrie eleison.*	Lord, have mercy.
80 60 1:35	Three voice parts begin at same time; other three voice parts join in turn. Voices imitate each other. Sustained chord, pause.	2. *Christe eleison.*	Christ, have mercy.
81 61 3:29	Soprano phrase quickly imitated in turn by three lower voice parts; two other voice parts join. Voices imitate each other.	3. *Kyrie eleison.*	Lord, have mercy.
4:35	Sustained chord ends *Kyrie.*		

3 Secular Music in the Renaissance

Vocal Music

During the Renaissance, secular vocal music became increasingly popular. Throughout Europe, music was set to poems in various languages, including Italian, French, Spanish, German, Dutch, and English.

The development of music printing helped spread secular music, and thousands of song collections became available. Music was an important leisure activity; every educated person was expected to play an instrument and read notation. The Elizabethan composer Thomas Morley describes the embarrassment of being unable to participate in after-dinner music making: "But supper being ended, and Musicke bookes (according to the custome) being brought to the tables, the mistresse of the house presented me with a part, earnestly requesting me to sing. But when, after many excuses, I protested unfainedly that I could not: every one began to wonder. Yea, some whispered to others, demanding how I was brought up."

Renaissance secular music was written for groups of solo voices and for solo voice with the accompaniment of one or more instruments. Word painting—musical illustration of a text—was common. Composers delighted in imitating natural sounds such as birdcalls and street cries. In a famous piece entitled *La Guerre* (*The War*), the Frenchman Clément Janequin (about 1485–1560) vividly imitated battle noises, drumbeats, and fanfares. Secular music contained more rapid shifts of mood than sacred music. As Morley advised one composer, "You must in your music be wavering like the wind, sometimes wanton, sometimes drooping, sometimes grave and staid; . . . and the more variety you show the better shall you please."

The Renaissance Madrigal An important kind of secular vocal music during the Renaissance was the *madrigal,* a piece for several solo voices set to a short poem, usually about love. A madrigal, like a motet, combines homophonic and polyphonic textures. But the madrigal uses word painting and unusual harmonies more often.

The Renaissance madrigal originated in Italy around 1520, during a creative explosion in Italian poetry. Madrigals were published by the thousands in sixteenth-century Italy, where they were sung by cultivated aristocrats. Among the many Italian madrigalists were Luca Marenzio (1553–1599) and Carlo Gesualdo (about 1560–1613), the infamous prince of Venosa who had his wife and her lover murdered after finding them together in bed.

In 1588—the year of the defeat of the Spanish Armada—a volume of translated Italian madrigals was published in London. This inspired a spurt of madrigal writing by English composers, and for about thirty years there was a steady flow of English madrigals and other secular vocal music. The time of Queen Elizabeth I (1533–1603) and William Shakespeare (1564–1616) was as much a golden age in English music as it was in English literature. The impetus for both arts arose in Italy. But the English madrigal became lighter and more humorous than its Italian model, and its melody and harmony were simpler.

As Vesta Was Descending (1601), by Thomas Weelkes

Basic Set:

CD 1 82

Brief Set:

CD 1 62

Among the finest English madrigalists was Thomas Weelkes (about 1575–1623), an organist and church composer. Weelkes's *As Vesta Was Descending* comes from *The Triumphes of Oriana* (1601), an anthology of English madrigals written to honor Queen Elizabeth, who was often called Oriana. The text of this six-voice madrigal pictures Vesta (the Roman goddess of the hearth) coming down a hill with her attendants, "Diana's darlings." (Diana was the Roman goddess of chastity, hunting, and the moon.) At the same time, the "maiden queen," Oriana (Elizabeth), is climbing the hill with her shepherd gallants. Vesta's attendants desert her and race down the hill to join Oriana.

As Vesta Was Descending has the light mood typical of English madrigals. Word painting is plentiful. For example, the word *descending* is sung to downward scales, and *ascending* to upward ones.

When Vesta's attendants run down the hill, "first *two* by *two,* then *three* by *three together,* leaving their goddess all *alone,*" we hear first *two* voices, then *three* voices, then *six* voices, and finally a *solo* voice. In the extended concluding section, "*Long* live fair Oriana," a joyous phrase is imitated among the voices. And in the bass this phrase is sung in long notes, with the longest note on the word *long.*

VOCAL MUSIC GUIDE

WEELKES, *As Vesta Was Descending*

82 **62**

Descending scales.	As Vesta was from Latmos hill *descending,*
Ascending scales.	she spied a maiden queen the same *ascending,*
Rapid descending figures.	attended on by all the shepherds swain, to whom Diana's darlings came *running down* amain.
Two voices,	First *two* by *two,*
Three voices; all voices.	then *three* by *three together,*
Solo voice.	leaving their goddess *all alone,* hasted thither, and mingling with the shepherds of her train with mirthful tunes her presence entertain. Then sang the shepherds and nymphs of Diana,
Brief joyful phrase imitated among voices; long notes in bass.	*Long* live fair Oriana!

The Renaissance Lute Song

A simpler type of secular music than the madrigal is the song for solo voice and lute. The **lute,** which derives from the Arab instrument known as the *ʿūd* (literally, *the wood*), is a plucked string instrument with a body shaped like half a pear. The lute's versatility—like that of the guitar today—made it the most popular instrument in the Renaissance home. It could be used for solos or for accompaniments; to play chords, melodies, and rapid scales; and even in polyphonic music.

In England the lute song was widely cultivated from the late 1590s to the 1620s. In contrast to much Renaissance music, lute songs are mostly homophonic in texture. The lute accompaniment is secondary to the vocal melody. During the Renaissance, singers could accompany themselves, or have the lute accompaniment played by another musician.

Flow My Tears (about 1600), by John Dowland (1563–1626)

Basic Set:
CD 1 **83**

Brief Set:
CD 1 **63**

The leading English composer of lute songs was John Dowland, a virtuoso performer on the lute famous throughout Europe. His lute song *Flow My Tears* was extraordinarily popular in Shakespeare's time, and in our own day it has been recorded by many singers, including the rock star Sting.

Flow My Tears expresses the intense melancholy of someone whose happiness has been abruptly shattered. Such emotionally charged words as *tears, despair, woes, sighs, groans, fear, and grief* dominate the song's text, a poem that may have been written by Dowland himself. The expression of melancholy was a prominent feature of English literature and music in the time of Elizabeth I and Shakespeare. Dowland, especially, seems to have cultivated a melancholy public image, and he composed many pieces with sad titles such as *Semper Dowland semper dolens* (*Always Dowland, Always Sorrow*).

Flow My Tears consists of three brief musical sections (A, B, C) that are each immediately repeated: AA (stanzas 1 and 2), BB (stanzas 3 and 4), CC (stanza 5 repeated to the same melody). Dowland's music heightens the mood of grief through its slow tempo, minor key, and descending four-note melodic pattern that represents falling tears. This descending pattern appears throughout the song with variations of pitch and rhythm.

The opening four-note descent, in minor, on *Flow my tears,* is immediately repeated—with greater emotional intensity—on higher, slower notes to the words *fall from your springs.*

Part B begins with a contrasting major-key version of the four-note descent on the words *Never may my.*

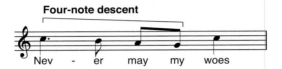

Dowland creates variety by opening part C with a stepwise *ascent,* turning the four-note pattern upside down on the words *Hark you shadows.*

In much of the song, the lute accompaniment is subordinate to the voice. However, in part B, the lute momentarily gains prominence as it imitates the voice's gasping upward skips on *and tears, and sighs,* heightening the agitated mood.

As Sting has observed, even though *Flow My Tears* is "a song about hopelessness, it is strangely uplifting."

VOCAL MUSIC GUIDE

DOWLAND, *Flow My Tears*

83 **63**	0:00	A	Minor key.	Flow my tears, fall from your springs,
				    Exiled for ever: Let me mourn
				where night's black bird her sad infamy sings,
				    there let me live forlorn.

	0:38	A	Minor.	Down vain lights, shine you no more,
				    No nights are dark enough for those
				That in despair their lost fortunes deplore,
				    light doth but shame disclose.

	1:18	B	Major.
			Minor.
			Lute imitates voice.
				Never may my woes be relieved,
				    since pity is fled,
				and tears, and sighs, and groans my weary days,
				    of all joys have deprived.

	1:55	B	Major.
			Minor.
			Lute imitates voice.
				From the highest spire of contentment,
				    my fortune is thrown;
				and fear, and grief, and pain for my deserts,
				    are my hopes since hope is gone

	2:31	C	Minor.	Hark you shadows that in darkness dwell,
				    learn to condemn light,
				Happy, happy they that in hell
				    feel not the world's despite.

	3:13	C	Minor.	Hark you shadows that in darkness dwell,
				    learn to condemn light,
				Happy, happy they that in hell
				    feel not the world's despite.

Instrumental Music

Though still subordinate to vocal music, instrumental music did become more important during the Renaissance. Traditionally, instrumentalists accompanied voices or played music intended for singing. Even in the early 1500s instrumental music was largely adapted from vocal music. Instrumental groups performed polyphonic vocal pieces, which were often published with the indication *to be sung or played.* Soloists used the harpsichord, organ, or lute to play simple arrangements of vocal works.

During the sixteenth century, however, instrumental music became increasingly emancipated from vocal models. More music was written specifically for instruments. Renaissance composers began to exploit the particular capacities of the lute or organ for instrumental solos. They also developed purely instrumental forms, such as theme and variations.

Much of this instrumental music was intended for dancing, a popular Renaissance entertainment. Every cultivated person was expected to be skilled in dance, which was taught by professional dancing masters. Court dances were often performed in pairs. A favorite pair was the stately *pavane,* or *passamezzo,* in duple meter, and the lively *galliard,* in triple meter. Dance music was performed by instrumental groups or by

A wide variety of instruments were used during the Renaissance. Hans Burgkmair's woodcut of the emperor Maximilian with his musicians (1505–1516) shows (left) an organ and a cornett; (center) a harp; (on floor) a drum, a kettledrum, a trumsheit (string instrument), and a sackbut; (on table) a viola da gamba, an oblong keyboard instrument, a flute, recorders, a cornett, and a krummhorn.

soloists like harpsichordists and lutenists. A wealth of dance music published during the sixteenth century has come down to us.

Renaissance musicians distinguished between loud, outdoor instruments like the trumpet and the *shawm* (a double-reed ancestor of the oboe), and soft, indoor instruments like the lute and the *recorder* (an early flute). The many instruments used in the Renaissance produced softer, less brilliant sounds than we hear from instruments today; most came in families of from three to eight instruments, ranging from soprano to bass. Among the most important Renaissance instruments were recorders, shawms, *cornetts* (wooden instruments with cup-shaped mouthpieces), *sackbuts* (early trombones), lutes, *viols* (bowed string instruments), organs, *regals* (small organs with reed pipes), and harpsichords. Often several members of the same instrumental family were played together, but Renaissance composers did not specify the instruments they wanted. A single work might be performed by recorders, viols, or several different instruments, depending on what was available. Today's standardized orchestra did not exist. Large courts might employ thirty instrumentalists of all types. On state occasions such as a royal wedding, guests might be entertained by woodwinds, plucked and bowed strings, and keyboard instruments all playing together.

Much instrumental music of the Renaissance was intended for dancing. This illustration is from a book of hours produced in Tours, France, c. 1530–1535.

Passamezzo and Galliard, by Pierre Francisque Caroubel, from *Terpsichore* (1612), by Michael Praetorius

This passamezzo and galliard illustrate the Renaissance practice of pairing contrasting court dances in duple and triple meter. These dances come from *Terpsichore*, a collection of over 300 dance tunes arranged for instrumental ensemble by Michael Praetorius (1571–1621), a German composer and theorist. (Terpsichore was the Greek muse, or goddess, of the dance.) A few dances in the collection, including the passamezzo and galliard studied here, were composed by the French violinist Pierre Francisque Caroubel (1576–1611). Both dance types originated in Italy and were popular during the sixteenth century and the early seventeenth century.

Basic Set:
CD 2

The passamezzo is a stately dance in duple meter and the galliard is a quick dance in triple meter. The dance-pair studied here is written for five unspecified instrumental parts. In our recording the two dances are performed by a Renaissance string ensemble including violins, violas, and bass violins (ancestors of the cello), lutes, and harpsichord. Both the passamezzo and galliard are made up of three brief sections (a, b, c). The two dances can be outlined as follows:

> Passamezzo: aa bb cc abc
> Galliard: aa bb cc

Basic Set:
CD 2

The music of the galliard is a variation of the preceding passamezzo, but sounds very different because its tempo is faster and its meter is triple rather than duple.

Gentile Bellini (c. 1429–1507), *Procession in St. Mark's Square*. The focal point for music in Venice was St. Mark's Cathedral.

In each dance, section b brings greater rhythmic animation. Section b of the passa-mezzo introduces quicker note values (eighth notes).

Section b of the galliard brings delightful rhythmic irregularity because $\frac{6}{4}$ meter alternates with the prevailing $\frac{3}{2}$ meter. That is, six fast pulses divide alternatively into *two* groups of three pulses (**1**-2-3 **4**-5-6) and *three* groups of two pulses (**1**-2 **3**-4 **5**-6).

A similar alternation can be heard in *America,* from Leonard Bernstein's *West Side Story,* studied in Part IX, Music for Stage and Screen.

4 | The Venetian School: From Renaissance to Baroque

During the sixteenth century, Venice—an independent city-state on the northeastern coast of Italy—became a center of instrumental and vocal music. Venice is a seaport built on tiny islands separated by canals; it was a thriving commercial center for trade between Europe and the near east. Venice proclaimed its importance both by means of magnificent processions and through its architecture and painting. Venetian painters such as Titian, Tintoretto, and Veronese were inspired by the city's special light and used rich, brilliant colors.

The focal point for music in Venice was St. Mark's Cathedral. The cathedral was colorful and wealthy, and it employed up to twenty instrumentalists and thirty singers for grand ceremonies within the cathedral and in St. Mark's Square. The music directors and organists at St. Mark's, such as Adrian Willaert (about 1490–1562), Andrea Gabrieli (about 1520–1586), and Andrea's nephew Giovanni Gabrieli, were among the finest composers of the Renaissance. They and their colleagues are called the *Venetian school.*

Venetian composers were stimulated by an architectural feature of St. Mark's Cathedral—two widely separated choir lofts, each with an organ—and wrote much music for several choruses and groups of instruments. Unlike most Renaissance choral music, Venetian choral music of the late sixteenth century often contains parts that are written exclusively for instruments. This conscious use of instrumental color brings some works of the Venetian school close to the early baroque style. Another early baroque feature of some Venetian music is a tendency toward homophonic texture, rather than the polyphonic texture typical of Renaissance music.

Giovanni Gabrieli and the Polychoral Motet

Giovanni Gabrieli (about 1555–1612), a native of Venice, was the most important Venetian composer of the late Renaissance. He studied with his uncle Andrea Gabrieli and was an organist at St. Mark's from 1585 until his death. His compositions include organ and instrumental ensemble works and *polychoral motets:* motets for two or more choirs, often including groups of instruments. Gabrieli's *Sonata pian e forte* (1597) is famous as one of the earliest instrumental ensemble pieces in which dynamics and instrumentation are specified by the composer. His polychoral motets for two to five choirs call for an unprecedentedly large number of performers and brilliantly exploit contrasts of register, sonority, and tone color.

Plaudite (Clap Your Hands; 1597)

Basic Set:

CD 2 ▪3▪

Giovanni Gabrieli's spectacular polychoral motet *Plaudite* was intended for a joyful ceremony at St. Mark's Cathedral. Its Latin text calls for praise of God. The motet is written for a large vocal and instrumental ensemble of twelve voice parts divided into three *choirs,* or performing groups, that contrast in register. It has one low choir, one choir in a middle register, and one high choir. The choice of instruments is left to the performers. In our recording, some voices are reinforced by three sackbuts, three cornetts, or an organ.

Gabrieli exploits the "stereophonic" possibilities of St. Mark's by rapidly tossing short phrases among the three separate choirs. Often the choirs combine to produce splendidly massive sonorities. Gabrieli unifies the motet by using the same music (A) for each of four short *alleluia* sections. These sections are in triple meter and contrast with the prevailing duple meter of the motet. With its homophonic texture and its flamboyant use of contrasting sonorities, *Plaudite* is at the border between the Renaissance and early baroque styles.

VOCAL MUSIC GUIDE

GIOVANNI GABRIELI, *Plaudite*

3	0:00		*Plaudite, Psallite, Jubilate Deo omnis terra:*	Clap your hands, sing praises, sing joyfully to God, all the earth.
	0:14	**A**	*alleluia,*	Alleluia.
			benedicant Dominum omnes gentes, collaudantes eum:	Let all the nations bless the Lord, together praising Him.
	0:50	**A**	*alleluia,*	Alleluia.
			quia fecit nobiscum Dominus misericordiam suam:	For the Lord hath acted in His mercy with us.
	1:28	**A**	*alleluia,*	Alleluia.
			et captivam duxit captivitatem, admirabilis et gloriosus in saecula:	And led captivity captive. Admirable and glorious He is forever.
	2:21	**A**	*alleluia.*	Alleluia.
	Climactic section in duple meter ends *Plaudite.*		*alleluia.*	Alleluia.

The Baroque Period

The figured bass is the most perfect foundation of music, being played with both hands in such a manner that the left hand plays the notes written down while the right adds consonances and dissonances, in order to make a well-sounding harmony to the Glory of God and the permissible delectation of the spirit.

— *Johann Sebastian Bach*

During the late baroque period, instrumental music became as important as vocal music for the first time. In *The Music Lesson* (1662–1665), by the Dutch painter Jan Vermeer, the instruments shown are a viola da gamba and a virginal, which is a type of small harpsichord.

TIME LINE

Baroque Period
1600–1750

1600–1680	1680–1750

Historical and Cultural Events

1607 Jamestown founded

1611 King James Bible

1610 Galileo confirms that the earth revolves around the sun

1618–1648 Thirty Years' War

1643–1715 Louis XIV reigns in France

1687 Newton, *Principia Mathematica*

1692 Witchcraft trials in Salem, Massachusetts

1715–1774 Louis XV reigns in France

1740–1786 Frederick the Great reigns in Prussia

Arts and Letters

1600 Shakespeare, *Hamlet*

1605 Cervantes, *Don Quixote*

1612–1615 Rubens, *Descent from the Cross*

1613 Gentileschi, *Judith Slaying Holofernes*

1623 Bernini, *David Slaying Goliath*

1630 Poussin, *Mars and Venus*

1659 Rembrandt, *Self-Portrait*

1667 Milton, *Paradise Lost*

1689 Locke, *Essay Concerning Human Understanding*

1717 Watteau, *The Embarkation for Cythera*

1719 Defoe, *Robinson Crusoe*

1726 Swift, *Gulliver's Travels*

Music

1607 Monteverdi, *Orfeo*

1642 Monteverdi, *The Coronation of Poppea*

1689 Purcell, *Dido and Aeneas*

1689 Corelli, Trio Sonata in A Minor, Op. 3, No. 10

c. 1709 Bach, Organ Fugue in G Minor (*Little Fugue*)

c. 1721 Bach, *Brandenburg* Concerto No. 5 in D Major

1725 Vivaldi, *La Primavera* (*Spring*), Concerto for Violin and Orchestra, Op. 8, No. 1

1731 Bach, Cantata No. 140: *Wachet auf, ruft uns die Stimme*

1741 Handel, *Messiah*

Though the word *baroque* has at various times meant bizarre, flamboyant, and elaborately ornamented, modern historians use it simply to indicate a particular style in the arts. An oversimplified but useful characterization of baroque style is that it fills space—canvas, stone, or sound—with action and movement. Painters, sculptors, and architects became interested in forming a total illusion, like a stage setting. Artists such as Caravaggio, Gentileschi, Bernini, Rubens, and Rembrandt exploited their materials to expand the dramatic potential of color, depth, and contrasts of light and dark; they wanted to create totally structured worlds.

Such a style was very well suited to the wishes of the aristocracy, who also thought in terms of completely integrated structures. In France, for example, Louis XIV held court in the palace of Versailles, a magnificent setting that fused baroque painting, sculpture, architecture, and garden design into a symbol of royal wealth and power.

The aristocracy was enormously rich and powerful during the seventeenth and eighteenth centuries. While most of the population barely managed to survive, European rulers surrounded themselves with luxury. There were many such rulers. Germany, for example, was divided into about 300 territories, each governed separately. Kings and princes proclaimed their greatness by means of splendid palaces and magnificent court entertainments like balls, banquets, ballets, operas, and plays. Indeed, entertainment was a necessity; most courtiers did no real work and tried to avoid boredom as much as possible.

The baroque period (1600–1750) is also known as the "age of absolutism" because many rulers exercised absolute power over their subjects. In Germany, for example, the duke of Weimar could throw his court musician Johann Sebastian Bach into jail for a month because Bach stubbornly asked to leave his job.

Judith Slaying Holofernes (c. 1612–1613) by the Italian painter Artemisia Gentileschi (1593–1652). Baroque artists emphasized motion and drama.

Bernini's *David Slaying Goliath* (1623) fills space with action and movement. It is far more dynamic than Michelangelo's *David* shown on page 95.

Along with the aristocracy, religious institutions powerfully shaped the baroque style. Churches used the emotional and theatrical qualities of art to make worship more attractive and appealing. During the baroque period, Europe was divided into Catholic and Protestant areas: France, Spain, Italy, and the Austrian empire were primarily Catholic; England, Holland, Denmark, Sweden, and parts of Germany were Protestant.

The middle class, too, influenced the development of the baroque style. In the Netherlands, for example, prosperous merchants and doctors commissioned realistic landscapes and scenes from everyday life.

It is also helpful to think of baroque style against the backdrop of scientific discoveries during the seventeenth and eighteenth centuries. The work of Galileo (1564–1642) and Newton (1642–1727) represented a new approach to science based on the union of mathematics and experiment; they discovered mathematical laws governing bodies in motion. Such scientific advances led to new inventions and the gradual improvement of medicine, mining, navigation, and industry during the baroque era.

Mars and Venus (c. 1630) by the French painter Nicholas Poussin. The subject matter, harmonious colors, and balanced composition reflect Poussin's love of classical antiquity and Renaissance art.

The Flemish painter Peter Paul Rubens used diagonal motion and theatrical lighting in *Descent from the Cross* (1612–1615). Baroque artists became interested in forming a total illusion, like a stage setting. Often baroque painting and baroque opera were created for the nobility and were designed to display magnificent extravagance.

Self-Portrait (1659) by Rembrandt van Rijn. Rembrandt's use of light and dark contributes to the poetry, drama, and psychological truth of his portraits.

The palace of Versailles, in France, fused baroque architecture, sculpture, and painting into a symbol of royal wealth and power.

1 Baroque Music
(1600–1750)

In music, the baroque style flourished during the period from 1600 to 1750. The two giants of baroque composition were George Frideric Handel and Johann Sebastian Bach. Bach's death in 1750 marks the end of the period. Other baroque masters— Claudio Monteverdi, Henry Purcell, Arcangelo Corelli, Antonio Vivaldi—were largely forgotten until the twentieth century. But the appearance of long-playing records in the late 1940s spurred a "baroque revival" that made these musicians familiar to many music lovers.

The baroque period can be divided into three phases: early (1600–1640), middle (1640–1690), and late (1690–1750). Though the baroque music best known today comes from the latest phase, the earliest was one of the most revolutionary periods in music history. Monteverdi (1567–1643), for instance, strove to create unprecedented passion and dramatic contrast in his works. In Italy, especially, music was composed for texts conveying extreme emotion, and the text ruled the music. With this stress on drama and text, it is not surprising that Italian composers of the early baroque created opera—a drama sung to orchestral accompaniment. Their melodic lines imitated the rhythms and inflections of speech.

Early baroque composers favored homophonic texture over the polyphonic texture typical of Renaissance music. They felt that words could be projected more clearly by using just one main melody with a chordal accompaniment. But note that this new emphasis on homophonic texture characterizes only the *early* baroque; by the *late* baroque period, polyphonic texture returned to favor.

To depict extreme emotions in their texts, early baroque composers used dissonance with a new freedom. Never before were unstable chords so prominent and emphatic. Contrasts of sound were stressed—one or more solo singers against a chorus, or voices against instruments. In Renaissance choral music, instruments—if used at all—duplicated a singer's melody. But in the early baroque, voices were accompanied by melodic lines designed for instruments.

During the middle phase of the baroque (1640–1690), the new musical style spread from Italy to practically every country in Europe. The medieval or church modes— scales that had governed music for centuries—gradually gave way to major and minor scales. By about 1690, major or minor scales were the tonal basis of most compositions. Another feature of the middle baroque phase was the new importance of instrumental music. Many compositions were written for specific instruments, the violin family being most popular.

We will focus mainly on the late baroque period (1690–1750), which produced most of the baroque music heard today. Many aspects of harmony—including an emphasis on the attraction of the dominant chord to the tonic—arose in this period. During the late baroque, instrumental music became as important as vocal music for the first time. Early baroque composers had emphasized homophonic texture; late baroque composers gloried in polyphony. Let's look more closely at some features of late baroque style. (From now on the word *baroque* will pertain to the late baroque phase.)

Characteristics of Baroque Music

Unity of Mood A baroque piece usually expresses one basic mood: what begins joyfully will remain joyful throughout. Emotional states like joy, grief, and agitation were represented—at the time, these moods were called *affections*. Composers molded a musical language to depict the affections; specific rhythms or melodic patterns were associated with specific moods. This common language gives a family resemblance to much late baroque music.

The prime exception to this baroque principle of unity of mood occurs in vocal music. Striking changes of emotion in a text may inspire corresponding changes in the music. But even in such cases, one mood is maintained at some length before it yields to another.

Rhythm   Unity of mood in baroque music is conveyed, first of all, by continuity of rhythm. Rhythmic patterns heard at the beginning of a piece are repeated throughout it. This rhythmic continuity provides a compelling drive and energy—the forward motion is rarely interrupted. The beat, for example, is emphasized far more in baroque music than in most Renaissance music.

Melody   Baroque melody also creates a feeling of continuity. An opening melody will be heard again and again in the course of a baroque piece. And even when a melody is presented in varied form, its character tends to remain constant. There is a continuous expanding, unfolding, and unwinding of melody. This sense of directed motion is frequently the result of a melodic sequence, that is, successive repetition of a musical idea at higher or lower pitches. Many baroque melodies sound elaborate and ornamental, and they are not easy to sing or remember. A baroque melody gives an impression of dynamic expansion rather than of balance or symmetry. A short opening phrase is often followed by a longer phrase with an unbroken flow of rapid notes.

Dynamics   Paralleling continuity of rhythm and melody in baroque music is continuity of dynamics: the level of volume tends to stay fairly constant for a stretch of time. When the dynamics do shift, the shift is sudden, like physically stepping from one level to another. This alternation between loud and soft is called *terraced dynamics. Gradual* changes through crescendo and decrescendo are *not* prominent features of baroque music. However, singers and instrumentalists no doubt made some subtle dynamic inflections for expressive purposes.

The main keyboard instruments of the baroque period were the organ and harpsichord, both well suited for continuity of dynamics. An organist or harpsichordist could not obtain a crescendo or decrescendo by varying finger pressure, as pianists today can. A third keyboard instrument, the *clavichord,* could make gradual dynamic changes, but only within a narrow range—from about *ppp* to *mp.* (The clavichord produced sound by means of brass blades striking the strings. It was usually not used in large halls, since its tone was too weak. But for home use by amateurs it was ideal; its cost was low and its expressive sound satisfying. It had especially wide popularity in Germany.)

Texture   We've noted that late baroque music is predominantly polyphonic in texture: two or more melodic lines compete for the listener's attention. Usually, the soprano and bass lines are the most important. Imitation between the various lines, or "voices," of the texture is very common. A melodic idea heard in one voice is likely to make an appearance in the other voices as well.

However, not all late baroque music was polyphonic. A piece might shift in texture, especially in vocal music, where changes of mood in the words demand musical contrast. Also, baroque composers differed in their treatment of musical texture. Bach inclined toward a consistently polyphonic texture, whereas Handel used much more contrast between polyphonic and homophonic sections.

Chords and the Basso Continuo   Chords became increasingly important during the baroque period. In earlier times, there was more concern with the beauty of individual melodic lines than with chords formed when the lines were heard together.

In a sense, chords were mere by-products of the motion of melodic lines. But in the baroque period chords became significant in themselves. As composers wrote a melodic line, they thought of chords to mesh with it. Indeed, sometimes they composed a melody to fit a specific chord progression. This interest in chords gave new prominence to the bass part, which served as the foundation of the harmony. The whole musical structure rested on the bass part.

The new emphasis on chords and the bass part resulted in the most characteristic feature of baroque music, an accompaniment called the ***basso continuo*** (Italian for *continuous bass*). The *continuo*—to use the common abbreviation for basso continuo— is usually played by at least two instruments: a keyboard instrument like an organ or a harpsichord and a low melodic instrument like a cello or bassoon. With the left hand the organist or harpsichordist plays the bass part, which is also performed by the cellist or bassoonist. With the right hand the keyboard player improvises chords following the indications of numbers (figures) above the bass part. This bass part with numbers (figures) is called a ***figured bass.*** The numbers specify only basic chords, not the exact way in which the chords should be played. Thus the performer is given a great deal of freedom. (This shorthand system is similar in principle to the chord indications found on the modern song sheets from which jazz pianists improvise.) Shown here is the beginning of the continuo part of Bach's *Brandenburg* Concerto No. 5, first movement (studied in Section 3), and one possible performance or *realization* of this part by a harpsichordist.

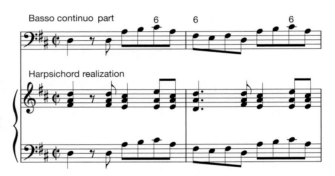

The basso continuo offered the advantage of emphasizing the all-important bass part, besides providing a steady flow of chords. Practically, the use of numbers, rather than chords with all their notes written out, saved time for busy baroque composers. It also saved paper during a period when paper was expensive.

Words and Music   Like their predecessors in the Renaissance, baroque composers used music to depict the meaning of specific words. *Heaven* might be set to a high tone, and *hell* to a low tone. Rising scales represented upward motion; descending scales depicted the reverse. Descending chromatic scales were associated with pain and grief. This descriptive musical language was quite standardized: a lament for a lost love might call forth the same descending chromatic scale used to depict suffering in the *Crucifixus* of the mass.

Baroque composers often emphasized words by writing many rapid notes for a single syllable of text; this technique also displayed a singer's virtuosity. The individual words and phrases of a text are repeated over and over as the music continuously unfolds.

The Baroque Orchestra

During the baroque period, the orchestra evolved into a performing group based on instruments of the violin family. By modern standards, the baroque orchestra was small, consisting of from ten to thirty or forty players. Its instrumental makeup was flexible and could vary from piece to piece. At its nucleus were the basso continuo (harpsichord plus cello, double bass, or bassoon) and upper strings (first and second violins and violas). Use of woodwind, brass, and percussion instruments was variable. To the strings and continuo could be added recorders, flutes, oboes, trumpets, horns, trombones, or timpani. One piece might use only a single flute, whereas another would call for two oboes, three trumpets, and timpani. Trumpets and timpani joined the orchestra mainly when the music was festive. This flexibility contrasts with the standardized orchestra of later periods, consisting of four sections: string, woodwind, brass, and percussion.

The baroque trumpet (like the early French horn) had no valves but was given rapid, complex melodic lines to play in a high register. Because the instrument was difficult to play and had a traditional association with royalty, the trumpeter was the aristocrat of the baroque orchestra. When prisoners of war were exchanged, trumpeters, if they had been captured, were treated like military officers.

Bach, Handel, Vivaldi, and others chose their orchestral instruments with care and obtained beautiful effects from specific tone colors. They loved to experiment with different combinations of instruments. However, in the baroque period tone color was distinctly subordinate to other musical elements—melody, rhythm, and harmony. Composers frequently rearranged their own or other composers' works for different instruments. A piece for string orchestra might become an organ solo, losing little in the process. Often, one instrument was treated like another. An oboe would play the same melody as the violins, or the flute and trumpet would imitate each other for extended sections of a piece.

Baroque Forms

It has been noted that a piece of baroque music—particularly instrumental music—usually has unity of mood. Yet many baroque compositions include a set of pieces, or movements, that contrast. A *movement* is a piece that sounds fairly complete and independent but is part of a larger composition. Usually, each movement has its own themes, comes to a definite end, and is separated from the next movement by a brief pause. Thus, a baroque composition in three movements may contain contrasts between a fast and energetic opening, a slow and solemn middle, and a conclusion that is quick, light, and humorous.

All the forms described in Part I, Section 9—"Musical Form"—appear in baroque music. Three-part form (A B A), two-part form (A B), and continuous or undivided form are all common. We'll consider examples of these and other forms in the sections that follow.

Regardless of form, baroque music features contrasts between bodies of sound. Often there is a quite regular alternation between a small and a larger group of instruments, or between instruments and voices with instrumental accompaniment. This exploration of contrasting sounds was pursued with great imagination and provides a key to the understanding and enjoyment of baroque music.

2 Music in Baroque Society

Before 1800, most music was written to order, to meet specific demands that came mainly from churches and aristocratic courts. Opera houses and municipalities also required a constant supply of music. In every case, the demand was for *new* music; audiences did not want to listen to pieces in an "old-fashioned" style.

Music was a main source of diversion in the courts of the aristocracy. One court might employ an orchestra, a chapel choir, and opera singers—the size of the musical staff depending on the court's wealth. Bach directed about eighteen players in the orchestra of a small German court in 1717, but a large court might have more than eighty performers, including the finest opera singers of the day. The music director supervised performances and composed much of the music required, including operas, church music, dinner music, and pieces for court concerts. This overworked musician also was responsible for the discipline of the other musicians, and for the upkeep of the instruments and the music library.

The music director's job had good and bad features. Pay and prestige were quite high, and anything the composer wrote would be performed. But no matter how great, the composer was still a servant who could neither quit nor even take a trip without the patron's permission. Like everyone in baroque society, musicians had to curry favor with the aristocracy.

It is in this light that we must understand dedications like the one which Bach addressed to a nobleman along with his *Brandenburg* Concertos: "Begging Your Highness most humbly not to judge their imperfection with the rigor of the fine and delicate taste which the whole world knows Your Highness has for musical pieces; but rather to infer from them in benign Consideration the profound respect and the most humble obedience which I try to show Your Highness." Yet sometimes musicians formed personal friendships with their patrons, as did Arcangelo Corelli, who thus gained a private apartment in a palace.

Some rulers were themselves good musicians. Frederick the Great, king of Prussia during the mid-eighteenth century, was a flutist and good composer, as well as a feared general. At his nightly court concerts, Frederick played his own works and some of the hundreds of pieces supplied by his flute teacher, Johann Quantz. (Quantz was "granted the privilege" of shouting "Bravo!" after a royal performance.)

During the baroque period, musicians often played with amateurs in music clubs or university music societies, getting together in private homes, coffeehouses, and taverns. *The Concert* by Nicholas Tournier (1590–1639) shows one such gathering.

Churches also needed music, and church music was often very grand. Along with an organ and a choir, many baroque churches had an orchestra to accompany services. Indeed, it was in church that most ordinary citizens heard music. There were few public concerts, and the populace was rarely invited to the palace. The music director of a church, like the music director at a court, had to produce a steady flow of new music and was also responsible for the musical training of choristers in the church school. Fine church music contributed to the prestige of a city, and cities often competed to attract the best musicians.

Still, church musicians earned less and had lower status than court musicians. Their meager income was supplemented by allotments of firewood and grain and by irregular fees for weddings and funerals. They suffered a financial pinch when a "healthy wind" blew and there were fewer funerals than usual, a situation Bach once complained about.

Large towns employed musicians for a variety of functions—to play in churches, in processions, in concerts for visiting dignitaries, and for university graduations. These town musicians often played with amateurs in music clubs or university music societies, getting together at private homes, coffeehouses, and taverns.

Some baroque musicians earned money by writing operas for commercial opera houses; such houses were located mainly in Italy. In Venice, a city of 125,000 people, six opera companies performed simultaneously between 1680 and 1700. In London, Handel became music director of a commercial opera company in 1719. Backed by English nobles, this company was a corporation with shares listed on the London stock exchange. When the company went bankrupt in 1728, Handel formed his own company, for which he wrote operas and served as conductor, manager, and impresario. In filling these many roles, Handel became one of the first great "freelance" musicians.

How did one become a musician in the baroque period? Often the art was handed from father to son; many leading composers—such as Bach, Vivaldi, Purcell, Couperin, and Rameau—were sons of musicians. Sometimes boys were apprenticed to a town musician and lived in his home. In return for instruction, the boys did odd jobs, such as copying music. Many baroque composers began their studies as choirboys, learning music in the choir school. In Italy, music schools were connected with orphanages. (*Conservatory* comes from the Italian for *orphans' home*.) There, orphans, foundlings, and poor children—boys and girls—were given thorough musical training, and some became the most sought-after opera singers and instrumentalists in Europe. Eminent composers such as Vivaldi were hired to teach and direct concerts in these schools. Vivaldi's all-female orchestra in Venice was considered one of the finest ensembles in Italy. During the baroque period, women were not permitted to be employed as music directors or as instrumentalists in court or opera orchestras. Nevertheless, a number of women—including Francesca Caccini, Barbara Strozzi, and Elisabeth-Claude Jacquet de la Guerre—succeeded in becoming respected composers.

To get a job, musicians usually had to pass a difficult examination, performing and submitting compositions. Sometimes there were nonmusical job requirements, too. An applicant might be expected to make a "voluntary contribution" to the town's treasury, or even to marry the daughter of a retiring musician. Bach and Handel turned down the same job because one of the conditions was marriage to the organist's daughter. Italian musicians held the best posts in most European courts and were frequently paid twice as much as local musicians.

Composers were an integral part of baroque society, working for courts, churches, towns, and commercial opera houses. Though they wrote their music to fit specific needs, its quality is so high that much of it has become standard in today's concert repertoire.

3 The Concerto Grosso and Ritornello Form

We've seen that the contrast between loud and soft sounds—between relatively large and small groups of performers—is a basic principle of baroque music. This principle governs the concerto grosso, an important form of orchestral music in the late baroque period. In a **concerto grosso**, a small group of soloists is pitted against a larger group of players called the **tutti** (*all*). Usually, between two and four soloists play with anywhere from eight to twenty or more musicians for the tutti. The tutti consists mainly of string instruments, with a harpsichord as part of the basso continuo. A concerto grosso presents a contrast of texture between the tutti and the soloists, who assert their individuality and appeal for attention through brilliant and fanciful melodic lines. The soloists were the best and highest-paid members of the baroque orchestra, because their parts were more difficult than those of the other players. Concerti grossi were frequently performed by private orchestras in aristocratic palaces.

A concerto grosso consists of *several movements that contrast in tempo and character.* Most often there are three movements: (1) fast, (2) slow, (3) fast. The opening movement is usually vigorous and determined, clearly showing the contrast between tutti and soloists. The slow movement is quieter than the first, often lyrical and intimate. The last movement is lively and carefree, sometimes dancelike.

The first and last movements of concerti grossi are often in **ritornello form,** which is based on alternation between tutti and solo sections. In ritornello form the tutti opens with a theme called the **ritornello** (*refrain*). This theme, always played by the tutti, returns in different keys throughout the movement. But it usually returns in fragments, not complete. Only at the end of the movement does the entire ritornello return in the home key. Although the number of times a ritornello (tutti) returns varies from piece to piece, a typical concerto grosso movement might be outlined as follows:

1. a. Tutti (f), ritornello in home key
   b. Solo
2. a. Tutti (f), ritornello fragment
   b. Solo
3. a. Tutti (f), ritornello fragment
   b. Solo
4. Tutti (f), ritornello in home key

In contrast to the tutti's ritornello, the solo sections offer fresh melodic ideas, softer dynamics, rapid scales, and broken chords. Soloists may also expand short melodic ideas from the tutti. The opening movement of Bach's *Brandenburg* Concerto No. 5 is a fine example of ritornello form in the concerto grosso.

Brandenburg Concerto No. 5 in D Major (about 1721), by Johann Sebastian Bach

With his set of six *Brandenburg* Concertos, Bach brought immortality to a German aristocrat, the margrave of Brandenburg. Bach and the margrave met in 1718, when Bach was music director for another patron. The margrave loved music and asked Bach to send him some original compositions. About three years later, Bach sent him the *Brandenburg* Concertos with the flattering dedication quoted in Section 2, probably hoping for money or favors in return. (We don't know whether he got any.) These concertos had actually been composed for, and performed by, the orchestra of Bach's employer, the prince of Cöthen. Each of the concertos is written for a different and unusual combination of instruments.

Brandenburg Concerto No. 5 uses a string orchestra and a group of soloists consisting of a flute, a violin, and a harpsichord. This was the first time that a harpsichord had been given the solo role in a concerto grosso. In 1719, the prince of Cöthen bought a new harpsichord; Bach probably wanted to show off this instrument (as well as his own skill as a keyboard player), and so he gave it a solo spot. The tutti is written for violins, violas, cellos, and double bass. During the tutti sections the solo violinist plays along, as does the harpsichordist, who realizes the figured bass.

Here, we'll focus on the first movement of *Brandenburg* Concerto No. 5; the second and third movements are discussed later in Section 12 (see pages 157–158).

First Movement:
Allegro

Basic Set:
CD 2 4

Brief Set:
CD 2 [1]

The allegro movement opens with the ritornello, which is an almost continuous flow of rapid notes. After the ritornello ends—very definitely—the soloists present short melodic ideas, the flute and violin imitating each other playfully. The appearance of the soloists brings a lower dynamic level and a new tone color—the flute. After a while, the tutti returns loudly with a brief fragment of the ritornello, only to give way again to the soloists. This alternation between brief, relatively loud ritornello fragments in the tutti and longer, softer solo sections continues throughout the movement.

The soloists' music tends to be brilliant, fanciful, and personal as compared with the more vigorous and straightforward tutti sections. Solo sections are also more polyphonic in texture than the tutti and stress imitation between the flute and violin. The soloists play new material of their own or varied fragments from the ritornello. These solo sections build tension and make the listener anticipate the tutti's return. Listen especially for the suspenseful solo section that begins with a new theme in minor and ends with long notes in the flute.

Only the harpsichord plays during the long final solo section. And it is spectacular! Bach builds to a tense high point for the movement through irresistible rhythm and dazzling scale passages that require a virtuoso's skill. His audience must have marveled at this brilliant harpsichord solo within a concerto grosso. Audiences are still dazzled by it.

LISTENING OUTLINE

BACH, *Brandenburg* Concerto No. 5

First Movement: Allegro

Ritornello form, duple meter ($\frac{2}{2}$), D major

Flute, violin, harpsichord (solo group); string orchestra, continuo (tutti)

(Duration, 9:58)

Tutti

4 **1** 0:00   **1. a.** Strings, *f*, ritornello.

Solo

5 **2** 0:20   **b.** Flute, violin, harpsichord, major key.

Tutti

6 **3** 0:44   **2. a.** Strings, *f*, ritornello fragment.

Solo

0:49   **b.** Flute, violin, harpsichord, varied ritornello fragment.

Tutti

1:09   **3. a.** Strings, *f*, ritornello fragment.

Solo

1:16   **b.** Violin, flute, harpsichord.

Tutti

1:36   **4. a.** Strings, *f*, ritornello fragment, minor.

Solo

1:42   **b.** Harpsichord, flute, violin.

Tutti

2:23   **5. a.** Strings, ***f***, ritornello fragment, major.

Solo

2:30   **b.** Flute, harpsichord, violin, varied ritornello fragment, ***pp***.

`7` `4`   2:55   **c.** New theme in minor, ***pp***, tossed between flute and violin.

Tension mounts, long notes in flute lead to

Tutti

4:11   **6. a.** Strings, ***f***, ritornello fragment, major.

Solo

4:16   **b.** Violin, flute, harpsichord.

Tutti

5:01   **7. a.** Strings, ***f***, longer ritornello fragment.

Solo

5:12   **b.** Violin, harpsichord, flute, varied ritornello fragment.

Tutti

5:40   **8. a.** Strings, ***f***, ritornello fragment.

Solo

5:47   **b.** Violin and flute play carefree idea with rapid harpsichord scales in background.

`8` `5`   6:24   **c.** Long harpsichord solo featuring virtuoso display. Mounting tension resolved in

Tutti

9:32   **9.** Strings, ***f***, ritornello.

4 The Fugue

One cornerstone of baroque music is the fugue, which can be written for a group of instruments or voices, or for a single instrument like an organ or harpsichord. A ***fugue*** is a polyphonic composition based on one main theme, called a ***subject***. Throughout a fugue, different melodic lines, called *voices,* imitate the subject. The top melodic line—whether sung or played—is the soprano voice, and the bottom is the bass. The texture of a fugue usually includes three, four, or five voices. Though the subject remains fairly constant throughout, it takes on new meanings when shifted to different keys or combined with different melodic and rhythmic ideas.

The form of a fugue is extremely flexible; in fact, the only constant feature of fugues is how they begin—the subject is almost always presented in a single, unaccompanied voice. By thus highlighting the subject, the composer tells us what to remember and listen for. In getting to know a fugue, try to follow its subject through the different levels of texture. After its first presentation, the subject is imitated in turn by all the remaining voices.

The opening of a fugue in four voices may be represented as follows:

Soprano	Subject	....etc.
Alto		Subject ....etc.
Tenor		Subject ....etc.
Bass		Subject ......etc.

In this case, the top voice announces the subject and then the lower voices imitate it. However, the subject may be announced by *any* voice—top, bottom, or middle—and the order in which the remaining voices imitate it is also completely flexible.

This may seem reminiscent of a round like *Row, Row, Row Your Boat,* but in a fugue the game of follow the leader (exact imitation of the subject) does not continue indefinitely. The dotted lines in the diagram indicate that *after a voice has presented the subject, it is free to go its own way with different melodic material.* The opening of a fugue differs from that of a round in another way: in a round, each voice presents the melody on the same tones. If the melody begins with the tones C–D–E, each voice will begin with these tones, whether at a higher or a lower register. But in the opening of a fugue, *the subject is presented in two different scales.* The first time, it is based on the notes of the *tonic scale.* But when the second voice presents the subject, it is in the *dominant scale*—five scale steps higher than the tonic—and it is then called the **answer.** A subject beginning with the notes C–D–E, for example, would be imitated by an answer five steps higher, on G–A–B. This alternation of subject and answer between the two scales creates variety.

In many fugues, the subject in one voice is constantly accompanied in another voice by a different melodic idea called a **countersubject.** A constant companion, the countersubject always appears with the subject, sometimes below it, sometimes above it.

After the opening of a fugue, when each voice has taken its turn at presenting the subject, a composer is free to decide how often the subject will be presented, in which voices, and in which keys. Between presentations of the subject, there are often transitional sections called **episodes,** which offer either new material or fragments of the subject or countersubject. Episodes do *not* present the subject in its entirety. They lend variety to the fugue and make reappearances of the subject sound fresh. Bach called one composer of fugues "pedantic" because he "had not shown enough fire to reanimate the theme by episodes."

Several musical procedures commonly appear in fugues. One is **stretto,** in which a subject is imitated before it is completed; one voice tries to catch the other. Another common procedure is **pedal point** (or **organ point**), in which a single tone, usually in the bass, is held while the other voices produce a series of changing harmonies against it. (The term is taken from organ music, where a sustained low tone is produced by the organist's foot on a key of the pedal keyboard.)

A fugue subject can be varied in four principal ways:

1. It can be turned upside down, a procedure known as **inversion.** If the subject moves *upward* by leap, the inversion will move *downward* the same distance; if the subject moves *downward* by step, the inversion will move *upward* by step. In inversion, each interval in the subject is reversed in direction.
2. The subject may be presented **retrograde,** that is, by beginning with the last note of the subject and proceeding backward to the first.

3. The subject may be presented in **augmentation,** in which the original time values are lengthened.

4. The subject may appear in **diminution,** with shortened time values.

Fugues usually convey a single mood and a sense of continuous flow. They may be written as independent works or as single movements within larger compositions. Very often an independent fugue is introduced by a short piece called a **prelude.**

Bach and Handel each wrote hundreds of fugues; their fugues represent the peak among works in the form. In the baroque period, as a friend of Bach's observed, "Skill in fugue was so indispensable in a composer that no one could have attained a musical post who had not worked out a given subject in all kinds of counterpoint and in a regular fugue." Fugal writing continued into the nineteenth and twentieth centuries. It is not used as frequently today as in the baroque period; yet to this day, as part of their training, musicians study how to write fugues.

Organ Fugue in G Minor (*Little Fugue;* about 1709), by Johann Sebastian Bach

Basic Set:

CD 2 17

Brief Set:

CD 2 6

One of Bach's best-known organ pieces is the *Little Fugue* in G Minor, so called to differentiate it from another, longer fugue in G minor. The opening section of the *Little Fugue* corresponds to the diagram on page 131. Each of the fugue's four voices takes its turn presenting the tuneful subject, which is announced in the top voice and then appears in progressively lower voices, until it reaches the bass, where it is played by the organist's feet on the pedal keyboard. Like many baroque melodies, the subject gathers momentum as it goes along, beginning with relatively long time values (quarter notes) and then proceeding to shorter ones (eighth and sixteenth notes). Starting with its second appearance, the subject is accompanied by a countersubject that moves in short time values.

After the opening section, the subject appears five more times, each time preceded by an episode. The first episode uses both new material and a melodic idea from the countersubject. This episode contains downward sequences, which are melodic patterns repeated in the same voice but at lower pitches.

For harmonic contrast, Bach twice presents the subject in major keys rather than minor. The final statement of the subject—in minor—exploits the powerful bass tones of the pedal keyboard. Though the fugue is in minor, it ends with a major chord. This was a frequent practice in the baroque period; major chords were thought more conclusive than minor chords.

LISTENING OUTLINE

BACH, Organ Fugue in G Minor (*Little Fugue*)

Fugue, quadruple meter ($\frac{4}{4}$), G minor

Organ

(Duration, 4:04)

17 **6** 0:00   **1. a.** Subject, soprano voice alone, minor key.

0:18   **b.** Subject in alto, countersubject in running notes in soprano.

0:41   **c.** Subject in tenor, countersubject above it.

0:58   **d.** Subject in bass (pedals), countersubject in tenor.

18 **7** 1:14   **e.** Brief episode, downward sequence.

1:24   **2. a.** Subject begins in tenor, continues in soprano, accompanied by sustained tone in bass; subject leads to

1:43	**b.**	Brief episode, running notes in a downward sequence.
19 **8** 1:52	**3. a.**	Subject in alto, major key; countersubject in soprano; subject leads to
2:08	**b.**	Episode in major, upward leaps and running notes.
2:20	**c.**	Subject in bass (pedals), major key, countersubject and long trill above it.
2:37	**d.**	Longer episode, downward sequence; begins in major, ends in minor.
2:54	**4. a.**	Subject in soprano, minor key, countersubject below it.
3:10	**b.**	Most extended episode, running notes in a downward sequence; upward sequences lead to sustained high tones which usher in
3:40	**c.**	Subject in bass (pedals), countersubject in soprano. Fugue ends with major chord.

5 The Elements of Opera

The baroque era witnessed the development of a major innovation in music—*opera,* or drama that is sung to orchestral accompaniment. This unique fusion of music, acting, poetry, dance, scenery, and costumes is a theatrical experience offering overwhelming excitement and emotion. Since its beginnings in Italy around 1600, opera has spread to many countries, and even today it remains a powerful form of musical theater. In Section 6, we'll look closely at opera in the baroque period; but first, a general discussion of opera is in order.

In an opera, characters and plot are revealed through song, rather than the speech used in ordinary drama. Once we accept this convention, opera provides great pleasure; its music both delights the ear and heightens the emotional effect of the words and story. Music makes even an unlikely plot believable by depicting mood, character, and dramatic action. The flow of the music carries the plot forward. In opera, the music *is* the drama.

Opera demands performers who can sing and act simultaneously. Onstage are star solo singers, secondary soloists, a chorus, and sometimes dancers—all in costume. Besides the chorus of professional singers, there may be "supers" (supernumeraries, or "extras"), who don't sing but who carry spears, fill out crowds, drink wine, or do other things that add to the effect. Scenery, lighting, and stage machinery are intricate and are used to create the illusion of fires, floods, storms, and supernatural effects. In the orchestra pit are the instrumentalists and the conductor, whose awesome responsibility it is to hold everything together. The personnel for a large opera—from conductor to stage director and assorted vocal coaches, rehearsal accompanists, technicians, and stagehands—may reach a startling total of several hundred people.

The capacity of this combined force to create spectacle and pageantry accounts for much of opera's appeal. Historically, opera has been associated with high social status. It originated in the courts of kings and princes (who could afford it) and long continued as a form of aristocratic entertainment. But as opera became more concerned with "real" people and less with royal figures, it attracted popular audiences. Today, radio and television broadcasts, videos, DVDs, and recordings have changed opera's image as an exotic and expensive diversion for the very rich. Millions of people from every economic background know opera for what it is: a powerful and pleasurable emotional experience.

The creation of an opera involves the joint efforts of a composer and a dramatist. The **libretto,** or text, of the opera is usually written by the **librettist,** or dramatist,

A scene from a production of *Aida* (1871), by Giuseppe Verdi, at the Théàtre Antique in Orange, France.

and set to music by the composer. But composers often collaborate with dramatists to ensure that the texts meet their musical needs. W. H. Auden once said that a good libretto "offers as many opportunities as possible for the characters to be swept off their feet by placing them in situations which are too tragic or too fantastic for words. No good opera plot can be sensible, for people do not sing when they are feeling sensible." And that is true—opera characters are people overwhelmed by love, lust, hatred, and revenge. They wear fantastic disguises and commit extraordinary acts of violence. Yet the music makes them human and real. It evokes the haughtiness of a countess or the simplicity of a peasant girl. It creates a dramatic entrance for an outraged father, depicts the tension behind sword thrusts in a duel, and portrays the bleakness of a winter dawn. A great opera composer is a master of musical timing and characterization and has a keen sense of theater, knowing just when to have a character sing a simple phrase or a soaring melody, when to provide a stirring chorus or a graceful dance. Through the music, the composer paces the drama, controlling the speed of gestures, entrances, exits, and stage movements.

Some operas are serious, some comic, some both. Operas may contain spoken dialogue, but most are entirely sung. (Spoken dialogue is used mainly in comic opera, where stage action must be performed quickly for the most humorous effect.) Since singing normally takes longer than speaking words, the text of a 3-hour opera is shorter than that of a 3-hour play. The librettist allows time for the composer's musical elaboration.

The range of characters found in opera is broad and varied; gods, empresses, dukes, servants, priests, prostitutes, peasants, clowns, and cowboys all make appearances. Opera soloists must create all these characters and so need acting skill as well as vocal artistry. During rehearsals, the stage director coaches the singers to move well, gesture meaningfully, and identify with their characters.

The basic voice ranges (soprano, alto, tenor, bass) are divided more finely in opera. Some of the *voice categories of opera* are as follows:

Coloratura soprano	Very high range; can execute rapid scales and trills
Lyric soprano	Rather light voice; sings roles calling for grace and charm
Dramatic soprano	Full, powerful voice; is capable of passionate intensity
Lyric tenor	Relatively light, bright voice
Dramatic tenor	Powerful voice; is capable of heroic expression
Basso buffo	Takes comic roles; can sing very rapidly
Basso profondo	Very low range, powerful voice; takes roles calling for great dignity

Like a play, an opera has from one to five acts subdivided into scenes. A single act presents a variety of vocal and orchestral contrasts. For example, a tenor solo might be followed by a duet for soprano and bass, and then by a chorus or an orchestral interlude. A section may end definitely—and provide an opportunity for applause—or it may be linked with the next section to form a continuous flow of music within the act.

The main attraction for many opera fans is the *aria,* a song for solo voice with orchestral accompaniment. It's an outpouring of melody that expresses an emotional state. In an aria, *I love you* might be sung ten times to accommodate the expansion of the idea. Often the action stops while the character's feelings are revealed through music. An aria usually lasts several minutes. It is a complete piece with a definite beginning, high point, and end. If the performance of an aria is brilliant, the audience responds with an ovation at its conclusion. This breaks the dramatic flow but allows the audience to release its feelings through applause and shouts of *bravo!* or *brava!*

Opera composers often lead into an aria with a *recitative,* a vocal line that imitates the rhythms and pitch fluctuations of speech. In a recitative (from the Italian word for *recite*), words are sung quickly and clearly, often on repeated tones. There is usually only one note to each syllable in a recitative—as opposed to an aria, where one syllable may be stretched over many notes. Recitative is used for monologues and dialogues that connect the more melodic sections of the opera. It carries the action forward and presents routine information quickly.

Besides arias, the soloists in an opera will sing compositions for two or more singers: duets (for two singers), trios (for three), quartets (for four), quintets (for five), and sextets (for six). When three or more singers are involved, the composition is called an *ensemble.* In a duet or ensemble, the performers either face the audience or move through action that develops the plot. Each character expresses his or her own feelings. Conflicting emotions like grief, happiness, and anger can be projected simultaneously when different melodies are combined. This special blend of feelings is the glory of opera and is possible only through music; it cannot be duplicated in spoken drama.

An opera *chorus* generates atmosphere and makes comments on the action. Its members might be courtiers, sailors, peasants, prisoners, ballroom guests, and so on. Their sound creates a kind of tonal background for the soloists.

Rising just over the edge of center stage, near the footlights, is the prompter's box. In this cramped space, invisible to the audience, is the *prompter,* who gives cues and reminds the singers of words or pitches if they momentarily forget. Occasional memory lapses are inevitable with so much activity onstage.

Dance in opera is generally incidental. It provides an ornamental interlude that contrasts with and relaxes the thrust of the plot. By and large, dance is used as part of the setting—in a ballroom, at a country fair, in a pagan court—while the soloists, downstage, advance the action of the plot and work out their destinies.

The nerve center of an opera in performance is the orchestra pit—a sunken area directly in front of the stage. An opera orchestra has the same instruments as a full symphony orchestra, but usually it has a smaller string section. Covered lights attached to the players' music stands leave the orchestra in a deep shadow that doesn't interfere with the audience's view of the stage. The orchestra not only supports the singers but depicts mood and atmosphere and comments on the stage action. During the performance, the conductor shapes the entire work. He or she sets tempos, cues in singers, and indicates subtle dynamic gradations.

Most operas open with a purely orchestral composition called an **overture** or a **prelude.** Since the eighteenth century, the music for an overture has been drawn from material heard later in the opera. The overture is thus a short musical statement that involves the audience in the overall dramatic mood. Orchestral introductions to acts in the opera other than the first are always called *preludes*. We've already discussed one of these, the Prelude to Act III of *Lohengrin,* where Wagner anticipates the wedding of the hero and heroine. Because overtures and preludes, like arias, are complete compositions, they frequently appear on symphony orchestra programs.

Should opera be translated? This question has long aroused controversy, and the battle continues. Most of the best-loved operas are in Italian, German, or French. Champions of translations into English argue that an audience should be able to understand the plot as it develops. Why tell jokes in a comic opera if they can't be understood? On the other hand, a composer takes pains to make a special fusion of pitch and the original words. This results in tonal color that seems absolutely right. But no matter how well a singer articulates, some words are bound to be lost, whatever the language. For example, a sung melody can stretch one vowel over many notes; it takes a while to get to the end of a word. If the melody is placed in a soprano's highest range, the listener is really aware only of the silvery vowel and not of the word as a whole. Some operas seem to work well in translation; others don't. Much depends on the style of the opera and on the sensitivity of the translator.

In many recent opera productions, a translation of the libretto is projected above the stage. This device—called *supertitles*—has also been a source of controversy. Its advocates say that it provides the best of both worlds, since it allows an opera to be sung in the original language while the audience is enabled to understand the words. But its opponents feel that it detracts from the music and the action onstage.

Before you attend a live opera performance, in any language and with or without supertitles, it's a good idea to read the libretto or a synopsis of the plot. Even better, watch a video or DVD, or listen to a recording while following the libretto. This way, you will be freer at the performance to appreciate the quality of production and interpretation.

6 Opera in the Baroque Era

Opera was born in Italy. Its way was prepared by musical discussions among a small group of nobles, poets, and composers who began to meet regularly in Florence around 1575. This group was known as the **Camerata** (Italian for *fellowship* or *society*) and included the composer Vincenzo Galilei, father of the astronomer Galileo.

The Camerata wanted to create a new vocal style modeled on the music of ancient Greek tragedy. Since no actual dramatic music had come down to them from the Greeks, they based their theories on literary accounts that had survived. It was believed that the Greek dramas had been sung throughout in a style that was midway between melody and speech. The Camerata wanted the vocal line to follow the rhythms and pitch fluctuations of speech. Because it was modeled after speech, the new vocal style became known as *recitative (recited).* It was sung by a soloist with only a simple chordal accompaniment. The new music was therefore homophonic in texture.

Much baroque opera was designed to display magnificent extravagance. Pietro Domenico Olivero's painting of the Royal Theater, Turin (1740), shows a performance of Francesco Feo's opera *Arsace*.

Polyphony was rejected by the Camerata because different words sounding simultaneously would obscure the all-important text.

Euridice by Jacopo Peri is the earliest opera that has been preserved. It was composed for the wedding of King Henri IV of France and Marie de' Medici and was performed in Florence in 1600. Seven years later Monteverdi composed *Orfeo*—the first *great* opera—for the court of the Gonzaga family in Mantua. Both these operas are based on the Greek myth of Orpheus's descent into Hades to bring back his beloved Eurydice.

Much baroque opera was composed for ceremonial occasions at court and was designed as a display of magnificence and splendor. The subject matter was drawn from Greek mythology and ancient history. Not only were aristocratic patrons of the baroque fascinated by the classical civilizations of Greece and Rome, but they identified with Greek and Roman heroes and divinities. Opera did indeed reflect the creative urge of composer and librettist, but it also was a way to flatter the aristocracy. The radiant appearance of Apollo (god of poetry, music, and the sun) might symbolize a prince's enlightened rule.

The first public opera house opened in Venice in 1637; now anyone with the price of admission could attend an opera performance. Between 1637 and 1700 there were seventeen opera houses in Venice alone, as well as many in other Italian cities—ample evidence that opera had been born in the right place at the right time. Hamburg,

Leipzig, and London had public opera houses by the early 1700s, but, on the whole, public opera outside Italy took longer to develop.

Venetian opera became a great tourist attraction. An English traveler wrote in 1645 about the opera and its "variety of scenes painted and contrived with no less art of perspective, and machines for flying in the air, and other wonderful motions; taken together, it is one of the most magnificent and expensive diversions the wit of man can invent." The stage machinery of baroque opera bordered on the colossal; stage effects might include gods descending on clouds or riding across the sky in chariots, ships tossing, boulders splitting. And set design was an art in itself. Painters turned backdrops into cities with arches and avenues that stretched into the distant horizon.

Baroque opera marked the rise of virtuoso singers. Chief among these was the *castrato,* a male singer who had been castrated before puberty. (Castration of boy singers was common in Italy from 1600 to 1800; it was usually done with the consent of impoverished parents who hoped their sons would become highly paid opera stars.) A castrato combined the lung power of a man with the vocal range of a woman. His agility, breath control, and unique sound (which was not like a woman's) intrigued listeners. Castrati received the highest fees of any musicians. With their soprano or alto vocal ranges, they played male roles such as Caesar and Nero—baroque audiences evidently were more interested in vocal virtuosity than dramatic realism. Some baroque operas cannot be performed today, because contemporary singers aren't able to manage the fiendishly difficult castrato parts.

During the late baroque, operas consisted largely of arias linked by recitatives. These recitatives were usually accompanied only by a basso continuo, in which case they are called *secco recitatives.* At emotional high points and moments of tension, however, they might be supported by the orchestra; they are then called *accompanied recitatives.*

All action stopped during the aria, when the singer faced the audience, expressed the feelings of the character, and displayed vocal virtuosity. The form of a typical late baroque aria is A B A. An aria in A B A form is called a *da capo aria:* after the B section, the term *da capo* is written; this means *from the beginning* and indicates a repetition of the opening A section. However, the repetition was usually not literal, because the singer was expected to embellish the returning melody with ornaments.

By combining virtuosity, nobility, and extravagance, baroque opera perfectly expressed the spirit of a grand age.

7 Claudio Monteverdi

Claudio Monteverdi (1567–1643), one of the most important composers of the early baroque era, was born in Cremona, Italy. He served at the court of Mantua for twenty-one years, first as a singer and violist, then as music director. For this court Monteverdi created the earliest operatic masterpiece, *Orfeo* (*Orpheus,* 1607). Though widely recognized as a leading composer in Mantua, Monteverdi received little pay or respect: "I have never suffered greater humiliation," he wrote, "than when I had to go and beg the treasurer to obtain what was due me."

Life improved for Monteverdi in 1613, when he was appointed music director at St. Mark's in Venice, the most important church position in Italy. He stayed at St. Mark's for thirty years, until his death in 1643. There he composed not only the required sacred music but also secular music for the aristocracy. He wrote operas for San Cassiano in Venice, the first public opera house in Europe. At the age of seventy-five, Monteverdi wrote his last opera, *L'incoronazione di Poppea* (*The Coronation of Poppea,* 1642).

Monteverdi is a monumental figure in the history of music. His works form a musical bridge between the sixteenth and seventeenth centuries and greatly influ-

Claudio Monteverdi (c. 1640), in a portrait by Bernardo Strozzi.

enced composers of the time. All his music—madrigals, church music, opera—is for voices, ordinarily supported by a basso continuo and other instruments.

Monteverdi wanted to create music of emotional intensity. He felt that earlier music had conveyed only moderate emotion, and he wanted to extend its range to include agitation, excitement, and passion. To achieve this intensity, he used dissonances with unprecedented freedom and daring. And to evoke the angry or warlike feelings in some of his texts, he introduced new orchestral effects, including pizzicato and tremolo.

Monteverdi was the first composer of operatic masterpieces. Only three of the twelve operas he wrote are preserved, but they truly blend music and drama. His vocal lines respond marvelously to the inflections of Italian while maintaining melodic flow.

Orfeo (Orpheus, 1607)

Fittingly enough, Monteverdi's first opera is about Orpheus, the supremely gifted musician of Greek myth. Orpheus, son of the god Apollo, is ecstatically happy after his marriage to Eurydice. But his joy is shattered when his bride is killed by a poisonous snake. Orpheus goes down to Hades hoping to bring her back to life. Because of his beautiful music, he is granted this privilege—on the condition that he not look back at Eurydice while leading her out of Hades. During a moment of anxiety, however, Orpheus does look back, and Eurydice vanishes. Nonetheless, there is a happy ending, of sorts. Apollo pities Orpheus and brings him up to heaven, where he can gaze eternally at Eurydice's radiance in the sun and stars.

Orpheus and Euridice (c. 1625), by Jacopo Vignali. The painting depicts Orpheus leading Eurydice out of Hades while a winged demon reaches out to her from behind.

Orfeo was composed in 1607 for the Mantuan court, and no expense was spared to make it a lavish production. There were star soloists, a chorus, dancers, and a large orchestra of about forty players. The aristocratic audience was wildly enthusiastic and recognized the historic significance of the performance.

Monteverdi creates variety in *Orfeo* by using many kinds of music—recitatives, arias, duets, choruses, and instrumental interludes. He uses the opera orchestra to establish atmosphere, character, and dramatic situations. With the simplest of musical means, Monteverdi makes his characters come alive. Through vocal line alone he quickly characterizes the hero's joy and despair. Monteverdi sets his text in a very flexible way, freely alternating recitatives with more melodious passages, depending on the meaning of the words.

We'll now consider one well-known passage from this opera, Orpheus's recitative *Tu se' morta* (*You are dead*).

Act II:
Recitative: *Tu se' morta* (*You are dead*)

Basic Set:
CD 2 [20]

Brief Set:
CD 2 [9]

Monteverdi's mastery of the then novel technique of recitative is shown in *Tu se' morta*, sung by Orpheus after he is told of Eurydice's death. Orpheus resolves to bring her back from Hades, and he bids an anguished farewell to the earth, sky, and sun. His vocal line is accompanied only by a basso continuo played by a small portable organ and a bass lute. (In modern performances, other instruments are sometimes substituted.)

The texture is homophonic: the accompaniment simply gives harmonic support to the voice. The vocal line is rhythmically free, with little sense of beat or meter, and its phrases are irregular in length. This flexible setting of text is meant to suggest the passionate speech of an actor declaiming his lines.

Monteverdi frequently uses word painting, the musical representation of poetic images that was favored by baroque composers. For example, words like *stelle* (*stars*) and *sole* (*sun*) are sung to climactic high tones, whereas *abissi* (*abysses*) and *morte* (*death*) are sung to somber, low tones. Three times during the recitative the melodic line rises to a climax and then descends. Through such simple means, Monteverdi expresses Orpheus's passion.

VOCAL MUSIC GUIDE

MONTEVERDI, *Tu se' morta* from *Orfeo*

[20] [9]		*Tu se' morta, se' morta, mia vita,*	You are dead, you are dead, my dearest,
		ed io respiro; tu se' da me partita,	And I breathe; you have left me,
		se' da me partita per mai più,	You have left me forevermore,
		mai più non tornare, ed io rimango—	Never to return, and I remain—
		no, no, che se i versi alcuna cosa	No, no, if my verses have any
		ponno,	power,
1:12	Low tone on *abissi.*	*n'andrò sicuro a' più profondi abissi,*	I will go confidently to the deepest abysses,
		e, intenerito il cor del re de l'ombre,	And, having melted the heart of the king of shadows,
1:38	High tone on *stelle.*	*meco trarotti a riverder le stelle,*	Will bring you back to me to see the stars again,
		o se ciò negherammi empio destino,	Or, if pitiless fate denies me this,
2:00	Low tone on *morte.*	*rimarrò teco in compágnia di morte.*	I will remain with you in the company of death.
2:17	High tone on *sole.*	*Addio terra, addio cielo, e sole, addio.*	Farewell earth, farewell sky, and sun, farewell.

8 Henry Purcell

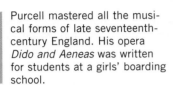
Purcell mastered all the musical forms of late seventeenth-century England. His opera *Dido and Aeneas* was written for students at a girls' boarding school.

Henry Purcell (about 1659–1695), called the greatest of English composers, was born in London; his father was a musician in the king's service. At about the age of ten, Purcell became a choirboy in the Chapel Royal, and by the time he was in his late teens his extraordinary talents were winning him important musical positions. In 1677, at about eighteen, he became composer to the king's string orchestra; two years later he was appointed organist of Westminster Abbey; and in 1682, he became an organist of the Chapel Royal. During the last few years of his short life, Purcell was also active composing music for plays.

Acclaimed as *the* English composer of his day, Purcell, who died at thirty-six, was buried beneath the organ in Westminster Abbey. He was the last native English composer of international rank until the twentieth century.

Purcell mastered all the musical forms of late seventeenth-century England. He wrote church music, secular choral music, music for small groups of instruments, songs, and music for the stage. His only true opera is *Dido and Aeneas* (1689), which many consider the finest ever written to an English text. His other dramatic works are spoken plays with musical numbers in the form of overtures, songs, choruses, and dances.

Few composers have equaled Purcell's handling of the English language. His vocal music is faithful to English inflection and brings out the meaning of the text. Purcell developed a melodious recitative that seems to grow out of the English language. His music is filled with lively rhythms and has a fresh melodic style that captures the spirit of English folk songs. He treated the chorus with great variety and was able to obtain striking effects through both simple homophonic textures and complex polyphony. His music is spiced with dissonances that seemed harsh to the generation of musicians who followed him. Some of Purcell's finest songs use a variation form found in many baroque works—a ground bass.

Ground Bass

Often in baroque works, a musical idea in the bass is repeated over and over while the melodies above it change. The repeated musical idea is called a **ground bass,** or **basso ostinato** (*obstinate* or *persistent bass*). The ground bass pattern may be as short as four notes or as long as eight measures. In this type of variation form, the constant repetition of the bass pattern gives unity, while the free flow of the melodic lines above it results in variety.

Composers have used a ground bass in both vocal and instrumental music. We'll hear a ground bass in Purcell's opera *Dido and Aeneas,* as well as in Bach's Mass in B Minor (Section 12).

Dido and Aeneas (1689)

Purcell's *Dido and Aeneas,* a masterpiece of baroque opera, was written for students at a girls' boarding school. It lasts only an hour, is scored only for strings and harpsichord continuo, and requires no elaborate stage machinery or virtuoso soloists. Most of its solo roles are for women. Purcell used many dances in *Dido and Aeneas,* because the director of the school was a dancing master who wanted to display the students' accomplishments. The chorus plays a prominent role, both participating in the action and commenting on it.

The libretto of *Dido and Aeneas,* by Nahum Tate, was inspired by the *Aeneid,* an epic poem by the Roman poet Virgil (70–19 B.C.). The opera's main characters are Dido, queen of Carthage; and Aeneas, king of the defeated Trojans. After the destruction of his native Troy, Aeneas has been ordered by the gods to seek a site for building a new city. He sets out on the search with twenty-one ships. After landing at Carthage, a north African seaport, Aeneas falls in love with Dido. A sorceress and two witches see this as an opportunity to plot Dido's downfall. (In Purcell's time, people really believed in witches: nineteen supposed "witches" were hanged in Massachusetts in 1692, three years after *Dido*'s first performance.) A false messenger tells Aeneas that the gods command him to leave Carthage immediately and renew his search. Aeneas agrees but is desolate at the thought of deserting Dido.

In the last act, which takes place at the harbor, Aeneas's sailors sing and dance before leaving, and the witches look on in glee. An emotional scene follows between Aeneas and Dido, who enters with her friend Belinda. Dido calls Aeneas a hypocrite and refuses his offer to stay. After he sails, Dido sings a noble, deeply tragic lament and kills herself. The opera concludes with the mourning of the chorus.

Now let's look at *Dido's Lament.*

Act III:
Dido's Lament

Basic Set:
CD 2 `21`

Brief Set:
CD 2 `10`

A melodic recitative accompanied only by the basso continuo sets the sorrowful mood for *Dido's Lament,* the climax of the opera. This aria is built on a chromatically descending ground bass that is stated eleven times. (In the baroque period, such chromatic ground basses were commonly used to show grief.) As shown in the music example, Dido's melody moves freely above this repeated bass line, creating touching dissonances with it.

Dido's repeated *Remember me* reaches the highest note of the aria and haunts the listener. The emotional tension is sustained in the orchestral conclusion, where a chromatically descending violin melody movingly expresses the tragedy of Dido's fate.

VOCAL MUSIC GUIDE

PURCELL, *Dido's Lament*

`21` `10` 0:00

Recitative, descending melody, basso continuo accompanies.

Thy hand, Belinda, darkness shades me,
On thy bosom let me rest;
More I would but Death invades me;
Death is now a welcome guest.

`22` `11` 0:46

Dido's Lament
(aria), lute introduces chromatically descending ground bass.

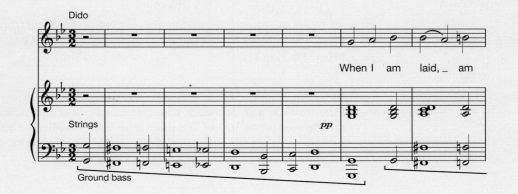

laid _____ in earth, may my wrongs ___ cre - ate

Upper strings join.

Orchestral conclusion,
violin melody descends
chromatically.

When I am laid, am laid in earth, may my wrongs create
No trouble, no trouble in thy breast.
Remember me! But ah! forget my fate.

9 The Baroque Sonata

Instrumental music gained importance rapidly and dramatically during the baroque period. One of the main developments in instrumental music was the ***sonata,*** a composition in several movements for one to eight instruments. (In later periods, the term *sonata* took on a more restricted meaning.)

Composers often wrote ***trio sonatas,*** so called because they had three melodic lines: two high lines and a basso continuo. Yet the word *trio* is misleading, because the "trio" sonata actually involves *four* instrumentalists. There are two high instruments (commonly, violins, flutes, or oboes) and two instruments for the basso continuo—a keyboard instrument (organ or harpsichord) and a low instrument (cello or bassoon).

The sonata originated in Italy but spread to Germany, England, and France during the seventeenth century. Sonatas were played in palaces, in homes, and even in churches—before, during, or after the service. Sometimes composers differentiated between the *sonata da chiesa* (church sonata), which had a dignified character and was suitable for sacred performance; and the *sonata da camera* (*chamber sonata*), which was more dancelike and was intended for performance at court.

10 Arcangelo Corelli

The most prominent Italian violinist and composer of string music around 1700 was Arcangelo Corelli (1653–1713). Corelli studied in Bologna but spent most of his adult life in Rome. He was friend and music director to Cardinal Ottoboni, in whose palace he lived. There he mingled with the intellectual and aristocratic elite of Rome.

As a teacher, Corelli instructed some of the most eminent musicians of his time and laid the foundations of modern violin technique. He was one of the first to write double stops and chords for the violin. He was unique among Italian composers of the period in that he wrote only instrumental music: sixty sonatas and twelve concertos, all for strings.

Though little is known about Corelli's personality, he is generally described as gentle and calm. But when he played, he seemed transformed. According to a contemporary report, "Whilst he was playing on the violin it was usual for his countenance to be distorted, his eyes to become as red as fire, and his eyeballs to roll as in an agony."

Trio Sonata in A Minor, Op. 3, No. 10 (1689)

Corelli's Trio Sonata in A Minor, Op. 3, No. 10, is written for two violins and basso continuo. The violins play the two upper lines in the same high register and are the center of attention; they seem to be rivals, taking turns at the melodic ideas, intertwining, and sometimes rising above each other in pitch. The basso continuo is for organ and cello or *theorbo* (bass lute), a plucked string instrument which is capable of producing chords as well as the bass line. Though the bass line is subordinate to the two upper voices, it is not merely an accompaniment. It imitates melodic ideas presented by the violins.

The sonata consists of four short movements:

1. Fast
2. Fast
3. Slow
4. Fast

All are in the same minor key, but they differ in meter, mood, and tempo. Each movement alone has only a single basic mood, as is typical in baroque instrumental music.

The lively opening movement is in quadruple meter and features dotted rhythms. It is played twice, each time ending with an incomplete cadence on the dominant that creates a feeling of expectancy.

First Movement:
Basic Set:
CD 2 23

Second Movement:
Basic Set:
CD 2 24

The second movement, a vigorous allegro, is fuguelike and also in quadruple meter. Fugal second movements were characteristic of baroque trio sonatas. The subject begins with a pervasive repeated-note motive.

This subject is introduced by the first violin and then is successively imitated in lower registers by the second violin and the cello (doubled by the organ). The second movement, like the first, ends with an incomplete cadence on the dominant that creates expectancy.

The third movement is songlike and soulful, a very brief adagio in triple meter. It opens with a descending leap in the first violin that is immediately imitated a step higher by the second violin.

The longest and most brilliant movement of this sonata is the concluding allegro, a dancelike piece in quadruple meter in which each beat is subdivided into three. This fourth movement is in two-part form, and each part is repeated: A A B B. Section B is three times longer than section A. At the end of section B, Corelli calls for the only dynamic change in the sonata: the concluding phrase is repeated more softly, like an echo.

11 Antonio Vivaldi

Antonio Vivaldi (1678–1741), a towering figure of the late Italian baroque, was born in Venice; his father was a violinist at St. Mark's Cathedral. Along with his musical training, Vivaldi prepared for the priesthood. He took holy orders at the age of about twenty-five, but poor health caused him to leave the ministry after a year. Because of his religious background and his red hair, Vivaldi was known as the "red priest" (*il prete rosso*).

For most of his life, Vivaldi was a violin teacher, composer, and conductor at the music school of the Pietà, an institution for orphaned or illegitimate girls in Venice.

Every Sunday and holiday, about forty young women presented a concert of orchestral and vocal music in the chapel. They were placed in a gallery, "hid from any distinct view of those below by a lattice of ironwork." It was for this all-female group—considered one of the finest orchestras in Italy—that Vivaldi composed many of his works. He also wrote for Venetian opera houses and sometimes took leave to visit foreign courts.

Vivaldi was famous and influential as a virtuoso violinist and composer. Bach arranged some of his concertos. Emperor Charles VI, a passionate music lover, was said to have talked longer to Vivaldi "alone in fifteen days, than he talked to his ministers in two years."

But Vivaldi's popularity waned shortly before his death in 1741, and he died in poverty. Although he had been acclaimed during his lifetime, he was almost forgotten for 200 years after his death. The baroque revival of the 1950s established his reputation among modern music lovers.

Although Vivaldi composed operas and fine church music, he is best known for his 450 or so concerti grossi and solo concertos. A **solo concerto** is a piece for a *single* soloist and an orchestra. Vivaldi exploited the resources of the violin as well as other instruments. (There are Vivaldi concertos for solo flute, piccolo, cello, bassoon, and even mandolin.) His fast movements feature tuneful themes in vigorous rhythms, and his slow movements have impassioned, lyrical melodies that would be appropriate in an opera aria.

Vivaldi's most popular work is the concerto *La Primavera (Spring)* from *The Four Seasons,* a set of four solo concertos for violin, string orchestra, and continuo.

La Primavera (*Spring*), Concerto for Violin and String Orchestra, Op. 8, No. 1, from *The Four Seasons* (1725)

Vivaldi's most popular work is the concerto *La Primavera* (*Spring*) from *The Four Seasons,* a set of four solo concertos for violin, string orchestra, and basso continuo. Each of these concertos depicts sounds and events associated with one of the seasons, such as the birdsong heard in spring and the gentle breezes of summer. The descriptive effects in the music correspond to images and ideas found in the sonnets that preface each of the four concertos. To make his intentions absolutely clear, Vivaldi placed lines from the poems at the appropriate passages in the musical score and even added such descriptive labels as *sleeping goatherd* and *barking dog*. The concertos *Spring, Summer, Autumn,* and *Winter* are examples of baroque *program music,* or instrumental music associated with a story, poem, idea, or scene. They are forerunners of the more elaborate program music that developed during the romantic period.

Spring was as popular in Vivaldi's time as it is in ours and was a special favorite of Louis XV, king of France. Once, when the violinist Guignon gave a concert at the court, the king asked for *Spring* as an encore. This posed a problem, since the king's orchestra was not present. Rising to the occasion, a group of nobles at the court volunteered to accompany the violin soloist. A Parisian newspaper reported that "this beautiful piece of music was performed perfectly."

Like most of Vivaldi's concertos, *Spring* has three movements: (1) fast, (2) slow, (3) fast. Both the first and last movements are in ritornello form.

First Movement:
Allegro

Spring has come, and joyfully,
The birds greet it with happy song.
And the streams, fanned by gentle breezes,
Flow along with a sweet murmur.
Covering the sky with a black cloak,
Thunder and lightning come to announce the season.
When these have quieted down, the little birds
Return to their enchanting song.

Basic Set:
CD 2 **25**

Brief Set:
CD 2 **12**

The allegro, in E major, opens with an energetic orchestral ritornello depicting the arrival of spring. Each of the ritornello's two phrases is played loudly and then repeated softly, in the terraced dynamics typical of baroque music. After the ritornello, the movement alternates between extended solo sections containing musical tone painting and brief tutti sections presenting part of the ritornello theme. In the first solo section, birdsongs are imitated by high trills and repeated notes played by the violin soloist and two violins from the orchestra. (A ***trill*** is an ornament consisting of the rapid alternation of two tones that are a whole or half step apart.) In the second descriptive episode, murmuring streams are suggested by soft running notes in the violins. The next solo section contains string tremolos and rapid scales representing thunder and lightning. Following the storm, the ritornello appears in minor instead of in major. All the pictorial passages in this movement provide contrasts of texture and dynamics between returns of the ritornello theme. The allegro's tunefulness, rhythmic vitality, and light, homophonic texture evoke the feeling of springtime.

LISTENING OUTLINE

VIVALDI, *La Primavera,* from *The Four Seasons*

First Movement: Allegro

Ritornello form, quadruple meter ($\frac{4}{4}$), E major
Solo violin, string orchestra, harpsichord (basso continuo)
(Duration, 3:38)

Spring has come

25 **12**   0:00   **1. a.** Tutti, ritornello opening phrase, ***f***, repeated ***p***

closing phrase with syncopations, *f*, repeated *p*, major key.

Song of the birds

`26` `13` 0:31

          b. Solo violin joined by two violins from orchestra, high trills and repeated notes.

     1:06   **2. a.** Tutti, ritornello closing phrase, *f*.

Murmuring streams

`27` `14` 1:14

          b. Violins, *p*, running notes, cellos, *p*, running notes below sustained tones in violins.

     1:38   **3. a.** Tutti, ritornello closing phrase, *f*.

Thunder and lightning

`28` `15` 1:46

          b. String tremolos, *f*, upward rushing scales introduce high solo violin, brilliant virtuoso passages answered by low string tremolos.

     2:15   **4. a.** Tutti, ritornello closing phrase in minor key, *f*.

Song of the birds

`29` `16` 2:23

          b. Solo violin joined by two violins from orchestra, high repeated notes and trills, minor key.

     2:43   **5. a.** Tutti, ritornello opening phrase varied, *f*, ends in major key.

     2:55   **b.** Solo violin, running notes accompanied by basso continuo.

     3:11   **6.** Tutti, ritornello closing phrase, *f*, repeated *p*, major key.

Second Movement: Largo e pianissimo sempre (very slow and very soft throughout)

> And then, on a pleasant meadow covered with flowers,
> Lulled by the soft murmuring of leaves and branches,
> The goatherd sleeps, his faithful dog at his side.

Basic Set:
CD 2 `30`

Brief Set:
CD 2 `17`

The peaceful slow movement, in C sharp minor, is much quieter than the energetic opening movement. It uses only the solo violin and the orchestral violins and violas, omitting the cellos, basses, and harpsichord. A tender, expansive melody for the solo violin depicts the goatherd's slumber, while a soft, rocking figure in the violins suggests the rustling of leaves. The violas imitate the barking of the goatherd's "faithful dog" with a repeated-note figure in short-long rhythm. The tranquillity of this pastoral scene is evoked by the movement's unchanging texture, rhythm, and dynamic level.

In the performance of this movement on our recordings, the violin soloist Jeanne Lamon decorates the melody with ornaments, or embellishing notes. During the baroque period, performers were often expected to add embellishments not indicated in the printed music. Vivaldi's notated melody and the decorated version of the melody you hear in the recording are shown in the following music examples.

(a) Notated melody

(b) Ornamented melody

(a)

(b)

Third Movement:
Danza pastorale (Pastoral Dance)

Basic Set:
CD 2 **31**

Brief Set:
CD 2 **18**

To the festive sounds of country bagpipes,
Dance nymphs and shepherds in their beloved fields,
When spring appears in all its brilliance.

Like the first movement, the concluding *Danza pastorale (Pastoral Dance)*, in E major, alternates between tutti and solo sections. The playful ritornello theme, with its dotted rhythms, suggests nymphs and shepherds dancing in the fields. Sustained tones in the lower strings imitate the drone of country bagpipes. The sections for solo violin contain brilliant passages with many melodic sequences, which are typical of baroque style.

The following outline will clarify the movement's ritornello form:

31 **18**	0:00	1. a. Tutti, ritornello, lilting melody in major.
	0:27	b. Solo violin accompanied by basso continuo.
32 **19**	0:49	2. a. Tutti, varied ritornello in minor.
	1:17	b. Solo violin joined by violin from orchestra, major.
	1:47	c. Solo violin, staccato, accompanied by violins, faster rhythms.
33 **20**	2:08	3. a. Tutti, ritornello, major, varied in minor.
	2:39	b. Solo violin accompanied by sustained tone in cellos and basses, minor.
	3:02	4. Tutti, ritornello in major.

Jeanne Lamon, Violinist, Plays and Conducts Vivaldi's Spring Concerto

One of the leading performers on the baroque violin is Jeanne Lamon, who conducts and directs the Canadian period-instrumental group Tafelmusik. During the past few decades, many performers of baroque music have chosen to use baroque instruments—originals and reproductions—rather than the later counterparts. Baroque instruments differ somewhat from their later counterparts in construction and in the way they are played. Baroque violins, for example, usually have strings of gut rather than metal. The strings are held under less tension and produce sounds that are softer and less brilliant.

Jeanne Lamon, who was raised in New York state, began to play the violin at age seven and later studied music at Brandeis University in Boston. After graduating, she studied baroque violin in the Netherlands, a center for the performance of early music. In 1973, she returned to North America, where she performed as soloist and concertmaster with many ensembles. Under her direction since 1981, Tafelmusik has made many award-winning recordings, including Vivaldi's *The Four Seasons* and Bach's *Brandenburg* Concertos.

In Lamon's performance of Vivaldi's *Spring* Concerto—included in the recordings—she conducts from the concertmaster's seat, playing the solo violin part at the same time. She points out that "most orchestral music of the baroque was led by the first violinist or the harpsichordist. This suits the music very well, as do the original instruments. It is in many ways easier for string players to follow a violinist than a conductor."

As we have seen, Vivaldi's *Spring* Concerto contains episodes suggesting birdsongs and murmuring streams. Lamon believes that such passages pose special problems for the performer: "How rhythmically strict should an imitation of birds be? How literally would Vivaldi have wished it to be played? Should the birdcalls be played as literally as possible, or should we take whatever freedom we see fit to make them as realistic as we can? I chose a middle ground, probably a bit more strict than free, but with the intention of applying humor and charm to this music. I see it not as literal music, but as playful and evocative."

In the peaceful second movement, Lamon enriches the written solo violin melody with decorative tones. She points out that she "chose to ornament in a way that was comfortable for me as a player and reflected the mood of the musical picture." The second movement poses special interpretive problems for the conductor. "The biggest challenge in this movement, writes Lamon, "is the viola part, which imitates dogs barking and is indicated *ff e strappato* ("very loud and ripped"). If we really do this, we hear nothing else, but the polite version where the violas play softly and roundly doesn't sound at all like dogs." Lamon's solution is to have the violists play *forte* rather than *fortissimo*. She thinks that Vivaldi marked the part *fortissimo* because he was "frustrated that his violists were playing too softly and without any edge or roughness (barking). Our violists are much meatier players perhaps!"

How can the performer breathe new life into such a well-known work as Vivaldi's *Spring* Concerto? Lamon answers, "Our challenge as performers is to keep sometimes very familiar works 'new' and fresh by remembering what was new and fresh about them: . . . when they were heard for the first time; what surprised the audience; what was innovative, shocking, humorous."

Johann Sebastian Bach

The masterpieces of Johann Sebastian Bach (1685–1750) mark the high point of baroque music. Bach came from a long line of musicians: his father, grandfather, and great-grandfather were all church organists or town musicians in Germany. In fact, so many members of the family were musicians that the name *Bach* became synonymous with *town musician*. Annual family gatherings might assemble more than a hundred Bachs to make music. Johann Sebastian Bach passed on this musical heritage—he had twenty children, of whom nine survived him and four became well-known composers.

In Eisenach, his birthplace, Bach probably received his first musical training from his father, the town musician; and his cousin, the church organist. But when he was nine, both his parents died and Johann went to live with his oldest brother, the organist in a nearby town. At fifteen, Bach left his brother's crowded home and moved to yet another town, where he went to school and supported himself by singing in the church choir and playing the organ and violin. By this time his love of music was so great that he would walk up to thirty miles to hear a famous organist.

When he was eighteen, Bach became church organist in Arnstadt, a town not far from his birthplace. Here he came into conflict with church authorities, because they felt that his music was too complicated; they also questioned his meeting a "strange maiden" in the empty church to accompany her singing. Bach resolved both issues when he was twenty-three by finding a better position at Mühlhausen and by marrying the "strange maiden," his cousin Barbara. His reputation as an organist was growing steadily through his virtuoso performances, which included improvising elaborate fugues and, reportedly, playing with his feet (on the pedal keyboard) better than many performers could play with their fingers.

Though recognized as the most eminent organist, harpsichordist, improviser, and master of the fugue, Bach was by no means considered the greatest composer of his day; his music was largely forgotten and remained unpublished for years after his death.

After these two jobs as church organist, Bach obtained a more important post in 1708 as court organist in Weimar. He stayed there for nine years, becoming concertmaster of the court orchestra, but decided to leave when he was passed over for promotion. The duke of Weimar was so annoyed at Bach's obstinacy in requesting dismissal that he put him in jail for a month. (Such was the power of a minor German aristocrat!) But all his life Bach kept demanding his rights, never fearing controversy.

Bach's most lucrative and prestigious post was as court conductor for the prince of Cöthen. His salary equaled that of the marshal of the court, the second highest official. But more important, this was the first time in Bach's career that he was not involved with church or organ music. The prince belonged to the Reformed (Calvinist) church, where only simple psalm singing was permitted in the service. For the six years from 1717 to 1723, Bach directed the prince's small orchestra of about eighteen players and composed music for it. The *Brandenburg* Concertos grew out of this productive period.

In 1720, Bach's wife died, leaving him with four young children. The next year, at thirty-six, he married a twenty-one-year-old singer at the court of Cöthen, and the second marriage was apparently as happy as the first.

Because he was an ardent amateur musician, the prince of Cöthen treated Bach as a friend. But the prince's interest waned when he married a woman who did not like music, and Bach decided to look for a new job.

He found one in 1723: the position of cantor (director of music) of St. Thomas Church in Leipzig, a position that involved responsibility for Leipzig's four main municipal churches. Bach remained here for the last twenty-seven years of his life. Though one of the most important church posts in Germany, the position carried less prestige and paid less than the one with the prince of Cöthen. But Bach was probably interested because it was in Leipzig, a comparatively large city of 30,000, where his children could receive a good Lutheran education and go to the university. Then, too, Bach was a deeply religious man. At the beginning of each sacred composition he wrote the letters *J.J.*, for *Jesu Juva* (*Jesus help*), and at the end he put *S.D.G.*, for *Soli Deo Gloria* (*to God alone the glory*).

At Leipzig, Bach rehearsed, conducted, and usually composed an extended composition for chorus, soloists, and orchestra for each Sunday and holiday of the church year. He was responsible for the musical education of some fifty-five students in the St. Thomas school. After some years in Leipzig he became director of the Leipzig Collegium Musicum, a student organization that gave concerts every Friday night at a coffeehouse. He was also an eminent teacher of organ and composition, gave organ recitals, and was often asked to judge the construction of organs. It's hard to imagine how he did all this while surrounded by children, relatives, and students—and living in the school building next to a classroom.

During the 1740s, Bach's eyesight deteriorated, yet he continued to compose, conduct, and teach. In 1750, the year of his death, he became blind.

Though recognized as the most eminent organist, harpsichordist, improviser, and master of the fugue, Bach was by no means considered the greatest composer of his day. He was little known outside Germany, and even his post in Leipzig was offered to him only after two other noted musicians had turned it down. By the time of Bach's maturity, the baroque style had begun to go out of fashion; people wanted light, uncomplicated music. Many thought his works too heavy, complex, and polyphonic.

Bach's music was largely forgotten and remained unpublished for years after his death. But a few composers of the generations following knew some of his compositions and were aware of his genius. In 1829, Felix Mendelssohn presented the *St. Matthew Passion,* and Bach's music has been the daily bread of every serious musician since then.

Bach's Music

Bach created masterpieces in every baroque form except opera. Throughout, he fused technical mastery and emotional depth. His instrumental music includes pieces for orchestra, for small groups, and for solo organ, harpsichord, clavichord, violin, and cello. The excellence and number of these works show how prominent instrumental music had become in the baroque period. Bach's vocal music—the bulk of his output—was written mostly for the Lutheran church and was often based on familiar hymns.

In forming his personal style, Bach drew on the musical resources of three different lands. He avidly studied Italian concertos and French dance pieces, as well as the church music of his native Germany.

Bach's music is unique in its combination of polyphonic texture and rich harmony. Several melodic lines of equal importance often occur at once; and so many things might go on at the same time that the music will convey an awesome complexity and elaboration. Yet even with the great interest that the individual voices convey, it is the progression of chords that directs the musical motion. Bach used complex and dissonant harmonies more imaginatively than his contemporaries. His works show an astounding mastery of harmony and counterpoint, and they are used as models by music students today.

Baroque music leans toward unity of mood, and this is particularly true of Bach, who liked to elaborate a single melodic idea in a piece. Bach's melodies can be intricate, unpredictable, and highly embellished, but unity of mood is created by an insistent rhythmic drive. Whether slow or fast, Bach's works generate perpetual motion.

By Bach's time there was little difference in style between secular and sacred music. In fact, he often created sacred music simply by rearranging instrumental pieces or works originally written for secular texts. His church music also uses operatic forms like the aria and recitative.

Bach liked to illustrate religious or pictorial ideas through musical symbolism. In an organ piece based on the hymn tune *Durch Adams Fall (Through Adam's Fall)*, Bach represents the serpent by twisting inner voices, and man's fall by downward leaps in the bass. And in one called *These Are the Holy Commandments*, Bach uses the theme exactly ten times. Sometimes Bach composed music to demonstrate what he could do with a specific musical form. His *Art of the Fugue,* for example, is a collection which displays all the resources of fugue writing.

Prelude and Fugue in C Minor from *The Well-Tempered Clavier*, Book I (about 1722)

In his collection of preludes and fugues, *The Well-Tempered Clavier*—which means, roughly, *The Well-Tuned Keyboard Instrument*—Bach explored with unprecedented thoroughness systems of tuning instruments that enabled a composer to write in all twenty-four keys, even keys with many sharps or flats. The collection is in two volumes (1722 and 1738–1742), each with twenty-four pairs of preludes—introductory pieces—and fugues, one pair in every major and minor key. On the title page of *The Well-Tempered Clavier,* Bach explains that the collection is "for the profit and use of musical youth desiring instruction, and especially for the pastime of those who are already skilled in this study." The word *clavier* in the title refers to keyboard instruments in general. In Bach's day, the preludes and fugues were probably played most often on the harpsichord and clavichord, but also on the organ and fortepiano (an early piano). Today the pieces are basic to the repertoire of keyboard players.

The Prelude and Fugue in C Minor from Book I is among Bach's most widely performed keyboard works. In the 1960s, millions heard recordings of an electronic version, *Switched-On Bach,* by Wendy Carlos; and a jazz-influenced vocal version, *Bach's Greatest Hits,* by the Swingle Singers. In our recording the Prelude and Fugue in C Minor is performed on a harpsichord.

Prelude in C Minor

Like many of the preludes in Bach's *Well-Tempered Clavier,* the Prelude in C Minor is a study in perpetual motion. This motion results from continuous running notes that appear almost without pause. Most of the prelude grows out of repeated patterns of eight rapid notes in both the right and the left hand. In the right hand, the first tone of the pattern is the highest of the eight notes. The succession of high notes forms a melodic line made up of short repeated tones (indicated by the asterisks in the music example for item 1*a* of the listening outline).

Toward the end of the prelude, the rhythmic drive is briefly interrupted by a slow ornamental passage in the style of an improvisation. As if waking from a reverie, the prelude soon returns to rapid running notes and concludes with a bright C major harmony.

LISTENING OUTLINE

BACH, Prelude in C Minor, from *The Well-Tempered Clavier*, Book I
Quadruple meter (4/4), C minor
Harpsichord
(Duration, 1:46)

34 0:00   **1. a.** Repeated pattern of running notes, successive high tones of pattern form melodic line.

0:10   Gradual descent of high notes of repeated pattern; brief melodic ascent leads to
35 0:54   **b.** New pattern of low running notes, single voice.

1:02   **c.** High running notes, lower running notes join.
36 1:16   **2. a.** Suddenly slow, ornamental, improvisatory style.

1:30   **b.** Fast running notes, major harmony at end.

Basic Set:
CD 2 **37**

Fugue in C Minor

The Fugue in C Minor is lighter in mood than Bach's Organ Fugue in G Minor (*Little Fugue*), studied in Section 4. Also, the C minor fugue is much shorter, has three voices rather than four, and has a more compact subject.

The subject grows out of a decisive five-note fragment—two short notes followed by three longer ones. In the opening section of the fugue, each of the three voices in turn—alto, soprano, bass—states the subject, which is introduced without accompaniment. Starting with its second appearance, the subject is accompanied by a countersubject that begins with a rapid descending scale. The fugue subject is stated eight times: seven times in minor and once in major.

Transitional episodes, which have a more continuous flow of rapid notes, precede several statements of the subject. In most of these episodes, the countersubject's rapid scale accompanies the subject's opening fragment. These melodic ideas are sequentially repeated and varied. For example, Bach sometimes transforms the rapid descending scale of the countersubject into an ascending version. The first episode quickly and almost imperceptibly leads to the subject in major (items 1e and 2a in the listening outline). This transition is particularly smooth because the beginning of the subject sounds like a continuation of the episode's downward sequence.

The last appearance of the subject sounds like an epilogue. The subject in the soprano is now accompanied by a pedal point—a low, sustained octave in the bass. Like its prelude, the Fugue in C Minor ends with a bright C major harmony.

LISTENING OUTLINE

BACH, Fugue in C Minor, from *The Well-Tempered Clavier*, Book I

Quadruple meter (4/4), C minor
Harpsichord
(Duration, 1:33)

37 0:00   **1. a.** Subject, alto voice alone, minor key.

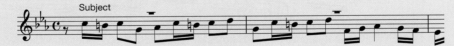

0:06   **b.** Subject in soprano, countersubject in alto.

0:12   **c.** Bridge, subject fragment, ascending sequence.
0:17   **d.** Subject in bass, countersubject in soprano.
38 0:23   **e.** Episode, subject fragments in soprano and alto against rapid downward scales in bass.

39 0:28   **2. a.** Subject in soprano, major key.

0:33   **b.** Episode, rapid upward scales in soprano.

0:39   **c.** Subject in alto, minor key; countersubject in soprano.

0:45   **d.** Longer episode, subject fragments and upward scale segments, ascending sequences.

40 0:53   **3. a.** Subject in soprano, countersubject in alto.

0:59   **b.** Longest episode, subject fragments in soprano and alto against rapid downward scales in bass; upward sequences and rapid bass scale introduce

1:11   **c.** Subject in low bass, countersubject in soprano, brief pause, cadence to

1:23   **d.** Subject in soprano, accompanied by held low octave in bass (pedal point), major chord at end.

Brandenburg Concerto No. 5 in D Major (about 1721)

Second Movement:
Affettuoso (affectionately, tenderly)

Basic Set:

CD 2 **9**

We have already examined the opening movement (allegro) of the Fifth *Brandenburg* Concerto in Section 3, "The Concerto Grosso and Ritornello Form." Here we'll study the two remaining movements of this concerto grosso for flute, violin, harpsichord, and orchestra.

In marked contrast to the vigorous opening movement, the affettuoso is slow, quiet, and in a minor key. It uses only the three solo instruments and a cello, which duplicates the bass line (left hand) of the harpsichordist. The movement is based on repeated alternation between a main theme and episodes. The main theme is serious and features a motive in dotted rhythm. It is presented alternately in minor and major keys and uses the harpsichord only as a basso continuo accompaniment to an imitative duet between violin and flute. In the recurring main theme, there is no notated part for the right hand; the harpsichordist is expected to improvise chords as guided by Bach's figured bass.

In contrast to the recurring main theme, the episodes present melodies played by the harpsichordist's right hand, and the harpsichord becomes a center of attention, a soloist along with the flute and violin. The episodes elaborate a gentle, two-note "sigh" motive as well as the dotted-rhythm motive of the main theme.

Bach creates melodic variety by turning both the dotted-rhythm motive and the "sigh" motive upside down. The following example shows the two motives and their inversions:

Here is an outline of the second movement:

9 0:00

10 0:57

11 1:57

12 3:10

13 4:31

1. Main theme (minor)—episode (harpsichord melody imitated by flute, violin; minor to major).
2. Main theme (major)—episode (harpsichord melody imitated by violin, flute; major to minor).
3. Main theme (minor)—episode (harpsichord melody answered by "sigh" motive in flute, violin; minor).
4. Main theme (major)—long episode (harpsichord melody answered by flute, violin; flute-violin duets answered by harpsichord melody; major to minor).
5. Main theme (minor).

Third Movement:
Allegro

Basic Set:
CD 2 **14**

The concluding allegro is dancelike in character. It is in A B A form; the A sections are in major, and the B section is in minor. The movement begins like a fugue, with a rollicking subject introduced by the solo violin and then imitated by the flute and harpsichord.

Section A
14 0:00

After a while, the instruments of the tutti—not heard since the opening movement—join in playing the subject.

The middle section, in minor, begins softly with a lyrical melody for the flute.

Section B
15 1:16

This melody starts like the main subject but contains long notes, which give it a songlike character. After the flute, the violin and harpsichord take turns playing this melody. The main subject also has a prominent role throughout the middle section and can be heard in a harpsichord solo. Bach achieves both unity and variety by combining within the middle section the main subject and the new lyrical melody related to it.

Return of Section A
16 3:45

A loud tutti signals the conclusion of the middle section. Then the solo violin, imitated by the flute, announces the return of the opening section A. The major key and lively rhythms seem even more joyful after the minor key and reflective quality of the middle section.

Mass in B Minor (Begun 1733)

Over a period of years, Bach, a pious Lutheran, composed what is probably the most monumental setting of the Roman Catholic mass. In 1733, he wrote the first two sections (the Kyrie and Gloria) and sent them to a Catholic monarch with a request for the honorary title of court composer. Years later, he finished the mass by composing new music and by fitting the Latin text to some of his earlier Lutheran church pieces. Bach probably never heard the entire work performed. Since it is far too long to be used in the Catholic service, Bach's reasons for creating it are unknown. He may simply have wanted to show what he could do with this ancient and imposing form.

Bach's B Minor Mass contrasts strikingly with the Renaissance mass studied in Part III. It has specific orchestral accompaniments for the voices. Also, each major section of Bach's mass—such as the Kyrie or Credo—is subdivided into arias, duets, and choruses. Thus this mass has more variety within each large section than a Renaissance mass has in its sections. Each part of Bach's B Minor Mass expresses the meaning and emotion of the text.

Let us explore two contrasting movements from the Credo: the *Crucifixus,* a profound expression of grief at Christ's crucifixion; and *Et resurrexit,* which expresses joy at Christ's resurrection.

Crucifixus

> Crucifixus etiam pro nobis sub
> Pontio Pilato, passus et sepultus est.

> And was crucified also for us under
> Pontius Pilate. He suffered and was
> buried.

The *Crucifixus* is scored for four voice parts and a small orchestra of strings, two flutes, and continuo. It is built on a chromatically descending ground bass, or basso ostinato, the traditional symbol of grief in baroque music. (You heard one in *Dido's Lament,* by Purcell.)

Over the constantly repeating ground bass, the soprano, alto, tenor, and bass sing ever-changing melodic lines that produce dissonant harmonies. Minor key, slow tempo, and hushed dynamics—together with the generally downward-moving melodies—contribute to a feeling of infinite sorrow. One particularly sublime moment occurs at the very end of this movement, when there is an unexpected shift from minor to major and the sopranos descend chromatically to their lowest tone. At this point of deepest sorrow, the major key implies hope.

Et Resurrexit

> Et resurrexit tertia die secundum
> scripturas. Et ascendit in coelum, sedet
> ad dexteram Dei Patris, et iterum
> venturus est cum gloria judicare vivos
> et mortuos, cujus regni non erit finis.

> And on the third day he rose again
> according to the scriptures. And
> ascended into Heaven. And sitteth at
> the right hand of God the Father.
> And he shall come again with glory
> to judge both the living and the dead;
> whose kingdom shall have no end.

The jubilant *Et resurrexit* fulfills the hope implied in the *Crucifixus.* Now Bach uses a chorus and full orchestra, including three trumpets, timpani, and two oboes. The movement is in major; a fast tempo and bright-sounding trumpets make it festive. Typically baroque is the rising melodic line on the words *Et resurrexit (and he rose).*

Et re-sur-re - xit, re-sur-re - xit,

Variety is achieved through repeated alternations between orchestral sections and sections using voices and instruments.

The Baroque Suite

Instrumental music has always been closely linked with dancing; in the past, much of it was written for use in palace ballrooms. During the Renaissance, dances often came in pairs—a dignified dance in quadruple meter was often followed by a lively one in triple meter. In the baroque period and later, music was written that—while meant for listening, not dancing—was related to specific dance types in tempo, meter, and rhythm.

Baroque composers wrote **suites,** which are sets of dance-inspired movements. Whether for solo instruments, small groups, or orchestra, a baroque suite is made up of movements that are all written in the same key but differ in tempo, meter, and character. The dancelike movements also have a variety of national origins: the moderately paced *allemande* (from Germany) might be followed by a fast *courante* and a moderate *gavotte* (from France), a slow and solemn *sarabande* (from Spain), and a fast *gigue* (jig, from England and Ireland). Suites were played in private homes, at court concerts, or as background music for dinner and outdoor festivities.

Dance pieces have a diverse past. Some began as folk dances, while others sprang from aristocratic ballrooms. Even the character of a dance might show dramatic evolution. The slow, solemn sarabande grew out of a sexually suggestive song and dance that a sixteenth-century moralist condemned as "so lascivious in its words, so ugly in its movements, that it is enough to inflame even very honest people." In the seventeenth century, however, the sarabande became respectable enough to be danced by a cardinal at the French court.

The movements of a suite are usually in two-part form with each section repeated; that is, in the form A A B B. The A section, which opens in the tonic key and modulates to the dominant, is balanced by the B section, which begins in the dominant and returns to the tonic key. Both sections use the same thematic material, and so they contrast relatively little except in key.

Suites frequently begin with a movement that is *not* dance-inspired. One common opening is the French overture, which is also the type of piece heard at the beginning of baroque oratorios and operas. Usually written in two parts, the **French overture** first presents a slow section with dotted rhythms that is full of dignity and grandeur. The second section is quick and lighter in mood, often beginning like a fugue. Sometimes part of the opening section will return at the end of the overture.

The suite was an important instrumental form in the baroque. Even compositions not called "suite" often have several dance-inspired movements. Music influenced by dance tends to have balanced and symmetrical phrases of the same length, because formal dancing has a set of steps in one direction symmetrically balanced by a similar motion in the opposite direction.

Bach wrote four suites for orchestra. We don't know exactly when they were composed, but it seems likely that the Collegium Musicum performed them in a coffeehouse in Leipzig.

Suite No. 3 in D Major (1729–1731), by Johann Sebastian Bach

First Movement: Overture

Suite No. 3 in D Major—scored for two oboes, three trumpets, timpani, strings, and basso continuo—opens with a majestic French overture, which exploits the bright sounds of trumpets. After a slow opening section with dotted rhythms, we hear the energetic fast section. This begins like a fugue, with an upward-moving theme introduced by the first violins and then imitated by the other instruments.

The fast section is like a concerto grosso in its alternation of solid tutti passages with lightly scored passages highlighting the first violins. After the fast section, the slow tempo, dotted rhythms, and majestic mood of the opening return.

Second Movement: Air
The second movement, the air, contains one of Bach's best-loved melodies. It is scored for only strings and continuo and is serene and lyrical, in contrast to the majestic and then bustling French overture. The title suggests that the movement is written in the style of an Italian aria. Like the opening movement, the air is not related to dance. It is in A A B B form, with the B section twice as long as the A section. The air combines a steadily moving bass (which proceeds in upward and downward octave leaps) with a rhapsodic and rhythmically irregular melody in the violins.

Third Movement: Gavotte
All the movements that follow the overture and the air are inspired by dance, beginning with the gavotte, which is written in duple meter and in a moderate tempo and uses the full orchestra again. It may be outlined as follows: gavotte I (A A B B); gavotte II (C C D D); gavotte I (A B). Notice the contrast between the sections for full orchestra and those without trumpets and timpani.

Fourth Movement: Bourrée
The bourrée is an even livelier dance, also in duple meter; it is the shortest movement of the suite. Its form is A A B B. Section A uses the full orchestra, including trumpets and timpani. Section B is three times as long as section A and alternates loud tutti passages with softer passages for strings and oboes.

Fifth Movement: Gigue
The suite concludes with a rollicking gigue in $\frac{6}{8}$ time, which is also in the form A A B B. Here, Bach's manner is simple and direct. Listen for the splendid effect when timpani and trumpets periodically join the rest of the orchestra.

14 The Chorale and Church Cantata

In Leipzig in Bach's time, the Lutheran church service on Sunday was the social event of the week: it started at seven in the morning and lasted about 4 hours. The sermon alone could take an hour.

Music was a significant part of the Lutheran service. Most religious services today use no more than a chorus and an organ, but Bach's church had a small orchestra of between fourteen and twenty-one players to accompany the twelve or so men and boys of the choir. The service was filled with music; single compositions might last half an hour.

Music was a significant part of the Lutheran church service in Germany during the baroque period. This engraving shows a performance of a cantata in Bach's time.

To further the direct communication that Lutheranism stressed between the believer and Christ, the rite was largely in the vernacular—German. Each service included several hymns, or chorales. The *chorale,* or hymn tune, was sung to a German religious text. Chorales were easy to sing and remember, having only one note to a syllable and moving in steady rhythm. They were tunes that had been composed in the sixteenth and seventeenth centuries or had been adapted from folk songs and Catholic hymns. The members of the congregation had sung these tunes since childhood, and each tune carried religious associations. Congregational singing of chorales was an important way for people to participate directly in the service. These melodies were often harmonized for church choirs. The hymn melody was sung in the top part, and the tones of the supporting harmonies were sung in the three lower parts.

New church music was often based on traditional melodies written as far back as two centuries earlier. Before the congregation began to sing a hymn, the organist might play a *chorale prelude,* a short composition based on the hymn tune that reminded the congregation of the melody. By using traditional tunes in their works, composers could involve the congregation and enhance the religious associations.

The Church Cantata

The principal means of musical expression in the Lutheran service, and one which used chorales, was the church **cantata.** *Cantata* originally meant a piece that was *sung,* as distinct from a sonata, which was *played.* Many kinds of cantatas were being written in Bach's day, but we shall focus only on the cantata designed for the Lutheran service in Germany in the early 1700s. It was usually written for chorus, vocal soloists, organ, and a small orchestra. It had a German religious text, either newly written or drawn from the Bible or familiar hymns. In the Lutheran services, there were different Gospel and Epistle readings for each Sunday and holiday, and the cantata text was related to them. In a sense, the cantata was a sermon in music that reinforced the minister's sermon, which was also based on the Gospel and Epistle readings. The cantata of Bach's day might last 25 minutes and include several different movements—choruses, recitatives, arias, and duets. You'll see that in its use of aria, duet, and recitative, the cantata closely resembled the opera of the time and thus is typical of the baroque fusion of sacred and secular elements in art and music.

The cantor, or music director, had to provide church cantatas for every Sunday and holiday. Bach wrote about 295; about 195 are still in existence. In his first few years as cantor in Leipzig, he composed cantatas at the staggering rate of almost three a month. During the remaining twenty-five years of his tenure, he was inclined to reuse cantatas, and so his output dropped.

Cantata No. 140: *Wachet auf, ruft uns die Stimme* (*Awake, a Voice Is Calling Us*; 1731) by Johann Sebastian Bach

Wachet auf, ruft uns die Stimme (Cantata No. 140) is Bach's best-known cantata. To fully appreciate it, we perhaps should imagine ourselves as pious Lutherans of his time. It was composed for the twenty-seventh Sunday after Trinity Sunday, when the Gospel reading was the parable of the wise and foolish virgins (Matthew, 25). The Christian believers are represented by virgins, and Christ by the bridegroom:

> Then shall the kingdom of heaven be likened unto ten virgins, which took their lamps and went forth to meet the bridegroom. And five of them were wise, and five were foolish. . . . And at midnight there was a cry made, Behold the bridegroom cometh; go ye out to meet him. Then all those virgins arose, and trimmed their lamps. And the foolish said unto the wise, Give us of your oil; for our lamps are gone out. But the wise answered, saying, Not so; lest there not be enough for us and you: but go ye rather to them that sell, and buy for yourselves. While they were away the bridegroom arrived; and those who were ready went in with him to the wedding; and the door was shut. . . . Keep awake then; for you never know the day or the hour. . . .

Bach based his cantata on the chorale tune *Wachet auf*, because its text was inspired by the Gospel for this particular Sunday. The text and melody of the chorale had been written by Philipp Nicolai (1556–1608) in about 1597—more than 130 years before Bach used it. This was a widely known chorale tune that had been used by other composers before Bach. The hymn has three stanzas, and all are sung to the same melody. Bach used the chorale melody and text in three of the seven movements in the cantata:

Movement	Use of Chorale	Content of Text
1. Chorus with orchestra.	Chorale stanza 1	Virgins awakened by watchmen announcing the coming of the bridegroom.
2. Recitative for solo tenor with continuo.		The bridegroom is coming.
3. Duet for soprano and bass with violino piccolo and continuo.		Dialogue between a longing soul (soprano) and Jesus (bass).
4. Tenors of chorus sing chorale in unison; strings and continuo.	Chorale, stanza 2	Zion (Christian believers) rejoices at the arrival of Lord Jesus, God's son.

5. Recitative for bass, accompanied by strings and continuo.

Jesus lovingly greets the bride.

6. Duet for soprano and bass with oboe and continuo.

Joyous union between Christ (bass) and Christian (soprano).

7. Chorus doubled by orchestra.

Chorale, stanza 3

Christians praise God and rejoice in union with him.

According to a Protestant theologian and music scholar, the chorale text interprets the relationship of the bridegroom and bride "as a picture of the union of God with his people, of Christ with the Church." The other texts of Cantata No. 140, for duets and recitatives, were written by an unknown author and depict "the relationship between Jesus and the pious individual soul." They are based on the Song of Songs (or Song of Solomon) in the Bible.

Before listening to Cantata No. 140, it's helpful to become acquainted with the chorale tune, which the last movement presents unadorned. The melody has the form A A B. (The text of the chorale is translated on page 168.)

Last movement
Basic Set:
CD 2 53

Brief Set:
CD 2 26

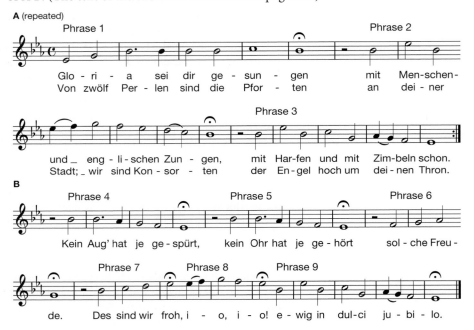

There are nine melodic phrases, of which the first three (making up the A section) are repeated immediately. The last phrase of the A section (phrase 3) reappears at the end of the B section (phrase 9) and beautifully rounds off the chorale melody.

Now let's consider movements 1, 4, and 7, which use the chorale melody in different ways.

First Movement: Chorus and Orchestra

Basic Set:
CD 2 47

The opening movement is scored for chorus and a small orchestra of two oboes, English horn, French horn, strings, and basso continuo (organ, bassoon, and cello). In the chorale text of this movement, watchmen on the towers of Jerusalem call on the wise virgins (Christians) to awake because the bridegroom (Christ) is coming. The movement opens with an orchestral ritornello that may have been intended to suggest a procession or march. As shown in the music example which follows, there are dotted rhythms (long-short, long-short), a rising figure with syncopation, and a series of rising scales.

At the ritornello's closing cadence the sopranos enter and sing the first phrase of the chorale in long notes. Soon the three lower voices engage in an imitative dialogue based on a new motive in shorter note values. Throughout, the orchestra continues to play still shorter notes.

Thus there are three layers of sound: the chorale phrases in long notes in the soprano; the imitative dialogue in shorter note values in the three lower voices; and the ever-busy orchestra playing motives from the ritornello in even shorter notes. The chorale tune (in the soprano) is presented not as a continuous whole but rather phrase by phrase, with breaks between phrases. After each phrase, the voices pause while the orchestra continues to play interludes made up of either the whole ritornello or sections from it. Sometimes the motives in the three lower voices illustrate the text, as when they have rising scale figures at the word *hoch* (high) and exclamations at the repeated *wo* (where).

Once during the movement, the three lower voices become emancipated from the soprano and jubilantly sing a melody in rapid notes on *Alleluja*. This, perhaps, is the most exciting moment in the movement.

VOCAL MUSIC GUIDE

BACH, *Wachet auf, ruft uns die Stimme*

First Movement

47 0:00
Orchestral ritornello.

48 0:28
Brief orchestral interlude.

	Wachet auf, ruft uns die Stimme	"Awake," the voice of watchmen

0:49
Rising scales in lower voices depict *hoch* (high). Brief orchestral interlude.

	der Wächter sehr hoch auf der Zinne	calls us from high on the tower,
	wach auf, du Stadt Jerusalem!	"Awake, you city of Jerusalem!"

1:32
Orchestral ritornello.

2:00	*Mitternacht heisst diese Stunde;*	Midnight is this very hour;

Brief orchestral interlude.

	sie rufen uns mit hellem Munde:	they call to us with bright voices:

Brief orchestral interlude.

	wo seid ihr klugen Jungfrauen?	"Where are you, wise virgins?"

3:04
Long orchestral interlude.

	Wohl auf, der Bräut'gam kömmt,	Take cheer, the Bridegroom comes,

Brief orchestral interlude.

49 3:56
Altos, jubilant melody in rapid notes. Imitation by tenors, then basses.

	steht auf, die Lampen nehmt!	arise, take up your lamps!
	Alleluja!	Hallelujah!

4:22
Sopranos, chorale in long notes.

Orchestral interlude.

	Alleluja!	Hallelujah!
	Macht euch bereit	Prepare yourselves

Orchestral interlude.		
Brief orchestral interlude.	*zu der Hochzeit*	for the wedding,
5:14	*ihr müsset ihm entgegen gehn.*	you must go forth to meet him.
Orchestral ritornello.		

Basic Set:
CD 2 **50**

Brief Set:
CD 2 **23**

Fourth Movement: Tenor Chorale

The fourth movement is scored for tenors; violins and violas in unison; and basso continuo. The chorale tune returns in this movement, the most popular of the cantata. Bach liked this section so much that toward the end of his life he rearranged it as a chorale prelude for organ. With miraculous ease, he sets two contrasting melodies against each other. First we hear the unison strings supported by the continuo playing the ritornello, a warm, flowing melody that Bach may have intended as a dancelike procession of the maidens as they "all follow to the joyful hall and share in the Lord's supper." This melody is repeated and varied throughout while the tenors sing the chorale tune against it.

Zi - on hört die Wäch-ter sin - gen

das Herz tut ihr __ vor Freu - den sprin - gen,

The chorale tune moves in faster rhythmic values here than in the opening movement, but, again, it is broken into component phrases linked by the instrumental melody. It's helpful to listen several times to this movement, focusing first on the rapid rhythms of the graceful string melody, then on the sturdy, slower rhythms of the chorale tune, and finally on all lines at once.

VOCAL MUSIC GUIDE

BACH, *Wachet auf, ruft uns die Stimme*

Fourth Movement

50 **23**   0:00
**String
ritornello.**

51 **24**   0:39

Zion hört die Wächter singen,	Zion hears the watchmen singing,
das Herz tut ihr vor Freuden springen,	for joy her very heart is springing,
sie wachet und steht eilend auf.	she wakes and rises hastily.

Ritornello.

1:52

Ihr Freund kommt von Himmel prächtig,	From heaven comes her friend resplendent,
von Gnaden stark, von Wahrheit mächtig,	sturdy in grace, mighty in truth,
Ihr Licht wird hell, ihr Stern geht auf.	her light shines bright, her star ascends.

Ritornello.

52 **25**   2:46

Nun komm, du werte Kron,	Now come, you worthy crown,
Herr Jesu, Gottes Sohn.	Lord Jesus, God's own Son.

3:04

Hosianna!	Hosanna!

Ritornello in minor.

3:28

Wir folgen all' zum Freudensaal	We all follow to the joyful hall
und halten mit das Abendmahl.	and share the Lord's Supper.

Ritornello.

**Basic Set:
CD 2** **53**

Brief Set:
CD 2 **26**

Seventh Movement: Chorale

Bach rounds off Cantata No. 140 by bringing back the chorale once more. For the first time since the first movement, all voices and instruments take part. Here the chorale is set in a relatively simple, homophonic texture for four voices, with the instruments simply doubling them, not playing melodies of their own. Now the chorale is heard as a continuous melody, without interludes between its phrases. The rich sound, full harmonies, and regular rhythms express praise of God, faith in him, and joy in being in his kingdom. No doubt the congregation joined in the singing of the final chorale, which so firmly expressed their unity and belief.

VOCAL MUSIC GUIDE

BACH, *Wachet auf, ruft uns die Stimme*

Seventh Movement

53 **26**

A

Gloria sei dir gesungen	Gloria be sung to you
mit Menschen- und englischen Zungen,	with men's and angel's tongues,
mit Harfen und mit Zimbeln schon.	with harps and beautiful cymbals.

A

Von zwölf Perlen sind die Pforten	Of twelve pearls are the gates
an deiner Stadt; wir sind Konsorten	at your city; we are consorts
der Engel hoch um deinen Thron.	of the angels high about your throne.

B		
Kein Aug' hat je gespürt,		No eye has ever sensed,
kein Ohr hat je gehört		no ear has ever heard
solche Freude.		such a delight.
Des sind wir froh,		Of this we rejoice,
io, io!		io, io!
ewig in dulci jubilo.		forever in sweet joy.

15 The Oratorio

Together with the opera and cantata, the oratorio stands as a major development in baroque vocal music. Like an opera, an **oratorio** is a large-scale composition for chorus, vocal soloists, and orchestra; it is usually set to a narrative text. Oratorio differs from opera in that it has no acting, scenery, or costumes. Most oratorios are based on biblical stories, but usually they are not intended for religious services. Today they are performed in either concert halls or churches.

An oratorio contains a succession of choruses, arias, duets, recitatives, and orchestral interludes. The chorus is especially important and serves either to comment on or to participate in the drama. A narrator's recitatives usually relate the story and connect one piece with another. Oratorios (which sometimes last over 2 hours) are longer than cantatas and have more of a story line.

Oratorios first appeared in early seventeenth-century Italy as musical dramatizations of biblical stories and were performed in prayer halls called *oratorios.* During the baroque period, the oratorio spread to other countries and assumed many forms. *Messiah,* by George Frideric Handel, has for decades been the best-known and most-loved oratorio.

16 George Frideric Handel

George Frideric Handel (1685–1759), a master of Italian opera and English oratorio, was born in Halle, Germany, one month before J. S. Bach. Handel was not from a musical family; his father was a barber-surgeon who wanted his son to study law, not music. By the time Handel was nine, however, his musical talent was so outstanding that his father relented somewhat and permitted him to study with the local organist, who was also a composer. By the age of eleven, Handel was able not only to compose but also to give organ lessons. Perhaps to honor the wishes of his father, who had died when Handel was twelve, he entered Halle University at seventeen to study law. But a year later he left the university and set out for Hamburg.

Handel was drawn to the renowned opera house in Hamburg. There he became a violinist and harpsichordist in the orchestra, and when he was twenty, one of his operas was successfully produced.

Handel was a man of temperament and conviction. At the Hamburg opera one incident almost cost him his life. The company was performing an opera by one of Handel's

Handel's triple career as impresario, composer, and performer brought him success and fame but led to political infighting and two nervous breakdowns.

friends, who insisted that he, not Handel, play the harpsichord. Handel refused to give up his post, and their argument led to a duel. A metal button on Handel's coat broke his opponent's sword. It was a button's great contribution to posterity.

Handel's good fortune continued. He went to Italy at twenty-one to establish his career and stayed for three highly productive years. There he wrote Italian operas that were acclaimed far and wide. He mingled with princes and famous musicians; even cardinals wrote librettos for him to set to music.

Returning to Germany in 1710, Handel took a well-paid position as music director for Elector Georg Ludwig of Hanover. After just a month, he asked for a leave to go to London, where his opera *Rinaldo* was being produced. *Rinaldo* was a triumph, and he returned to Hanover. A year later Handel again asked the elector for an English leave. It was granted on the condition that Handel stay only a reasonable length of time in London.

This turned out to be the next half century (1712–1759). Handel's fame in England grew as rapidly as it had grown in Italy. He became England's most important composer and a favorite of Queen Anne, who gave him a subsidy of £200 a year. On Queen Anne's death, a complicated arrangement made the elector of Hanover, Georg Ludwig, King George I of England (1714). Evidently the king had not taken offense at Handel's absence; the composer's subsidy was increased to £400 annually, and he taught music to the king's granddaughters.

Italian opera in London was an exotic entertainment for the pleasure of the aristocracy. Middle-class audiences had little desire to see works with mythological plots they considered absurd. Therefore a few aristocrats provided the base of support for opera in London. They ran a commercial opera company called the Royal Academy of Music; in 1719, Handel became its music director. After nine seasons the company folded because of inadequate support. But in that period Handel had composed a number of brilliant operas for outstanding sopranos and castrati.

Handel's reputation continued to grow, and after the collapse of the Royal Academy, he decided to form a company to produce his works. (For years he had a triple career as impresario, composer, and performer.) At the time, opera had become a political weapon. To spite him, a company called the Opera of the Nobility was formed. Its backers opposed the party in power, and Handel—a friend of the king and an establishment composer—became a scapegoat.

Both opera companies went bankrupt as a result of the competition, and Handel suffered a breakdown. He went to Germany to recuperate, and his condition moved the future king of Prussia to write, in 1737, "Handel's great days are over, his inspiration is exhausted, and his taste behind the fashion."

But the king of Prussia was mistaken. Handel recovered, returned to London, and—though heavily in debt—managed again to produce operas on his own. To these he added his oratorios, opening a glowing new chapter in music history.

For the English public, oratorios were a novelty. But the English people knew the Old Testament and liked hearing English onstage. Handel offered his oratorios during Lent, when operas were prohibited. Oratorios, unlike opera, required no expensive sets, stage machinery, or costumes, and were thus cheaper to produce. Even though Handel charged high prices, he attracted a new, middle-class audience.

In 1741, the year he composed *Messiah,* Handel stopped writing operas entirely. Oratorios poured from his pen. At first, some people were scandalized that biblical words were being sung in a public theater. One newspaper received a letter asserting that "the People of England were arriv'd to such a Height of *Impiety* and *Prophaneness,* that the most sacred *Things* were suffer'd to be us'd as *publick Diversions.*"

Despite the sniping, the oratorio seasons were acclaimed; they had the added attraction of Handel himself performing his organ concertos between acts. But too much success can bring trouble. Some aristocrats began to plot Handel's ruin. To them, the idea of a foreign-born musician's attaining power and prominence was too much. Concert posters were torn down, hired hoodlums robbed and assaulted concertgoers, and aristocrats made a point of giving private concerts and balls on oratorio evenings. Gradually, all this simmered down, but not before Handel had another breakdown. Again, he recovered rapidly and went on producing oratorios.

By 1753, Handel was still conducting and giving organ concerts, though he was almost blind. During his lifetime a statue of him was erected in a public park, and when he died in 1759, 3,000 mourners attended his funeral in Westminster Abbey. He was wealthy, generous, cultivated—and stubborn. But above all, he was a master composer whose dramatic sense has rarely been equaled.

Handel's Music

Handel shares Bach's stature among composers of the late baroque. Although he wrote a great deal of instrumental music—suites, organ concertos, concerti grossi—the core of his huge output consists of Italian operas and English oratorios.

Handel's thirty-nine Italian operas, almost all written in London, are not as well known today as his oratorios. But after two centuries of neglect, these operas are being revived successfully by modern opera companies. Handel's operas are nearly all serious. They are based on ancient Greek and Roman history or mythology. The heroes and heroines are royal figures like Julius Caesar and Cleopatra. Most noteworthy in Handel's operas are the arias, which are connected by long passages of recitative in which the plot develops. The arias show Handel's outstanding ability to evoke a mood or emotion. They were often written to display the virtuosity of singers, some of whom were castrati.

Handel's English oratorios are usually based on stories from the Old Testament and have titles like *Israel in Egypt, Saul, Joshua,* and *Judas Maccabaeus.* They are *not* church music, however; they were composed to entertain paying audiences in public theaters. Most have plots and characters, even though they are performed without acting, scenery, or costumes. As we'll see, *Messiah* is an exception, in that it deals with a New Testament subject and is without a plot.

The chorus is the focus of Handel's oratorios. Sometimes the chorus participates in the narrative, representing the Israelites or their heathen enemies. But it also comments on the action, lamenting or exulting. Handel treats the combination of chorus and orchestra with flexibility and imagination. In his hands, a chorus can project delicacy, drama, or grandeur. Even Beethoven marveled at Handel's ability to "achieve great effects with simple means."

Handel never hesitated to reinforce an idea in his text by interrupting a polyphonic flow of music with a series of chords. Changes in texture are more frequent in his music than in Bach's. And he liked to present two different melodic ideas and then combine them polyphonically. Handel achieved sharp changes of mood by shifting between minor keys and major keys.

Messiah (1741)

Messiah lasts about 2½ hours and was composed in just twenty-four days. Handel wrote it before going to Ireland to attend performances of his own works that were being given to dedicate a concert hall. About five months after his arrival in Dublin (in 1742), Handel gave the first performance of *Messiah;* the occasion was a benefit for people languishing in debtors' prisons. The rehearsals attracted wide attention: one newspaper commented that *Messiah* was thought "by the greatest Judges to be the finest Composition of Musick that ever was heard." Normally, the concert hall held 600 people; but to increase the capacity, women were asked not to wear hoopskirts, and men were asked to leave their swords at home.

Although the premiere was a success, the first performance in London (1743) was poorly received, mainly because of religious opposition to using a Christian text in a theater. It took *Messiah* almost a decade to find popularity in London. Not until it was performed yearly at a benefit for a London orphanage did it achieve its unique status. A contemporary wrote that *Messiah* "fed the hungry, clothed the naked, fostered the orphan."

Messiah is in three parts. Part I starts with the prophecy of the Messiah's coming and makes celestial announcements of Christ's birth and the redemption of humanity through his appearance. Part II has been aptly described by one Handel scholar as "the accomplishment of redemption by the sacrifice of Jesus, mankind's rejection of God's offer and mankind's utter defeat when trying to oppose the power of the Almighty." Part III expresses faith in the certainty of eternal life through Christ as redeemer.

Unlike most of Handel's oratorios, *Messiah* is meditative rather than dramatic; it lacks plot, action, and specific characters. *Messiah* is Handel's only English oratorio that uses the New Testament as well as the Old. Charles Jennings, a millionaire and amateur literary man, compiled the text by taking widely separated passages from the Bible—Isaiah, Psalms, and Job from the Old Testament; Luke, I Corinthians, and Revelations from the New.

Over the years, Handel rewrote some movements in *Messiah* for different performers and performances. In his own time, it was performed with a smaller orchestra and chorus than we are used to. His chorus included twenty singers, all male; and his small orchestra had only strings and continuo, with trumpets and timpani used in some sections. Today we sometimes hear arranged versions; Mozart made one, and still later versions are often played by orchestras of one hundred and choruses of several hundred.

Messiah has over fifty movements, and Handel ensures variety by skillfully contrasting movements and grouping them. He achieves profound effects through simple alternations of major and minor. We will focus on movements 1, 2, 3, and 12 from Part I, and on the *Hallelujah* Chorus, which ends Part II.

Sinfonia for Strings and Continuo (French Overture)
Grave; Allegro moderato (moderate allegro)

Messiah opens with a French overture in minor. As is customary, a slow section featuring dotted rhythms is followed by a quite rapid section beginning like a fugue. A lively subject is passed from higher instruments to lower.

Basic Set:
CD 3 ▮1▮
Grave
▮1▮ 0:00
Allegro moderato
▮2▮ 1:20

After this, the imitation mainly involves fragments of the subject. Near the end of the movement is a feature typical of Handel: energetic orchestral motion is suddenly broken off by a brief pause that ushers in a closing cadence of slow chords. It's as though Handel had applied a brake to bring the music to a decisive end.

Comfort Ye, My People
Accompanied recitative for tenor, strings, and continuo
Larghetto (slow, but less so than largo)

Basic Set:

CD 3 3

In *Comfort Ye, My People,* the vocal line is something between a recitative and an aria, more lyrical than the one, less elaborate than the other. Such a melodic accompanied recitative is called an **arioso.** *Comfort Ye, My People* is based on verses from Isaiah (40:1–3) which console Jerusalem by announcing that the exile of her people will soon end because they have atoned for their sins. A heavenly voice commands that a road be prepared for the exiles to return through the desert. *Comfort Ye* opens with a string ritornello in major that does seem "comforting" after the overture's minor key. The beginning of this ritornello often reappears during the piece, and the entire ritornello returns near the end in a different key. The tenor's opening *Comfort ye* pattern (long-short-long) is echoed by the strings, which repeat it reassuringly throughout. At the end, when a heavenly voice is heard (*The voice of him that crieth in the wilderness*), the vocal line becomes pure recitative.

VOCAL MUSIC GUIDE

HANDEL, *Comfort Ye*, from *Messiah*

3	0:14	Strings, ritornello.	
		Tenor alone.	Comfort ye,
	0:22	Strings imitate *comfort ye.*	
		Strings, tenor.	comfort ye my people,
		Strings, *comfort ye* pattern.	
	0:38	Tenor alone.	comfort ye,
		Strings, tenor.	comfort ye my people,
		Strings, *comfort ye* pattern.	
	1:02	Tenor, strings.	saith your God, saith your God;
		Strings, ritornello fragment.	
	1:19	Tenor, strings.	speak ye comfortably to Jerusalem,
		Tenor alone.	and cry unto her that her
		Tenor, strings, ritornello fragment.	warfare is accomplish'd,
			that her iniquity is pardon'd.
		Strings, ritornello.	
4	2:32	Tenor recitative, short string chords accompany	The voice of him that crieth in the wilderness, Prepare ye the way of the Lord, make straight in the desert a highway for our God.

Ev'ry Valley Shall Be Exalted
Aria for tenor, strings, and continuo Andante

Basic Set:
CD 3 **5**

Brief Set:
CD 2 **27**

The aria *Ev'ry Valley Shall Be Exalted* is based on a verse from Isaiah (40:4) describing the creation of a desert highway on which God will lead his people back to their homeland. Like many baroque arias, it opens and closes with a string ritornello. This aria is striking in its vivid word painting, so characteristic of baroque music. On a single syllable of *exalted* (*raised up*), forty-six rapid notes form a rising musical line.

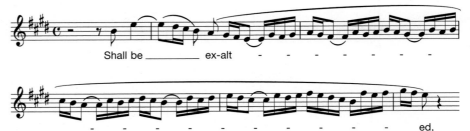

Notice, too, the rising and falling direction of the phrase *and every mountain and hill made low*:

The crooked straight is represented as follows:

In the line *and the rough places plain*, the word *plain* (*smooth* or *level*) is expressed by sustained tones and a long, legato melodic line.

VOCAL MUSIC GUIDE

HANDEL, *Ev'ry Valley Shall Be Exalted,* from *Messiah*

5 **27**	Orchestral ritornello.	
0:20	Voice alone.	Ev'ry valley
	Orchestra imitates voice.	
	Ascending rapid notes on *exalted.*	Ev'ry valley shall be exalted,
0:54	High tone on *mountain.*	and ev'ry mountain
	Low tone on *low.*	and hill made low,
	Wavy melody on *crooked.*	the crooked straight,
	Legato melody on *plain.*	and the rough places plain.
	Orchestra alone, cadence.	
	New word painting on	Ev'ry valley shall be exalted,
1:37	*exalted, mountain, low.*	and ev'ry mountain and hill
	crooked, plain.	made low, the crooked straight,
		and the rough places plain.
2:46	Slow, ornamented	The crooked straight,
	vocal cadence.	and the rough places plain.
	Orchestral ritornello.	

For unto Us a Child Is Born
Chorus, strings, continuo

Basic Set:
CD 3 **6**

The twelfth movement, *For unto Us a Child Is Born,* is among Handel's most joyful music. This chorus is based on a verse from Isaiah (9:6) that celebrates the birth of a royal child whose names predict salvation. The texture is light, often with only one or two voices singing at a time. Handel uses a transparent polyphonic texture for the words *For unto us a Child is born, unto us a Son is given.* He sets two contrasting ideas against each other. One voice part sings fifty-six rapid notes on the single syllable of *born* while another sings *unto us a Son is given,* with one note to each syllable.

The words *and the government shall be upon His shoulder* bring a new melodic idea in dotted rhythm:

Handel keeps the dynamics subdued until the striking chordal outburst on *Wonderful, Counsellor*. This change from *p* to *ff* and from polyphonic to homophonic texture is a masterstroke.

For unto Us a Child Is Born divides into four sections, each with the same text and musical ideas. The first three sections all begin with a light texture, but the climactic final section uses the full chorus almost from the very beginning.

With such a close fusion of words and music, it may be disconcerting to learn that most of the melodic ideas in this chorus came from Handel's Italian duet for the words *No, I will not trust you, blind love, cruel Beauty! You are too treacherous, too charming a deity!* (The musical idea for *Wonderful* is new.) But remember that in Handel's time there was little difference in style between sacred and secular music. Amorous joy and religious joy could therefore be conveyed in the same manner.

VOCAL MUSIC GUIDE

HANDEL, *For unto Us a Child Is Born,* from *Messiah*

6	0:00	Strings, ritornello.	
	0:13	Sopranos. is given,	For unto us a Child is born, unto us a Son
	0:26	Tenors imitate. Sopranos, rapid notes (*born*) against tenors (*unto us a Son is given*). Altos, basses, rapid notes (*born*) against altos (*unto us a Son is given*).	
7	0:57	Tenors, dotted rhythm.	and the government shall be upon His shoulder,
		Sopranos, tenors and basses imitate.	and His Name shall be called:
8	1:12	Full chorus, *ff*, chordal texture.	Wonderful, Counsellor, the Mighty God, the Everlasting Father, the Prince of Peace.
	1:23	Altos imitated by tenors.	(For) unto us a Child is born, unto us a Son is given,
		Sopranos.	unto us a Child is born,
		Basses.	unto us a Son is given,
	1:36	Altos, dotted rhythm.	and the government shall be upon His shoulder,
	1:46	Basses imitate. Choral dialogue.	and His Name shall be called:
		Full chorus, *ff*, chordal texture.	Wonderful, Counsellor, the Mighty God, the Everlasting Father, the Prince of Peace.
	2:01	Tenors, imitated by sopranos, basses, altos, rapid notes (*born*) against basses (*unto us*).	(For) unto us a Child is born, unto us a Son is given,
	2:19	Tenors, dotted rhythm.	and the government shall be upon His shoulder
		Sopranos imitate, altos and basses imitate.	

2:31	All voices. Full chorus, *ff*, chordal texture.	and His Name shall be called: Wonderful, Counsellor, the Mighty God, the Everlasting Father, the Prince of Peace.
2:45	Basses, other voices join Sopranos and altos, rapid notes (*born*) against tenors and basses (*unto us*). All voices together.	(For) unto us a Child is born, unto us a Son is given,
3:02	Sopranos, dotted rhythm, altos, tenors and basses imitate. All voices.	and the government shall be upon His shoulder, and His Name shall be called:
3:14	Full chorus, *ff*, chordal texture.	Wonderful, counsellor, the Mighty God, the Everlasting Father, the Prince of Peace.
3:31	Strings, ritornello.	

Hallelujah Chorus

Basic Set:
CD 3 9

Brief Set:
CD 2 28

The *Hallelujah* Chorus is one of the world's most famous choral pieces. In this vigorous chorus, Handel offers sweeping variety by sudden changes among monophonic, polyphonic, and homophonic textures. The monophonic texture is very full-sounding as all the voices and instruments perform in unison at the proclamation *for the Lord God Omnipotent reigneth*. The texture becomes polyphonic when this majestic proclamation is set against joyful repeated exclamations of *Hallelujah* in quick rhythms. Polyphony gives way to homophony as the chorus sings *The kingdom of this world* to hymnlike music.

In the *Hallelujah* Chorus, words and phrases are repeated over and over, as has been common practice in choral music for several centuries. (In the following text, braces connect lines sung at the same time.) Handel took his text from the Revelation of St. John, which celebrates God as the almighty and everlasting ruler.

VOCAL MUSIC GUIDE

HANDEL, *Hallelujah* Chorus, from *Messiah*

9 28		Orchestral introduction.	
		Chorus joins, homophonic, quick exclamations.	Hallelujah!
10 29	0:23	Monophonic, longer notes.	for the lord God Omnipotent reigneth;
		Homophonic, quick exclamations.	Hallelujah!
		Monophonic, longer notes.	for the Lord God Omnipotent reigneth;
		Homophonic, quick exclamations.	Hallelujah!
11 30	0:44	Longer-note melody against quick exclamations, polyphonic.	{ for the Lord God Omnipotent reigneth; Hallelujah!
12 31	1:09	Hymnlike in longer notes, homophonic.	The kingdom of this world is become the Kingdom of our Lord and of His Christ:
13 32	1:26	Bass melody, monophonic. Other voices imitate, polyphonic.	and He shall reign for ever and ever,
14 33	1:48	Long repeated tones against quick exclamations; phrases repeated at higher pitches.	{ King of Kings, and Lord of Lords, for ever and ever, Hallelujah, Hallelujah!
	2:28	Polyphonic, imitation.	and He shall reign for ever and ever,
	2:40	Long repeated tones against quick exclamations. Polyphonic.	King of Kings, and Lord of Lords, for ever and ever, Hallelujah, Hallelujah! and He shall reign for ever and ever,
	2:55	Homophonic. Polyphonic.	King of Kings, and Lord of Lords, and He shall reign for ever and ever.
	3:10	Quick exclamations.	{ King of Kings, and Lord of Lords, for ever and ever, for ever and ever, Hallelujah, Hallelujah, Hallelujah, Hallelujah!
		Pause.	
	3:20	Sustained chords, homophonic.	Hallelujah!

The Baroque Period Summary

Music in Society

- Music was composed to order for specific events.
- The primary areas of employment for musicians were in aristocratic courts, the church, and the opera house. Composers working in aristocratic courts were considered servants.
- Some aristocrats became accomplished musicians.
- Large towns employed musicians for a variety of functions.

Important Style Features

Mood and Emotional Expression

- In instrumental music, a section or entire movement will express one basic mood throughout ("unity of mood").
- In vocal music, changes of mood in the text are often accompanied by changes in the music.

Rhythm

- Rhythmic patterns heard at the beginning of a piece are often repeated throughout.
- The rhythmic pulse is regular, consistent, and strong, typically featuring a constantly moving bass line, even when the music is in a slow tempo.
- The unity of rhythm provides compelling drive and energy that are characteristic of baroque music.

Dynamics

- Terraced dynamics change suddenly rather than gradually and are a major feature of baroque music.

Tone Color

- The basso continuo—consisting of a bass melodic instrument, such as the cello or bassoon; and a keyboard instrument, such as the organ or harpsichord—is one of the most distinctive instrumental features of baroque music.
- The instruments of baroque orchestras, typically ten to forty players, vary from piece to piece.
- Stringed instruments predominate, along with the basso continuo. Woodwind, brass, and percussion instruments are optional and variable in number when used.
- Purely instrumental music grows in importance as a genre throughout the baroque period.

Melody and Harmony

- Melodies are often complex and are not easy to remember on one hearing.
- Melodies recur as a whole or in part throughout a movement or aria.
- Melodies give an impression of continuous expansion, even within a slow tempo.
- Vocal melodies frequently use wide leaps and contain striking chromatic intervals.
- Harmony is based on major and minor scales but may contain passages of striking chromaticism.

Texture

- In late baroque music, the texture is predominantly polyphonic, with an emphasis on the lowest and highest melodic lines.

- The bass line provides a harmonic foundation for the music, often written as a figured bass that encouraged improvisation.
- Imitation between the individual melodic lines of music is very common.

Baroque Performance Practice

- Performers of baroque music face numerous choices about how they are going to play the music written on the page. Their decisions greatly affect the music you hear.
- Baroque musical scores often do not specify either the instruments to be used in a performance or the exact numbers of performers required, especially in early baroque music. Pay careful attention to the types and number of instruments or voices you hear.
- Improvisation and virtuosity by instrumentalists and vocalists were both expected and greatly prized by baroque audiences. Performing or "realizing" a basso continuo line relies heavily on this practice. Listen carefully for the distinctive sound of the basso continuo, or note if the soloist embellishes the music if a section is repeated.
- Performers of baroque music must choose to perform on either "authentic" period instruments that are typical of those used during the baroque era, or modern instruments that utilize technological advances made since the music was composed.

FEATURED GENRES

- Concerto grosso, p. 128
- Fugue, p. 131
- Opera, p. 135
- Sonata, p. 145
- Trio sonata, p. 145
- Solo concerto, p. 147
- Prelude and fugue, p. 154
- Mass, p. 158
- Suite, p. 160
- Cantata, p. 162
- Oratorio, p. 169

FEATURED COMPOSERS

- Johann Sebastian Bach (1685–1750)
- Claudio Monteverdi (1567–1643)
- Henry Purcell (1659–1695)
- Arcangelo Corelli (1653–1713)
- Antonio Vivaldi (1678–1741)
- George Frideric Handel (1685–1759)

Beyond the Classroom: Attending an Opera

Opera was one of the most important genres invented during the baroque era. Thousands of operas have been composed since then, and they remain one of the most popular forms of entertainment today. When you attend a live opera performance or listen to a recording, you will notice that certain aspects do not change regardless of when the music was composed, whereas other features vary considerably. Pay attention to these similarities and differences. Newer productions now may incorporate computer-generated projections to the set and scenery, demonstrating opera's great ability to adapt to the times. To more fully enjoy an opera performance, ask yourself the following questions:

- What features of the music might indicate when it was composed? For example, if you are listening to an opera from the baroque period, do you notice recitatives accompanied by a basso continuo? Do any of the arias repeat the opening section, as in a da capo aria, and if so, is the repeated music ornamented by the singer?
- What are the voice types of the lead singers and any secondary characters?

- Is there a chorus, and if so, what role does the chorus play in the drama?
- Are there any duets, trios, or larger ensembles of singers?
- What number and kinds of instruments are used in the orchestra?
- Does the opera feature dancing at any point?
- Are the scenery and costumes characteristic of the period and locale, or do they represent another time and place?
- Are computer-generated projections used to create scenery? Do you notice any other digital enhancements added to the projection?
- Is the opera sung in its original language or in English translation?
- If there are supertitles above the stage, are they helpful or distracting?
- Did you notice a prompter?
- Did the performance appear to go as rehearsed, or did you notice anything unusual or notable about it?

The
Classical
Period

I am never happier than when I have something to compose, for that, after all, is my sole delight and passion.

—*Wolfgang Amadeus Mozart*

During the classical period, many members of the aristocracy and the wealthy middle class were good musicians. Jean-Honoré Fragonard (1732–1806), *The Music Lesson*.

TIME LINE
Classical Period (1750–1820)

1750–1770	1770–1820

Historical and Cultural Events

1756–1763 Seven Years' War

1769 Watt invents steam engine

1774–1792 Louis XVI reigns in France

1776 American Declaration of Independence

1780–1790 Joseph II reigns in Austria

1789 French Revolution begins

1799 Napoleon becomes first consul of France

1803–1815 Napoleonic Wars

1814–1815 Congress of Vienna

Arts and Letters

1751 Publication of the French *Encyclopedia* begins

1759 Voltaire, *Candide*

1762 Rousseau, *The Social Contract*

c. 1771–1773 Fragonard, *The Lover Crowned*

1787 David, *Death of Socrates*

1800 David, *Napoleon at St. Bernard*

1808 Goethe, *Faust*

1813 Austen, *Pride and Prejudice*

1814 Goya, *The Third of May, 1808*

1819 Scott, *Ivanhoe*

Music

c. 1757 Haydn, String Quartets, Op. 1

1759 Haydn, Symphony No. 1 in D Major

1764 Mozart, Symphony No. 1 in E♭ Major, K. 16

1772 Haydn, Symphony No. 45 in F♯ Minor (*Farewell*)

1787 Mozart, *Don Giovanni* and *Eine kleine Nachtmusik*

1788 Mozart, Symphony No. 40 in G Minor, K. 550

1791 Haydn, Symphony No. 94 (*Surprise*)

1796 Haydn, Trumpet Concerto in E♭ Major

1798 Beethoven, Piano Sonata in C Minor, Op. 13 (*Pathétique*)

1808 Beethoven, Symphony No. 5 in C Minor

1824 Beethoven, Symphony No. 9 in D Minor (*Choral*)

THE CLASSICAL ERA (1750–1820)

In looking at the baroque era, we found that the scientific methods and discoveries of geniuses like Galileo and Newton vastly changed people's view of the world. By the middle of the eighteenth century, faith in the power of reason was so great that it began to undermine the authority of the social and religious establishment. Philosophers and writers—especially Voltaire (1694–1778) and Denis Diderot (1713–1784)—saw their time as a turning point in history and referred to it as the "age of enlightenment." They believed in progress, holding that reason, not custom or tradition, was the best guide for human conduct. Their attacks on the privileges of the aristocracy and clergy reflected the outlook of the middle class, which was struggling for its rights.

The ideas of enlightenment thinkers were implemented by several rulers during the eighteenth century. For example, Emperor Joseph II of Austria, who reigned from 1780 to 1790, abolished serfdom, closed monasteries and convents, and eliminated the nobility's special status in criminal law. He discouraged elaborate religious ceremonies and decreed that burials be simple; though this decree was soon revoked, modest funerals became customary in Vienna. In 1791, Wolfgang Amadeus Mozart—one of the greatest composers of the classical period—was buried in a sack in an unmarked communal grave.

Violent political and social upheaval marked the seventy-year period from 1750 to 1820. These years were convulsed by the Seven Years' War, the American and French revolutions, and the Napoleonic Wars. Political and economic power shifted from the aristocracy and church to the middle class. Social mobility increased to a point that Napoleon could become emperor of France by his own genius rather than as a birthright. "Subversive" new slogans like *Liberty, equality, fraternity!* sprang from the people's lips. All established ideas were being reexamined, including the existence of God.

Revolutions in thought and action were paralleled by shifts in style in the visual arts. During the early eighteenth century, the heavy, monumental baroque style gave way to the more intimate *rococo* style, with its light colors, curved lines, and graceful ornaments. The painters Antoine Watteau (1684–1721) and Jean-Honoré Fragonard (1732–1806) depicted an enchanted world peopled by elegant men and women in constant pursuit of pleasure. But by the later eighteenth century there was yet another change in taste, and rococo art was thought frivolous, excessively ornamented, and lacking in ethical content. The rococo style was superseded by the *neoclassical* style, which attempted to recapture the "noble simplicity and calm grandeur" of ancient Greek and Roman art. Neoclassical artists emphasized firm lines, clear structure, and moralistic subject matter. The painter Jacques-Louis David (1748–1825), who took

The rococo painter Jean-Honoré Fragonard showed the game of love in *The Lover Crowned* (c. 1771–1773).

Death of Socrates (1787) by Jacques-Louis David. By the late eighteenth century, the rococo style had been superseded by the neoclassical style, which attempted to recapture the "noble simplicity and calm grandeur" of ancient Greek and Roman art. Neoclassic artists, such as the French painter David, emphasized firm lines, clear structure, and moralistic subjects.

Monticello, Thomas Jefferson's home, shows the influence of ancient Greek and Roman architecture.

part in the French Revolution, sought to inspire heroism and patriotism through his scenes of ancient Rome.

The artistic response to the decline of traditional power is evidenced further by the English painter William Hogarth (1697–1764), whose socially conscious paintings satirized the manners and morals of the British aristocracy and middle class; and by the Spanish painter Francisco Goya (1746–1828), who used his highly personal vision to create art that lashed out against hypocrisy, oppression, and inhumanity.

Napoleon at St. Bernard (1800) by Jacques-Louis David. Beethoven originally planned to name his Third Symphony (*Eroica,* 1803–1804) "Bonaparte," because he saw Napoleon as an embodiment of heroism; but when he learned that Napoleon had proclaimed himself emperor, Beethoven tore out the title page and later renamed the symphony "Heroic Symphony composed to celebrate the memory of a great man."

The Third of May, 1808 by the Spanish artist Francisco Goya. The classical period was a time of violent political and social upheaval, witnessing the American Revolution, the French Revolution, and the Napoleonic wars. In 1814 Goya painted this vivid scene of the execution of Spanish hostages by Napoleon's soldiers.

1 The Classical Style
(1750–1820)

In music history, the transition from the baroque style to the full flowering of the classical is called the *preclassical* period; it extends from roughly 1730 to 1770. The shift in musical taste parallels the similar, earlier trend in the visual arts. It was developing even as Bach and Handel were creating baroque masterpieces. Among the important pioneers in this new style were Bach's sons Carl Philipp Emanuel (1714–1788) and Johann Christian (1735–1782). Around the middle of the eighteenth century, composers concentrated on simplicity and clarity, discarding much that had enriched late baroque music. Polyphonic texture was neglected in favor of tuneful melody and simple harmony. Carl Philipp Emanuel Bach described music with strict polyphonic imitation as "dry and despicable pieces of pedantry." Mid-eighteenth-century composers entertained their listeners with music offering contrasts of mood and theme. The term *style galant* (*gallant style*) was applied to this light, graceful music. The *style galant* in music is comparable to the rococo style in art.

The term *classical* is confusing because it has so many different meanings. It may refer to Greek or Roman antiquity, or it may be used for any supreme accomplishment of lasting appeal (as in the expression *movie classic*). Many people take *classical music* to mean anything that is not rock, jazz, folk, or popular music.

Music historians have borrowed the term *classical* from art history, where it is more appropriate. The painting, sculpture, and architecture of the late eighteenth century and the early nineteenth century were often influenced by Greek and Roman models. But the music of this period shows little direct relation to antiquity. The significant parallel between "classical" music and "neoclassical" art is a common stress on balance and clarity of structure. These traits can be found in the fully developed classical style in music, which we will focus on. That style flourished from about 1770 to 1820, and its master composers were Joseph Haydn (1732–1809), Wolfgang Amadeus Mozart (1756–1791), and Ludwig van Beethoven (1770–1827). First, we'll study the characteristics of their work.

Characteristics of the Classical Style

Contrast of Mood Great variety and contrast of mood received new emphasis in classical music. Whereas a late baroque piece may convey a single emotion, a classical composition will fluctuate in mood. Dramatic, turbulent music might lead into a carefree dance tune. Not only are there contrasting themes within a movement, but there may also be striking contrasts within a single theme.

Mood in classical music may change gradually or suddenly, expressing conflicting surges of elation and depression. But such conflict and contrast are under the firm control of the classical composer. Masters like Haydn, Mozart, and Beethoven were able to impart unity and logic to music of wide emotional range.

Rhythm Flexibility of rhythm adds variety to classical music. A classical composition has a wealth of rhythmic patterns, whereas a baroque piece contains a few patterns that are reiterated throughout. Baroque works convey a sense of continuity and perpetual motion, so that after the first few bars one can predict pretty well the rhythmic character of an entire movement. But the classical style also includes unexpected pauses, syncopations, and frequent changes from long notes to shorter notes. And the change from one pattern of note lengths to another may be either sudden or gradual.

Texture   In contrast to the polyphonic texture of late baroque music, classical music is basically homophonic. However, texture is treated as flexibly as rhythm. Pieces shift smoothly or suddenly from one texture to another. A work may begin homophonically with a melody and simple accompaniment but then change to a more complex polyphonic texture that features two simultaneous melodies or melodic fragments imitated among the various instruments.

Melody   Classical melodies are among the most tuneful and easiest to remember. The themes of even highly sophisticated compositions may have a folk or popular flavor. Occasionally, composers simply borrowed popular tunes. (Mozart did, in his variations on the French song *Ah, vous dirai-je, maman,* which we know as *Twinkle, Twinkle, Little Star.*) More often, however, they wrote original themes with a popular character.

Classical melodies tend to sound balanced and symmetrical because they are frequently made up of two phrases of the same length. The second phrase in such melodies may begin like the first, but it ends more conclusively. Such a melodic type, which may be diagrammed a a′, is easy to sing. (It is frequently found in nursery tunes such as *Mary Had a Little Lamb.*) Baroque melodies, on the contrary, tend to be less symmetrical, more elaborate, and harder to sing.

Dynamics and the Piano   Classical composers' interest in expressing shades of emotion led to the widespread use of gradual dynamic change—crescendo and decrescendo. These composers did not restrict themselves to the terraced dynamics (abrupt shifts from loud to soft) characteristic of baroque music. Crescendos and decrescendos were an electrifying novelty; audiences sometimes rose excitedly from their seats.

During the classical period, the desire for gradual dynamic change led to the replacement of the harpsichord by the piano. By varying the finger pressure on the keys, a pianist can play more loudly or softly. Although the piano was invented around 1700, it began to replace the harpsichord only around 1775. Most of the mature keyboard compositions of Haydn, Mozart, and Beethoven were written for the piano, rather than for harpsichord, clavichord, and organ, which had been featured in baroque music. The late eighteenth-century piano—called a *fortepiano*—weighed much less than the modern piano and had thinner strings held by a frame made of wood rather than metal. Its pitch range was smaller, and its tone was smaller and lasted a shorter time.

The End of the Basso Continuo   The basso continuo was gradually abandoned during the classical period. In Haydn's or Mozart's works, a harpsichordist did not need to improvise an accompaniment. One reason why the basso continuo became obsolete was that more and more music was written for amateurs, who could not master the difficult art of improvising from a figured bass. Also, classical composers wanted more control; they preferred to specify an accompaniment rather than trust the judgment of improvisers.

The Classical Orchestra

A new orchestra evolved during the classical period. Unlike the baroque orchestra, which could vary from piece to piece, it was a standard group of four sections: strings, woodwinds, brass, and percussion. In the late instrumental works of Mozart and Haydn, an orchestra might consist of the following:

> *Strings:* 1st violins, 2d violins, violas, cellos, double basses
> *Woodwinds:* 2 flutes, 2 oboes, 2 clarinets, 2 bassoons
> *Brass:* 2 French horns, 2 trumpets
> *Percussion:* 2 timpani

Notice that woodwind and brass instruments are paired and that clarinets have been added. Trombones were also used by Haydn and Mozart, but only in opera and church music, not in solely instrumental works.

The number of musicians was greater in a classical orchestra than in a baroque group, though practice varied considerably from place to place. Haydn directed a private orchestra of only twenty-five players from 1761 to 1790. But for public concerts in London in 1795, he led an orchestra of sixty.

Classical composers exploited the individual tone colors of orchestral instruments. Unlike baroque composers, they did not treat one instrument like another. Classical composers would not let an oboe duplicate the violin melody for the entire length of a movement. A classical piece has greater variety—and more rapid changes—of tone color. A theme might begin in the full orchestra, shift to the strings, and then continue in the woodwinds.

Each section of the classical orchestra had a special role. The strings were the most important section, with the first violins taking the melody most of the time and the lower strings providing an accompaniment. The woodwinds added contrasting tone colors and were often given melodic solos. Horns and trumpets brought power to loud passages and filled out the harmony, but they did not usually play the main melody. Timpani were used for rhythmic bite and emphasis. As a whole, the classical orchestra had developed into a flexible and colorful instrument to which composers could entrust their most powerful and dramatic musical conceptions.

Classical Forms

Instrumental compositions of the classical period usually consist of several movements that contrast in tempo and character. There are often four movements, arranged as follows:

1. Fast movement
2. Slow movement
3. Dance-related movement
4. Fast movement

Classical symphonies and string quartets usually follow this four-movement pattern, while classical sonatas may consist of two, three, or four movements. A *symphony* is written for orchestra; a *string quartet* for two violins, viola, and cello; and a **sonata** for one or two instruments. (The classical symphony, string quartet, and sonata are more fully described in Sections 3 to 7 and 9.)

In writing an individual movement of a symphony, string quartet, or sonata, a classical composer could choose from several different forms. One movement of a composition might be in A B A form, while another might be a theme and variations. The sections that follow will describe some forms used in classical movements, but now let's look at a few general characteristics of classical form.

Classical movements often contrast themes vividly. A movement may contain two, three, or even four or more themes of different character. This use of contrasting themes distinguishes classical music from baroque music, which often uses only one main theme. The classical composer sometimes uses a brief pause to signal the arrival of a new theme.

The larger sections of a classical movement balance each other in a satisfying and symmetrical way. Unstable sections that wander from the tonic key are balanced by stable sections that confirm it. By the end of a classical movement, musical tensions have been resolved.

Though we speak of the classical style, we must remember that Haydn, Mozart, and Beethoven were three individuals with dissimilar personalities. While Haydn's and Mozart's works may sound similar at first, deeper involvement reveals striking personal styles. Beethoven's music seems more powerful, violent, and emotional when compared with the apparently more restrained and elegant works of the earlier masters. But Haydn and Mozart also composed music that is passionate and dramatic. We'll see that all three composers used similar musical procedures and forms, yet their emotional statements bear the particular stamp of each.

2 Composer, Patron, and Public in the Classical Period

Haydn, Mozart, and Beethoven—three of the world's greatest composers—worked during a period of violent political and social upheaval, as we have seen in the opening of Part V (page 185). Like everyone else, musicians were strongly affected by changes in society, and in the careers of the three classical masters we can trace the slow emancipation of the composer. First came Joseph Haydn (1732–1809), who was content to spend most of his life serving a wealthy aristocratic family. His contract of employment (1761) shows that he was considered a skilled servant, like a gardener or gamekeeper. He had to wear a uniform and "compose such music as His Highness shall order"—and was warned to "refrain from vulgarity in eating, drinking, and conversation." Wolfgang Amadeus Mozart (1756–1791), born just twenty-four years later, could not bear being treated as a servant; he broke from his court position and went to Vienna to try his luck as a freelance musician. For several years, he was very successful, but then his popularity declined; he died in debt. Ludwig van Beethoven (1770–1827) fared better than Mozart. Only a few years after Mozart's death, Beethoven was able to work as an independent musician in Vienna. His success was gained through a wider middle-class market for music and a commanding personality that prompted the nobility to give him gifts and treat him as an equal.

As the eighteenth century advanced, more people made more money. Merchants, doctors, and government officials could afford larger homes, finer clothes, and better food. But the prospering middle class wanted more than material goods; it also sought aristocratic luxuries like theater, literature, and music. In fact, during the classical period, the middle class had a great influence on music. Because palace concerts were usually closed to them, townspeople organized public concerts, where, for the price of admission, they could hear the latest symphonies and concertos. During the second half of the eighteenth century, public concerts mushroomed throughout Europe. In London, a concert series ran from 1765 to 1781, codirected by one of Bach's sons, Johann Christian Bach, who had settled in England. In Paris, around the same time, a concert organization called the *Concert des Amateurs* assembled a large orchestra, conducted during the 1770s by the Chevalier de Saint-Georges (1739–1799), a black composer and violinist who was a champion fencer as well.

But merchants and lawyers were not content to hear music only in concerts. They wanted to be surrounded by music at home. They felt that their sons and daughters deserved music lessons as much as the children of aristocrats did. Indeed, if middle-class children played instruments well enough, they might be invited to palaces and eventually marry into the aristocracy. In any event, the demand for printed music, instruments, and music lessons had vastly increased.

Composers in the classical period took middle-class tastes into account. They wrote pieces that were easy for amateur musicians to play and understand. They turned from serious to comic opera, from the heroic and mythological plots dear to the nobility to middle-class subjects and folklike tunes. Their comic operas sometimes even ridiculed the aristocracy, and their dance movements became less elegant and courtly, more vigorous and rustic.

Serious composition was flavored by folk and popular music. The classical masters sometimes used familiar tunes as themes for symphonies and variations. Mozart was delighted that people danced to waltzes arranged from melodies in his operas. Haydn, Mozart, and Beethoven all wrote dance music for public balls in Vienna.

Most of Haydn's music was composed for a wealthy aristocratic family. Shown here is a performance of a comic opera by Haydn in 1775 at the palace Eszterháza.

Vienna

Vienna was one of the music centers of Europe during the classical period, and Haydn, Mozart, and Beethoven were all active there. As the seat of the Holy Roman Empire (which included parts of modern Austria, Germany, Italy, Hungary, and the Czech Republic), it was a bustling cultural and commercial center with a cosmopolitan character. Its population of almost 250,000 (in 1800) made Vienna the fourth largest city in Europe. All three classical masters were born elsewhere, but they were drawn to Vienna to study and to seek recognition. In Vienna, Haydn and Mozart became close friends and influenced each other's musical style. Beethoven traveled to Vienna at sixteen to play for Mozart; at twenty-two, he returned to study with Haydn.

Aristocrats from all over the empire would spend winters in Vienna, sometimes bringing their private orchestras. Music was an important part of court life, and a good orchestra was a symbol of prestige. Many of the nobility were excellent musicians. For instance, Empress Maria Theresa had sung in palace musicales when she was young, Emperor Joseph II was a competent cellist, and Archduke Rudolf was Beethoven's longtime student of piano and composition.

Much music was heard in private concerts, where aristocrats and wealthy commoners played alongside professional musicians. Mozart and Beethoven often earned money by performing in these intimate concerts. The nobility frequently hired servants who could double as musicians. An advertisement in the *Vienna Gazette* of 1789 reads: "Wanted, for a house of the gentry, a manservant who knows how to play the violin well."

In Vienna there was also outdoor music, light and popular in tone. Small street bands of wind and string players played at garden parties or under the windows of people likely to throw down money. A Viennese almanac reported that "on fine summer nights you may come upon serenades in the streets at all hours." Haydn and Mozart wrote many outdoor entertainment pieces, which they called *divertimentos* or *serenades*. Vienna's great love of music and its enthusiastic demand for new works made it the chosen city of Haydn, Mozart, and Beethoven.

3 Sonata Form

An astonishing amount of important music from the classical period to the twentieth century was composed in sonata form (sometimes called *sonata-allegro form*). The term **sonata form** refers to the form of a *single* movement. It should not be confused with the term *sonata,* which is used for a whole composition made up of *several* movements. The opening fast movement of a classical symphony, sonata, or string quartet is usually in sonata form. This form is also used in slow movements and in fast concluding movements.

A sonata-form movement consists of three main sections: the exposition, where the themes are presented; the development, where themes are treated in new ways; and the recapitulation, where the themes return. These three main sections are often followed by a concluding section, the coda (Italian for *tail*). Remember that these sections are all within *one movement.* A *single* sonata-form movement may be outlined as follows:

Exposition
First theme in tonic (home) key
Bridge containing modulation from home key to new key
Second theme in new key
Closing section in key of second theme

Development
New treatment of themes; modulations to different keys

Recapitulation
First theme in tonic key
Bridge
Second theme in tonic key
Closing section in tonic key

Coda
In tonic key

A fast movement in sonata form is sometimes preceded by a slow introduction that creates a strong feeling of expectancy.

Exposition

The **exposition** sets up a strong conflict between the tonic key and the new key, and between the first theme (or group of themes) and the second theme (or group of themes). It begins with the first theme in the tonic, or home, key. Then comes a **bridge,** or **transition,** leading to the second theme, which is in a new key. The modulation from the home key to a new key creates a feeling of harmonic tension and forward motion. The second theme often contrasts in mood with the first theme. A closing section ends the exposition in the key of the second theme. At the end of a classical exposition there is usually a repeat sign (:‖) to indicate that the whole exposition is to be played again.

Development

The *development* is often the most dramatic section of the movement. The listener may be kept off balance as the music moves restlessly through several different keys. Through these rapid modulations, the harmonic tension is heightened.

In this section, themes are *developed,* or treated in new ways. They are broken into fragments, or *motives,* which are short musical ideas developed within a composition. A motive may take on different and unexpected emotional meanings. One fragment of a comic theme, for example, may be made to sound aggressive and menacing through changes of melody, rhythm, or dynamics. Themes can be combined with new ideas or changed in texture. A complex polyphonic texture can be woven by shifting a motive rapidly among different instruments. The harmonic and thematic searching of the development builds tension that demands resolution.

Recapitulation

The beginning of the *recapitulation* brings resolution, as we again hear the first theme in the tonic key. In the recapitulation, the first theme, bridge, second theme, and concluding section are presented more or less as they were in the exposition, with one crucial difference: all the principal material is now in the tonic key. Earlier, in the exposition, there was strong contrast between the first theme in the home key and the second theme and closing section in a new key; that basis for tension is resolved in the recapitulation by presenting the first theme, second theme, and closing section all in the tonic key.

Coda

An even more powerful feeling of conclusion is attained by following the recapitulation with yet another section. The *coda* rounds off a movement by repeating themes or developing them further. It always ends in the tonic key.

The amazing durability and vitality of sonata form result from its capacity for drama. The form moves from a stable situation toward conflict (in the exposition), to heightened tension (in the development), and then back to stability and resolution of conflict. The following illustration shows an outline.

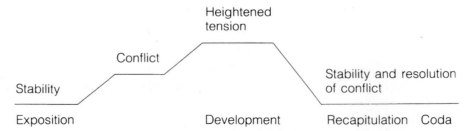

A movement in sonata form proceeds from a stable situation toward conflict, to heightened tension, and then back to stability.

Sonata form is exceptionally flexible and subject to endless variation. It is not a rigid mold into which musical ideas are poured. Rather, it may be viewed as a set of principles that serve to shape and unify contrasts of theme and key. Haydn, Mozart, and Beethoven used sonata form repeatedly, yet each maintained individuality. Movements in sonata form may differ radically in character, in length, and in the number and treatment of themes. Sonata form is so versatile that it is no surprise to find its use spanning more than two centuries.

Symphony No. 40 in G Minor, K. 550 (1788), by Wolfgang Amadeus Mozart

Fourth Movement:
Allegro assai (very fast)

The rapid sonata-form last movement of Mozart's Symphony No. 40 in G Minor, K. 550, conveys a feeling of controlled tension. The opening theme, in the tonic key of G minor, offers brusque contrasts of dynamics and rhythm. A soft upward arpeggio (broken chord) alternates repeatedly with a loud rushing phrase.

Excitement is maintained throughout the long bridge, which is based on the loud rushing phrase of the first theme. The bridge ends clearly with a brief pause, as do other sections in this movement.

The tender second theme, in the new key of B flat major, is a lyrical contrast to the brusque opening theme. It is softer, flows more smoothly, and uses longer notes.

Mozart weaves almost the entire development section from the upward arpeggio of the first theme. During the opening few seconds, there is an eruption of violence as the orchestra, in unison, plays a variation of the arpeggio and a series of jagged downward leaps. As the development continues, the texture becomes polyphonic and contrasts with the homophony of the exposition. Arpeggios press on each other in quick imitation. Rapid shifts of key create restless intensity.

In the recapitulation, both the first and the second themes are in the tonic key, G minor. This minor key now adds a touch of melancholy to the tender second theme, which was heard in major before. The passion and violence of this movement foreshadow the romantic expression to come during the nineteenth century.

LISTENING OUTLINE

MOZART, Symphony No. 40 in G Minor

Fourth Movement: Allegro assai (very fast)

Sonata form, duple meter ($\frac{2}{2}$), G minor

Flute, 2 oboes, 2 clarinets, 2 bassoons, 2 French horns, 1st violins, 2d violins, violas, cellos, double basses

(Duration, 4:38)

Exposition

First theme

`30`   0:00

1. Upward arpeggio, ***p***, explosive rushing phrase, ***f***, minor key.

High repeated tones, ***f***, upward arpeggio, ***p***, rushing phrase, ***f***, leads into

Bridge

`31`   0:27

2. Long passage of continuously rushing notes, strings, ***f***.

Second theme

`32`   1:00

3. a. Tender melody in violins, ***p***, major key.

1:14

b. Clarinet, ***p***, tender melody somewhat varied.

Closing section

`33`   1:29

4. Suddenly loud, continuously rushing notes in strings, ***f***.

Development

`34`   1:49

1. Orchestra in unison, ***f***, upward arpeggio, jagged downward leaps.

1:57

2. Suddenly soft, upward arpeggio lightly tossed between violins and woodwinds.

2:09

3. Suddenly loud, string arpeggios interwoven with rushing notes. Arpeggios press upon each other in quicker imitation. Woodwinds rejoin imitative dialogue.

Recapitulation

First theme

35 3:03

1. Upward arpeggio, *p*, explosive rushing phrase, *f*, minor key. High repeated tones, *f*, upward arpeggio, *p*, rushing phrase, *f*, leads into

Bridge

3:15

2. Passage of continuously rushing notes, strings, *f*.

Second theme

36 3:38

3. a. Tender melody in violins, *p*, minor key.

3:51

  b. Woodwinds, *p*, tender melody somewhat varied.

Closing section

4:07

4. Suddenly loud, continuously rushing notes, full orchestra. Cadence.

4 Theme and Variations

The form called *theme and variations* was widely used in the classical period, either as an independent piece or as one movement of a symphony, sonata, or string quartet. In a **theme and variations,** a basic musical idea—the theme—is repeated over and over and is changed each time. This form may be outlined as theme (A)—variation 1 (A′)—variation 2 (A″)—variation 3 (A‴), and so on; each prime mark indicates a variation of the basic idea. (Another way of indicating variations is A^1, A^2, etc.)

Each variation, though usually about the same length as the theme, is unique and may differ in mood from the theme. Changes of melody, rhythm, harmony, accompaniment, dynamics, or tone color may be used to give a variation its own identity. The core melody may appear in the bass, or it may be repeated in a minor key instead of a major key. It may be heard together with a new melody. The variations may be connected to each other or separated by pauses. For the theme itself, a composer may invent an original melody or borrow someone else's. Beethoven once borrowed a little waltz tune and put it through thirty-three brilliant variations. More modest examples of theme and variations have as few as three variations.

Symphony No. 94 in G Major (*Surprise*; 1791), by Joseph Haydn

Second Movement: Andante

Basic Set:

CD 3 **45**

Brief Set:

CD 2 **43**

The second movement (andante) of Haydn's Symphony No. 94 in G Major (*Surprise* Symphony) is a theme and variations. The folklike, staccato theme begins softly but is punctuated by a sudden loud chord—this is the "surprise." There are four variations, in which the theme is changed in tone color, dynamics, rhythm, and melody. Sometimes the original melody is accompanied by a new one called a **countermelody.** Such combinations of two distinctive melodies result in a polyphonic texture. In one variation the theme is presented in minor instead of major. The last variation is followed by a closing section in which a gently dissonant accompaniment momentarily darkens the mood of the carefree theme.

The theme consists of two parts, sections a and b, each of which is repeated. This pattern is usually retained in the variations.

LISTENING OUTLINE

HAYDN, Symphony No. 94 in G Major (*Surprise*)

Second Movement: Andante

Theme and variations, duple meter ($\frac{2}{4}$), C major

2 flutes, 2 oboes, 2 bassoons, 2 French horns, 2 trumpets, timpani, 1st violins, 2d violins, violas, cellos, double basses

(Duration, 6:14)

Theme

Section a

45 **43** 0:00   Violins, ***p***, staccato theme.

Section a repeated, ***pp***, with pizzicato string accompaniment. Surprise chord, ***ff***.

Section b   Violins, ***p***, continuation of theme.

Section b repeated with flute and oboe.

Variation 1

46 **44** 1:06   **a.** Theme begins, ***f***, higher countermelody in violins, ***p***. Section a repeated.

b. Violins, ***p***, continuation of theme and higher countermelody. Section b repeated.

Variation 2

47 **45** 2:13   **a.** Theme in minor, ***ff***, violin phrase in major, ***p***. Section a repeated.

b. Violins, ***f***, rapid downward scales, orchestra ***f***. Violins alone, ***p***, lead into

Variation 3

  3:21

a. Oboe, *p*, theme in faster repeated notes, major key.

Flute and oboe, *p*, legato countermelody above staccato theme in violins, *p*.

b. Continuation of theme and countermelody. Section b repeated.

Variation 4

  4:28

a. Theme in brasses and woodwinds, *ff*, fast notes in violins, *ff*. Violins, *p*, legato version of theme, dotted rhythm (long-short).

b. Violins, *p*, continuation of theme, dotted rhythm. Full orchestra, *ff*, triumphant continuation of theme leads to suspenseful chord, *ff*, sudden *p*.

Closing section

  5:52

Theme in oboe, *p*, gently dissonant chords in strings, flute joins, very soft, conclusion.

5 Minuet and Trio

The form known as ***minuet and trio,*** or ***minuet,*** is often used as the third movement of classical symphonies, string quartets, and other works. Like the movements of the baroque suite, the minuet originated as a dance. It first appeared at the court of Louis XIV of France around 1650 and was danced by aristocrats throughout the eighteenth century. The minuet was a stately, dignified dance in which the dancing couple exchanged curtsies and bows.

The minuet movement of a symphony or string quartet is written for listening, not dancing. It is in triple meter (¾) and usually in a moderate tempo. The movement is in A B A form: minuet (A), trio (B), minuet (A). The trio (B) is usually quieter than the minuet (A) section and requires fewer instruments. It often contains woodwind solos. The trio section got its name during the baroque period, when a set of two dances would be followed by a repetition of the first dance. The second dance was known as a "trio" because it was usually played by three instruments. Classical composers did not restrict themselves to three instruments in the B sections of their minuets, but the name *trio* remained.

The A (minuet) section includes smaller parts a, b, and a′ (variation of a). In the opening A (minuet) section, all the smaller parts are repeated, as follows: a (repeated) ba′ (repeated). (In the musical score, the repeat sign :‖ indicates each repetition.) The B (trio) section is quite similar in form: c (repeated) dc′ (repeated). At the close of the B (trio) section, the repetition of the entire A (minuet) section is indicated by the words ***da capo*** (*from the beginning*). This time, however, the minuet is played straight through without the repetitions: a ba′. The whole movement can be outlined like this:

Minuet	Trio	Minuet
A	B	A
a (repeated) ba′ (repeated)	c (repeated) dc′ (repeated)	a ba′

With its A B A form and its many repeated parts, the minuet is structurally the simplest movement of a symphony or string quartet.

In many of Beethoven's compositions, the third movement is not a minuet but a related form called a *scherzo*. Like a minuet, a ***scherzo*** is usually in A B A form and triple meter, but it moves more quickly, generating energy, rhythmic drive, and rough humor. (*Scherzo* is Italian for *joke*.)

Eine kleine Nachtmusik (*A Little Night Music; 1787*), K. 525, by Wolfgang Amadeus Mozart

Third Movement: Minuet (Allegretto)

Basic Set:
CD 3 [51]

Brief Set:
CD 2 [49]

Mozart's *Eine kleine Nachtmusik* is a **serenade,** a work that's usually light in mood, meant for evening entertainment. It is written for a small string orchestra or for a string quartet plus a double bass. (The double bass plays the cello part an octave lower.) The third movement is a courtly minuet in A B A form. The A (minuet) section is stately, mostly loud and staccato, with a clearly marked beat. In contrast, the B (trio) section is intimate, soft, and legato. Its murmuring accompaniment contributes to the smooth flow of the music.

LISTENING OUTLINE

MOZART, *Eine kleine Nachtmusik*

Third Movement: Minuet (Allegretto)

A B A form, triple meter ($\frac{3}{4}$), G major

1st violins, 2d violins, violas, cellos, double basses

(Duration, 2:03)

Minuet (A)

[51] [49]   0:00   **1.** Stately melody, *f*, predominantly staccato. Repeated.

Legato phrase, *p*, leads to stately staccato phrase, *f*. Repeated.

Trio (B)

52 **50** 0:42

2. Gracious legato melody, *p*, murmuring accompaniment. Repeated.

Climbing legato phrase, *f*, leads to legato melody, *p*. Repeated.

Minuet (A)

53 **51** 1:39

3. Stately melody, *f*, predominantly staccato.

Legato phrase, *p*, leads to stately staccato phrase, *f*.

6 Rondo

Many classical movements are in rondo form. A ***rondo*** features a tuneful main theme (A) which returns several times in alternation with other themes. Common rondo patterns are A B A C A and A B A C A B A. The main theme is usually lively, pleasing, and simple to remember, and the listener can easily recognize its return. Because the main theme is usually stated in the tonic key, its return is all the more welcome. The rondo can be used either as an independent piece or as one movement of a symphony, string quartet, or sonata. It often serves as a finale, because its liveliness, regularity, and buoyancy bring a happy sense of conclusion.

Rondo form is often combined with elements of sonata form to produce a sonata-rondo. The ***sonata-rondo*** contains a development section like that in sonata form and is outlined A B A—development section—A B A.

The popularity of the rondo did not end with the classical period. It was used by twentieth-century composers such as Igor Stravinsky and Arnold Schoenberg.

String Quartet in C Minor, Op. 18, No. 4 (1798–1800), by Ludwig van Beethoven

Fourth Movement:
Rondo (Allegro)

Basic Set:
CD 3 **54**

Brief Set:
CD 3 **1**

The exciting rondo movement from Beethoven's String Quartet in C Minor, Op. 18, No. 4, may be outlined A B A C A B A. Its lively main theme, A, in the style of a Gypsy dance, is made up of two repeated parts: a a b b. An unexpected held tone in part b suggests the improvisatory playing of a Gypsy fiddler. The main theme, in minor, contrasts with the other themes, which are in major. Theme B is a lyrical legato melody. Theme C is playful, with quick upward rushes. At its final return, the main theme (A) has a faster tempo, prestissimo, and leads into a frenzied concluding section.

LISTENING OUTLINE

BEETHOVEN, String Quartet in C Minor,
Op. 18, No. 4

Fourth Movement: Rondo (Allegro)

Duple meter (²⁄₂), C minor

1st violin, 2d violin, viola, cello

(Duration, 4:08)

A

54 1 0:00   **1.** Lively main theme in 1st violin, minor key.

B

55 2 0:29   **2.** Lyrical melody, legato, major key.

A

56 3 1:14   **3.** Lively main theme, minor key. Theme becomes more agitated.

C

57 4 1:42   **4.** Upward rushes in each instrument, playful downward phrase in 1st violin, major key.

A

2:05   **5.** Lively main theme, minor key. Crescendo to held chord, *ff*.

B

2:43   **6.** Lyrical melody, legato, major key. Melody repeated an octave higher. Playful phrases in violins, crescendo to *f*, sustained tones in 1st violin.

A

3:26   **7.** Lively main theme, *ff*, faster tempo (prestissimo), minor key. Concluding section builds, downward staccato scale, high repeated tones, *p*. Upward rushes, *ff*, at end.

7 The Classical Symphony

The great contribution of the classical period to orchestral music is the symphony. Haydn wrote at least 104 symphonies, Mozart over forty, and Beethoven nine. Most of Haydn's symphonies were composed for his employers, who required a steady flow of works for their palace concerts. Beethoven, on the other hand, wrote a symphony only when inspired. His symphonies are longer than Haydn's or Mozart's and were conceived for performance in large concert halls.

A *symphony* is an extended, ambitious composition typically lasting between 20 and 45 minutes, exploiting the expanded range of tone color and dynamics of the classical orchestra. A classical symphony usually consists of four movements which evoke a wide range of emotions through contrasts of tempo and mood. A typical sequence is (1) a vigorous, dramatic fast movement; (2) a lyrical slow movement; (3) a dancelike movement (minuet or scherzo); and (4) a brilliant or heroic fast movement.

The opening movement is almost always fast and in sonata form. It is usually the most dramatic movement and stresses an exciting development of short motives. Sometimes a slow introduction leads to the opening fast movement and creates a feeling of anticipation.

It is in the slow second movement that we are most likely to find broad, songlike melodies. This movement, by and large, is in either sonata form, A B A form, or theme-and-variations form. Unlike the other movements in the symphony, the slow movement is generally *not* in the tonic key. For example, if the first, third, and fourth movements are in the tonic key of C major, the second movement may be in F major. The new key points up the expressive contrast of the slow movement.

In the symphonies of Haydn and Mozart, the third movement is generally a minuet and trio, which may be in a moderate or fairly quick tempo. This movement varies in character from a courtly dance to a peasant romp or a vigorous piece that is hardly dancelike. Beethoven liked fast, energetic scherzos for his third movements.

The fourth, concluding movement of a symphony by Haydn or Mozart is fast, lively, and brilliant, but somewhat lighter in mood than the opening movement. (The agitated final movement of Mozart's Symphony No. 40 in G minor is not typical.) Beethoven's concluding movement tends to be more triumphant and heroic in character and is sometimes meant as the climax of the whole symphony. The final movement of a classical symphony is most often in sonata or sonata-rondo form.

In most classical symphonies, each movement is a self-contained composition with its own set of themes. A theme in one movement will only rarely reappear in a later movement. (Beethoven's Fifth and Ninth Symphonies are exceptions.) But a symphony is unified partly by the use of the same key in three of its movements. More important, the movements balance and complement each other both musically and emotionally.

The importance of the symphony lasted through the twentieth century and into the twenty-first. Its great significance is reflected in such familiar terms as *symphonic music, symphony hall,* and *symphony orchestra.*

8 | The Classical Concerto

A classical *concerto* is a three-movement work for an instrumental soloist and orchestra. It combines the soloist's virtuosity and interpretive abilities with the orchestra's wide range of tone color and dynamics. Emerging from this encounter is a contrast of ideas and sound that is dramatic and satisfying. The soloist is very much the star, and all of his or her musical talents are needed in this challenging dialogue.

The classical love of balance can be seen in the concerto, because soloist and orchestra are equally important. Between them, there's an interplay of melodic lines and a spirit of give-and-take. One moment the soloist plays the melody while the orchestra accompanies. Then the woodwinds may unfold the main theme against rippling arpeggios (broken chords) played by the soloist. Mozart and Beethoven—the greatest masters of the classical concerto—often wrote concertos for themselves to play as piano soloists; the piano is their favored solo instrument. But other solo instruments used in classical concertos include violin, cello, horn, trumpet, clarinet, and bassoon.

Like symphonies, concertos can last anywhere from 20 minutes to 45 minutes. But instead of the symphony's four movements, a classical concerto has three: (1) fast, (2) slow, and (3) fast. A concerto has no minuet or scherzo.

In the first movement and sometimes in the last movement, there is a special unaccompanied showpiece for the soloist, the *cadenza* (Italian for *cadence*). Near the end of the movement, the orchestra suspends forward motion by briefly sustaining a dissonant chord. This is indicated in the score by a *fermata* (⌢), a sign meaning *pause*, which is placed over the chord. The suspense announces the entry of the soloist's cadenza. For several minutes, the soloist, *without orchestra,* displays virtuosity by playing dazzling scale passages and broken chords. Themes of the movement are varied and presented in new keys. At the end of a cadenza, the soloist plays a long trill followed by a chord that meshes with the reentrance of the orchestra.

In the classical era, the soloist, who was often the composer, generally improvised the cadenzas. In this case, the score contained only the fermata, indicating where the cadenza should be inserted. But after the eighteenth century, the art of improvisation declined, and composers began to write cadenzas directly into the score. This gave them more control over their compositions.

Today, performers of eighteenth-century concertos may have a choice of cadenzas. For some concertos, composers wrote cadenzas for their own performance or for that of a student. Also, many nineteenth-, twentieth-, and early twenty-first-century musicians later provided cadenzas for classical concertos. These are best when their style matches that of the concerto. For example, the cadenzas Beethoven composed for Mozart's D Minor Piano Concerto are so strong and so much in the spirit of the work that pianists still use them today.

A classical concerto begins with a movement in sonata form of a special kind, containing *two* expositions. The first is played by the orchestra, which presents several themes in the home key. This opening section sets the mood for the movement and leads us to expect the soloist's entrance. The second exposition begins with the soloist's first notes. Music for the solo entry may be powerful or quiet, but its effect is dramatic because suspense has been built. Together with the orchestra, the soloist explores themes from the first exposition and introduces new ones. After a modulation from the home key to a new key, the second exposition then moves to a development section, followed by the recapitulation, cadenza, and coda. The slow middle movement may take any one of several forms, but the finale is usually a quick rondo or sonata-rondo.

9 Classical Chamber Music

Classical *chamber music* is designed for the intimate setting of a room (chamber) in a home or palace, rather than for a public concert hall. It is performed by a small group of two to nine musicians, with one player to a part. Chamber music is lighter in sound than classical orchestral music. During the classical period, it was fashionable for an aristocrat or a member of the well-to-do middle class to play chamber music with friends and to hire professional musicians to entertain guests after dinner.

Chamber music is subtle and intimate, intended to please the performer as much as the listener. A chamber music group is a team. Each member is essential, and each may have an important share of the thematic material. Therefore much give-and-take is called for among the instruments. Classical chamber music does not need a conductor; instead, each musician must be sensitive to what goes on and must coordinate dynamics and phrasing with the other musicians. In this respect, a chamber ensemble is like a small jazz group.

The most important form in classical chamber music is the *string quartet,* written for two violins, a viola, and a cello. Haydn, Mozart, and Beethoven wrote some of their most important music in this form. The string quartet can be compared to a conversation among four lively, sensitive, and intelligent people. It's not surprising that the string quartet evolved when conversation was cultivated as a fine art.

Like a symphony, a string quartet usually consists of four movements: (1) fast, (2) slow, (3) minuet or scherzo, (4) fast. (Sometimes the second movement is a minuet or a scherzo and the slow movement is third.)

Other popular forms of classical chamber music are the sonata for violin and piano; the piano trio (violin, cello, and piano); and the string quintet (two violins, two violas, and cello).

Today, as in the eighteenth century, much chamber music is performed by amateurs. By consulting the Internet or the directory *Amateur Chamber Music Players,* one can find partners for chamber music almost anywhere in the United States.

10 Joseph Haydn

The first of the three classical masters, Joseph Haydn (1732–1809), was born in a tiny Austrian village called Rohrau. His father made wagon wheels, and until he was six, Haydn's musical background consisted of the folk songs his father loved to sing and the peasant dances that whirled about him on festive occasions. (This early contact with folk music later had an influence on his style.) Haydn's eager response to music was recognized, and he was sent to live with a relative who gave him basic music lessons for two years. At the age of eight, he went to Vienna to serve as a choirboy in the Cathedral of St. Stephen. There, though his good voice was appreciated, he had no chance for composition lessons or for perfecting an instrumental technique. And when his voice changed, Haydn was dismissed from St. Stephen's and turned out on the street without a penny. "I barely managed to stay alive by giving music lessons to children for about eight years," he wrote. Throughout those years he struggled to teach himself composition and also took odd jobs, including playing violin in the popular Viennese street bands that offered evening entertainment.

Haydn was a pathfinder for the classical style, a pioneer in the development of the symphony and string quartet.

Gradually, aristocratic patrons of music began to notice Haydn's talent. For a brief time he was music director at the court of a Bohemian count, though the orchestra was then dissolved because of his patron's financial problems. When he was twenty-nine, Haydn's life changed for the better, permanently.

In 1761, Haydn entered the service of the Esterházys, the richest and most powerful of the Hungarian noble families. For almost thirty years, from 1761 to 1790, most of his music was composed for performance in the palaces of the family. Haydn spent much of his time at Eszterháza, a magnificent but isolated palace in Hungary that contained an opera house, a theater, two concert halls, and 126 guest rooms.

As a highly skilled servant, Haydn was to compose all the music requested by his patron, conduct the orchestra of about twenty-five players, coach singers, and oversee the condition of instruments and the operation of the music library. He was also required to "appear daily in the antechamber before and after mid-day and inquire whether His Highness is pleased to order a performance of the orchestra." The amount of work demanded of Haydn as assistant music director and later as music director was staggering; there were usually two concerts and two opera performances weekly, as well as daily chamber music in the prince's apartment. Since Nicholas Esterházy played the baryton (a complicated string instrument now obsolete), Haydn wrote over 150 pieces with a baryton part.

Though today it seems degrading for a genius to be dependent on the will of a prince, in the eighteenth century patronage was taken for granted. Composers found definite advantages in it: they received a steady income and their works were performed. And though Haydn felt restricted by his job from time to time, he later wisely said, "Not only did I have the encouragement of constant approval, but as conductor of an orchestra I could make experiments, observe what produced an effect and what weakened it, and was thus in a position to improve, alter, make additions or omissions, and be as bold as I pleased. I was cut off from the world; there was no one to confuse or torment me, and I was forced to become original."

Despite an unhappy marriage, Haydn was good-humored and unselfish. He was conscientious about his professional duties, and he cared about the personal interests of his musicians. Prince Nicholas loved Eszterháza and once stayed at the palace longer than usual. The orchestra members came to Haydn and asked to return to Vienna; they were tired of being isolated in the country, away so long from their wives and children. Haydn obliged by composing his Symphony in F Sharp Minor, now known as the *Farewell*. At its first performance for the prince, the musicians followed the indications in the score: during the last movement, one after another stopped playing, put out his candle, and quietly left the hall. By the time that only Haydn and the first violinist remained, Nicholas took the hint; the next day he ordered the household to return to Vienna.

Haydn met the younger Mozart in the early 1780s, and they became close friends. To someone finding fault with one of Mozart's operas, Haydn replied, "I cannot settle this dispute, but this I know: Mozart is the greatest composer the world possesses now."

Over a period of twenty years, word spread about the Esterházys' composer, and Haydn's music became immensely popular all over Europe. Publishers and concert organizations sent commissions for new works. After the death of Prince Nicholas Esterházy in 1790, Haydn was free to go to London, where a concert series was planned around his compositions. He had been asked by the concert manager Johann Peter Salomon to write and conduct new symphonies for performance at public concerts. Six were composed for a first visit in 1791–1792 and six more for a second visit in 1794–1795. The twelve became known as the *Salomon* or *London* symphonies.

Reports of the time say that Haydn's appearances were triumphs. By the end of the eighteenth century, London was the largest and richest city in the world. Its concert life was unusually active and attracted many foreign musicians. The acclaim at Haydn's concerts was so overwhelming that some movements of his symphonies had to be repeated. One listener noted that there was "an electrical effect on all present and such a degree of enthusiasm as almost amounted to a frenzy."

A performance of Haydn's oratorio *The Creation* at the University of Vienna in 1808.

And so a servant became a celebrity. Haydn was wined and dined by the aristocracy, given an honorary doctorate at Oxford, and received by members of the royal family. And, as though to balance out earlier personal unhappiness, he had a love affair with a rich English widow. After his thirty years of service to the Esterházys, Haydn's reception by the English moved him to write, "How sweet is some degree of liberty. The consciousness of no longer being a bond servant sweetens all my toil."

Haydn returned to Vienna in 1795, rich and honored, and maintained good relations with Eszterháza. The new prince, Nicholas II, did not have his father's wide musical interests and liked only religious music. Haydn's agreement specified that he would compose a mass a year. He wrote six, and all reflect the mature, brilliant writing of the London symphonies. In this period, when he was in his late sixties, Haydn composed two oratorios, *The Creation* (1798) and *The Seasons* (1801). They were so popular that choruses and orchestras were formed at the beginning of the nineteenth century for the sole purpose of performing them.

Haydn died in 1809, at the age of seventy-seven, while Napoleon's army was occupying Vienna. The wide recognition he had attained could be seen in a memorial service held for him: joining the Viennese were French generals and an honor guard of French soldiers.

Haydn's Music

Haydn was a pathfinder for the classical style, a pioneer in the development of the symphony and string quartet. Both Mozart and Beethoven were influenced by his style. Haydn's music, like his personality, is robust and direct; it radiates a healthy optimism.

Haydn never forgot the peasant dances and songs of his childhood in a small village, and many of his works have a folk flavor. He quoted actual peasant tunes and composed original melodies in a folklike style. The minuets often romp and stomp rather than bow and curtsy. *The Creation* and *The Seasons,* Haydn's late oratorios, reflect his love of nature. There are vivid and humorous musical descriptions of storms, hail, animals, birds, and fish.

Haydn was a master at developing themes. He would split them into small fragments to be repeated quickly by different instruments. His skill at development made it possible for him to build a whole movement out of a single main theme. In such movements, contrast of mood results from changes in texture, key, rhythm, dynamics, and orchestration. The contagious joy that springs from his lively rhythms and vivid contrasts makes it clear why London went wild.

"I prefer to see the humorous side of life," Haydn once said. He produced comic effects from unexpected pauses and tempo changes and from sudden shifts in dynamics and pitch. We've heard one of his musical jokes in the second movement of the *Surprise* Symphony, where a soft theme is suddenly punctuated by a loud chord.

Haydn's enormous output revolves around his 104 symphonies, which span a period of over forty-five years, from about 1758 to 1795. For a long time, the last twelve symphonies (Nos. 93 to 104), composed for public concerts in London during the 1790s, were the only symphonies by Haydn regularly performed. Now, thanks to venturesome scholars and performers, the earlier symphonies composed for Eszterháza and other castles are heard more often. Many of Haydn's popular symphonies have nicknames, such as *Surprise* (No. 94), *Military* (No. 100), *Clock* (No. 101), and *Drum Roll* (No. 103).

Haydn's symphonies and his sixty-eight string quartets are considered his most important works. Some scholars believe that Haydn invented the string quartet form. He began writing string quartets for a good reason—only three other musicians were on hand during the summer of 1757, when he was invited to take part, as violist, in chamber music performances at a castle. The steward of the aristocratic host and the parish priest each played a violin, and there was a cellist named Albrechtsberger. Spurred by necessity, the twenty-five-year-old Haydn wrote the first of his lifelong series of string quartets.

Haydn's output also includes piano sonatas, piano trios, divertimentos, concertos, operas, and masses. The variety in his works is astounding. He was a great innovator and experimenter who hated arbitrary "rules" of composition. "What is the good of such rules? Art is free, and should be fettered by no such mechanical regulations. The educated ear is the sole authority in all these questions, and I think that I have as much right to lay down the law as anyone."

Symphony No. 94 in G Major (*Surprise;* 1791)

Haydn composed his most famous symphony, Symphony No. 94 in G Major (*Surprise*), in 1791, during his first visit to London. It was performed at a public concert on March 23, 1792, by an orchestra of forty players, a large group for the time. The London *Diary* reported that the new symphony was "of extraordinary merit. It was simple, profound and sublime. The andante movement was particularly admired."

The nickname *Surprise,* coined by Haydn's contemporaries, comes from the sudden loud chord that punctuates the soft theme of the andante (as we've seen on page 197). "It was my wish to surprise the public with something new," Haydn once explained, "and to make a debut in a brilliant manner." Typical of Haydn are the musical surprises, folklike tunes, and vivid contrasts of tone color and dynamics in Symphony No. 94.

First Movement:
Adagio (slow introduction);
Vivace assai (very lively)

Basic Set:
CD 3 37

The slow introduction to the first movement begins with a peaceful melody that is divided between woodwinds and strings:

The mood soon becomes serious, as a pulsating rhythm, a crescendo, and chromatic harmonies create a momentary feeling of uncertainty.

The uncertainty of the introduction is resolved in the vivace assai, a very rapid, joyful movement in sonata form.

The first theme is a brief dance tune that is played softly by the violins:

38 1:12

39 1:41
2:00

It is followed by a loud, energetic section for full orchestra. After a restatement of the soft opening theme, the exposition continues with a long, powerful bridge section for full orchestra. During the bridge, the soft opening theme is heard once again, this time slightly varied and in a new key:

40 2:15

A carefree waltz melody serves as the second theme of the exposition:

41 2:32

It begins with a syncopated repetition of a single tone and is played softly by the violins with an "oom-pah-pah" accompaniment in the other strings. Haydn rounds off the exposition with a gracious closing theme that is introduced by the strings and continued by the woodwinds:

Repeat of exposition
42 3:10
Development
43 5:08

Soon the remaining instruments join in and bring the exposition to a rousing finish. The exposition is repeated.

The development begins softly as Haydn reveals the potential of his lilting first theme. In the agitated continuation of the development, tension is built through motives from the bridge section, which move restlessly through minor keys. After a sudden **p**, the development concludes with repeated notes that lead into the recapitulation.

Recapitulation
44 6:08

For a while, all is "normal" in the recapitulation; we hear the first theme, a shortened form of the bridge, and the second theme. But before letting us hear the closing theme, Haydn expands the recapitulation through a rich polyphonic development of the first theme. The return of the closing theme brings a feeling of relaxation, and the movement ends jubilantly.

Basic Set:
CD 3 45

Brief Set:
CD 2 43

Second Movement:
Andante
The second movement of the symphony is the well-known theme and variations already discussed in Section 4.

Third Movement:
Minuet (Allegro molto)
With its heavily marked "oom-pah-pah" beat and unusually fast tempo, the minuet of Symphony No. 94 sounds more like a boisterous peasant romp than an elegant court dance. This movement is written in the customary A B A minuet form:

Minuet	Trio	Minuet
A	B	A
a (repeated) ba′ (repeated)	c (repeated) dc′ (repeated)	a ba′

The high-spirited A (minuet) section is mostly loud and played by the full orchestra, but there are softer interludes played by strings and woodwinds.

The minuet section concludes with a soft flute phrase that is repeated loudly by the whole orchestra.

In contrast to the A section, the trio (B) section is intimate, with softer dynamics, fewer instruments (only strings and bassoon), and a less strongly emphasized beat.

Fourth Movement:
Finale (Allegro di molto)

The symphony's very rapid and brilliant finale is a sonata-rondo. It imaginatively combines the thematic development typical of sonata form with the recurring main theme found in rondo form.

The movement may be outlined as A B A′ (shortened)—development section—A′ (shortened)—development section—A B coda. Its playful main theme, A, is soft but lively:

Theme B is a gentle, lilting melody:

At its first two returns the main theme is shortened and leads immediately into a bustling development section. With great wit, Haydn prepares for the second return of the main theme by repeating its upbeat beginning over and over.

The *Surprise* Symphony is an example of Haydn's genius for making rich, complex music from the simplest phrases and themes.

Trumpet Concerto in E Flat Major (1796)

Haydn's Trumpet Concerto in E Flat Major has a remarkable history. After its premiere in 1800, it was forgotten for almost 130 years. It was first published only in 1929, and in the 1930s a phonograph recording brought it to a wide audience. Now, it may well be Haydn's most popular work.

Haydn wrote the concerto in 1796 for a friend, a trumpeter at the Viennese court who had recently invented a keyed trumpet that could produce a complete chromatic scale. The keyed trumpet was intended to replace the natural trumpet, which could produce only a restricted number of tones. But the keyed trumpet had a dull sound and was supplanted by the valve trumpet around 1840. Today, the concerto is performed on a valve trumpet. Like most concertos, it has three movements: (1) fast, (2) slow, (3) fast. We'll examine the third movement.

Third Movement:
Allegro

Basic Set:
CD 3 58

The third movement is a dazzling sonata-rondo in which Haydn gives the trumpeter's virtuosity free rein. The movement combines the recurring main theme characteristic of rondo form with the development section found in sonata form. It may be outlined as A B A B′ A—development section—A B″—coda. Themes A and B are introduced by the orchestra and are then presented mainly by the trumpet, with orchestral support. The main theme, A, is a high-spirited melody that is well suited to the trumpet. Theme B is playful; it contains a short, downward-moving phrase that is repeated several times. Haydn's fondness for musical surprises is reflected in the coda, which contains sudden changes of dynamics, unexpected harmonic twists, and a suspenseful long pause.

LISTENING OUTLINE

HAYDN, Trumpet Concerto in E Flat Major

Third Movement: Allegro

Sonata-rondo form, duple meter ($\frac{2}{4}$), E flat major

Solo trumpet, 2 flutes, 2 oboes, 2 bassoons, 2 French horns, 2 trumpets, timpani, 1st violins, 2d violins, violas, cellos, double basses

(Duration, 4:35)

A

58   0:00

1. **a.** Main theme in violins, ***p***.

b. Main theme in full orchestra, ***f***, violins, running notes and rising scale lead to

B

59   0:23

c. Violins, ***f***, downward short phrase, repeated ***p***,

orchestra, ***f***, brass fanfares, cadence, pause.

A

60   0:38

2. Main theme in trumpet, strings accompany, trumpet repeats main theme, orchestra, ***f***, violins, ***p***, lead to

B′

61 1:08

3. Trumpet, held tone, ushers in downward short phrases, upward phrases with trills, downward legato phrases, trumpet trill to cadence, trumpet fanfares, orchestra, *f*.

A

62 1:48

4. a. Trumpet, held tone, ushers in main theme.

   b. Main-theme phrase in full orchestra, *f*.

Development

63 2:06

5. Trumpet, main-theme phrases, *p*, violins, *p*, main-theme phrases in minor with trumpet fanfares, running notes in violins, *f*, trumpet and brasses join, suddenly soft, violins introduce

A

64 2:40

6. a. Trumpet, held tone, ushers in main theme.

   b. Orchestra, *f*, running notes and rising scale lead to

B″

2:58

7. a. Trumpet, downward short phrases, downward broken chords, octave leaps, trill to cadence.

   b. Violins, *p*, high woodwinds, *p*, trumpet fanfares, violins, *p*, lead to

Coda

3:33

8. a. Trumpet, main-theme phrase, strings, *p*, trumpet, downward chain of trills.

   b. Suddenly loud, full orchestra, sudden *pp*, string tremolos, suddenly loud, full orchestra, repeated notes in trumpet, long pause.

   c. Trumpet, main-theme phrases, orchestra, *p*, crescendo to *ff*, repeated notes in trumpet, closing chords in orchestra.

11 Wolfgang Amadeus Mozart

Wolfgang Amadeus Mozart (1756–1791), one of the most amazing child prodigies in history, was born in Salzburg, Austria. By the time he was six, he could play the harpsichord and violin, improvise fugues, write minuets, and read music perfectly at first sight. At the age of eight, he wrote a symphony; at eleven, an oratorio; at twelve, an opera. By his early teens, Mozart had behind him many works that would have brought credit to a composer three times his age.

Mozart's father, Leopold, who was a court musician, was understandably eager to show him off and went to great lengths to do so. Mozart spent almost half his time between the ages of six and fifteen on tour in Europe and England. He played for Empress Maria Theresa in Vienna, for Louis XV at Versailles, for George III in London, and for innumerable aristocrats along the way. On his trips to Italy he was able to study and master the current operatic style, which he later put to superb use. Mozart was in

Mozart was among the most versatile of all composers; he wrote masterpieces in all the musical forms of his time.

Rome during Holy Week when he was fourteen, and he went to hear the famous choir of the Sistine Chapel performing a work that was its treasured property. Anyone caught copying this choral piece was to be punished by excommunication. Mozart heard it once, wrote it out afterward almost completely, returned with his manuscript to make a few additions—and was discovered. For anyone to copy the music was a crime; for anyone to hear it and remember it so accurately seemed incredible. Mozart not only escaped punishment but was knighted by the pope for his musical accomplishments.

When he was fifteen, Mozart returned to Salzburg, which was ruled by a new prince-archbishop, Hieronymus Colloredo. The archbishop was a tyrant who did not appreciate Mozart's genius, and he refused to grant him more than a subordinate seat in the court orchestra. With his father's help, Mozart tried repeatedly over the next decade to find a suitable position elsewhere, but with no success.

The tragic irony of Mozart's life was that he won more acclaim as a boy wonder than as an adult musician. His upbringing and personality were partly to blame. In his childhood, his complete dependence on his father gave him little opportunity to develop initiative. Even when Mozart was twenty-two, his mother tagged along when he went to Paris to seek recognition and establish himself. A Parisian observed that Mozart was "too good-natured, not active enough, too easily taken in, too little concerned with the means that may lead him to good fortune."

Unlike Haydn, Mozart began his professional life as an international celebrity, pampered by kings. He could not tolerate being treated like a servant and eating with valets and cooks, and his relations with his patron went from bad to worse. Mozart became totally insubordinate when the prince-archbishop forbade him to give concerts or perform at the houses of the aristocracy. After an ugly confrontation, Mozart wrote: "He lied to my face that my salary was five hundred gulden, called me a scoundrel, a rascal, a vagabond. At last my blood began to boil, I could no longer contain myself, and I said, 'So Your Grace is not satisfied with me?'" The archbishop answered, "What, you dare to threaten me—you scoundrel? There is the door!" On his third attempt to request dismissal, Mozart was thrown out of the room by a court official and given a kick.

By 1781, when he was twenty-five, Mozart could stand it no longer. He broke free of provincial Salzburg and traveled to Vienna, intending to be a freelance musician.

To reassure his father, he wrote: "I have the best and most useful acquaintances in the world. I am liked and respected in the best houses, and all possible honors are given me, and moreover I get paid for it. I guarantee you I'll be successful."

Indeed, Mozart's first few years in Vienna were successful. His German opera *Die Entführung aus dem Serail* (*The Abduction from the Seraglio*, 1782) was acclaimed. Concerts of his own music were attended by the emperor and the nobility. Pupils paid him high fees, his compositions were published, and his playing was heard in palace drawing rooms. He even went against his father's wishes by marrying Constanze Weber, who had no money and was as impractical as he. Contributing to the brightness of these years was Mozart's friendship with Haydn, who told Leopold, "Your son is the greatest composer that I know, either personally or by reputation; he has taste and, what is more, the most profound knowledge of composition."

Then, in 1786, came Mozart's opera *Le Nozze di Figaro* (*The Marriage of Figaro*). Vienna loved it, and Prague was even more enthusiastic. "They talk about nothing but *Figaro*. Nothing is played, sung, or whistled but *Figaro*," Mozart joyfully wrote. This success led an opera company in Prague to commission *Don Giovanni* (*Don Juan*) the following year. *Don Giovanni* was a triumph in Prague, but it pushed the Viennese too far. Emperor Joseph II acknowledged that it was a masterwork, but not appropriate for his pleasure-loving subjects. Dark qualities and dissonance did not appeal to them.

Mozart's popularity in Vienna began to decline. It was a fickle city; one was society's darling for a few seasons and then was suddenly ignored. And Mozart's music was considered complicated and hard to follow, too "highly spiced" with dissonance. A publisher warned him: "Write in a more popular style, or else I can neither print nor pay for any more of your music!" His pupils dwindled, and the elite snubbed his concerts. In desperate financial straits, he wrote to friends, "Great God, I would not wish my worst enemy to be in this position. . . . I am coming to you not with thanks but with fresh entreaties."

Many of Mozart's letters have been published. These span his life, and it is sad to move from the colorful, witty, and keenly observant notes of a prodigy on tour through his initial optimism about Vienna to the despair of "I cannot describe what I have been feeling. . . . A kind of longing that is never satisfied."

During his last year, Mozart was happier and more successful. He was delighted to receive a commission from a Viennese theater for a German comic opera, *Die Zauberflöte* (*The Magic Flute*). While hard at work, Mozart was visited by a stranger who carried an anonymous letter commissioning a requiem, a mass for the dead. Mozart could not begin the requiem, because he had to finish *The Magic Flute* and compose another opera, *La Clemenza di Tito* (*The Clemency of Titus*), which was performed in Prague on September 6, 1791. On September 30, two months before his death, *The Magic Flute* was premiered to resounding praise in Vienna. Its success probably would have brought large financial rewards, but it came too late. Mozart died of rheumatic fever on December 5, 1791, shortly before his thirty-sixth birthday, leaving the requiem unfinished. On the day of his burial, a Vienna newspaper reported, "His works, which are loved and admired everywhere, are proof of his greatness—and they reveal the irreplaceable loss which the noble art of music has suffered through his death."

Mozart's Music

Mozart was among the most versatile of all composers; he wrote masterpieces in all the musical forms of his time. His symphonies are as profound as his string quartets, his piano concertos as dramatic and lyrical as his operas. All his music sings: even his instrumental melodies seem to grow out of the human voice. His works convey a feeling of ease, grace, and spontaneity, as well as balance, restraint, and perfect proportion. Yet mysterious harmonies bring dark moods that contrast with the lyricism. Mozart fuses power and elegance in a unique way. However passionate and intense, his works are always sensuous and beautiful. He believed that music "must never offend the ear, but must please the hearer, or in other words, must never cease to be *music*."

Not only do Mozart's compositions sound effortless; they were created with miraculous ease and rapidity. For example, he completed his last three symphonies in only six weeks! And he composed extended works completely in his mind. He could even converse while notating a score.

Mozart's more than 600 compositions were cataloged during the nineteenth century by Ludwig von Köchel. Hence, it is customary to refer to a Mozart work by the "K." number that indicates its chronological place in his output. For example, his Piano Concerto No. 23 in A Major (1786) is K. 488, and his Symphony No. 40 in G Minor (1788)—composed two years later—is K. 550.

In Mozart's hands, the classical concerto was raised to its highest level. Many of his concertos are among his greatest works. Particularly important are the more than twenty piano concertos that Mozart—a brilliant virtuoso—composed mainly for his own performances. He also wrote several violin concertos and horn concertos, two flute concertos, and one concerto each for bassoon, oboe, and clarinet. The concertos, as well as his other works, show a sensitivity to woodwind tone colors that is unmatched by earlier composers. The clarinet, especially, came into its own through Mozart. His Concerto for Clarinet, K. 622 (1791), written in the last year of his life, remains the finest ever composed for that instrument.

Mozart was a master of opera; few composers have matched his ability to coordinate music and stage action. His dramatic works reveal a keen sense of theater, an inexhaustible gift of melody, and a genius for creating characters through tone. Most of his operas are comedies, composed to librettos in German or in Italian, which was the international language of music in Mozart's time. While the Italian operas are entirely sung, the German operas include spoken dialogue, as was customary in German opera at the time. Mozart's three masterpieces of Italian comic opera are *The Marriage of Figaro* (1786), *Don Giovanni* (1787), and *Così fan tutte* (*All Women Behave Like This*, 1790); they were all composed to librettos by Lorenzo da Ponte. Mozart's finest opera in German is *The Magic Flute* (1791); its wide range of style embraces folk song and fugue, farcical comedy, and solemn hymns about the brotherhood of man.

The comic operas contain both humorous and serious characters. The major characters are not mere stereotypes but human beings who think and feel. Even when six characters sing together in a complex ensemble, the individuality of each shines through. Mozart once tried to explain how he depicted emotion in an aria: "Would you like to know how I have expressed it—and even indicated his throbbing heart? By two violins playing octaves. You feel the trembling—the faltering—you see how his throbbing breast begins to swell; this I have expressed by a crescendo. You hear the whispering and sighing—which I have indicated by the first violins with mutes and a flute playing in unison." Emotions in Mozart's arias and ensembles are not static; they continuously evolve and change. A character may feel one way at the beginning of an ensemble and entirely differently at its end. In a duet from *Don Giovanni,* for example, the feelings of a peasant girl change as she gradually gives in to the charm of the aristocrat Don Giovanni.

Throughout his life, Mozart learned from other composers. As a boy, he was influenced by Italian operas and the graceful style of one of Bach's sons, Johann Christian Bach. The strongest influence on his later works came from J. S. Bach, dead and nearly forgotten; and from Haydn, the most famous composer at the time. From Bach, Mozart learned to write intricate polyphonic textures that flow smoothly. He arranged Bach's and Handel's works for performances at private concerts sponsored by Baron Gottfried van Swieten, a Viennese who was a passionate music lover. From Haydn's works, Mozart learned ways to develop themes. But his musical relationship with Haydn was not one-sided. Some compositions by Haydn show traces of Mozart's melodic and orchestral style.

"I am never happier," Mozart once wrote his father, "than when I have something to compose, for that, after all, is my sole delight and passion." Mozart's "delight and passion" are communicated in his works, which represent late eighteenth-century musical style at its highest level of perfection.

Don Giovanni (1787)

Don Giovanni (*Don Juan*) is a unique blend of comic and serious opera, combining seduction and slapstick with violence and the supernatural. The old tale of Don Juan, the legendary Spanish lover, had attracted many playwrights and composers before Mozart. Mozart's Don Giovanni is an extremely seductive but ruthless nobleman who will stop at nothing to satisfy his sexual appetite. Don Giovanni's comic servant, Leporello, is a grumbling accomplice who dreams of being in his master's place.

The Don attempts to rape a young noblewoman, Donna Anna; her father, the Commendatore (Commandant), challenges him to a duel. Don Giovanni kills the old man, causing Donna Anna and her fiancé, Don Ottavio, to swear revenge. Pursued by his enemies, Don Giovanni deftly engages in new amorous adventures. During one of them, he hides in a cemetery, where he sees a marble statue of the dead Commandant. The unearthly statue utters threatening words, but Don Giovanni brazenly invites it to dinner. When the statue appears at the banquet hall, it orders the Don to repent. Don Giovanni defiantly refuses and is dragged down to hell.

Overture

Mozart plunges us into a dark atmosphere at the beginning of the overture with awesome D minor chords, anxious syncopations, and sinister scale passages; there is a hair-raising effect when this slow, ominous music returns at the end of the opera for the statue's confrontation with Don Giovanni in the banquet hall. The overture continues with a fast sonata-form movement in D major, which has the energy and swagger of the opera's leading character. This contrast of minor and major, mystery and brilliance, foretells the tremendous range of emotions to come.

Act I:
Introduction

The overture leads directly into the action-packed opening scene. In breathless succession we witness Leporello keeping guard, Don Giovanni struggling with Donna Anna, the Commandant dueling with the Don, and the Commandant's agonized last gasps. Mozart's music vividly depicts the characters and pushes the action forward. (In the vocal music guide, braces indicate that characters sing at the same time. *Etc.* indicates that previous lines of text are repeated.)

connect

A video clip of this excerpt is available in *Connect Kamien.*

Basic Set:
CD 4 **1**

Brief Set:
CD 3 5

VOCAL MUSIC GUIDE

MOZART, *Don Giovanni*

Act I: Excerpt from Opening Scene

1 5 0:00
Orchestral introduction,
molto allegro;
sudden fortes
suggest pacing
and abrupt turns.

(Late evening outside the Commandant's palace in Seville. Don Giovanni, concealing his identity, has stolen into Donna Anna's room for an amorous adventure. Leporello paces back and forth.)

Leporello

0:15	*Notte e giorno faticar,*	Night and day I slave
	Per chi nulla sa gradir;	For one who does not appreciate it.

0:29	*Piova e vento sopportar,*	I put up with wind and rain,
	Mangiar male e mal dormir!	Eat and sleep badly.
	Voglio far il gentiluomo,	I want to be a gentleman
	E non voglio più servir,	And to give up my servitude.
	No, no, no, no, no, no,	No, no, no, no, no, no,
	Non voglio più servir!	I want to give up my servitude.
0:46	*Oh che caro galantuomo!*	Oh, what a fine gentleman!
	Voi star dentro colla bella	You stay inside with your lady
0:58	*Ed io far la sentinella!*	And I must play the sentinel!
	Voglio far il gentiluomo, ecc.	Oh, what a fine gentleman, etc.
1:24	*Ma mi par che venga gente . . .*	But I think someone is coming!
	Non mi voglio far sentir, ecc.	I don't want them to hear me, etc.

1:41
Orchestral
crescendo.

Leporello hides to one side. Don Giovanni and Donna Anna come down the palace stairs struggling. The Don hides his face to prevent her from recognizing her.)

Donna Anna

1:47	*Non sperar, se non m'uccidi.*	There's no hope, unless you kill me
	Ch'io ti lasci fuggir mai!	That I'll ever let you go!

Don Giovanni

	Donna folle, indarno gridi:	Idiot! You scream in vain.
	Chi son io tu non saprai.	Who I am you'll never know!

Donna Anna

Non sperar, ecc. — There's no hope, etc.

Don Giovanni

1:58   *Donna folle! ecc.* — Idiot! etc.

Leporello

Che tumulto! Oh ciel, che gridi!	What a racket! Heavens, what screams!
Il padron in nuovi guai.	My master in another scrape.

Donna Anna

2:07   *Gente! Servi! Al traditore!* — Help! Everyone! The betrayer!

Don Giovanni

Taci, e trema al mio furore! — Keep quiet! Beware my wrath!

Donna Anna

Scellerato! — Scoundrel!

Don Giovanni

Sconsigliata! — Fool!

Donna Anna

Scellerato! — Scoundrel!

Don Giovanni

Sconsigliata! — Fool!

Leporello

Sta a veder che il malandrino	We will see if this rascal
Mi farà precipitar.	Will be the ruin of me!

Donna Anna

Gente! Servi! — Help! Everyone!

Don Giovanni

Taci, e trema!   Keep quiet!

Donna Anna

2:18 *Come furia disperata*   Like a desperate fury
Ti saprò perseguitar! ecc.   I'll know how to pursue you! etc.
Scellerato! Gente! Servi!   Scoundrel! Help! Everyone!
Come furia disperata, ecc.   Like a desperate fury, etc.

Don Giovanni

Questa furia disperata   This desperate fury
Mi vuol far precipitar! ecc.   Is aimed at destroying me!
Sconsigliata! Taci, e trema!   Fool! Keep quiet!
Questa furia disperata, ecc.   This desperate fury, etc.

Leporello

Che tumulto! Oh ciel, che gridi!   What a racket! Heavens, what screams!
Sta a veder che il malandrino, ecc.   We will see if this rascal, etc.

2 **6** 3:02
String tremolo, *ff*,   (Donna Anna hears the Commandant; she leaves Don Giovanni and goes into the house.
shift to minor key.   The Commandant appears.)

Commandant

3:10 *Lasciala, indegno! Battiti meco!*   Leave her alone, wretch, and defend
                                           yourself.

Don Giovanni

Va, non mi degno di pugnar teco.   Go away! I disdain to fight with you.

Commandant

Così pretendi da me fuggir?   Thus you think to escape me?

Leporello

Potessi almeno di qua partir.   If I could only get out of here!

Don Giovanni

3:23

Va, non mi degno, no!   Go away! I disdain you!

Commandant

Così pretendi da me fuggir?   Thus you think to escape me!

Leporello

Potessi almeno di qua partir!   If I could only get out of here!

Commandant

3:31 *Battiti!*   Fight!

Don Giovanni

Misero! Attendi, se vuoi morir!   So be it, if you want to die!

Dueling music, 3:47   (They duel. The Commandant is fatally wounded.)
upward sweeps in
strings. Death blow,
suspenseful,
held chord.

3 **7** 4:06   **Commandant**
andante, *pp*,   Help! I've been betrayed!
pathetic minor   *Ah, soccorso! son tradito!*   The assassin has wounded me!
phrases.   *L'assassino m'ha ferito,*   And from my heaving breast
                    E dal seno palpitante   I feel my soul escaping!
                    Sento l'anima partir.

Don Giovanni

Ah! già cade il sciagurato!	Ah, already the wretch has fallen,
Affannosa e agonizzante	And he gasps for air.
Già dal seno palpitante	From his heaving breast I already
Veggo l'anima partir, ecc.	See his soul escaping, etc.

Leporello

Qual misfatto! Qual eccesso!	What a misdeed! What a crime!
Entro il sen dallo spavento	I can feel my heart
Palpitar il cor mi sento!	Beating hard from fright!
Io non sò che far, che dir, ecc.	I don't know what to do or say, etc.

(The Commandant dies.)

4 8 5:18

Recitative, harpsichord accompanies.

Don Giovanni

Leporello, dove sei?	Leporello, where are you?

Leporello

Son qui, per mia disgrazia. E voi?	I'm here, unfortunately, and you?

Don Giovanni

Son qui.	Over here.

Leporello

Chi è morto, voi, o il vecchio?	Who's dead, you or the old man?

Don Giovanni

Che domanda da bestia! Il vecchio.	What an idiotic question! The old man.

Leporello

5:29

Bravo! Due imprese leggiadre,	Well done! Two misdeeds!
Sforzar la figlia, ed ammazzar	First you raped the daughter, then
il padre!	murdered the father!

Don Giovanni

L'ha voluto, suo danno.	He asked for it; too bad for him.

Leporello

Ma Donn' Anna cosa ha voluto?	And Donna Anna, did she ask for it too?

Don Giovanni

Taci, non mi seccar!	Keep quiet and don't bother me.
Vien meco, se non vuoi qualche	Now come along, unless you're
cosa ancor tu.	anxious for something for yourself.

Leporello

Non vo' nulla, signor, non parlo	I have no desires, sir, and no more to
più.	say.

connect

A video clip of this excerpt is available in *Connect Kamien*.

Basic Set:
CD 4 5

Act I:
Leporello's catalog aria (*Madamina*)

Not long after the opening scene, Leporello sings his famous "catalog" aria (*Madamina*) to Donna Elvira, a woman whom Don Giovanni has earlier seduced and deserted and who has now appeared on the scene. In mocking "consolation," Leporello tells her that she is but one of many and displays a fat catalog of his master's conquests. The music bubbles with Leporello's delight as he reels off the amazing totals: 640 in Italy, 231 in Germany, 100 in France, 91 in Turkey, and in Spain, 1,003! Mozart makes the most of comic description as Leporello proceeds to list the Don's seduction techniques for different types of women.

VOCAL MUSIC GUIDE

MOZART, *Madamina* from *Don Giovanni*

5 0:00
Allegro.

Madamina, il catalogo è questo
Delle belle, che amò il padron mio;
Un catalogo egli è, che ho fatt'io,
Osservate, leggete con me.

My dear lady, this is a list
Of the beauties my master has loved,
A list which I have compiled.
Observe, read along with me.

0:21
Staccato woodwind chuckles.

In Italia seicento e quaranta,

In Italy, six hundred and forty;

In Almagna duecento a trentuna,

In Germany, two hundred and thirty-one;

Cento in Francia, in Turchia novantuna,

A hundred in France; in Turkey ninety-one.

0:37
Longer notes.
0:54
Shorter notes.

Ma in Ispagna son già mille e tre!

In Spain already one thousand and three!

V'han fra queste contadine,
Cameriere, cittadine,
V'han contesse, baronesse,
Marchesine, principesse,
E v'han donne d'ogni grado,
D'ogni forma, d'ogni età!
In Italia seicento e quaranta, ecc.

Among these are peasant girls
Maidservants, city girls,
Countesses, baronesses,
Marchionesses, princesses,
Women of every rank,
Every shape, every age.
In Italy six hundred and forty, etc.

6 2:05
Andante con moto, courtly minuet.

Nella bionda egli ha l'usanza
Di lodar la gentilezza;

With blonds it is his habit
To praise their kindness;

2:25
Mock-heroic flourish.

Nella bruna, la costanza;

In brunettes, their faithfulness;

2:35
Suave melodic phrase.

Nella bianca la dolcezza;
Vuol d'inverno la grassotta,
Vuol d'estate la magrotta;

In the very blond, their sweetness.
In winter he likes fat ones,
In summer he likes thin ones.

2:57
Crescendo, melody slowly rises to high held tone.

È la grande maestosa,

He calls the tall ones majestic.

3:20
Sprightly quick notes.

La piccina è ognor vezzosa;

The little ones are always charming.

Delle vecchie fa conquista
Pel piacer di porle in lista.

He seduces the old ones
For the pleasure of adding to the list.

Sua passion predominante	His greatest favorite
È la giovin principiante.	Is the young beginner.
Non si picca se sia ricca,	It doesn't matter if she's rich,
Se sia brutta, se sia bella,	Ugly, or beautiful;
Se sia ricca, brutta, se sia bella;	If she is rich, ugly, or beautiful.
Purchè porti la gonnella,	If she wears a petticoat,
Voi sapete quel che fa!	*You* know what he does.
Purchè porti la gonnella, ecc.	If she wears a petticoat, etc.

connect

A video clip of this excerpt is available in *Connect Kamien*.

Basic Set:
CD 4 7

Act I:
Duet: *Là ci darem la mano*
(There you will give me your hand)

The Don's seduction technique is put to use in the lovely duet *Là ci darem la mano*. Don Giovanni persuades the pretty peasant girl Zerlina to come to his palace, promising to marry her and change her life. The music magically conveys his persuasiveness and her gradual surrender, as the voices become more and more intertwined. Forgetting her fiancé, Masetto, Zerlina throws herself into the Don's arms and they sing together, "Let us go, my beloved."

As they go off together, Donna Elvira suddenly intercepts them, denounces Don Giovanni, and protectively leads Zerlina away. During the opera, all of Don Giovanni's attempts at seduction or rape are frustrated.

The Korean soprano Hei-Kyung Hong as Zerlina and the Welsh baritone Bryn Terfel as Don Giovanni in a production of *Don Giovanni* at the Metropolitan Opera.

VOCAL MUSIC GUIDE

MOZART, *Là ci darem la mano*, from *Don Giovanni*

7 0:00
Andante, $\frac{2}{4}$,
legato melody.

Don Giovanni

Là ci darem la mano,

There you will give me your hand,

Là mi dirai di sì.
Vedi, non è lontano;
Partiam, ben mio, da qui.

There you will tell me "yes."
You see, it is not far;
Let us leave, my beloved.

Zerlina

0:20
Legato melody
repeated.

Vorrei e non vorrei;
Mi trema un poco il cor.
Felice è ver, sarei,
Ma può burlarmi ancor.

I'd like to, but yet I would not.
My heart trembles a little.
It's true I would be happy,
But he may just be tricking me.

8 0:45
Quicker
interchange
between voices.

Vieni, mio bel diletto!

Don Giovanni

Come, my dearly beloved!

Zerlina

Mi fa pietà Masetto!

I'm sorry for Masetto

Don Giovanni

Io cangierò tua sorte.

I will change your life!

Zerlina

Presto, non son più forte!

Soon I won't be able to resist.

Don Giovanni

Vieni! Vieni!
Là ci darem la mano!

Come! Come!
There you will give me your hand.

9 1:14
Legato melody now
shared by both voices.

Zerlina

Vorrei, e non vorrei!

I'd like to, but yet I would not.

Don Giovanni

Là mi dirai di sì.

There you will tell me "yes."

Zerlina

Mi trema un poco il cor!

My heart trembles a little.

Don Giovanni

Partiam, mio ben, da qui!

Let us leave, my beloved.

Zerlina

Ma può burlarmi ancor!

But he may just be tricking me.

Don Giovanni

1:41

Vieni, mio bel diletto!

Come, my dearly beloved!

Zerlina

Voices overlap.

Mi fa pietà Masetto!

I'm sorry for Masetto.

Don Giovanni

	Io cangierò tua sorte.	I will change your life.

Zerlina

Presto, non son più forte!   Soon I won't be able to resist.

Don Giovanni

1:58   *Andiam! Andiam!*   Let us go!

Zerlina

Andiam!   Let us go!

10 2:09   **Don Giovanni and Zerlina**

Allegro, ₵; together
they sing a new,
joyous tune.

Andiam, andiam, mio bene,   Let us go, let us go, my beloved,
A ristorar le pene   To soothe the pangs
D'un innocente amor! ecc.   Of an innocent love, etc.

Act II:
Finale

The finale of Act II, the concluding section of the opera, opens as Don Giovanni enjoys good food and good music; it closes with a sextet celebrating his horrible punishment. Mozart's genius fuses these dissimilar events into a coherent whole. Don Giovanni dines in his banquet hall while watching Leporello's comic antics and listening to his private band play three hit tunes. The third tune is from Mozart's *Marriage of Figaro,* and Leporello comments, "This I know only too well." The frivolous mood evaporates when Donna Elvira bursts in and begs the Don to mend his ways. Terror strikes as the Commandant's marble statue enters, accompanied by the awesome opening of the overture, in D minor. Mozart uses this return to weld a powerful sense of unity within the opera. As the orchestra plays the dueling music from Act I, the statue commands, "Repent, change your life, it is your last moment!" Defiant to the end, Don Giovanni shouts, "No, no, I do not repent!" Flames and smoke surround the Don. He cries out in agony as a chorus of demons sing of his eternal damnation. With a hideous shriek, Don Giovanni is engulfed by the flames of hell.

An epilogue in a lighter mood follows this scene of terror. The other characters, learning of Don Giovanni's fate, form a sextet and jubilantly sing a moral to the audience: "This is how evildoers end up!"

Symphony No. 40 in G Minor, K. 550 (1788)

Mozart's Symphony No. 40 in G Minor is the most passionate and dramatic of his symphonies. Although the work is classical in form and technique, it is almost romantic in emotional intensity. It staggers the imagination that Mozart could compose the G minor and two other great symphonies—No. 39 in E Flat and No. 41 in C (*Jupiter*)—during the short period of six weeks. They are his last three symphonies.

Like most classical symphonies, Symphony No. 40 in G Minor has four movements: (1) fast, (2) slow, (3) minuet, (4) fast.

Basic Set:
CD 3 **15**

Brief Set:
CD 2 **34**

First Movement:
Molto allegro

A quiet but agitated opening theme in the violins sets the mood for the entire first movement, which is in sonata form. A throbbing accompaniment in the violas contributes to the feeling of unrest. Dominating the violin melody is the rhythmic pattern short-short-long, first heard in the opening three-note motive.

The persistence of this rhythmic pattern gives the music a sense of urgency. Yet the melody is balanced and symmetrical. Questioning upward leaps are answered by downward scales, and the second phrase of the melody is a sequential repetition of the first, one step lower. The exposition continues with a bridge section that presents a new staccato motive played loudly by the violins.

The lyrical second theme, in B flat major, contrasts completely with the agitated G minor opening. Mozart exploits the expressive resources of tone color by dividing the theme between strings and woodwinds. In the closing section of the exposition, Mozart uses a fragment from the opening theme to achieve a different emotional effect. The three-note motive now sounds gentle and plaintive as it is passed between clarinet and bassoon against a background of sighing strings.

In the development, the movement becomes feverish. The opening theme is led into different keys and is cut into smaller and smaller pieces. The development begins mysteriously as the opening phrase ends in an unexpected way and sinks lower and lower. Then a sudden explosion of polyphonic texture increases the excitement and complexity. Mozart brusquely shifts the opening phrase between low and high strings while combining it with a furious staccato countermelody. Soon after, he demolishes the opening phrase: we hear the beginning of the theme without its upward leap.

Then the final note is lopped off.

Finally, we are left with the irreducible minimum of the original theme, the three-note motive.

The tension resolves only with the entrance of the entire opening theme in the tonic key.

In the recapitulation, exposition material is given new expressive meaning. The bridge is expanded and made more dramatic. The lyrical second theme, now in G minor, is touching and sad.

LISTENING OUTLINE

MOZART, Symphony No. 40 in G Minor

First Movement: Molto allegro

Sonata form, duple meter (2/2), G minor

Flute, 2 oboes, 2 clarinets, 2 bassoons, 2 French horns, 1st violins, 2d violins, violas, cellos, double basses

(Duration, 8:12)

Exposition

First theme

15 **34** 0:00   **1. a.** Main theme in violins, *p*, throbbing accompaniment in violas, minor key.

b. Full orchestra, *f*.

Bridge

16 **35** 0:23   **2. a.** Violins, *p*, main theme takes new turn to
                          b. Full orchestra, *f*, major key, staccato motive and insistent upward scales in violins. Pause.

Second theme

17 **36** 0:52   **3. a.** Lyrical melody, *p*, major key, strings and woodwinds.

            1:01   **b.** Woodwinds and strings, *p*, lyrical melody somewhat varied. Crescendo in full orchestra.
                          c. Staccato phrase, *f*, downward scale, *p*, to

Closing section

18 **37** 1:28   **4. a.** String sighs, *p*, three-note motive in woodwinds, violins, *f*. Varied repetition of string sighs and three-note motive.
                          b. Downward scales, *f*, full orchestra, cadence in major key.

19 **38** 2:02   Exposition is repeated.

Development

20 **39** 4:05   **1. a.** High woodwinds, *p*, lead to
                          b. Violins, *p*, main-theme phrase repeated on lower pitches.
            4:21   **2.** Sudden *f*, full orchestra, main-theme phrase combined with rapid countermelody.
            4:49   **3. a.** Sudden *p*, high violins and woodwinds, three-note motive.
                          b. Sudden *f*, full orchestra, three-note motive.
                          c. Sudden *p*, high flutes and clarinets, three-note motive carried down to

Recapitulation

First theme

21 **40** 5:21   **1. a.** Main theme in violins, *p*, throbbing accompaniment in violas, minor key.
                          b. Full orchestra, *f*.

Bridge

5:46   **2. a.** Violins, *p*, main theme takes new turn to
      b. Full orchestra, *f*, staccato motive in violins and cellos. Insistent upward scales in violins, *f*. Pause.

Second theme

22 **41** 6:37   **3. a.** Lyrical melody, *p*, minor key, strings and woodwinds.
6:46   **b.** Woodwinds and strings, *p*, lyrical melody somewhat varied. Crescendo in full orchestra.
      c. Staccato phrase, *f*, downward scale, *p*, to

Closing section

7:19   **4. a.** String sighs, *p*, three-note motive in woodwinds, violins, *f*. Varied repetition of string sighs and three-note motive.
      b. Downward scales, *f*, full orchestra.

Coda

23 **42** 7:49   **1. a.** Sudden *p*, main-theme motive in strings.
      b. Full orchestra, *f*, cadence in minor key.

Second Movement:
Andante

The mood of the andante hovers between gentleness and longing. The andante is written in sonata form and is the only movement of this symphony in major (it is in E flat). This movement develops from a series of gently pulsating notes in the opening theme.

Basic Set:
CD 3 **24**

Exposition
24 0:00
Development
25 3:39
Recapitulation
26 5:03

Andante
Violas

p

As the theme continues, the violins introduce an airy two-note rhythmic figure that will appear—with changes of dynamics and orchestration—in almost every section of the andante. The rhythmic figure will be, at different times, graceful, insistent, and forceful.

Later, Mozart uses the airy figures as a delicate countermelody to the repeated-note idea. Floating woodwinds interwoven with strings reveal Mozart's sensitivity to tone color as an expressive resource.

Third Movement:
Menuetto (Allegretto)

Basic Set:
CD 3 **27**

The minuet, in G minor, is serious and intense; it does not sound like an aristocratic dance. The form of the minuet is A B A:

Minuet	**Trio**	**Minuet**
A	B	A
a (repeated) ba' (repeated)	c (repeated) dc' (repeated)	a ba'

Section A
27 0:00

Powerful syncopations give a fierce character to the A section (the minuet), which is predominantly loud and in minor.

Section B
28 1:54

Later, Mozart increases the tension through polyphonic texture and striking dissonances. At the end of the A section, there is a sudden drop in dynamics; the flute, supported by oboes and a bassoon, softly recalls the opening melody of the minuet.

The trio section (B) brings a shift from minor to major, from fierce energy to graceful relaxation.

Return of section A
29 3:57

This change of mood is underscored by a soft dynamic level and pastoral woodwind interludes. After the trio, a sudden forte announces the return of the fierce A section.

Fourth Movement:
Allegro assai
Mozart ends the symphony with the tense movement already described in Section 3.

Basic Set:
CD 3 **30**

Piano Concerto No. 23 in A Major, K. 488 (1786)

Mozart's Piano Concerto in A Major—completed on March 2, 1786—dates from a very productive and successful period in his life. Between October 1785 and May 1786, he taught piano and composition; conducted operas; performed in concerts; and composed *The Marriage of Figaro,* the comic one-act opera *The Impresario,* two other great piano concertos (K. 482 in E Flat and K. 491 in C Minor), Quartet for Piano and Strings (K. 478), and *Masonic Funeral Music* (K. 477).

Mozart thought highly of the A Major piano concerto. In a letter to the court chamberlain of a prospective patron, he included it among "the compositions which I keep for myself or for a small circle of music-lovers and connoisseurs. . . ." Today, it is one of the best-known of his piano concertos.

Like all classical concertos, this one has three movements. The grace of the opening movement and the high spirits of the finale contrast with the melancholy of the middle movement. This concerto stresses poetry and delicacy rather than pianistic virtuosity or orchestral power. It is scored for an orchestra without trumpets or timpani and highlights the clarinets, flute, and bassoon. Mozart associated its key—A major—with tenderness, lyricism, and elegance. (He also used this key for the Clarinet Concerto and the duet between Don Giovanni and Zerlina in *Don Giovanni.*)

First Movement:
Allegro
Basic Set:
CD 4 **11**

Brief Set:
CD 3 **9**

The gentle opening movement blends lyricism with a touch of sadness, owing to many shifts between major and minor. Two main lyrical themes introduced by the orchestra in the first exposition are restated by the piano and orchestra in the second exposition. The development section is based on a new legato theme that is unexpectedly introduced by the orchestra after a dramatic pause. (In the listening outline, this is called the *development theme.*) Mozart creates a dramatic confrontation by juxtaposing fragments of this new theme, played by the woodwinds, with restless ideas in the piano and orchestra.

Toward the end of the allegro is a cadenza—an unaccompanied showpiece for the soloist. Exceptionally, Mozart notated the cadenza directly into the score, instead of leaving it to be improvised by the soloist. With its rapid sweeps up and down the keyboard, its alternation between brilliant and tender passages, and its concluding trill, this cadenza gives us some idea of how Mozart himself must have improvised.

LISTENING OUTLINE

MOZART, Piano Concerto No. 23 in A Major

First Movement: Allegro

Sonata form, quadruple meter (⁴/₄), A major

Solo piano, flute, 2 clarinets, 2 bassoons, 2 French horns, 1st violins, 2d violins, violas, cellos, double basses

(Duration, 11:36)

First exposition

First theme

11 **9** 0:00   **1. a.** Strings, *p*, gracious main melody, legato, major key,

          staccato ascent.

       0:16   **b.** Winds, *p*, repeat opening of main melody an octave higher. Strings, *f*, answered by winds; cadence to

Bridge

12 **10** 0:34   **2.** Full orchestra, *f*, vigorous bridge theme,

          running notes in violins, *f*. Brief pause.

Second theme group

13 **11** 0:58   **3. a.** Violins, *p*, tender second theme, repeated notes in dotted rhythm.

          b. Violins and bassoon, *p*, repeat second theme, flute joins.
          c. Agitated rhythms in minor lead to
      1:34   **d.** Full orchestra, *f*, major; winds alternate with violins, minor, crescendo to
          e. Full orchestra, *f*, major, cadence. Brief pause.
          f. High woodwind phrase, *p*, orchestral chords, *f*. Brief pause.

Second exposition

First theme

14 **12** 2:11   **1. a.** Piano solo, main melody, low strings join, violins introduce
          b. Piano, varied repetition of main melody, rapid downward and upward scales.

Bridge

      2:40   **2. a.** Full orchestra, *f*, bridge theme.
          b. Piano, running notes, with string accompaniment. High staccato violins, high staccato winds, downward scale in piano. Brief pause.

Second theme group

3:11   **3. a.** Piano solo, second theme, dolce.

      b. Violins and flute repeat second theme, piano joins.

3:42   **c.** Piano and orchestra.

3:53   **d.** Violins alternate with piano, minor.

      e. Piano, major. Long passage of running notes in piano culminating in short trill closing into

4:25   **4.** Full orchestra, opening of bridge theme. Sudden pause.

Development

15 **13** 4:39   **1. a.** Strings, *p*, legato development theme.

      b. Piano solo, development theme embellished by rapid notes.

5:05   **2. a.** Clarinet, fragment of development theme in minor, answered by piano and staccato strings.

5:13   **b.** Flute, fragment of development theme in major, answered by piano and staccato strings.

5:21   **c.** High woodwinds, development theme fragment in minor answered by piano, strings join with development theme fragment.

5:33   **3.** Piano continues with running notes; clarinet and flute, imitations of development theme fragment.

5:48   **4.** Strings, minor, repeatedly alternate with piano and woodwinds.

6:10   **5.** Piano solo, orchestra joins. Long descents and ascents, rising chromatic scale leads into

Recapitulation

First theme

16 **14** 6:30   **1. a.** Strings, *p*, main melody, woodwinds join.

      b. Piano *p*, with woodwinds, ornamented repeat of main melody in higher octave; piano scales lead to

Bridge

7:00   **2. a.** Full orchestra, *f*, bridge theme.

      b. Piano, running notes, strings accompany; staccato violins, high staccato winds, upward scale in piano. Brief pause.

Second theme group

7:30   **3. a.** Piano solo, second theme.

      b. Winds repeat second theme an octave higher, piano joins.

8:00   **c.** Piano and orchestra.

8:12   **d.** Violins alternate with piano, minor.

8:20   **e.** Piano, major, running-note passage interrupted by brief pause.

8:35   **4. a.** Piano alone, development theme.

      b. Clarinets and bassoons repeat development theme, accompanied by running notes in piano, staccato winds join, piano trill meshes with entrance of

9:19   **5. a.** Full orchestra, *f*, bridge theme; sudden brief pause.

9:32   **b.** Strings and winds, *p*, development theme. Full orchestra, *f*, dotted rhythm, briefly held chord.

Cadenza

17 **15** 9:48   **c.** Extended piano solo; long trill closes into

Coda

11:05   **6. a.** Full orchestra, *f*, cadence.

      b. High woodwind phrase, *p*; full orchestra; sudden *p* ending, trills in flutes and violins.

PERFORMANCE PERSPECTIVES

Murray Perahia, Pianist, Playing and Conducting the First Movement of Mozart's Piano Concerto in A Major, K. 488

Murray Perahia, one of the world's leading pianists, was born in New York City in 1947. Though he began to play the piano at age four, his major musical interest during his teens was conducting and composition, which he studied at Mannes College of Music in New York. His career as a piano soloist soared in 1972, when he became the first American to win the Leeds International Piano Competition in England. Starting in the 1980s, Perahia began to conduct from the piano in performances and recordings of works including the piano concertos of Mozart. (His performance of the first movement of Mozart's Piano Concerto in A Major, K. 488, is included in the recordings.)

In the early 1990s, a serious thumb injury forced Perahia to stop performing for several years. "You get very depressed when you can't play, because it's your way of communicating," he later recalled. "Bach was a solace to me. . . . There is something in his music that is life-fulfilling, life-affirming." After recovering from his injury, he made a series of award-winning Bach recordings. In 2004, Perahia was knighted for his musical achievements by Queen Elizabeth II in London, where he now lives.

Perahia feels that great "music has to appeal at many different levels—intellectually, emotionally, metaphysically, spiritually. Every note has to have a reason for being. A masterpiece must be inevitable." He believes that a sense of direction is crucially important in music. Music must not be static: "It should sound spontaneous, so that it never seems mechanical. And at the same time, it must have an inner logic."

Concerning the Piano Concerto in A Major, K. 488, Perahia emphasizes that it is very different from other concertos Mozart composed at that time (1786): "They were all more symphonic in dimension, military-sounding, and they had very virtuosic piano writing—robust and strong." By contrast, in the first movement of the Piano Concerto in A Major, "the piano writing is more melodic, more obviously lyrical." The movement's "passion and ardor" are akin to the world of romantic love depicted in operas by Mozart, such as *Così fan tutte.* "There is a constant give-and-take with the orchestra, the piano decorating ideas first stated by the orchestra." The movement evokes a world "in perfect concord, an idealized world—soon to be shattered by a slow movement whose depth of pain and despair is matched by its sublimity."

Second Movement:

Adagio

The extraordinary melancholy of this adagio is matched by its even more unusual key, F sharp minor. It is in three-part form: A (minor)—B (major)—A′ (minor)—coda. The piano alone introduces a sad main theme characterized by the dotted rhythmic pattern long-short-long and by expressive upward and downward leaps.

The orchestra continues with a minor-key theme of its own, imitated among the clarinet, bassoon, and flute.

Rounding off the A section is a touching piano melody that grows out of the themes heard earlier.

The sad mood of the second movement is somewhat lightened by its middle section, which begins with a graceful new theme in major played by the flute and clarinets.

A varied return of the opening section (A′) is followed by a reflective coda in which pizzicato strings accompany a piano melody that shifts expressively between high and low pitches.

Third Movement:
Allegro assai

The melancholy of the adagio is immediately dispelled by the exhilarating opening of the very rapid finale, which brings a return to major. This movement is in a special type of rondo form favored by Mozart: A B A′ (highly abridged) C B A. Each large section (A, B, and C) contains a rich variety of musical ideas and begins with a theme introduced by the piano and continued by the orchestra.

The exuberant main theme of section A opens with a three-note idea (short-short-long) that leaps downward and then upward.

In sections B and C there are delightful shifts between major and minor, and between piano and orchestra; and there are tuneful themes and running passages. Woodwinds are often given virtuoso passages. Section B contrasts a graceful opening idea in major presented by the piano

with a wistful contrasting theme in minor, introduced by the flute and bassoon.

Section C begins with a stormy piano passage in minor, but the mood changes when we hear a new playful theme in major, as though a comic character has come onstage.

The movement concludes brilliantly with a long-awaited return of A, in which the piano is more active. It is typical for late eighteenth-century music to end happily.

Requiem in D Minor, K. 626 (1791)

Although Mozart did not live to complete his monumental Requiem—a *requiem* is a mass for the dead—it is one of the finest sacred choral works of the classical period. It was commissioned anonymously by an unscrupulous nobleman who meant to claim the work as his own composition. In the last two months of his life, Mozart composed nine movements of the Requiem and part of a tenth. Reportedly, as his health grew worse, Mozart came to believe that the Requiem was for himself and tried to finish it on his deathbed. After Mozart died, his friend and pupil Franz Xaver Süssmayr filled out the often sketchy orchestration, completed the fragmentary section, and added four other movements. We do not know to what extent these additions represent the intentions of the dying Mozart. Süssmayr may have used sketches by Mozart which have not survived.

Mozart associated the Requiem's key of D minor with moods of foreboding, conflict, and tragedy. (He had used it in *Don Giovanni* for the somber opening of the overture and for the appearance of the statue of the Commandant at the end of the opera.) The solemnity is deepened by the dark colors in the orchestra, which is restricted to basset horns (low clarinets), bassoons, trumpets, trombones (traditional in sacred music), timpani, strings, and organ—with no lighter-sounding woodwinds such as flutes or clarinets. Mozart's Requiem includes movements for chorus, for soloists, and for a combination of both. It draws on a wide range of styles, from baroque fugues to almost operatic solos and ensembles.

We'll focus on the third movement, the *Dies irae* in D minor for chorus and orchestra.

Dies irae

Basic Set:
CD 4 [18]

Brief Set:
CD 3 [16]

The dramatic *Dies irae* (*Day of wrath*) is based on a thirteenth-century text which vividly describes the last judgment. Enormous tension is created by the key of D minor, by stormy rushing notes in the violins, and by the distinctive rhythmic pattern (long-long-short-short) of the opening phrase, which intensifies the word *irae* (*wrath*).

Most of the *Dies irae* is homophonic in texture, with all the voices singing in the same rhythm simultaneously. As the movement progresses, however, Mozart uses a change of texture to heighten the tension. A trill-like idea in the basses of the chorus in unison with the orchestra, representing the fearful trembling of *Quantus tremor est futurus* (*How great the trembling shall be*), is answered by the three higher voices in chords on *Dies irae* (*Day of wrath*).

Though it could have been written by no one but Mozart, the *Dies irae* has a baroque flavor and reflects his great admiration for Handel, whose *Messiah* he conducted and reorchestrated.

VOCAL MUSIC GUIDE

MOZART, *Dies irae,* from Requiem in D Minor

18 **16**

Chorus		*Dies irae, dies illa*	Day of wrath, day of mourning
		Solvet seculum in favilla:	Earth in smouldering ashes lying:
		Teste David cum Sibylla.	So spake David and the Sybil.
Orchestra briefly alone.			
	0:17	*Quantus tremor est futurus.*	How great the trembling shall be
		Quando judex est venturus,	when the judge shall come
		Cuncta stricte discussurus!	by whose sentence all shall be bound!
Orchestra alone.	0:32		
	0:38	*Dies irae, dies illa*	Day of wrath, day of mourning
		Solvet seculum in favilla:	Earth in smouldering ashes lying:
		Teste David cum Sibylla.	So spake David and the Sybil.
Orchestra briefly alone.			
	0:53	*Quantus tremor est futurus.*	How great the trembling shall be
		Quando judex est venturus,	when the judge shall come
		Cuncta stricte discussurus!	by whose sentence all shall be bound!
Basses, "trembling" figure twice answered by higher voices.	1:10	*Quantus tremor est futurus.*	How great the trembling shall be.
		Dies irae, dies illa	Day of wrath, day of mourning,
Basses answered by full chorus, "trembling" figure.	1:24	*Quantus tremor est futurus,*	How great the trembling shall be,
		Quantus tremor est futurus,	How great the trembling shall be
	1:32	*Quando judex est venturus,*	when the judge shall come
		Cuncta stricte discussurus!	by whose sentence all shall be bound!
Syncopated phrase exchanged between high and low voices.	1:40	*Cuncta stricte discussurus!*	by whose sentence all shall be bound!
Agitated orchestral close.	1:54		

Apart from Mozart's Requiem, the best-known requiem masses were written in the nineteenth century by the French composers Hector Berlioz and Gabriel Fauré, and the Italian composer Giuseppe Verdi. The term *requiem* has also been applied to choral works that honor the dead but are not masses, such as Johannes Brahms's *A German Requiem* (1868), which will be discussed in Part VI (Section 16); and Benjamin Britten's *War Requiem* (1962).

12 Ludwig van Beethoven

For many people, Ludwig van Beethoven (1770–1827) represents the highest level of musical genius. His unique stature is comparable to Shakespeare's in literature and Michelangelo's in painting and sculpture. He opened new realms of musical expression and profoundly influenced composers throughout the nineteenth century.

Beethoven was born on December 16, 1770, in Bonn, Germany. Like Bach and Mozart before him, he came from a family of musicians. His grandfather, also named Ludwig, was music director at the court at Bonn. His father, Johann, was a tenor who held a low position in the court and who saw his talented son as a profitable prodigy like Mozart. It's told that Johann van Beethoven and a musician friend would come home from the local tavern late at night, rouse young Ludwig from sleep, and make him practice at the keyboard until morning. At the age of eleven, Beethoven served as assistant to the court organist, and at twelve he had several piano compositions published.

Beethoven went to Vienna when he was sixteen to improvise for Mozart. Mozart reportedly said, "Keep your eyes on him; someday he will give the world something to talk about." Beethoven then returned to Bonn, because his mother was critically ill. She died shortly after. His father, who had become an alcoholic, was soon dismissed from the court choir. Beethoven, at eighteen, became the legal guardian of his two younger brothers. By now, Beethoven had become a court organist and violist and was responsible for composing and performing; suddenly, he was also head of a family.

Shortly before his twenty-second birthday, Beethoven left Bonn to study with Haydn in Vienna, where he spent the rest of his life. In 1792, Haydn was at the height of his fame, too busy composing to devote much time or energy to teaching. As a result, he overlooked errors in Beethoven's counterpoint exercises, and Beethoven felt compelled to go secretly to another teacher. (Haydn never learned of this.) Beethoven's drive for thoroughness and mastery—evident throughout his life—is shown by his willingness to subject himself to a strict course in counterpoint and fugue after he had already composed fine works.

Beethoven's first seven years in Vienna brought hard work, growing confidence, a strong sense of identity, and public praise. His letters of introduction from members of the aristocracy in Bonn opened the doors of the social and cultural elite in this music-loving city. People were dazzled by his piano virtuosity and moved by his improvisations. "He knew how to produce such an impression on every listener," reports a contemporary, "that frequently there was not a single dry eye, while many broke out into loud sobs, for there was a certain magic in his expression." Beethoven rebelled against social convention, asserting that an artist deserved as much respect as the nobility. Once, while playing in an aristocratic drawing room, he was disturbed by the loud conversation of a young count. Beethoven jumped up from the piano, exclaiming, "I will not play for such swine!" For a long time he was a guest of Prince Karl von Lichnowsky, who told his personal servant that if ever he and Beethoven rang at the same time, Beethoven should be served first. Aristocrats showered Beethoven with gifts, and he earned good fees from piano lessons and private concerts. Publishers were quick to buy his compositions, even though some critics complained that they were "bizarre" and "excessively complicated."

Disaster struck during his twenty-ninth year: Beethoven felt the first symptoms of deafness. Doctors could do nothing to halt its progress or to relieve Beethoven's physical and emotional torment. In 1801 he wrote despairingly, "For two years I have avoided almost all social gatherings because it is impossible for me to say to people 'I am deaf.' If I belonged to any other profession it would be easier, but in my profession it is a terrible handicap." On October 6, 1802, Beethoven was in Heiligenstadt, a village outside Vienna where he sought solitude during the summer. That day he expressed

Beethoven opened new realms of musical expression that profoundly influenced composers throughout the nineteenth century.

his feelings in what is now known as the *Heiligenstadt testament,* a long, agonized letter addressed to his brothers. Beethoven wrote, "I would have ended my life—it was only my art that held me back. Ah, it seemed to me impossible to leave the world until I had brought forth all that I felt was within me."

Beethoven's victory over despair coincided with an important change in his musical style. Works that he created after his emotional crisis have a new power and heroism. In 1803 he composed the gigantic Third Symphony, the *Eroica,* a landmark in music history. It is longer than any previous symphony written by him or by any other composer. At first, he planned to name it *Bonaparte,* after Napoleon, the first consul of the French Republic. Beethoven saw Napoleon as the embodiment of heroism and the champion of the principles underlying the French Revolution. *Liberty, equality, fraternity* were stirring words that expressed Beethoven's democratic ideals. But when he learned that Napoleon had proclaimed himself emperor of the French, Beethoven reportedly "flew into a rage and cried out, 'He too is nothing but an ordinary man! Now he will trample underfoot all the rights of man and only indulge his ambition. He will exalt himself above all others and become a tyrant!'" Sometime later Beethoven crossed out the words "titled Bonaparte" on his score, and when the symphony was published in 1806, it bore the title "Heroic Symphony composed to celebrate the memory of a great man."

In 1812, Beethoven met Johann Wolfgang von Goethe, the great German poet he had long worshipped. He played for Goethe, and the two artists walked and talked together. Shortly after this meeting, Goethe described Beethoven to a friend as "an utterly untamed personality." To his wife, the poet wrote, "Never before have I seen an artist with more power of concentration, more energy, more inwardness."

Despite such descriptions by people who knew him, Beethoven remains a mystery. He was self-educated and had read widely in Shakespeare and the ancient classics, but he was weak in elementary arithmetic. He claimed the highest moral principles, but he was often unscrupulous in dealing with publishers. Although orderly and methodical when composing, Beethoven dressed sloppily and lived in incredibly messy apartments. During his thirty-five years in Vienna, he changed dwellings about forty times.

Beethoven fell in and out of love with several women, mostly of noble birth, but was never able to form a lasting relationship. He wrote a passionate letter to a woman referred to as the "immortal beloved"; it was found in a drawer after his death. Only in 1972 did a Beethoven scholar establish her identity as the Viennese aristocrat Antonie Brentano. Beethoven took consolation from nature for disappointments in his personal life. Ideas came to him while he walked through the Viennese countryside. His Sixth Symphony, the *Pastoral,* beautifully expresses his recollections of life in the country.

Beethoven was never in the service of the Viennese aristocracy. A growing musical public made it possible for him to earn a fairly good income by selling compositions to publishers. His stature was so great that when he threatened to accept a position outside Austria in 1809, three nobles made a special arrangement to keep him in Vienna. Prince Kinsky, Prince Lobkowitz, and Archduke Rudolf—who was the emperor's brother and Beethoven's pupil—committed themselves to give Beethoven an annual income. Their only condition was that Beethoven continue to live in the Austrian capital—an unprecedented arrangement in music history.

As Beethoven's hearing weakened, so did his piano playing and conducting. By the time he was forty-four, this once brilliant pianist was forced to stop playing in public. But he insisted on conducting his orchestral works long after he could do it efficiently. The players would become confused by his wild gestures on the podium, and performances were often chaotic. His sense of isolation grew with his deafness. Friends had to communicate with him through an ear trumpet, and during his last eight years he carried notebooks in which people would write questions and comments.

In 1815, his brother Caspar died, leaving a nine-year-old son, Karl, to whom Beethoven and Caspar's widow became co-guardians. Young Karl was the object of a savage tug-of-war. For five years, Beethoven fought legal battles for exclusive custody of his nephew; he finally won. This "victory" was a disaster for everyone. Growing up in the household of a deaf, eccentric bachelor uncle is not easy at best, and for Karl it was complicated by Beethoven's craving for love and companionship. The young man attempted suicide, and Beethoven, whose health was already poor, was shattered.

During the first three years of legal battles over Karl, Beethoven composed less, and the Viennese began to whisper that he was finished. Beethoven heard the rumor and said, "Wait awhile; they'll soon learn differently!" And they did. After 1818, Beethoven's domestic problems did not prevent a creative outburst that produced some of his greatest works: the late piano sonatas and string quartets, the *Missa solemnis,* and the Ninth Symphony—out of total deafness, new realms of sound.

Beethoven's Music

"I must despise the world which does not know that music is a higher revelation than all wisdom and philosophy." For Beethoven, music was not mere entertainment, but a moral force capable of creating a vision of higher ideals. His music directly reflects his powerful, tortured personality. In both art and life, his heroic struggle resulted in victory over despair.

Beethoven's demand for perfection meant long and hard work. Unlike Mozart, he couldn't dash off three great symphonies in six weeks. Sometimes he worked for years on a single symphony, writing other works during the same period of time. He carried music sketchbooks everywhere, jotting down new ideas, revising and refining old ones. These early notes often seem crude and uninspired when compared with the final versions of his works, which were often hammered out through great labor.

Beethoven mostly used classical forms and techniques, but he gave them new power and intensity. The musical heir of Haydn and Mozart, he bridged the classical and romantic eras. Many of his innovations were used by composers who came after him.

In his works, great tension and excitement are built up through syncopations and dissonances. The range of pitch and dynamics is greater than ever before, so that contrasts of mood become more pronounced. Accents and climaxes seem titanic. Tiny rhythmic ideas are often repeated over and over to create momentum. Greater tension called for a larger musical framework, and so Beethoven expanded his forms. For example, as mentioned above, the Third Symphony (*Eroica*) is far longer than any symphony by Haydn or Mozart; it takes almost 50 minutes to perform. Beethoven was a musical architect who was unsurpassed in his ability to create large-scale structures in which every note seems inevitable. In describing Beethoven's music, it is perhaps too easy to give the impression that all of it is stormy and powerful. A lot is; but much is gentle, humorous, noble, or lyrical. His range of expression is enormous. Tempo, dynamic, and expressive indications are marked far more extensively in his scores than in those of earlier composers. For example, one direction reads, "Somewhat lively and with deepest feeling." Characteristic of his explicit dynamic markings is ⏝ *p*, a gradual increase in loudness followed by sudden softness.

More than his predecessors, Beethoven tried to unify the contrasting movements of a symphony, sonata, or string quartet. Musical continuity is heightened in his works in several ways. Sometimes one movement leads directly into the next, instead of ending with a pause, as was traditional. In the Fifth Symphony, for example, the last two movements are linked by a suspenseful bridge section. A musical bond between different movements of the same work is also created when their themes resemble each other. In a few compositions (the Fifth and Ninth Symphonies, for example), a theme from one movement is quoted in a later movement.

Like Haydn and Mozart, Beethoven wrote many movements in sonata form. In his works, however, the development section is greatly expanded and becomes even more dramatic. It often contains a powerful crescendo that leads to a climactic return of the first theme at the start of the recapitulation. The coda is also expanded and serves to develop themes still further. Its length balances what has come before and affirms the victory of the tonic key over the many new keys in the development section.

As the third movement of a symphony or string quartet, Beethoven most often used a scherzo rather than the traditional minuet. Where earlier composers had used a courtly dance, Beethoven composed a rapid movement with rhythmic drive. The character of the scherzo in Beethoven is flexible. In the Fifth Symphony, it's an ominous force, but in the Sixth Symphony (*Pastoral*), it depicts peasants' merrymaking. Beethoven's works often have a climactic, triumphant finale, toward which the previous movements seem to build. Beethoven's finales mark an important departure from the light, relaxed ending movement favored by Haydn and Mozart.

Beethoven's most popular works are the nine symphonies, which were conceived for larger orchestras than Haydn's or Mozart's. For greater power and brilliance, Beethoven sometimes added the trombone, piccolo, and contrabassoon—instruments that had not previously been used in symphonies. All the orchestral instruments must play difficult music. For example, the French horn has prominent melodies, and the timpani participate in the musical dialogue, rather than merely mark the beat.

Each of Beethoven's symphonies is unique in character and style. There is a curious alternation of mood between his odd-numbered symphonies (Symphonies No. 3, 5, 7, and 9), which tend to be forceful and assertive, and his even-numbered ones (Symphonies No. 4, 6, and 8), which are calmer and more lyrical. In the finale of the Ninth Symphony (*Choral*), Beethoven took the unprecedented step of using a chorus and four solo vocalists. They sing the text of Schiller's *Ode to Joy,* a poem about human brotherhood.

A hint of the virtuosity and improvisation that so astounded the Viennese can be found in Beethoven's thirty-two piano sonatas, which are far more difficult than the sonatas of Haydn and Mozart. They exploit the stronger, tonally improved piano of Beethoven's time. Beethoven drew many new effects from the piano, ranging from massive chords to the hollow, mystical sounds produced when the right and left hands play far apart on the keyboard. In the piano sonatas, he experimented with compositional techniques that he would later expand in the symphonies and string quartets.

Beethoven's sixteen string quartets, which span his entire career, are among the greatest music composed. They are unsurpassed in sheer invention, thematic treatment, and heartrending expressiveness. In three of the last quartets, Beethoven again stepped beyond the conventions of classical form: he used five, six, and seven movements (in Op. 132, Op. 130, and Op. 131, respectively), which he connected in subtle ways.

He also wrote five superb piano concertos, each remarkable in its individuality. In the Fourth and Fifth Piano Concertos, the opening movement begins with a brief piano solo rather than the traditional orchestral exposition.

While most of Beethoven's important works are for instruments, his sense of drama was also expressed in vocal music. In his only opera, *Fidelio,* a wife's heroism enables justice to triumph over tyranny. Beethoven also composed two masses. His *Missa solemnis (Solemn Mass,* 1819–1823) is one of the most monumental and expressive settings of this sacred text.

Beethoven's total output is usually divided into three periods: early (up to 1802), middle (1803–1814), and late (1815–1827). The music of Haydn and Mozart influenced some works of the early period, but other pieces clearly show Beethoven's personal style. The compositions of the middle period are longer and tend to be heroic in tone. And the sublime works of the last period well up from the depths of a man almost totally deaf. During this period Beethoven often used the fugue to express new musical concepts. The late works contain passages that sound surprisingly harsh and "modern." When a violinist complained that the music was very difficult to play, Beethoven reportedly replied, "Do you believe that I think of a wretched fiddle when the spirit speaks to me?"

Piano Sonata in C Minor, Op. 13 (*Pathétique;* 1798)

The title *Pathétique,* coined by Beethoven, suggests the tragically passionate character of his famous Piano Sonata in C Minor, Op. 13. Beethoven's impetuous playing and masterful improvisational powers are mirrored in the sonata's extreme dynamic contrasts, explosive accents, and crashing chords. At the age of twenty-seven, during his early period, Beethoven had already created a powerful and original piano style that foreshadowed nineteenth-century romanticism.

First Movement:
Grave (solemn, slow introduction);
Allegro molto e con brio (very fast and brilliant allegro)

Basic Set:
CD 4 19

The *Pathétique* begins in C minor with an intense, slow introduction, dominated by an opening motive in dotted rhythm: long-short-long-short-long-long.

19 0:00

This six-note idea seems to pose a series of unresolved questions as it is repeated on higher and higher pitch levels. The tragic mood is intensified by dissonant chords, sudden contrasts of dynamics and register, and pauses filled with expectancy. The slow introduction is integrated in imaginative and dramatic ways into the allegro that follows it.

20 1:41

The tension of the introduction is maintained in the allegro con brio, a breathless, fast movement in sonata form. The opening theme, in C minor, begins with a staccato idea that rapidly rises up a 2-octave scale. It is accompanied by low broken octaves, the rapid alternation of two tones an octave apart.

1:57

Growing directly out of the opening theme is a bridge that is also built from a climbing staccato motive.

This bridge motive has an important role later in the movement.

21 2:08

The contrasting second theme, which enters without a pause, is spun out of a short motive that is repeatedly shifted between low and high registers.

This restless idea begins in E flat minor but then moves through different keys. The exposition is rounded off by several themes, including a high running passage and a return of the opening staccato idea in E flat major.

22 2:53

23 3:11

The development section begins with a dramatic surprise: Beethoven brings back the opening bars of the slow introduction. This reappearance creates an enormous contrast of tempo, rhythm, and mood. After four bars of slow music, the fast tempo resumes as Beethoven combines two different ideas: the staccato bridge motive and a quickened version of the introduction motive. The introduction motive is presented in a rhythmically altered form: short-short-short-long-long.

3:54

The bridge motive is then developed in the bass, played by the pianist's left hand while the right hand plays high broken octaves. After several high accented notes, the brief development concludes with a running passage that leads down to the recapitulation.

For a while, the recapitulation runs its usual course as themes from the exposition are presented in the tonic key of C minor. But Beethoven has one more surprise for the coda—after a loud dissonant chord and a brief pause, he again brings back the opening of the slow introduction. This time the slow music is even more moving, as it is punctuated by moments of silence. Then the fast tempo resumes, and the opening staccato idea and powerful chords bring the movement to a decisive close.

Second Movement:
Adagio cantabile (lyrical adagio)

The second movement, in A flat major, is slow, intimate, and songlike. It is in rondo form and may be outlined A B A C A—coda. The legato main theme (A), played in the piano's rich middle register, is one of Beethoven's most lyrical melodies.

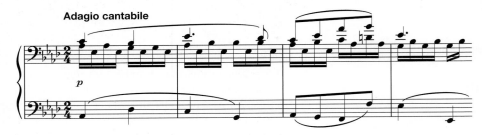

This melody is immediately repeated an octave higher with fuller harmony.

Section B
27 1:11

Section C
28 2:42

Return of Section A
29 3:44

Section B is also legato and maintains the opening mood while introducing a new accompaniment of repeated chords. Section C is a duet between tender legato phrases in the top part and more animated staccato replies in the bass. This section brings some contrast with a shift to minor, a powerful crescendo, and a triplet rhythm in the accompaniment. On its last return, the main melody sounds more flowing, because it is now accompanied by a rocking figure in triplet rhythm. The movement is rounded off by a poetic coda that descends leisurely to soft concluding chords.

Third Movement:
Rondo (Allegro)

The last movement, in C minor, is a rapid and energetic rondo. It is outlined A B A C A B A—coda. The lively main theme (A), in minor, contrasts with the other sections, which are in major.

Section B
31 0:25

Section C
32 1:26

End of coda
33 3:50

The B section includes several lyrical themes. The C section is polyphonic and contains ideas that are shifted from one hand to the other. Sections B and C both end with a sustained dominant chord that creates expectancy for the return of the main theme and key. Toward the end of the stormy coda, a sustained chord is followed unexpectedly by the opening notes of the main theme, in major rather than minor.

But the consolation of major is brief, as a rapid downward scale brings the movement to a powerful close in C minor.

Symphony No. 5 in C Minor, Op. 67 (1808)

The Fifth Symphony opens with one of the most famous rhythmic ideas in all music, a short-short-short-long motive. Beethoven reportedly explained this four-note motive as "fate knocking at the door." It dominates the first movement and also plays an important role later in the symphony. The entire work can be seen as an emotional progression from the conflict and struggle of the first movement, in C minor, to the exultation and victory of the final movement, in C major. The finale is the climax of the symphony; it is longer than the first movement and more powerful in sound.

Through several different techniques, Beethoven brilliantly welds four contrasting movements into a unified work. The basic rhythmic motive of the first movement (short-short-short-long) is used in a marchlike theme in the third movement. And this third-movement theme is later quoted dramatically within the finale. The last two movements are also connected by a bridge passage.

Beethoven jotted down a few themes for the Fifth Symphony in 1804 but mainly worked on it during 1807 and 1808, an amazingly productive period when he also composed his Mass in C Major; Sonata for Cello and Piano, Op. 69; and Symphony No. 6.

First Movement:
Allegro con brio (allegro with vigor)

Basic Set:
CD 4 **34**

Brief Set:
CD 3 17

The allegro con brio is an enormously powerful and concentrated movement in sonata form. Its character is determined by a single rhythmic motive, short-short-short-long, from which Beethoven creates an astonishing variety of musical ideas. Tension and expectation are generated from the very beginning of the movement. Three rapid notes of the same pitch are followed by a downward leap to a held, suspenseful tone. This powerful idea is hammered out twice by all the strings in unison; the second time, it is a step lower in pitch.

As the opening theme continues in C minor, Beethoven maintains excitement by quickly developing his basic idea. He crowds varied repetitions of the motive together and rapidly shifts the motive to different pitches and instruments.

The second theme, in E flat major, dramatically combines different ideas. It begins with an unaccompanied horn call that asserts the basic motive in a varied form (short-short-short-long-long-long).

This horn-call motive announces a new legato melody, which is calm and contrasts with the preceding agitation. Yet even during this lyrical moment, we are not allowed to forget the basic motive; now it is muttered in the background by cellos and double basses.

Beethoven generates tension in the development section by breaking the horn-call motive into smaller and smaller fragments until it is represented by only a single tone. Supported by a chord, this tone is echoed between woodwinds and strings in a breathtaking decrescendo. The recapitulation comes as a tremendous climax as the full orchestra thunders the basic motive. The recapitulation also brings a new expressive oboe solo at the end of the first theme. The heroic closing section of the recapitulation, in C major, moves without a break into a long and exciting coda in C minor. This coda is like a second development section in which the basic motive creates still greater power and energy.

LISTENING OUTLINE

BEETHOVEN, Symphony No. 5

First Movement: Allegro con brio

Sonata form, duple meter (2/4), C minor

2 flutes, 2 oboes, 2 clarinets, 2 bassoons, 2 French horns, 2 trumpets, timpani, 1st violins, 2d violins, violas, cellos, double basses

(Duration, 7:07)

Exposition

First theme

34 **17** 0:00   **1. a.** Basic motive, *ff*, repeated a step lower, strings in unison.

0:08   **b.** Sudden *p*, strings quickly develop basic motive, minor key, powerful chords, high held tone.

Bridge

35 **18** 0:20   **2. a.** Basic motive, *ff*, orchestra in unison.

0:24   **b.** Sudden *p*, strings quickly develop basic motive, crescendo, *ff*, powerful chords.

Second theme

36 **19** 0:44   **3. a.** Solo French horns, *ff*, horn-call motive.

0:47   **b.** Violins, *p*, lyrical melody in major. Basic motive accompanies in low strings.

Crescendo to

37 **20** 1:06   **4. a.** Triumphant melody, *ff*, violins.

38	**21**	1:15

1:24

b. Woodwinds and horns, basic motive rushes downward. Cadences in basic rhythm. Pause. Exposition is repeated.

Development

39	**22**	2:48

1. a. Basic motive, **_ff_**, horns, strings.

  b. Sudden **_p_**, strings and woodwinds, basic motive quickly developed. Motive climbs to rapidly repeated chords, **_ff_**.

3:22

2. a. Violins, **_ff_**, horn-call motive, low strings, descending line.

3:32

  b. High woodwinds, **_ff_**, in dialogue with lower strings, **_ff_**. Horn-call motive broken into tiny fragments. Decrescendo to **_pp_**.

3:52

  c. Sudden **_ff_**, horn-call rhythm.

  d. Sudden **_pp_**, woodwinds echoed by strings.

  e. Sudden **_ff_**, repeated motive drives into

Recapitulation

First theme

40	**23**	4:05

1. a. Climactic basic motive, full orchestra, **_ff_**, repeated a step lower.

  b. Sudden **_p_**, strings quickly develop basic motive, minor key, chords lead to

4:21

  c. Oboe solo.

Bridge

4:38

2. Basic motive quickly developed in strings, crescendo to **_ff_**, full orchestra.

Second theme

4:58

3. a. Horn-call motive, solo bassoons, **_ff_**.

  b. Lyrical major melody, **_p_**, violins and flutes alternate. Basic motive accompanies in timpani, **_p_**. Crescendo to

5:25

4. a. Triumphant melody, **_ff_**, violins.

  b. Woodwinds, basic motive rushes downward. Cadences in basic rhythm.

Coda

41	**24**	5:41

1. a. Rapidly repeated chords, **_ff_**.

5:55   **b.** Horn-call motive, lower strings, *f*, with higher violin melody, minor.

            Descending violin melody, staccato, leads to
6:10   **2. a.** New, rising theme in strings, legato and staccato.

6:20   **b.** High woodwinds, *ff*, answered by lower strings in powerful interchange. Rapidly repeated
            notes lead to
6:42   **3. a.** Basic motive, *ff*, repeated a step lower, full orchestra.
            b. Sudden *p*, basic motive quickly developed in strings and woodwinds.
            c. Sudden *ff*, powerful concluding chords.

Second Movement:
Andante con moto (moderately slow, with movement)

The second movement, in A flat major, is mostly relaxed and lyrical, but it includes moments of tension and heroism. It is an extended set of variations based on two themes. The main theme (A), softly introduced by the cellos and violas, is a long, legato melody of great nobility. The second theme (B) begins very gently in the clarinets but soon brings a startling contrast of mood. The full orchestra suddenly bursts in, and the clarinet melody is transformed into a triumphant trumpet fanfare. A hushed transitional passage then leads back to the main theme, presented now in quicker notes.

After several variations, there is a middle section in which fragments of the themes are treated in new ways. Woodwind instruments are featured, and there is a brief episode in minor. The movement concludes with a final variation of the main melody—now majestically proclaimed by the full orchestra—and a coda that poetically recalls what has come before.

Basic Set:
CD 4 42

Brief Set:
CD 3 25

LISTENING OUTLINE

BEETHOVEN, Symphony No. 5

Second Movement: Andante con moto

Theme and variations, triple meter ($\frac{3}{8}$), A flat major

2 flutes, 2 oboes, 2 clarinets, 2 bassoons, 2 French horns, 2 trumpets, timpani, 1st violins, 2d violins, violas, cellos, double basses

(Duration, 9:58)

Theme A

`42` `25` 0:00

1. Lyrical melody, violas and cellos, *p*.

Melody continues in higher register, violins alternate with flute.

Theme B

`43` `26` 0:55

2. a. Clarinets, *p*, rising phrases.

Violins, *pp*, sudden *ff*, full orchestra.

1:17   **b.** Trumpets, *ff*, rising phrases.

Violins, *pp*, sustained notes.

Variation A¹

`44` `27` 2:02

3. Violas and cellos, *p*, lyrical melody in even-flowing rhythm.

Melody continues in higher register, violins alternate with flute.

Variation B¹

2:54   **4. a.** Clarinets, *p*, rising phrases. Violins, *pp*, sudden *ff*, full orchestra.

3:16   **b.** Trumpets, *ff*, rising phrases. Violins, *pp*, sustained notes, cellos, low repeated notes.

Variation A²

`45` `28` 4:01

5. a. Violas and cellos, *p*, lyrical melody decorated by quick, even-flowing notes.

4:18   **b.** Violins, *pp*, repeat decorated melody in higher register.

4:38   **c.** Loud repeated chords, decorated melody in cellos and double basses. Upward scales lead to high held tone.

Middle Section

`46` `29` 5:03

6. Sudden *pp*, repeated string chords, clarinet phrase passed to bassoon and flute. High woodwind interlude leads to

5:58	**7. a.** Full orchestra, ***ff***, rising phrases, timpani rolls.
6:22	**b.** Strings, ***p***, repeated short figure.
6:44	**8. a.** Woodwinds, ***p***, staccato variation of lyrical melody, minor key.
7:05	**b.** Rising scales in flute, strings. Crescendo.

Variation A³

47 **30** 7:25   **9.** Full orchestra, ***ff***, lyrical melody in high register, major key, rising scales. Flute and violins, ***p***, continue melody.

Coda

8:13	**10. a.** Più mosso (faster tempo), bassoon, ***p***, variation of lyrical phrase. Violins, crescendo.
8:38	**b.** Original tempo, flute and strings, ***pp***, conclusion of lyrical melody.
9:09	**c.** Clarinets, ***p***, variation of lyrical phrase, low strings, crescendo. Cadence in full orchestra, ***ff***.

Basic Set:
CD 4 **48**

Brief Set:
CD 3 **31**

Section A
48 **31** 0:00

Section B
49 **32** 1:48

Section A'
50 **33** 3:15

Bridge
51 **34** 4:27

Third Movement:
Allegro (scherzo)

The rapid third movement is a scherzo, in C minor, with three sections: A (scherzo) B (trio) A′ (scherzo). The scherzo opens with a hushed, mysterious broken-chord theme played by cellos and double basses in a low register.

Soon, in sharp contrast, a bold repeated-note theme is hammered out loudly by the horns.

This theme is dominated by the rhythmic pattern short-short-short-long and recalls the basic motive of the first movement.

The B section (trio), in major, brings a gruff, hurried theme, played by cellos and double basses.

This theme is imitated, in the style of a fugue, by each of the higher strings. The bustling rhythmic motion of the B section has a feeling of energy and rough humor.

When the scherzo section (A′) returns, it is hushed and ominous throughout, sounding like a ghost of its former self. The mysterious opening theme is now played pizzicato rather than legato. The repeated-note theme is completely transformed in mood; it is no longer proclaimed by horns but is whispered by clarinets, plucked violins, and oboe.

One of the most extraordinary passages in the symphony follows the scherzo section (A′): a bridge leading from the dark, mysterious world of the scherzo to the bright sunlight of the finale. It opens with a feeling of suspended animation as the timpani softly repeat a single tone against a sustained chord in the strings. Over the timpani pulsation, the violins hesitantly play a fragment of the mysterious scherzo theme. Tension mounts as this fragment is carried higher and higher, until a sudden crescendo climaxes with the heroic opening of the finale.

Fourth Movement:
Allegro

The fourth movement, in sonata form, is the climax of the symphony. It brings the victory of C major over C minor, of optimism and exultation over struggle and uncertainty. For greater power and brilliance, Beethoven enlarged the orchestra in the finale to include three trombones, a piccolo, and a contrabassoon. Brass instruments are especially prominent and give a marchlike character to much of the movement.

The exposition is rich in melodic ideas; even the bridge has a theme of its own, and there is also a distinctive closing theme. The triumphant opening theme begins with the three tones of the C major triad, brilliantly proclaimed by the trumpets.

Basic Set:
CD 4 52

Brief Set:
CD 3 35

52 35 0:00

53 36 0:36

A bridge theme, similar in mood to the opening theme, is announced by the horns and continued by the violins.

54 37 1:05

Triplets lend a joyous quality to the second theme, which contrasts loud and soft phrases.

55 38 1:34

Two powerful chords and a brief pause announce the closing theme of the exposition. This melody, composed of descending phrases, is first played by the strings and woodwinds and then forcefully repeated by the entire orchestra.

56 39 2:07
57 40 3:47

The development focuses mainly on the second theme and its triplet rhythm. A huge climax at the end of the development is followed by one of the most marvelous surprises in all music. Beethoven dramatically quotes the whispered repeated-note theme (short-short-short-long) of the preceding scherzo movement. This ominous quotation is like a sudden recollection of past anxiety, and it creates a connection between the last two movements. Leading into the powerful recapitulation of the fourth movement, it prepares for the renewal of the victory over uncertainty.

Recapitulation
4:18

Coda
58 41 6:26

During the long coda of the finale, earlier themes are heard in altered and quickened versions. Several times, the music keeps going even though the listener thinks it's coming to an end. Over and over, Beethoven affirms the tonic key and resolves the frenzied tensions built up during the symphony. Such control over tension is an essential element of Beethoven's genius.

The Classical Period: Summary

Music in Society

- Composers strove to write music that would appeal simultaneously to amateurs and learned connoisseurs.
- The growing middle class, who had greater access to education, financial stability, and leisure time than ever before, fueled a demand for public concerts.
- Composers increasingly broke from the patronage system to seek their fortune as freelance musicians.
- The aristocracy and middle class considered training in music an important educational skill.
- Music making in the home became increasingly important.

Important Style Features

Mood and Emotional Expression

- Classical music features fluctuations of mood within a movement.
- Changes in mood may occur gradually or suddenly, but are always firmly controlled by the composer and typically fall within a tastefully acceptable emotional range.
- Music was expected to be immediately appealing, pleasing, natural-sounding, and tasteful.

Rhythm

- Numerous rhythmic patterns provide variety and contrast.
- Unexpected pauses, syncopations, and frequent changes between long notes and shorter notes also provide variety and contrast.
- Rhythmic changes occur suddenly or gradually.

Dynamics

- Dynamics change gradually or suddenly, enabling the expression of highly varied emotional nuances within one movement.

Tone Color

- The characteristic sound of an orchestra with four families of instruments (strings, woodwinds, brass, and percussion) of approximately twenty-five to sixty players gradually became the standard.
- Wind and brass instruments were used in the orchestra to provide contrasts of timbre.
- The most important form of classical chamber music was the string quartet, written for two violins, viola, and cello.

Melody and Harmony

- Melodies are tuneful and easily remembered after one or two hearings.
- Phrases often occur in pairs, with the first phrase ending with an incomplete cadence and the second phrase ending more conclusively.
- Classical melodies may be broken into fragments or motives that undergo development to explore different moods.
- Harmonies are based on major and minor scales.
- Dissonance is used to provide contrast, suspense, or excitement.

Texture

- Texture is predominantly homophonic.
- Fluctuations of texture occur to provide contrasts; a piece may shift gradually or suddenly from one texture to another.

Performance Practice

- During the classical era, the use of the characteristic baroque basso continuo was gradually abandoned.
- The piano, able to create subtle dynamic changes through varied finger pressure on the keys, became favored over the harpsichord.
- An increase in the number of amateur musicians, unable to improvise an accompaniment at the keyboard from a figured bass, led to simpler accompaniments written out by the composer.
- Audiences were keenly aware of differences in musical style, and they expected music to be composed for specific performers so as to capitalize on their musical strengths.
- Regarding cadenzas in concertos for solo instrument by Mozart, performers must choose between using one composed by Mozart (if one exists), using one by another composer, or creating one.

FEATURED FORMS

- Sonata form, p. 193
- Theme and variations, p. 197
- Minuet and trio, p. 199
- Scherzo, p. 200
- Rondo, p. 201
- Sonata-rondo, p. 201

MAJOR COMPOSERS

Three composers, all of whom were active in Vienna at some time during their lives, dominate the classical era:

- Joseph Haydn (1732–1809)
- Wolfgang Amadeus Mozart (1756–1791)
- Ludwig van Beethoven (1770–1827)

Beyond the Classroom: Attending an Orchestra Concert

Haydn, Mozart, Beethoven, and their contemporaries established and developed the symphony by composing numerous symphonies that are still performed today, but later eras adapted the model to fit their own aesthetic vision, producing a symphonic repertoire that today is vast and richly diverse. On any given evening, thousands of people around the world can be found at concerts featuring symphony orchestras, many of which have their own unique and distinctive histories extending back more than a century.

When you attend an orchestra concert, check to see if a program is available. Usually the program specifies the name of the orchestra, its conductor, and any featured soloists, as well as the specific repertoire programmed for that evening. Some programs even list the specific instrumentation for each selection. Pay close attention to what you hear at any moment, and ask yourself the following questions:

- Does the program include a symphony, a concerto, or some other type of orchestral work? Does a work contain separate movements?
- Does the program include classical composers other than the "big three"?
- What is the specific orchestration of each selection? Pay particular attention to see if the number and kind of instruments change between different compositions.
- Are there any sections where one instrument within the orchestra plays a memorable melody or is featured in some special way?
- Is a soloist featured on the program, and if so, who is performing and on which instrument? If a concerto is on the program, do the program notes indicate which cadenza is being used?
- In a piano concerto, is the work played on a modern piano or on a replica of an early piano (fortepiano)?

The Romantic Period

The prevailing qualities of my music are passionate expressiveness, inner fire, rhythmic drive, and unexpectedness.

—*Hector Berlioz*

Romantic painters and musicians often saw political revolution as a reflection of their own struggles for artistic freedom. In *Liberty Leading the People* (1830), the French painter Eugène Delacroix combined a realistic description of street fighting in Paris during the July Revolution of 1830 with a symbolic representation of liberty.

251

Romantic Period (1820–1900)

1820–1850	1850–1900

Historical and Cultural Events

1823 Monroe Doctrine

1830 Revolutions in France, Belgium, Poland

1837–1901 Queen Victoria reigns in England

1848 Revolutions in Europe

1848 Marx and Engels, *The Communist Manifesto*

1859 Darwin, *Origin of Species*

1861–1865 American Civil War

1870 Franco-Prussian War

1876 Bell invents telephone

1898 Spanish-American War

Arts and Letters

1819 Keats, *Ode to a Nightingale*

1822 Delacroix, *Dante and Virgil in Hell*

1830 Delacroix, *Liberty Leading the People*

1831 Hugo, *The Hunchback of Notre Dame*

1835 Friedrich, *The Evening Star*

1837 Dickens, *Oliver Twist*

1840 Turner, *The Slave Ship*

1844 Dumas, *The Three Musketeers*

1845 Poe, *The Raven*

1857 Millet, *The Gleaners*

1866 Dostoevsky, *Crime and Punishment*

1874 Monet, *Impression, Sunrise*

1877 Cézanne, *Still Life with Apples*

1877 Tolstoy, *Anna Karenina*

1884 Twain, *The Adventures of Huckleberry Finn*

1889 van Gogh, *The Starry Night*

1893 Munch, *The Scream*

Music

1815 Franz Schubert, *Erlkönig*

1830 Berlioz, *Symphonie fantastique*

1831 Chopin, Nocturne in E♭ Major, Op. 9, No. 2

c. 1831 Chopin, Étude in C Minor, Op. 10, No. 12 (*Revolutionary*)

1835 Robert Schumann, *Carnaval*

1839 Clara Wieck Schumann, Romance in E♭ Minor for Piano, Op. 11, No. 1

1842 Chopin, Polonaise in A♭ Major, Op. 53

1844 Mendelssohn, Violin Concerto in E Minor, Op. 64

1851 Liszt, *Transcendental* Étude in F Minor

1851 Verdi, *Rigoletto*

1856 Wagner, *Die Walküre*

1868 Brahms, *German Requiem*

1870 Tchaikovsky, *Romeo and Juliet*

1874 Smetana, *The Moldau*

1893 Dvořák, Symphony No. 9 in E Minor (From *the New World*)

1896 Puccini, *La Bohème*

ROMANTICISM (1820-1900)

The early nineteenth century brought the flowering of romanticism, a cultural movement that stressed emotion, imagination, and individuality. In part, romanticism was a rebellion against the neoclassicism of the eighteenth century and the age of reason. Romantic writers broke away from time-honored conventions and emphasized freedom of expression. Romantic painters used bolder, more brilliant colors and preferred dynamic motion to gracefully balanced poses.

But romanticism was too diverse and complex to be defined by any single formula. It aimed to broaden horizons and encompass the totality of human experience. The romantic movement was international in scope and influenced all the arts.

Emotional subjectivity was a basic quality of romanticism in art. "All good poetry is the spontaneous overflow of powerful feelings," wrote William Wordsworth, the English romantic poet. And "spontaneous overflow" made much romantic literature autobiographical; authors projected their personalities in their work. Walt Whitman, the American poet, expressed this subjective attitude beautifully when he began a poem, "I celebrate myself, and sing myself."

In exploring their inner lives, the romantics were especially drawn to the realm of fantasy: the unconscious, the irrational, the world of dreams. Romantic fiction includes tales of horror and the supernatural, such as *The Cask of Amontillado,* by Edgar Allan Poe; and *Frankenstein,* by Mary Wollstonecraft Shelley. The writer Thomas De Quincey vividly describes his drug-induced dreams in *Confessions of an English Opium-Eater:* "I was buried, for a thousand years, in stone coffins, with mummies and sphinxes. I was kissed, with cancerous kisses, by crocodiles." The visual arts also depict nightmarish visions. In an etching called *The Sleep of Reason Breeds Monsters,* the Spanish painter Francisco Goya shows batlike monsters surrounding a sleeping figure. The realm of the unknown and

Romantic artists often depicted scenes of extreme violence and suffering. In *The Raft of the Medusa* (1819), the French painter Théodore Géricault conveyed the epic tragedy of a contemporary shipwreck. The ship captain—appointed only because of his noble birth—saved himself and other officers, while abandoning many other survivors to their horrible fate on a primitive raft.

Emotional subjectivity was a basic quality of romanticism. A portrait of the Polish composer and pianist Frédéric Chopin by Eugène Delacroix.

The Gleaners (1857) by Jean-François Millet. The industrial revolution caused vast social and economic changes and awakened interest in the poor. The French painter Millet portrayed the labor of peasant women picking up leftover grain in the fields.

Eugène Delacroix's painting *Dante and Virgil in Hell* (1822) depicts the agony of the damned. The romantics were also drawn to the realm of the supernatural and took inspiration from literary works such as Dante's *Inferno.*

The Evening Star (1830–1835), by the German painter Caspar David Friedrich. The romantics were especially drawn to the realm of fantasy: the unconscious, the irrational, and the world of dreams.

Salisbury Cathedral from the Meadows, Royal Academy, 1831, by John Constable. Of all the inspirations for romantic art, none was more important than nature.

the exotic also interested the French artist Eugène Delacroix, who often depicted violent scenes in far-off lands.

The romantic fascination with fantasy was paired with enthusiasm for the Middle Ages, that time of chivalry and romance. Whereas neoclassicists had thought of the medieval period as the "dark ages," the romantics cherished it. They were inspired by medieval folk ballads and by tales of fantasy and adventure. Romantic novels set in the Middle Ages include *Ivanhoe* (1819), by Walter Scott; and *The Hunchback of Notre Dame* (1831), by the French writer Victor Hugo. Gothic cathedrals, which had long gone unappreciated, now seemed picturesque and mysterious. A "gothic revival" in architecture resulted in the construction of buildings such as the houses of Parliament in London (1836–1852) and Trinity Church in New York (1839–1846).

Of all the inspirations for romantic art, none was more important than nature. The physical world was seen as a source of consolation and a mirror of the human heart. Wordsworth, for example, thought of nature as "the nurse,/the guide, the guardian of my heart, and soul." One of his poems begins:

> There was a time when meadow,
>   grove, and stream,
>   The earth, and every common
>   sight,
>   To me did seem
>   Apparelled in celestial light,
> The glory and the freshness of a
>   dream.

The romantic sensitivity to nature is revealed in landscape painting, which attained new importance. Artists like John Constable and J. M. W. Turner in England were masters at conveying movement in nature: rippling brooks, drifting clouds, stormy seas. In Turner's seascapes, the sweep of waves expresses not only the grandeur of nature, but human passion as well.

Romanticism coincided with the industrial revolution, which caused vast social and economic changes. Many writers and painters recorded the new social realities of their time. The novels of Charles Dickens and the paintings of Honoré Daumier reflect an interest in the working class and the poor.

Subjectivity, fantasy, and enthusiasm for nature and the Middle Ages are only a few aspects of romanticism in literature and painting. We'll now focus on romanticism in music.

1 Romanticism in Music
(1820–1900)

The romantic period in music extended from about 1820 to 1900. Among the most significant romantic musicians were Franz Schubert, Robert Schumann, Clara Wieck Schumann, Frédéric Chopin, Franz Liszt, Felix Mendelssohn, Hector Berlioz, Peter Ilyich Tchaikovsky, Bedřich Smetana, Antonin Dvořák, Johannes Brahms, Giuseppe Verdi, Giacomo Puccini, Richard Wagner, and Gustav Mahler. The length of this list—and some important composers have been omitted from it—testifies to the richness and variety of romantic music and to its continuing impact on today's concert and operatic repertoire.

Composers of the romantic period continued to use the musical forms of the preceding classical era. The emotional intensity associated with romanticism was already present in the work of Mozart and particularly in that of Beethoven, who greatly influenced composers after him. The romantic preference for expressive, songlike melody also grew out of the classical style.

Nonetheless, there are many differences between romantic and classical music. Romantic works tend to have greater ranges of tone color, dynamics, and pitch. Also, the romantic harmonic vocabulary is broader, with more emphasis on colorful, unstable chords. Romantic music is linked more closely to the other arts, particularly to literature. New forms developed, and in all forms there was greater tension and less emphasis on balance and resolution. But romantic music is so diverse that generalizations are apt to mislead. Some romantic composers, such as Mendelssohn and Brahms, created works that were deeply rooted in classical tradition; other composers, such as Berlioz, Liszt, and Wagner, were more revolutionary.

Characteristics of Romantic Music

Individuality of Style Romantic music puts unprecedented emphasis on self-expression and individuality of style. There is "not a bar which I have not truly felt and which is not an echo of my innermost feelings," wrote Tchaikovsky of his Fourth Symphony. A "new world of music" was the goal of the young Chopin. Many romantics created music that sounds unique and reflects their personalities. As Robert Schumann observed, "Chopin will soon be unable to write anything without people crying out at the seventh or eighth bar, 'That is indeed by him.'" And today, with some listening experience, a music lover can tell within a few minutes—sometimes within a few seconds—whether a piece is by Schumann or Chopin, Tchaikovsky or Brahms.

Expressive Aims and Subjects The romantics explored a universe of feeling that included flamboyance and intimacy, unpredictability and melancholy, rapture and longing. Countless songs and operas glorify romantic love; often, the lovers are unhappy and face overwhelming obstacles. Fascination with the fantastic and diabolical is expressed in music like the *Dream of a Witches' Sabbath* from Berlioz's *Symphonie fantastique* (*Fantastic Symphony*). All aspects of nature attracted romantic musicians. In different sections of Part VI we'll study music that depicts shepherds' pipes and distant thunder (Berlioz's *Fantastic Symphony*), a wild horseback ride on a stormy night (Schubert's *Erlkönig,* or *Erlking*), the flow of a river (Smetana's *Moldau*), and a walk in the countryside (Mahler's *Ging heut' Morgen über's Feld*). Romantic composers also dealt with subjects drawn from the Middle Ages and from Shakespeare's plays.

Nationalism and Exoticism Nationalism was an important political movement that influenced nineteenth-century music. Musical **nationalism** was expressed when romantic composers deliberately created music with a specific national identity, using the folk songs, dances, legends, and history of their homelands. This national flavor of romantic music—whether Polish, Russian, Bohemian (Czech), or German—contrasts with the more universal character of classical music.

Fascination with national identity also led composers to draw on colorful materials from foreign lands, a trend known as musical *exoticism.* For instance, some composers wrote melodies in an Asian style or used rhythms and instruments associated with distant lands. The French composer Georges Bizet wrote *Carmen,* an opera set in Spain; the Italian Giacomo Puccini evoked Japan in his opera *Madame Butterfly;* and the Russian Rimsky-Korsakov suggested an Arabian atmosphere in his orchestral work *Scheherazade.* Musical exoticism was in keeping with the romantics' attraction to things remote, picturesque, and mysterious.

Program Music The nineteenth century was the great age of **program music,** instrumental music associated with a story, poem, idea, or scene. The nonmusical element is usually specified by a title or by explanatory comments called a **program.** A programmatic instrumental piece can represent the emotions, characters, and events of a particular story, or it can evoke the sounds and motion of nature. For example, in Tchaikovsky's *Romeo and Juliet,* an orchestral work inspired by Shakespeare's play, agitated music depicts the feud between the rival families, a tender melody conveys young love, and a funeral-march rhythm suggests the lovers' tragic fate. And in *The Moldau,* an orchestral work glorifying the main river of Bohemia, Smetana uses musical effects that call to mind a flowing stream, a hunting scene, a peasant wedding, and the crash of waves.

Program music in some form or another has existed for centuries, but it became particularly prominent in the romantic period, when music was closely associated with literature. Many composers—Berlioz, Schumann, Liszt, and Wagner, for example—were prolific authors as well. Artists in all fields were intoxicated by the concept of a "union of the arts." Poets wanted their poetry to be musical, and musicians wanted their music to be poetic.

Expressive Tone Color Romantic composers reveled in rich and sensuous sound, using tone color to obtain variety of mood and atmosphere. Never before had timbre been so important.

In both symphonic and operatic works, the romantic orchestra was larger and more varied in tone color than the classical orchestra. Toward the end of the romantic era, an orchestra might include close to 100 musicians. (There were twenty to sixty players in the classical ensemble.) The constant expansion of the orchestra reflected composers' changing needs as well as the growing size of concert halls and opera houses. The brass, woodwind, and percussion sections of the orchestra took on a more active role. Romantic composers increased the power of the brass section to something spectacular, calling for trombones, tubas, and more horns and trumpets. In 1824, Beethoven had broken precedent by asking for nine brasses in the Ninth Symphony; in 1894, the Austrian composer Gustav Mahler demanded twenty-five brass instruments for his Second Symphony. The addition of valves had made it easier for horns and trumpets to cope with intricate melodies.

The woodwind section took on new tone colors as the contrabassoon, bass clarinet, English horn, and piccolo became regular members of the orchestra. Improvements in the construction of instruments allowed woodwind players to perform more flexibly and accurately. Orchestral sounds became more brilliant and sensuously appealing through increased use of cymbals, the triangle, and the harp.

New sounds were drawn from all instruments of the nineteenth-century orchestra. Flutists were required to play in the breathy low register, and violinists were asked to strike the strings with the wood of their bows. Such demands compelled performers to attain a higher level of technical virtuosity.

Composers sought new ways of blending and combining tone colors to achieve the most poignant and intense sound. In 1844, Hector Berlioz's *Treatise on Modern Instrumentation and Orchestration* signaled the recognition of orchestration as an art in itself.

The piano, the favorite instrument of the romantic age, was vastly improved during the 1820s and 1830s. A cast-iron frame was introduced to hold the strings under greater tension, and the hammers were covered with felt. Thus the piano's tone became more "singing." Its range was also extended. With a stronger instrument, the pianist could produce more sound. And use of the damper ("loud") pedal allowed a sonorous blend of tones from all registers of the piano.

Colorful Harmony In addition to exploiting new tone colors, the romantics explored new chords and novel ways of using familiar chords. Seeking greater emotional intensity, composers emphasized rich, colorful, and complex harmonies.

There was more prominent exploitation of *chromatic harmony,* which uses chords containing tones not found in the prevailing major or minor scale. Such chord tones come from the chromatic scale (which has twelve tones), rather than from the major or minor scales (which have seven different tones). Chromatic chords add color and motion to romantic music. Dissonant, or unstable, chords were also used more freely than during the classical era. By deliberately delaying the resolution of dissonance to a consonant, or stable, chord, romantic composers created feelings of yearning, tension, and mystery.

A romantic piece tends to have a wide variety of keys and rapid modulations, or changes from one key to another. Because of the nature and frequency of these key shifts, the tonic key is somewhat less clear than in classical works. The feeling of tonal gravity tends to be less strong. By the end of the romantic period, even more emphasis was given to harmonic instability and less to stability and resolution.

Expanded Range of Dynamics, Pitch, and Tempo Romantic music also calls for a wide range of dynamics. It includes sharp contrasts between faint whispers and sonorities of unprecedented power. The classical dynamic extremes of *ff* and *pp* didn't meet the needs of romantics, who sometimes demanded *ffff* and *pppp*. Seeking more and more expressiveness, nineteenth-century composers used frequent crescendos and decrescendos, as well as sudden dynamic changes.

The range of pitch was expanded, too, as composers reached for extremely high or low sounds. In search of increased brilliance and depth of sound, the romantics exploited instruments like the piccolo and contrabassoon, as well as the expanded keyboard of the piano.

Changes of mood in romantic music are often underlined by accelerandos, ritardandos, and subtle variations of pace: there are many more fluctuations in tempo than there are in classical music. To intensify the expression of the music, romantic performers made use of *rubato,* the slight holding back or pressing forward of tempo.

Form: Miniature and Monumental The nineteenth century was very much an age of contradictions. Romantic composers characteristically expressed themselves both in musical miniatures and in monumental compositions. On the one hand are piano pieces by Chopin and songs by Schubert that last but a few minutes. Such short forms were meant to be heard in the intimate surroundings of a home; they met the needs of the growing number of people who owned pianos. The romantic genius for creating an intense mood through a melody, a few chords, or an unusual tone color found a perfect outlet in these miniatures. On the other hand, there are gigantic works by Berlioz and Wagner that call for a huge number of performers, last for several hours, and were designed for large opera houses or concert halls.

Romantic composers continued to write symphonies, sonatas, string quartets, concertos, operas, and choral works, but their individual movements tended to be longer than Haydn's and Mozart's. For example, a typical nineteenth-century symphony might last about 45 minutes, as opposed to 25 minutes for an eighteenth-century symphony. And as the romantic period drew to a close, compositions tended to become ever more extended, more richly orchestrated, and more complex in harmony.

New techniques were used to unify such long works. The same theme or themes might occur in several different movements of a symphony. Here composers followed the pioneering example of Beethoven's Fifth Symphony, where a theme from the scherzo is quoted within the finale. When a melody returns in a later movement or section of a romantic work, its character may be transformed by changes in dynamics, orchestration, or rhythm—a technique known as *thematic transformation.* A striking use of thematic transformation occurs in Berlioz's *Symphonie fantastique* (*Fantastic Symphony,* 1830), where a lyrical melody from the opening movement becomes a grotesque dance tune in the finale.

Different movements or sections of a romantic work can also be linked through transitional passages; one movement of a symphony or concerto may lead directly into the next. Here, again, Beethoven was the pioneer. And nineteenth-century operas are unified by melodic ideas that reappear in different acts or scenes, some of which may be tied together by connecting passages.

In dealing with an age that so prized individuality, generalizations are especially difficult. The great diversity found in romantic music can best be appreciated, perhaps, by approaching each piece as its composer did—with an open mind and heart.

2 Romantic Composers and Their Public

The composer's role in society changed radically during Beethoven's lifetime (1770–1827). In earlier periods, part of a musician's job had been the composition of works for a specific occasion and audience. Thus Bach wrote cantatas for weekly church services in Leipzig, and Haydn composed symphonies for concerts in the palaces of the Esterházy family. But Beethoven, as we have seen, was one of the first great composers to work as a freelance musician outside the system of aristocratic or church patronage.

The image of Beethoven as a "free artist" inspired romantic musicians, who often composed to meet an inner need rather than fulfill a commission. Romantic composers were interested not only in pleasing their contemporaries but also in being judged favorably by posterity. The young Berlioz wrote to his father, "I want to leave on this earth some trace of my existence." It became common for romantics to create extended works with no immediate prospects for performance. For example, Wagner wrote *Das Rheingold* (*The Rhine Gold*), a 2½-hour opera, and then had to wait fifteen years before seeing its premiere.

Sometimes the romantic composer was a "free artist" by necessity rather than choice. Because of the French Revolution and the Napoleonic wars (from 1789 to 1814), many aristocrats could no longer afford to maintain private opera houses, orchestras, and "composers in residence." Musicians lost their jobs when many of the tiny princely states of Germany were abolished as political units and merged with neighboring territories. (In Bonn, Germany, the court and its orchestra were disbanded; Beethoven

Romantic composers wrote primarily for a middle-class audience. In this picture by Moritz von Schwind, Franz Schubert is shown at the piano accompanying the singer Johann Michael Vogl.

could not have returned to his position there even if he had wanted to.) Many composers who would have had modest but secure incomes in the past had to fight for their livelihood and sell their wares in the marketplace.

Romantic composers wrote primarily for a middle-class audience whose size and prosperity had increased because of the industrial revolution. During the nineteenth century, cities expanded dramatically, and a sizable number of people wanted to hear and play music.

The needs of this urban middle class led to the formation of many orchestras and opera groups during the romantic era. Public concerts had developed during the eighteenth century, but not until the nineteenth century did regular subscription concerts become common. The London Philharmonic Society was founded in 1813, the Paris Société des Concerts du Conservatoire was founded in 1828, and the Vienna Philharmonische Konzerte and the New York Philharmonic were founded in 1842.

The first half of the nineteenth century also witnessed the founding of music conservatories throughout Europe. In the United States, conservatories were founded in Chicago, Cleveland, Boston, Oberlin (Ohio), and Philadelphia during the 1860s. More young men and women than ever before studied to be professional musicians. At first women were accepted only as students of performance, but by the late 1800s they could study musical composition as well.

The nineteenth-century public was captivated by virtuosity. Among the musical heroes of the 1830s were the pianist Franz Liszt and the violinist Niccolò Paganini (1782–1840), who toured Europe and astonished audiences with their feats. Never before had instrumental virtuosity been so acclaimed. After one concert by Liszt in Budapest, Hungarian nobles presented him with a jeweled sword, and a crowd of thousands formed a torchlight parade to escort him to his dwelling. Following Liszt's example, performers like the pianist Clara Wieck Schumann and the violinist Joseph Joachim began to give solo recitals in addition to their customary appearances with orchestras.

The needs of the urban middle class led to the formation of many orchestras during the romantic era. This engraving shows Louis Jullien conducting an orchestra and four military bands at Covent Garden Theater in London in 1846.

Private music making also increased during the romantic era. The piano became a fixture in every middle-class home, and there was great demand for songs and solo piano pieces. Operas and orchestral works were transcribed, or arranged, so that they could be played on a piano in the home.

Romantic composers came from the social class that was their main audience. Berlioz was the son of a doctor; Schumann was the son of a bookseller; Mendelssohn was the son of a banker. This was a new situation. In earlier periods, music, like cabinet-making, had been a craft passed from one generation to another. Bach, Mozart, and Beethoven were all children of musicians. But the romantics often had to do a great deal of persuading before their parents permitted them to undertake a musical career. Berlioz wrote to his reluctant father in 1824: "I am voluntarily driven toward a magnificent career (no other term can be applied to the career of an artist) and I am not in the least headed toward damnation. . . . This is the way I think, the way I am, and nothing in the world will change me."

Middle-class parents had reason for concern when their children wanted to be musicians. Few romantic composers were able to support themselves through composition alone. Only a very successful opera composer like Verdi could become wealthy by selling music to opera houses and publishers. Most composers were forced to work in several areas at once. Some were touring virtuosos like Paganini and Liszt. Many taught; Chopin charged high fees for giving piano lessons to rich young women in Paris. Music criticism was a source of income for Berlioz and Schumann. (And Berlioz bitterly resented having to waste time reviewing compositions by nonentities.) Some of the finest conductors of the romantic period were composers, among them Mendelssohn and Mahler. Only a few fortunates, such as Tchaikovsky and Wagner, had wealthy patrons to support them while they created.

3 The Art Song

One of the most distinctive forms in romantic music is the **art song,** a composition for solo voice and piano. Here, the accompaniment is an integral part of the composer's concept, and it serves as an interpretive partner to the voice. Although they are now performed in concert halls, romantic songs were written to be sung and enjoyed at home.

Poetry and music are intimately fused in the art song. It is no accident that this form flowered with the emergence of a rich body of romantic poetry in the early nineteenth century. Many of the finest song composers—Schubert, Schumann, and Brahms, for example—were German or Austrian and set poems in their native language. Among the poets favored by these composers were Johann Wolfgang von Goethe (1749–1832) and Heinrich Heine (1797–1856). The German word *Lied* (*song*) is commonly used for a song with German text. (*Lied* is pronounced *leet;* its plural, *Lieder,* is pronounced *leader.*)

Yearning—inspired by a lost love, nature, a legend, or other times and places—haunted the imagination of romantic poets. Thus art songs are filled with the despair of unrequited love; the beauty of flowers, trees, and brooks; and the supernatural happenings of folktales. There are also songs of joy, wit, and humor. But by and large, romantic song was a reaching out of the soul.

Song composers would interpret a poem, translating its mood, atmosphere, and imagery into music. They created a vocal melody that was musically satisfying and perfectly molded to the text. Important words were emphasized by stressed tones or melodic climaxes.

The voice shares the interpretive task with the piano. Emotions and images in the text take on an added dimension from the keyboard commentary. Arpeggios in the piano might suggest the splashing of oars or the motion of a mill wheel. Chords in a low register might depict darkness or a lover's torment. The mood is often set by a brief piano introduction and summed up at the end by a piano section called a **postlude.**

Strophic and Through-Composed Form

When a poem has several stanzas, the musical setting must accommodate their total emotional impact. Composers can use **strophic form,** repeating the same music for each stanza of the poem. Strophic form makes a song easy to remember and is used in almost all folk songs. Or composers might use **through-composed form,** writing new music for each stanza. (*Through-composed* is a translation of the German term *durchkomponiert.*) Through-composed form allows music to reflect a poem's changing moods.

The art song is not restricted to strophic or through-composed form. There are many ways that music can be molded to the structure and feeling of a poem. A three-stanza poem is frequently set as follows: A (stanza 1)—B (stanza 2)—A (stanza 3). This might be called a **modified strophic form,** since two of the three stanzas are set to the same music.

The Song Cycle

Romantic art songs are sometimes grouped in a set, or **song cycle.** A cycle may be unified by a story line that runs through the poems, or by musical ideas linking the songs. Among the great romantic song cycles are *Winterreise* (*Winter's Journey,* 1827) by Schubert, and *Dichterliebe* (*Poet's Love,* 1840) by Schumann.

In many of their art songs, romantic composers achieved a perfect union of music and poetry. They created an intensely personal world with a tremendous variety of moods. These miniatures contain some of the most haunting melodies and harmonies in all music.

4 Franz Schubert

The career of Franz Schubert (1797–1828), the earliest master of the romantic art song, was unlike that of any great composer before him. He never held an official position as musical director or organist, and he was neither a conductor nor a virtuoso. He was the first Viennese composer whose income came entirely from musical composition. "I have come into the world for no other purpose but to compose," he told a friend. The full measure of his genius was recognized only years after his tragically early death.

Schubert was born in Vienna, the son of a schoolmaster. Even as a child, he had astounding musical gifts. "If I wanted to instruct him in anything new," recalled his amazed teacher, "he knew it already. Therefore I gave him no actual instructions but merely talked to him and watched him in silent astonishment." At eleven, Schubert became a choirboy in the court chapel and won a scholarship to the Imperial Seminary, an exclusive boarding school, where he played first violin and occasionally conducted the orchestra. Schubert so loved music that he once sold his schoolbooks to buy a ticket for a performance of Beethoven's opera *Fidelio*.

Schubert managed to compose an extraordinary number of masterpieces in his late teens while teaching at his father's school, a job he hated. His love of poetry led him to the art song, a form that Haydn, Mozart, and Beethoven had only touched on. Inflamed by the poetry and passion of Goethe's *Faust,* the seventeen-year-old Schubert composed his first great song, *Gretchen am Spinnrade* (*Gretchen at the Spinning Wheel*). The next year he composed 143 songs, including *The Erlking.* When he was nineteen, his productivity rose to a peak: he composed 179 works, including two symphonies, an opera, and a mass.

When he was twenty-one, Schubert gave up teaching school to devote himself entirely to music. He associated with a group of Viennese poets and artists who admired his compositions. "We often wandered about town until three in the morning," recalled a friend. "One of us not seldom would sleep in the apartment of another. We were not particular about comfort in those days. Whoever happened to have money paid for us all." Schubert often lived with friends because he did not have money to rent a room of his own.

Working with incredible speed, Schubert turned out one piece after another. He worked from seven o'clock in the morning until one or two in the afternoon; then he spent

Franz Schubert did not mingle with the aristocracy, preferring instead the company of poets, painters, and other musicians.

his afternoon in cafés, drinking coffee, playing billiards, reading newspapers, and talking with friends. His evenings were spent at "Schubertiads," parties where only his music was played. He accompanied the songs and played his delightful waltzes while his friends danced. Most of his works were composed for performances in the homes of Vienna's cultivated middle class. Unlike Beethoven, Schubert did not mingle with the aristocracy.

At the age of twenty-five, Schubert contracted a venereal disease and became moody and prone to despair. "Think of a man," he wrote of himself at the time, "whose health can never be restored, . . . of a man whose brightest hopes have come to nothing, to whom love and friendship are but torture. . . ." He applied for musical positions several times during his last years but never received them. The publication and performance of his songs brought him some recognition, but his two most important symphonies—the *Unfinished* and the *Great* C Major—were not performed in public during his lifetime.

Schubert was thirty-one when he died of syphilis in 1828, a year after Beethoven's funeral. His reputation was mainly that of a fine song composer, until the *Unfinished* Symphony was performed almost forty years later. Then the world began to recognize Schubert's comprehensive greatness.

Schubert's Music

It is amazing how original, varied, and numerous Schubert's works are. Along with over 600 songs, Schubert left symphonies, string quartets, chamber music for piano and strings, piano sonatas, short piano pieces for two and four hands, masses, and operatic compositions.

The songs embrace an enormous variety of moods and types. Some are very short, others very long; their forms include strophic, modified strophic, and through-composed. Many deal with nature—the flow of a brook, the mystery of the night—or with unhappy love. The songs amply display Schubert's melodic genius. His melodies range from simple, folklike tunes to complex lines that suggest impassioned speech. His piano accompaniments are equally rich and evocative. Many songs draw emotional power from the relentless repetition of a rhythmic idea or from a shattering climax.

Schubert's imaginative harmonies provide some of the most poetic moments in music. He uses unexpected dissonances to capture a mood, and he shifts abruptly to contrasting keys. In Schubert's hands, even the simple change from minor to major can evoke a sudden thought of love or an illusion of light breaking through clouds.

The spirit of song permeates Schubert's instrumental music, too. Many of his symphonies and chamber works have long, lyrical melodies, and often Schubert writes variations on his own songs. For instance, the fourth movement of the *Trout* Quintet, for piano and strings, is a set of variations on his song *Die Forelle* (*The Trout*). And his short piano pieces such as the *Moments musicaux* (*Musical Moments*) and *Impromptus* are true "songs without words."

Schubert wrote a number of symphonies and chamber works that are comparable in power and emotional intensity to those of his idol, Beethoven. The *Unfinished* Symphony (1822) and the *Great* C Major Symphony (1825–1826) use French horns, trombones, and woodwinds with a new feeling for their poetic capacities. The *Unfinished* Symphony, Schubert's most popular orchestral work, was written six years before his death; we probably will never learn why it has only two movements rather than the usual four. The *Great* C Major Symphony was discovered ten years after Schubert's death by Robert Schumann, who was ecstatic about the work. "It is not possible to describe it to you," he wrote to his fiancée. "All the instruments are human voices; . . . and this length, this heavenly length. . . ." Reviewing the first public performance of this symphony, Schumann made an observation that is true of much of Schubert's music: "It bears within it the seeds of everlasting youth."

Erlkönig (The Erlking; 1815)

Basic Set:
CD 5 **1**

Brief Set:
CD 3 **42**

Schubert's song *Erlkönig* (*The Erlking*) is one of the earliest and finest examples of musical romanticism. It is a musical setting of a narrative ballad of the supernatural by Goethe. A friend of Schubert's tells how he saw the eighteen-year-old composer reading Goethe's poem. "He paced up and down several times with the book; suddenly he sat down, and in no time at all (just as quickly as he could write) there was the glorious ballad finished on the paper." Goethe's ballad, in dialogue almost throughout, tells of a father riding on horseback through a storm with his sick child in his arms. The delirious boy has visions of the legendary Erlking, the king of the elves, who symbolizes death.

Schubert uses a through-composed setting to capture the mounting excitement of the poem. The piano part, with its rapid octaves and menacing bass motive, conveys the tension of the wild ride.

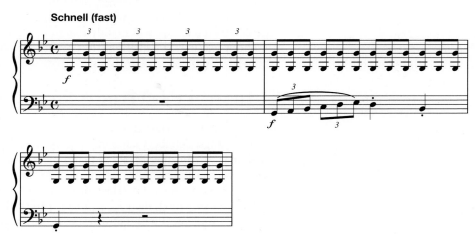

The piano's relentless triplet rhythm unifies the episodes of the song and suggests the horse's gallop.

By imaginatively varying the music, Schubert makes one singer sound like several characters in a miniature drama. The terrified boy sings in a high register in minor. Three times during the poem, he cries out, "My father, my father." Each time, the boy sings a musical outcry that is intensified through dissonant harmonies.

Mein Va - ter, mein Va - ter,

To convey mounting fear, Schubert pitches the boy's outcry higher and higher each time. The reassuring father sings in a low register that contrasts with the high-pitched outcries of his child. The Erlking, who tries to entice the boy, has coy melodies in major keys.

Du lie - bes Kind, komm, geh mit mir! gar schö-ne Spie-le spiel' ich mit dir;

The deeply moving climax of *The Erlking* comes when father and son arrive home and the galloping accompaniment gradually comes to a halt. In a bleak, heartbreaking recitative that allows every word to make its impact, the narrator tells us, "In his arms the child was dead!"

VOCAL MUSIC GUIDE

SCHUBERT, *Erlkönig*

1 **42** 0:00
Piano introduction,
rapid octaves,
f, bass motive,
minor key.

Narrator

Wer reitet so spät durch Nacht und Wind?	Who rides so late through the night and the wind?
Es ist der Vater mit seinem Kind;	It is the father with his child;
Er hat den Knaben wohl in dem Arm,	he holds the boy close in his arms,
Er fasst ihn sicher, er hält ihn warm.	he clasps him securely, he holds him warmly.

2 **43** 0:56
Low register.

Father

"Mein Sohn, was birgst du so bang dein Gesicht?"	"My son, why do you hide your face so anxiously?"

3 **44** 1:04
Higher register

Son

"Siehst, Vater, du den Erlkönig nicht?	"Father, don't you see the Erlking?
Den Erlenkönig mit Kron' und Schweif?"	The Erlking with his crown and his train?"

1:20
Low register

Father

"Mein Sohn, es ist ein Nebelstreif."	"My son, it is a streak of mist."

4 **45** 1:29
Coaxing tune,
pp, higher
register, major.

Erlking

"Du liebes Kind, komm, geh mit mir!	"Dear child, come, go with me!
Gar schöne Spiele spiel' ich mit dir,	I'll play the prettiest games with you.
Manch bunte Blumen sind an dem Strand,	Many colored flowers grow along the shore;
Meine Mutter hat manch gülden Gewand."	My mother has many golden garments."

5 **46** 1:51
Outcry, *f*, minor.

Son

"Mein Vater, mein Vater, und hörest du nicht,	"My father, my father, and don't you hear
Was Erlenkönig mir leise verspricht?"	the Erlking whispering promises to me?"

2:03
Low register.

Father

"Sei ruhig, bleibe ruhig, mein Kind:	"Be quiet, stay quiet, my child;
In dürren Blättern säuselt der Wind."	the wind is rustling in the dead leaves."

2:13
Playful tune,
pp, major.

Erlking

"Willst, feiner Knabe, du mit mir gehn?	"My handsome boy, will you come with me?
Meine Töchter sollen dich warten schön;	My daughters shall wait upon you;
Meine Töchter führen den nächtlichen Reihn	my daughters lead off in the dance every night,
Und wiegen und tanzen und singen dich ein."	and cradle and dance and sing you to sleep."

6 **47** 2:30

Son

Outcry, *f*, higher than before, minor.

"Mein Vater, mein Vater, und siehst du nicht dort
Erlkönigs Töchter am düstern Ort?"

"My father, my father, and don't you see there
the Erlking's daughters in the shadows?"

2:43
Lower register.

Father

"Mein Sohn, mein Sohn, ich seh' es genau:
Es scheinen die alten Weiden so grau."

"My son, my son, I see it clearly;

the old willows look so gray."

Erlking

"Ich liebe dich, mich reizt deine schöne Gestalt;
Und bist du nicht willig, so brauch' ich Gewalt."

"I love you, your beautiful figure delights me!
And if you are not willing, then I shall use force!"

3:11
Outcry, *f*, highest yet.

Son

"Mein Vater, mein Vater, jetzt fasst er mich an!
Erlkönig hat mir ein Leids getan!"

"My father, my father, now he is taking hold of me!
The Erlking has hurt me!"

Narrator

3:24

Dem Vater grauset's, er reitet geschwind,
Er hält in Armen das ächzende Kind,
Erreicht den Hof mit Mühe und Not;

The father shudders, he rides swiftly on;
he holds in his arms the groaning child,
he reaches the courtyard weary and anxious:

Piano stops.
Recitative.

In seinen Armen das Kind war tot.

in his arms the child was dead.

Die Forelle (The Trout; 1817)

Basic Set:
CD 5 **7**

One of Schubert's most famous songs, *Die Forelle* (*The Trout*) reflects the romantics' attraction to nature and to folklike simplicity. The text—by Christian Daniel Schubart (1739–1791)—tells of a trout that swims merrily in a brook but is then caught by a clever fisherman. *Die Forelle* is in modified strophic form: A (stanza 1)—A (stanza 2)—BA' (stanza 3). It begins with a short piano introduction, which reappears as an interlude after the first and second stanzas and as a postlude after the third stanza. The first two stanzas of the poem, which describe the fish happily swimming, are both sung to the same lighthearted melody (A). Repeated-note patterns (as on *einem* and *Bächlein*) contribute to the melody's folklike quality.

In ei - nem Bäch-lein hel - le da schoss in fro - her _ Eil'

The piano accompaniment is pervaded by a short ascending figure which depicts the trout's leaps and twists.

New music (B) is used for most of the last stanza, which tells how the trout is caught.

Doch end - lich ward dem Die - be   die Zeit zu lang,

The change to a more dramatic mood is conveyed by a momentary shift from major to minor and the appearance of a more agitated accompaniment in place of the repeated rising "trout" figure. To round off the song, Schubert brings back the last phrase (A′) of the opening melody for the concluding line, *Und ich mit regem Blute/Sah die Betrogne an* (*and I, with my pulse beating high, watched the betrayed one*).

VOCAL MUSIC GUIDE

SCHUBERT, *Die Forelle*

7 0:00
Piano
introduction,
major

A

	In einem Bächlein helle,	In a clear brooklet,
	Da schoss in froher Eil'	with happy haste,
	Die launische Forelle	a capricious trout
	Vorüber wie ein Pfeil.	darted about like an arrow.
	Ich stand an dem Gestade,	I stood on the bank
	und sah in süsser Ruh'	and contentedly watched
	Des muntern Fischleins Bade	the merry fish bathe
	Im klaren Bächlein zu.	in the clear brooklet.

Piano
interlude
    0:42

A

	Ein Fischer mit der Rute,	A fisherman with his rod
	Wohl an dem Ufer stand,	stood on the bank
	Und sah's mit kaltem Blute,	and looked on cold-bloodedly
	Wie sich das Fischlein wand.	as the fish wriggled about.
	So lang dem Wasser helle,	So long as the clear water,
	So dacht' ich, nicht gebricht,	I thought, is not disturbed,
	So fängt er die Forelle	he will not catch the trout
	Mit seiner Angel nicht.	with his hook.

8 1:18
B, minor

	Doch endlich ward dem Diebe	But suddenly the thief
	Die Zeit zu lang. Er macht	got tired of waiting. He
	Das Bächlein tückisch trübe,	slyly muddied up the brook,
	Und eh' ich es gedacht;	and before I realized it
	So zuckte seine Rute,	he jerked his rod
	Das Fischlein zappelt dran,	and the fish struggled on the line,

1:37
A′, major

	Und ich mit regem Blute	and I, with my pulse beating high,
	Sah die Betrogne an.	watched the betrayed one.

Piano
postlude

Piano Quintet in A Major (*Trout;* 1819)

Fourth Movement

Basic Set:
CD 5 **9**

Among the best-loved of all chamber works is the *Trout* Quintet, which was commissioned in 1819 by an amateur cellist who admired Schubert's song *Die Forelle* (*The Trout*) and asked the composer to write variations on it. The theme and variations is the fourth of five movements in this quintet, which is scored for the unusual combination of piano, violin, viola, cello, and double bass. Schubert gives each player a chance to present the main melodic line.

The strings alone introduce the theme, a charming melody in D major marked *andantino* (*moderately slow*). The six variations that follow embellish the theme and combine it with countermelodies. The first three variations build in rhythmic animation and brilliance of sound, but in them the original melody is altered very little. Variation 4 is a dramatic climax: the key shifts to D minor and the theme is changed radically in melody, rhythm, and dynamics. Variation 5 is in the new key of B flat major, and the theme is transformed into an intense legato melody that sounds almost new. The concluding variation brings back the original D major melody in a faster tempo (allegretto). The music sounds fresh and sparkling as Schubert introduces a new accompaniment figure that he had used in the original song to suggest the brook trout's leaps and twists.

The theme is in the two-part form aa b. This pattern is retained in most of the variations.

LISTENING OUTLINE

SCHUBERT, Piano Quintet in A Major (*Trout*)

Fourth Movement: Andantino

Theme and variations, duple meter ($\frac{2}{4}$), D major

Piano, violin, viola, cello, double bass

(Duration, 8:18)

Theme
(andantino)

9 0:00   Violin, ***pp***, theme, strings accompany.

Variation 1

10 1:19   Piano enters, ***p***, theme decorated by trills; strings accompany with broken chords, high violin trills.

Variation 2

11 2:21   Viola, ***p***, theme; higher flowing countermelody in violin, ***p***; piano echoes phrases of theme.

Variation 3

12 3:21   Piano, *f*, rapid countermelody above bass and cello, *p*, staccato theme in low register.

Variation 4 (minor)

13 4:15   Piano and strings, *ff*, repeated chords in minor alternate with high violin phrase, *p*, in major. Trills in piano and violin, *pp*; songlike phrases in cello, viola, and violin, *p*; variation ends in minor.

Variation 5

14 5:21   Cello, *p*, theme transformed into lyrical legato melody; accompanying strings joined by piano in high register.

Long cello melody followed by brief dialogue with violin. Cello leads to

**Variation 6
(allegretto)**

15 6:59
    a. Violin, *p*, theme in faster tempo; piano accompanies with *trout* figure.
    b. Cello, *p*, theme; violin, *trout* figure.
    c. Violin, *p*, theme continues; piano accompanies with *trout* figure.
    d. Cello, *p*, theme; violin, *trout* figure.
    e. Violin and cello, *p*, theme; *trout* figure in piano; then cello, *pp*, brings movement to gentle close.

5 Robert Schumann

Robert Schumann (1810–1856) in many ways embodied musical romanticism. His works are intensely autobiographical, and they are usually linked with descriptive titles, texts, or programs. He expressed his essentially lyrical nature in startlingly original piano pieces and songs. As a gifted writer and critic, he also discovered and made famous some of the leading composers of his day.

Schumann was born in Zwickau, Germany. His father was a bookseller, from whom he acquired a love of literature. As a youth, Schumann wrote poetry, composed short pieces, and played the piano fairly well. To please his mother, he studied law at Leipzig University; but he rarely attended lectures and devoted his time instead to literature and music.

At the late age of twenty, Schumann decided to become a piano virtuoso. Around that time, he developed serious problems with the fingers of his right hand. In search of a cure, he used a mechanical gadget designed to stretch and strengthen the fingers. But neither this device nor various medical treatments alleviated his condition: one finger was permanently crippled, and his hopes of becoming a virtuoso were dashed. "Don't worry about my finger," he wrote to his mother. "I can compose without it."

Indeed, in his twenties he composed many poetic piano works which are a basic part of the pianist's repertoire even today. In Schumann's time, however, many considered his compositions too unconventional, too personal. Schumann admitted that his works were autobiographical: "I am affected by everything that goes on in the world—politics, literature, people—I think it over in my own way, and then I long to express my feelings in music."

Robert Schumann's works are intensely autobiographical and are usually linked with descriptive titles, texts, or programs.

During his twenties, too, Schumann founded and edited the twice-weekly *New Journal of Music* to promote musical originality and combat the commercial trash that flooded the market. In his essays, Schumann invented an imaginary "league of David" fighting against musical "philistines," lovers of the conventional. He often signed his articles "Florestan" or "Eusebius," names of imaginary characters who represented, respectively, the outgoing and introspective sides of his personality. The *New Journal* grew to be influential and contained Schumann's appreciative reviews of "radical" young composers like Chopin and Berlioz.

While studying piano, Schumann became acquainted with his teacher's daughter and prize pupil, Clara Wieck. Schumann was eighteen when they met, and Clara was a nine-year-old prodigy who was already a well-known pianist. The two were engaged when Clara was seventeen, despite bitter opposition from her father, who did not want his daughter's brilliant career to be hampered by marriage to an impoverished musician. Since Clara was not of age, the couple fought bitter court battles against Wieck before they could be married. Their marriage turned out to be a happy one that produced eight children. Clara, herself a composer, was the ideal interpreter of her husband's piano works and introduced many of them to the public.

Schumann was temperamentally ill-suited for a regular musical position. He taught in the newly established Leipzig Conservatory of Music, but only for a short time. He was a failure as municipal music director at Düsseldorf because of his inability to control an orchestra and chorus. During his later years his mental and physical health progressively deteriorated, and in 1854 he attempted suicide by throwing himself from a bridge into the Rhine. At his own request, he was committed to an asylum, where he died two years later.

Schumann's Music

Schumann's genius is most characteristically expressed in his songs and short piano pieces, both of which he usually organized into sets or cycles. The titles of these sets— *Carnaval* (*Carnival*), *Kinderscenen* (*Scenes of Childhood*), *Nachtstücke* (*Night Pieces*), *Dichterliebe* (*Poet's Love*), *Fantasiestücke* (*Fantasy Pieces*)—provide insight into his imagination. Schumann thought of music in emotional, literary, and autobiographical terms; his work is full of extramusical references.

During the first ten years of his creative life, Schumann published only piano pieces. His basic musical style seems to grow out of piano improvisation, and these short pieces are like mosaics of vivid musical fragments. Each expresses a single mood through an intensely sensitive melody. Dance rhythms such as the waltz are prominent, as are syncopations and dotted rhythms. Schumann's cycles of short pieces are unified through a story, through a title, or through thematic connections.

In 1840, the year of his marriage, Schumann composed many art songs. The songs, like the piano pieces, reveal Schumann's great gift for melody. Many of the songs have a piano postlude which sums up the message of the text. Schumann's song texts suit his feelings, and he often changes a poem by repeating words, lines, and even whole stanzas.

After 1840, Schumann turned to symphonies and chamber music. This direction may well have resulted from Clara's influence, for she wrote in her diary, "I am infinitely delighted that Robert has at last found the sphere for which his great imagination fits him." Schumann's four symphonies are romantic in their emphasis on lyrical second themes, in their use of thematic transformation, and in their connections between movements.

Carnaval (Carnival; 1834–1835)

Carnaval is a cycle of twenty-one brief pieces with descriptive titles evoking a festive masked ball, with its varied characters, moods, and activities. This "musical picture gallery," as Schumann called it, includes sketches of fellow musicians, young women in the composer's life, stock characters from *commedia dell'arte* (Italian improvised theater), and self-portraits representing the introverted and outgoing sides of his own personality (Eusebius and Florestan).

Carnaval was inspired partly by Schumann's brief engagement to Ernestine von Fricken, an eighteen-year-old pianist who studied with Clara Wieck's father. In 1834, Schumann wrote that he had "just discovered that the name Asch [Ernestine's birthplace] is very musical and contains letters that also occur in my name [SCHumAnn]. They are musical symbols." In German, B natural is known as H, and so the letters A S C H refer to the four notes A–E flat–C–B natural, if the S is read as Es (German for E flat); or to the three notes A flat–C–B natural, if A and S are compressed to As (German for A flat). Schumann used these four-note or three-note groups to open most of the pieces in *Carnaval,* creating musical links between them. However, these links are quite concealed, because the same notes are presented in ever-changing rhythms, melodic shapes, and harmonies. By using musical ideas related to himself and his fiancée, Schumann permeated *Carnaval* with autobiographical references.

We will now focus on four pieces from this best-known of Schumann's extended piano works. The four successive pieces *Chiarina, Chopin, Estrella,* and *Reconnaissance* (Nos. 11–14) illustrate the contrasting moods within *Carnaval.* The first and third of these are in minor keys, and the second and fourth are in major. *Chiarina, Estrella,* and *Reconnaissance* all open with the same three-note group, A flat–C–B natural (see the letters at the beginning of the music examples).

Chiarina

Chiarina (Little Clara) refers to the fifteen-year-old piano virtuoso Clara Wieck. Schumann must have thought that the young Clara had a passionate nature, because he associated her with an agitated piece in minor, marked *passionato* and including prominent dissonances. *Chiarina* is in triple meter and elaborates a single dotted rhythmic pattern (long-short-long-short) throughout—one of Schumann's stylistic trademarks.

Chiarina may be outlined as follows:

1. Phrase A, ascending and descending, dotted rhythm, phrase A′ louder with melody in octaves and conclusive ending.
2. a. Phrase B, softer beginning, dotted rhythm, melody with repeated high note.
   b. Phrases A and A′ return.

Part 2 is repeated.

Basic Set:

CD 5 [16]

[16] 0:00

[17] 0:19

    0:29

    0:49

Chopin

Chopin is in the style of a nocturne, or "night piece," by Frédéric Chopin. A lyrical legato melody is accompanied by flowing arpeggios which emphasize the $\frac{6}{4}$ meter (**1**-2-3-4-5-6).

Characteristic of Chopin's style are the slight changes in tempo and the filigree of high ornamental tones. *Chopin* is in major and may be outlined A A: the melody is first played loudly and then repeated softly.

Estrella

Estrella, marked *con affecto* (*with feeling*), is a sketch of Schumann's fiancée Ernestine von Fricken. The composer thought of Estrella as "the kind of name one would put under a portrait to fix it more clearly in one's memory." Perhaps understandably, *Estrella* shares some features with *Chiarina,* the other portrait of a young woman in Schumann's life: each is impassioned, in minor, and in triple meter. Yet the pieces sound quite different, partly because *Estrella* includes a variety of rhythmic patterns and has a waltzlike accompaniment.

Section A
19 **48** 0:00

Section B
20 **49** 0:15

Section A'
0:29

Estrella is in A B A' (abridged) form. The outer sections, which are consistently forceful, contrast with the middle section, which begins softly. Section B is permeated by syncopations—accents on the second and third beats—a distinctive feature of Schumann's music.

Reconnaissance (Reunion)

Reconnaissance is a lyrical piece, which Schumann described as a "scene of reunion." In A B A' form, it is longer than any of the three preceding miniatures. Schumann's style of piano writing is highly original here. In the outer (A) sections, which are in major, the pianist's right hand simultaneously plays two versions of the same melody an octave apart: the higher melody is legato, whereas the lower one is decorated with fast, staccato, repeated notes.

Perhaps these pulsating repeated notes represent the throbbing hearts of the reunited lovers.

Section B

22 **51** 0:44

The calmer middle section (B) brings a new major key and a shift from homophonic to polyphonic texture. The original melody is presented in the top part and imitated in the bass. Rhythmic excitement is maintained by a syncopated accompaniment in the middle parts.

Section A'

1:36

The concluding A' section is a shortened and slightly varied version of the opening A section.

Together, *Chiarina, Chopin, Estrella,* and *Reconnaissance* reveal different facets of Schumann's musical personality.

6 Clara Wieck Schumann

One of the leading concert pianists of the nineteenth century, Clara Wieck Schumann (1819–1896) premiered many works by her husband Robert Schumann and by her close friend Johannes Brahms. Born in Leipzig, Germany, she was the daughter of Marianne Wieck, a singer and pianist; and Friedrich Wieck, a well-known piano pedagogue. Her father trained her to be a child prodigy who would both earn money and demonstrate the superiority of his teaching methods. Between the ages of twelve and twenty she performed throughout Europe to great acclaim, usually programming one or more of her own compositions.

Clara Wieck married Robert Schumann the day before her twenty-first birthday, despite her father's opposition. During their fourteen-year marriage she continued to concertize and compose—though on a reduced scale—while caring for seven children (one of the Schumanns' children had died in infancy) and catering to the needs of her hypersensitive husband. The year 1853 was particularly important for Clara Schumann. The twenty-year-old composer Johannes Brahms came to play his works for the Schumanns, beginning a friendship with Clara that would last until her death in 1896. In the same year, she also met the famous violinist Joseph Joachim, with whom she would often give chamber music concerts.

After her husband's death, Clara Schumann expanded her performing activities, became renowned as a teacher, and edited his collected works. She helped refine the tastes of concert audiences by performing serious works by earlier composers such as Bach, Mozart, and Beethoven as well as works by her late husband and her friend Brahms.

Clara Schumann considered herself primarily a performing artist. "I feel I have a

Clara Wieck Schumann was one of the leading concert pianists of the nineteenth century and a composer of songs, piano pieces, and chamber music.

mission to perform beautiful works, Robert's above all," she once wrote. "The practice of my art . . . is the very air I breathe." She was less confident about her creative ability and stopped composing when she was thirty-six, after she had become a widow. Her self-doubt was perhaps influenced by the predominantly negative attitude toward women composers and by her relationship with overwhelming geniuses like Robert Schumann and Brahms.

Until recently, Clara Schumann was known mainly as a famous pianist who had been the wife of one great composer and the close friend of another. But in the last decade, her compositions have been increasingly recorded and performed. These include songs; a piano concerto; a trio for piano, violin, and cello; and piano pieces, one of which will be studied here.

Basic Set:
CD 5 **23**

Brief Set:
CD 3 **52**

Romance in E Flat Minor for Piano, Op. 11, No. 1 (1839)

Clara Wieck composed the *Three Romances* for Piano, Op. 11, when she was nineteen, during a six-month stay in Paris—far distant from her fiancé, Robert, who was in Vienna. The term **romance** (*Romanze* in German) was often used during the nineteenth century for short, lyrical pieces for piano.

Clara's *Three Romances* expressed her intimate feelings for Robert, and as each was finished she sent him a copy to get his opinion. "I wrote a little piece but don't know what to call it," she wrote in April 1839. "I had so many feelings as I wrote it—so intimate and heartfelt—won't you find a name for it for me?" In July, Clara sent Robert a copy of another *Romance* and wrote that he should "play it very freely, at times passionately, at times melancholy again. . . ." Robert responded, "In your *Romance* I heard anew that you complement me as a composer just as I do you." Inspired by Clara's *Three Romances*—dedicated to him—Robert wrote his own *Three Romances* for Piano, Op. 28, dedicated to her, soon after.

We'll focus on Clara's Romance in E Flat Minor, Op. 11, No. 1, which evokes a mood of sweet melancholy. Contributing to this mood are the minor key, moderate tempo (andante), and mostly soft dynamic level.

Like many short pieces of the romantic period, this Romance is in A B A'—coda form. The A section creates a sense of longing through a melody spun out of the rhythmic idea short-short-short-long. Throughout the section, this melody is accompanied by rippling sixteenth notes.

A brief transition smoothly links section A with section B, which brings a shift from major to minor, from sweet melancholy to relaxed optimism. The melody of B flows evenly and continuously in the top part and includes many decorative tones. In our recording the pianist Pierre-Alain Volondat heightens the emotional effect of this section by dynamically emphasizing accompanying melodic ideas in lower parts of the musical texture. Near the end of section B, the short-short-short-long rhythm reappears to lead into section A', a varied and abridged repetition of section A. A brief coda rounds off the Romance with a slowing of tempo and two questioning minor chords.

LISTENING OUTLINE

CLARA WIECK SCHUMANN, Romance in E Flat Minor, Op. 11, No. 1

Andante, triple meter ($\frac{3}{4}$), A B A'—coda form

Piano

(Duration 2:57)

A

 52 0:00   **1. a.** Accompaniment introduces main melody, short-short-short-long rhythm, minor key.

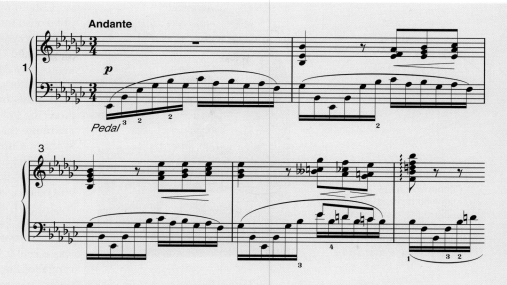

0:23 **b.** Varied repeat of main melody in lower register, smooth transition to

B

24 53 0:44   **2. a.** New flowing melody in high register, major key.

0:59   **b.** Flowing melody repeated in lower register, tempo slows.

1:20   **c.** Downward sequence of even-flowing melody; short-short-short-long rhythm and slowing of tempo introduce

A′

25 54 1:45   **3. a.** Main melody, minor key, short-short-short-long rhythm; gradual descent of melody from high register to low chords separated by pauses.

Coda

26 55 2:24   **b.** Slowing of tempo, short-short-short-long rhythm in low register, two questioning minor chords at close.

7 Frédéric Chopin

Frédéric Chopin (1810–1849), called the poet of the piano, was the only great composer who wrote almost exclusively for the piano.

Chopin was a shy, reserved man who disliked crowds and preferred to play in salons rather than in public concert halls. Photograph of Chopin by L. A. Bisson, Paris, 1849.

Chopin was brought up in Warsaw, the son of a Polish mother and a French father. When he was very young, his highly original style of playing and composing astonished the Polish aristocracy. After graduating from the Warsaw Conservatory, he toured Austria and Germany, playing his own compositions. While he was away, the Poles revolted against the Russians. Learning that the Russians had conquered Warsaw, Chopin was filled with despair and guilt: "They have burnt down the town, . . . and here I am—doing nothing, only heaving sighs and pouring out my grief at the piano."

In 1831, the twenty-one-year-old Chopin arrived in Paris, which would be his home for the rest of his short life. In the 1830s Paris was a center of romanticism and the artistic capital of Europe. Chopin met such writers as Victor Hugo, Balzac, and Heine. The painter Delacroix was Chopin's close friend, as were Liszt and Berlioz.

Chopin's playing quickly gained him access to the aristocratic salons of Paris. Liszt provides a vivid description of the kind of people who attended Chopin's rare concerts: "Numerous carriages brought . . . the most elegant ladies, the most fashionable of young men, the richest financiers, the most illustrious great lords, . . . an entire aristocracy of birth, fortune, and beauty."

Chopin was a shy, reserved man who disliked crowds and preferred to play in salons rather than in public concert halls. It was for such intimate gatherings that he conceived short pieces like the nocturnes, preludes, and waltzes.

Chopin's frail physique made it difficult for him to draw big sounds from the piano. The fascination of his playing lay, rather, in his beautiful tone, rhythmic flexibility, atmospheric use of the pedal, and poetic subtleties of dynamics. Chopin is the only pianist in history to have achieved a legendary reputation on the basis of only thirty or so public performances. He earned a good living by teaching piano to the daughters of the rich. Chopin was an elegant and fashionable man of the world and lived in luxury.

Chopin's life took an increasingly productive turn after he met Aurore Dudevant, a well-known novelist whose pen name was George Sand. She was a feminist who often wore men's clothing, smoked cigars, and fought for sexual freedom. Chopin and Sand became lovers when he was twenty-eight and she thirty-four. He thrived on her care, composing many of his greatest works during the nine years they lived together. After they separated, his health declined rapidly and he composed very little.

Before dying of tuberculosis at thirty-nine, Chopin asked that Mozart's Requiem be played at his funeral. The mourners also heard Chopin's own *Funeral March* from his Piano Sonata in B Flat Minor.

Chopin's Music

By the age of eighteen, Chopin had evolved an utterly personal and original style. Compared with other great composers, he wrote few works, but almost all of them remain in the pianist's repertoire. Most of his pieces are short. But in these exquisite miniatures, Chopin evokes an infinite variety of moods, from melancholy to heroism. His music is always elegant and graceful. Even the virtuoso passages are melodic, not intended merely for display.

Chopin expressed his love of Poland in mazurkas and polonaises. In these stylized dances, he captured the spirit of the Polish people without actually using folk tunes. Unlike Schumann, Chopin did not attach literary programs or titles to his pieces.

No composer has made the piano sound as beautiful as Chopin. His unique melodic gift creates the illusion that the piano is singing. In repeating a melody, Chopin adds delicate and graceful ornamental tones, similar to the vocal decorations heard in the Italian opera of his time. Many of Chopin's most poetic effects come from the sensitive exploitation of the damper ("loud") pedal. He blends harmonies like washes of color. The pedal connects widely spaced tones in the left-hand accompaniment. Chopin's treatment of harmony was highly original and influenced later composers.

Chopin's compositions allow a pianist to heighten expression by slightly speeding up or slowing down the tempo, or by holding a note longer than the music actually indicates. This use of rubato lends a poetic and improvisatory quality to his music.

Nocturne in E Flat Major, Op. 9, No. 2 (1830–1831)

Basic Set:
CD 5 **27**

Brief Set:
CD 3 **56**

Chopin composed his popular Nocturne in E Flat Major, Op. 9, No. 2, when he was about twenty. A **nocturne,** or *night piece,* is a slow, lyrical, intimate composition for piano. Like much of Chopin's music, this nocturne is tinged with melancholy.

Nocturne in E Flat Major opens with a legato melody containing graceful upward leaps, which become increasingly wide as the line unfolds. This melody is heard again three times during the piece. With each repetition, it is varied by ever more elaborate decorative tones and trills. The nocturne also includes a subordinate melody, which is played with rubato—slight fluctuations of tempo.

A sonorous foundation for the melodic line is provided by the widely spaced notes in the accompaniment, connected by the damper ("loud") pedal. The waltzlike accompaniment gently emphasizes the $\frac{12}{8}$ meter, 12 beats to the measure subdivided into four groups of 3 beats each.

The nocturne is reflective in mood until it suddenly becomes passionate near the end. The new concluding melody begins softly but then ascends to a high register and is played forcefully in octaves. After a brilliant trill-like passage, the excitement subsides; the nocturne ends calmly.

LISTENING OUTLINE

CHOPIN, Nocturne in E Flat Major, Op. 9, No. 2

Andante, $\frac{12}{8}$ meter
Piano
(Duration, 4:05)

27 **56**   0:00   **1. a.** Main melody, dolce, espressivo, waltzlike accompaniment.

28 **57** 0:25   **b.** Main melody, ***p***, embellished with decorative notes and trills.

29 **58** 0:51   **2. a.** Subordinate melody, ***p***, played with rubato;

crescendo to

1:18   **b.** Main melody, with more elaborate decorative notes and trills; chromatic descent leads to cadence.

1:44   **c.** Subordinate melody, ***p***, played with rubato; crescendo to

2:11   **d.** Main melody with more elaborate decorative notes and trills; chromatic descent leads to cadence.

2:39   **3. a.** Concluding melody, ***p***, then ***pp***.

3:10   **b.** Concluding melody varied, crescendo with ascent to high register, melody played forcefully in octaves, ***ff***; high trill-like figure, decrescendo and descent to gentle, rocking close, ***pp***, then ***ppp***.

Étude in C Minor, Op. 10, No. 12 (*Revolutionary*; 1831?)

Basic Set:
CD 5 **30**

Brief Set:
CD 3 **59**

The Russian takeover of Warsaw in 1831 may have inspired Chopin to compose the blazing and furious *Revolutionary* Étude in C Minor, Op. 10, No. 12. An ***étude*** is a study piece designed to help a performer master specific technical difficulties. The *Revolutionary* Étude, for example, develops speed and endurance in the pianist's left hand, which must play rapid passages throughout. Chopin's études reach beyond mere exercises in technique to become masterpieces of music, exciting to hear as well as to master.

The *Revolutionary* Étude, in A A'—coda form, begins with a dramatic outburst. High, dissonant chords and downward rushing passages lead to the main melody, marked *appassionato* (*impassioned*), which is played in octaves by the right hand. Tension mounts because of the melody's dotted rhythms and its tempestuous accompaniment. After a climax at the end of section A', the coda momentarily relaxes the tension. Then a torrential passage sweeps down the keyboard to come to rest in powerful closing chords.

LISTENING OUTLINE

CHOPIN, Étude in C Minor, Op. 10, No. 12 (*Revolutionary*)

Allegro con fuoco (allegro with fire), duple meter ($\frac{2}{2}$)

Piano

(Duration, 2:42)

A

30 **59** 0:00   **1.** **a.** High accented chords, ***f***, answered by downward rushing passages; low running notes introduce

0:16   **b.** Passionate main melody in octaves, ***f***, dotted rhythm, minor,

decrescendo to

0:32   **c.** Repetition of main melody, ***p***, with different continuation, syncopated chords, crescendo to cadence in major.

0:46   **d.** Lyrical melody in dotted rhythm, minor, crescendo and downward running notes; very high descending phrases lead to return of

A'

1:00   **2.** **a.** High accented chords, ***f***, answered by downward rushing passages; low running notes introduce

1:22   **b.** Passionate main melody intensified, ***f***, decrescendo; low running notes introduce

1:40   **c.** Repetition of intensified main melody leading to

1:47   **d.** Majestic downward phrases in major, ***ff***, decrescendo, ***p***, return to minor, low running notes rise and fall, ritardando to

Coda

2:10   **e.** Gentle upward phrase repeated with ritardando. Sudden ***ff***, downward rushing passage, powerful closing chords, ***fff***.

Polonaise in A Flat Major, Op. 53 (1842)

Basic Set:
CD 5 **31**
Introduction
31 0:00
Section A
32 0:28

The *polonaise,* a piece in triple meter, originated as a stately processional dance for the Polish nobility. Chopin's heroic polonaises evoke the ancient splendor of the Polish people.

His Polonaise in A Flat Major is majestic and powerful, with moments of lyrical contrast. It may be outlined as follows: introduction—A B A'—coda. Its main theme makes a grand entrance.

The majesty of this theme is enhanced by intervals of thirds in the right hand and by the resonant, wide-ranging accompaniment. After the main theme is repeated twice with an even richer texture, Chopin offers the contrasting middle section (B). This is a marchlike melody accompanied by relentlessly repeated rapid octaves in the left hand. This section tests a pianist's strength and endurance. Powerful crescendos bring mounting excitement. Then Chopin gradually relaxes the mood to prepare for the final return of the heroic main theme (A').

Section B
33 2:48
Section A'
34 5:17

8   Franz Liszt

During the 1840s, a handsome, long-haired, magnetic young man performed super-human feats at the piano and overwhelmed the European musical public. An incredible showman and irresistible to women, Franz Liszt (1811–1886) left a trail of broken hearts from Paris to Moscow. Musicians were as impressed as the concertgoing public. Brahms said, "Whoever has not heard Liszt cannot speak of piano playing." Chopin wished he could play his own piano études the way Liszt played them. Robert Schumann wrote that Liszt "enmeshed every member of the audience with his art and did with them as he willed. Within a few seconds tenderness, boldness, exquisiteness, wildness succeed one another; the instrument glows and flashes under the master's hands."

Franz Liszt, an outstanding pacesetter in the history of music, was born in Hungary. His father was an administrator for the same Esterházy family that Haydn had served. As a boy of eleven, Liszt studied in Vienna, where he met Schubert and Beethoven.

Paris, a city where romanticism flourished and a magnet for virtuoso performers, was Liszt's home during his teens and twenties. When he was nineteen and already acclaimed as a brilliant pianist, Liszt was overwhelmed by the virtuosity of the great violinist Paganini. The unheard-of effects Paganini drew from his violin drove audiences into a frenzy; people half suspected he had been taught by the devil. Young Liszt was determined to become the Paganini of the piano. He withdrew from the concert stage for a few years, practiced from eight to twelve hours a day, and emerged as probably the greatest pianist of his time.

To display his own incomparable piano mastery, Liszt composed his *Transcendental* Études and made piano transcriptions of Paganini's violin pieces. "My piano," he

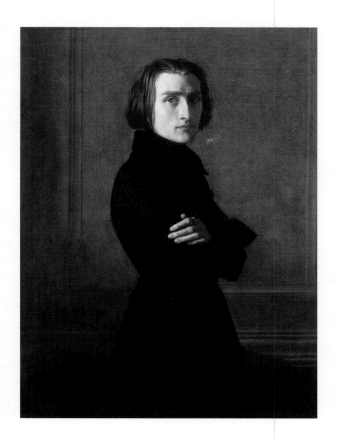

Franz Liszt—handsome, long-haired, magnetic—performed superhuman feats at the piano and overwhelmed the European musical public.

wrote, "is my very self, my mother tongue, my life. . . . A man's ten fingers have the power to reproduce the harmonies which are created by hundreds of performers." Once, following an orchestral performance of a movement from Berlioz's *Fantastic Symphony*, Liszt played his own piano arrangement of the movement and made a more powerful effect than the entire orchestra. He toured Europe tirelessly between 1839 and 1847, playing mainly his own piano music and receiving unprecedented public adulation.

But Liszt wanted recognition as a serious composer, too. At thirty-six, he abandoned his career as a traveling virtuoso to become court conductor for the grand duke in Weimar. He composed many orchestral pieces during the years that followed and developed a new form of program music that influenced later composers. Weimar had become a center for modern music, and Liszt conducted works by such contemporaries as Berlioz, Schumann, and Wagner. One of the most unselfish and generous musicians who ever lived, he provided musical and financial support crucial to Wagner's success. Hundreds of gifted pianists flocked to Weimar, and he taught them free of charge.

Liszt was also an active writer, publishing music criticism as well as books on Chopin and Gypsy music. His literary efforts were aided by two women with whom he had long-term relationships. Both were aristocrats and writers. The first, Countess Marie d'Agoult, left her husband to live with Liszt. (One of their three children, Cosima, later left her own husband to marry Richard Wagner.) Liszt's companion in Weimar was the Russian Princess Carolyne Sayn-Wittgenstein, a deeply religious woman who wrote a twenty-four-volume study entitled *Interior Causes of the External Weakness of the Church.*

Liszt's many-sided career took another abrupt turn in 1861. Dissatisfied with conditions at Weimar, he resigned and went to Rome to pursue religious studies. In 1865 he took minor holy orders, becoming Abbé Liszt. Contemporaries were stunned by the seeming incongruity: a notorious Don Juan and diabolical virtuoso had become a churchman. In Rome, Liszt composed oratorios and masses, feeling that he had a mission to reform and renew church music.

During the last seventeen years of his life, Liszt traveled between Rome, Weimar, and Budapest, where he was president of the new Academy of Music. Now he began to write curious, experimental piano pieces that foreshadowed some features of twentieth-century music. Though these late works went unappreciated, Liszt had become a living legend. The grand duke who had once employed him said, "Liszt *was* what a prince *ought* to be."

Liszt's Music

Liszt's music is controversial. Some consider it vulgar and bombastic; others revel in its extroverted romantic rhetoric. Yet few would deny Liszt's originality, his influence, or his importance as the creator of the symphonic poem.

Liszt found new ways to exploit the piano; under his hands it could give the impression of an entire orchestra. In the *Hungarian Rhapsodies,* which influenced a generation of nationalist composers, Liszt made the piano sound at times like a cimbalom (a Hungarian instrument in which strings are struck by hammers held in the hand) and at other times like an entire Gypsy band. Liszt's piano works demand an unprecedented range of dynamics, from a whispered *ppp* to a thunderous *fff*. He requires the pianist to play rapid octaves and daring leaps. Lyrical melodies are embellished with rapid runs, and melodies in the middle register are sometimes surrounded by garlands of arpeggios which create the impression that three hands are playing, not two. Before the age of phonograph records and frequent concerts, Liszt's transcriptions of operas and symphonies made it possible for people to play great orchestral works on their own pianos.

Liszt created the symphonic poem, or tone poem, a one-movement orchestral composition based to some extent on literary or pictorial ideas (see Section 10). In his symphonic poems and other works, Liszt unified contrasting moods through thematic transformation: a single musical idea recurs throughout a work but is varied so that its character is transformed. For example, in his most famous symphonic poem, *Les Préludes,* a basic motive is treated as a majestic melody in one section, a love theme in another, and a march in the concluding section. Liszt's music can stand by itself without a program, as can most program music. However, he no doubt felt that particular influences from literature should be cited to make his musical processes very clear. Liszt broke away from the standard four-movement symphony and from the sonata form as it was used by the classical masters.

Among Liszt's favorite inspirations were the literary works of Goethe (on which he based his *Faust* Symphony, 1854) and Dante (which inspired the *Dante* Symphony, 1856). Many of his compositions are concerned with the devil or death and bear titles like *Mephisto Waltz, Totentanz (Dance of Death),* or *Funérailles (Funeral Ceremony).* Continual changes of tempo and mood and alternations between diabolical fury and semireligious meditation contribute to a feeling of improvisation.

Liszt's music influenced many composers, including Wagner, who admitted to him: "When I compose and orchestrate, I always think only of you." As a stupendous performer, innovative composer, and charismatic personality, Liszt typified the romantic movement.

Transcendental Étude No. 10 in F Minor (1851)

Basic Set:
CD 5 35

As dazzling, passionate, and poetic as Liszt himself, the *Transcendental* Étude No. 10 in F Minor is one of the finest virtuoso pieces of the romantic era. Liszt had written an early, simpler version of this piece in 1824, when he was only thirteen, and included it in a group of twelve studies. Fifteen years later, at the peak of his career as a virtuoso, he published a revised version that demanded transcendent, almost superhuman technical skill from the pianist. (Schumann was so overwhelmed by Liszt's études that he described them as "studies in storm and dread meant to be played by, at most, ten or twelve players in the world.") In 1851, after retiring from the concert stage, Liszt dedicated a third and final version—which we'll study—to his piano teacher Carl Czerny (1791–1857) "as a token of esteem, gratitude, and friendship."

The étude taxes the player with left-hand passages that require rapid skips and changes of hand position. Though written in A B A'—coda form, it almost seems like an improvisation, owing to its frequent alternations between brilliant virtuoso passages and more melodic ideas. The A section contains three themes. The first, in minor, is fragmentary and syncopated. The second, in major, is more lyrical and in a high register, with dotted rhythms, and with rapid notes in the accompaniment. The third, which has a processional character, is a transformation of the second. (In the listening outline, this is called the *processional theme*.) A melody that was introduced in major in a high register is now presented in minor, in a low register set against higher arpeggios. Yet another thematic transformation takes place in the coda, which is based on a speeded-up variant of the syncopated main theme.

LISTENING OUTLINE

LISZT, *Transcendental* Étude No. 10 in F Minor
Allegro agitato molto (very agitated allegro), duple meter ($\frac{2}{4}$), A B A'—coda form, F minor
Piano
(Duration, 4:44)

A

35 0:00   **1. a.** Rapid falling chords and syncopated fragment, *p*; rapid falling chords, syncopated main theme.

Gradual ascent and crescendo to

0:17   **b.** Abrupt outbursts, *f*, alternating with upward sweeps; descent to rapid falling chords, decrescendo, slight ritardando.

0:29   **c.** Syncopated main theme, ascent and crescendo to

36 0:42   **2. a.** Very high lyrical theme in octaves, *ff*, major, dotted rhythm, rapid accompaniment.

High syncopated octaves in melody, close into

1:00   **b.** Abrupt outbursts, *f*, alternating with upward sweeps, *ff*, slight ritardando.

37 1:14   **3.** Low "processional theme," *ff*, in minor, against higher rapid arpeggios.

B

38 1:26   **4. a.** Sudden *p*, syncopated main theme varied, crescendo, ascending phrases lead to *ff* climax, downward sweeps, slight ritardando.

    1:49   **b.** Breathless staccato syncopated chords, ascent with crescendo and accelerando to high chord, *ff*. Rapid falling chords, decrescendo, and ritardando introduce

A′

39 2:04   **5.** Syncopated main theme, *p*, gradual ascent, crescendo and ritardando to high octaves.

    2:22   **6. a.** Very high lyrical theme in minor, *p*, accompanied by rapid arpeggios; gradual crescendo builds to high repeated octaves, *ff*, climax on

    3:04   **b.** Syncopated octave descending melody in minor, *ff*, ritardando; cadence to

    3:22   **c.** Abrupt outbursts, *f*, alternating with upward sweeps, *ff*; high broken octaves descend to

    3:36   **7. a.** Low minor "processional theme," *ff*, against higher rapid arpeggios; ascent to dissonant held chord.

                b. High broken chords ascend chromatically. Brief pause.

Coda

40 4:05   **8. a.** Faster tempo, furiously syncopated octaves,

crescendo, close into

                b. Rising octave leaps, concluding massive chords.

9 Felix Mendelssohn

Felix Mendelssohn (1809–1847) was a romantic whose music was deeply rooted in classical tradition. He was born in Hamburg, Germany, to a wealthy and famous family. His father was a banker, and his grandfather was the distinguished Jewish philosopher Moses Mendelssohn. Felix, a brother, and two sisters were raised in the Protestant faith.

Mendelssohn's talent was as phenomenal and precocious as Mozart's. By the age of nine, he was a brilliant pianist; by age thirteen, he had written symphonies, concertos, sonatas, and vocal works. And the quality of this youthful work is even more astounding than its quantity. His Overture to *A Midsummer Night's Dream* (1826), which he composed when he was seventeen, is a masterpiece of startling originality. As a teenager, Mendelssohn tried out his compositions with a private orchestra in the family dining room at a series of Sunday musicales. These gatherings were attended by the intellectual and artistic elite of Berlin, where the Mendelssohns had settled.

In 1829, at twenty, Mendelssohn conducted Bach's *St. Matthew Passion* in its first performance since the composer's death. This historic concert rekindled interest in Bach's music and earned Mendelssohn an international reputation. He often performed as a pianist, an organist, and a conductor in Germany and in England, where his own music was especially popular. When only twenty-six, Mendelssohn became conductor of the Leipzig Gewandhaus Orchestra and transformed it into one of the finest performing groups in Europe. He directed the posthumous premiere of Schubert's *Great* C Major Symphony, which his friend Robert Schumann had discovered, as well

Besides his musical achievements, Felix Mendelssohn was a talented painter, a fine writer, and a brilliant conversationalist in four languages.

as the first performances of two Schumann symphonies. As though all these accomplishments weren't enough, Mendelssohn founded the Leipzig Conservatory when he was thirty-three.

Besides his musical achievements, Mendelssohn was a talented painter, a fine writer, and a brilliant conversationalist in four languages. He was extremely polished and charming and felt at ease in aristocratic salons. In England, Mendelssohn often visited the young Queen Victoria, who sang his songs while he accompanied her on the piano. His personal life was more conventional than that of many romantics; he was happily married and the father of four children.

The high point of Mendelssohn's career was the triumphant premiere of his oratorio *Elijah* in Birmingham, England, in 1846. The London *Times* reported that "the last note of 'Elijah' was drowned in a long-continued unanimous volley of plaudits, vociferous and deafening." But constant travel and exhausting work sapped Mendelssohn's strength. The death of his beloved sister Fanny in 1847 was a violent shock, and he himself died five months later at the age of thirty-eight.

Mendelssohn's Music

Mendelssohn's music radiates the elegance and balance of his personality. It evokes a variety of moods but avoids emotional extremes. His pieces typically convey an elfin quality through rapid movement, lightness, and transparent orchestral texture. He was a musical landscapist who could depict a particular atmosphere in orchestral program works. For example, the *Hebrides* Overture (1830–1832; also called *Fingal's Cave*) suggests an agitated sea through swells and surges of sound. But even when Mendelssohn evokes something extra musical, his compositions have a logical form, and we can enjoy them without knowing their sources of inspiration.

Mendelssohn wrote an enormous amount of music in all the forms of his day except opera. Today, only a few of his works are in the concert repertoire, but these are extremely popular. Among his best-known compositions are the Violin Concerto—which we'll study—the *Midsummer Night's Dream* and *Hebrides* overtures, the *Italian* and *Scotch* symphonies (1833, 1842), the oratorio *Elijah*, and Trio in D Minor for Violin, Cello, and Piano (1839). His collection of short piano pieces *Songs without Words* (1829–1845) has now returned to favor after a period of neglect. These pieces convey youthful dash and vigor as well as lyricism tinged with melancholy, basic qualities of Mendelssohn's art.

Concerto for Violin and Orchestra in E Minor, Op. 64 (1844)

Mendelssohn's Violin Concerto in E Minor, Op. 64, was inspired by his friendship with the concertmaster of his orchestra, the famous violinist Ferdinand David. "I should like to make a violin concerto for you next winter," Mendelssohn wrote. "One in E minor runs in my head and its beginning gives me no rest." With David as soloist, the Violin Concerto met with great success at its premiere in 1845. Ever since, its unique fusion of lyricism and virtuosity has made it one of the best-loved concertos.

The concerto's three movements are played without pause, in a characteristic linking technique used by romantic composers. Mendelssohn's love of balance is reflected in the cooperation and interplay between soloist and orchestra. Themes pass from one to another, producing a beautiful contrast of tone color and expression. At one moment, the violinist plays a melody while the orchestra discreetly accompanies; at another, the woodwinds present thematic fragments while the soloist has dazzling running passages.

First Movement:
Allegro molto appassionato (very impassioned allegro)

Though Mendelssohn is usually considered a conservative composer, a "classical romantic," his opening movement departs from classical concerto form. Traditionally, the opening movement of a concerto began with an extended section for orchestra. But Mendelssohn's first movement begins with the soloist, who presents the main theme. This ardent, expansive melody is heard high above a murmuring string accompaniment. The orchestra then expands the violin's theme and introduces a new, flowing melody that begins the bridge section of this sonata-form movement. Toward the end of the bridge, the excitement is gradually relaxed to prepare for the second theme, a tranquil woodwind melody which the soloist accompanies with a single sustained tone. This unusual combination of instruments produces a delicate, intimate sound. Following this, the violin reclaims the spotlight and sings the tranquil theme while the woodwinds support it.

The cadenza has a new function in this movement. In classical concertos, the cadenza was improvised by the soloist and played near the end of the movement. Here, the composer has written it out and placed it at the end of the development section as a transition to the recapitulation. Mendelssohn wanted the cadenza to be an integral part of the movement, not merely something tacked on to display the soloist's virtuosity. Listen for the magical moment when the violinist's rapid arpeggios are joined by the orchestra softly playing the first theme of the recapitulation.

Basic Set:
CD 5 **41**

Brief Set:
CD 4 **1**

LISTENING OUTLINE

MENDELSSOHN, Concerto for Violin and Orchestra in E Minor

First Movement: Allegro molto appassionato

Sonata form, duple meter ($\frac{2}{2}$), E minor

Solo violin, 2 flutes, 2 oboes, 2 clarinets, 2 bassoons, 2 French horns, 2 trumpets, timpani, 1st violins, 2d violins, violas, cellos, double basses

(Duration, 12:01)

Exposition

First theme

41 **1** 0:00   **1. a.** Strings, **_p_**, introduce solo violin. Main melody in minor, high register, legato.

0:29   **b.** Running notes in solo violin. Crescendo, climbing phrases.
0:53   **c.** Orchestra, **_ff_**, main melody. Increased rhythmic motion leads to cadence.

Bridge

42 **2**   1:22

2. a. Violins, flowing bridge theme. Solo violin repeats bridge theme an octave higher.

1:35

b. Solo violin phrases sweep downward and upward through wide range. Flute joins. Crescendo. Running passage rises and falls. Decrescendo, mood calms.

Second theme

43 **3**   2:34

3. a. Clarinets and flutes, ***pp***, calm melody in major. Solo violin accompanies with sustained tone.

2:49

b. Solo violin, ***pp***, calm theme expanded. Woodwinds, then strings accompany.

3:53

4. a. Main melody in solo violin, major. Brilliant running passages, pizzicato accompaniment. Crescendo.

4:40

b. Climactic orchestral trills alternate with solo violin, opening of main melody. Decrescendo.

Development

44 **4**   5:00

1. a. Solo violin, ***p***, flowing bridge theme. Violins, ***f***.

5:13

b. Running passage in solo violin and fragments of main melody in orchestra.

5:38

2. Solo violin, ***p***, main melody varied. Decrescendo. Violin melody slowly descends. Orchestral crescendo to ***ff***.

Cadenza

45 **5**   6:27

3. Unaccompanied solo violin, broken chords. Ascents to high tones, trills, fragment of main melody. Rapid broken chords lead into

Recapitulation

First theme

46 **6**   8:01

1. Main melody in orchestra, ***p***. Broken chords continue in solo violin. Crescendo.

Bridge

8:18

2. a. Orchestra, ***ff***, bridge theme.

b. Solo violin, ***mf***, bridge theme carried downward. Decrescendo.

Second theme

8:48

3. a. Woodwinds, ***pp***, calm melody in major. Solo violin accompanies with sustained tone.

9:02

b. Solo violin, ***pp***, calm theme expanded. Woodwinds, then strings accompany.

10:09

4. a. Brilliant running passages in solo violin. Pizzicato accompaniment. Crescendo.

10:55

b. Climactic orchestral trills alternate with solo violin, opening of main melody. Decrescendo.

Coda

11:14

5. Solo violin, bridge theme. Tempo becomes faster. Crescendo. Brilliant running passages. Full orchestra, ***ff***.

Hilary Hahn, Violinist, Playing the First Movement of Mendelssohn's Violin Concerto in E Minor, Op. 64

Hilary Hahn is one of the most prominent concert violinists of our time. In 1999, when she was nineteen, *Time* Magazine called her "America's best" young classical musician.

As with most concert artists, Hahn's extraordinary musical talent was recognized at a very early age. When not quite four, she began studying violin, and at age ten she was accepted at the Curtis Institute of Music in Philadelphia. At sixteen, she signed a recording contract, made her debut at Carnegie Hall with the Philadelphia Orchestra, and completed the requirements for her bachelor of music degree. However, she chose to delay her graduation from Curtis for three years: "I loved the school, so I stayed as long as I could. There were a lot of classes that interested me that I hadn't taken yet; for extra electives, I enrolled in poetry- and fiction-writing workshops and several literature classes, in addition to continuing with German."

For Hahn, "communicating music to people is something that I feel very lucky to be able to do." She writes her own liner notes for her recordings and maintains an online journal (on her Web site, HilaryHahn.com) of her experiences in cities where she performs. To expand children's musical horizons, Hahn often plays in grade schools. "I always play solo Bach, a slow and a fast movement. The music casts a spell. They really like it."

Hahn enjoys music in a wide range of styles, from blues and world music to trip-hop and classical. Her prizewinning recordings include works by Mendelssohn, Bach, Beethoven, and Bernstein, and she performs on the sound track of the M. Night Shyamalan film *The Village,* as well as on an album by Austin alt-rockers . . . *And You Will Know Us by the Trail of Dead.*

Hahn learned the Mendelssohn Violin Concerto when she was eleven and performed excerpts with the Curtis Orchestra the following year. (Her performance of the first movement of the concerto is included in the recordings.) "Not long after, I performed the entire concerto with a chamber orchestra in Florida, and since then the Mendelssohn concerto has been a staple of my repertoire." For Hahn, the first movement of the concerto is full of "lyricism, fire, drama, and contrast."

Hahn observes that performing a concerto requires close cooperation with the conductor and members of the orchestra. "Sometimes the conductor and I will disagree about something and meet in the middle. There's a system of give-and-take, opinions, and compromise—though as a musician, you try to never be compromised or compromise someone else's interpretation. Musicians inevitably interact with each other, so we have to be aware of what the others are doing. For example, if I share a solo line with the flute, I will pay attention to how the flutist plays the line so that it sounds like a duet. The conductor coordinates some of that, but in a concerto, the minutiae are really decided by the musicians, by listening to each other and reacting to the musical ideas that we hear."

For Hahn, playing before a live audience is very different from recording in a studio. "The audience influences performing to a large extent because the presence of people affects the way the concert hall sounds. The energy in the hall is hard to describe, but there is a different feeling when you know people are there to absorb the music (both acoustically and psychologically). It's quite energizing and inspiring. In recording, you have a limited time and an empty hall—any tiny noise can ruin a take, so no audience is allowed in the studio—and you have to get it right, so that situation takes a different approach. I try to keep the feeling as similar as possible, though, by imagining an audience listening in the hall, or in their car, or to their stereo."

Second Movement:
Andante

A single bassoon tone links the brilliant opening movement with the hushed intro-duction to the slow second movement. The C major andante is a songlike, intimate piece in A B A′ form. Its opening section (A) features a warm, expansive melody in the solo violin's high register; a string accompaniment gently emphasizes the ⅜ meter (1–2–3–4–5–6). The middle section (B) becomes more agitated, and the accompaniment is rhythmically more active. The orchestra plays a more important role as it engages in dialogue with the soloist. Mendelssohn requires the solo violinist to play a melody and a trembling accompaniment figure at the same time. The soloist also presents the melody in full-sounding octaves. The transition to the concluding A′ section is very smooth because the trembling accompaniment figure is maintained. The andante ends quietly with a tender epilogue for solo violin and woodwinds.

Third Movement:
Allegretto non troppo (transitional section);
Allegro molto vivace (very lively allegro)

A pensive transitional section for solo violin and strings connects the andante with the concluding movement of the concerto. The very rapid finale, in sonata form, creates the lightness, joy, and brilliance so typical of Mendelssohn's art. Forceful chords in the woodwinds and upward solo figures usher in the playful and mostly staccato opening theme of the exposition; it is presented by the solo violin and high woodwinds.

A dazzling series of running passages and a long upward scale lead directly into the second theme, which is also a carefree one. With great effect, it combines a loud, marchlike phrase by the full orchestra with a softer motive from the opening theme.

In the development, the woodwinds softly present the marchlike phrase while the soloist plays brilliant running passages. A highlight of the development comes when the violinist presents a new legato melody which the strings lightly accompany with fragments of the opening theme.

Then there is a reversal of roles: the strings sing the lyrical melody while the soloist gracefully presents the fragment of the opening theme.

At the beginning of the recapitulation, the two themes are combined once again. The French horn and lower strings play the warm legato melody while the soloist brings back the sparkling first theme. After a return of the second theme, the move-ment builds to an exciting climax in the coda, which is fuller in sound than anything that has come before.

10 | Program Music

Romantic composers were particularly attracted to *program music*—instrumental music associated with a story, poem, idea, or scene. Programmatic orchestral works such as Berlioz's *Fantastic Symphony*, Tchaikovsky's *Romeo and Juliet*, and Smetana's *Moldau* depict the emotions, characters, and events of particular stories or the sounds and motions of nature. Such nonmusical ideas are usually specified by the title or by the composer's explanatory comments (*program*) in the concertgoer's program.

Program music draws on the capacity of music to suggest and evoke. It is obvious that music can imitate certain sounds—birdsongs, the rumble of thunder, the clang of bells, or the howling of the wind. But "sound effects" are only part of the descriptive resources of music. A composer can also exploit the correspondence between musical rhythm and objects in motion. A continuous flow of rapid notes, for example, can evoke a running stream or the rise and fall of waves. Most important, though, is the ability of music to create mood, emotion, and atmosphere. An agitated theme can represent a feud between rival families, just as a lyrical melody can symbolize youthful love.

Apart from the sound effects just described, music alone makes no definite reference to ideas, emotions, and objects. Music cannot identify anything. It is the title or a verbal explanation that lets us fully grasp a composer's source of inspiration. We know that the agitated theme in Tchaikovsky's *Romeo and Juliet* is meant to suggest a feud between rival families, but in another piece the same theme could as easily evoke a king's rage or a cavalry charge.

The aim of most program music is expression more than mere description. Beethoven explicitly stated this aim when he referred to his *Pastoral* Symphony (his Symphony No. 6) as "an expression of feeling rather than painting." Even the most "realistic" episodes in program music can also serve a purely musical function, as in the slow movement of the *Pastoral, By the Brook,* where the songs of a nightingale, quail, and cuckoo are realistically imitated. (The names of these birds are even written in the score.) These birdcalls provide a point of rest near the end of the movement and flow logically from what has come before.

Generally, we can appreciate a descriptive piece as pure music, without knowing its title or program. We can enjoy the lyrical theme of Tchaikovsky's *Romeo and Juliet,* for example, without associating it with young love. The forms used for program music are similar to those used for nonprogram music, or *absolute music.* A programmatic work can be heard simply as an example of rondo, fugue, sonata form, or theme and variations. But our pleasure may be greater when we can relate music to literary or pictorial ideas. Romantic composers were well aware that verbal explanations helped listeners follow the flow of music. Occasionally, they even added titles or programs to finished works. Musicians and audiences in the romantic period liked to read stories into all music, whether intended by the composer or not.

Clearly, the distinction between program music and absolute music is not always useful. A composition entitled simply Symphony No. 6 might have a program that its composer chooses not to reveal. Here are Tchaikovsky's comments about his Sixth Symphony (*Pathétique*): "This time a program symphony—but with a program which shall remain an enigma for everyone—let them puzzle their heads over it. This program is subjective through and through, and during my journey, while composing it in my mind, I often wept bitterly."

Most romantic program music was written for piano or for orchestra. Schumann's *Carnaval* (1835) and Mussorgsky's *Pictures at an Exhibition* (1874)—each a set of short pieces—are well-known descriptive compositions for piano. But program music found its most varied expression in the coloristic resources of the romantic orchestra. The main forms of orchestral program music are the program symphony, the concert overture, the symphonic poem (tone poem), and incidental music.

A ***program symphony*** is a composition in several movements—as its name implies, a symphony with a program. Usually, each movement has a descriptive title. For example, Berlioz's *Fantastic Symphony* has five movements: (1) *Reveries, Passions,* (2) *A Ball,* (3) *Scene in the Country,* (4) *March to the Scaffold,* and (5) *Dream of a Witches' Sabbath.* (This work is discussed in Section 11.)

A ***concert overture*** has one movement, usually in sonata form. The romantic concert overture was modeled after the opera overture, a one-movement composition that establishes the mood of an opera. But the concert overture is *not* intended to usher in a stage work; it is an independent composition. Well-known concert overtures include Mendelssohn's *Hebrides* Overture and Tchaikovsky's *Overture 1812* and *Romeo and Juliet* Overture, which is studied in Section 13.

A ***symphonic poem,*** or ***tone poem,*** is also a one-movement composition. Symphonic poems take many traditional forms—sonata form, rondo, or theme and variations—as well as irregular forms. This flexibility of form separates the symphonic poem from the concert overture, which is usually in sonata form. Franz Liszt developed the symphonic poem in the late 1840s and 1850s, and it became the most important type of program music after 1860. Well-known tone poems include *Les Préludes,* (1854) and *Hamlet* (1858), by Liszt; *Danse macabre* (1874), by Camille Saint-Saëns (1835–1921); and *The Sorcerer's Apprentice* (1897), by Paul Dukas (1865–1935). A leading composer of tone poems at the end of the nineteenth century was Richard Strauss (1864–1949). His tone poems—characterized by brilliant orchestration—include *Don Juan* (1889), *Till Eulenspiegel's Merry Pranks* (1895), and *Also sprach Zarasthustra (So Spoke Zoroaster;* 1896), which was used in the film *2001: A Space Odyssey.* During the late nineteenth century, symphonic poems became an important means of expression for nationalism in music. In Section 14, we'll consider a nationalistic tone poem, Smetana's *Moldau,* depicting the longest river of Bohemia (a region which became part of the modern Czech Republic) as it winds through the countryside.

Incidental music is music that is intended to be performed before and during a play. It is "incidental" to the staged drama, but it sets the mood for certain scenes. Interludes, background music, marches, and dances are all incidental music (as are today's movie scores). Mendelssohn's incidental music for *A Midsummer Night's Dream* includes his famous *Wedding March.*

11 Hector Berlioz

Hector Berlioz (1803–1869), one of the first French romantic composers and a daring creator of new orchestral sounds, was born in a small town near Grenoble. Berlioz was twenty before he could devote himself to music. His father, a physician, sent him to Paris to study medicine, but Berlioz was "filled with horror" by the dissecting room. He shocked his parents by abandoning his medical studies to pursue a career in music.

It did not take long for Berlioz to fill the gaps in his musical knowledge. He studied at the Paris Conservatory, analyzed musical scores, haunted the opera house, and composed. He memorized many operas and became furious if a conductor tampered with the orchestration. This fiery young fanatic would stand during a performance and shout, "Not two flutes, you scoundrels! Two piccolos! Two piccolos!"

When he was twenty-three, Berlioz was overwhelmed by the works of Shakespeare. He also fell madly in love with Harriet Smithson, a Shakespearean actress whose portrayals of Ophelia and Juliet had captivated the Parisian public. Berlioz wrote Harriet

The French composer Hector Berlioz was a daring creator of new orchestral sounds and one of the first great orchestra conductors.

such wild and impassioned letters that she thought he was a lunatic and refused to see him. He grieved: "If she could for one moment conceive all the poetry, all the infinity of such a love, she would fly into my arms." Instead, Harriet Smithson left Paris without meeting Berlioz. That came later.

To depict his "endless and unquenchable passion," Berlioz wrote the *Symphonie fantastique* (*Fantastic Symphony*) in 1830. Parisians were startled by the sensationally autobiographical program for the symphony, its amazingly novel orchestration, and its vivid depiction of the weird and diabolical. At twenty-six, Berlioz had become the musical counterpart of such revolutionary French romantics as Victor Hugo and Delacroix.

In 1830, too, Berlioz won the Prix de Rome (Rome Prize), the highest award of the Paris Conservatory. The prize subsidized two years' study in Rome. When he returned to Paris from his studies in Rome, Berlioz presented a concert featuring his *Fantastic Symphony*. In the audience was Harriet Smithson. When she realized that Berlioz's music depicted her, "she felt the room reel about her; she heard no more but sat in a dream." The next day, they met, and a year later they were married. Alas, the fantasy was more successful than reality—they separated after only a few years.

Berlioz's unconventional music irritated the directors of the main opera house and concert society in Paris. To get a hearing for his works, Berlioz had to arrange concerts at his own expense. This involved hiring a hall, rounding up hundreds of musicians, writing publicity, getting the music copied, and countless other petty chores; it drained Berlioz financially, physically, and emotionally. "The main reason for the long war against me," he wrote when he was fifty-four, "lies in the antagonism existing between my musical feeling and that of the great mass of the Parisian public." He complained that "all music off the beaten track . . . seemed to these people the music of madness." Berlioz was not completely unappreciated in Paris. He had a following of about 1,200 who faithfully bought tickets to his concerts. Nevertheless, this was not enough support for a composer of difficult and monumental works requiring much rehearsal time and hundreds of performers. To support his family, Berlioz turned to musical journalism. He was one of the most brilliant and witty music critics who ever lived. He made it his mission to convince the Parisian public that music was not merely a form of entertainment but dramatic emotional expression.

Outside France, Berlioz's stock was higher. Liszt directed a German orchestra in several "Berlioz weeks," performing nothing but Berlioz's works. After 1840, Berlioz was in demand throughout Europe, conducting his own music and that of others. As one of the first great orchestral conductors, he influenced a whole generation of musicians. In 1860, Wagner wrote to Liszt, saying that the three greatest composers of the time were Wagner, Liszt, and Berlioz.

Berlioz's later years were bitter. He was repeatedly passed over for important conducting positions and academic honors. He composed very little during the six years before his death at sixty-five.

Berlioz's Music

"The prevailing qualities of my music," wrote Berlioz, "are passionate expressiveness, inner fire, rhythmic drive, and unexpectedness." Above all, Berlioz's music sounds unique. It includes abrupt contrasts between high woodwinds and low strings, snarling brass, and rumbling percussion. The dynamics fluctuate continually, and the tempo changes many times.

Berlioz was extraordinarily imaginative in treating the orchestra, creating tone colors never before heard. At a time when the average orchestra contained about sixty players, Berlioz often assembled hundreds of musicians to achieve an enormous range of power and instrumental timbre. More than any earlier composer, he made tone color a basic part of his musical language. A list of orchestral effects in the *Fantastic Symphony* alone would include four kettledrums combining to play a chord, bells combined with brasses, and violinists striking the strings with the bow stick.

Berlioz's compositions are full of long melodies that take unexpected turns and are irregular and asymmetrical in construction. To critics who complained that his works lacked melodies, Berlioz replied, "To deny their existence is unfair and absurd. But as they are often on a large scale, an immature or unappreciative mind cannot appreciate their forms."

Most of Berlioz's works are for orchestra, or for orchestra with chorus and vocal soloists. All his major works are dramatic in nature and relate either to a literary program or to a text. He invented new forms: his "dramatic symphony" *Romeo and Juliet* (1839) is for orchestra, chorus, and vocal soloists; and his "dramatic legend" *The Damnation of Faust* (1846) combines opera and oratorio. Berlioz wrote three operas: *Benvenuto Cellini* (1838), *The Trojans* (1856–1858), and *Beatrice and Benedict* (1860–1862). Some of his works, such as his Requiem (1837), are grandiose and monumental. He knew he was a pioneer in this territory: "In the Requiem, for example, I employ four distinct brass orchestras, answering each other at certain distances around the main orchestra and chorus. The result of this immensity of form is that one either entirely misses the drift of the music or is crushed by a tremendous emotion. . . . I have seen one man listening in terror, shaken to the depths of his soul, while his next neighbor could not catch an idea, though trying with all his might to do so."

Symphonie fantastique (Fantastic Symphony; 1830)

The astonishing *Symphonie fantastique* (*Fantastic Symphony*), a five-movement program symphony, is a romantic manifesto. Both the symphony and Berlioz's program reflect the twenty-six-year-old composer's unrequited passion for the actress Harriet Smithson:

> A young musician of extraordinary sensibility and abundant imagination, in the depths of despair because of hopeless love, has poisoned himself with opium. The drug is too feeble to kill him but plunges him into a heavy sleep accompanied by weird visions. His sensations, emotions, and memories, as they pass through his affected mind, are transformed into musical images and ideas. The beloved one herself becomes to him a melody, a recurrent theme (*idée fixe*) which haunts him continually.

A single melody, which Berlioz called the ***idée fixe,*** or *fixed idea,* is used to represent the beloved. It appears in all five movements and unifies the contrasting episodes of the symphony. This recurrence of the same theme in every movement of a symphony was a striking novelty in Berlioz's day. The theme changes in character during the work, sounding, in turn, exultant, waltzlike, and vulgar.

Another innovation in the symphony is its use of a very large and colorful orchestra: piccolo, 2 flutes, 2 oboes, English horn, 2 clarinets, 4 bassoons, 4 French horns, 2 cornets, 2 trumpets, 3 trombones, 2 tubas, 4 timpani, bass drum, snare drum, cymbals, bells, 2 harps, and strings. (Beethoven, for one, had not used the English horn, tuba, bells, cornet, or harp in his symphonies.) Berlioz saves the heaviest orchestration for the last two movements, where he depicts the fantastic and diabolical. Though the macabre and supernatural had long been dealt with in opera (for example, in Mozart's *Don Giovanni*), this is its first expression in an important symphony.

First Movement: *Reveries, Passions*
Largo (slow introduction); Allegro agitato e appassionato assai (agitated and very impassioned allegro)

> First he remembers that weariness of the soul, that indefinable longing, that somber melancholia, and those objectless joys which he experienced before meeting his beloved. Then, the volcanic love with which she suddenly inspired him, his delirious suffering, his return to tenderness, his religious consolations.

The symphony opens with an extended slow introduction—almost a movement in itself—in which fluctuations of tempo and mood help create a dreamlike atmosphere. A long muted violin melody expresses, in Berlioz's words, "the overpowering sadness of a young heart first caught in the toils of a hopeless love."

The allegro movement following the introduction is written in a modified sonata form. Its first theme, played by the violins and flutes, is the *idée fixe* (*fixed idea*). Berlioz described this expansive, upward-groping melody as "passionate but at the same time noble and shy."

In the development, Berlioz uses a fragment of the *idée fixe* and builds tension through rising and falling chromatic scales played by staccato strings. A shattering climax is followed by a pregnant moment of silence. Yet another climax occurs toward the end of the movement, when the full orchestra plays the *idée fixe* in a hysterically jubilant transformation. The movement concludes with slow chords that evoke the "religious consolations" mentioned in the program.

Second Movement: *A Ball*
Allegro non troppo

> He finds his beloved again at a ball in the midst of the tumult of a brilliant party.

The second movement is a waltz, the most popular dance of the romantic era. Its form may be outlined as introduction—A B A'—coda. A shimmering atmosphere is created in the introduction by string tremolos and delicate harp arpeggios. The lilting waltz theme (the A section) is introduced by the violins.

The B section brings a return of the *idée fixe,* now transformed into a waltz played by woodwinds.

The *idée fixe* is soon joined by an oom-pah-pah accompaniment and intertwined with fragments of the lilting waltz theme.

In the coda, Berlioz builds to a climax that is suddenly interrupted by yet another reminiscence of the *idée fixe*—this time played soulfully by a solo clarinet. The movement concludes brilliantly.

Third Movement: *Scene in the Country*
Adagio

On a summer evening in the country, he hears two herders calling each other with their shepherd melodies. The pastoral duet in such surroundings, the gentle rustle of the trees softly swayed by the wind, some reasons for hope which had come to his knowledge recently—all unite to fill his heart with a rare tranquillity and lend brighter colors to his ideas. But his beloved appears anew, spasms contract his heart, and he is filled with dark premonitions. What if she were deceiving him? One of the shepherds resumes his rustic tune; the other does not reply. The sun sets. Far away there is rumbling thunder—solitude—silence.

Like the preceding waltz movement, the adagio has the form introduction—A B A′—coda. In the introduction, Berlioz evokes a mood of loneliness in the midst of nature: a solo English horn is echoed by an oboe an octave higher. No previous symphonic movement had ever begun with a duet between these two instruments. The A section opens with an extended melody for flute and violins—"delightful reverie."

The *idée fixe* returns in the B section. It is now played by the oboe and flute against an agitated low countermelody in the cellos and basses. This combination of contrasting melodies in widely separated registers and different tone colors is a typically brilliant stroke. At the end of the coda, we again hear the English horn solo, but this time the oboe does not answer. Instead, four timpani suggest the rumbling of distant thunder. Berlioz explains that his aim is not merely to imitate thunder "but rather to make silence more perceptible, and thus to increase the impression of uneasy sadness and painful isolation."

Fourth Movement: *March to the Scaffold*
Allegretto non troppo

He dreams that he has murdered his beloved, that he has been condemned to death and is being led to the scaffold. The procession moves forward to the sounds of a march that is now somber and fierce, now brilliant and solemn, in which the muffled sounds of heavy steps give way without transition to the noisiest outbursts. At the end, the *idée fixe* returns for a moment, like a last thought of love interrupted by the death blow.

Basic Set:
CD 5 47

Brief Set:
CD 4 7

"The *March to the Scaffold* is fifty times more frightening than I expected," Berlioz gleefully observed after the first rehearsals of the *Fantastic Symphony*. It is not until this fiendish fourth movement that all the brass and percussion instruments enter the action. Berlioz creates a menacing atmosphere with the opening orchestral sound, a unique combination of muted French horns, timpani tuned a third apart, and basses playing pizzicato chords.

Two contrasting themes alternate within *March to the Scaffold*. The first theme, described as "somber and fierce" in Berlioz's program, is introduced by cellos and basses and moves down the scale for two octaves. This scalewise melody appears both in minor and in major and is combined with countermelodies. It is also inverted, moving upward rather than downward. The second theme, described as "brilliant and solemn" in the program, is a syncopated march tune blared by the brasses and woodwinds. At the end of the march a solo clarinet begins to play the *idée fixe* but is savagely interrupted by a very loud chord representing the fall of the guillotine's blade. The following string pizzicato may well have been intended to suggest the bouncing of the severed head.

LISTENING OUTLINE

BERLIOZ, *Symphonie fantastique*

Fourth Movement: *March to the Scaffold*

Allegretto non troppo

2 flutes, 2 oboes, 2 clarinets, 4 bassoons, 2 trumpets, 2 cornets, 4 French horns, 3 trombones, 2 tubas, timpani, bass drum, snare drum, cymbals, 1st violins, 2d violins, violas, cellos, double basses

(Duration 4:48)

47 **7** 0:00   **1.** Timpani, pizzicato basses, ***pp***; syncopations in muted French horns, ***p***, crescendo to ***ff*** chord.

48 **8** 0:27   **2. a.** Basses and cellos alone, ***ff***, downward scalewise melody, minor, decrescendo.

Allegretto non troppo

0:41   **b.** Downward melody repeated with countermelody in high bassoons.

0:54   **c.** High violins, ***f***, downward melody, major, accompanied by staccato lower strings. Sudden ***ff***. Melody repeated by violins, ***f***.

1:19   **d.** Staccato bassoons, ***p***, together with pizzicato strings, minor, decrescendo to ***pp***, quick crescendo to

49 **9** 1:39   **3.** Brasses and woodwinds, ***f***, syncopated march tune, major. March tune repeated.

2:04   **4. a.** Very loud brass and woodwind fanfare introduces

2:11   **b.** Splintered downward melody, pizzicato and bowed strings, staccato winds, minor. Pizzicato violins and timpani, crescendo to

2:22   **c.** Brasses, woodwinds, ***f***, syncopated march tune, major, active string accompaniment. March tune repeated.

2:46
2:54   **d.** Very loud brass and woodwind fanfare introduces

3:02   **e.** Splintered downward melody, pizzicato and bowed strings, staccato winds, minor.

3:16   **f.** Brasses, ***mf***, shortened downward melody repeated on higher pitches, active string accompaniment, crescendo.

3:27   **5. a.** Whole orchestra, downward melody, ***ff***, timpani, cymbals, minor, decrescendo to ***pp***.

   b. Sudden ***ff***, whole orchestra, upward scalewise melody, major, timpani, cymbals.

Staccato strings alone, orchestral punctuation, *ff*, excited dotted rhythm in strings, repeated figure in brasses and woodwinds; downward staccato strings, *ff*, lead to

4:01   **c.** Wind and string chords alternate, *f*, decrescendo to *pp*. Sudden *ff*, full orchestra.

50 **10** 4:14   **d.** Solo clarinet, *idée fixe,*

*pp dolce assai
ed appassionato*

interrupted by

4:24   **e.** Short orchestral chord, *ff* (fall of guillotine blade), and string pizzicato (bouncing of severed head), powerful timpani roll, *ff*, brasses and woodwinds *f*, repeated major chord, strings, *ff*, cymbals, ending chord by full orchestra, *ff*.

Fifth Movement: *Dream of a Witches' Sabbath*
Larghetto; Allegro

He sees himself at a witches' sabbath in the midst of a hideous crowd of ghouls, sorcerers, and monsters of every description, united for his funeral. Strange noises, groans, shrieks of laughter, distant cries, which other cries seem to answer. The melody of the loved one is heard, but it has lost its character of nobleness and timidity; it is no more than a dance tune, ignoble, trivial, and grotesque. It is she who comes to the sabbath! . . . A howl of joy greets her arrival. . . . She participates in the diabolical orgy. . . . The funeral knell, burlesque of the *Dies irae.* Witches' dance. The dance and the *Dies irae* combined.

Dream of a Witches' Sabbath is the most "fantastic" movement of the symphony; it depicts a series of grotesque events. Its slow, hushed introduction (larghetto) immediately draws the listener into the realm of the macabre and supernatural, evoking "strange noises, groans, shrieks of laughter" and "distant cries." Eerie tremolos in high muted strings and menacing low tones of cellos and basses begin a succession of fragmentary ideas in starkly contrasting tone colors, registers, and dynamics. In the exploratory spirit of his romantic age, Berlioz dared to create sounds that are weird rather than conventionally pleasing.

In the allegro section, the beloved is revealed to be a witch. Her theme, the once "noble and timid" *idée fixe,* is transformed into a dance tune that is "trivial and grotesque." Played shrilly by a high-pitched clarinet, the tune moves in quick notes decorated by trills.

A "funeral knell" of sonorous bells (chimes) lends an awesome atmosphere to the next part of the movement. Tubas and bassoons intone a solemn low melody in long, even notes. This melody is the medieval chant *Dies irae (Day of wrath),* traditionally sung in the mass for the dead. Berlioz quotes it here as a symbol of eternal damnation. Soon the chant melody is shifted up to a high register and played by woodwinds and pizzicato strings in a quick dancelike rhythm. Thus Berlioz dared to parody a sacred chant by transforming it into a trivial tune, as he had just done moments earlier with the *idée fixe.*

Berlioz conveys the frenzy of a witches' dance in a fuguelike section. The fugue subject (the witches' dance) is introduced by the lower strings and then imitated by other instruments. A crescendo builds to a powerful climax in which the rapid witches' dance, played in the strings, is set against the slower-moving *Dies irae,* proclaimed by the brasses and woodwinds. This musical nightmare ends in an orgy of orchestral power.

LISTENING OUTLINE

BERLIOZ, *Symphonie fantastique*

Fifth Movement: *Dream of a Witches' Sabbath*

Larghetto; Allegro

Piccolo, flute, 2 oboes, 2 clarinets, 4 bassoons, 2 trumpets, 2 cornets,
4 French horns, 3 trombones, 2 tubas, timpani, bass drum, bells (chimes),
1st violins, 2d violins, violas, cellos, double basses

(Duration, 9:47)

Larghetto
Strange noises

51 0:00   **1. a.** High string tremolo, ***pp***, joined by low repeated figure in cellos and basses; high descending staccato strings, ***ppp***; staccato brasses, ***f***; sudden low chord.

0:28   **b.** High woodwinds, short repeated notes, ***mf***, echoed in lower register by muted horn, ***ppp***, ascent to

0:47   **c.** High string tremolo, ***pp***, joined by low repeated figure in cellos and basses; high staccato strings descend to rumble in low strings; sudden loud chord.

1:07   **d.** High woodwinds, short repeated notes, ***mf***, echoed in lower register by muted horn, ***pppp***.

Allegro
Beloved as witch

1:21   **2. a.** Clarinet, part of *idée fixe* as dance tune, timpani accompany, full orchestra interrupts, ***ff***.

52 1:39   **b.** High clarinet, joined by piccolo, *idée fixe* as dance tune, woodwinds accompany; high violins join, leading to

high repeated figure in strings, ***ff***; orchestral chord ***ff***, staccato chromatic descent; repeated chords and string descent lead to

2:28   **c.** Violins, ***p***, rapid ascent and crescendo, cellos and basses, ***p***, descend; long low tones introduce

Funeral knell

2:56   **3.** Bell tolls (chimes) alternating with violas, beginning of witches' dance.

53 3:22   **4. a.** Low tubas and bassoons, ***f***, beginning of *Dies irae* in long even notes, bells (chimes) accompany.

3:43   **b.** Higher horns and trumpets, beginning of *Dies irae* played faster.

54 3:54   **c.** High woodwinds, beginning of *Dies irae* as fast staccato dance tune.

4:00   **5. a.** Low tubas and bassoons, continuation of *Dies irae* in long even notes, bells (chimes) accompany.

4:12   **b.** Higher horns and trumpets, continuation of *Dies irae* played faster.

4:18   **c.** High woodwinds, continuation of *Dies irae* as fast dance tune.

4:22   **6. a.** Low tubas and bassoons, *f*, conclusion of *Dies irae* in long even notes.

4:41   **b.** Higher horns and trumpets, conclusion of *Dies irae* played faster.

4:50   **c.** High woodwinds, conclusion of *Dies irae* as fast dance tune.

4:57   **d.** Strings, beginning of witches' dance with brass interruptions; crescendo to *ff*, full orchestra.

Witches' dance
(fuguelike section)
55 5:14   **7. a.** Witches' dance introduced by cellos and double basses, imitated in violins, then high woodwinds.

5:42   **b.** Violin syncopations, piccolo; strings alternate between *ff* and *p*; crescendo to *ff* repeated chords.

6:01   **c.** Witches' dance introduced in woodwinds, imitated in low strings, then violins.

6:17   **d.** Rapid brass chords, *ff*, bass drum, repeatedly answered by descending high woodwinds; decrescendo to

6:42   **e.** Pizzicato cellos and basses, varied witches' dance, imitations by bassoon, horn punctuations.

6:58   **f.** Low strings, *mf*, *Dies irae* phrases in brasses.

7:14   **g.** Very soft, witches' dance rhythm passed from low to high strings, long crescendo; orchestra, *ff*, repeated syncopated chords.

56 7:52   **8. a.** Witches' dance, strings in unison, *ff*, joined by *Dies irae* in brasses and woodwinds, *ff*.

8:20   **b.** Sudden *p*; *ff* repeated figure in strings and woodwinds, high strings struck with wood of bow joined by

8:31   **c.** Woodwinds, *mf*, varied witches' dance with trills.

8:43   **d.** Staccato woodwinds, *pp*; full orchestral chords, *ff*, alternate with high woodwind trills; sudden *pp*, crescendo to *ff*.

9:05   **e.** Bass drum, *Dies irae* phrase in tubas, played faster by higher brasses and woodwinds; fast and powerful orchestral conclusion.

12 Nationalism in Nineteenth-Century Music

During the nineteenth century, Europeans felt strongly that their homelands merited loyalty and self-sacrifice. These nationalistic feelings were awakened during the upheavals of the French Revolution and the Napoleonic wars (1789–1814), when French armies invaded much of Europe. In many countries, military resistance to Napoleon aroused the citizens' sense of national identity. Common bonds of language, culture, and history were strengthened, since now battles were fought by soldiers drawn from the general population—not by mercenaries, as in the past. Patriotic feeling was intensified, too, by romanticism, which glorified love for one's national heritage.

As a revolutionary political movement, nationalism led to the unification of lands—like Germany and Italy—that had previously been divided into tiny states. It spurred revolts in countries under foreign rule, such as Poland and Bohemia (later part of the Czech Republic).

Nationalism was a potent cultural movement as well, particularly regarding language. In lands dominated by foreign powers, the national language was used increasingly in textbooks, newspapers, and official documents. For example, in Bohemia there was a revival of the Czech language, which before 1800 had lost ground to the German spoken by Austrian rulers. By the 1830s and 1840s, important textbooks on astronomy and chemistry were written in Czech, and there were many collections of Czech folk poetry. In every land, the "national spirit" was felt to reside in the "folk," the peasantry. The national past became a subject of intense historical investigation, and there was new enthusiasm for folk songs, dances, legends, and fairy tales.

Nationalism influenced romantic music, as composers deliberately gave their works a distinctive national identity. They used folk songs and dances and created original melodies with a folk flavor. Nationalist composers wrote operas and program music inspired by the history, legends, and landscapes of their native lands. Their works bear titles like *Russian Easter* Overture (Rimsky-Korsakov), *Finlandia* (Sibelius), and *Slavonic Dances* (Dvořák). But a genuine feeling of national style does not come merely through the use of folk songs or patriotic subjects. A piece of music will *sound* French, Russian, or Italian when its rhythm, tone color, texture, and melody spring from national tradition. There were regional traits in music before the romantic period, but never had differences of national style been emphasized so strongly or so consciously.

In these revolutionary times, musical compositions could symbolize nationalist yearnings and sometimes stirred audiences to violent political demonstrations. The Italian opera composer Giuseppe Verdi deliberately chose librettos that fanned public hatred for the Austrian overlords; censors constantly pressured him to change scenes that might be interpreted as anti-Austrian or antimonarchical. A twentieth-century parallel occurred when the Nazis banned performances of Smetana's symphonic poem *The Moldau* in Prague, the composer's home city.

The strongest impact of nationalism was felt in lands whose own musical heritage had been dominated by the music of Italy, France, Germany, or Austria. During the romantic period, Poland, Russia, Bohemia, the Scandinavian countries, and Spain produced important composers whose music had a national flavor. Early in the nineteenth century, Chopin transformed his native Polish dances into great art. After about 1860, groups or "schools" of composers consciously declared their musical independence and established national styles. Among the leading musical nationalists were Mussorgsky, Rimsky-Korsakov, and Borodin from Russia; Smetana and Dvořák from Bohemia; Edvard Grieg (1843–1907) from Norway; Jean Sibelius (1865–1957) from Finland; and Isaac Albéniz (1860–1909) from Spain.

Nationalism had an impact on American music as well. Around the middle of the nineteenth century, the leading nationalist composer in the United States was Louis Moreau Gottschalk (1829–1869), the first American concert pianist to gain international recognition. Born in New Orleans and trained in Paris, Gottschalk used African American, Cuban, and Puerto Rican melodies and rhythms in such works as *Bamboula: African-American Dance* and the symphony *A Night in the Tropics* (1858–1859). During the 1890s and the first decade of the twentieth century, Edward MacDowell (1860–1908)—composer, pianist, and teacher—was the outstanding musical figure in America. His best-known compositions incorporating American folk material are the orchestral work *Indian Suite* (1896)—based on Native American melodies—and a set of piano pieces called *Woodland Sketches* (1896). A leading American composer and conductor of band music was John Philip Sousa (1854–1932), whose works include *The Stars and Stripes Forever,* studied in Part I, Section 2.

We will focus on the most important of the national schools, the Russian.

The Russian Five

The most distinctive national music arose in Russia, where folk songs pervaded everyday life. "Every muzhik, carpenter, bricklayer, doorkeeper, cabman; every peasant woman, laundry-maid and cook, every nurse and wet nurse—all bring the folk songs of their villages with them to Petersburg, Moscow, to each and every city, and we hear them the whole year round," wrote a nineteenth-century Russian music critic. The folk music of Russia sounds different from that of western Europe. It is often based on ancient church modes, rather than on major or minor scales. (Although church modes, like major and minor scales, consist of eight tones within an octave, they have different patterns of whole and half steps.) Russian folk tunes also tend to be irregular in meter. A measure may contain 5 beats ($\frac{5}{4}$ time), instead of the customary 2, 3, 4, or 6. And the meter may change within a song so that two bars in $\frac{3}{4}$ time will be followed by one bar in $\frac{5}{4}$. Russian nationalist composers thus were able to draw on folk music that was both distinctive and highly varied.

Before 1800, there were no important Russian composers of art music. Czars imported Italian and German composers to provide music at the court. But in the early 1800s a composer emerged who is considered the father of Russian music—Mikhail Glinka (1804–1857). His opera *A Life for the Czar* (1836) incorporated peasant and folk tunes in a convincing way and laid the groundwork for a national style.

Still, it was only in the 1860s that a true "school" of national music came into being. (This decade also saw the appearance of the great Russian novels *Crime and Punishment,* by Dostoevsky; and *War and Peace,* by Tolstoy.) Five young men, whom we now know as the "Russian five," met together in St. Petersburg (later Leningrad, and now St. Petersburg again) with the aim of creating a truly Russian music. They criticized each other's works and asserted the necessity of breaking from some of the traditional techniques of German, Italian, and French composers. Remarkably, all but one began as amateurs; most had nonmusical jobs and could compose only in their spare time. At first, the only professional musician was Mily Balakirev (1837–1910). The other members were César Cui (1835–1918), an army engineer; Alexander Borodin (1833–1887), a chemist; Nikolai Rimsky-Korsakov (1844–1908), a naval officer; and Modest Mussorgsky, a civil servant. Mussorgsky was the most original and probably the greatest of the Russian five. We'll focus on his *Pictures at an Exhibition,* a masterpiece of musical nationalism.

Pictures at an Exhibition (1874), by Modest Mussorgsky; Arranged for Orchestra by Maurice Ravel (1922)

The son of a wealthy landowner, Modest Mussorgsky (1839–1881) was educated in a military academy and became an army officer when he was seventeen. After two years he left the army to devote himself to music. But the emancipation of the Russian serfs in 1861 caused financial hardship for his family, and Mussorgsky had to find a job. He became a government clerk in St. Petersburg and remained in that position for most of his life.

Though a competent pianist, Mussorgsky had little training in composition. He taught himself, except for occasional advice from Balakirev—one of the Russian five. Mussorgsky was plagued by severe psychological problems and eventually became an alcoholic. When he died at forty-two, he left relatively few compositions. These include the symphonic poem *Night on Bald Mountain* (1867), some songs, and the opera *Boris Godunov* (1874).

Pictures at an Exhibition (1874) originated as a cycle of piano pieces inspired by pictures in a memorial exhibition honoring Mussorgsky's recently deceased friend, the Russian architect and artist Victor Hartmann (1842–1873). Apart from the introduction, *Promenade,* ten pieces of the set have descriptive titles related to specific drawings and paintings by Hartmann in the exhibition: (1) *Gnome—Promenade,* (2) *The Old Castle—Promenade,* (3) *Tuileries: Dispute between Children at Play,* (4) *Bydlo* (Polish Oxcart)—*Promenade,* (5) *Ballet of the Unhatched Chicks,* (6) *Samuel Goldenberg and Schmuyle—Promenade,* (7) *The Marketplace at Limoges,* (8) *Catacombs: Roman Burial Place—Promenade: Con mortuis in lingua mortua (With the Dead in a Dead Language),* (9) *The Hut on Hen's Feet: Baba-Yaga,* (10) *The Great Gate of Kiev.* The introduction, *Promenade,* reappears in varied forms to unify the cycle and to represent Mussorgsky's changing moods as he walks through the exhibition. Parts of the work express the composer's Russian nationalism. *The Hut on Hen's Feet: Baba-Yaga* depicts a witch in Russian fairy tales, and *The Great Gate of Kiev* includes a Russian hymn melody. Mussorgsky sometimes creates the feeling of Russian folk music by using modal melodies with changing meters and narrow ranges.

Pictures at an Exhibition was not performed in public during the composer's lifetime; it found favor with pianists only around the middle of the twentieth century. Today, the work is best-known in its brilliant orchestral arrangement (1922) by the

A source of inspiration for the finale of Mussorgsky's *Pictures at an Exhibition* was *The Great Gate of Kiev* by Victor Hartmann.

French composer Maurice Ravel (Part VII, Section 5). We'll focus on the climactic finale of *Pictures at an Exhibition, The Great Gate of Kiev,* in Ravel's orchestral version.

The Great Gate of Kiev

Basic Set:
CD 5 **57**

The grandiose *Great Gate of Kiev* was inspired by Hartmann's design—never executed—for a monumental entrance to the city of Kiev. This ancient city was the birthplace of Christianity and church music in Russia.

The Great Gate of Kiev begins with a processional main theme that recurs several times with changes in orchestration, dynamics, accompaniment, tempo, and rhythm. Two other themes appear as well. One is soft and solemn, Mussorgsky's adaption of the Russian hymn *As You Are Baptized in Christ.* The second is the assertive *Promenade* theme, which has been heard several times previously. This theme is now accompanied by spectacular bell sounds. Bells were a characteristic feature of czarist Russia and were linked with events that marked the passage of time—births, deaths, weddings, and coronations.

LISTENING OUTLINE

MUSSORGSKY-RAVEL, *Pictures at an Exhibition*

The Great Gate of Kiev

Piccolo, 3 flutes, 3 oboes, English horn, 2 clarinets, bass clarinet, 4 French horns, 3 trumpets, 3 trombones, tuba, timpani, bass drum, cymbals, glockenspiel, bells, 2 harps, 1st violins, 2d violins, violas, cellos, double basses

(Duration, 6:29)

57 0:00   **1. a.** Majestic main melody, *f*, brasses and woodwinds;

                     suddenly softer, crescendo.

0:42   **b.** Main melody repeated, *ff*, full orchestra, cymbal crashes.

58 1:01   **2.** Sudden *p*, Russian hymn, clarinets and bassoons.

1:37   **3. a.** Sudden *f*, full orchestra, main melody in low brasses, accompanied by high fast scales.

1:52   **b.** Main melody repeated in high brasses, accompanied by low fast scales

2:12   **4.** Sudden *p*, Russian hymn, clarinets and bassoons; flutes join.

59 2:47   **5. a.** Bell tolls, *mf*, alternating with gong, cymbals, and tuba, steady beat; high soft violin pulsations join.

60 3:17   **b.** Trumpets, glockenspiel, *f*, promenade theme;

                     bell tolls, crescendo, rapid descending scales in strings, *ff*, brief pause.

3:51   **6. a.** Main theme in slow tempo, full orchestra, *ff*, brass fanfares in triple meter; suddenly softer, pulsations in strings, gradual crescendo builds to *ff*, full orchestra, timpani rolls, cymbal crashes.

5:17   **b.** Main theme phrase in very slow tempo, *ff*, full orchestra, bells, gong, cymbals, bass drum. Triumphant concluding chords.

13 Peter Ilyich Tchaikovsky

Peter Ilyich Tchaikovsky (1840–1893), the most famous Russian composer, came from the small town of Votkinsk, where his father was a mining inspector. When he was ten, he and his family moved to St. Petersburg, where he studied at the School of Jurisprudence. After graduating at nineteen, Tchaikovsky became a government clerk. He began to study music theory at the relatively late age of twenty-one. While keeping his government position, he entered the newly established St. Petersburg Conservatory, the first college-level music school in Russia. Two days after the opening of the conservatory, he wrote to his sister: "Sooner or later I shall abandon my present job for music. . . . Of course, I won't resign from my present job till I'm certain that I'm no longer a clerk, but a musician." The next year he did resign. So rapid was his progress in music that after graduating he became professor of harmony at the new Moscow Conservatory, a position he held for twelve years. As though to make up for his late start, Tchaikovsky composed furiously; a symphony, an opera, and a tone poem flowed from his pen, and by the age of thirty he had composed his first great orchestral work, *Romeo and Juliet.*

Peter Ilyich Tchaikovsky was the most famous Russian composer of the nineteenth century.

The year 1877 was bitterly dramatic. Tchaikovsky took the disastrous step of marrying a twenty-eight-year-old conservatory student who adored him and his music. Tchaikovsky seems to have married only to conceal his homosexuality. A few days after the wedding, he was writing of "ghastly spiritual torture." Two weeks later he waded into the icy Moscow River, intending to commit suicide by getting pneumonia. But a strong constitution saved him, and he fled to St. Petersburg, where a nervous collapse put him into a coma for two days. He separated from his wife and never saw her again.

In 1877 Tchaikovsky also acquired a benefactress, Nadezhda von Meck, a very rich widow of forty-six with eleven children. Madame von Meck passionately loved Tchaikovsky's music. She gave him an annuity that allowed him to quit his conservatory position and devote himself to composition. For fourteen years they corresponded, but they agreed never to meet. "I prefer to think of you from afar," she wrote, "to hear you speak in your music and to share your feelings through it." After so many years of this curious but intimate friendship, Tchaikovsky was deeply hurt when she abruptly cut off the annuity and stopped writing to him. "This situation lowers me in my own eyes," he wrote to her son-in-law; "it makes the memory of the money I accepted from her almost unbearable."

During these years, Tchaikovsky conducted his own works more and more, achieving success throughout Europe. Yet success did not bring spiritual peace. His brother observed, "The weariness and suffering which sprang up in Tchaikovsky's soul . . . reached their greatest intensity at the moment of his greatest triumphs." In 1891 he was invited to the United States, where he participated in four concerts inaugurating Carnegie Hall in New York and two concerts of his music in Baltimore and Philadelphia.

On October 28, 1893, Tchaikovsky conducted the premiere of his last great work, his Symphony No. 6 (*Pathétique*), which ends unconventionally with a slow, despairing finale. Nine days later, he died at the age of fifty-three.

Tchaikovsky's Music

"I grew up in the backwoods, filling myself from earliest childhood with the inexplicable beauty of the characteristic traits of Russian folk music. . . . I passionately love the Russian element in all its manifestations." Tchaikovsky thought of himself as *"Russian in the fullest sense of the word."* But Russian folk song was only one influence on his art. His style also contains elements of French, Italian, and German music.

Tchaikovsky's works are much more in the western tradition than are the compositions of his contemporaries, the Russian five. He fused national and international elements to produce intensely subjective and passionate music. "At the moment of composing," Tchaikovsky wrote, "when I am aglow with emotion, it flashes across my mind that all who will hear my music will experience some reflection of what I am feeling myself." And indeed, the brooding melancholy that plagued Tchaikovsky is a prominent feature in much of his music.

Tchaikovsky was a prolific composer of both instrumental and vocal works. Among his most popular orchestral compositions are the Fourth, Fifth, and Sixth (*Pathétique*) Symphonies (1877, 1888, and 1893); Piano Concerto No. 1 in B Flat Minor (1875); the Violin Concerto (1878); and the overture-fantasy *Romeo and Juliet* (1869), which we'll study. Tchaikovsky wrote some of his best music for ballet: *Swan Lake* (1876), *Sleeping Beauty* (1889), and *The Nutcracker* (1892). He reworked these ballet scores into concert suites, of which the suite from *The Nutcracker* is best-known. The spirit of ballet permeates much of Tchaikovsky's music. Of his eight operas, *Eugene Onegin* (1877–1878) and *Pique Dame* (*The Queen of Spades;* 1890) are performed with some frequency. He also wrote the orchestral showpieces *Marche slave* (*Slavic March*) and *Overture 1812.*

All of Tchaikovsky's music contains beautiful melodies that stretch and leap widely, like dancers. He repeats melodies over and over, sometimes transforming an intimate, lyrical utterance into an intense outcry by means of louder dynamics and fuller orchestration. His treatment of the orchestra is extremely colorful, marked by striking contrasts and alternations of strings, woodwinds, and brasses. The emotional quality of his music results from sharp contrasts of tempo, dynamics, and thematic material, as well as from powerful climaxes.

Romeo and Juliet, Overture-Fantasy (1869)

Basic Set:

CD 6 **1**

Romantic composers felt an artistic kinship with Shakespeare because of his passionate poetry, dramatic contrasts, and profound knowledge of the human heart. Shakespeare's plays inspired some of the finest nineteenth-century compositions. Among these were *Macbeth* and *Othello,* set as operas by Verdi; and *A Midsummer Night's Dream,* depicted in incidental music by Mendelssohn. *Romeo and Juliet* inspired both a "dramatic symphony" by Berlioz and a concert overture by Tchaikovsky.

Tchaikovsky composed *Romeo and Juliet* at twenty-nine, near the beginning of his musical career. Although it is now one of the best-loved works, *Romeo and Juliet* was a dismal failure at its premiere in 1870. "After the concert we dined. . . . No one said a single word to me about the overture the whole evening. And yet I yearned so for appreciation and kindness." Tchaikovsky decided to revise the overture. He composed a new theme to represent Friar Laurence, adopting a suggestion made by his friend Balakirev. Despite this, the work remained unappreciated. Only about twenty years later, after further revisions, did it achieve worldwide popularity.

Like Shakespeare's play, Tchaikovsky's *Romeo and Juliet* glorifies a romantic love powerful enough to triumph over death. Tchaikovsky captures the essential emotions of Shakespeare's play without defining the characters or the exact course of events. Highly contrasted themes are used to express the conflict between family hatred and youthful love. Tchaikovsky also depicts the gentle and philosophical Friar Laurence, intermediary between the lovers and the harsh outside world.

Romeo and Juliet is a concert overture consisting of a slow introduction followed by a fast movement in sonata form. (Tchaikovsky's title—Overture-Fantasy—implies that he treated the musical material in a free and imaginative way.) We can enjoy *Romeo and Juliet* as an exciting orchestral piece without knowing the play. However, a new dimension is added to our listening experience when we associate the music with the drama.

Tchaikovsky opens the overture with the Friar Laurence theme, a solemn, hymn-like melody. As the slow introduction unfolds, brooding strings set an atmosphere of impending tragedy. The clash of swords and the anger of the feud between the Montagues and the Capulets are suggested by the violent first theme of the allegro. Syncopations, rushing strings, and massive sounds create enormous excitement. The second theme of the exposition, a tender love theme, is expressively scored for English horn and muted violas. When the love theme returns in the recapitulation, it has a new, exultant character, as Tchaikovsky envelops the listener in opulent sound. There are long crescendos as the melody is led higher and higher to ever more passionate orchestral climaxes.

In the coda, Tchaikovsky transforms the love theme into a song of mourning, while timpani softly beat the rhythm of a funeral march. Then, a new hymn and a tender reminiscence of the love theme suggest that Romeo and Juliet are reunited in death.

LISTENING OUTLINE

TCHAIKOVSKY, *Romeo and Juliet,* Overture-Fantasy

Andante non tanto quasi moderato (andante, almost a moderate tempo, slow introduction); Allegro giusto (moderate allegro)

Sonata form, quadruple meter ($\frac{4}{4}$), B minor

Piccolo, 2 flutes, 2 oboes, English horn, 2 clarinets, 2 bassoons, 4 French horns, 2 trumpets, 3 trombones, tuba, timpani, cymbals, bass drum, harp, 1st violins, 2d violins, violas, cellos, double basses.

(Duration, 19:21)

Introduction

Andante non tanto
quasi moderato

| **1** | 0:00 | **1. a.** Low clarinets and bassoons, ***p***, hymnlike Friar Laurence theme. |

	0:37	**b.** Strings and French horns, ***p***, sustained tones. Basses.
	1:10	**c.** Woodwinds and strings, crescendo. Harp, ***mf***, flutes, ***p***.
	2:03	**2. a.** Pizzicato strings accompany high woodwinds, ***p***, Friar Laurence theme.
	2:34	**b.** Strings and French horns, ***p***, sustained tones. Basses.
	3:05	**c.** Strings and woodwinds, crescendo. Harp, ***mf***, violins, ***p***.
	3:57	**3. a.** Strings answered by high woodwinds, ***mf***. Crescendo to ***ff***, full orchestra, accelerando.
	4:26	**b.** Timpani roll, decrescendo, much slower tempo; strings, ***p***, answered by woodwind chords, ***pp***. Crescendo and accelerando to

Allegro giusto

Exposition

First theme

| **2** | 5:16 | **1. a.** Orchestra, ***f***, feud theme, minor. |

	5:31	**b.** Cellos imitated by piccolo, ***f***, feud motive.
	6:04	**c.** Cymbal crashes against rushing notes in strings. Crescendo to ***ff***.
	6:16	**d.** Full orchestra, ***ff***, feud theme. Cymbal crashes.

Bridge

| **3** | 6:38 | **2.** Suddenly soft, woodwinds. Basses and French horns, ***pp***, rhythm slows. |

Second theme

| **4** | 7:28 | **3. a.** English horn and muted violas, love theme, major. |

5   7:48

b. Muted violins, *pp*, gently pulsating melody.

Crescendo.

c. High woodwinds, *p*, love theme extended.

Closing section

4. Harp, *p*, accompanies muted strings, bassoon, English horn, *p*.

Development

6   10:32

1. Strings, woodwinds, *p*, feud motive. Crescendo, rushing notes in strings, *f*.

2. a. French horns, *p*, Friar Laurence theme, strings accompany. Violins, *pp*, high repeated notes, brass, woodwind chords, *pp*.

b. Horns, *p*, Friar Laurence theme. Crescendo, rushing notes in strings, *f*.

c. Horns, *p*, Friar Laurence theme, strings accompany. Violins, *pp*, high repeated notes, brass, woodwind chords, *pp*.

d. Horns, *p*, Friar Laurence theme.

11:46

3. Low strings, *f*, answered by woodwinds, *f*, feud motive. Crescendo to *ff*, cymbal crashes.

4. a. Trumpets, *ff*, Friar Laurence theme.

12:09

b. Strings, *ff*, rushing notes, cymbal crashes.

Recapitulation

First theme

7   12:35

1. Full orchestra, *ff*, feud theme, minor, cymbal crashes. Downward rushing notes in strings, decrescendo.

Second theme

8   12:57

2. Oboes, *p*, gently pulsating melody, major. Violins accompany *pp*. Crescendo.

9   13:34

3. a. Strings, *f*, love theme extended. Crescendo to *ff*. Love theme repeated. Decrescendo.

b. Cellos, woodwinds, *mf*, love-theme phrases. French horn. Crescendo.

c. Strings, *ff*, love theme. Feud motive, cymbal crashes.

15:14

4. a. Full orchestra, *ff*, feud theme, cymbal crashes.

b. Brasses, *ff*, Friar Laurence theme.

c. Full orchestra, *ff*, feud theme, cymbal crashes.

d. Brasses, *ff*, Friar Laurence theme.

e. Full orchestra, *ff*, cymbal crashes. Cellos and basses, timpani roll, decrescendo to *p*.

Coda

10   16:24

1. Timpani, *p*, funeral-march rhythm. Strings, *mf*, love theme transformed into song of mourning. Very moderate tempo.

2. Woodwinds, *pp*, hymnlike melody. Harp.

3. Violins, *mf*, love theme varied. Timpani roll, crescendo.

4. Full orchestra, *ff*, repeated chords.

14 Bedřich Smetana

Bedřich Smetana (1824–1884) was the founder of Czech national music. His works are steeped in the folk songs, dances, and legends of his native Bohemia (which became part of the Czech Republic). When Smetana was growing up, Bohemia was under Austrian domination, and the official language in Prague's schools and government bureaus was German, not Czech. The young Smetana's feelings of national identity were inflamed during the revolutions of 1848, when Czech radicals fought for political freedom and the abolition of serfdom. As a member of the armed Citizen Corps, he was probably on the barricades when the Austrians bombarded Prague. The insurrection was a failure and resulted in a harsh reaction from Austria; censorship was increased, and patriots were imprisoned.

In this repressive atmosphere, Smetana's musical nationalism could make little headway. Though he was recognized as a pianist, his compositions were scorned by those opposed to nationalism or "modernity" of any variety. In 1856, Smetana emigrated to Sweden, where he taught, conducted, and composed symphonic poems in the style of Franz Liszt. He did not return to Prague until 1862, when Austria's military defeats had resulted in some liberal concessions. Political prisoners were released, Czech-language newspapers were established, and Czech theaters for drama and opera were allowed to open. It was for one of these theaters that Smetana wrote *The Bartered Bride,* his most famous opera, based on Bohemian legend and folk material. Smetana was active in Prague not only as a composer but as a pianist, conductor, teacher, and tireless propagandist for Czech musical nationalism.

At age fifty, Smetana suffered the same fate as Beethoven—he became completely deaf. Yet some of his finest works followed, including *Má Vlast (My Country;* 1874–1879), a cycle of six symphonic poems glorifying Bohemian history and legend, the fertile Czech countryside, and peasant songs and dances. Smetana passed his last ten years in acute physical and mental torment caused by syphilis. He died in an insane asylum at age sixty.

The Moldau (1874)

Basic Set:
CD 6 ▪11▪

Brief Set:
CD 4 ▪11▪

"Today I took an excursion to the St. John Rapids where I sailed in a boat through huge waves. . . . The view of the landscape was both beautiful and grand." Smetana's trip inspired his famous symphonic poem *The Moldau,* which depicts Bohemia's main river as it flows through the countryside. This orchestral work, part of the cycle *Má Vlast (My Country),* is both a romantic representation of nature and a display of Czech nationalism. *The Moldau* was written in three weeks shortly after Smetana became deaf, but its fresh, optimistic mood gives no hint of the composer's anguish and despair.

Smetana wrote the following program to preface his score:

> The composition depicts the course of the river, beginning from its two small sources, one cold the other warm, the joining of both streams into one, then the flow of the Moldau through forests and across meadows, through the countryside where merry feasts are celebrated; water nymphs dance in the moonlight; on nearby rocks can be seen the outline of ruined castles, proudly soaring into the sky. The Moldau swirls through the St. John Rapids and flows in a broad stream toward Prague. It passes Vyšehrad [where an ancient royal castle once stood], and finally the river disappears in the distance as it flows majestically into the Elbe.

The Moldau falls into contrasting musical sections that represent different scenes and episodes described in the program. Hunting along the riverbank is suggested by horn fanfares; a peasant wedding by a rustic polka, the Bohemian dance; and a moonlit night by shimmering woodwinds and a serene melody in high muted strings. An expansive

311

folklike theme that recurs several times symbolizes the river. Smetana unifies the symphonic poem with running notes evoking the movement of water, sometimes rippling, sometimes turbulent.

LISTENING OUTLINE

SMETANA, *The Moldau*

Allegro commodo non agitato (unhurried allegro, not agitated), sextuple meter ($\frac{6}{8}$), E minor

Piccolo, 2 flutes, 2 oboes, 2 clarinets, 2 bassoons, 4 French horns, 2 trumpets, 3 trombones, tuba, timpani, bass drum, triangle, cymbals, harp, 1st violins, 2d violins, violas, cellos, double basses

(Duration, 11:35)

Two springs

11 11 0:00

1. **a.** Flutes, *p*, running notes. Harp, pizzicato violins.

Clarinets, *p*, join, running notes.

b. Lower strings, *p*, running notes lead to

The river

12 12 1:10

2. Violins, songlike river theme, minor key. Running-note accompaniment in strings.

1:39 River theme extended.

Forest hunt

13 13 3:00

3. **a.** French horns and trumpets, *f*, hunting calls. Strings, running notes. Crescendo to *ff*.

b. Decrescendo to *ppp*.

Peasant wedding

14 14 3:57

4. **a.** Strings, *p*, polka.

Crescendo to *f*, triangle strokes.

b. Decrescendo to *ppp*, melody descends.

Moonlight: dance of water nymphs

15 15 5:19

5. **a.** Woodwinds, *pp*, sustained tones. Flutes, *p*, running notes lead to

5:42 **b.** High muted violins, *pp*, serene legato melody, flutes and harp accompany, *p*.

6:58 **c.** Brasses, *pp*. Gentle staccato chords join accompaniment to violin melody.

7:36 **d.** Crescendo. Woodwinds, running notes lead to

The river

7:59 6. Violins, river theme. Running-note accompaniment in strings.

The rapids
16 16 8:40

7. **a.** Full orchestra, *ff*. Brasses, timpani roll, piccolo, cymbal crashes.

   b. Strings, *pp*. Quick crescendo.

The river at its
widest point
17 17 9:53

8. Full orchestra, *ff*, river theme in major key. Faster tempo.

Vyšehrad, the
ancient castle
10:21

9. **a.** Brasses and woodwinds, *ff*, hymnlike melody. Cymbal crashes.

   b. Decrescendo. Violins, *ppp*. Full orchestra, *ff*, closing chords.

15 Antonin Dvořák

Antonin Dvořák (1841–1904) followed Smetana as the leading composer of Czech national music. He infused his symphonies and chamber music with the spirit of Bohemian folk song and dance.

Dvořák's father was a poor innkeeper and butcher in a small town near Prague. After working in his father's butcher shop, Dvořák left home at the age of sixteen to study music in Prague. For years he earned a meager living by playing in an opera orchestra under Smetana's direction. He was little known as a composer until his works came to the attention of the German master Brahms, who recommended Dvořák to his own publisher: "I took much pleasure in the works of Dvořák of Prague. If you play them through, you will enjoy them as much as I have done. Decidedly he is a very talented man."

From this time on—Dvořák was then about thirty-six—his fame spread rapidly. He was invited several times to England, where the melodiousness of his symphonies, chamber music, Slavonic dances, and choral works appealed to the English love for folk music and the countryside. Although Dvořák rarely quoted actual folk tunes, his works breathe a folk quality and express a cheerful and direct personality.

In 1892, Dvořák went to New York, where he was to spend almost three years as director of the National Conservatory of Music. He received a salary of $15,000, about twenty times what he was earning as a professor at the Prague Conservatory. Besides his urban impressions, Dvořák learned about the American heartland by spending a summer in Spillville, Iowa, where there was a colony of Czechs.

Dvořák encouraged American composers to write nationalistic music. He had become interested in Native American melodies and African American spirituals, which he learned about from his student Henry T. Burleigh, a black composer and baritone. Dvořák told a reporter from the New York *Herald* that in the spirituals he had "found a secure basis for a new national musical school. America can have her own music, a fine music growing up from her own soil and having its own character—the natural voice of a free and great nation."

In 1895 Dvořák returned to his homeland and rejoined the faculty of the Prague Conservatory, becoming its director six years later.

Symphony No. 9 in E Minor
(*From the New World;* 1893)

Dvořák wrote his *New World* Symphony, Symphony No. 9 in E Minor, during his first year in the United States. One of the best-known of all symphonies, it glorifies the American and the Czech folk spirit. Its popular character grows out of Dvořák's use of syncopations, **pentatonic** (five-note) **scales,** and modal scales often found in folk music. Colorful orchestration and melodious thematic material add to the attractiveness of the *New World* Symphony. Its four contrasting movements are unified through quotation of thematic material: themes from the first movement are recalled in the second and third movements, and the finale brings back themes from all three preceding movements.

First Movement:
Adagio (slow introduction); Allegro molto

The slow introduction to the first movement builds great tension and contains an ominous low motive foreshadowing the opening theme of the energetic allegro that follows. In the exposition of this sonata-form movement, there are three distinctive themes. The first begins in minor with a syncopated arpeggio motive that dominates the entire symphony. The dancelike second theme, also in minor, is gentler than the first and narrower in range. Dvořák shifts to a major key for the third theme, a gracious melody which resembles the spiritual *Swing Low, Sweet Chariot.* (In the listening outline this is called the *Swing Low theme,* but with no implication that Dvořák meant it to recall the spiritual.) Between these themes come beautiful bridge passages that rise to a climax and then calm down to usher in new melodic material. In his development, Dvořák concentrates on the first and third themes, which he varies and combines. The recapitulation of all three themes is followed by a coda, which brings the first movement to a climactic close.

Basic Set:
CD 6 `18`

Brief Set:
CD 4 `18`

LISTENING OUTLINE

DVOŘÁK, Symphony No. 9 in E Minor (*From the New World*)

First Movement: Adagio (slow introduction); Allegro molto

Sonata form, duple meter ($\frac{2}{4}$), E minor

Piccolo, 2 flutes, 2 oboes, 2 clarinets, 2 bassoons, 4 French horns, 2 trumpets, 3 trombones, timpani, 1st violins, 2d violins, violas, cellos, double basses

(Duration, 9:00)

Adagio (slow
introduction)

`18` `18` 0:00   **1. a.** Cellos, ***pp***, downward phrases. French horns.

0:32   **b.** Flute, ***p***, downward phrases.

0:55   **2. a.** Strings, ***ff***, alternate with timpani, woodwinds, horns, ***ff***.

           b. Cellos and basses, ***pp***.

           c. High woodwinds alternate with low strings, bass motive.

           d. Full orchestra, crescendo, timpani roll, violin tremolo, ***pp***.

Allegro molto

Exposition

First theme

`19` `19` 1:53

1. a. Horns, arpeggio motive. Woodwinds, *p*, playful rhythm, minor key.

  b. Oboes, arpeggio motive. Woodwinds, playful rhythm.

  c. Strings, *ff*, arpeggio motive developed. Crescendo.

Bridge

`20` `20` 2:25

2. Brasses, *ff*, arpeggio motive. Strings, playful rhythm developed. Decrescendo.

Second theme

`21` `21` 2:57

3. a. Flute and oboe, *p*, dancelike tune.

  b. Violins, *ppp*, dancelike tune developed, crescendo to *f*. Decrescendo.

Third theme

`22` `22` 4:03

4. a. Flute, *p*, *Swing Low* theme, major.

  b. Violins, *Swing Low* theme. Crescendo to *ff*, full orchestra.

Development

`23` `23` 4:32

1. Strings, decrescendo.

  4:45

2. a. Horn, *p*, *Swing Low* motive, piccolo. Crescendo.

  b. Trumpets, *f*, *Swing Low* motive. Trombones, *f*, arpeggio motive. Horns, *ff*. Strings, *ff*.

  c. Trombones, *ff*, arpeggio motive. High violins, *ff*. Rhythm quickens.

  5:52

3. Oboes, *p*, arpeggio motive, flute. Crescendo.

Recapitulation

First theme

`24` `24` 6:08

1. a. Horns, *mf*, arpeggio motive. Woodwinds, *p*, playful rhythm, minor.

  b. Oboes, arpeggio motive. Woodwinds, *p*, playful rhythm.

  c. Strings, *ff*, arpeggio motive developed. Decrescendo.

Second theme

  6:48

2. a. Flute, *p*, dancelike tune.

  b. Woodwinds, *p*, dancelike tune. Strings, dancelike tune developed, crescendo to *ff*. Decrescendo.

Third theme

  7:50

3. a. Flute, *p*, *Swing Low* theme, major.

  b. Violins, *Swing Low* theme. Crescendo.

Coda

  8:18

1. Full orchestra, *fff*. *Swing Low* and arpeggio motives, minor.

2. Repeated chords, *ff*, at end.

The music for this movement is available in Connect Kamien.

Second Movement:
Largo

After several introductory chords, we hear the famous largo melody, which has a nostalgic quality heightened by the timbre of the English horn. Dvořák uses tone color expressively throughout the second movement, frequently passing musical ideas among different instruments. The largo is in the form A B—bridge—A'. Its gentle mood is broken only in the bridge, which contains a climactic quotation of motives from the first movement.

LISTENING OUTLINE

DVOŘÁK, Symphony No. 9 in E Minor (*From the New World*)

Second Movement: Largo

A B—bridge—A' form, quadruple meter (⁴/₄), D flat major

2 flutes, 2 oboes, English horn, 2 clarinets, 2 bassoons, 4 French horns, 2 trumpets, 3 trombones, tuba, timpani, 1st violins, 2d violins, violas, cellos, double basses

Introduction

1. Brasses and woodwinds, *pp*, solemn chords. Crescendo and decrescendo.
2. Muted strings, *ppp*.

A

1. **a.** English horn, *p*, main melody, major key.

   b. Clarinet, *pp*, repeats ending notes of melody.
2. High woodwinds, *pp*, solemn chords, crescendo. Brasses, timpani, *ff*, decrescendo.
3. Muted strings, *ppp*, extension of main melody.
4. **a.** English horn, *p*, concluding phrases of main melody. Clarinet, violins softly repeat ending notes of melody.

   b. Muted French horns, *p*, opening notes of melody.

B

1. Oboe and flute, *pp*, minor melody, a little faster tempo than before. Tremolo strings accompany.

2. **a.** Clarinets, *pp*, hymnlike minor melody, a little slower tempo. Pizzicato basses accompany.

   b. Flutes and oboes, *p*, hymnlike melody continued. Pizzicato basses accompany.
3. Muted violins, *pp*, minor melody, a little faster tempo. Countermelody in oboe and flute. Strings, decrescendo.
4. Muted violins, *pp*, hymnlike minor melody, a little slower tempo. Tremolo strings accompany. Strings, *pp*, major chord.

Bridge

A′

5. **a.** Staccato oboe, *p*, flute trills, *p*.

  b. Crescendo to *ff*, full orchestra. Arpeggio and *Swing Low* motives from first movement combined with opening of largo melody. Decrescendo.

1. **a.** English horn, main melody, original tempo, major.

  b. Muted strings, *pp*, main melody broken up by pauses.

  c. Solo violin and solo cello, *pp*.

  d. Strings, concluding phrases of main melody. Clarinet, *p*, repeats ending notes of melody. Violins, decrescendo to *ppp*.

2. Brasses, *pp*, solemn chords. Crescendo. Decrescendo. Strings, *pp*, melody rises to high, sustained chord, *pp*. Ending chords in double basses, *pp*.

Third Movement:
Scherzo (Molto vivace)

The exciting scherzo breathes the spirit of dancing. Its form is outlined A (scherzo)—bridge—B (trio)—bridge—A (scherzo)—coda. Motives from the first movement are recalled in the bridge to the trio and in the coda. The opening part of the scherzo (A) section, in minor, has great rhythmic drive and features a short motive which chases itself in close imitation.

Dvořák then relaxes the tension with a lilting legato melody in a major key; the charm is heightened by delicate strokes of the triangle.

In the bridge to the trio (B), the cellos recall the arpeggio motive from the first movement.

The trio (B) section, in major, features two staccato dance tunes that might be performed by a town band. The first is played softly by the woodwinds with the triangle accompanying.

The second tune, graced by delightful trills, alternates between violins and woodwinds.

The scherzo section (A) is played again, and then we hear a dramatic string tremolo that ushers in the coda. Horns vigorously recalling the arpeggio motive are whimsically answered by woodwinds, *p*, playing the scherzo motive. The movement fades into silence before ending with a powerful chord for full orchestra.

Fourth Movement:
Allegro con fuoco (allegro with fire)

The *New World* Symphony ends with a sonata-form finale of great power and splendor. Dvořák skillfully combines the themes of the finale with motives from the three earlier movements.

After a brief string introduction, the horns and trumpets proclaim the first theme, which sounds like a proud march song.

A solo clarinet presents the yearning second theme, accompanied by a cello countermelody in faster time values.

The third theme, jubilant and folklike, ends with a three-tone descending figure that resembles *Three Blind Mice*.

Dvořák plays with the three-tone figure, shifting it from low to high instruments and embellishing it with humorous variations.

In the development, motives from preceding movements are quoted and varied. Flutes and clarinets softly recall the largo melody, which is combined with the marchlike finale theme and reminiscences of the scherzo. A crescendo builds to the opening of the recapitulation, as brasses proclaim the marchlike theme. The remainder of the recapitulation is subdued in dynamics, and from it the coda emerges as a passionate and triumphant summary of the whole symphony.

16 | Johannes Brahms

Johannes Brahms (1833–1897) was a romantic who breathed new life into classical forms. He was born in Hamburg, Germany, where his father made a precarious living as a string bass player. At thirteen, Brahms led a double life: during the day he studied piano, music theory, and composition; at night he played dance music in cafés. Brahms's first concert tour, when he was twenty, gave him a chance to meet two of the greatest composers then living—Liszt and Schumann. The contact with Liszt was not helpful. Brahms, a product of a conservative musical education, was repelled by what he considered the bombast and lack of form in Liszt's music. Schumann, on the other hand, was to shape the course of Brahms's artistic and personal life.

Moments after presenting himself at Schumann's home, Brahms began to play one of his own piano sonatas. At the end of the first movement, Schumann called his wife, Clara, the famous piano virtuoso, and they listened enthusiastically to Brahms's music for hours. Four weeks later, Schumann published a magazine article hailing young Brahms as a musical messiah "called to give ideal expression to his time." Brahms was both overjoyed and apprehensive about his overnight fame. "The open praise which you gave me," he wrote Schumann, "has probably excited the expectations of the public to such a degree that I don't know how I can come anywhere near fulfilling them."

As Brahms was preparing new works for an eager publisher, Schumann had a recurrence of his nervous illness and tried to drown himself. He was committed to an asylum, leaving Clara Schumann with seven children to support. Brahms rushed to her aid and helped care for the children while she went on concert tours to earn money. For two years Brahms lived in the Schumann home, becoming increasingly involved with Clara, who was fourteen years older than he. The conflict between his loyalty to Robert and his passion for Clara may well have accounted for the stormy music he wrote at the time. Robert Schumann's death left Brahms and Clara Schumann free to marry, yet they did not. Since they destroyed many of their letters, we'll never know what passed between them. A few months later they separated, although they remained lifelong intimate friends. Brahms never married; for him, Clara Schumann was "the most beautiful experience of my life."

Brahms desperately wanted to become conductor of the Philharmonic Orchestra in Hamburg, his birthplace. When he was passed over for the post in 1862, the disappointment was overwhelming. "For me this was much sadder even than you can possibly imagine," he wrote to Clara Schumann, "perhaps even sadder than you can understand." He left his native city to settle in Vienna, where he spent the last thirty-five years of his life. For several years he conducted a Viennese musical society and introduced many forgotten masterpieces by Bach, Handel, and Mozart to the public. Brahms had a wide knowledge of older music; he edited baroque and classical compositions, and he was an ardent collector of music manuscripts.

Brahms's intimate knowledge of past masterpieces made him extremely critical of his own work. Once, after a violinist had played a Bach piece, Brahms threw his own music to the floor, exclaiming, "After that, how could anyone play such stuff as this!" Brahms was obsessed by Beethoven. "You have no idea," he told a friend, "how the likes of us feel when we hear the tramp of a giant like him behind us." He worked at his own First Symphony on and off for twenty years and completed it only when he was forty-three. Brahms endlessly revised compositions and sent them to friends for advice and criticism. He sent some songs to Clara Schumann with the request, "Write me if possible one short word about each, . . . such as: No. 5, bad; No. 6, shameful; No. 7, ridiculous."

In 1879, an honorary doctoral degree from Breslau University calling Brahms "the first among today's masters" provoked a venomous attack from Richard Wagner, who

Brahms was a romantic who breathed new life into classical forms.

sneered, "Compose, compose, even if you don't have the slightest of ideas!" Music critics of the time pitted Brahms's fondness for traditional forms against Wagner's innovative music dramas. Actually, their musical paths hardly ever crossed; Brahms never ventured into opera, Wagner's special territory.

Brahms always lived frugally, even though he earned a good income from publishers and from playing and conducting his works. He hid a shy, sensitive nature behind a mask of sarcasm and rudeness. Once, on leaving a party, he reportedly announced, "If there is anyone here I have not insulted, I apologize!" Yet this gruff bear could be extremely generous to talented young musicians. He helped Dvořák find a publisher, and the grateful Czech composer wrote: "I am so overcome by his kindness that I cannot help but love him! What a warm heart and great spirit there is in that man!"

When Brahms's beloved Clara Schumann lay dying in 1896, his grief found expression in the haunting *Four Serious Songs,* set to biblical texts. Not long after, it was discovered that he had cancer. On March 7, 1897, he dragged himself to hear a performance of his Fourth Symphony; the audience and orchestra gave him a tremendous ovation. Less than a month later, at the age of sixty-four, he died.

Brahms's Music

Brahms created masterpieces in all the traditional forms except opera. His varied output includes four symphonies, two concertos for piano and one for violin, short piano pieces, over 200 songs, and some magnificent choral music, such as the *German Requiem* (1868; we'll study its fourth movement). Some of Brahms's finest music may be found in the two dozen chamber works written for many different instrumental combinations, including duo sonatas for cello and piano (Op. 38 and Op. 99); a trio for violin, horn, and piano (Op. 40); and a quintet for clarinet and strings (Op. 115).

Brahms's works, though very personal in style, are rooted deeply in the music of Haydn, Mozart, and Beethoven. Brahms reinterprets classical forms while using the harmonic and instrumental resources of his own time. He was the greatest master of theme-and-variations form since Beethoven: he wrote variations that sound completely different from their thematic source, while retaining the theme's basic structure.

Brahms's music embraces a range of moods, but particularly it has an autumnal or mellow feeling and a sense of lyrical warmth. Lyricism pervades even the rich polyphonic textures he was so fond of. One Brahms scholar has aptly observed, "It is possible to sing every Brahms movement from beginning to end as though it were a single, uninterrupted melody. Through all its polyphonic intricacies, the clear flow of invention always remains distinctly recognizable." We'll study the lyrical aspect of Brahms's art as represented in the third movement of his Third Symphony.

Among romantics, Brahms is outstanding in his ability to make intricate polyphonic texture sound natural and spontaneous. When he was in his twenties, he and a violinist friend gave each other difficult contrapuntal exercises to correct. "Why shouldn't we two serious and intelligent people," Brahms wrote, "be able to teach each other better than some professor could?"

All of Brahms's music is rhythmically exciting. Contrasting rhythmic patterns are set against one another; one instrument plays two even notes to the beat, while another plays three. The use of "2 against 3," as this rhythmic technique is called, is one of Brahms's trademarks. He also delights in all sorts of syncopations and in phrases of irregular length that push against the prevailing meter.

The quality of sound in Brahms's music is very special. He liked rich, dark tone colors. In his orchestral music, he usually blended the different instrumental choirs, favoring mellow instruments like the viola, clarinet, and French horn. (It's characteristic of Brahms's feeling for tradition that he preferred the old-fashioned hunting-type horn to the modern horn with valves.) The rich sound often results from his practice of doubling melodies in thirds and sixths; the same melody is duplicated at the interval of a third or sixth.

Brahms's music always radiates the security and solidity of a complete master. He justified Schumann's prediction of greatness for the "young eagle."

Symphony No. 3 in F Major, Op. 90

Shortly after completing his Third Symphony during the summer of 1883, Brahms was visited in Vienna by the younger composer Antonin Dvořák, whose *New World* Symphony was studied in Section 15. "At my request to hear something of his new symphony," Dvořák reported later, Brahms "was immediately forthcoming" and played two movements on the piano. Dvořák's reaction was ecstatic: "What magnificent melodies are to be found! It is full of love, and it makes one's heart melt."

The briefest of Brahms's symphonies, the Third Symphony is characterized by thematic connections among its four movements and pervasive contrasts between major and minor. At the very end of the last movement, for example, the impassioned opening of the symphony, which combines F major and F minor harmonies, is gently recalled in F major. We'll focus on the third movement, a short interlude between the slow movement and the climactic finale.

Third Movement:
Poco Allegretto

Basic Set:
CD 6 25

Brief Set:
CD 4 25

Instead of using a rapid scherzo, standard in nineteenth-century symphonies, Brahms created a unique kind of third movement that is moderate in tempo (poco allegretto) and intensely lyrical in character. Brahms enhanced the intimate mood of the poco allegretto by reducing the size of its orchestra, which does not include the trumpets, trombones, contrabassoon, and timpani heard in the outer movements. Though romantic in style, the poco allegretto reflects Brahms's strong feeling for musical tradition: it has the triple meter, ternary form, and relaxed middle section typical of third movements in classical symphonies.

The poco allegretto contains one of Brahms's most haunting melodies. (In 1999, this melody was used by Carlos Santana and Dave Matthews in their song *Love of My Life*, from the album *Supernatural*.) The melody's yearning mood is created by its minor key and by its three-note dotted-rhythmic motive (long-short-long) that rises on the upbeat and falls on the downbeat.

Poco allegretto

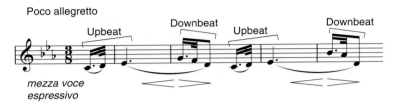

mezza voce
espressivo

In the poco allegretto, Brahms creates variety by presenting the main melody in different tone colors and in successively higher octaves. In the opening section (A), the melody is introduced by the cellos, playing expressively (*espressivo*) and softly in an intimate "half voice" (*mezza voce*). Then it is heard in the violins, and—after an interlude—in the flute. When the opening section returns (A′), Brahms reorchestrates the main melody, which now is presented first by the French horn, then by the oboe, and finally by the high violins, as the climax of the movement.

The middle section (B) brings a shift from minor to major, from yearning to graciousness. Section B opens with a lilting waltzlike melody in the winds, accompanied by a staccato syncopated figure in the cellos. Later, Brahms creates a contrast of mood and tone color by introducing a new expressive melody in the strings alone. A hushed transition smoothly links the middle section (B) to the concluding A′ section. Brahms prepares beautifully for the return of the main melody with an upward sequence in the woodwinds of the melody's initial dotted-rhythm motive (long-short-long). After the reorchestrated repetition of the opening section (A′), we hear a coda in which the dotted-rhythm motive flowers into an eloquent phrase that epitomizes the movement's intense lyricism.

LISTENING OUTLINE

BRAHMS, Symphony No. 3 in F Major

Third Movement: Poco allegretto

A B A′ Coda form, triple meter ($\frac{3}{8}$), C minor

2 flutes, 2 oboes, 2 clarinets, 2 bassoons, 2 French horns, 1st violins, 2d violins, violas, cellos, double basses

(Duration, 5:45)

A (minor)

 0:00   **1. a.** Cellos, ***p***, yearning main melody in minor, middle register, strings and pizzicato basses accompany; ends with incomplete cadence.

Cellos

0:25   **b.** Violins, *p*, repeat main melody an octave higher, string accompaniment more animated; ends with complete cadence.

0:49   **c.** Cellos, *p*, new flowing idea in major, imitated in violins,

downward sequence in violins, quick rising arpeggios in cellos and clarinets introduce

1:19   **d.** Flute, oboe, *mp*, main melody in minor, at even higher octave, accompanied by strings, winds, and pizzicato basses; complete cadence, winds, soft sustained chord introduces

B (Major)

26 26 1:45   **2. a.** Flutes and clarinets, *p*, lilting waltzlike melody in major, cellos accompany with syncopated staccato figure.

1:59   **b.** Winds, *p*, repeat waltzlike melody, violins and cellos accompany with syncopated staccato arpeggios.

2:13   **c.** Strings alone, *pp*, new expressive legato melody, crescendo to *f*, decrescendo to *p*.

2:32   **d.** Winds, soft waltzlike melody, accompanied by syncopated staccato arpeggios in violins and cellos.

2:46   **e.** Strings alone, *p*, expressive legato melody, decrescendo to *pp*, woodwinds, *p*, upward sequence of opening dotted-rhythm motive from main melody, sustained chord.

A' (Minor)

27 27 3:23   **3. a.** French horn, *p*, main melody in minor, middle register, strings and pizzicato basses accompany, ends with incomplete cadence.

3:50   **b.** Oboe, *p*, repeats main melody an octave higher, strings accompany, ends with complete cadence.

4:12   **c.** High bassoon, *p*, flowing idea in major, imitated in clarinet, downward sequence in winds; clarinets and bassoons alone, quick rising arpeggios in strings and flute introduce

4:43   **d.** Violins, **_mp_**, main melody in minor at even higher octave, accompanied by strings, winds, pizzicato basses; complete cadence.

Coda

5:08   **4. a.** Winds, soft sustained chords.

5:17   **b.** Strings and winds, **_pp_**, repeat soft chords, eloquent rising and falling phrase in dotted rhythm, cadence;

soft sustained wind chord, pizzicato strings close movement.

Ein Deutsches Requiem
(*A German Requiem;* 1868)

A masterpiece of romantic choral music, the *German Requiem* established Brahms, at thirty-four, as a leading composer of his time. Scored for chorus, baritone and soprano soloists, and orchestra, it consists of seven movements and lasts more than an hour. Brahms entitled the work *Ein Deutsches Requiem—A German Requiem—*because he had chosen texts relating to death and resurrection from Luther's German translation of the Bible. He meant to distinguish his composition from the Latin requiem, or mass for the dead, which includes a vivid depiction of the last judgment (as in the *Dies irae* from Mozart's Requiem, studied in Section 11 of Part V).

Fourth Movement: *How Lovely Is Thy Dwelling Place*
Chorus and orchestra

Basic Set:
CD 6 28

Brahms sent the manuscript of this movement to Clara Schumann, who wrote back, "The chorus from the Requiem pleases me very much; I imagine it must sound beautiful." The predominantly lyrical music subtly reflects the text, which is from Psalm 84, verses 2, 3, and 5. For example, the word *lieblich* (*lovely*) is increasingly emphasized within the movement, and the excitement of *Meine Seele verlanget und sehnet* (*My soul longs and faints*) is expressed through quicker rhythms and polyphonic imitations.

Like the rest of the *German Requiem,* this movement shows Brahms's masterful vocal writing, gained from his wide experience as a choral conductor performing works by Bach and Handel. The rich variety of choral colors in the *German Requiem* is created by skillful alternation among homophonic, monophonic, and polyphonic textures. There is frequent interplay between chorus and orchestra. For example, the fourth movement opens with an introductory downward phrase in the high wood-winds, which is immediately inverted, or turned upside-down, to become the magical rising opening phrase with which the sopranos enter.

Soon after, a second idea in long notes is introduced by the violins and immediately imitated by the tenors.

VOCAL MUSIC GUIDE

BRAHMS, *How Lovely Is Thy Dwelling Place* from *A German Requiem*

28 0:00
Woodwinds, ***p***, downward phrase introduces sopranos, upward phrase.

Wie lieblich sind deine Wohnungen, Herr Zebaoth!

How lovely is thy dwelling place, O Lord of Hosts!

Woodwinds repeat upward phrase.

    0:28

deine Wohnungen Herr Zebaoth!

thy dwelling place O Lord of Hosts!

    0:41
High violins, long-note theme, imitated by tenors, basses, sopranos; *lieblich (lovely)* emphasized.

Wie lieblich sind deine Wohnungen,

How lovely is thy dwelling place,

Herr Zebaoth!
Wie lieblich sind deine Wohnungen,
Herr Zebaoth!

O Lord of Hosts!
How lovely is thy dwelling place,
O Lord of Hosts!

    1:19
Pizzicato strings introduce chorus.

    1:26
Imitation, basses, tenors, altos, sopranos; quicker notes; crescendo to ***f***.

Meine Seele verlanget und sehnet sich

My soul longs and faints

p, homophonic, pizzicato accompaniment. Oboe echo.

nach den Vorhöfen des Herrn.

for the courts of the Lord.

2:02 String accents.	*Mein Leib und Seele freuen sich in dem lebendigen Gott.* *Mein Leib und Seele freuen sich in dem lebendigen Gott.*	My body and soul rejoice in the living God. My body and soul rejoice in the living God.
2:36 Violins, woodwinds, *p*, downward phrase introduces sopranos, *p*; upward phrase.	*Wie lieblich sind deine Wohnungen, Herr Zebaoth!*	How lovely is thy dwelling place O Lord of Hosts!
Woodwinds, upward phrase.	*deine Wohnungen, Herr Zebaoth!*	thy dwelling place O Lord of Hosts!
3:20 High violins, long-note theme.	*Wohl denen,*	Blessed are those
3:35 Chorus, *p*, long-note theme, crescendo.	*Wohl denen, die in deinem Hause wohnen,*	Blessed are those who dwell in thy house
3:50 Extended fugal imitation, *f*; quicker rhythms, staccato strings.	*die loben dich immerdar,*	who praise Thee evermore.
4:36 Sudden *p*, low, extended tones.	*immerdar.*	evermore.
4:43 Woodwinds, downward phrase. Sopranos, tenors imitated by altos, basses. Sopranos, *p*, rise to *f* peak and gently descend. Soft orchestral close.	*Wie lieblich* *Wie lieblich sind deine Wohnungen!*	How lovely How lovely is thy dwelling place!

17 Giuseppe Verdi

Giuseppe Verdi (1813–1901), the most popular of all opera composers, was born in a tiny Italian village. As a boy, he had such an intense love of music that his parents bought him a piano—an unusual acquisition in nineteenth-century Italy. At the age of ten, Verdi went to live in a nearby town, Busseto, to study music and go to school. Every Sunday for nine years, he walked three miles barefoot to serve as church organist in his own village, carrying his shoes to preserve them. A wealthy music patron took Verdi into his home and later supported Verdi's studies in Milan. After finishing his music education at twenty-two, Verdi returned to Busseto and became municipal music director. Thus assured of a regular income, he was able to marry his patron's daughter, a young woman he had known and loved since childhood.

But the small town couldn't fulfill Verdi's needs for long. After three years he returned to Milan with the score of his first opera, *Oberto* (1839). With the help of an influential friend, the young provincial's work was produced at La Scala, the most important opera house in Italy. Though the response to *Oberto* was only modest, it was enough to win Verdi a contract for three more operas. Just when Verdi's future seemed bright, however, disaster struck. While he was working on his next opera—a comedy—his wife fell ill and died. This tragedy completed the destruction of his family, since two infant children had died within the previous two years. Verdi managed to complete the opera, but it understandably lacked inspiration and was greeted by boos and hisses. In despair, he vowed to compose no more.

He changed his mind after reading a libretto about the ancient Jews exiled from their homeland. Verdi was an ardent nationalist who yearned to see the Italian people freed from Austrian domination and unified into one nation. For him, the ancient Jews symbolized the enslaved Italians. He quickly composed *Nabucco* (*Nebuchadnezzar,* king of Babylon), which was an enormous success. One chorus, *Oh, my country so beautiful and*

Giuseppe Verdi was one of the greatest opera composers and an ardent Italian nationalist.

lost! became a national liberation hymn sung by all Italian patriots. From that time on, Verdi and his operas symbolized a free and united Italy. A poet wrote that "the very soul of Italy . . . has today its voice in the name of Giuseppe Verdi." As Italy approached war with Austria, the cry *Viva Verdi* stood also for the patriotic slogan, *Vittorio Emmanuele, Re D'Italia (Victor Emmanuel, king of Italy).*

In his late thirties, Verdi composed *Rigoletto* (1851), *Il Trovatore* (1853), and *La Traviata* (1853), the first of his operas which are now universally known. Although the public loved these works, critics were often scandalized by their subject matter. *Rigoletto* seemed to condone rape and suicide, and *La Traviata* apparently glorified free love and made a heroine out of a kept woman. But Verdi was a fiercely independent man who himself lived openly with his second wife for ten years before marrying her.

After these successes had made him wealthy, Verdi bought an estate at Busseto. In 1861 he was elected deputy to the first Italian parliament to convene after Italy had become a nation. Verdi was Italy's most famous native son when he wrote *Aïda* (1871), an opera commissioned to commemorate the opening of the Suez Canal. In 1874 he wrote his most important nonoperatic work, a gigantic Requiem to honor the memory of the Italian poet and novelist Alessandro Manzoni (1785–1873). In 1887, Verdi, then seventy-three, had a triumphant success with *Otello (Othello)*, one of his greatest operas. Even this masterpiece did not still his creative urge. Remarkably, at the age of seventy-nine, Verdi completed *Falstaff* (1893), his only comedy since the failure of his second opera fifty years earlier.

Verdi's Music

"In the theater," Verdi once wrote, "lengthy is synonymous with boring, and of all styles the boring style is the worst." He composed not for the musical elite, but for a mass public whose main entertainment was opera. Verdi wanted subjects that were "original, interesting . . . and passionate; passions above all!" An aria "needs the greatest variety of mood; irony, contempt, rage, all thrown into sharp profile." Almost all of Verdi's mature works are serious and end unhappily. The operas move quickly and involve characters who are plunged into extremes of hatred, love, jealousy, and fear. His powerful music summons up heroes and villains and vividly underlines dramatic situations. Expressive vocal melody is the soul of a Verdi opera. No matter how elaborate or atmospheric the orchestral part, the musical center lies in the voice. There are many duets, trios, and quartets, in which each character is given melodies superbly tailored to the emotions depicted. Choruses—of Gypsies, Egyptian priests, conspirators, and monks, for example—play an important role in his operas.

In the course of his long life, Verdi's style became less conventional, more subtle and flexible. His later works have greater musical continuity. He used fewer pauses between sections and lessened the difference between aria and recitative. His orchestration became more imaginative and the accompaniments richer.

Verdi's last three operas are perhaps his greatest. *Aïda* is a true "grand opera" with spectacular pageants, ballets, and choruses. Yet for all its spectacle, there are many scenes of tender and intimate beauty. *Otello* and *Falstaff*, the operas of Verdi's old age, have marvelous librettos based on plays by Shakespeare. The librettist was Arrigo Boito, himself a gifted opera composer. For *Otello*, the seventy-three-year-old Verdi wrote sensuous, overpowering music that completely fuses with the poetry and action. The opera rivals Shakespeare's play in its dramatic force and lyricism. Verdi's last opera, *Falstaff*, is incomparably witty, imaginative, and sparkling. The aged composer ended this comic masterwork with a carefree fugue to the words *All the world's a joke!*

Rigoletto (1851)

Verdi dared to create an operatic hero out of a hunchbacked court jester—Rigoletto—whose only redeeming quality is an intense love for his daughter, Gilda. Rigoletto's master, the licentious Duke of Mantua, has won Gilda's love while posing as a poor student. When the Duke seduces the innocent girl, Rigoletto plots his death. Gilda loves the Duke even after learning about his dissolute character, and she ultimately sacrifices her own life to save his. Vice triumphs in this powerful drama.

Act III:
La donna è mobile and Quartet

Basic Set:
CD 6 `29`

Act III of *Rigoletto* contains two of the most popular pieces in opera, the Duke's aria *La donna è mobile* and the Quartet. The scene is a run-down inn where the Duke has come to meet Maddalena, the voluptuous sister of the cutthroat Sparafucile.

The carefree and tuneful *La donna è mobile* (*Woman is fickle*) perfectly expresses the Duke's pleasure-loving personality. Even before the premiere of *Rigoletto*, which was to take place in Venice, Verdi knew that *La donna è mobile* would be a hit. Afraid that his catchy tune would leak out during rehearsals and be sung by every Venetian gondolier, he waited until the last possible moment before giving the manuscript to the tenor who was to sing the aria.

The Quartet is sung as Rigoletto and Gilda peer through a crack in the wall of the inn, observing the Duke flirting with Maddalena. Verdi projects four conflicting emotions at one time, characterizing each singer with an appropriate melodic line. The Duke attempts to seduce Maddalena with a suave and ardent legato melody. Maddalena coquettishly repels his advances with quick, staccato laughs. Outside the inn, Gilda laments her fate with anguished sobs punctuated by rests, while Rigoletto curses and mutters threats of vengeance in repeated notes. Verdi lets us hear each of the four voices separately before combining them in a glorious ensemble.

VOCAL MUSIC GUIDE

VERDI, *Rigoletto*

La donna è mobile and Quartet

`29` 0:00
Aria. Orchestra
introduces
Duke's melody.

Duke

La donna è mobile	Woman is fickle
Qual piuma al vento,	Like a feather in the wind,
Muta d'accento	She changes her words
E di pensiero.	And her thoughts.

Allegretto

La don - na è mo - bi - le   qual piu - ma al ven - to,

mu - ta d'ac - cen - to   e di pen - sie - ro.

Sempre un amabile	Always a lovable
Leggiadro viso,	And lovely face,
In pianto o in riso,	Weeping or laughing,
È menzognero.	Is lying.
La donna è mobile, ecc.	Woman is fickle, etc.

1:00
Orchestra.
Duke's melody
repeated with
different
words.

È sempre misero
Chi a lei s'affida,
Chi le confida
Mal cauto il core!
Pur mai non sentesi
Felice appieno
Chi su quel seno
Non liba amore!
La donna è mobile, ecc.

The man's always wretched
Who believes in her,
Who recklessly entrusts
His heart to her!
And yet one who never
Drinks love on that breast
Never feels
Entirely happy!
Woman is fickle, etc.

2:04
Duke's melody
in orchestra,
decrescendo.

(Sparafucile comes back in with a bottle of wine and two glasses, which he sets on the table; then he strikes the ceiling twice with the hilt of his long sword. At this signal, a laughing young girl, in a Gypsy dress—Maddalena—leaps down the stairs: the Duke runs to embrace her, but she escapes him. Meanwhile Sparafucile has gone out into the road, where he says softly to Rigoletto:)

Sparafucile

È là vostr'uomo . . .
viver dee o morire?

Your man is there . . .
Must he live or die?

Rigoletto

Più tardi tornerò l'opra a compire.

I'll return later to complete the deed.

Brief pause.

(Sparafucile goes off behind the house toward the river. Gilda and Rigoletto remain in the street, the Duke and Maddalena on the ground floor.)

30 2:47
Allegro

Duke

Un dì, se ben rammentomi,
O bella, t'incontrai . . .
Mi piacque di te chiedere,
E intesi che qui stai.
Or sappi, che d'allora
Sol te quest'alma adora!

One day, if I remember right,
I met you, O beauty . . .
I was pleased to ask about you,
And I learned that you live here.
Know then, that since that time
My soul adores only you!

Gilda

Iniquo!

Villain!

Maddalena

Ah, ah! . . . e vent'altre appresso
Le scorda forse adesso?
Ha un'aria il signorino
Da vero libertino . . .

Ha, ha! . . . And does it now perhaps
Forget twenty others?
The young gentleman looks like
A true libertine . . .

Duke
(starting to embrace her)

Si . . . un mostro son . . .

Yes . . . I'm a monster . . .

Gilda

Ah padre mio!

Ah, Father!

Maddalena

Lasciatemi, stordito.

Let me go, foolish man!

Duke

Ih, che fracasso!

Ah, what a fuss!

Maddalena

Stia saggio.

Be good.

Duke

Rhythm slows.

E tu sii docile,	And you, be yielding,
Non fare tanto chiasso.	Don't make so much noise.
Ogni saggezza chiudesi	All wisdom concludes
Nel gaudio e nell'amore.	In pleasure and in love.
	(He takes her hand.)

Quick rhythm resumes.

La bella mano candida! What a lovely, white hand!

Maddalena

Scherzate voi, signore. You're joking, sir.

Duke

No, no. No, no.

Maddalena

Son brutta. I'm ugly.

Duke

Abbracciami. Embrace me.

Gilda

Iniquo! Villain!

Maddalena

Ebro! You're drunk!

Duke

D'amor ardente! With ardent love!

Maddalena

Signor l'indifferente, My indifferent sir,
Vi piace canzonar? Do you enjoy teasing?

Duke

No, no, ti vo'sposar. No, no, I want to marry you.

Maddalena

Ne voglio la parola. I want your word.

Duke

(ironic)

Amabile figliuola! Lovable maiden!

Rigoletto

(to Gilda, who has seen and heard all)

E non ti basta ancor? Isn't that enough for you yet?

Gilda

Iniquo traditor! Villainous betrayer!

Characters sing simultaneously.

Maddalena

Ne voglio la parola. I want your word.

Duke

Amabile figliuola! Lovable maiden!

Rigoletto

E non ti basta ancor? Isn't that enough for you yet?

Short pause.

31 4:14
Quartet, andante.

Duke

Bella figlia dell'amore, Beautiful daughter of love,
Schiavo son de' vezzi tuoi; I am the slave of your charms;

Con un detto sol tu puoi	With a single word you can
Le mie pene consolar.	Console my sufferings.

Bel - la fi - glia del - l'a - mo - re, schia - vo son de'

vez - zi tuo - i; con un det - to, un det - to sol tu

puo - i le mie pe - ne, le mie pe - ne _ con - so - lar.

Vieni, e senti del mio core	Come, and feel the quick beating
Il frequente palpitar . . .	Of my heart . . .
Con un detto sol tu puoi	With a single word you can
Le mie pene consolar.	Console my sufferings.

Maddalena

Ah! ah! rido ben di core,	Ha! Ha! I laugh heartily,
Chè tai baie costan poco.	For such tales cost little.

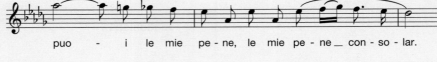

Ah! ah! ri - do ben di co - re, chè tai ba - ie cos - tan po - co;

Gilda

Ah! così parlar d'amore . . .	Ah! To speak thus of love . . .

Ah! ___ co - sì ___ par - lar _ d'a - mo - re!

Maddalena

Quanto valga il vostro gioco,	Believe me, I can judge
Mel credete, so apprezzar.	How much your game is worth.

Gilda

. . . a me pur l'infame ho udito!	. . . I too have heard the villain so!

Rigoletto
(to Gilda)

Taci, il piangere non vale.	Hush, weeping is of no avail.

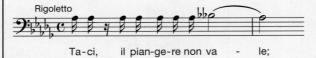

Ta - ci, il pian - ge - re non va - le;

Gilda

Infelice cor tradito,	Unhappy, betrayed heart.
Per angoscia non scoppiar. Ah, no!	Do not burst with anguish. Ah, no!

Characters sing simultaneously.		

Maddalena

Son avvezza, bel signore,	I'm accustomed, handsome sir,
Ad un simile scherzare.	To similar joking.
Mio bel signor!	My handsome sir!

Duke

Bella figlia dell'amore, ecc.	Beautiful daughter of love, etc.
Vieni!	Come!

Rigoletto

Ch'ei mentiva sei sicura.	You are sure that he was lying.
Taci, e mia sarà la cura	Hush, and I will take care
La vendetta d'affrettar.	To hasten vengeance.
Sì, pronto fia, sarà fatale,	Yes, it will be swift and fatal,
Io saprollo fulminar.	I will know how to strike him down.
Taci taci . . .	Hush, hush . . .

18 Giacomo Puccini

Some of the best-loved operas were created by Giacomo Puccini (1858–1924), who succeeded Verdi as the most important Italian opera composer of his time. Puccini came from a long line of composers and church organists. During his student years at the Milan Conservatory (1880–1883), he lived a hand-to-mouth existence, usually eating on credit at a restaurant fittingly named Aïda. The success of Puccini's first opera, written shortly after his graduation, brought him to the attention of Italy's leading music publisher, who commissioned new works and gave him an annual income.

In 1893 Puccini became well known throughout Italy for his opera *Manon Lescaut,* and after 1896 he was wealthy and world-famous from the enormous success of *La Bohème,* which portrays a "bohemian" life similar to his own life as an impoverished music student. *La Bohème,* along with two other very popular operas, *Tosca* (1900) and *Madame Butterfly* (1904), was written in collaboration with the librettists Luigi Illica and Giuseppe Giacosa. Puccini was very much concerned with the literary and dramatic qualities of his librettos, often demanding endless changes from his collaborators. He spent as much time polishing the librettos as he did composing the music. His last opera, *Turandot,* was based on a Chinese fairy tale. He died before finishing it; the work was completed from Puccini's sketches by a friend, Franco Alfano.

Puccini's marvelous sense of theater has given his operas lasting appeal. He knew just when to introduce new musical material or a moment of silence, and he was able to provide smooth transitions from one scene or mood to

Giacomo Puccini.

another. His melodies have short, easily remembered phrases and are intensely emotional. He used the orchestra to reinforce the vocal melody and to suggest atmosphere, landscape, and mood. As Verdi did in his late works, Puccini minimized the difference between aria and recitative, creating a continuous flow of music. He also achieved unity and continuity by using the same material in different acts, particularly at moments when his characters reflect on past events or emotions.

Some of Puccini's operas, notably *Tosca,* reflect an artistic trend of the 1890s known as *verismo—realism,* or the quality of being "true to life." Operas coming out of this realistic movement deal with ordinary people rather than kings, gods, or great heroes and often contain shockingly violent scenes set to music of raw emotional power. *Cavalleria rusticana* (*Rustic Chivalry,* 1890), by Pietro Mascagni; and *I Pagliacci* (*The Clowns,* 1892), by Ruggiero Leoncavallo, are other famous examples of *verismo.* Puccini's operas also feature exoticism. *Madame Butterfly* is set in Japan and *Turandot* in China, and in both Puccini used melodic and rhythmic elements derived from Japanese and Chinese music. His melodies cast a romantic glow over any subject matter, realistic or exotic.

La Bohème (1896)

La Bohème (*Bohemian Life*) takes place in the Latin Quarter of Paris around 1830. Its hero is Rodolfo, a young poet who shares a garret with Marcello, a painter; Colline, a philosopher; and Schaunard, a musician. Mimi, the heroine, is a poor, tubercular seamstress who lives in the same building. The simple, touching plot has been aptly summarized as "boy meets girl, boy loses girl, boy and girl are reunited as girl dies of consumption in boy's arms and curtain falls." Everyone can relate to the characters and emotions of this enchanting opera. Though there are many realistic touches in this picture of bohemian life, it is seen through a romantic haze.

connect

A video of this scene is available in *Connect Kamien.*

Basic Set:
CD 7 **1**

Brief Set:
CD 4 **28**
(Ends after Rodolfo's aria)

Act I:
Scene between Rodolfo and Mimi

Mimi and Rodolfo meet and fall in love toward the end of Act I, which takes place on a cold Christmas eve. Her candle has blown out, and she knocks on his door asking for a light. At Rodolfo's insistence, Mimi enters, but she suddenly has a coughing fit and faints in his arms. She revives after Rodolfo sprinkles water on her face. She then leaves, her candle alight, but she returns immediately, for she has lost her key. They must search for the key in the dark—a gust of wind has extinguished their candles. When their hands touch, Rodolfo sings the aria *Che gelida manina* (*How cold your little hand is!*). He sings about himself, his dreams, and his fantasies. Mimi responds with a poetic description of her simple life in the aria *Michiamano Mimì* (*They call me Mimì*). Under the spell of their newfound love, they join in a duet which closes the act.

Puccini's sensuous melody casts a glow over the entire scene. His music has an improvisatory quality, with many fluctuations of tempo that reflect changes of mood and dramatic action. In the musical dialogue between Mimi and Rodolfo, Puccini easily alternates between speechlike and melodic phrases. When Mimi enters, the orchestra murmurs a touching phrase—Mimi's theme—which suggests her fragility and tenderness. Mimi coughing fit is evoked by agitated music and her fainting by a poignant oboe solo. When Mimi returns to get her key, she introduces a new melody in a faster tempo.

Each of the two arias begins simply, almost conversationally. Then the melody grows warmer until it reaches a climax in a broad, passionate phrase. The climactic phrase of Rodolfo's aria, sung to the words *Talor dal mio forziere* (*My hoard of treasure is robbed by two thieves: a pair of beautiful eyes*), is the love theme of the whole opera. Mimi's emotional high point is reached when she dreams about the end of winter (*ma quando vien la sgelo*), when "the first kiss of April" is hers. Returning to reality at the end of her aria, she sings in conversational repeated tones.

Veronica Villaroel as Mimi and Roberto Aronica as Rodolfo in a performance of *La Bohème* at the San Francisco Opera.

The mood changes momentarily as Rodolfo goes to the window and has a brief exchange with his friends in the courtyard—an example of Puccini's theatrical timing, for he provides a moment of relaxation before the lovers join in the closing duet. First, Rodolfo sings alone; then both voices unite beautifully in a declaration of love.

VOCAL MUSIC GUIDE

PUCCINI, *La Bohème*

Excerpt from Act I

1 **28** 0:00

Flute melody.	(Rodolfo closes the door, sets his light on the table, and tries to write. But he tears up the paper and throws the pen down.)	
		Rodolfo
	Non sono in vena.	I'm not in the mood.
		(A timid knock at the door.)
Speechlike.	*Chi è la?*	Who's there?
		Mimi
	Scusi.	Excuse me.
		Rodolfo
	Una donna!	A woman!
		Mimi
Mimi's theme,	*Di grazia, me si è spento*	I'm sorry . . . my light
pp, in orchestra.	*Il lume.*	Has gone out.

Rodolfo

(opens the door)

Ecco.   Here.

Mimi

(in the doorway, with a candlestick and a key)

Vorrebbe . . . ?   Would you . . . ?

Rodolfo

S'accomodi un momento.   Come in for a moment.

Mimi

Non occorre.   There's no need.

Rodolfo

La prego, entri.   Please . . . come in.

(Mimi enters, has a fit of coughing.)

Rodolfo

Si sente male?   You're not well?

Mimi

No . . . nulla.   No . . . it's nothing.

Rodolfo

Impallidisce!   You're pale!

Mimi

È il respir . . . quelle scale . . .   I'm out of breath . . . the stairs . . .

1:04

Oboe.

(She faints, and Rodolfo is just in time to support her and help her to a chair. The key and the candlestick fall from her hands.)

Rodolfo

Ed ora come faccio?   Now what shall I do?

(He gets some water and sprinkles her face.)

Pizzicato violins.

Così.   So.

Che viso d'ammalata!   How ill she looks!

1:28

Staccato
muted strings.

(Mimi comes to.)

Si sente meglio?   Are you better now?

Mimi

Sì.   Yes.

Rodolfo

Qui c'è tanto freddo.   It's so cold here.

Segga vicino al fuoco.   Come and sit by the fire.

(He helps her to a chair by the stove.)

Aspetti . . . un po' di vino.   Wait . . . some wine.

Mimi

Grazie.   Thank you.

Rodolfo

A lei.   Here.

Mimi

Poco, poco.   Just a little.

Rodolfo

Così.   There.

Mimi

Grazie.   Thank you.

Rodolfo

(Che bella bambina!)   (What a lovely creature!)

Mimi
(rising)

Ora permetta	Now, please,
Che accenda il lume.	Relight my candle.
È tutto passato.	I'm better now.

Rodolfo

Tanta fretta. — Such a hurry!

Mimi

Sì. — Yes.

(Rodolfo lights her candle for her.)

Mimi

Grazie. Buona sera. — Thank you. Good evening.

Rodolfo

Buona sera. — Good evening.

(Mimi goes out, then reappears at the door.)

Mimi

Oh! sventata, sventata,	Oh! foolish me! . . .
La chiave della stanza	Where have I left
Dove l'ho lasciata?	The key to my room?

Rodolfo

Non stia sull'uscio:	Don't stand in the door:
Il lume vacilla ai vento.	The wind makes your light flicker.

(Her candle goes out.)

Mimi

Oh Dio! Torni ad accenderlo. — Heavens! Will you relight it?

(Rodolfo rushes to her with his light, but when he reaches the door, his candle goes out, too. The room is dark.)

Rodolfo

Oh Dio! Anche il mio s'è spento. — Heavens! Now mine's out, too.

Mimi

Ah! E la chiave ove sarà? — Ah! And where can my key be?

Rodolfo

Buio pesto! — Pitch-dark!

Mimi

Disgraziata! — Unlucky me!

Rodolfo

Ove sarà? — Where can it be?

Mimi

Importuna è la vicina . . . — You've a bothersome neighbor . . .

Rodolfo

Ma le pare! — Not at all.

Mimi

Importuna è la vicina . . . — You've a bothersome neighbor . . .

Rodolfo

Cosa dice, ma le pare! — What do you mean? Not at all!

Mimi

Cerchi. — Search.

Rodolfo

Cerco. — I'm searching.

(They both grope on the floor for the key.)

Mimi

Ove sarà? — Where can it be?

2:28
A little faster. Tuneful vocal melody.

Rodolfo
(finds the key, pockets it)

Ah!	Ah!

Mimi

L'ha trovata?	Did you find it?

Rodolfo

No.	No.

Mimi

Mi parve . . .	I thought . . .

Rodolfo

In verità!	Truthfully!

Mimi

Cerca?	Are you hunting?

Rodolfo

Cerco.	I'm hunting for it.

3:50
Orchestra
alone, tempo slows.

(Guided by her voice, Rodolfo pretends to search as he draws closer to her. Then his hand meets hers, and he holds it.)

Mimi
(surprised)

Ah!	Ah!

(They rise. Rodolfo continues to hold Mimi's hand.)

2 **29** 4:14
Rodolfo's aria.

Rodolfo

Che gelida manina,	How cold your little hand is!
Se la lasci riscaldar.	Let me warm it for you.

Che ge - li - da ma - ni - na,   se la la - sci ri - scal - dar.

Harp.

Cercar che giova? Al buio	What's the use of searching?
Non si trova. Ma per fortuna	We'll never find it in the dark.
È una notte di luna,	But luckily there's a moon,
E qui la luna l'abbiamo vicina.	And she's our neighbor here.
Aspetti, signorina,	Just wait, my dear young lady,
Le dirò con due parole chi son,	And meanwhile I'll tell you
Chi son, e che faccio, come vivo.	In a word who and what I am.
Vuole?	Shall I?

(Mimi is silent.)

Chi son? Chi son? Son un poeta.	Who am I? I'm a poet.
Che cosa faccio? Scrivo.	My business? Writing.
E come vivo? Vivo.	How do I live? I live.
In povertà mia lieta	In my happy poverty
Scialo da gran signore	I squander like a prince
Rime ed inni d'amore.	My poems and songs of love.
Per sogni e per chimere	In hopes and dreams
E per castelli in aria	And castles in air,
L'anima ho milionaria.	I'm a millionaire in spirit.

6:42
Love theme.

Talor dal mio forziere	My hoard of treasure
Ruban tutti i gioielli	Is stolen by two thieves:
Due ladri: gli occhi belli.	A pair of beautiful eyes.

Ta - lor dal mio for - zie - re _____ ru-ban tut-ti i gio-

iel - li due la - dri: gli oc - chi bel - li.

V'entrar con voi pur ora	They came in now with you
Ed i miei sogni usati,	And all my lovely dreams,
Ed i bei sogni miei	My dreams of the past,
Tosto si dileguar!	Were soon stolen away.
Ma il furto non m'accora	But the theft doesn't upset me,
Poichè, poichè v'ha preso stanza	Since the empty place was filled
La speranza.	With hope.
Or che mi conoscete	Now that you know me,
Parlate voi, deh! parlate.	It's your turn to speak.
Chi siete? Vi piaccia dir?	Who are you? Will you tell me?

3 8:49

Mimi's aria.

	Mimi
Sì.	Yes.
Mi chiamano Mimì,	They call me Mimi,
Ma il mio nome è Lucia.	But my real name is Lucia.

Andante lento

Mi chia-ma-no Mi - mì, ma il mio no-me è Lu - ci - a. ___

La storia mia è breve.	My story is brief.
A tela o a seta	I embroider silk and satin
Ricamo in casa e fuori.	At home or outside.
Son tranquilla e lieta,	I'm tranquil and happy,
Ed è mio svago	And my pastime
Far gigli e rose.	Is making lilies and roses.
Mi piaccion quelle cose	I love all things
Che han si dolce malia,	That have a gentle magic,
Che parlano d'amor, di primavere,	That talk of love, of spring,
Che parlano di sogni e di chimere,	That talk of dreams and fancies—
Quelle cose che han nome poesia . . .	The things called poetry . . .
Lei m'intende?	Do you understand me?

	Rodolfo
Sì.	Yes.

10:49

	Mimi
Mi chiamano Mimì—	They call me Mimi—
Il perchè non so.	I don't know why.
Sola, mi fo il pranzo	I live all by myself
Da me stessa.	And I eat all alone.
Non vado sempre a messa,	I don't often go to church,
Ma prego assai il Signor.	But I like to pray.
Vivo sola, soletta,	I stay all alone
Là in una bianca cameretta;	In my tiny white room,
Guardo sui tetti e in cielo.	I look at the roofs and the sky.

Ma quando vien lo sgelo	But when the thaw comes
Il primo sole è mio,	The first sunshine is mine,
Il primo bacio	The first kiss
Dell'aprile è mio!	Of April is mine!
Il primo sole è mio!	The first sunshine is mine!
Germoglia in un vaso una rosa.	A rose blossoms in my vase,
Foglia a foglia l'aspiro.	I breathe in its perfume,
Così gentil è il profumo d'un fior.	Petal by petal. So lovely,
Ma i fior ch'io faccio, ahimè,	So sweet is the flower's perfume.
I fior ch'io faccio,	But the flowers I make,
Ahimè non hanno odore.	Alas, have no scent.
Altro di me non le saprei narrare.	What else can I say?
Sono la sua vicina	I'm your neighbor,
Che la vien fuori d'ora a importunare.	Disturbing you at this impossible hour.

4   14:03

Schaunard

(from below)

Eh! Rodolfo!	Hey! Rodolfo!

Colline

Rodolfo!	Rodolfo!

Marcello

Olà! Non senti?	Hey! Can't you hear?
Lumaca!	You snail!

Colline

Poetucolo!	You fake!

Schaunard

Accidenti al pigro!	To hell with that lazy one!

(Rodolfo, impatient, goes to the window to answer. When the window is opened, the moonlight comes in, lighting up the room.)

Rodolfo

Scrivo ancora tre righe a volo.	I've a few more words to write.

Mimi

Chi son?	Who are they?

Rodolfo

Amici.	Friends.

Schaunard

Sentirai le tue.	You'll hear about this.

Marcello

Che te ne fai lì solo?	What are you doing there alone?

Rodolfo

Non son solo. Siamo in due.	I'm not alone. There's two of us.
Andate da Momus, tenete il posto.	Go to Momus and get a table.
Ci saremo tosto.	We'll be there soon.

Marcello, Schaunard, Colline

Momus, Momus, Momus,	Momus, Momus, Momus.
Zitti e discreti audiamocene via.	Quietly, discreetly, we're off.
Momus, Momus, Momus.	Momus, Momus, Momus.
Trovò la poesia.	He's found his poem at last.

(Turning, Rodolfo sees Mimi wrapped in a halo of moonlight. He contemplates her, in ecstasy.)

14:48

Duet.

Rodolfo

O soave fanciulla, o dolce viso	Oh! lovely girl, oh! sweet face
Di mite circonfuso alba lunar,	Bathed in the soft moonlight.
In te, ravviso il sogno	I see in you the dream

	Ch'io vorrei sempre sognar!	I'd dream forever!
Voices unite, love theme.	Fremon già nell'anima	Already I taste in spirit
	Le dolcezze estreme,	The heights of tenderness!
	Amor nel bacio freme!	Love trembles in our kiss!

Mimi

Ah, tu sol comandi, amore. . . .   Ah! Love, you rule alone. . . .
Oh! come dolci scendono   How sweet his praises
Le sue lusinghe al core. . . .   Enter my heart. . . .
Tu sol comandi, amore!   Love, you alone rule!

(Rodolfo kisses her.)

Mimi

No, per pietà!   No, please!

Rodolfo

Sei mia!   You're mine!

Mimi

V'aspettan gli amici. . . .   Your friends are waiting.

Rodolfo

Già mi mandi via?   You send me away already?

Mimi

Vorrei dir . . . ma non oso.   I daren't say what I'd like . . .

Rodolfo

Di'.   Tell me.

Mimi

Se venissi con voi?   If I came with you?

Rodolfo

Che? Mimì!   What? Mimi!
Sarebbe così dolce restar qui.   It would be so fine to stay here.
C'è freddo fuori.   Outside it's cold.

Mimi

Vi starò vicina!   I'd be near you!

Rodolfo

E al ritorno?   And when we come back?

Mimi

Curioso!   Who knows?

Rodolfo

Melody from   Dammi il braccio, o mia piccina . . .   Give me your arm, my little one . . .
Rodolfo's aria.

Mimi

Obbedisco, signor!   Your servant, sir . . .

Rodolfo

Che m'ami . . . di' . . .   Tell me you love me!

Mimi

Io t'amo.   I love you.

Rodolfo

Amor!   My love!

Mimi

Amor!   My love!

Rodolfo and Mimi

Amor!   Beloved!

Luciano Pavarotti, Tenor, Singing the Part of Rodolfo in Puccini's La Bohème

The operatic tenor Luciano Pavarotti (1935–2007) was probably the world's best-known classical performer during the late twentieth century. He appeared frequently not only on operatic and concert stages, but in stadiums, on television, and in movies. In June 1993, more than 500,000 fans attended his performance in New York's Central Park and millions more watched on television. In July 1994, he participated in the second of several "Three Tenors" concerts—together with Placido Domingo and José Carreras—in Dodger Stadium, Los Angeles; it was seen on television by an estimated billion people in 107 countries.

Pavarotti was born in Modena, Italy, in 1935. As a boy, he listened avidly to recordings of tenors brought home by his father, an amateur singer. At nineteen Pavarotti began serious vocal study, and at twenty-five he won a singing competition that led to his operatic debut as Rodolfo in Puccini's La Bohème. Pavarotti later recalled the thrill of "singing for the first time with a full orchestra. All those years of studying and thinking of yourself as a singer—there is always an orchestra there, in your mind. But the first time it is *really* there—it is an experience, impossible to describe to someone who hasn't dreamed for years of becoming an opera singer." From then on his career rose rapidly: he made his debut at Milan's La Scala—Italy's most important opera house—in 1965, and his debut at New York's Metropolitan Opera in 1968.

Pavarotti wrote insightfully on his approach to Rodolfo's aria *Che gelida manina* from Puccini's *La Bohème* (included in the video clip found on the CD-ROM accompanying this book). "For me the most difficult notes for the tenor in *La Bohème* are in Act I when Rodolfo sings to Mimi, '*Che gelida manina.*' . . . Those quiet low notes must have a big rich sound—a steady, pure sound that floods the opera house. They may be soft notes, but they must have behind them all your power as a singer. They must have the same amount of support from your diaphragm that you give the big notes."

Pavarotti was inspired by the great conductors with whom he worked: they revealed deeper aspects of the drama, and they influenced him to try new approaches "to passages I had sung many times in a different way." When the conductor Carlos Kleiber directed a performance of *La Bohème* at La Scala, "difficult places in the score that had caused me problems before, I found myself singing without effort. As an example, it is traditional to transpose '*Che gelida manina*' down a half tone to spare the tenor the difficult high C at the end. Although few people were aware of it, most of the great tenors of the past had done this. But Kleiber made me sing the aria in the original key. Somehow I soared up to the high C with no strain. It may seem like superstition, but I am sure that was due to the inspiration of working with him and the way he conducted." No one did more than Pavarotti to introduce listeners to the magic of opera.

19 | Richard Wagner

Few composers have had so powerful an impact on their time as Richard Wagner (1813–1883). During the last decades of the nineteenth century, his operas and artistic philosophy influenced not only musicians, but also poets, painters, and playwrights. Such was his preeminence that an opera house of his own design was built in Bayreuth, Germany, solely for performances of his music dramas.

Wagner was born in Leipzig and grew up in a theatrical atmosphere. His stepfather and two of his sisters were actors, and another sister was an opera singer. His boyhood dream was to be a poet and playwright. But at fifteen he was overwhelmed by the power of Beethoven's music, and he decided to become a composer. The young Wagner taught himself by studying scores. He never tried to master an instrument, though he did have almost three years of formal training in music theory.

When he was seventeen, Wagner enrolled in Leipzig University, where he was more interested in riotous student club life than in academic studies. His family thought him good for nothing because of his dueling, drinking, and gambling. The pattern continued throughout his life; Wagner shamelessly lived off other people and accumulated enormous debts that he never repaid.

During his early twenties, Wagner conducted in small German theaters, wrote several operas, and married Minna Planer, a beautiful and well-known actress. In 1839 he decided to try his luck in Paris, then the center of grand opera. Unpaid debts prevented him from getting a passport, and so he and Minna crossed the frontier illegally. Their two years in Paris were miserable. Unable to get an opera performed, Wagner was reduced to musical hackwork. He ran up so many bills that he was briefly confined to a debtors' prison.

Wagner returned to Germany in 1842 to supervise the production of his opera *Rienzi* at the Dresden opera. The work was immensely successful, and Wagner was appointed conductor of the Dresden opera; the job paid a good salary and was to have been a lifetime position. He spent six years there, becoming famous both as an

Richard Wagner's operas and artistic philosophy had a powerful impact on musicians, poets, painters, and playwrights.

opera composer and as a conductor. Wagner demanded that his orchestra play with enormous dynamic subtlety and rhythmic freedom. "When he conducts," a musician observed, "he is almost beside himself with excitement. . . . Every sinew in his body speaks. His whole appearance is of arrogance and despotism personified."

The revolutions of 1848 swept across Europe like a forest fire and marked a turning point in Wagner's career. His life in Dresden had become increasingly difficult because he had again accumulated debts (he owed more than ten times his annual salary). Hoping that a new society would wipe out his debts and produce conditions favorable to his art, Wagner participated in the insurrection in Dresden. He ordered hand grenades and tried to incite disobedience among the king's soldiers. When a warrant was issued for his arrest, Wagner fled to Switzerland.

For several years Wagner did no composing; instead he worked out theories of art in essays such as *Art and Revolution* (1849), *The Artwork of the Future* (1850), and *Opera and Drama* (1851). More important, he completed the librettos to *Der Ring des Nibelungen* (*The Ring of the Nibelung*), a set of four operas based on Nordic mythology. The *Ring* was to occupy Wagner for a quarter of a century. He began the text in 1848 and finished the music in 1874. Wagner's amazing self-confidence and belief in his own greatness enabled him to compose one gigantic opera after another, with no prospect of performance. He composed the first opera of the *Ring* cycle, *Das Rheingold* (*The Rhine Gold*, 1853–1854); the second, *Die Walküre* (*The Valkyrie*, 1854–1856); and the first two acts of the third, *Siegfried* (1856–1857)—and then he interrupted his work to compose *Tristan and Isolde* (1857–1859), which he hoped would have a better chance for performance. In *Tristan and Isolde,* sexual passion is presented musically with unprecedented power and vividness.

Wagner had several bad years after finishing *Tristan.* His opera *Tannhäuser* was a failure in a revival at the Paris Opera in 1861, and *Tristan* was abandoned by the Vienna Opera after many rehearsals. Creditors pounded on his door, demanding payment for the silks, satins, laces, and perfumes he "needed" as part of his lifestyle.

In 1864 Wagner was rescued from his desperate situation by King Ludwig of Bavaria, an eighteen-year-old fanatical Wagnerian who was determined to help Wagner produce his operas and complete the *Ring.* All the resources of the Munich Opera were put at Wagner's disposal. *Tristan* and *Die Meistersinger von Nürnberg* (*The Mastersingers of Nuremberg,* 1862–1867) were lavishly produced in Munich. Wagner completed *Siegfried* (1869–1870) and composed the final opera of the *Ring, Götterdämmerung* (*The Twilight of the Gods,* 1869–1874).

During this period, Wagner fell in love with Cosima von Bülow. She was Liszt's daughter and the wife of Hans von Bülow, Wagner's close friend and favorite conductor. Cosima gave birth to two of Wagner's children while still married to von Bülow. Shortly after Wagner's first wife died, he married Cosima.

In Richard Wagner, towering musical genius was allied with utter selfishness, ruthlessness, and an absolute conviction about his place in history. He was a rabid German nationalist; he wrote in his diary, "I am the most German of beings. I am the German spirit." He bent people to his will, and he forged an audience for his complex music dramas from a public accustomed to conventional opera.

Wagner designed a theater to suit performances of the *Ring.* With the help of King Ludwig and contributions from Wagner clubs which had been formed all over Germany, Wagner's festival theater was constructed in Bayreuth, a small Bavarian town. The premiere of the *Ring* cycle in 1876 was perhaps the single most important musical event of the century. Sixty newspaper correspondents from all over the world attended, including two from the United States. Though some critics still found his music too dissonant, heavily orchestrated, and long-winded, Wagner was generally acclaimed the greatest composer of his time. A year after completing *Parsifal* (1877–1882), his last opera, Wagner visited Venice, where he died at the age of sixty-nine.

Wagner's Music

For Wagner, an opera house was a temple in which the spectator was to be overwhelmed by music and drama. He wrote his own librettos, which he based on medieval Germanic legends and myths. His characters are usually larger than life—heroes, gods, demigods.

Wagner called his works *music dramas* rather than operas, to emphasize the close relationship in them between music and drama. He envisioned music drama as a "universal artwork" (*Gesamtkunstwerk* in German) in which all the arts—music, drama, dance, painting—are fused. Today, however, many people find Wagner's music more exciting than his rather static drama. For long stretches of time his characters exult, lament, or relate what has happened to them.

Within each act, there is a continuous musical flow, which Wagner described as "unending melody." The music is not broken into traditional arias, recitatives, and duets. He achieves musical and dramatic continuity by smoothly connecting each section to the next. There are no breaks where applause can disturb the listener's concentration. Wagner conceived his vocal line as a "speech song" combining the speechlike quality of a recitative with the lyricism of an aria. The vocal line is inspired by rhythms and pitch fluctuations in the German text.

Wagner revolutionized opera by shifting the musical center of gravity from the voice toward the orchestra. His expanded and colorful orchestration brilliantly expresses the drama and reveals characters' thoughts and feelings. He treats the orchestra symphonically, always developing, transforming, and intertwining musical ideas. Many long orchestral interludes graphically depict scenic effects such as floods, sunrises, and flames.

Wagner loved to exploit the rich power of the brasses. The *Ring* calls for eight French horns and four new brass instruments (called *Wagner tubas*) that he designed. The orchestral sound is so full that only singers with unusually powerful voices, such as a "Wagnerian soprano" or a "heroic tenor," can cut through it.

Wagner spins an orchestral web out of recurrent musical ideas called *leit motifs*, or *leading motives*. A **leitmotif** is a short musical idea associated with a person, an object, or a thought in the drama. When the text refers to Siegfried, for example, his leitmotif is usually heard in the orchestra. Leitmotifs are sometimes also heard in the vocal parts. They are varied and transformed to convey the evolving dramatic situation and changes of character. When Siegfried is murdered, his leitmotif is set against strident dissonant harmonies. As Wagner develops his leitmotifs, he often sets one against another to suggest the clash of two persons or ideas. The leitmotifs unify Wagner's greatly extended music dramas.

The emotional tension of Wagner's music is heightened by chromatic and dissonant harmonies. He creates motion and color through rapid shifts from one key to another and through many chromatic chords in each key. The listener often expects a resolution to a stable chord, only to hear yet another dissonance. Wagner's chromatic harmony ultimately led to the breakdown of tonality and to the new musical language of the twentieth century.

Die Walküre (The Valkyrie; 1856)

Die Walküre (*The Valkyrie*) is the second and most widely performed of the four music dramas in Wagner's gigantic cycle *Der Ring des Nibelungen* (*The Ring of the Nibelung*). Despite its gods, giants, dwarfs, and magic fire, the *Ring* is really about Wagner's view of nineteenth-century society. He uses Nordic mythology to warn that society destroys itself through lust for money and power. It is fitting that Wagner first sketched the plot of the *Ring* in 1848, the year that brought Marx's *Communist Manifesto* and revolutions throughout Europe.

Basic Set:
CD 7 **5**

Brief Set:
CD 4 **30**

Act I:
Love scene (conclusion)

Wagner builds the first act of *Die Walküre* to an overwhelming climax in the passionate love scene which concludes it. To grasp this scene fully, it's helpful to know what has happened earlier in the *Ring*.

A Nibelung dwarf, Alberich, has stolen gold belonging to the Rhine maidens, mermaids in the Rhine River. From this gold, the dwarf fashions a ring that can bestow immense power on anyone who wears it and is willing to renounce love. The dwarf, in turn, is robbed of his prize by Wotan, king of the gods. (*Wednesday* comes from *Wotan's day*.) Soon Wotan himself is forced to give up the ring; he then lives in fear that Alberich will get it back and use it to destroy him. Hoping to protect himself, he surrounds his castle, Valhalla, with a bodyguard of heroes. His daughters, goddesses called *Valkyries*, swoop over battlefields on horseback and bear away the dead bodies of the bravest warriors. The Valkyrie of the opera's title is Brünnhilde, Wotan's favorite daughter.

Seeking to create a hero who can help him regain the ring, Wotan takes a human wife and fathers the Volsung twins—a son, Siegmund; and a daughter, Sieglinde. The twins know their father as Wälse, unaware that he is the god Wotan. They are separated as children when a hostile clan kidnaps Sieglinde and kills their mother. Siegmund becomes an outlaw and Sieglinde is eventually forced to marry the warrior-chief Hunding, whom she hates. During the wedding feast in Hunding's home, Wotan appears, disguised as an old man dressed in gray. He thrusts a magic sword into the tree around which the house is built, and proclaims that the weapon belongs to the one who can draw it out. Hunding and his followers try but are unable to withdraw the sword.

Jeannine Altmeyer as Sieglinde and Peter Hoffmann as Siegmund in the love scene from Act I of *Die Walküre.*

The first act of *Die Walküre* begins as Siegmund, weaponless and pursued by enemies, unwittingly takes refuge in the house of Hunding, who is away hunting. Sieglinde and Siegmund almost immediately fall in love, unaware that they are brother and sister. Hunding returns and soon realizes that the stranger—who identifies himself as *Wehwalt (Woeful)*—is an enemy of his clan. He says that Siegmund is his guest for the night, but the next day they must do battle. Sieglinde gives her husband a sleeping potion and tells Siegmund that her shame and misery will be avenged by the hero who can withdraw the sword from the tree. As they embrace passionately, the door of the hut suddenly opens, allowing the moonlight of a beautiful spring night to shine on them.

The following excerpt occurs at the end of the love scene, when Siegmund and Sieglinde gradually become aware of their amazing resemblance to each other and finally realize that they are brother and sister. Since her beloved no longer wants to be called *Wehwalt*, Sieglinde renames him *Siegmund (Victor)*. With a powerful effort, Siegmund withdraws the sword from the tree and the lovers rapturously embrace. (The offspring of this unlawful union will be Siegfried, the human hero of the *Ring* cycle. In the mythology and folklore of many lands, heroes are often born of incestuous love.)

In the excerpt which we'll study, Wagner creates a continuous musical flow that depicts the surging passions of the lovers through frequent changes of tempo, dynamics, and orchestral color. Typically, the vocal lines range from speechlike to highly melodic and closely reflect the inflections and meaning of the text. For example, the word *Notung (Needy)*—the name of the sword—is powerfully emphasized when it is sung to the downward leap of an octave.

Several leitmotifs are heard, sometimes together. In this excerpt, the leitmotif *Valhalla*—Wotan's castle—is first presented when Sieglinde looks at Siegmund and later returns when she recalls how their father (Wotan disguised as the old man) gazed at her during her marriage feast. The very important *sword* leitmotif is barely noticeable when it first appears, as Sieglinde refers to the fire in Siegmund's eyes. It is presented ***pp***, in combination with the leitmotif *Volsung* (the people to which Siegmund and Sieglinde belong). Later, the sword motif is very prominent when it is proclaimed by the brasses as Siegmund draws the sword out of the tree and as the lovers embrace during the orchestral conclusion of the act. Other leitmotifs heard in our excerpt are *love* and *spring*.

VOCAL MUSIC GUIDE

WAGNER, *Die Walküre*

Act I, Love Scene, Conclusion

(Sieglinde pushes Siegmund's hair back from his brow and looks at him with astonishment.)

Sieglinde

5 | **30** | 0:00

Wie dir die Stirn so offen steht,
der Adern Geäst in den Schläfen sich
schlingt!
Mir zagt es vor der Wonne, die mich
entzückt!

Look how your forehead broadens out,
and the network of veins winds into
your temples.
I tremble with the delight that
enchants me.

6 | **31** | 0:19

Valhalla,
French horns,
p.

	Ein Wunder will mich gemahnen: den heut zuerst ich erschaut, mein Auge sah dich schon!	It brings something strange to my mind: though I first saw you today, I've set eyes on you before.

Siegmund

| 0:45 | Ein Minnetraum gemahnt auch mich: in heissem Sehnen sah ich dich schon! | A dream of love comes to my mind as well: burning with longing I have seen you before. |

Sieglinde

| 1:04 | Im Bach erblickt' ich mein eigen Bild und jetzt gewahr ich es wieder: wie einst dem Teich es enttaucht, bietest mein Bild mir nun du! | In the stream I've seen my own likeness; and now I see it again. As once it appeared in the water so now you show me my likeness. |

Siegmund

| ■ 7 32 1:28 *Love*, voice. | Du bist das Bild, das ich in mir barg. | You are the likeness that I hid in myself. |

Sieglinde

| *Love*, French horn, ***p***. | O still! Lass mich der Stimme lauschen: mich dünkt, ihren Klang hört' ich als Kind. | Hush! let me listen to your voice. Its sound, I fancy, I heard as a child, |
| 2:00 | Doch nein! Ich hörte sie neulich, als meiner Stimme Schall mir widerhallte der Wald. | but no! I heard it recently— when the echo of my voice sounded back through the forest. |

Siegmund

| | O lieblichste Laute, denen ich lausche! | O loveliest sound for me to hear! |

| ■ 8 33 2:24 *Volsung*, low strings, ***pp***, together with *Sword*, bass trumpet, ***pp***. | | |

Sieglinde

2:34 *Valhalla*. French horns, ***pp***, then strings, ***pp***. Pause.	Deines Auges Glut erglänzte mir schon: so blickte der Greis grüssend auf mich, als der Traurigen Trost er gab.	The fire in your eyes has blazed at me before: So the old man gazed at me in greeting when to my sadness he brought comfort.
	An dem Blick erkannt' ihn sein Kind. schon wollt' ich beim Namen ihn nennen!	By his look his child recognized him, I even wanted to call him by name.
3:04	Wehwalt heisst du fürwahr?	Are you really called Woeful?

Siegmund

| | Nicht heiss ich so, seit du mich liebst: nun walt ich der hehrsten Wonnen! | I am not called that since you love me: Now I am full of purest rapture. |

Sieglinde

| 3:23 | Und Friedmund darfst du froh dich nicht nennen? | And "Peaceful" may you not, being happy, be named? |

Siegmund

	Nenne mich du, wie du liebst, dass ich heisse:	Name me what you love to call me.
	den Namen nehm ich von dir!	I take my name from you.

Sieglinde

| 3:42 | *Doch nanntest du Wolfe den Vater?* | But did you name Wolf as your father? |

Siegmund

	Ein Wolf war er feigen Füchsen!	A Wolf he was to craven foxes!
	Doch dem so stolz strahlte das Auge,	But he whose proud eyes shone
	wie, Herrliche, hehr dir es strahlt,	as grandly as yours, you marvel,
	der war: Wälse genannt.	his name was "Volsa."

Sieglinde

4:03	*War Wälse dein Vater, und bist du ein Wälsung,*	If "Volsa" was your father and you are a "Volsung,"
	stiess er für dich sein Schwert in den Stamm,	it was for you he thrust his sword into the tree—
	so lass mich dich heissen, wie ich dich liebe:	so let me call you by the name I love:
	Siegmund: so nenn ich dich!	Siegmund (Victor)—so I name you.

Siegmund

4:27	*Siegmund heiss ich und Siegmund bin ich!*	Siegmund I am called and Siegmund I am,
	Bezeug es dies Schwert, das zaglos ich halte!	let this sword, which I fearlessly hold, bear witness.
	Wälse verhiess mir, in höchster Not	Volsa promised me that in deepest distress
4:42	*fänd' ich es einst: ich fass es nun!*	I should one day find it. Now I grasp it.
	Heiligster Minne höchste Not,	Holiest love's deepest distress,
	sehnender Liebe sehrende Not	yearning love's scorching desire,
	brennt mir hell in der Brust,	burn bright in my breast,
	drängt zu Tat und Tod:	urge me to deeds and death.

9 **34** 5:20
Voice, downward octave leaps.

	Notung! Notung! so nenn ich dich,	"Needy," "Needy," I name you,
	Schwert.	sword.
	Notung, Notung! neidlicher Stahl!	"Needy," "Needy," precious blade,
	Zeig deiner Schärfe schneidenden Zahn:	show your sharpness and cutting edge:
	heraus aus der Scheide zu mir!	come from your scabbard to me!

10 **35** 5:50
Sword, the trumpets, **ff**.

(With a powerful effort, Siegmund pulls the sword from the tree, showing it to astonished and delighted Sieglinde.)

6:07
Volsung, trumpets, **pp**.

	Siegmund, den Wälsung, siehst du, Weib!	You see Siegmund, the Volsung, woman!
	Als Brautgabe bringt er dies Schwert:	As wedding gift he brings this sword;
	so freit er sich	so he weds
	die seligste Frau;	the fairest of women;

		dem Feindeshaus entführt er dich so.	he takes you away from the enemy's house.
		Fern von hier folge mir nun,	Now follow me far from here,

11 **36** 6:41
Spring, voice.

fort in des Lenzes lachendes Haus: out into springtime's smiling house.

fort in des Len - zes la - chen-des Haus;

		dort schützt dich Notung, das Schwert,	For protection you'll have "Needy" the sword,
		wenn Siegmund dir liebend erlag!	even if Siegmund expires with love.

Sieglinde

7:10

Bist du Siegmund, den ich hier sehe, Are you Siegmund whom I see here?
Sieglinde bin ich, die dich ersehnt: I am Sieglinde who longed for you:
die eig'ne Schwester your own sister
gewannst du zu eins mit dem Schwert! you have won and the sword as well.

Siegmund

Braut und Schwester bist du dem Bruder, Wife and sister you'll be to your brother.

so blühe denn Wälsungen-Blut! So let the Volsung blood increase!

12 **37** 7:39
Sword,
brasses, ***ff***.
Passionate
orchestral
conclusion.

(He draws her to him with passionate fervor.)

20 Gustav Mahler

Gustav Mahler (1860–1911) was the last great Austrian romantic composer. He opened new realms of orchestral sound that influenced composers of the early twentieth century, but his works were not fully appreciated until half a century after his death.

Mahler was born in Bohemia and grew up in a small town where his father was a tavern keeper. His musical environment included Bohemian peasant songs and dances, and marches played by a local military band. (This early contact with folk music and marches later had an influence on his style.) As a boy, he studied piano and composed constantly. At fifteen, he entered the Vienna Conservatory, where he studied for three years. He also took courses in history, Greek art, and ancient literature at the University of Vienna. At twenty he began his conducting career, directing musical comedies at a summer resort. In the years that followed, Mahler steadily gained in professional status, working as an opera conductor in several theaters, each more important than the last. By the time he was twenty-eight, he was director of the Budapest Opera. Brahms heard one of his performances there and declared that to hear "the true *Don Giovanni*" you had to go to Budapest. Mahler's ambition as a performer was to direct the Vienna Opera, but there was one obstacle: he was Jewish. However, in

1897, at thirty-seven, he converted to Roman Catholicism and became director of the Vienna Opera, a position he held for ten years. Mahler brought the Vienna Opera to new heights of excellence, supervising every aspect of its performances: music, acting, costumes, and scenery. He was uncompromising in artistic matters, with the result that many performers regarded him as a tyrant.

Although Mahler quickly won fame as a conductor, he had to struggle for recognition as a composer. Performances of his symphonies often met with a mixed reception. Critics would acknowledge his talent but complain about his harsh dissonances, over-elaborate orchestration, and confusing shifts of mood. Mahler composed much of his music during summer vacations, since he was preoccupied with his feverish activity as a conductor during most of the year. In addition to his directorship of the Vienna Opera, he also conducted the Vienna Philharmonic orchestra.

At the age of forty-two, Mahler married the beautiful and musically talented Alma Schindler, who was nineteen years his junior. Two daughters were born to the couple within the first two years of their marriage. Tragically, Maria ("Puzi"), the older daughter, died of scarlet fever at the age of four, leaving Mahler a broken man.

In 1908, Mahler traveled to the United States to become principal conductor of the Metropolitan Opera in New York. The next year he was elected director of the New York Philharmonic orchestra. Mahler's experiences in New York were not happy. His own works were received coolly, he aroused the dislike of many of his players, and he was unable to get along with the socialites who supported the orchestra. In 1911 he became seriously ill and returned to Europe. He died in Vienna at the age of fifty.

Mahler was a passionately intense man, full of conflicts and contradictions. He was an active leader and administrator, but he often craved solitude. His mood frequently shifted from exaltation to despair. He could be cruel to his players, and yet he gave generous support to young musicians—for example, the conductor Bruno Walter and the composer Arnold Schoenberg.

Mahler's Music

Mahler's music is often programmatic and reflects his constant search for the meaning of life. His output consists basically of nine symphonies (plus an unfinished Tenth Symphony that is also performed) and several song cycles for voice and orchestra, including *Lieder eines fahrenden Gesellen* (*Songs of a Wayfarer,* 1883–1885), which we'll study; and his monumental masterpiece *Das Lied von der Erde* (*The Song of the Earth,* 1908). "The symphony is the world!" Mahler once explained. "The symphony must embrace everything." Following the example of Beethoven's Ninth Symphony, Mahler used voices in four of his symphonies. And his symphonies are often monumental in length and in their performing forces. His Eighth Symphony (*Symphony of a Thousand,* 1907), for example, lasts about an hour and a half and calls for eight vocal soloists, a boys' choir, two choruses, and a gigantic orchestra. Yet Mahler often uses his gigantic orchestra to achieve delicate chamber music effects in which only a few instruments are heard at a time. He created polyphonic textures in which several themes are presented simultaneously in contrasting tone colors. His use of unconventional instruments—including cowbells, celesta, guitar, and mandolin—influenced twentieth-century Viennese composers such as Arnold Schoenberg, Anton Webern, and Alban Berg.

Mahler's instrumental music, like that of Schubert—whose music was a source of inspiration—is permeated with the spirit of song. Many of Mahler's symphonic movements are based on themes from his own songs. Mahler loved to use folklike tunes and march music, perhaps remembering his childhood in a small Bohemian town. But sometimes he parodies a tune by giving it an unusual twist or a grotesque *glissando* (a continuous slide in pitch up or down the scale), and there are many sudden and extreme shifts of mood in his music—an intensely emotional section may be interrupted by something light and frivolous.

Lieder eines fahrenden Gesellen (*Songs of a Wayfarer*; Composed 1883–1885, Orchestrated 1891–1896)

Mahler's first masterpiece was *Lieder eines fahrenden Gesellen* (*Songs of a Wayfarer*), a cycle of four songs for voice and orchestra. He wrote both the words and the music of this autobiographical song cycle at the age of twenty-four, under the impact of an unhappy love affair with Johanna Richter, a soprano in the opera company where he was a conductor. "What can these songs tell her that she does not know already?" Mahler confided to a friend. "The cycle deals with a young wayfarer ill-treated by destiny, who sets out in the wide world and wanders about aimlessly."

Mahler's depiction of an alienated wanderer, a frequent theme in German romantic poetry, was probably influenced by Schubert's song cycle *Winterreise* (*Winter's Journey*; 1827). To convey a feeling of restlessness, Mahler begins and ends each song of his cycle in a different key. He would later use melodies from the second and fourth of the *Songs of a Wayfarer* as themes in his next work, his First Symphony (1885–1888). We'll focus on the second song of the cycle.

Ging heut' Morgen über's Feld (*This Morning I Went through the Fields*)

Basic Set:
CD 7 🔳13

Ging heut' Morgen über's Feld reflects Mahler's attraction to nature and to folklike simplicity. The song is in modified strophic form, with brief orchestral interludes connecting the different stanzas. In the first three stanzas of the poem the wayfarer tells how he walks through the fields on a beautiful spring morning and is greeted merrily by the flowers and birds. The final stanza brings a darkening of mood with the wanderer's realization that happiness is beyond his reach.

The first two stanzas are sung to the same lighthearted melody (A) in folk style. The last two stanzas begin with varied forms of the opening phrase of A in a new major key, but then continue with different music. The sadness of the last stanza is conveyed by a slow tempo, which contrasts with the moderate tempo of the carefree earlier stanzas. Mahler expresses the pain of the wayfarer's final realization—"No! No! What I love can never bloom for me!"—by a whispered high melody with poignant dissonances on the words *nimmer* (*never*) and *blühen* (*bloom*). An orchestral postlude featuring harp and solo violin rounds off the song on a note of unfulfilled longing.

VOCAL MUSIC GUIDE

MAHLER, *Ging heut' Morgen über's Feld*

🔳13 0:00
At a comfortable
pace; flutes, repeated
notes, introduce

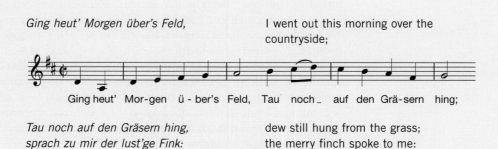

A

| *Ging heut' Morgen über's Feld,* | I went out this morning over the countryside; |

Ging heut' Mor-gen ü-ber's Feld, Tau noch _ auf den Grä-sern hing;

| *Tau noch auf den Gräsern hing,* | dew still hung from the grass; |
| *sprach zu mir der lust'ge Fink:* | the merry finch spoke to me: |

"Ei, du! Gelt? Guten Morgen!
Wird's nicht eine schöne Welt?
Zink! Zink! Schön und fink!
Wie mir doch die Welt gefällt!"

"Oh, it's you, is it! Good morning!
Is it not a lovely world?
Chirp! Chirp! Pretty and lively!
How the world delights me!"

String interlude,
crescendo, trumpet.
14 0:41

A

Auch die Glockenblum' am Feld

The bluebells in the meadow also

Cellos, ***p***, imitate
voice. Glockenspiel.

hat mir lustig, guter Ding',
mit den Glöckchen, klinge, kling,
ihren Morgengruss geschellt:
"Wird's nicht eine schöne Welt!?
Kling, kling! Schönes Ding!
Wie mir doch die Welt gefällt!
Heia!"

rang merrily and cheerfully for me
with their little bells, ring-a-ring,
rang their morning greeting:
"Is it not a lovely world!?
Ring, ring! Pretty thing!
How the world delights me!
Ho!"

String interlude,
clarinets and
harp introduce
15 1:29
Opening of A in
new key, with high
sustained tone
in voice.

Und da fing im Sonnenschein

And then in the sunshine

gleich die Welt zu funkeln an;
Alles, alles Ton und Farbe
gewann im Sonnenschein!
Blum' und Vogel, Gross und Klein!
"Guten Tag, guten Tag!
Ist's nicht eine schöne Welt?
Ei, du! Gelt? Ei, du Gelt? Schöne
Welt!?"

the world at once began to sparkle,
everything, everything took on
sound and color in the sunshine!
Flower and bird, the large and the small!
"Good day! good day!
Isn't it a lovely world?
Don't you agree? Don't you agree?
Lovely world!"

Tempo slows, repeated
notes in cellos introduce
16 2:34
Opening of A in
voice, slow tempo,
imitated by oboe
and muted cellos.
Flutes, clarinets,
timpani, ***pp***.

Nun fängt auch mein Glück wohl an?!
Nun fängt auch mein Glück wohl an?!

Now surely my happiness also begins?!
Now surely my happiness also begins?!

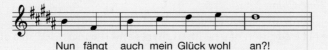

Nein! Nein! Das ich mein',
mir nimmer nimmer blühen kann!

No! No! What I love
can never, never bloom for me!

Postlude:
harp, muted
solo violin,
ppp ending.

The Romantic Period: Summary

Music in Society

- A large and growing urban middle class wanted to hear and play music; this trend resulted in the formation of numerous orchestras, opera companies, and music societies.
- Subscription concerts became common.
- The nineteenth-century musical public was captivated by virtuoso performers.
- Numerous music conservatories were founded in Europe and the United States.
- Women assumed greater roles as performers, composers, and patrons in professional music making.
- Music making in the home took on great importance.
- The piano became a regular fixture in middle-class and upper-class homes, used both for entertainment and for educating children, particularly girls.

Important Style Features

Mood and Emotional Expression

- Music of the romantic era is closely related to the other arts, particularly literature.
- Art forms, including music, exhibited extreme interest in subjects related to nature, death, the fantastic, the macabre, and the diabolical.
- Unprecedented emphasis was placed on self-expression and the development of a uniquely personal musical style.
- Music explored a universe of feeling that included flamboyance and intimacy, unpredictability and melancholy, rapture and longing, the mysterious and the remote.
- Some composers wrote music evoking a specific national identity ("nationalism") or an exotic location ("exoticism").

Rhythm

- Rhythm is extremely diverse.
- Tempos are flexible and may change frequently.
- Tempo rubato permitted greater expressivity and freedom in performance.

Dynamics

- Dynamic changes can be sudden or gradual.
- Extremely wide dynamic ranges, from very soft to very loud, add considerably to emotional excitement and intensity.

Tone Color

- Romantic music exhibits a wide range of expressive tone color and sensuous sound.
- The addition of new instruments and the increased size of the orchestra led to new and varied timbres.
- Woodwinds, brass, and percussion instruments played prominent roles in orchestral and operatic works. Composers experimented with timbre through unusual combinations of instruments or by having instruments play in unusual ways.

Melody and Harmony

- Melodies are often long, complex, and highly expressive.
- Recurring melodies and thematic transformation unify longer works.
- Prominent use of chromatic harmony based on pitches that lie outside the prevailing major or minor scale results in harmonies that are rich, colorful, and complex.

- Dissonance is used more freely; resolutions are often delayed to create feelings of yearning, tension, and mystery.
- A wide range of keys and frequent modulations sometimes obscure the sense of an overall tonic or home key.

Texture
- Texture is generally homophonic, but fluctuations of texture may occur to provide contrasts.
- A piece may shift gradually or suddenly from one texture to another.

Form
- Forms are rooted in the classical tradition, but now are more expansive and treated freely.
- New forms and genres were developed, such as the symphonic poem.
- Symphonies are typically longer than those of the classical era.
- Less emphasis is placed on balance, proportion, and resolution of tension than in the classical era.
- Works can be very brief (e.g., Chopin's *Minute* Waltz, Op. 64, No. 1) or long and monumental (e.g. Wagner's four-evening opera cycle *Der Ring des Nibelungen*).

Romantic Performance Practice

- Philharmonic societies appeared, and concert halls grew in size and number.
- Larger concert halls required a greater number of performers to fill the space with sound. Orchestras grew to 100 or more musicians, reflecting the desire for greater varieties of orchestral timbres and bigger sounds to fill large concert halls.
- Significant technological advances resulted in instruments that could be played louder, higher, lower, and faster than ever before. Performers capitalized on these advances to satisfy audiences who lavished praise on virtuoso performances.
- Cadenzas in concertos were usually written out rather than improvised.

FEATURED COMPOSERS

The romantic period in music lasted from about 1820 to 1900. The long list of important romantic-period composers whose music is still heard today testifies to the richness and variety of this music.

- Franz Schubert (1797–1828)
- Robert Schumann (1810–1856)
- Clara Wieck Schumann (1819–1896)
- Frédéric Chopin (1810–1849)
- Franz Liszt (1811–1886)
- Felix Mendelssohn (1809–1847)
- Hector Berlioz (1803–1869)
- Modest Mussorgsky (1839–1881)
- Peter Ilyich Tchaikovsky (1840–1893)
- Bedřich Smetana (1824–1884)
- Antonín Dvořák (1841–1904)
- Johannes Brahms (1833–1897)
- Giuseppe Verdi (1813–1901)
- Giacomo Puccini (1858–1924)
- Richard Wagner (1813–1883)
- Gustav Mahler (1860–1911)

Beyond the Classroom: Attending a Chamber Music Concert

Watching a small number of musicians in an intimate setting where one can see the interaction of performers as they gesture and glance at one another reveals energy and excitement during the performance that are almost palpable. Some chamber music concerts are held in large concert halls where this give-and-take between the musicians is lost, owing to the distance between the performers and the audience; but in a smaller setting, the audience feels as if it were one with the musicians.

Students often are stunned by the intensity of focus at these concerts. Playing chamber music is difficult, but fun, too. It demands extraordinary coordination among the players and great individual concentration. The slightest mistake is glaringly apparent. The audience is intently focused on the players, since everything is revealed by the intimacy of the event.

Before attending a chamber music concert, do some research on the composers and the selections on the program. If possible, listen to a recording of the selections beforehand. Doing so will increase your enjoyment of the live event. Unlike popular music that is instantly appealing on one hearing, chamber music unfolds its glories through repeated listening.

When attending a chamber music concert, ask yourself the following questions:

- Who composed the selections that you are hearing? When were the works composed? Might you be able to predetermine some of the stylistic features of the music by considering the composer and the composition date?
- How many movements are within each selection? Can you recognize any familiar forms, such as sonata form, theme and variations, minuet and trio, or rondo?
- How many musicians are performing, and what instruments do they play?
- Listen carefully to the interaction between the performers. Does one player have most of the melodic interest, or is this shared by the ensemble?
- Does one musician in the group, such as the first violinist in a string quartet, function as a kind of conductor?
- Do you notice instances of great technical virtuosity by one or more of the players?
- If you are listening to chamber music composed during the twentieth century, are the musicians asked to provide any unusual sound effects with their instruments or by some other means?

The Twentieth Century and Beyond

We find ourselves confronted with a new logic of music that would have appeared unthinkable to the masters of the past. This new logic has opened our eyes to riches whose existence we never suspected. *—Igor Stravinsky*

Music was a favorite subject of cubist artists. In Pablo Picasso's *Three Musicians* (1921), two comic characters from Italian popular theater are combined with a monklike figure. Picasso painted two versions of *Three Musicians.* In the version shown here, Harlequin (left) plays a violin, Pierrot (center) plays a recorder, and the monk (right) holds an accordion. A year before Picasso painted *Three Musicians,* he designed the costumes for *Pulchinella* (1920), a ballet with music by Igor Stravinsky.

Twentieth Century and Beyond (1900–2009)

TIME LINE

1900–1945

1945–2009

Historical and Cultural Events

1900 Freud, *Interpretation of Dreams*

1905 Einstein, special theory of relativity

1914–1918 First World War

1917 Russian Revolution begins

1929 Great Depression begins

1929–1953 Stalin dictator of Soviet Union

1933 Franklin D. Roosevelt inaugurated

1933 Hitler appointed chancellor of Germany

1939–1945 Second World War

1945 Atomic bomb destroys Hiroshima

1950–1953 Korean War

1953 Crick and Watson discover the structure of DNA

1955–1975 Vietnam War

1959 Fidel Castro becomes premier of Cuba

1963 President Kennedy assassinated

1969 American astronauts land on the moon

1974 President Nixon resigns

1981 Ronald Reagan inaugurated

1989 George Bush inaugurated

1990 Reunification of Germany

1991 Dissolution of the Soviet Union

1993 Bill Clinton inaugurated

1994 Mandela elected president of South Africa

2001 George W. Bush inaugurated

2001 Terrorist attacks in United States on September 11, 2001

2003 War in Iraq begins

2004 Tsunami in Asia

2005 New Orleans flooded

2007 Worldwide recession

2009 Barack Obama inaugurated

Arts and Letters

1907 Picasso, *Les Demoiselles d'Avignon*

1913 Kirchner, *Street, Berlin*

1914 Kandinsky, *Panels for Edward R. Campbell*

1915 Kafka, *The Metamorphosis*

1922 Eliot, *The Waste Land*

1922 Joyce, *Ulysses*

1929 Faulkner, *The Sound and The Fury*

1932 Picasso, *Girl before a Mirror*

1940–1941 Lawrence, *The Migration Series*

1942 Camus, *The Stranger*

1946 Sartre, *Existentialism and Humanism*

1948 Mailer, *The Naked and the Dead*

1950 Pollock, *One*

1951 Salinger, *Catcher in the Rye*

1955 Baldwin, *Notes of a Native Son*

1962 Warhol, *Campbell's Soup Cans*

1964 Riley, *Hesitate*

1967 Frankenthaler, *Flood*

1974 Solzhenitsyn, *The Gulag Archipelago*

1988 Morrison, *Beloved*

1990 Hockney, *Thrusting Rocks*

1996 Larson, *Rent*

2002 Kiefer, *The Sky Palace*

2002 Parks, *Topdog/Underdog*

2003 Gehry, Walt Disney Concert Hall

2005 Rowling, *Harry Potter and the Half-Blood Prince*

2007 Rowling, *Harry Potter and the Deathly Hollows*

Music

1894 Debussy, *Prelude to the Afternoon of a Faun*

1911–1913 Webern, *Five Pieces for Orchestra*

1912 Schoenberg, *Pierrot lunaire*

1913 Stravinsky, *The Rite of Spring*

1917–1922 Berg, *Wozzeck*

1924 Gershwin, *Rhapsody in Blue*

1926 Bessie Smith, *Lost Your Head Blues*

1927 Armstrong, *Hotter Than That*

1930 Stravinsky, *Symphony of Psalms*

1931 Still, *Afro-American Symphony*

1941 Ginastera, *Estancia* Suite

1942 Ellington, *C-Jam Blues*

1943 Bartók, Concerto for Orchestra

1943–1944 Copland, *Appalachian Spring*

1945 Parker, KoKo

1946 Benjamin Britten, *Young Person's Guide to the Orchestra*

1946–1948 Cage, *Sonatas and Interludes*

1947 Schoenberg, *A Survivor from Warsaw*

1957 Bernstein, *West Side Story*

1958 Varèse, *Poème électronique*

1960 Penderecki, *Threnody: To the Victims of Hiroshima*

1961 Carter, Double Concerto

1967 The Beatles, *Sgt. Pepper's Lonely Hearts Club Band*

1970 Crumb, *Ancient Voices of Children*

1976 Philip Glass, *Einstein on the Beach*

1985 Zwilich, *Concerto Grosso 1985*

1986 Adams, *Short Ride in a Fast Machine*

1996 Walker, *Lilacs*

1997 Carter, *Shard*

2004 Reich, *You Are (Variations)*

2005 Adams, *Dr. Atomic*

2007 Glass, *Appomattox*

2008 Zwilich, Symphony No. 5

2008 Carter, *Interventions* for Piano and Orchestra

2009 Adams, *City Noir*

TWENTIETH-CENTURY DEVELOPMENTS

Extremes of violence and progress marked the twentieth century. During the first half of the century, two world wars—in 1914–1918 and 1939–1945—unleashed new weapons of unprecedented destructive force. Between the wars, dictatorships and a global depression caused massive hardship. The second half of the century saw the breakup of colonial empires, an extended cold war between the United States and the Soviet Union (a nation that later dissolved), and armed conflicts around the world. At the same time, rapid economic growth propelled prosperity for many. The principle of equal rights gained ground after protracted struggles by women, African Americans, and others.

Extraordinarily accelerated developments in technology and science transformed politics and society. The Wright brothers made the first powered flight in 1903; sixty-six years later, humans walked on the moon. A flood of new technologies like sound recordings, movies, radio, satellites, computers, and the Internet triggered a continuous revolution in communications. Albert Einstein reshaped our understanding of the universe with his theory of relativity, Sigmund Freud probed the unconscious, and Francis Crick and James Watson discovered the structure of DNA, the basic material of heredity.

Rapid changes and radical breaks with earlier traditions characterized the arts. Shock as a goal was a twentieth-century phenomenon.

In the decade before World War I, Isadora Duncan's modern dance clashed with conventions of classical ballet; Pablo Picasso's cubist paintings distorted figures and objects, showing them from several angles at one time; and Wassily Kandinsky's abstract paintings no longer tried to represent the visual world at all.

In the arts, as in other aspects of life, there was an increased emphasis on pluralism and diversity. Contradictory styles and tendencies coexisted, as conservative and avant-garde works appeared at the same time. Moreover, individual artists, such as Picasso and the composer Igor Stravinsky, often alternated between radical and more traditional styles.

Summarizing such an incredibly diverse cultural landscape is difficult, yet any overview must include the following developments:

In *Dance* (1909), by Henri Matisse, there is little sense of perspective or realistic detail. The five dancers are flattened to silhouettes, and colors are mainly limited to large areas of green, blue, and flesh tones.

In the cubist painting *Violin and Grapes* by Pablo Picasso, the violin is flattened into fragmented planes.

Girl Before a Mirror (1932) by Pablo Picasso. The young girl on the left looks at an older, troubled reflection of herself. Here, Picasso reinterprets a traditional theme: a woman seeing a death's-head in her mirror. Twentieth-century composers such as Stravinsky have also reinterpreted earlier musical forms and styles.

1. The United States powerfully shaped world culture and entertainment, as well as politics and economics. Cities like Paris and Vienna that had so dominated nineteenth-century and early twentieth-century culture were supplanted by New York and Hollywood.
2. Nonwestern cultures and thought had wide and profound effects on all the arts. Examples include the impact of African sculpture on Picasso, of Japanese design on the architect Frank Lloyd Wright, and of Indian philosophy on the composer John Cage.
3. New technologies stimulated many artists. Sculptors used such materials as plastic, fluorescent lights, and television monitors; architects called for reinforced concrete and steel girders; and musicians exploited audiotape, electric guitars, and computers.
4. Artists explored the varieties of human sexuality with extraordinary frankness.
5. The concerns of women, African Americans, and other minorities were more powerfully represented in the arts than ever before.
6. Many artists expressed alienation, antirationality, nihilism, and dehumanization in their works, partly in reaction against catastrophic wars and massacres. The antihero became a prominent feature of novels, plays, and musical compositions.
7. Since the 1960s, many painters, architects, writers, and musicians have rejected the seriousness of

Panel for Edwin R. Campbell, No. 3 (left) and *Panel for Edwin R. Campbell, No. 1* (right), by Wassily Kandinsky (1914). Kandinsky stated that his abstract paintings were a "graphic representation of a mood and not of objects."

Street, Berlin (1913) by Ernst Ludwig Kirchner. German expressionist painters used deliberate distortion and violent colors to communicate the tension and anguish of the human psyche. Expressionist composers include Arnold Schoenberg, Alban Berg, and Anton Webern.

modernism in favor of more pluralistic approaches. "Postmodern" artists have combined different styles, blurred the boundaries between elite and popular culture, and used pre-existing images and texts from history, advertising, and the media. The pop artist Andy Warhol, for example, painted multiple Campbell's soup cans and heads of Marilyn Monroe.

Panel 58, "In the North the African American had more educational opportunities," from *The Migration Series* (1940–1941) by the history painter Jacob Lawrence. In his depictions of black experiences in the United States, Lawrence was influenced by the Harlem Renaissance, a cultural movement of the 1920s and 1930s that included African American writers, artists, and musicians. An important musical voice of this movement was William Grant Still, who often made use of spirituals, ragtime, and blues.

1 Musical Styles: 1900–1945

In music, as in the other arts, the early twentieth century was a time of revolt. The years following 1900 saw more fundamental changes in the language of music than any time since the beginning of the baroque era. There were entirely new approaches to the organization of pitch and rhythm and a vast expansion in the vocabulary of sounds, especially percussive sounds. Some compositions broke with tradition so sharply that they were met with violent hostility. The most famous riot in music history occurred in Paris on May 29, 1913, at the premiere of Igor Stravinsky's ballet *Le Sacre du printemps* (*The Rite of Spring*). Police had to be called in as hecklers booed, laughed, made animal noises, and actually fought with those in the audience who wanted to hear Stravinsky's evocation of primitive rites. One music critic complained that *The Rite of Spring* produced a "sensation of acute and almost cruel dissonance" and that "from the first measure to the last, whatever note one expects is never the one that comes." Another wrote, "To say that much of it is hideous in sound is a mild description. . . . It has no relation to music at all as most of us understand the word."

Today, we are amused by the initial failure of some music critics to understand this composition, now recognized as a masterpiece. Chords, rhythms, and percussive sounds that were baffling in 1913 are now commonly heard in jazz, rock, and music for movies and television. But the hostile critics of the early 1900s were right in seeing that a great transformation in musical language was taking place.

From the late 1600s to about 1900, musical structure was governed by certain general principles. As different as the works of Bach, Beethoven, and Brahms may be, they share fundamental techniques of organizing pitches around a central tone. Since 1900, however, no single system has governed the organization of pitch in all musical compositions. Each piece is more likely to have its own unique system of pitch relationships.

In the past, composers depended on the listener's awareness—conscious or unconscious—of the general principles underlying the interrelationship of tones and chords. For example, they relied on the listener's expectation that a dominant chord would normally be followed by a tonic chord. By substituting another chord for the expected one, the composer could create a feeling of suspense, drama, or surprise. Twentieth-century music relies less on preestablished relationships and expectations. Listeners are guided primarily by musical cues within an individual composition. This new approach to the organization of sound makes twentieth-century music fascinating. When we listen openly, with no assumptions about how tones "should" relate, modern music is an adventure.

1900–1945: An Age of Musical Diversity

The range of musical styles during the first half of the twentieth century was vast. The stylistic diversity in the works of Claude Debussy, Maurice Ravel, Igor Stravinsky, Arnold Schoenberg, Alban Berg, Anton Webern, Béla Bartók, Dmitri Shostakovich, Charles Ives, George Gershwin, William Grant Still, Aaron Copland, and Alberto Ginastera—to name only composers studied here—is a continuation and intensification of the diversity we've seen in romantic music. During the twentieth century, differences among styles were so great that it seems as though composers used different musical languages, not merely different dialects of the same musical language. Radical changes of style occur even within the works of individual composers.

This great variety of musical styles reflected the diversity of life during the early twentieth century. More people were free to choose where to live, how to earn a living, and how to spend their time. The automobile, airplane, telephone, phonograph, movies, and radio all made the world more accessible and expanded the range of experiences.

Through the work of scholars and performers, a wider range of music became available. Composers drew inspiration from an enormous variety of sources, including folk and popular music; the music of Asia, Africa, and Latin America; and European art music from the Middle Ages through the nineteenth century.

Elements of folk and popular music were often incorporated within personal styles. Composers were especially attracted to unconventional rhythms, sounds, and melodic patterns that deviated from the common practice of western music. Folk music was studied more systematically than before, partly because scholars could now record the actual sounds of peasant songs. One of the greatest twentieth-century composers, Béla Bartók, was also a leading scholar of the peasant music of his native Hungary and other parts of eastern Europe. "Studies of folk music in the countryside," he wrote, "are as necessary to me as fresh air is to other people." Bartók's imagination was fired by Hungarian, Bulgarian, and Romanian folk songs, and he believed that peasant music provided "the ideal starting point for a musical renaissance." Other composers stimulated by folklore were Stravinsky, who drew on the folk songs of his native Russia; and Charles Ives, who used American revival hymns, ragtime, and patriotic songs.

During the early twentieth century, non-European music had a deep influence on the music of the west. Western composers and painters were more receptive and sympathetic to Asian and African cultures than they had been earlier. For example, in 1862, Hector Berlioz could say that "the Chinese sing like dogs howling, like a cat screeching when it has swallowed a toad." But in 1889, Debussy was delighted by the Javanese music he heard at the Paris International Exhibition. "If we listen without European prejudice to the charm of their percussion," he wrote later, "we must confess that our percussion is like primitive noises at a country fair." Echoes of the gamelan (Indonesian orchestra) can be heard in the bell-like sounds and five-tone melodic patterns of Debussy's piano piece *Pagodes (Pagodas, 1903)*. Another French composer influenced by Asian culture was Olivier Messiaen (1908–1992); Messiaen's novel rhythmic procedures grew out of his study of Indian music.

American jazz was another non-European influence on twentieth-century composers. Musicians were fascinated by its syncopated rhythms and improvisational quality, as well as by the unique tone colors of jazz bands. Unlike a string-dominated symphony orchestra, a jazz band emphasizes woodwinds, brasses, and percussion.

Jazz elements were used in works as early as Debussy's *Golliwogg's Cake-Walk* (from the suite *Children's Corner*, 1908) and Stravinsky's *Ragtime* (from *The Soldier's Tale*, 1918). But the peak of jazz influence came during the 1920s and 1930s, with works such as the ballet *Le Création du monde (The Creation of the World, 1923)* by Darius Milhaud, the Piano Concerto (1926) by Aaron Copland, and the *Afro-American Symphony* (1931) by William Grant Still. For Americans, jazz idioms represented a kind of musical nationalism, a search for an "American sound." For European composers, the incorporation of jazz rhythms and tone colors represented a kind of musical exoticism. During the 1920s and 1930s, popular composers such as George Gershwin (1898–1937) used jazz and popular elements within "classical" forms. Gershwin's *Rhapsody in Blue* (1924) and his opera *Porgy and Bess* (1934–1935) are well known.

Modern composers can also draw inspiration from a wider historical range of music. During the twentieth century, music from remote times was unearthed by scholars and then published, performed, and recorded. There was a rediscovery of earlier masters such as Perotin and Machaut from the medieval period, Josquin Desprez and Gesualdo from the Renaissance, and Purcell and Vivaldi from the baroque. Some important modern composers have been music historians, like Anton Webern; or experts in the performance of "old" music, like Paul Hindemith.

Music from the past is a fruitful source of forms, rhythms, tone colors, textures, and compositional techniques. Baroque dances like the gavotte and gigue and forms like the passacaglia and concerto grosso are being used again. The long-forgotten harpsichord has been put to new use in compositions such as Elliott Carter's Sonata for Flute, Oboe, Cello, and Harpsichord (1952). In the *Classical Symphony* (1917) by the Russian composer Sergei Prokofiev (1891–1953), a classical orchestra is used, and the texture is light and transparent like much late eighteenth-century music. Occasionally twentieth-century composers used themes of earlier composers, as Benjamin Britten did in *The Young Person's Guide to the Orchestra,* which is based on a theme by Henry Purcell (about 1659–1695).

Modern compositions may be inspired by older music, but this does not mean that they simply imitate past styles. Instead, a traditional form might be used with harmonies, rhythms, melodies, and tone colors that would have been inconceivable before the twentieth century.

Modern composers were also influenced by the music of the immediate past. Nineteenth-century composers such as Wagner, Brahms, Mahler, Richard Strauss, and Mussorgsky were musical points of departure for composers of the early twentieth century. Wagner's music, in particular, was as potent an influence as Beethoven's was for romantic musicians. Composers took Wagner's style as a point of departure, or else they reacted violently against all he stood for.

Characteristics of Twentieth-Century Music

Having reviewed some of the sources of inspiration for twentieth-century music, let's now examine some of its characteristics.

Tone Color During the twentieth century, tone color became a more important element of music than it ever was before. It often had a major role, creating variety, continuity, and mood. In Webern's Orchestral Piece, Op. 10, No. 3 (1913), for example, the use of eerie, bell-like sounds at the beginning and end is vital to the form. If this composition were altered in tone color—say, by being played on a piano—it would lose much. An orchestral work from an earlier period, like Beethoven's Fifth Symphony, suffers less in a piano arrangement.

In modern music, noiselike and percussive sounds are often used, and instruments are played at the very top or bottom of their ranges. Uncommon playing techniques have become normal. For example, the *glissando,* a rapid slide up or down a scale, is more widely used. Woodwind and brass players are often asked to produce a fluttery sound by rapidly rolling their tongues while they play. And string players frequently strike the strings with the stick of the bow, rather than draw the bow across the strings.

Percussion instruments have become prominent and numerous, reflecting the twentieth-century interest in unusual rhythms and tone colors. Instruments that became standard during the 1900s include the xylophone, celesta, and wood block, to name a few. Composers occasionally call for noisemakers—typewriters, sirens, automobile brake drums. A piano is often used to add a percussive edge to the sound of an orchestra. Modern composers often draw hard, drumlike sounds from the piano, in contrast to the romantics, who wanted the instrument to "sing." Besides expanding the percussion section of the orchestra, early twentieth-century composers wrote works for unconventional performing groups in which percussion plays a major role. Well-known examples are Stravinsky's *Les Noces* (*The Wedding,* 1914–1923), for vocal soloists, chorus, four pianos, and percussion; Bartók's Music for Strings, Percussion, and Celesta (1936); and Edgard Varèse's *Ionisation* (1931), which was one of the first works for percussion ensemble.

Modern orchestral and chamber works often sound transparent; individual tone colors are heard clearly. To bring out the individuality of different melodic lines that are played simultaneously, a composer will often assign each line to a different timbre. In general, there is less emphasis on blended sound than there was during the romantic period. Many twentieth-century works are written for nonstandard chamber groups made up of instruments with sharply contrasting tone colors. Stravinsky's *L'Histoire du soldat* (*The Soldier's Tale,* 1918), for example, is scored for violin, double bass, clarinet, bassoon, cornet, trombone, and percussion. Even orchestral works often sound as though they are scored for a group of soloists.

Harmony

Consonance and Dissonance The twentieth century brought fundamental changes in the way chords are treated. Up to about 1900, chords were divided into two opposing types: consonant and dissonant. A consonant chord was stable; it functioned as a point of rest or arrival. A dissonant chord was unstable; its tension demanded onward motion, or resolution to a stable, consonant chord. Traditionally, only the triad, a three-tone chord, could be consonant. All others were considered dissonant. In the nineteenth century, composers came to use ever more dissonant chords, and they treated dissonances with increasing freedom. By the early twentieth century, the traditional distinction between consonance and dissonance was abandoned in much music. A combination of tones that earlier would have been used to generate instability and expectation might now be treated as a stable chord, a point of arrival. In Stravinsky's words, dissonance "is no longer tied down to its former function" but has become an entity in itself. Thus "it frequently happens that dissonance neither prepares nor anticipates anything. Dissonance is thus no more an agent of disorder than consonance is a guarantee of security."

This "emancipation of dissonance" does not prevent composers from differentiating between chords of greater or lesser tension. Relatively mild-sounding chords may be goals of motion, while harsher chords are used for transitional sounds. But no longer is there a general principle that determines whether a chord is stable or not. It is now entirely up to the composer's discretion. "We find ourself confronted with a new logic of music that would have appeared unthinkable to the masters of the past," wrote Stravinsky. "This new logic has opened our eyes to riches whose existence we never suspected."

New Chord Structures Before 1900, there were general principles governing chord construction: certain combinations of tones were considered chords, while others were not. At the core of traditional harmony is the triad. A triad might be made up of alternate tones of a major scale, such as the first (*do*), third (*mi*), and fifth (*sol*). Within a triad, there are two intervals of a third:

Although the triad often appears in twentieth-century music, it is no longer so fundamental.

Some twentieth-century composers create fresh harmonies by placing one traditional chord against another. Such a combination of two chords heard at the same time is called a **polychord.**

Copland, *Appalachian Spring*

E major chord
A major chord

A polychord can be heard either as a single block of sound or as two distinct layers, depending on whether the two combined chords contrast in tone color and register.

Another development in twentieth-century music was the use of chordal structures *not* based on triads. One used commonly is the ***fourth chord,*** in which the tones are a fourth apart, instead of a third. (From *do* to *fa,* or from *re* to *sol,* is an interval of a fourth.)

Ives, *The Cage*

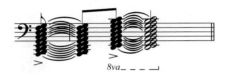

Harmonic resources were also extended through the ***tone cluster,*** a chord made up of tones only a half step or a whole step apart. A tone cluster can be produced on a piano by striking a group of adjacent keys with the fist or forearm.

Ives, *The Majority*

Alternatives to the Traditional Tonal System In addition to creating new chord structures, twentieth-century composers explored alternatives to the traditional tonal system. This system of tonal gravity, known as *tonality* or *key,* governed the organization of pitch from the 1600s to about 1900. By the late nineteenth century, the gravitational pull of a central tonality had been weakened by rapid and frequent key shifts. After 1900, some composers continued to use the traditional system, but others modified it greatly and still others discarded it entirely.

Before looking at new approaches to pitch organization, recall the basic principles of the traditional tonal system. As we saw in Part I (Elements), *tonality,* or *key,* refers to the use of a central tone, scale, and chord within a composition. The central tone, called the *tonic* or *keynote* (*do*), is the composition's resting point. The tonic major or minor scale and the tonic triad are built on this tone. Since the tonic triad is stable and restful, compositions almost always ended with it. Next in importance to the tonic triad is the *dominant chord,* which is built on the fifth tone (*sol*) of the tonic scale. There is a special gravitational pull from the dominant chord toward the tonic chord, and the motion from dominant to tonic is the essential chord progression of the tonal system. This cadence provides a strong sense of conclusion, and traditionally it was used to round off melodies, sections, and entire pieces. In summary, the tonal system is based on a central tone, a major or minor scale, and a triad; and there is a special relationship between the tonic and dominant chords.

After 1900, this system was modified in many different ways. The new techniques of pitch organization are so varied as to resist easy generalization. Some compositions have a central tone but are missing other traditional elements, such as the tonic triad, the central major or minor scale, or the dominant-tonic relationship.

This modified approach to tonality is reflected even in the titles of compositions, which are less likely to include the terms *major* or *minor.* For example, one piano piece by Stravinsky is entitled *Serenade in A* to show that it revolves around the tone A but is not in a major or minor key.

To create fresh sounds, composers used scales other than major or minor. For example, they breathed new life into the church modes—scales that had been used widely before 1600 as well as in folk songs of every period. Other scales were borrowed from the musical tradition of lands outside western Europe, and still others were invented by composers.

Twentieth-century compositions are often organized around a central chord other than the triad. Thus, the basic chord may well be one that was considered a dissonance earlier. In some works, the traditional relationship between dominant and tonic triads is replaced by other chord relationships. Melodies, sections, or entire pieces are rounded off not by the usual dominant-tonic cadence, but by other chord progressions.

Another twentieth-century approach to pitch organization is the use of two or more keys at one time: *polytonality.* When only two different keys are used at once—as is most common—the technique is called *bitonality.* A famous bitonal passage occurs in Stravinsky's ballet *Petrushka,* when one clarinet plays in C major and another plays in F sharp major:

In general, the greater the contrast of tone color, register, and rhythm between the different layers of sound, the more we can hear the different keys.

A further departure from tradition is *atonality,* the absence of tonality or key. Atonality was foreshadowed in nineteenth-century works such as Wagner's *Tristan and Isolde,* where the pull of a central key is weakened by frequent modulations and by liberal use of all twelve tones in the chromatic scale. Arnold Schoenberg wrote the first significant atonal pieces around 1908. He avoided traditional chord progressions in these works and used all twelve tones without regard to their traditional relationship to major or minor scales. But atonality is not a specific technique of composition; each atonal work is structured according to its own needs. (Though the word *atonality* is imprecise and negative, no other term has yet come into general use.)

Before long, Schoenberg felt the need for a more systematic approach to atonal composition, and during the early 1920s he developed the *twelve-tone system,* a new technique of pitch organization. This system gives equal prominence to each of the twelve chromatic tones, rather than singling out one pitch, as the tonal system does. For about twenty years, only Schoenberg and a few disciples used the twelve-tone system, but during the 1950s it came to be used by composers all over the world.

Rhythm The new techniques of organizing pitch were accompanied by new ways of organizing rhythm. The rhythmic vocabulary of music was expanded, with increased emphasis on irregularity and unpredictability. Rhythm is one of the most striking elements of twentieth-century music; it is used to generate power, drive, and excitement.

In the twentieth century, new rhythmic procedures were drawn from many sources, including jazz, folk music from all over the world, and European art music from the Middle Ages through the nineteenth century. The syncopations and complex rhythmic combinations of jazz fired the imagination of Stravinsky and Copland. Béla Bartók used the "free and varied rhythmic structures" of east European peasant music. And irregular phrase structures in Brahms's music inspired rhythmic innovations in Schoenberg's works.

Rapidly changing meters are characteristic of twentieth-century music, whereas baroque, classical, or romantic music maintains a single meter throughout a movement or section. Before the twentieth century, beats were organized into regularly recurring groups; the accented beat came at equal time intervals. Rhythmic irregularities such as syncopations or accents on weak beats were heard against a pervasive meter. But in many twentieth-century compositions, beats are grouped irregularly, and the accented beat comes at unequal time intervals. In some modern music the meter changes with almost every bar, so that we might count *1–2–3, 1–2–3–4–5, 1–2–3–4–5, 1–2–3, 1–2–3–4, 1–2–3–4–5, 1–2–3–4–5–6, 1–2–3–4–5, 1–2, 1–2–3–4–5–6*:

Basic Set:
CD 7 44

Brief Set:
CD 5 7

Stravinsky, *Ritual of Abduction* from *The Rite of Spring*

Count this again quickly and experience some of the rhythmic excitement of twentieth-century music, which often has a rapid and vigorous beat with jolting accents at unexpected times.

The rhythmic resources of twentieth-century music were also expanded through unconventional meters. Along with traditional meters such as duple and triple, modern composers use meters with five or seven beats to the measure. The pulses within a measure of any length may be grouped in irregular, asymmetrical ways. For example, eight quick pulses in a measure may be subdivided 3 + 3 + 2, or **1**–2–3–**4**–5–6–**7**–8, **1**–2–3–**4**–5–6–**7**–8. This meter, common in east European folk music, is used by Bartók in one of his *Six Dances in Bulgarian Rhythm:*

Twentieth-century music often has two or more contrasting, independent rhythms at the same time; this is called **polyrhythm.** Each part of the musical texture goes its own rhythmic way, often creating accents that are out of phase with accents in the other parts. Different meters are used at the same time. For example, one instrument may play in duple meter (*1–2, 1–2*) while another plays in triple meter (*1–2–3, 1–2–3*). Although polyrhythm occasionally occurs in classical and romantic music, it became more common and more complex after 1900. The polyrhythms of jazz strongly influenced composers in the 1920s and 1930s.

Rhythmic repetition of a group of pitches is a unifying technique widely used in twentieth-century music. Many modern compositions contain an **ostinato,** a motive or phrase that is repeated persistently at the same pitch throughout a section. The ostinato may occur in the melody or in the accompaniment. (The accompaniment for the example from Bartók's *Six Dances* has an eight-note ostinato: **1**–2–3–**4**–5–6–**7**–8.) Ostinatos can be found in music from various periods and cultures. In twentieth-century music, they usually serve to stabilize particular groups of pitches.

Melody The new techniques of pitch and rhythmic organization that we've surveyed had a strong impact on twentieth-century melody. Melody is no longer necessarily tied to traditional chords or to major and minor keys. It may be based on a wide variety of scales, or it may freely use all twelve chromatic tones and have no tonal center. Melody often contains wide leaps that are difficult to sing. Rhythmic irregularity and changing meters tend to make twentieth-century melodies unpredictable. They often consist of a series of phrases that are irregular in length. In general, twentieth-century music relies less than classical and romantic music on melodies that are easy to sing and remember. Melody is as rich and varied as twentieth-century music itself; neither can be classified easily.

2 Music and Musicians in Society

The twentieth century and the early twenty-first century have seen dramatic changes in how music reaches its listeners. Recordings, radio, television, and the Internet have brought a wider variety of music to more people than ever before. By the end of the twentieth century, the repertoire of recorded music included not only familiar classics, but also medieval, Renaissance, early baroque, nonwestern, and unconventional modern works—music not often played in concert. Recordings of such lesser-known music multiplied with the appearance of long-playing discs in 1948. But as early as 1904, composers' interpretations of their own works were recorded, giving composers an unprecedented opportunity to communicate precisely their intentions about phrasing, dynamics, and tempo.

Radio broadcasts of live or recorded music began to reach a large audience during the 1920s. In the 1930s, radio networks in several countries formed orchestras specifically to broadcast live music. The best-known American ensemble of this kind was the NBC Symphony Orchestra, directed by Arturo Toscanini. In addition to such radio-sponsored groups, regular broadcasts of the Saturday matinee performances of the Metropolitan Opera made opera available to millions of people.

With television, broadcast music performances could be seen as well as heard. Christmas Eve, 1951, brought the premiere of the first opera created for television, *Amahl and the Night Visitors,* by the Italian-American composer Gian-Carlo Menotti (1911–2007). Other television highlights included appearances of Leonard Bernstein conducting the New York Philharmonic orchestra. Apart from such notable exceptions, commercial television devoted little time to opera and symphonic music. Public television, however, brought a wide range of music to home viewers; successful music programming included *Live from Lincoln Center* and *Live from the Met.* In addition, music videos of operas, symphonies, and solo performances became popular.

In the first half of the twentieth century, the concert and operatic repertoire was dominated by music from earlier periods rather than by contemporary works. This was a new situation in music history. In Mozart's time, for instance, audiences demanded and got the latest music, not operas by Handel or cantatas by Bach. Even during the romantic period, when interest in past music was high, concert programs consisted mainly of recent works.

After 1900, however, listeners and performers were often baffled by the dissonances, percussive sounds, and irregular rhythms in some of the new music. (Remember the riot at the first performance of Stravinsky's *Rite of Spring.*) To avoid alienating audiences, many conductors chose not to perform "difficult" contemporary works, but favored works that were relatively accessible in style. One result was that some of the most innovative twentieth-century composers—Ives, Webern, and Varèse, for example—were neglected.

After World War I, organizations were formed for the specific purpose of giving the public a greater opportunity to hear new music. The International Society for Contemporary Music was the most influential, with branches in many countries.

Starting in the 1950s, major orchestras and opera companies began to program more twentieth-century music. Long-playing recordings gave listeners access to works that had seemed incomprehensible; these works could now be played repeatedly until they were understood and enjoyed. Musicians themselves grew more accustomed to intricate modern rhythms and thus were better able to perform them.

Many modern compositions were commissioned by ballet and opera companies, foundations, orchestras, performers, film studios, and wealthy music lovers. Developments in dance had an especially strong impact on twentieth-century music. A single company, Sergei Diaghilev's Russian Ballet, provided the impetus for masterpieces such as Stravinsky's *Petrushka* (1911), Ravel's *Daphnis et Chloé* (1912), and Debussy's *Jeux* (1913). Films provided a new stimulus for music, too. Though most film scores were merely background music, some, like Prokofiev's *Lieutenant Kijé* (1934), were enjoyed apart from the movie. Philanthropic foundations became significant music patrons. One, most active in the field of chamber music, was established by Elizabeth Sprague Coolidge in 1925 at the Library of Congress in Washington. Her generosity spurred the creation of many fine compositions, including Bartók's Fifth String Quartet (1934) and Schoenberg's Fourth String Quartet (1936). Yet, however important commissions were in the twentieth century, few serious musicians could live on them alone. Most composers were, and still are, also teachers, conductors, or performers. Recently, some have become "composers in residence" with symphony orchestras. They advise music directors on the contemporary repertoire and compose works for performance by the host orchestra.

The twentieth century saw the emergence of important composers from Latin America. The earliest to achieve international recognition was the Brazilian Heitor Villa-Lobos (1887–1959), a nationalist who fused contemporary musical techniques with the rhythms and tone colors of folk and popular music from his homeland. Villa-Lobos's best known work is *Bachianas brasileiras No. 5,* for soprano solo and eight cellos. Other prominent Latin American composers include the Mexicans Silvestre Revueltas (1898–1940) and Carlos Chávez (1899–1978), and the Argentinians Alberto Ginastera (1916–1983) and Astor Piazzolla (1921–1992). Ginastera's exciting *Final Dance: Malambo* will be studied in Section 18.

In the twentieth century, more women than ever before became active as composers, virtuoso soloists, and music educators. The most noted women among American composers include Amy Beach (1867–1944), Ruth Crawford Seeger (1901–1953), Miriam Gideon (1906–1996), Vivian Fine (1913–1996), Pauline Oliveros (b. 1932), Joan Tower (b. 1938), Ellen Taaffe Zwilich (b. 1939), Barbara Kolb (b. 1940), Shulamit Ran (b. 1949), and Jennifer Higdon (b. 1962), to name only a few. The French musician Nadia Boulanger (1887–1979) was among the most important teachers of musical composition in the twentieth century. And in the years after World War II (1939–1945), women joined professional orchestras as instrumentalists and conductors.

African American composers and performers—both women and men—became increasingly prominent during the twentieth century. One of the pioneer black composers was William Grant Still (1895–1978), who often made use of spirituals, ragtime, and blues. Other leading African American composers include Howard Swanson (1907–1978), Ulysses Kay (1917–1995), Olly Wilson (b. 1937), Tania Léon (b. 1943), and George Walker (b. 1922), who won a Pulitzer Prize in 1996 for *Lilacs,* a work for soprano and orchestra based on a poem by Walt Whitman.

For many years African American musicians were admitted as students in music schools but were barred as performers and conductors in established opera companies and symphony orchestras. Color barriers in major American opera companies were not broken until the baritone Todd Duncan performed at the New York City Opera company in 1945 and the contralto Marian Anderson sang at the Metropolitan Opera in 1955. During the 1950s and 1960s black conductors like Dean Dixon and Everett Lee had to go to Europe to find permanent positions. But starting in the 1970s, important conducting posts were occupied by such musicians as Henry Lewis, who directed the New Jersey Symphony; and James DePriest, who led the Quebec Symphony.

Like all people, musicians were affected by the political, economic, and social upheavals of the twentieth century. The violence and chaos of the Russian Revolution (1917) caused many musicians—including the composer Sergei Rachmaninoff (1873–1943)—to leave Russia. Under Stalin's totalitarian regime in the Soviet Union—most of which (including Russia) later became the Commonwealth of Independent States—musicians' lives and careers were strictly controlled. Starting in the 1930s, the Communist Party demanded that Soviet composers reject modernism and write optimistic, accessible music that praised the regime. Dmitri Shostakovich (1906–1975), for example, wrote an oratorio, *Song of the Forests* (1949), glorifying the government's reforestation plan.

Hitler's rise to power in Germany in 1933 had an especially dramatic impact on musicians. Avant-garde, socialist, and Jewish musicians were abruptly ousted from their jobs, and their works were no longer performed. Dictatorship, persecution, and the onset of World War II led to the largest migration of artists and intellectuals in history. Many composers, including Stravinsky, Bartók, Schoenberg, and Hindemith, left Europe for the United States. Such distinguished refugees made enormous contributions to American musical culture. Schoenberg and Hindemith, for example, taught in universities and helped train some of the finest composers in the United States.

During the twentieth century, the United States became a potent force in music. American jazz and popular music swept the world. After 1920 the country produced a large group of composers representing a wide spectrum of contemporary styles. In addition, the United States now has more first-rank symphony orchestras than any other country.

American colleges and universities have played an unusually vital role in our musical culture. They have trained and employed many of our leading composers, performers, and scholars. Music courses have expanded the horizons and interests of countless students. And since the 1950s, many universities have sponsored performing groups specializing in contemporary music. In addition, they have housed most of the electronic music studios. Thus American colleges and universities have indirectly become patrons of music, much as the church and nobility were in earlier times.

3 Impressionism and Symbolism

Many different musical styles coexisted around the beginning of the twentieth century. Among the most important was *impressionism,* best represented by the music of the French composer Claude Debussy (1862–1918). We'll look closely at musical impressionism in Section 4; but first, two related, though slightly earlier, artistic movements in France demand our attention: impressionist painting and symbolist poetry.

French Impressionist Painting

In 1874, a group of French painters including Claude Monet (1840–1926), Auguste Renoir (1841–1919), and Camille Pissarro (1830–1903) had an exhibition in Paris. One painting by Monet entitled *Impression: Sunrise*—a misty scene of boats in port—particularly annoyed an art critic, who wrote, "Wallpaper in its embryonic state is more finished than that seascape." Using Monet's title, the critic mockingly called the

Impression: Sunrise (1874) by Claude Monet. At an exhibition in Paris in 1874, this painting annoyed a critic who saw it as a formless collection of tiny colored patches. Using Monet's own title, he mockingly called the entire show the "exhibition of the impressionists." Like the impressionist painters, the French composer Claude Debussy was a master at evoking a fleeting mood and misty atmosphere.

entire show "the exhibition of the impressionists." The term *impressionist* stuck, but it eventually lost its derisive implication.

Today most of us appreciate impressionist paintings, which colorfully depict the joys of life and the beauties of nature. But during the 1870s, they were seen as formless collections of tiny colored patches—which they are when viewed closely. From a distance, however, the brushstrokes blend and merge into recognizable forms and shimmering colors. Impressionist painters were concerned primarily with effects of light, color, and atmosphere—with impermanence, change, and fluidity. Monet created a series of twenty paintings (1892–1894) showing Rouen Cathedral at different times of the day, from dawn to dusk. In this series, the cathedral's stone facade is desolidified and looks like colored mist. Many impressionist painters preferred to work in the open air rather than in a studio. They were fascinated by outdoor scenes from contemporary life, picnics in the woods, and crowds on Parisian boulevards. But most of all, the impressionists were obsessed with water. Using light pastel colors, they depicted the ripples and waves of the ocean and sailboats on the river Seine.

French Symbolist Poetry

As impressionist painters broke from traditional depictions of reality, writers called *symbolists* rebelled against the conventions of French poetry. Like the painters, poets such as Stéphane Mallarmé (1842–1898), Paul Verlaine (1844–1896), and Arthur Rimbaud (1854–1891) emphasized fluidity, suggestion, and the purely musical, or sonorous, effects of words. "To *name* an object," insisted Mallarmé, "is to suppress three-quarters of the enjoyment of a poem, which is made up of gradually guessing; the dream is to *suggest* it."

Claude Debussy was a close friend of many symbolist poets, especially Mallarmé, whose poem *L'Après-midi d'un faune* (*The Afternoon of a Faun*) inspired Debussy's most famous orchestral work. Many poems by Verlaine became texts for Debussy's songs. (And, more personally, Verlaine's mother-in-law was Debussy's first piano teacher.) Impressionist painting and symbolist poetry were an impetus for many developments during the twentieth century. Section 4 describes their effect on music.

Claude Debussy

The French impressionist composer Claude Debussy (1862–1918) linked the romantic era with the twentieth century. He was born in St. Germain-en-Laye, a small town near Paris. At the early age of ten, he entered the Paris Conservatory, where he studied until he was twenty-two. (While Debussy was at the Conservatory, the impressionists were exhibiting their paintings in Paris.) Debussy's teachers regarded him as a talented rebel who improvised unorthodox chord progressions of dissonances that did not resolve.

In his late teens, Debussy worked summers as pianist for Nadezhda von Meck, the Russian patroness of Tchaikovsky. During his stays in Russia, Debussy's lifelong interest in Russian music took root. In 1884, he won the highest award in France for composers, the Prix de Rome, which subsidized three years of study in Rome. But he left Italy after only two years, because he lacked musical inspiration away from his beloved Paris.

When Debussy returned to Paris in 1887, the music and ideas of Richard Wagner were having a profound influence on French composers and writers. Many of Debussy's friends wrote articles for *La Revue Wagnérienne* (*The Wagnerian Review*), a periodical devoted to the German master. During the summers of 1888 and 1889, Debussy traveled to Bayreuth, Germany, to hear Wagner's music dramas. They were memorable events for Debussy, who was both attracted and repelled by Wagner's music.

The Asian music performed at the Paris International Exposition of 1889 also had a strong impact on Debussy. "Do you not remember the Javanese music," he wrote to a friend, "able to express every shade of meaning, . . . which makes our tonic and dominant seem like ghosts?"

The impressionist Claude Debussy was a master at evoking a fleeting mood and misty atmosphere.

For years, Debussy led an unsettled life, earning a small income by teaching piano. His friends were mostly writers, such as Stéphane Mallarmé, whose literary gatherings Debussy attended regularly. In cafés and cabarets he mingled with jockeys and entertainers like those immortalized in the paintings of Toulouse-Lautrec. Until the age of thirty-one, Debussy was little known to the musical public and not completely sure of himself. "There are still things that I am not able to do—create masterpieces, for example," he wrote in 1893. But that same year Debussy did complete a masterpiece, his String Quartet. And in 1894 he created another, the tone poem *Prelude to the Afternoon of a Faun,* which has become his most popular orchestral work.

A dramatic turning point in Debussy's career came in 1902, with his opera *Pelléas et Mélisande.* Critics were sharply divided. Some complained about the absence of melody and the harmonies that broke traditional rules; others were delighted by the poetic atmosphere and subtle tone colors. The opera soon caught on, however, and Debussy was recognized as the most important living French composer. Musicians all over the world imitated his style.

This artistic triumph contrasted with a personal life filled with financial and emotional crises. Debussy constantly borrowed money for luxuries he craved: fine food, beautiful clothes, and artworks. The attempted suicides of two women in his life were major scandals in Paris. His longtime mistress shot herself when he left her for Rosalie Texier, a milliner who became his first wife. Then Rosalie Texier, in turn, shot herself when Debussy left *her* for Emma Bardac, an intelligent, talented, and rich society woman.

Debussy's marriage to Emma Bardac necessitated his undertaking concert tours to maintain their high standard of living. Though he was not gifted as a conductor and hated appearing in public, he presented his music throughout Europe. The onset of World War I in 1914 heightened his sense of nationalism, and he began to sign his works "Claude Debussy, French musician." He had developed cancer at the age of fifty, and he died in Paris on March 25, 1918, while the city was being shelled by German artillery.

Debussy's Music

Like the French impressionist painters and symbolist poets, Debussy was a master at evoking a fleeting mood and misty atmosphere. His interest in the effects of fluidity, intangibility, and impermanence is mirrored even in his titles: *Reflets dans l'eau* (*Reflections in the Water*), *Nuages* (*Clouds*), and *Les Sons et les parfums tournent dans l'air du soir* (*Sounds and Perfumes Swirl in the Evening Air*). Literary and pictorial ideas often inspired Debussy, and most of his compositions have descriptive titles. His music sounds free and spontaneous, almost improvised. He once wrote, "I am more and more convinced that music is not, in essence, a thing which can be cast into a traditional and fixed form. It is made up of colors and rhythms." This stress on tone color, atmosphere, and fluidity is characteristic of *impressionism* in music.

Tone color truly gets unprecedented attention in Debussy's works. His subtle changes of timbre are as crucial to his music as thematic contrasts are to earlier music. The sound he sought is sensuous and beautiful—never harsh. The entire orchestra seldom plays together to produce massive sound. Instead, there are brief but frequent instrumental solos. The woodwinds are especially prominent and are used in unusual registers. (The velvety low register of the flute is featured in *Prelude to the Afternoon of a Faun.*) Strings and brasses are often muted; their sound seems to come from far off. Atmosphere is created through the shimmer of a string tremolo or the splash of a harp.

Debussy wrote some of his finest music for piano, again creating new sonorities. His frequent use of the damper pedal, which allows a pianist to sustain tones after the keys are released, results in hazy sounds. Chords are often blended together, and the pianist is directed to let the sounds vibrate. The rich variety of bell- and gonglike sounds in Debussy's piano works may reflect the influence of Asian music he heard at the Paris International Exposition in 1889.

Debussy's treatment of harmony was a revolutionary aspect of musical impressionism. He tends to use a chord more for its special color and sensuous quality than for its function in a standard harmonic progression. He uses successions of dissonant chords that do not resolve. (As a young man, Debussy was once asked which harmonic rules he followed; he replied, simply, "My pleasure.") He freely shifts a dissonant chord up or down the scale; the resulting parallel chords characterize his style:

Debussy, *La Cathédrale engloutie* (*The Sunken Cathedral*)

molto diminuendo

Debussy's harmonic vocabulary is large. Along with traditional three- and four-note chords, he uses five-note chords with a lush, rich sound. Chord progressions that were highly unorthodox when Debussy wrote them soon came to seem mild and natural.

"One must drown the sense of tonality," Debussy wrote. Although he never actually abandoned tonality, Debussy weakened it by deliberately avoiding chord progressions that would strongly affirm any key. The traditional dominant-tonic cadence is relatively rare in his music. He also "drowns" tonality by using scales in which the main tone is less emphasized than it is in major or minor scales. He turned to the medieval church modes, which he knew from Gregorian chant. He also used the **pentatonic,** or five-tone, scales heard in Javanese music. These pentatonic scales lend an Asian atmosphere to some of Debussy's music. (A pentatonic scale is produced by five successive black keys of the piano—for example, F♯–G♯–A♯–C♯–D♯.)

Debussy's most unusual and tonally vague scale is the **whole-tone scale,** made up of six different notes each a whole step away from the next (C–D–E–F♯–G♯–A♯–C). Unlike major or minor, the whole-tone scale has no special pull from *ti* to *do,* since its tones are all the same distance apart. And because no single tone stands out, the whole-tone scale creates a blurred, indistinct effect.

The pulse in Debussy's music is sometimes as vague as the tonality. "Rhythms cannot be contained within bars," he wrote. He avoids recurring strong accents that coincide with the bar line. His rhythmic flexibility reflects the fluid, unaccented quality of the French language. In fact, few composers have set French to music as sensitively as Debussy. He composed fifty-nine art songs, many of which are set to symbolist poems by Charles Baudelaire, Paul Verlaine, and Stéphane Mallarmé. His only opera, *Pelléas et Mélisande,* is an almost word-for-word setting of a symbolist play by the Belgian poet Maurice Maeterlinck. This great and highly original opera is the essence of musical impressionism. Its vague, mysterious plot includes characters who barely communicate with each other. There are no arias, and the melodic line is almost entirely speechlike. The play's dreamlike atmosphere is magically evoked by an orchestral accompaniment that is discreet and understated; it's as though Debussy had consciously sought to avoid the powerful sound of Wagner's orchestral parts.

Although not large, Debussy's output is remarkably varied. Along with his opera, he contributed masterpieces to the literature of the piano, orchestra, chamber ensemble, and art song. Since Debussy's music is tonally vague and has an improvisational, floating quality, it's not surprising that he avoided sonata form, which traditionally calls for a clear contrast of keys and systematic development of themes. One section of Debussy's music melts into the next; melodic lines tend to be brief and fragmentary.

Echoes of Debussy's music can be heard in the works of many composers during the first two decades of the twentieth century. However, no other important musician can so fairly be described as an impressionist. Even the composer most similar to

Debussy, his younger French contemporary Maurice Ravel (1875–1937), wrote music with greater clarity of form. Debussy's impressionist style was both a final expression of romanticism and the beginning of a new era. His use of tone color as a vital element of form and his novel harmonic techniques made him the immediate forerunner of later twentieth-century musicians. Igor Stravinsky was perceptive when he remarked, "I and the members of my generation owe most to Debussy."

Prélude à l'Après-midi d'un faune (Prelude to the Afternoon of a Faun; 1894)

Basic Set:
CD 7 17

Brief Set:
CD 4 38

"The music of this Prelude," wrote Debussy of his *Prelude to the Afternoon of a Faun*, "is a very free illustration of the beautiful poem by Stéphane Mallarmé, *The Afternoon of a Faun*." This poem evokes the dreams and erotic fantasies of a pagan forest creature who is half man, half goat. While playing a "long solo" on his flute, the intoxicated faun tries to recall whether he actually carried off two beautiful nymphs or only dreamed of doing so. Exhausted by the effort, he falls back to sleep in the sunshine.

Debussy intended his music to suggest "the successive scenes through which pass the desires and dreams of the faun in the heat of this afternoon." The subtle, sensuous timbres of this miniature tone poem were new in Debussy's day. Woodwind solos, muted horn calls, and harp glissandos create a rich variety of delicate sounds. The dynamics are usually subdued, and only rarely does the entire orchestra—from which trombones, trumpets, and timpani are excluded—play at one time. The music often swells sensuously and then subsides in voluptuous exhaustion.

The prelude begins with an unaccompanied flute melody; its vague pulse and tonality make it dreamlike and improvisatory. This flute melody is heard again and again, faster, slower, and against a variety of lush chords. Though the form of the prelude may be thought of as A B A', one section blends with the next. It has a continuous ebb and flow. The fluidity and weightlessness typical of impressionism are found in this music. We are never tempted to beat time to its subtle rhythms. The prelude ends magically with the main melody, played by muted horns, seeming to come from far off. The bell-like tones of antique cymbals finally evaporate into silence. With all its new sounds and musical techniques, the piece has aptly been described as a "quiet revolution" in the history of music.

LISTENING OUTLINE

DEBUSSY, *Prélude à l'Après-midi d'un faune*

At a very moderate tempo, A B A' form, E major

3 flutes, 2 oboes, 1 English horn, 2 clarinets, 2 bassoons, 4 French horns, 2 harps, antique cymbals, 1st violins, 2d violins, violas, cellos, double basses

(Duration, 9:40)

A

17 38 0:00   **1. a.** Solo flute, ***p***, main melody.

Harp glissando; soft horn calls. Short pause. Harp glissando; soft horn calls.

18 **39** 0:43   **b.** Flute, ***p***, main melody; tremolo strings in background. Oboe, ***p***, continues melody. Orchestra swells to ***f***. Solo clarinet fades into

19 **40** 1:35   **c.** Flute, ***p***, main melody varied and expanded; harp and muted strings accompany. Flute melody comes to quiet close.

        2:48   **2. a.** Clarinet; harp and cellos in background.

20 **41** 3:16   **b.** New oboe melody.

Violins take up melody, crescendo and accelerando to climax. Excitement subsides. Ritardando. Clarinet, ***p***, leads into

B

21 **42** 4:33   **3. a.** Woodwinds, ***p***, legato melody in long notes. Crescendo.

        5:16   **b.** Strings repeat melody; harps and pulsating woodwinds in background, crescendo. Decrescendo. Horns, ***p***, solo violin, ***p***, clarinet, oboe.

A′

22 **43** 6:21   **4. a.** Harp accompanies flute, ***p***, main melody in longer notes. Oboe, staccato woodwinds.

        6:56   **b.** Harp accompanies oboe, ***p***, main melody in longer notes. English horn, harp glissando.

23 **44** 7:39   **5. a.** Antique cymbals, bell-like tones. Flutes, ***p***, main melody. Solo violins, ***pp***, in high register.

        8:16   **b.** Flute and solo cello, main melody; harp in background.

        8:45   **c.** Oboe, ***p***, brings melody to close. Harps, ***p***.

        9:10   **d.** Muted horns and violins, ***ppp***, beginning of main melody sounding far off. Flute, antique cymbals, and harp; delicate tones fade into silence.

Voiles (*Sails*), from Preludes for Piano, Book I (1910)

**Basic Set:
CD 7** **24**

In this short piano piece, Debussy exploits the blurred and tonally vague quality of the whole-tone scale to suggest the gentle rocking of sails in the wind. (However, Debussy's title may also refer to veils, a second meaning of the French word *voiles*.) *Voiles* is subdued in dynamics, moderate in tempo, and the composer indicates that it should be played "in a rhythm that is caressing and not strict." Debussy uses the piano's damper pedal to create lingering vibrations that suggest a misty atmosphere. Contributing to the impression of motion in place is a low repeated tone, B flat, that serves as a pedal point in all three sections of the piece.

Debussy, *Voiles (Sails)*

The opening section, which is longest, uses the whole-tone scale almost exclusively. It is based on three main ideas. One is a short melodic figure, the *sails* motive, in parallel thirds that is first presented alone, and then with accompaniment.

The second idea is a stepwise melody that is heard first in soft octaves in a low register

and later in a high register doubled by parallel chords in a middle register.

This use of chords moving in parallel motion—with the same chord structure shifted to different pitch levels—is characteristic of impressionist style.

The third idea of the opening section is a figure that turns around a single note.

In the brief but animated middle section, contrast is created by a shift from the whole-tone to the pentatonic (five-tone) scale: E♭–G♭–A♭–B♭–D♭. This scale is used for rapid upward rushes.

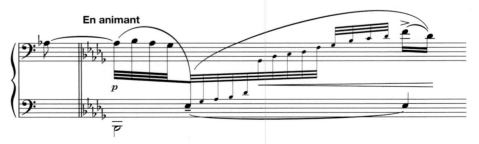

The concluding section brings a return of the whole-tone scale, the stepwise melody, and the *sails* motive. But now the upward melody is presented in a high register, in single notes—rather than in octaves or chords—and accompanied by gliding upward whole-tone-scale figures. At the end of *Voiles* there is no sense of harmonic resolution; we are left drifting in a sonorous haze.

5 Maurice Ravel

The French composer Maurice Ravel (1875–1937) was a master of orchestral and pianistic tone color. Like his older contemporary Debussy, Ravel grew up in Paris and studied piano and composition for many years at the Paris Conservatory. But unlike Debussy, Ravel never succeeded in winning the Prix de Rome, despite five attempts. His last failure—at age thirty, when he was already a recognized composer—caused a scandal that led to a change of administration at the Conservatory. It was perhaps owing to his lingering resentment of the musical establishment that he refused the Legion of Honor when it was offered to him, as France's most famous living composer, in 1920.

Though he is often described as an impressionist and paired with Debussy, Ravel does not fit neatly into any stylistic category. It is true that some of his music—such as the piano piece *Jeux d'eaux* (*Fountains,* 1901) and the ballet *Daphnis and Chloé* (1909–1912)—has the fluid, misty, atmospheric quality associated with impressionism. And subtle changes of tone color are indeed extremely important in Ravel's works, as in the impressionist music of Debussy. Yet much music by Ravel is too clearly defined in form and tonality and classically balanced in phrase structure to be considered impressionist. His lyrical melodic lines, though individual in style, are closely related to melodies by nineteenth-century French composers such as Georges Bizet. However, Ravel's melodies are often based on modes, which sometimes make them suggest music from a foreign land or from the distant past. His music is often characterized by a clear beat, and rhythmic patterns are often obsessively repeated.

Above all, Ravel was a master craftsman; he once said, "My objective is technical perfection." He worked unceasingly to produce a relatively small number of vocal and instrumental works (for piano, orchestra, and chamber groups) that are almost all widely performed and recorded. His highly original piano pieces contain novel sonorities and extend the virtuoso style of Liszt. They were a proving ground for compositional procedures he later used in orchestral compositions. In fact, a considerable proportion of his orchestral works—including *Alborada del gracioso* (*Jester's Dawn Song*) and *Le Tombeau de Couperin* (*The Tomb of Couperin*)—are orchestrations of piano pieces; and his orchestral transcription of Mussorgsky's piano piece *Pictures at an Exhibition* is very popular (see Part VI, section 12). Ravel was extremely sensitive to the technical and expressive capacities of orchestral instruments and created many fresh combinations of tone colors.

Ravel had a taste for exotic musical idioms. Many of his works have a Spanish flavor; examples are the one-act opera *L'Heure espagnole* (*The Spanish Hour,* 1907–1909) and the orchestral works *Rhapsodie espagnole* (*Spanish Rhapsody,* 1908) and *Bolero.* He exploited the rhythms and tone colors of American jazz in such works of the 1920s as Piano Concerto in G major, Piano Concerto for the Left Hand (commissioned by the one-armed pianist Paul Wittgenstein), and the *Blues* movement of Sonata for Violin and Piano. Ravel was also fascinated by dance and wrote several ballets, including *Daphnis and Chloé,* which he later arranged as two concert suites for orchestra. Stylized dance rhythms pervade much of his music: the Renaissance pavane in *Pavane pour une infante défunte* (*Pavane for a Dead Princess,* 1899); the baroque forlane, rigaudon, and minuet in *Le Tombeau de Couperin* (1914–1917); the Viennese waltz in *Valses nobles et sentimentales* (*Noble and Sentimental Waltzes,* 1911) and *La Valse* (*The Waltz,* 1919–1920); and the Spanish bolero in *Bolero.*

Bolero (1928)

Basic Set:
CD 7 31

One of the best-known of all orchestral works, *Bolero* reflects Ravel's fascination with tone color, Spanish music, and obsessive rhythmic repetition. It originated as a ballet commissioned by the dancer Ida Rubinstein and was introduced by her at the Paris Opera in 1928. Set in a dimly lit Spanish café, the ballet centers on a young Gypsy woman dancing a bolero on a table surrounded by men. Her movements become increasingly lively, and the excitement and tension of the onlookers culminate in violence. The ballet was a success, but soon *Bolero* became more famous internationally as a concert piece. After its American premiere by Arturo Toscanini and the New York Philharmonic in 1929, a critic wrote that "*Bolero* brought shouts and cheers from the audience."

Ravel modestly described Bolero as an "experiment" consisting of "one long, very gradual crescendo." Its theme and rhythm "were deliberately given a Spanish character" and "repeated to the point of obsession." *Bolero* is unusual in form, consisting of an extended, exotic-sounding theme that is heard over and over with increasingly rich and brilliant orchestration. Ravel creates movement and growth through changes of tone color, as Stravinsky does in the *Firebird* Suite and *The Rite of Spring.* The theme is first presented by solo woodwind instruments, including the unusual oboe d'amore, which is lower than the oboe but higher than the English horn. As the volume gradually increases, brass instruments and tenor and sopranino saxophones—rare in a symphony orchestra—are given the theme. Novel tone colors result from unusual doublings, such as muted trumpet and flute, as though Ravel were inventing new instruments. Sometimes the melody is doubled at different pitch levels, a device which results in sliding parallel chords.

Only after the dynamic level has reached f is the melody presented by the violins and doubled by woodwinds and brasses.

Bolero's accompaniment is even more obsessive than its melody. From beginning to end, a two-bar bolero rhythmic pattern is repeated in the snare drum, which is progressively doubled by more and more instruments. Moreover, in the bass of virtually every bar we hear a three-note ostinato played pizzicato by the lower strings. Also contributing to the hypnotic effect is the insistence on the key of C major, which persists until an electrifying climax—resulting from a sudden, momentary upward shift to the brighter key of E major—and a violently dissonant ending.

The theme of *Bolero* is made up of two extended parts which are each heard twice with varied orchestration: A A B B. This A A B B pattern is presented four times, gradually building in power. Finally, Ravel compresses the theme to A B. Thus *Bolero* can be outlined A A B B—A A B B—A A B B—A A B B—A B. The bolero rhythmic pattern and the accompanying bass ostinato are presented alone—without the melody—as an introduction to each A and B, with gradually increasing volume and richness of sound.

In part A, the melody is fairly narrow in range and uses only the notes of the C major scale. It has two phrases, the first ending with a questioning upward skip to an incomplete cadence, and the second ending with a complete cadence as if giving an answer.

Part B of the theme is also made up of two phrases, but it is wider in range and darker in mood because it combines elements of major, minor, and modal scales. After ascending to a climactic tone that is repeated with hypnotic insistence, the melody gradually moves downward a long distance until it reaches a cadence.

LISTENING OUTLINE

RAVEL, *Bolero*

Tempo di bolero, moderato assai (tempo of a bolero, very moderate), triple meter ($\frac{3}{4}$)

2 piccolos, 2 flutes, 2 oboes (one doubling on oboe d'amore), English horn, E flat clarinet, 2 B flat clarinets, bass clarinet, 3 saxophones (sopranino, soprano, tenor), 2 bassoons, contrabassoon, 4 French horns, 1 small trumpet in D, 3 trumpets, 3 trombones, tuba, harp, 3 timpani, cymbals, tam-tam, celesta, 2 snare drums, 1st violins, 2d violins, violas, cellos, double basses

(Duration, 15:05)

31 0:00

1. a. Bolero rhythm in snare drum, ***pp***, accompanied by ostinato in pizzicato violas and cellos.

pizzicato

0:10

b. Part A, flute, ***pp***, extended melody with two phrases.

pp

Bolero rhythm in flute, ***pp***, introduces

0:58 **c.** Part A repeated, clarinet, ***p***. Bolero rhythm in flute, ***pp***, introduces

32 1:46 **d.** Part B, bassoon, ***mp***, enters in high register, extended exotic-sounding melody with two phrases.

mp

Harp, ***pp***, and bolero rhythm in flute, ***pp***, introduce

2:35 **e.** Part B, repeated an octave higher, high (E flat) clarinet, ***p***. Bolero rhythm in high bassoon, ***mp***, introduces

33 3:24 **2. a.** Part A, oboe d'amore, ***mp***. Bolero rhythm in French horn, ***p***, introduces

4:13 **b.** Part A repeated, muted trumpet, ***mp***, doubled an octave higher by flute, ***p***. Pizzicato violins, bolero rhythm in muted trumpet, ***mp***, introduce

34 5:00 **c.** Part B, tenor saxophone, ***mp***, melody decorated by slides. Pizzicato violins, bolero rhythm in muted trumpet, ***mp***, introduce

5:48 **d.** Part B repeated an octave higher, sopranino saxophone, ***mf***. Harp, bolero rhythm in French horn, ***mf***, introduce

35 6:37 **3. a.** Part A, French horn, ***mf***, doubled at higher pitches by piccolos. Pizzicato strings, bolero rhythm in muted trumpets, ***mf***, introduce

7:24 **b.** Part A repeated in woodwinds, ***mf***. Harp, bolero rhythm in violas and French horns, ***mf***, introduce

8:10 **c.** Part B, trombone, ***mf***, melody decorated by slides. Bolero rhythm in trumpets, ***f***, introduces

8:59 **d.** Part B repeated in high woodwinds, ***mf***, with melody in parallel chords, ***f***. Bolero rhythm in French horns, ***f***, introduces

36 9:46 **4. a.** Part A, violins, ***f***, and woodwinds. Bolero rhythm in French horns, ***f***, introduces

10:33 **b.** Part A, repeated in violins, ***f***, and woodwinds, with melody in parallel chords. Bolero rhythm in French horns, ***f***, introduces

11:20 **c.** Part B, violins, woodwinds, and trumpet, ***f***. Bolero rhythm in strings, woodwinds, and French horns, ***f***, introduces

12:02 **d.** Part B repeated in strings, woodwinds, and trombone, ***f***, with melody in parallel chords. Bolero rhythm in strings, woodwinds, and French horns, ***ff***, introduces

37 12:56 **5. a.** Part A, violins, trumpets, and woodwinds, ***ff***, with melody in parallel chords. Bolero rhythm in strings, woodwinds, and French horns, ***ff***, introduces

13:44 **b.** Part B, violins, woodwinds, and brasses, ***ff***, with melody in parallel chords; melody changes with shift to new key, closes with return to original key. Bolero rhythm in whole orchestra; percussion, ***ff***, cymbal crashes, dissonant concluding chords.

6 Neoclassicism

From about 1920 to 1950, the music of many composers, including Igor Stravinsky and Paul Hindemith (1895–1963), reflected an artistic movement known as **neoclassicism.** Neoclassicism is marked by emotional restraint, balance, and clarity; neoclassical compositions use musical forms and stylistic features of earlier periods, particularly of the eighteenth century. Stravinsky summed it up: "I attempted to build a new music on eighteenth-century classicism." Neoclassical music is not merely a revival of old forms and styles; it uses earlier techniques to organize twentieth-century harmonies and rhythms.

"Back to Bach" was the slogan of this movement, which reacted against romanticism and impressionism. (Since many neoclassical compositions were modeled after Bach's music, the term *neobaroque* might have been more appropriate.) Neoclassical composers turned away from program music and the gigantic orchestras favored at the turn of the century. They preferred absolute (nonprogrammatic) music for chamber groups. This preference for smaller performing groups partly reflected economic necessity: during the post–World War I period, economic conditions were so bad in parts of Europe that there was little money to hire large orchestras. Favoring clear polyphonic textures, composers wrote fugues, concerti grossi, and baroque dance suites. Most neoclassical music was tonal and used major and minor scales. Still, neoclassicism was more an attitude than a style. Schoenberg wrote minuets and gigues using his twelve-tone system. And though neoclassical composers referred to many past styles, their works sound completely modern. They play on the delightful tension between our expectations about old forms and styles and the novel harmonies and rhythms. In Section 7, we'll study a neoclassical work by Stravinsky, *Symphony of Psalms* (1930).

Neoclassicism was an important trend in other arts, too. The poet T. S. Eliot often quoted and alluded to earlier writers. Picasso, who designed sets for Stravinsky's first neoclassical work, *Pulcinella* (1920), went through a phase during which he created paintings that show the influence of ancient Greek art. Picasso described the neoclassical attitude by saying that artists "must pick out what is good for us where we find it. When I am shown a portfolio of old drawings, for instance, I have no qualms about taking anything I want from them."

7 Igor Stravinsky

Even before his death at the age of eighty-eight, Igor Stravinsky (1882–1971) was a legendary figure and was regarded as the world's greatest composer. His once revolutionary works were modern classics; he was a restless innovator who influenced three generations of composers and inspired many painters, writers, and choreographers. Cultural giants like Picasso and T. S. Eliot were his friends; President John F. Kennedy honored him at a White House dinner in his eightieth year.

Stravinsky, who was born in a small town near St. Petersburg, Russia, grew up in a musical atmosphere. His father was a leading singer at the St. Petersburg opera. Despite Stravinsky's obvious talent, his parents insisted that he study law at the University of St. Petersburg. Soon he began to neglect his studies and devote himself to composition. At the age of twenty-one, he became a private student of Nikolai Rimsky-Korsakov.

Stravinsky's life took a sudden turn in 1909, when the great impresario Sergei Diaghilev heard his music at a concert in St. Petersburg. Diaghilev was director of

Igor Stravinsky in a sketch by Picasso.

the Russian Ballet. This troupe, based in Paris, had a powerful impact not only on Stravinsky but on the entire cultural scene in Europe from 1909 to 1929. It employed great masters in all arts. Its dancers included Vaslav Nijinsky, and the choreographers Michel Fokine and George Balanchine created works for the troupe. It commissioned stage designs from great painters like Picasso and ballet music from outstanding musicians like Stravinsky, Debussy, Ravel, and Prokofiev. Diaghilev asked the twenty-six-year-old Stravinsky to orchestrate piano pieces by Chopin as ballet music for the first season of the Russian Ballet in 1909. In 1910, Stravinsky was commissioned to compose an original ballet, *The Firebird*. The immense success of this ballet, which was based on a Russian fairy tale, immediately established Stravinsky as a leading young composer. His second ballet, *Petrushka* (1911), was performed a year later, and at the age of twenty-nine Stravinsky was hailed as a modern master. His incisive rhythms, witty musical satire, and brilliant orchestral colors delighted sophisticated Parisians.

A now-legendary riot erupted in the audience when Stravinsky's third ballet, *The Rite of Spring,* was performed in Paris in 1913. Spectators hissed and booed at the music's "primitive" evocation of pagan fertility rites, its harshly insistent dissonance, its percussiveness, and its pounding rhythms. One member of the audience reported that someone excitedly "began to beat rhythmically on top of my head with his fists. My emotion was so great that I did not feel the blows." Soon after, however, the ballet was recognized as a masterpiece; it influenced composers all over the world.

The outbreak of World War I in 1914 forced Stravinsky to seek refuge in neutral Switzerland, where he lived for six years with his wife and children. When the Russian Revolution of 1917 ended his private income, he faced financial difficulties for the first time in his life. To "escape from this alarming situation," he wrote *The Soldier's Tale* (1918), a theatrical work that required few performers and was easy to present under wartime conditions.

After the armistice in 1918, Stravinsky moved to France, which remained his home until the onset of World War II. Now Stravinsky was an international figure, constantly touring Europe and the United States to play and conduct his music. His voluntary exile from Russia coincided with his turning away from Russian folk music as a source of inspiration. Stravinsky's works in the 1920s and 1930s seemed excessively cool and objective to some music lovers, who preferred the early, Russian-flavored ballets.

Unlike his contemporaries Schoenberg and Bartók, Stravinsky got well-paying commissions for his work and was an astute businessman. He described himself as composing "every day, regularly, like a man with banking hours." His love of order and discipline was reflected in his studio, which had, in the words of a friend, "all the instruments needed for writing, copying, drawing, pasting, cutting, clipping, filing, sharpening, and gluing that the combined effects of a stationery and hardware store can furnish."

World War II caused Stravinsky to settle in yet another country, the United States. He lived outside Los Angeles, not far from Arnold Schoenberg, but the two never visited each other. Their different musical philosophies created an unbridgeable gulf, and each had his own group of loyal disciples.

In 1948, Stravinsky engaged Robert Craft, a twenty-four-year-old conductor, as his musical assistant. Craft encouraged Stravinsky to become more familiar with the works of Schoenberg, Berg, and Webern. By the 1950s, all three composers were dead, and Stravinsky astonished his followers by adopting Schoenberg's twelve-tone system.

And in his seventies and eighties, despite physical pain, this incredible man toured the world from Chile to Tahiti, conducting his rich and intense late works. He also, for the first time in fifty years, returned to Russia and bared his soul to a group of Soviet composers: "The smell of the Russian earth is different. . . . A man has one birthplace, one fatherland, one country."

Stravinsky's Music

Stravinsky had an enormous influence on twentieth-century music. His innovations in rhythm, harmony, and tone color inspired musicians throughout the world. No contemporary contributed so many masterpieces to the international repertoire. Stravinsky's extensive output includes music of almost every kind, for both voices and instruments. His many works for the stage include thirteen ballet scores.

Like that of his friend Picasso, Stravinsky's development shows dramatic changes of style. His three early ballets—*The Firebird* (1910), *Petrushka* (1911), and *The Rite of Spring* (1913)—call for very large orchestras and draw on Russian folklore and folk tunes. During World War I, Stravinsky abandoned the large orchestra and wrote for small chamber groups with unconventional combinations of instruments. Ragtime rhythms and popular dances (for example, the tango) were used in such works as *The Soldier's Tale* (1918). From about 1920 to 1951 (described earlier, in Section 6, as the period of neoclassicism), he gradually turned from Russian folklore and drew inspiration largely from eighteenth-century music. First came the ballet *Pulcinella* (1920), based partly on the music of Giovanni Battista Pergolesi, an Italian composer of the early eighteenth century; this phase ended with his opera *The Rake's Progress* (1951), modeled after Mozart's operas. Emphasizing emotional restraint, balance, and wit, Stravinsky's work at this time was far removed from the violence and "primitivism" of *The Rite of Spring*. Many pieces feature woodwind and brass instruments, which Stravinsky felt to be less "romantic" in sound than strings. Some works are based on subjects from antiquity, like the opera-oratorio *Oedipus Rex* (1927); others were inspired by sacred texts, like *Symphony of Psalms* (1930).

Whatever Stravinsky's current style, he had always written music with a clear tonal center, and so the musical world was startled when he shifted from tonality to the twelve-tone system. This dramatic change of approach came during the 1950s, when Stravinsky was in his seventies. Taking inspiration from the music of Anton Webern (1883–1945), Stravinsky now wrote brief works in which melodic lines were "atomized" into short fragments in continually changing tone colors and registers.

Despite such stylistic changes, all of his music has an unmistakable "Stravinsky sound." His tone colors tend to be dry and clear, while his beat is strong and regular.

Stravinsky's rhythmic imagination was one of the most fertile in the twentieth century. His music abounds in changing and irregular meters; sometimes several meters are heard at once. Ostinatos, or repeated rhythmic patterns, frequently unify sections of a piece. They also accompany melodies with highly irregular phrase structures.

Stravinsky's treatment of musical form is also unique. Rather than connecting themes with bridge passages, he shifts abruptly from one section to the next. One idea is repeated and varied for a while, only to be broken off by something new. "Here, you see, I cut off the fugue with a pair of scissors," he remarked of a fugue that is repeatedly punctuated by contrasting material. But despite all the sudden changes, Stravinsky's music sounds unified and continuous.

Tone color is an integral part of his work. The effectiveness of his rhythms, chords, and melodies depends largely on how they are orchestrated. Much of his music is scored for unconventional groups of instruments. Highly contrasting tone colors are often combined: a violin is set against a trumpet, or a piano against a trombone. Instruments play in unusual registers, too. For example, *The Rite of Spring* opens with the highest tones of a solo bassoon. Stravinsky uses percussion instruments imaginatively, often giving them solo roles. He even acquired percussion instruments so that he could personally try out his drum parts. The writer who collaborated with Stravinsky on *The Soldier's Tale* reported that he and Stravinsky met almost daily "surrounded by side drums, kettledrums, bass drums, and every kind of percussion instrument."

Stravinsky's music has rich, novel harmonies, such as the famous "Petrushka chord," a bitonal combination of a C major triad with an F sharp major triad. He makes even conventional chords sound unique through spacing, doubling, and the orchestration of their tones. The spirit of this composer's approach is seen in his exclamation about one such novel-sounding harmony: "How happy I was when I discovered this chord!"

Stravinsky often used existing music to create original compositions. He drew on a vast range of styles, from Russian folk songs to baroque melodies, from Renaissance madrigals to tango rhythms. Sometimes he gave another composer's melody new harmonies and orchestration. But more often the music is entirely Stravinsky's, while vaguely suggesting a past style. Stravinsky spoke of a "lifelong need for outside nourishment." He believed that tradition is "a living force that animates and informs the present. . . . It appears as an heirloom, a heritage that one receives on condition of making it bear fruit before passing it on to one's descendants."

Le Sacre du printemps (The Rite of Spring, 1913)

Few compositions have had so powerful an impact on twentieth-century music as *Le Sacre du printemps* (*The Rite of Spring*), Stravinsky's third ballet score for the Russian Ballet. Its harsh dissonances, percussive orchestration, rapidly changing meters, violent offbeat accents, and ostinatos fired the imagination of many composers. The idea for *The Rite of Spring* came to Stravinsky as a "fleeting vision," while he was completing *The Firebird* in St. Petersburg in 1910. "I saw in imagination a solemn pagan rite: wise elders, seated in a circle, watching a young girl dance herself to death. They were sacrificing her to propitiate the god of spring." Later in life, Stravinsky remarked that the "most wonderful event" of every year of his childhood was the "violent Russian spring that seemed to begin in an hour and was like the whole earth cracking."

Stravinsky's interest in so-called primitive or preliterate culture was shared by many artists and scholars in the early 1900s. In 1907, Picasso's violent and pathbreaking painting *Les Demoiselles d'Avignon* reflected the influence of African sculpture. In 1913—the same year as *The Rite of Spring*—Freud published *Totem and Taboo*, a study of "resemblances between the psychic lives of savages and neurotics." But *primitivism*—the deliberate evocation of primitive power through insistent rhythms and percussive sounds—did not have a lasting impact on early twentieth-century music. Stravinsky never again wrote anything like *The Rite of Spring*; and with the exception of works like *Allegro barbaro* (1911), a piano piece by Bartók, few primitivistic compositions have entered the repertoire.

The Rite of Spring has two large parts, which are subdivided into sections that move at varying speeds. These subsections follow each other without pause. The titles of the dances suggest their primitive subject matter. Part I, *The Adoration of the Earth,* consists of (1) *Introduction;* (2) *Omens of Spring: Dances of the Youths and Maidens;* (3) *Ritual of Abduction;* (4) *Spring Rounds;* (5) *Games of the Rival Tribes;* (6) *Procession of the Wise Elder;* (7) *Adoration of the Earth;* (8) *Dance of the Earth.* Part II, *The Sacrifice,* consists of (1) *Introduction;* (2) *Mysterious Circles of the Young Girls;* (3) *Glorification of the Chosen Maiden;* (4) *Evocation of the Ancestors;* (5) *Ritual of the Ancestors;* (6) *Sacrificial Dance.* Each of the two large parts begins with a slow introduction and ends with a frenzied, climactic dance.

The Rite of Spring is written for an enormous orchestra including eight horns, four tubas, and a very important percussion section made up of five timpani, bass drum, tambourine, tam-tam, triangle, antique cymbals, and a guiro (a notched gourd scraped with a stick). The melodies of *The Rite of Spring* are folklike. Like ancient Russian folk tunes, they have narrow ranges, and they are made up of fragments that are repeated with slight changes in rhythm and pitch. Many individual chords are repeated, and

Les Demoiselles d'Avignon (1907) by Picasso reflects the influence of African sculpture.

each change of harmony produces a great impact. This melodic and harmonic repetition gives the music a ritualistic, hypnotic quality. Rhythm is a vital structural element in *The Rite of Spring;* it has a life of its own, almost independent of melody and harmony. Today, *The Rite of Spring* is performed more frequently as a concert piece than as a ballet.

We'll now take a closer look at four sections of *The Rite of Spring: Introduction, Omens of Spring—Dances of the Youths and Maidens,* and *Ritual of Abduction,* which open Part I; and *Sacrificial Dance,* which concludes Part II.

Part I:
Introduction

Basic Set:
CD 7 [38]

Brief Set:
CD 5 [1]

For Stravinsky, the *Introduction* to Part I represented "the awakening of nature, the scratching, gnawing, wiggling of birds and beasts." It begins with the strangely penetrating sound of a solo bassoon straining at the top of its register. As though improvising, the bassoon repeats a fragment of a Lithuanian folk tune in irregular ways.

Soon other woodwind instruments join the bassoon with repeated fragments of their own. The impression of improvisation is strengthened by the absence of a clearly defined pulse or meter. Dissonant, unconventional chord structures are used. Toward the end of the *Introduction,* different layers of sounds—coming mostly from woodwinds and brasses—are piled on top of each other, and the music builds to a piercing climax. But suddenly, all sound is cut off; only the solo bassoon forlornly repeats its opening melody. Then the violins, playing pizzicato, introduce a repeated four-note "ticking" figure. This figure later serves as an ostinato in *Omens of Spring—Dances of the Youths and Maidens,* which immediately follows the *Introduction.*

Basic Set:
CD 7 **40**

Brief Set:
CD 5 **3**

Part I:
Omens of Spring—Dances of the Youths and Maidens

Sounding almost like drums, the strings pound out a dissonant chord. There are unexpected and irregular accents whose violence is heightened by jabbing sounds from the eight horns. This is the way the passage might be counted (with a rapid pulse): 1–2–3–**4**, 1–2–3–4, 1–**2**–3–**4**, 1–2–3–4, 1–**2**–3–4, **1**–2–3–4, **1**–2–3–4, **1**–2–3–4. The unchanging dissonant harmony is a polychord that combines two different traditional chords. Successive melodic fragments soon join the pounding chord and other repeated figures. The melodic fragments, played by brass and woodwind instruments, are narrow in range and are repeated over and over with slight variations. The rhythmic activity is ceaseless and exciting, and gradually more and more instruments are added.

It's interesting to contrast Stravinsky's musical techniques in *Dances of the Youths and Maidens* with those of a classical movement in sonata form. A classical movement grows out of conflicts between different keys; this section of *The Rite of Spring* is based almost entirely on repetition of a few chords. Themes in a classical movement are developed through different keys, varied, and broken into fragments that take on new emotional meanings. In *Dances of the Youths and Maidens,* Stravinsky simply repeats melodic fragments with relatively slight variation. To create movement and growth, he relies instead on variations of rhythm and tone color—a technique that can be traced back to nineteenth-century Russian musical tradition.

Basic Set:
CD 7 **44**

Brief Set:
CD 5 **7**

Part I:
Ritual of Abduction

The frenzied *Ritual of Abduction* grows out of the preceding section and is marked by violent strokes on the timpani and bass drum. Enormous tension is generated by powerful accents and rapid changes of meter (see the music example on page 369). This section of *The Rite of Spring* closes with high trills in the strings and flutes.

LISTENING OUTLINE

STRAVINSKY, *Le Sacre du printemps*

Part I: *Introduction, Omens of Spring—Dances of the Youths and Maidens, Ritual of Abduction*

2 piccolos, 3 flutes, alto flute, 4 oboes, English horn, E flat clarinet, 3 clarinets, 2 bass clarinets, 4 bassoons, 2 contrabassoons, 8 French horns, small trumpet in D, 4 trumpets, 3 trombones, 3 tubas, timpani, bass drum, triangle, antique cymbals, 1st violins, 2d violins, violas, cellos, double basses

(Duration, 7:24)

Introduction

38 **1** 0:00   **1. a.** High solo bassoon, repeated folk song fragment in changing meters, joined by French horn, ***mp***, then clarinets and bass clarinets, ***p***.

0:43   **b.** English horn, new melodic fragment; high bassoon; English horn, melodic fragment, bassoons accompany in faster rhythm.

1:12   **c.** Pizzicato strings, oboe, repeated notes introduce high clarinet melody.

1:24   **d.** Oboe phrase, ***f***, high flutes accompany; English horn phrase, ***mf***, bass clarinets accompany; flutes and English horn move in even rhythm; violin trill joins.

	1:53	**e.** Pizzicato cello pulsations, rhythmic activity quickens, rapid shifts between large and small wind groups; clarinet, repeated descending phrase.
	2:18	**f.** Oboe with rapid alto flute accompaniment; piercing high clarinet, *ff*, joins; music builds to *ff* climax, different layers of woodwind and brass sound piled on each other.
	2:52	**2. a.** Sudden *p*, solo high bassoon, opening fragment; clarinet trill, joined by
39 ☐2	3:03	**b.** Pizzicato violins, "ticking" ostinato figure.

Low held tone in bass clarinet; high chord in violins; pizzicato violins, "ticking" ostinato figure.

Omens of Spring—Dances of the Youths and Maidens

40 ☐3	3:22	**3. a.** Sudden *f*, strings, repeated dissonant polychord with punctuations in French horns, irregular accents, moderate tempo, duple meter.

	3:29	**b.** English horn, *mf*, "ticking" ostinato figure.
	3:39	**c.** Strings, *f*, repeated dissonant polychord with punctuations in French horns; piccolos, trumpets, oboes join.
	3:49	**d.** Pizzicato basses and cellos introduce loud, rapid interjections in high trumpet and piccolos;
	3:54	**e.** Strings, *f*, repeated dissonant polychord with punctuations in French horns.
41 ☐4	4:02	**f.** Bassoons join with melodic fragment played staccato, string pulsations; trombone joins;

Bassoons repeat staccato melodic fragment; oboes, flute, and trombone imitate;

	4:28	**g.** Sudden break in pulse, French horns, *f*, sustained tone, timpani strokes, tubas, *ff*, low sustained tone;
	4:33	**h.** High "ticking" ostinato figure descends to English horn, *mf*, trills in winds and strings; loud "ticking" ostinato in violins and trumpet.
42 ☐5	4:49	**i.** French horn, *mp*, joins with legato melody; flute answers;

descending figure in oboes and trumpet.

	5:07	**j.** Legato melody in alto flute; legato melody in high flutes, pizzicato strings accompany.
43 ☐6	5:20	**k.** Trumpets join with repeated-note melody; triangle joins.

5:34   **I.** Sudden p, strings and syncopated accents introduce piccolo, high legato melodic fragment; full orchestra, melodic figures repeated with long crescendo to

Ritual of Abduction

44 **7** 6:10   **4. a.** Sustained brass chord, violent strokes on timpani and bass drum; high trumpet, rapid-note fanfare, very fast tempo, changing meters.

6:23   **b.** Horn calls, f, alternate with piccolo and flutes, rapid-note fanfare; timpani, bass drum join; crescendo to

6:43   **c.** High woodwinds and brasses, $f\!f$, staccato passage in changing meters; horn calls; full orchestra, $f\!f$.

45 **8** 6:59   **d.** Timpani accents punctuate staccato phrases with changing meters in trumpets and high winds; timpani accents punctuate repeated rapid figure in strings.

7:18   **e.** Trill in violins, $f\!f$, accented chords; trill in flutes, p.

Part II: *Sacrificial Dance*

Sacrificial Dance is the overwhelming climax of the work. It consists of sections that can be outlined as follows: A B A′ C A″ (very brief) C A‴. In the opening section (A), explosive, percussive chords fight brutal blows on the timpani. The time signature changes with almost every bar: $\frac{3}{16}$ $\frac{2}{16}$ $\frac{3}{16}$ $\frac{2}{8}$ $\frac{2}{16}$ $\frac{3}{16}$. The rapid pulse and irregular, jolting accents create intense excitement.

The second section (B) begins with a sudden drop in dynamic level as a single chord is repeated obsessively. Brief silences between these repeated chords urge the listener to supply accents.

Section C features brasses and percussive sounds from five timpani, a tam-tam (gong), and a bass drum. *Sacrificial Dance* glorifies the power of rhythm, as does the entire *Rite of Spring*.

Symphony of Psalms (1930)

Symphony of Psalms, a masterpiece from Stravinsky's "neoclassical period," was written for the fiftieth anniversary of the Boston Symphony Orchestra in 1930. It has three movements and is scored for chorus and orchestra. The Latin text is taken from three psalms in the Vulgate Bible. Stravinsky chose the Latin version to evoke the feeling of an ancient and solemn ritual. An austere, archaic quality is also communicated through chantlike melodies that are sometimes restricted to one or two tones.

The neoclassical features of *Symphony of Psalms* include its use of tonality, major and minor triads, and fugue, and its deliberate evocation of the past. Yet the music sounds completely of the twentieth century. As in many works by Stravinsky, the orchestra is highly unconventional. There are no violins, violas, or clarinets; instead, the sounds of woodwinds, brasses, and two pianos predominate. Stravinsky intended the voices and instruments to "be on an equal footing, neither of them outweighing the other." He uses the term *symphony* not in its usual sense, but simply to indicate a work in several movements that calls for an orchestra. The three movements are related motivically and are performed without interruption. We'll focus on the first movement.

First Movement: Psalm 38 (Vulgate), Verses 13–14*

The brief opening movement, based on a psalm beginning "Hear my prayer, O Lord," is a prelude to the successively longer movements that follow. First, a staccato orches-

---

*Psalm 38 in the Vulgate is Psalm 39 in the King James Version.

tral chord repeatedly punctuates woodwind solos. Although it is a standard E minor triad, this chord sounds unique because its tones are spaced and orchestrated in a novel way. After this orchestral introduction, the alto voices of the chorus sing a chantlike melody composed of just two notes that alternate.

E - xau - di ____ o - ra - ti - o - nem me - am, Do - mi - ne, __

This chantlike theme is supported by ostinatos in the woodwinds:

The first part of the movement is marked by abrupt contrasts between the staccato chord, woodwind interludes, and brief passages for chorus and orchestra. The second part of the movement is more continuous, as the chorus and orchestra are always heard together. The movement ends in triumph, with a sustained G major triad that has a great impact because it is the movement's only *major* triad; it vividly contrasts with the staccato minor triads heard earlier.

VOCAL MUSIC GUIDE

STRAVINSKY, *Symphony of Psalms*

First Movement

49

Orchestral introduction; loud staccato chord punctuates solos by oboe, bassoon.

Piano. High cello.

Altos, chantlike theme.	*Exaudi orationem meam, Domine,*	Hear my prayer, O Lord,
Full chorus. Oboe.	*et deprecationem meam;*	and my supplication;
Altos, chantlike theme.	*auribus percipe lacrimas meas.*	give ear to my tears.

Staccato chord.		
Tenors and altos, *f*; staccato chord.	*Ne sileas,*	Be not silent:
Altos, basses.	*quoniam advena ego*	for I am a stranger
Other voices join.	*sum apud te,*	with thee,
Crescendo to *ff*.	*et peregrinus*	and a sojourner
	sicut omnes patres mei.	as all my fathers were.
	Remitte mihi,	O forgive me,
Suddenly softer, chantlike theme in tenors and sopranos.	*(remitte mihi,)*	(O forgive me,)
	ut refrigerer	that I may be refreshed,
	priusquam abeam	before I go hence,
Major chord, *ff*	*et amplius non ero.*	and be no more.

8 Expressionism

Much music of the twentieth century reflects an artistic movement called ***expressionism,*** which stressed intense, subjective emotion. It was largely centered in Germany and Austria from 1905 to 1925. Expressionist painters, writers, and composers explored inner feelings rather than depicting outward appearances. They used deliberate distortion to assault and shock their audience, to communicate the tensions and anguish of the human psyche. Expressionism grew out of the same intellectual climate as Freud's studies of hysteria and the unconscious. German expressionist painting was in part a reaction against the pleasant subjects, delicate pastel colors, and shimmering surfaces of French impressionism.

The expressionists rejected conventional prettiness. Their works may seem "ugly" in their preoccupation with madness and death. Expressionist painters such as Ernst Ludwig Kirchner, Emil Nolde, Edvard Munch, and Oskar Kokoschka often use jarring colors and grotesquely distorted shapes. Expressionist art tends to be fragmentary; the scenes of an expressionist play may be episodic and discontinuous. Expressionism is also an art concerned with social protest. It movingly conveyed the anguish felt by the poor and oppressed. Many expressionists opposed World War I and used art to depict their horror of bloodshed.

There was close communication among expressionist writers, painters, and musicians. Many were creative in more than one art form. The painter Wassily Kandinsky wrote essays, poetry, and plays; the composer Schoenberg painted and even participated in the shows of expressionist artists.

The Scream (1893), by the Norwegian expressionist Edvard Munch. Expressionist painters reacted against French impressionism; they often used jarring colors and grotesquely distorted shapes to explore the subconscious.

Twentieth-century musical expressionism grows out of the emotional turbulence in the works of romantics like Wagner and Mahler. Immediate precedents for expressionism are the operas *Salome* (1905) and *Elektra* (1908) by Richard Strauss, in which extremely chromatic and dissonant music depicts perversion and murder. In Sections 9, 10, and 11, we'll study four expressionistic compositions: *Pierrot lunaire*, Op. 21 (*Moonstruck Pierrot,* 1912), and *A Survivor from Warsaw,* Op. 46 (1947), by Schoenberg; the opera *Wozzeck* (1917–1922), by Alban Berg; and Five Pieces for Orchestra, Op. 10 (1911–1913), by Anton Webern. These works all stress harsh dissonance and fragmentation, and exploit extreme registers and unusual instrumental effects. All four avoid tonality and traditional chord progressions. Both *A Survivor from Warsaw* and *Wozzeck* depict a nightmarish world and express a profound empathy with the poor and tormented.

9 Arnold Schoenberg

Arnold Schoenberg (1874–1951) was born in Vienna, the city of Mozart, Beethoven, and Brahms. Unlike such earlier masters, he was an almost entirely self-taught musician. "I began studying the violin at eight and almost immediately started composing," he later recalled. Schoenberg acquired his profound knowledge of music by studying scores, by playing in amateur chamber groups, and by going to concerts. His first musical hero was Brahms, then considered the greatest living German composer. He soon became an "equally confirmed addict" of Wagner; he saw each of Wagner's operas from twenty to thirty times.

Arnold Schoenberg developed the twelve-tone system, which offered the composer a new way of organizing pitch in a composition.

When Schoenberg was sixteen, his father died, and he had to work for several years as a bank clerk. When he lost that job at twenty-one, he decided to devote himself to music. He earned a poor living by conducting a choir of metalworkers in an industrial center outside Vienna. He also orchestrated operettas written by popular composers of the time. Performances of his own early works met with hostility from the conservative Viennese public. One music critic suggested that Schoenberg be put in an insane asylum without music paper.

Schoenberg began to teach music theory and composition in Vienna in 1904. His personality inspired love and loyalty among his students. Two of his disciples, Alban Berg and Anton Webern, themselves became leading composers.

Around 1908 Schoenberg took the revolutionary step of abandoning the traditional tonal system. "I already feel the opposition that I shall have to overcome," he wrote in a program note for his first atonal works. Schoenberg was a man possessed. "I have a mission. I have a task. . . . I am but the loudspeaker of an idea." His productivity between 1908 and 1915 was incredible. Besides creating many dazzlingly original works at lightning speed, he published a harmony textbook, wrote his own librettos, and entered his paintings in exhibitions of the German expressionists.

Following this fertile period came a span of eight years, encompassing World War I and the difficult postwar period, when Schoenberg published nothing. He searched for a way to organize the new musical resources he had discovered. Finally, in the summer of 1921, he told a student, "I have made a discovery which will ensure the supremacy of German music for the next hundred years." From 1923 to 1925 Schoenberg published compositions using his newly developed twelve-tone system. Although his music did not find a large audience, many important musicians respected it. At the age of fifty-one, Schoenberg received an important academic post: director of the master class in musical composition at the Prussian Academy of Arts in Berlin.

This period of official recognition was cut short in 1933, when the Nazis seized power in Germany. Schoenberg was dismissed from the faculty of the Prussian Academy. This shattering experience caused him to return to Judaism. (He had converted to Protestantism when he was eighteen.) The same year, he and his family left Germany for the United States, where he soon joined the music faculty at the University of California in Los Angeles. But Schoenberg felt neglected in his adopted country. His music was rarely performed, and he was refused a grant from the Guggenheim Foundation. At the age of seventy he was forced to retire from UCLA with a pension of less than $40 a month. "I am quite conscious," he wrote in 1947, "that a full understanding of my work cannot be expected before some decades, . . . and I know that—success or not—it is my historic duty to write what my destiny orders me to write." But appreciation came earlier than Schoenberg had anticipated. After his death in 1951, the twelve-tone system was adopted increasingly by composers throughout the world. It remains an important influence to this day.

Schoenberg's Music

"I claim the distinction of having written a truly new music which, based upon tradition as it is, is destined to become tradition." This proud assertion by Schoenberg contains a great deal of truth. His musical language was indeed new, yet it was rooted in the past and resulted from a gradual stylistic evolution. And his musical system *was* eventually adopted by many other composers.

Schoenberg's point of departure was the music of Wagner, Brahms, and Mahler. His early works, like the string sextet *Verklärte Nacht* (*Transfigured Night,* 1899), show many features of the late romantic style. The music is emotionally intense and often has a literary program. Some early compositions use the gigantic orchestra favored by late nineteenth-century composers. For example, the immense cantata *Gurrelieder* (*Songs of Gurre,* 1901; orchestration, 1911) calls for five vocal soloists, a speaker-narrator, four choruses, and a greatly expanded orchestra including about fifty woodwind and brass players. A feeling of subjectivity is generated through dissonances that resolve in unexpected ways and through angular melodies that have wide ranges and big leaps. There is prominent use of chromatic harmony, or chords with tones that do not belong to the prevailing major or minor scale. The pull of the central tonality is weakened because the music moves rapidly through remote keys.

During the years 1903 to 1907, Schoenberg moved farther from the harmonic language of the late romantics. In compositions such as *Chamber Symphony,* Op. 9 (1906), for fifteen solo instruments, he uses whole-tone scales and fourth chords.

Atonality Around 1908, Schoenberg finally began to write atonal music. Although it was a revolutionary development, *atonality*—the absence of key—evolved from Schoenberg's earlier emphasis on chromatic harmony and liberal use of all twelve tones in the chromatic scale. But in his atonal works, all twelve tones are used without regard for their traditional relationship to major or minor scales. Dissonances are "emancipated" from the necessity of resolving to consonances. Schoenberg explained atonality as a style based on "emancipation of the dissonance"; it "treats dissonances like consonances and renounces a tonal center. By avoiding the establishment of a key, modulation is excluded, since modulation means leaving an established tonality and establishing another tonality." In Schoenberg's atonal music from 1908 to 1914, triads and the traditional vocabulary of chord progressions are deliberately avoided, as are major and minor scales. But the word *atonality* does not imply a single system of composition. Each atonal composition has its own means of achieving unity. A piece usually grows out of a few short motives that are transformed in many different ways.

Among the best-known of Schoenberg's atonal compositions are Five Pieces for Orchestra, Op. 16 (1909); and *Pierrot lunaire,* Op. 21 (*Moonstruck Pierrot,* 1912), a setting of twenty-one poems, which we'll study. The jagged melodies, novel instrumental effects, and extreme contrasts of dynamics and register in Schoenberg's music are like the distorted figures and shocking colors in expressionist paintings. The texture is polyphonic and very complex. Phrases are of irregular length, and melodic repetition is avoided. Some pieces by Schoenberg embody his concept of a **tone-color melody** (*Klangfarbenmelodie* in German), a succession of varying tone colors used as a musical idea in a composition. *Pierrot lunaire* and other works by Schoenberg call for an unusual style of vocal performance halfway between speaking and singing. In German this is called **Sprechstimme,** a term that literally means *speech-voice.* The vocal part is written in music notation, but small *x*'s on the note stems indicate that the pitches are only approximate.

Schoenberg's atonal language was soon adopted by his students Berg and Webern. Their early atonal works, like Schoenberg's, tended to be extremely emotional and very short. Without a musical system like tonality, the three composers could create extended compositions only when they had a long text to serve as an organizing force.

The Twelve-Tone System During the years 1914 to 1920, Schoenberg finished very few works as he tried to develop a more systematic method of organizing atonal music. In the early 1920s, he finally developed what he called the "method of composing with twelve tones." He partly applied this new technique in Five Piano Pieces, Op. 23, and Serenade, Op. 24, and then fully elaborated it in Suite for Piano, Op. 25. All were composed from 1920 to 1923. These and some other works of the 1920s are less subjective and expressionistic than Schoenberg's earlier and later music. They use traditional forms (such as sonata form) and eighteenth-century dance types (minuet and trio, gavotte, and gigue).

The twelve-tone system enabled Schoenberg to write more extended compositions than he had written when using free atonality. In 1928 he composed the monumental Variations for Orchestra, and in the years 1930 to 1932 he wrote the opera *Moses und Aron* (*Moses and Aaron*). Though he never finished the third act of this masterpiece, the opera has an overwhelming impact. From the time of his arrival in the United States in 1933 to his death in 1951, Schoenberg used the twelve-tone system in many rich and varied works, including his Violin Concerto, Op. 36 (1936); Fourth String Quartet, Op. 37 (1936); and Piano Concerto, Op. 42 (1942); as well as his cantata *A Survivor from Warsaw,* Op. 46 (1947).

The **twelve-tone system** offers the composer a new way of organizing pitch in a composition. It is a twentieth-century alternative to tonality. Unlike the tonal system, which emphasizes one central tone, the twelve-tone system gives equal importance to each of the twelve chromatic tones. The twelve-tone method is a systematized form of atonality. It grew out of Schoenberg's desire to structure his music "*consciously* on a unifying idea."

In a twelve-tone composition, all pitches are derived from a special ordering of the twelve chromatic tones. This ordering or unifying idea is called a **tone row, set,** or **series.** * The composer creates a unique tone row for each specific piece. (Schoenberg's opera *Moses and Aaron* is based entirely on a single tone row.) The choice of rows is practically limitless, since there are 479,001,600 possible arrangements of the twelve chromatic tones. The tone row must be constructed with great care because it vitally affects the total sound and is the source of every melody and chord in a piece. Here is an example of a row, the one used by Schoenberg in his Suite for Piano, Op. 25:

E	F	G	D♭	G♭	E♭	A♭	D	B	C	A	B♭
1	2	3	4	5	6	7	8	9	10	11	12

Notice that no pitch occurs more than once within a row. This prevents any single tone from receiving too much emphasis.

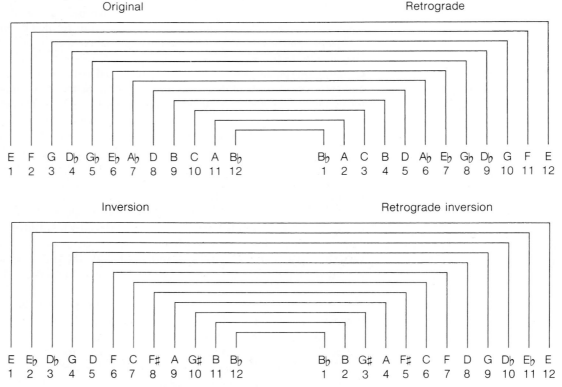

Forms of a tone row: original, retrograde, inversion, and retrograde inversion.

---

*Because of its systematic use of a *series* of tones, the twelve-tone method is also referred to as *serial technique.*

An entire composition is built by manipulating a single twelve-tone row. As shown in the illustration on the previous page, the row may be presented in four basic forms: forward (original form), backward (retrograde), upside down (inversion), and backward and upside down (retrograde inversion). The retrograde (backward) form simply presents the original tone row in reverse. The inverted (upside down) form keeps the original sequence of intervals between tones, but the intervals move in the opposite direction. For example, the original row begins by moving *up* a half step from E to F. The inversion begins by moving *down* a half step from E to E flat:

The retrograde inversion (backward and upside down) presents the tones of the inversion in reverse.

A tone row may be shifted to any pitch level. That is, it may begin on any of the twelve chromatic tones while keeping the original pattern of intervals. This applies to all four forms of the row: original, retrograde, inversion, and retrograde inversion. Since a row may begin on any one of twelve pitches and exist in four forms, there are forty-eight (twelve times four) possible versions of a row. This gives the composer a great deal of flexibility.

Each tone of a row may also be placed in any register, allowing an enormous variety of melodic shapes to be drawn from a single row. For example, given a row that begins with tones E–F–G, a composer could have the tones move upward by step (example *a*) or could have the E leap up to a high F and the F leap down to a low G (example *b*):

This further increases the flexibility of the system and may partially explain why so many twelve-tone melodies have unusually wide leaps. The tones of a row may be presented one after another, to form a melodic line; or at the same time, to form chords. Here is the same row treated in two different ways.

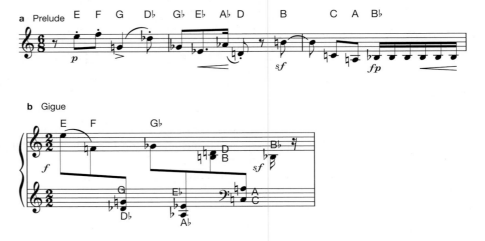

We'll now study two works by Schoenberg: the "freely" atonal *Pierrot Lunaire*, Op. 21 (*Moonstruck Pierrot;* 1912); and the twelve-tone cantata *A Survivor from Warsaw*, Op. 46 (1947), composed almost thirty-five years later.

Pierrot Lunaire, Op. 21 (*Moonstruck Pierrot;* 1912)

Like Stravinsky's *The Rite of Spring*, composed around the same time, Schoenberg's *Pierrot lunaire*, or *Moonstruck Pierrot*, is a revolutionary masterpiece that profoundly influenced twentieth-century music. It is a cycle of twenty-one songs for female voice and an ensemble of five musicians who play eight instruments: piano, cello, violin-viola, flute-piccolo, clarinet–bass clarinet. The instrumental ensemble varies with each piece. For example, *The Sick Moon* (No. 7) uses only the flute; *Prayer to Pierrot* (No. 9) uses the piano and clarinet; and *O Ancient Scent* (No. 21) uses all eight instruments. A song cycle accompanied by a chamber music ensemble—rather than by piano alone—represented a departure from convention. Another novelty was the pervasive use of *Sprechstimme,* the technique of half speaking, half singing developed by Schoenberg. The rhythms and pitches of the words are precisely notated, but the voice touches the notated pitch only momentarily and then departs from it.

Pierrot lunaire is based on weird poems written in 1884 by the Belgian poet Albert Giraud and later translated into German by Schoenberg's friend Otto Erich Hartleben. Many of the poems deal with the puppet Pierrot, a tragic clown character derived from the centuries-old *commedia dell'arte* (Italian improvised theater). Pierrot, who represented the isolated modern artist, was a favorite subject for artists, writers, and musicians of the late nineteenth century and the early twentieth century.

The cycle divides into three groups of seven songs that evoke a surrealistic night vision. In the first group, Pierrot, a poet, drunk on moonlight, becomes increasingly deranged. The second group is a nightmare filled with images of death and martyrdom. In the third group, Pierrot seeks refuge from the nightmare through clowning, sentimentality, and nostalgia. *Pierrot lunaire* is expressionist in its weird text, eerie *Sprechstimme,* unique instrumental effects, and atonal musical language. We'll focus on the opening piece of the cycle, *Mondestrunken* (*Moondrunk*).

Mondestrunken (*Moondrunk*)

Basic Set:
CD 8 **1**

Brief Set:
CD 5 **9**

Scored for voice, piano, flute, violin, and cello, *Mondestrunken* (*Moondrunk*) begins the fantastic nocturnal journey. Its text depicts moonlight as a sacramental "wine we drink through the eyes." The poet (Pierrot) becomes intoxicated as moonlight floods the still horizon with desires that are "horrible and sweet." Like the other poems in *Pierrot lunaire, Mondestrunken* is a rondeau—a verse form—of thirteen lines in which lines 1–2 reappear as lines 7–8 and line 1 repeats as line 13.

Mondestrunken is mostly soft and light in texture. It opens with a high seven-note motive that hypnotically repeats in the piano and evokes a feeling of moonlight.

The pervasive varied recurrence of this ostinato motive in different instruments unifies the piece. Schoenberg's music parallels the changing images of the text. The wine that "the moon pours down in torrents," for example, is depicted by a descending sequence of the motive in the piano and flute.

The poet's intoxication from "the holy drink" is suggested by a sudden *forte,* thick piano chords, and the first appearance of the cello. *Mondestrunken* rounds off with a final appearance of the motive at a slower tempo in the piano and flute.

VOCAL MUSIC GUIDE

SCHOENBERG, *Pierrot lunaire (Moonstruck Pierrot)*

No. 1, *Mondestrunken (Moondrunk)*

1 **9**

Piano, ***pp***, high repeated motive.		
Flute	*Den Wein, den man mit Augen trinkt,*	The wine that with eyes is drunk,
	Giesst Nachts der Mond in Wogen nieder,	at night the moon pours down in waves,
	Und eine Springflut überschwemmt	and a spring-flood overflows
	Den stillen Horizont.	the silent horizon.
Long flute melody, high piano		
	Gelüste, schauerlich und süss.	Desires shuddering and sweet
	Durchschwimmen ohne Zahl die Fluten!	swim countless through the floods!
Piano, flute, motive descends	*Den Wein, den man mit Augen trinkt,*	The wine that with eyes is drunk
	Giesst Nachts der Mond in Woge nieder.	at night the moon pours down in waves.
Sudden ***f***, cello enters.	*Der Dichter, die den Andacht treibt*	The poet, whom devotion inspires
	Berauscht sich an dem heiligen Tranke,	made drunk by the sacred drink,
High violin.	*Gen Himmel wendet er verzückt*	toward heaven he turns
	Das Haupt und taumelnd saugt und schlürft er	his entranced head and, reeling, sucks and slurps
	Den Wein, den man mit Augen trinkt.	the wine that with eyes is drunk.
Piano motive, flute imitates.		

A Survivor from Warsaw, Op. 46 (1947)

Basic Set:
CD 8 **2**

Brief Set:
CD 5 **10**

A Survivor from Warsaw, a dramatic cantata for narrator, male chorus, and orchestra, deals with a single episode in the murder of 6 million Jews by the Nazis during World War II. Schoenberg wrote the text himself, basing it partly on a direct report by one of the few survivors of the Warsaw ghetto. Over 400,000 Jews from this ghetto died in extermination camps or of starvation; many others perished during a heroic revolt against the Nazis in 1943.

The narrator's text is spoken in English, except for some terrifying Nazi commands, which are shouted in German. The narrator's part is a kind of *Sprechstimme,* the novel speech-singing developed by Schoenberg. The rhythms of the spoken words are precisely notated, but their pitch fluctuations are indicated only approximately.

I can-not re-mem-ber ev-'ry-thing,   I must have been un - con-scious most of the time;

Besides English and German, the text includes Hebrew. These were the three languages of Schoenberg's life: German, his native tongue; English, his adopted language in the United States; and Hebrew, the language of the faith to which he returned. The 6-minute cantata builds to an overwhelming conclusion when the male chorus sings in unison the Hebrew words of the prayer *Shema Yisroel* (*Hear, O Israel*). For centuries this has been the prayer of Jewish martyrs in their last agonized moments.

A Survivor from Warsaw is a twelve-tone composition written in 1947, when Schoenberg was seventy-two. The music vividly sets off every detail in the text.

A Survivor from Warsaw opens with a brief orchestral introduction that captures the nightmarish atmosphere which prevailed as Nazi soldiers awakened the Warsaw Jews for transport to death camps. We hear a weirdly shrill reveille in the trumpet and fragmentary sounds in the military drum and high xylophone.

During the narrator's opening lines, Schoenberg already prepares for the concluding Hebrew prayer. As the narrator speaks of "the old prayer they had neglected for so many years," a French horn softly intones the beginning of the melody that is later proclaimed by the chorus.

French horn

pp

An especially vivid musical description comes when the narrator tells how the Nazis counted their victims: "They began again, first slowly: One, two, three, four, became faster and faster. . . ." The music itself becomes faster and louder, building to the powerful entrance of the chorus.

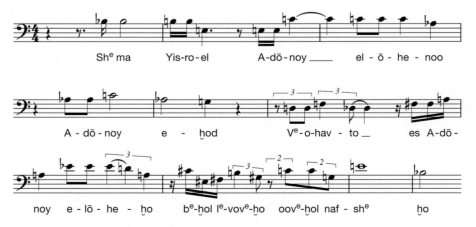

Sh^e ma   Yis-ro-el   A-dō - noy _____   el - ō - he - noo

A - dō - noy   e - hod   V^e-o-hav - to _   es A-dō -

noy   e - lō - he - ho   b^e-hol l^e-vov^e-ho oov^e-hol naf - sh^e   ho

The sung Hebrew contrasts dramatically with the spoken English and German that comes before, and it is the first extended melody in the work.

VOCAL MUSIC GUIDE

SCHOENBERG, *A Survivor from Warsaw*

2 [10]

Orchestral introduction

French
horn, *pp*.

I cannot remember everything. I must have been unconscious most of the time;
I remember only the grandiose moment when they all started
to sing, as if prearranged, the old prayer they had neglected for so
many years—the forgotten creed!

But I have no recollection how I got underground to live in the sewers of Warsaw so
long a time.

The day began as usual. Reveille when it still was dark—get out whether you slept or
whether worries kept you awake the whole night: you had been separated from your children, from your wife, from your parents, you don't know what happened to them; how
could you sleep?

They shouted again: "Get out! The sergeant will be furious!" They came out; some
very slow, the old ones, the sick men, some with nervous agility. They fear the sergeant.
They hurry as much as they can. In vain! Much too much noise, much too much com-
motion and not fast enough!

The Feldwebel shouts: *"Achtung! Still gestanden! Na wird's mal, oder soll ich mit dem
Gewehrkolben nachhelfen? Na jut; wenn Ihr's durchaus haben wollt!"* ("Attention! Stand
still! How about it, or should I help you along with the butt of my rifle? Oh well, if you
really want to have it!")

The sergeant and his subordinates hit everyone: young or old, strong or sick, guilty or
innocent—it was painful to hear the groaning and moaning.

I heard it though I had been hit very hard, so hard that I could not help falling down.
We all on the ground who could not stand up were then beaten over the head.

I must have been unconscious. The next thing I knew was a soldier saying, "They are
all dead!" Whereupon the sergeant ordered to do away with us.

There I lay aside half conscious. It had become very still—fear and pain—Then I
heard the sergeant shouting: *"Abzählen!"* ("Count off!")

3 [11]

They started slowly, and irregularly: One, two, three, four, *"Achtung."* The sergeant
shouted again: *"Rascher! Nochmals von vorn anfangen! In einer Minute will ich wissen
wieviele ich zur Gaskammer abliefere! Abzählen!"* ("Faster! Once more, start from the
beginning! In one minute I want to know how many I am going to send off to the gas
chamber! Count off!")

Accelerando,
crescendo.

They began again, first slowly: one, two, three, four, became faster and faster, so fast
that it finally sounded like a stampede of wild horses, and all of a sudden, in the middle
of it, they began singing the *Shema Yisroel*.

4 [12]

Chorus

*Shema Yisroel Adonoy elohenoo Adonoy eḥod. Veohavto es Adonoy eloheḥo beḥol
levoveḥo oovehol nafsheḥo oovehol meodeḥo. Vehoyoo haddevoreem hoelleh asher
onoḥee metsavveḥo hayyom al levoveḥo. Veshinnantom levoneḥo vedibbarto bom
beshivteḥo beveteḥo oovelehteḥo baddereḥ ooveshoḥbeḥo oovekoomeḥo.* ("Hear,
O Israel, the Lord our God, the Lord is One! And thou shalt love the Lord thy God
with all thy heart, and with all thy soul, and with all thy might. And these words,
which I command thee this day, shall be in thy heart. And thou shalt teach them
diligently unto thy children, and speak of them when thou sittest in thy house, and
when thou goest on the way, and when thou liest down, and when thou risest up."
[Deuteronomy 6:4–9])

10 Alban Berg

Alban Berg (1885–1935), a student of Schoenberg, wrote music that is a unique synthesis of traditional and twentieth-century elements. He combines romantic sounds and time-honored forms with the techniques of free atonality and the twelve-tone system. A wide audience has been attracted by the lyrical warmth, vivid tone colors, and theatrical qualities of Berg's compositions.

Like his teacher, Berg was born in Vienna. He began studying privately with Schoenberg at nineteen and continued working with him from 1904 to 1911. After serving in the Austrian army during World War I, he became codirector (with Schoenberg) of the Society for Private Musical Performances in Vienna. The goal of the society, which lasted from 1918 to 1921, was to "give artists and music-lovers a real and exact knowledge of modern music" through repeated and well-rehearsed performances.

Berg first attracted international attention in 1925, when his opera *Wozzeck* premiered in Berlin. Though its atonality baffled many critics, *Wozzeck* made such a powerful impression on the public that it was soon performed throughout Europe and in the United States.

Perhaps because of chronic ill health, Berg did not perform or conduct, and he composed relatively few works. From the time he finished *Wozzeck* (1922) until his death at the age of fifty, his works include *Chamber Concerto,* for piano, violin, and thirteen winds (1925); *Lyric Suite,* for string quartet (1926); the opera *Lulu* (1929–1935, orchestration not completed); and the Violin Concerto (1935).

Wozzeck (1917–1922)

Wozzeck is the tragic story of a soldier who is driven to murder and madness by a hostile society. An antihero obsessed by strange visions, Wozzeck is persecuted by his sadistic captain, used as a guinea pig by a half-demented doctor, and betrayed by the woman with whom he lives, Marie. Wozzeck stabs Marie to death and drowns while trying to wash her blood from his hands.

Berg's musical imagination was fired in 1914 when he saw *Woyzeck,* a play by the German dramatist and revolutionary Georg Büchner (1813–1837). Though written in the early 1830s, the play is amazingly modern in its starkly realistic dialogue and disconnected scenes. Berg adapted the play into an opera while in the Austrian army in World War I. His own traumatic army experiences may well have deepened his sympathy for Wozzeck.

The opera's nightmarish atmosphere makes it a musical counterpart of expressionist painting and literature. Berg conveys the tensions and torments of the unconscious through harsh dissonances and grotesque distortions. The range of emotions and styles in the music is tremendous. Though most of *Wozzeck* is freely atonal—it does not use the twelve-tone system—major and minor keys occasionally add contrast. The vocal line includes speaking, shrieking, *Sprechstimme,* distorted folk songs, and melodies with wide leaps that are difficult to sing. The gigantic orchestra closely parallels the dialogue and stage action. Descriptive effects include vivid orchestral depictions of the moon rising, frogs croaking, and water engulfing the drowning Wozzeck. Berg's music rapidly shifts between very high and very low registers, between *ffff* and *pppp*.

Wozzeck has three acts, each with five scenes. Connecting the scenes are short orchestral interludes that comment musically on the preceding action and serve as preparation for what is to come. As in Wagner's music dramas, there is a continuous musical flow within each act, and characters are associated with specific musical ideas. A novel feature of *Wozzeck* is that the music for each scene is a self-contained composition with a particular form (passacaglia, sonata form, etc.) or of a definite type (military march, lullaby). The five scenes of the last act—we'll study scenes 4 and 5—are organized as (1) variations on a theme, (2) variations on a single tone, (3) variations on a rhythmic pattern, (4) variations on a chord, and (5) variations on continuous running notes. But Berg did not intend for the listener to concentrate on or even be aware of these unifying techniques. He wanted the audience to be caught up in the opera's dramatic flow.

In Act II, Wozzeck has been driven to desperation by Marie's infidelity and by a savage beating from the man who has slept with her. Near the beginning of Act III, Wozzeck stabs Marie to death as they walk along a forest path near a pond.

Act III: Scenes 4 and 5

Basic Set:
CD 8 5

Scene 4: A path near a pond Wozzeck returns to the scene of the crime to dispose of his knife. Berg's orchestra vividly evokes the dark forest scene as a background to Wozzeck's anguished shrieks. Rising harp tones suggest the blood-red moon coming up through the clouds. Wozzeck goes mad and drowns in the pond while trying to wash the blood from his hands. Soft chromatic slides depict the engulfing water as the Captain and the Doctor, Wozzeck's tormentors, indifferently comment that someone is drowning. As Wozzeck drowns, the slides become slower and narrower in range.

The long orchestral interlude that follows is a deeply moving expression of grief for Wozzeck's tragic fate. It recalls the musical themes associated with his life. Berg described it as "a confession of the author stepping outside the dramatic events of the theater and appealing to the public as representing mankind." For this outpouring of compassion, Berg returns to tonality (the interlude is in D minor) and the musical language of late romanticism.

Basic Set:
CD 8 9

Scene 5: A street before Marie's door Children are playing in front of Marie's house; bright sunshine brings a glaring contrast to the darkness of the preceding scenes. One of the children cruelly tells Wozzeck's son: "Hey! Your mother is dead." The boy rides off on his hobby horse with the other children to see the body. The orchestra is reduced in size to produce delicate sounds that match the children's high voices, and a continuous rhythm symbolizes their utter indifference.

The opera does not end with a conclusive chord. It simply breaks off as though to suggest that the tragedy could begin again.

The concluding scene of *Wozzeck* in a production by the Metropolitan Opera.

VOCAL MUSIC GUIDE

BERG, *Wozzeck,* Act III, scenes 4 and 5

Scene 4

5   0:00

Winds, *p*,
repeated chord.

(Forest path by the pond. Moonlit night as before. Wozzeck staggers on hastily, and then stops as he searches for something.)

Wozzeck

Spoken
(*Sprechstimme*).

Das Messer? Wo ist das Messer? Ich hab's dagelassen . . . Näher, noch näher. Mir graut's! Da regt sich was. Still! Alles still und tot . . .

The knife! Where's the knife?
I left it somewhere here . . . Somewhere . . .
It's terrifying! Something's moving
Silence . . . Everything's silent and dead!

Shouted.

Mörder! Mörder! Ha! Da ruft's. Nein, ich selbst.

Murder! Murder! Someone called . . .
No, it was me

(Still searching, he staggers forward a few more steps, and comes on the corpse.)

Marie! Marie! Was hast du für eine rote Schnur um den Hals? Hast Dir das rote Halsband verdient, wie die Ohrringlein, mit Deiner Sünde! Was hängen Dir die schwarzen Haare so wild? Mörder! Mörder! Sie werden nach mir suchen . . .
Das Messer verrät mich!

Marie! Marie! What is that
red cord round your neck? Did you
earn this red necklace, like those gold
earrings? A reward for your sins?
Why is your lovely dark hair so
unruly? Murder! Murder! They'll be
looking for me
that knife will betray me
(*seeks it feverishly*)

Da, da ist's. So! Da hinunter. Es taucht ins dunkle Wasser wie ein Stein.

Ah, here it is! (At the pond) Into the
water! (Throws the knife in) It sinks into
the dark water like a stone.

6   1:55

Rising harp
tones, *pp*.

(The moon comes up blood-red through the clouds.)

Aber der Mond verrät mich . . . der Mond ist blutig. Will denn die ganze Welt es ausplaudern?!—Das Messer, es liegt zu weit vorn, sie finden's beim Baden oder wenn sie nach Muscheln tauchen. Ich find's nicht . . . Aber ich muss mich waschen. Ich bin blutig. Da ein Fleck . . . und noch einer. Weh! Weh!
Ich wasche mich mit Blut!

But the moon betrays me
The moon is bloody. Will the whole
world be talking about it? The knife
It's too near the shore, they'll find it
while swimming Or when they look
for mussels. (Wades in) I can't find it
I must wash myself. I'm all bloody
There's a spot here . . . and here!
Woe! Woe!
I'm washing myself in blood!

7   3:03

Water music.
Upward orchestral
slides, *pp*. Rhythm
gradually slows.

Das Wasser is Blut . . . Blut . . .

The water is blood . . . blood . . .
(He drowns.)

(After a short time the Doctor enters, followed by the Captain.)

Captain

Spoken.

Halt!

Stop!

Doctor

(Stands still)

Hören Sie? Dort!

Do you hear? Over there!

Captain
(Stands still)

Jesus! Das war ein Ton.	Jesus! I heard a sound.

Doctor
(Pointing to the pond.)

Ja, dort!	Yes, over there.

Captain

Es ist das Wasser im Teich. Das Wasser ruft. Es ist schon lange Niemand ertrunken. Kommen Sie, Doktor! Es ist nicht gut zu hören.	It's the water in the pond. The water calls out. It's a long time since anyone drowned here. Come away, Doctor! It's not good to hear it.

(He tries to drag the Doctor off.)

Doctor
(Stands still and listens.)

Das stöhnt . . . als stürbe ein Mensch. Da ertrinkt Jemand!	It groans . . . It sounds like a dying man . . . Someone's drowning there.

3:59
Celesta.

Captain

Unheimlich! Der Mond rot und die Nebel grau. Hören Sie? . . . Jetzt wieder das Ächzen.	It's eerie . . .The moon is red and the mist is . . . gray. Did you hear? It's groaning again.

Doctor

Stiller, . . . jetzt ganz still.	It's fainter. . . . and now quite silent.

Captain

Kommen Sie! Kommen Sie schnell.	Come away! Hurry!

(Drags the Doctor off with him.)

8 **4:40**
Extended
orchestral
interlude.

Scene 5

(Street before Marie's door. Bright morning. Sunshine. Children are playing and shouting. Marie's child is riding a hobbyhorse.)

Children

9 **7:40**

Ringel, Ringel, Rosenkranz, Ringel-reih'n! Ringel, Ringel, Rosenkranz, Rin . . .	Ring around the rosie Ring around the rosie

(They stop, and other children come rushing on.)

One of them

Du Käthe! . . . Die Marie . . .	Hey, Katie! You know about Marie?

Second Child

Was is?	What?

First Child

Weisst' es nit? Sie sind schon Alle'naus.	I don't know, they've all gone there.

Third Child
(To Marie's child.)

Du! Dein Mutter ist tot!	Hey, you! Your mother's dead.

Marie's Child
(Still riding his horse.)

Hopp, hopp! Hopp, hopp! Hopp, hopp!   Hop, hop! Hop, hop! Hop, hop!

Second Child

Wo is sie denn?   So where is she?

First Child

Draus' leigt sie, am Weg, neben dem   She's over there, by the pond, lying on the
Teich.   path.

Third Child

Kommt, anschaun!   Come, let's have a look!
(All the children run off.)

Marie's Child
(Continues to ride.)

Hopp, hopp! Hopp, hopp! Hopp, hopp!   Hop, hop! Hop, hop! Hop, hop!
Music breaks off.   (He hesitates for a moment, then rides off after the other children.)

11 Anton Webern

Neglected during his lifetime, Anton Webern (1883–1945) did not live to see his music influence composers throughout the world during the 1950s and 1960s.

Webern was born in Vienna, the son of a mining engineer. As a young man, he composed constantly and studied piano, cello, and music theory. At eighteen, he entered the University of Vienna, and later he earned a doctorate in music history. While at the university, he studied composition privately with Arnold Schoenberg.

After finishing his studies with Schoenberg, Webern earned a modest living conducting various orchestras and choruses. His career was solid but unspectacular. His most important position was as director of the Vienna Workers' Symphony Concerts, where traditional and contemporary compositions were performed for a working-class audience. The rare performances of his own works were usually met with ridicule.

Webern was a shy man, devoted to his wife and children. He was a Christian mystic who loved to commune with nature while mountain-climbing in the Austrian Alps. "It is not the beautiful landscape, the beautiful flowers in the usual romantic sense, that moves me," he wrote to his friend Alban Berg. "My object is the deep, bottomless, inexhaustible meaning in all. I love all nature, but most of all that which is found in the mountains."

With the rise of Nazism in Austria in 1934, Webern's orchestra and chorus—which had been sponsored by the Social Democratic party—were dissolved. In 1938, when Nazi Germany annexed Austria, Webern lost his job with the government radio, and his music was banned. He had to earn a living by proofreading for his Viennese publisher.

Webern's life seems ordinary enough, but his death was a bizarre tragedy. Toward the end of World War II, he took refuge from the bombing of Vienna in the small Austrian town of Mittersill. His daughter lived there with her husband and three children.

In 1945, victorious American soldiers occupied the town; on the night of September 15 they arrested Webern's son-in-law, who was suspected of dealing in the black market. During the questioning, Webern and his wife—who were unaware of their son-in-law's activities—went into the bedroom, where their grandchildren were sleeping. Later, Webern stepped outside the house to smoke a cigar without disturbing the children. Minutes later, an American soldier left the house and bumped into Webern in the darkness. Nervous because he was in a hostile foreign country, the soldier mistakenly thought he was being attacked. He fired three shots, and Webern was dead.

Webern's Music

Poetic lyricism pervades Webern's music, which is amazingly original in its brevity, quietness, and concentration. Webern distills a musical universe into miniatures lasting only 2 or 3 minutes; every single tone is of crucial importance, so that the listener experiences time with a new intensity. Schoenberg aptly observed that Webern "expressed a novel in a single gesture, a joy in a breath."

Rarely has a composer achieved such worldwide influence on the basis of so little music; virtually all of Webern's mature music can be played in less than 3½ hours. Choral works and songs make up about half of his output. The rest is music written for chamber orchestra or small chamber groups (as in his Quartet for Clarinet, Tenor Saxophone, Violin, and Piano, Op. 22, 1930). Webern's first atonal works date from 1908 to 1909, around the same time as Schoenberg's. He adopted the twelve-tone system in the late 1920s, not long after his teacher had developed it.

Webern exploited Schoenberg's idea of a "melody built of tone colors." His melodic lines are "atomized" into two- or three-note fragments which are presented in continually changing tone colors and registers. He forces us to focus on the tone color, dynamic level, and register of each note. At first his music may seem like isolated wisps of sound, but repeated hearings reveal that the fragments add up to a unified whole.

The texture of Webern's music is delicate and transparent; usually not more than a few solo instruments play at once. In his twelve-tone works, there is often strict polyphonic imitation among the lines of the texture. This technique may well reflect Webern's profound knowledge of Renaissance choral music, in which polyphonic imitation is so important. Texture, tone color, and dynamics play a crucial role in creating form in Webern's music.

Composers in the 1950s and 1960s used Webern's special way of manipulating a tone row as a musical point of departure. They were fascinated by his use of texture, tone color, dynamics, and register as unifying elements, and they often imitated the deceptively "cool" sound of his later music. Works that appealed to very few during Webern's lifetime have become a source of inspiration since his death.

Five Pieces for Orchestra, Op. 10 (1911–1913)

Webern's unique style is fully revealed in his early, atonal Five Pieces for Orchestra, Op. 10, composed before he adopted the twelve-tone system. These five "expressions of musical lyricism," as Webern called them, are among the shortest orchestral compositions ever written. The fourth piece is only 6⅓ measures long and lasts less than 30 seconds. Webern's chamber orchestra of eighteen soloists includes unconventional instruments like the mandolin, guitar, cowbells, and harmonium (a small organ with metal reeds). Each piece (we'll consider the third) is scored for a different number and combination of instruments.

Melodic fragments are whispered by ever-changing solo instruments and framed by poetic silences. Tone-color melodies replace "tunes" in this music. There are few notes, but each is crucial. The tempo continually fluctuates. Brasses and strings are usually muted.

Basic Set:
CD 8 **10**

Brief Set:
CD 5 [13]

Third Piece:
Very slow and extremely calm

With its bell sounds coming as though from far off, the third piece has a feeling of solitude and eerie stillness. The dynamics never rise above ***pp***. The sustained bell-like sounds—produced by mandolin, celesta, guitar, harp, glockenspiel, cowbells, chimes, and harmonium—are heard both at the beginning and at the end. This creates a vague A B A′ effect. Melodic fragments in ever-changing solo instruments are set apart from one another by brief moments of near silence.

LISTENING OUTLINE

WEBERN, Third Piece from Five Pieces for Orchestra

Clarinet, muted French horn, muted trombone, harmonium, mandolin, guitar, celesta, harp, bass drum, snare drum, chimes, cowbells, violin, muted viola, muted cello

Very slow and extremely calm

(Duration, 1:28)

10 [13] 0:00	**1. a.**	Pulsating bell-like sounds, ***ppp***.
	b.	Violin, ***pp***, pulsating bell-like sounds, ***ppp***.
	c.	Muted horn, ***pp***, chimes, ***ppp***.
0:38	**2.**	Quicker notes in clarinet. Muted viola.
0:47	**3. a.**	Pulsating bell-like sounds, ***ppp***.
	b.	Muted trombone, ***ppp***; pulsating bell-like sounds, ***ppp***. Snare drum roll, extremely soft.

12 Béla Bartók

Béla Bartók (1881–1945), whose music is infused with the spirit of east European folk song, was born in the Hungarian town of Nagyszentmiklós. When Bartók was seven, his father died; his mother was forced to move with her son from town to town while she earned a living as a schoolteacher. She gave him his first lessons on the piano, an instrument which had an important role in his career. For twenty-seven years (1907–1934), Bartók taught piano at his alma mater, the Budapest Academy of Music, and gave recitals throughout Europe.

During the early 1900s, Bartók was influenced by the nationalist movement that swept Hungary. He came to love the music of Hungarian peasants, and he spent most of his free time in tiny villages recording folk songs on a cylinder phonograph. Bartók became a leading authority on the peasant music of the Magyars, Romanians, Slovaks, and Turks, and the Arabs of north Africa. Soon his own music was profoundly affected by the folk music he knew so well.

Though Bartók was recognized abroad as an important composer early in his career, he was neglected in Hungary. For a time after 1911, he even refused to play in Hungary because of the "indifference and animosity" of the Hungarians. It was only after the successful Budapest premiere of his ballet *The Wooden Prince* in 1917 that Bartók's music gained acceptance in his homeland.

Béla Bartók.

During the 1920s, he performed his own works throughout Europe. He also made a tour of the United States in 1927 and 1928; one American newspaper warned readers: "Hungarian modernist advances upon Los Angeles to convince scoffers." By 1939 he was able to report gleefully to his son, "Since 1934, I have worked almost exclusively upon commissions!"

Hitler's rise posed a serious problem for Bartók, who was vehemently anti-Nazi. After the annexation of Austria by Germany in 1938, Bartók wrote to a friend: "There is the imminent danger that Hungary will also surrender to this system of robbery and murder. How I could then continue to live or—which amounts to the same thing—work in such a country is quite inconceivable." Bartók did not allow his music to be performed in Germany or on any radio station that could be heard in Germany or Italy.

In 1940, Bartók emigrated to the United States, where he was to spend the last five years of his life. This was a bleak period for him; he had little money, he was in poor health, and he felt isolated and neglected.

"My career as a composer is as much as finished," he wrote in 1942. "The quasi boycott of my works by the leading orchestras continues. . . ." For three years he stopped composing. He held a position as a research scholar in folk music at Columbia University, but his grant ended before he could finish his work. In 1943, his health declined

Caught up in the nationalist movement that swept Hungary, Bartók spent most of his free time in tiny villages recording folk songs on a cylinder phonograph.

alarmingly. After his weight fell to 87 pounds, he entered a New York hospital; while there, he unexpectedly received a commission for the Concerto for Orchestra, which is now his best-known work. The success of its first performance in 1944 resulted in a series of commissions for the once ignored composer. Tragically, Bartók had only a year to live and could write just two more compositions, his Sonata for Solo Violin (1944) and Third Piano Concerto (1945).

Soon after his death in New York in 1945, Bartók became one of the most popular twentieth-century composers.

Bartók's Music

"I do not reject any influence," wrote Bartók, "whether its source be Slovak, Romanian, Arab, or some other; provided this source be pure, fresh and healthy." But he emphasized that the "Hungarian influence is the strongest."

Bartók evolved a completely individual style that fused folk elements, classical forms, and twentieth-century sounds. He believed that peasant music helped liberate him from the "exclusive rule of the major or minor system." Most folk melodies, he observed, "adhere to the old church modes or the ancient Greek modes and certain still older modes (especially pentatonic), and moreover display extremely free and varied rhythmic structures and changes of meter. . . ." Bartók arranged many Hungarian and Romanian folk tunes, often giving them highly dissonant accompaniments. In most of his works, however, Bartók does not quote folk melodies; he uses original themes that have a folk flavor. His aim was to "assimilate the idiom of peasant music so completely" that he could "forget all about it and use it as his mother tongue."

Bartók's genius found its most characteristic expression in instrumental music. He wrote many works for piano solo, six string quartets, other chamber music, three concertos for piano, two concertos for violin, and several compositions for orchestra. Bartók's music embraces a wide range of emotions and is deeply expressive. Fast movements can convey a primitive brutality or the vitality and swing of a peasant dance. Slow movements often suggest feelings of bleakness and profound pessimism. They frequently contain atmospheric, almost impressionistic music suggesting nocturnal insect noises and the chirping of birds. Such mysterious passages are known as Bartók's "night music."

Bartók revitalized and reinterpreted traditional forms such as the rondo, fugue, and sonata form. He unifies the contrasting movements of a composition by bringing back a theme in transformed versions. He also creates formal unity by beginning and ending a movement in the same way. For example, the second movement of his Concerto for Orchestra (1943) opens and closes with a solo on the side drum (without snares). Polyphonic imitation and motivic development often generate tension and excitement.

Bartók always organized his works around a tonal center. Within this tonal framework, he often used harsh dissonances, polychords, and tone clusters—although in some of his late works he returned to a more traditional and less dissonant vocabulary. Rhythmically, Bartók's music is characterized by a powerful beat, unexpected accents, and changing meters. The irregular meters and asymmetrical rhythmic patterns of east European folk music are used imaginatively. (See the example from Bartók's *Six Dances in Bulgarian Rhythm* in Section 1, page 369.)

Bartók was also imaginative in his use of tone colors, particularly of percussion instruments. In works such as Music for Strings, Percussion, and Celesta (1936) and Sonata for Two Pianos and Percussion (1937), he drew unusual sounds from the xylophone and timpani. Bartók was especially fond of glissandos on the timpani (this sliding effect is produced by a pedal mechanism). Like many twentieth-century composers, Bartók drew percussive, drumlike sounds from the piano as well.

Bartók's six string quartets are widely thought to be among the finest since those of Beethoven. The works abound in exciting glissandos and in pizzicatos that produce a "snap" when the string rebounds against the fingerboard. But Bartók's string quartets are more than a collection of novel sounds; they reflect the composer's profundity and nobility of spirit.

Concerto for Orchestra (1943)

The commission that led to Bartók's Concerto for Orchestra was offered to him in 1943, while he was hospitalized in New York City. Serge Koussevitzky, the conductor of the Boston Symphony Orchestra, offered him $1,000 for a new work. While recuperating at Saranac Lake, New York, Bartók was able to work "practically day and night" on his new composition. He finished it in six weeks. Concerto for Orchestra was an enormous success at its premiere in Boston in 1944 and has since become Bartók's most popular work.

"The general mood of the work," wrote Bartók, "represents, apart from the jesting second movement, a gradual transition from the sternness of the first movement and the lugubrious death-song of the third, to the life-assertion of the last one." Bartók explained that the unusual title reflects the work's "tendency to treat the single orchestral instruments in a *concertant* or soloistic manner."

Indeed, Concerto for Orchestra is a showpiece for an orchestra of virtuosos. It is romantic in spirit because of its emotional intensity, memorable themes, and vivid contrasts of mood. Though its melodies were created by Bartók, they have a distinct folk flavor. The concerto is an example of Bartók's mellow "late" style, which is characterized by more frequent use of traditional chords. In all five movements, time-honored procedures like A B A form, sonata form, and fugue are fused with twentieth-century rhythms and tone colors. We'll focus on the first and second movements.

First Movement: *Introduction*
Andante non troppo; Allegro vivace

Basic Set:

CD 8 **11**

The concerto begins with an extended slow introductory section based on two melodic ideas that grow in intensity as they are varied. Low cellos and double basses mysteriously introduce the first idea, a short phrase that climbs and then falls. This phrase returns twice, each time ascending higher before it descends. The flute then softly introduces the second thematic idea, an exotic-sounding figure that circles around a single tone. This theme also returns twice. First it is varied and expanded by the trumpets playing very softly, and then it is transformed into a passionate outcry by the strings.

The allegro vivace is in a kind of sonata form. Themes are broken into fragments that are shifted among different instruments. In this movement there are frequent alternations between fast, powerful sections featuring strings and brasses and slower, calmer sections in which woodwinds are most prominent.

The assertive opening theme of the exposition is marked by the rapidly changing meter so typical of twentieth-century music.

Its descending second phrase is an inversion, or upside-down form, of the ascending first phrase.

Before the contrasting second theme enters, the trombone plays a somber phrase. This has an important role later in the movement. The atmosphere of the middle east is evoked by the plaintive second theme, which is first played by the oboe. It features an alternation between two tones, and it has the static, dronelike accompaniment common in folk music.

In the development section, the trombone motive from the exposition grows into an exciting brass fanfare. It is polyphonically imitated among the trombones, trumpets, French horns, and tuba. The recapitulation of the movement is unusual because the second theme comes before—rather than after—the first theme. The allegro vivace ends decisively with the trombone motive, played in unison by all the brasses.

LISTENING OUTLINE

BARTÓK, Concerto for Orchestra

First Movement: *Introduction* (Andante non troppo; Allegro vivace)

Sonata form

Piccolo, 3 flutes, 3 oboes, English horn, 3 clarinets, bass clarinet, 3 bassoons, 4 French horns, 3 trumpets, 3 trombones, tuba, timpani, cymbals, 2 harps, 1st violins, 2d violins, violas, cellos, double basses

(Duration, 10:14)

Andante non troppo (slow introduction)

11 0:00   **1. a.** Low strings, ***p***, ascending and descending phrase. High string tremolo, ***pp***, flutes.

0:35   **b.** Low strings, ***p***, phrase ascends higher, then descends. High string tremolo, ***pp***, flutes.

1:06   **c.** Low strings, phrase ascends still higher, then descends.

12 1:27   **2. a.** Flute, ***p***, new phrase. Strings, ***p***.

1:59   **b.** Trumpets, ***pp***, new phrase varied and extended. Strings in background.

2:35   **c.** Violins, ***f***, new phrase transformed into forceful melody.

13 2:57   **d.** Crescendo, bass motive repeated faster and faster, leading into

Allegro vivace

Exposition

First theme

14 3:28   **1. a.** Violins, ***f***, main theme. Fast tempo. Violin melody becomes slightly softer. Crescendo to ***f***.

15 4:17   **b.** Trombone motive, ***mf***. Flute, ***p***, descending melody.

Second theme

16 4:35   **2. a.** Oboe, ***p***, folklike melody, slower tempo. Strings and harp accompany.

4:57   **b.** Folklike melody repeated and extended by clarinets, flutes, ***p***. Strings and harp accompany.

Development

17 5:51   **1.** Orchestra, *f*, fragments of main theme in imitation. Allegro vivace. Crescendo to *ff*.

6:27   **2.** Clarinet, *p*, new legato melody, slower tempo. Melody extended by English horn, flute, *p*.

18 7:05   **3.** Strings, *ff*. Brasses, trombone motive in imitation. Allegro vivace. Orchestra, *fff*, high sustained tone.

Recapitulation

Second theme

19 8:06   **1. a.** Clarinet, *p*, folklike melody, slower tempo. Strings and harp accompany.

8:30   **b.** Folklike melody repeated and extended by flutes, oboe, *p*. Strings and harp accompany.

9:12   **c.** Low strings alternate with higher woodwinds. Crescendo and accelerando to

First theme

9:30   **2.** Orchestra, *ff*, main theme. Allegro vivace. Brasses, *ff*, trombone motive ends movement.

Basic Set:
CD 7 20

Brief Set:
CD 5 **14**

Second Movement: *Game of Pairs* Allegretto scherzando

The jesting second movement, *Game of Pairs,* which is in A B A' form, is a "game" involving different pairs of woodwind and brass instruments. The melodic lines of each pair are in parallel motion and are separated by a distinctive pitch interval.

In the opening section (A), pairs of bassoons, oboes, clarinets, flutes, and muted trumpets play a chain of five melodies consecutively. The contrasting middle section (B) is a hymnlike melody played softly by brass instruments. When the opening section returns (A'), it has a more active accompaniment. The incisive sound of a side drum (without snares) is prominent throughout the movement. It plays syncopated solos at the beginning and the end, as well as in the hymnlike middle section.

LISTENING OUTLINE

BARTÓK, Concerto for Orchestra

Second Movement: *Game of Pairs* (Allegretto scherzando)

A B A' form, duple meter ($\frac{2}{4}$)

2 flutes, 2 oboes, 2 clarinets, 3 bassoons, 4 French horns, 2 trumpets, 2 trombones, tuba, timpani, side drum, 2 harps, 1st violins, 2d violins, violas, cellos, double basses

(Duration, 6:40)

A

20 **14** 0:00   **1.** Solo side drum (without snares), *mf*.

0:12   **2.** Two bassoons, *p*, accompanied by pizzicato strings.

21 **15** 0:36   **3. a.** Two oboes, *p*, in higher register. Pizzicato strings accompany.

b. Low strings, pizzicato, while oboes sustain tones.

22 **16** 1:05   **4. a.** Two clarinets.

b. Low strings, accented notes.

23 **17** 1:27   **5. a.** Two flutes, *mf*, in higher register.

b. Low strings, pizzicato, while flutes sustain tones.

24 **18** 2:14   **6.** Two muted trumpets, *p*. Muted string tremolos, *pp*, in background.

B

25 19 3:02   **1. a.** Brasses, *mf*, hymnlike legato melody. Side drum accompanies.
                        b. French horns, *p*, conclude hymnlike melody and sustain chord.
                    2. Oboe, flute, and clarinet, *p*, lead to

A′

26 20 4:09   **1.** Two bassoons, *p*, opening melody. Staccato third bassoon in background.
        4:33   **2. a.** Two oboes, *p*, in higher register. Clarinets and strings in background.
                        b. Low strings, pizzicato, while oboes sustain tones.
        4:50   **3. a.** Two clarinets. Flutes and strings in background.
                        b. Low strings, accented notes.
        5:19   **4. a.** Two flutes, *mf*, in higher register. Woodwinds and strings in background.
                        b. Low strings, pizzicato, while flutes sustain tones.
        5:44   **5.** Two muted trumpets, *mf*. Harp glissandos and muted string tremolos in background.
        6:20   **6.** Woodwinds, *p*, repeated chord; solo side drum, decrescendo, ends *Game of Pairs*.

13 Dmitri Shostakovich

The career of Dmitri Shostakovich (1906–1975), one of the leading composers of the Soviet Union, illustrates the dilemma that confronted artists who lived under a totalitarian regime. Starting around 1929, the Soviet dictator Joseph Stalin used terror, show trials, labor camps, and mass murder to promote rapid industrialization and collectivization of agriculture. Artistic expression, like other kinds of human activity, came increasingly under the domination of the Communist Party. Composers were obliged to follow the doctrine of "socialist realism," which demanded that they reject modernism and emphasize everything that is "heroic, bright, and beautiful." Music had to be accessible and melodic, and avoid excessive dissonance and complexity. Leading composers like Prokofiev and Shostakovich were highly honored members of Soviet society, but—like everyone else—they were forced to follow the dictates of the Communist Party. Today a debate rages about whether Shostakovich was a devoted servant of the Communist regime or a secret dissident whose music conveys a revolt that could not be expressed in words.

Shostakovich began his advanced musical studies after the Russian Revolution (1917). At the early age of thirteen he entered the Petrograd Conservatory, where his enormous talents as pianist and composer were immediately recognized. (The city Petrograd was later renamed Leningrad and today is known as St. Petersburg, its name before the Russian Revolution.) Three years later, his father died and the young Shostakovich played piano for silent movies to support his mother and two sisters. His First Symphony (1926), written as a graduation piece, won great acclaim at its Russian premiere and was soon performed by major orchestras in Germany and the United States.

In 1934, the opera *Lady Macbeth of the Mtsensk District* established Shostakovich as a major figure in twentieth-century music. Though the opera was "modernistic" in its dissonance, violence, pessimism, and sexual explicitness, it had an extraordinary initial success in the Soviet Union and was soon performed throughout the world. However, in 1936, two years after its premiere, Stalin walked out on a performance of the opera. Soon afterward, a vicious editorial in the official Communist Party paper

Pravda denounced *Lady Macbeth* as "chaos instead of music," and the work was withdrawn from the stage. Shostakovich regained official favor in 1937 as a result of the extraordinary success and accessible style of his Fifth Symphony (which we'll study).

Hitler's attack on the Soviet Union and the siege of Leningrad in 1941 spurred Shostakovich to compose his Seventh (*Leningrad*) Symphony. Even before its premiere in Leningrad, millions of Americans heard the Seventh Symphony in a radio broadcast by the NBC Symphony, and orchestras around the world performed it as a symbol of the Soviet resistance against Nazi Germany. Shostakovich's picture was even on the cover of *Time* magazine in 1942.

In 1948, however, Shostakovich again fell into official disfavor. Together with Prokofiev and other leading Soviet composers, he was accused of following "the cult of atonality, dissonance, and discord." His compositions were blacklisted, he was forced to repent publicly, and he was dismissed from his teaching post. A year later he returned to favor after Stalin personally asked him to represent the Soviet Union at a World Peace Congress in New York.

Stalin's death in 1953 and the Soviet leader Nikita Khrushchev's revelations of Stalin's crimes in 1956 led the Communist Party to slightly relax its iron grip on the arts. Nevertheless, in 1962, Shostakovich angered the authorities when he used *Babi Yar,* a poem by the Russian poet Yevgeny Yevtushenko about Jews massacred by the Nazis in Kiev, as the text of the opening movement of his Thirteenth Symphony, for bass soloist, chorus of basses, and orchestra. Because of Soviet anti-Semitism, the poet and composer had to alter the text of *Babi Yar,* and few Russian conductors at that time dared to program the Thirteenth Symphony.

Shostakovich composed an enormous quantity of music in almost every genre, including fifteen symphonies, fifteen string quartets, chamber music with piano, concertos, piano music, operas, songs, and film music. His highly personal works encompass a wide variety of styles but are generally rooted in tonality. Often, his music shifts suddenly from satire to lyricism, from marchlike episodes to grotesquely humorous passages.

The Seventh (*Leningrad*) Symphony by Dmitri Shostakovich became a symbol of the Soviet Union's resistance against Nazi Germany, and the composer's picture appeared on the cover of *Time* magazine in 1942.

Symphony No. 5 in D Minor

The Fifth Symphony (1937), now Shostakovich's most popular work, rehabilitated Shostakovich after he was officially denounced for the modernism of his opera *Lady Macbeth of the Mtsensk District* (1934), as we have seen. In 1938, Shostakovich—or someone writing in his name—described the symphony as "a Soviet artist's practical creative response to just criticism." Indeed, the Fifth Symphony has wide appeal because of its lyrical melodies, exciting climaxes, and accessible musical language.

The symphony has four movements. In the opening sonata-form movement, Shostakovich transforms a lyrical melody from the first theme group into an aggressive march within the development section. The second movement, which we'll study, is a scherzo. The third movement is an extended, mournful largo. The driving finale is in minor but ends with a powerful coda in major.

Second Movement: Allegretto

Basic Set:
CD 8 **27**

The second movement, a scherzo in A B A' form, conveys the sarcastic humor characteristic of Shostakovich's music. Shostakovich creates effects of mockery from contrasts between low and high registers, from instruments like the xylophone and a shrill piccolo, from staccato and pizzicato melodies, and from phrases that include slides between tones (glissandos). The opening section of the movement (A) includes two extended themes, each in a minor key. A brusque phrase in the cellos and double basses introduces the first theme, which is lightly orchestrated. The second theme is a grotesque waltz played by the full orchestra.

The middle section (B) brings a shift from minor to major, from the boisterousness of the full orchestra to the relaxed playfulness of a lilting melody played by a solo violin and flute. Glissandos (slides) in the violin melody create a feeling of parody.

When the opening section returns (A'), it is initially hushed, sounding like a ghost of its former self, as in the scherzo of Beethoven's Fifth Symphony. Its introductory phrase is played *p* by staccato bassoon and contrabassoon, in contrast to the *ff* of the cellos and basses at the opening of section A. The first theme is now presented entirely by pizzicato violins and cellos, rather than by the high clarinet and bassoons. Shostakovich rounds off the movement with a coda that mockingly recalls the lilting phrase opening the middle section (B). Now played by the oboe, the varied phrase appears in minor rather than in major.

LISTENING OUTLINE

SHOSTAKOVICH, Symphony No. 5 in D Minor

Second Movement: Allegretto

A B A' coda form, triple meter ($\frac{3}{4}$), A minor

Piccolo, 2 flutes, 2 oboes, 3 clarinets, 2 bassoons, contrabassoon, 4 French horns, 3 trumpets, 3 trombones, tuba, timpani, snare drum, cymbals, 2 harps, 1st violins, 2d violins, violas, cellos, double basses

(Duration 4:50)

A

27 0:00   **1. a.** Cellos and basses in unison, *ff*, introductory phrase, heavy detached notes,

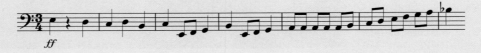

French horns, *f*.

28 0:14
b. First theme in minor, staccato, high clarinet,

theme continues in bassoons, then in violins, crescendo to

29 0:50
2. a. Grotesque waltz theme in minor, high woodwinds, *f*, cymbals punctuate;

French horns, *ff*, martial tune, timpani, snare drum.

1:11
b. High violins, *f*, repeat waltz theme; French horns, *ff*, martial tune; orchestra unison, *ff*, staccato French horns introduce

B
30 1:37
3. a. Solo violin, *p*, lilting melody in major with glissandos (slides), harp, pizzicato cellos accompany.

1:59
b. Flute, *p*, repeats lilting melody, accompanied by bassoons and pizzicato strings; sudden *f*, staccato strings in unison; French horns, *ff*.

2:29
c. Sudden *p*, flowing violin line joined by lilting melody phrase in woodwinds; sudden *ff* in orchestra; high, staccato woodwinds in unison, *ff*, French horns, *ff*.

2:51
d. Sudden *p*, flowing violin line joined by lilting melody phrase in woodwinds; sudden *ff* in orchestra, decrescendo to

A′
31 3:03
4. a. Bassoon and contrabassoon in unison, *p*, introductory phrase, staccato.

b. First theme in minor, high pizzicato violins, *p*, theme continues in pizzicato cellos, *p*, then in pizzicato violins, *p*, crescendo to *f*, ascent to

3:51
5. a. Grotesque waltz theme, high woodwinds and xylophone, *f*, trumpets, *ff*, martial tune, timpani, snare drum.

b. High violins, *f*, repeat waltz theme; French horns, *ff*, martial tune; orchestral unison, *ff*, timpani solo introduce

Coda
32 4:29
c. Oboe, *p*, altered lilting phrase in minor,

sudden *ff*, full orchestra.

14 Charles Ives

The American composer Charles Ives (1874–1954) wrote startlingly original music that was far ahead of its time. He was born in Danbury, Connecticut, the son of a bandmaster who loved to experiment with unusual sounds. "Pa taught me what I know," Ives later recalled. He learned to play many instruments and to follow the "rules" of harmony and counterpoint. But when Charles was ten, his father also encouraged his independence of mind and ear by instructing him to sing a tune in one key while being accompanied in another. At thirteen, Ives held a regular job as church organist, and his compositions were performed publicly. Still, he was prouder of his baseball than of his music. Once, when asked what he played, he gruffly replied "Shortstop!"

When he was twenty, Ives entered Yale University to study musical composition. His conservative teacher, Horatio Parker, frowned on his musical experimentation. Faced with choosing a profession on graduating, Ives decided that he could keep his music "stronger, cleaner, bigger, and freer" if he did not try to make a living out of it. He knew that his unconventional music would not be popular, and he did not want to raise a family that might "starve on his dissonances." Ives therefore went into the insurance business, starting out as a clerk in a New York firm. Eventually he founded a successful insurance agency and became very wealthy. Ives, a creative businessman, invented the concept of estate planning and wrote a textbook widely used by insurance agents.

Ives composed furiously each day after business until two or three in the morning, and on weekends and holidays as well. During the years he composed, he was isolated from the music world and almost completely unknown; none of his major works was publicly performed. His scores accumulated in the barn of his Connecticut farm. Musicians for whom he occasionally played his compositions commented: "It is not music," "It makes no sense," or "How can you like horrible sounds like that?" They urged him to write more conventionally, but his wife—a clergyman's daughter appropriately named Harmony—believed in his genius and supported his refusal to compromise.

The participation by the United States in World War I in 1917 and 1918 dampened Ives's creative urge. "I did practically nothing in music. I did not seem to feel like it," he recalled. "We were very busy at the office at this time with the extra Red Cross and Liberty Loan drives, and all the problems that the war brought on." Then, in October

The American composer Charles Ives knew that his unconventional music would not be popular, and he became a businessman so that his family would not "starve on his dissonances."

1918, shortly before the end of the war, the forty-four-year-old Ives had a heart attack from which he never completely recovered. He composed almost nothing after 1921. Instead, he began to make his compositions known to the public.

From 1920 to 1922, Ives privately printed his monumental *Concord* Sonata for piano, his explanatory *Essays before a Sonata,* and his collection *114 Songs* and sent them to musicians, critics, and libraries. At first, the volumes aroused little more than ridicule. ("It was the fate of many of them," wrote Henry Cowell, Ives's biographer, "to be used to adjust the height of the piano bench" in the studio of more than one well-known musician.) Gradually a few young composers and performers recognized that Ives was enormously original. In 1939, when Ives was sixty-four, his *Concord* Sonata (1909–1915) received an ovation at its first complete New York performance. By the 1940s, many thought Ives to be the first great composer from the United States. In 1947 he won a Pulitzer Prize for his Third Symphony (1904–1911), written some forty years earlier. Newspapers and magazines all over the country took up the story of the businessman who had lived a secret life as a composer. Ives's typically gruff reaction to the Pulitzer Prize was, "Prizes are for boys. I'm grown up."

A few years before his death, Ives received a letter from Arnold Schoenberg's widow, who had found the following note among her husband's papers: "There is a great Man living in this Country—a composer. He has solved the problem how to preserve one's self and to learn. He responds to negligence by contempt. He is not forced to accept praise or blame. His name is Ives."

Ives's Music

Though experimental and far ahead of their time, Ives's compositions are deeply rooted in the folk and popular music he knew as a boy: revival hymns and ragtime, village bands and church choirs, patriotic songs and barn dances. Ives was inspired by "unconventional" features of the American tradition: the village fiddler playing slightly out of tune, the cornetist a fraction ahead of the rest of the band, the church organist accidentally holding one chord while the choir sings another. Earlier American composers had made folk material conform to academic "rules," but Ives reveled in its irregular rhythms and asymmetrical melodies. His polyrhythms, polytonality, and tone clusters grew out of the music he knew.

To evoke nostalgic memories, Ives often quotes snatches of familiar tunes—*Yankee Doodle; Columbia, the Gem of the Ocean; America*—along with revival hymns and college songs. These snatches are not merely quoted but developed and integrated within his music. Even the titles of his works evoke Ives's New England heritage: the Second Piano Sonata is subtitled *Concord, Mass. 1840–60;* its movements are *Emerson, Hawthorne, The Alcotts,* and *Thoreau.* We'll study one movement from a set of orchestral pieces entitled *Three Places in New England.* Ives's large and varied output includes five symphonies and other orchestral music; music for piano, chorus, and chamber ensembles; and over 200 songs. Many of his instrumental works have philosophical or descriptive programs. *The Unanswered Question,* for example—a work for chamber orchestra—depicts a search for the meaning of life.

A boyhood incident seems to have had an important influence on Ives. Two bands playing different music passed each other as they marched by him in different directions. Their dissonant clash fascinated the young boy. In later works Ives simultaneously presents musical events that seem unrelated: two bands play in different keys; consonant chords are set against dissonant chords; conflicting meters and rhythmic patterns are intertwined.

Ives's music shows a wide range of emotions, styles, and musical techniques. It includes mild-sounding consonant chords and earsplitting dissonances that caused his contemporaries to think of him as a crank. Ives scorned those who couldn't take dissonance. "Beauty in music," he wrote, "is too often confused with something that lets the ears lie back in an easy chair." Once, when the dissonant music of his friend Carl Ruggles was hissed at a concert, Ives jumped up and shouted, "You goddamn sissy. . . . When you hear strong masculine music like this, get up and use your ears like a man!" Interested only in satisfying his inner ear, Ives created music that is extraordinarily difficult to perform. "The impossibilities of today are the possibilities of tomorrow," he wrote.

Putnam's Camp, Redding, Connecticut (1912), from *Three Places in New England* (1908?–1914)

Basic Set:
CD 8 33

Putnam's Camp, Redding, Connecticut (1912), is part of *Three Places in New England,* a set of three pieces for orchestra evoking American history, life, and landscape. Though completed around 1914, *Three Places in New England* was not performed until 1930. Today it is one of Ives's most popular works and is considered a landmark in American music.

The daring and brilliant second movement, *Putnam's Camp,* is a child's impression of a Fourth of July picnic. Ives recaptures his boyhood memory of two marching bands clashing dissonantly as they play different tunes. His quotations of snatches of marches and patriotic songs contribute to the piece's popular flavor. Like much of his music, *Putnam's Camp* shifts abruptly between conventional harmonies and harsh "modern" dissonances.

Ives prefaced his score with a literary program for the movement. "Near Redding Center, Conn., is a small park preserved as a Revolutionary Memorial; for here General Israel Putnam's soldiers had their winter quarters in 1778–1779." One Fourth of July, "a child went there on a picnic held under the auspices of the First Church and the Village Cornet Band." The child wanders "away from the rest of the children past the camp ground into the woods. As he rests on the hillside of laurel and hickories, the tunes of the band and the songs of the children grow fainter. . . ." He falls asleep and dreams of "a tall woman standing . . . the Goddess of Liberty . . . pleading with the soldiers not to forget their 'cause.' . . . But they march out of the camp with fife and drum to a popular tune of the day. Suddenly a new national note is heard. Putnam is coming over the hills from the center—the soldiers turn back and cheer. The little boy awakes, he hears the children's songs and runs down past the monument to 'listen to the band' and join in the games and dances."

Putnam's Camp is in three sections (free A B A′) that parallel the descriptive program. The first section (A) evokes the gaiety and confusion of a picnic. Based on a march tune composed by Ives, it also includes a parody of *Yankee Doodle* and a passage that sounds as though two bands are playing against each other. A sentimental violin melody probably represents the child, whose falling asleep is suggested when the music becomes softer and slows to a halt.

The middle section (B) represents the child's dream. The goddess of liberty pleading with the soldiers is suggested by the impression of two bands playing in different tempos. One band begins with a sad oboe melody accompanied by strings, the other with a march rhythm in the piano and snare drum. A quotation of *The British Grenadiers,* a favorite tune of the Revolutionary army, represents the army marching out of the camp. In the riotous concluding section (A′), Ives creates deliberate melodic and rhythmic confusion as the main march theme is combined with *The British Grenadiers* and other fragments.

LISTENING OUTLINE

IVES, *Putnam's Camp, Redding, Connecticut*

2 flutes, 2 clarinets, 2 bassoons, 2 trumpets, 4 French horns, 3 trombones, tuba, snare drum, bass drum, cymbals, piano, 1st violins, 2d violins, violas, cellos, double basses

A B A′ form

(Duration, 5:35)

Section A (Allegro: quickstep time)

Child's impression of picnic on Fourth of July.

33 0:00   **1. a.** Orchestra *ff*, descending dissonant chords, drums, cymbals, repeated notes in strings introduce

0:10   **b.** Violins, *f*, march theme,

dissonant piano chords, flute, *f*, *British Grenadiers* fragment, violin melody continues against brass fragments.

0:43   **c.** Trumpet repeated notes and drums introduce

0:48   **2. a.** Orchestra, *ff*, march theme, drums; trumpet melody *Battle Cry of Freedom* introduces

34 0:59   **b.** *Yankee Doodle* shared by trumpet, flute, violins.

Child wanders into woods, band becomes fainter, child falls asleep.

1:04   **c.** Solo violin melody, *p*, piano and high strings, *ppp*; flute and piano introduce

1:22   **d.** Violins, *ff*, syncopations, tempo gradually slows, bass drum punctuations, descrescendo, low strings slowly descend to sustained tone in double bass.

2:01   **e.** High held strings, *ppp*, and broken chord in piano.

Section B (Andanto animato)

Child's dream: goddess of liberty pleads with soldiers, but they march away.

35 2:08   **3. a.** Flute introduces extended oboe melody, joined by low, soft piano chords and snare drum in a different tempo; trumpet, *British Grenadiers* fragments; high violins and woodwinds, descending chromatic fragments, lead to

2:47   **b.** Clarinet melody in dotted rhythm, decrescendo.

36 3:03   **c.** Brass melody, *mf*, faster tempo, offbeat drums, introduce flute, *British Grenadiers*.

Cymbals and bass drum join, high violins lead to

General Putnam comes over the hills.

3:27   **d.** Trumpets, repeated-note melody, *ff*, crescendo to orchestral pandemonium, *fff*.

Child awakens and runs to hear the band.

3:47   **e.** Sudden *pp*, violin melody; clarinet, *f*, and crescendo to syncopated orchestral chords, *ff*, introduce

Section A′

Picnic on Fourth of July.

37 4:06   **4. a.** Full orchestra, *ff*, trombone melody against march theme.

4:19   **b.** Trumpet, *f*, *British Grenadiers* joins full orchestra.

4:30   **c.** Trumpet and French horn "fanfare," *ff*, introduces

4:39   **d.** Full orchestra, *fff*, march theme in trumpet, collage of melodies and scales builds to final *ffff* chord.

15 | George Gershwin

Popular songs and musical comedies as well as jazz-flavored orchestral works and opera won worldwide fame for the American composer George Gershwin (1898–1937). Born in Brooklyn of Russian-Jewish immigrant parents, he grew up on the lower east side of Manhattan. "Music never really interested me," said Gershwin of his childhood. "I spent most of my time with the boys in the street, skating and, in general, making a nuisance of myself." His first attraction to music came when he was ten, while he was standing outside Public School 25 and heard, through an open window, Dvořák's *Humoresque* played by a young violinist at a school assembly. Possibly inspired by this "flashing revelation of beauty," he taught himself to play hit tunes of the day on a neighbor's piano. Another musical turning point came three years later, when Gershwin began studying with a teacher who recognized his amazing talent and introduced him to piano works ranging from Bach to Liszt and Debussy.

When he was fifteen, Gershwin left high school to become a "piano pounder," a pianist demonstrating new songs in the salesrooms of a music publisher in Tin Pan Alley—a neighborhood in Manhattan where the popular music business was centered. (The name *Tin Pan Alley* was also used for the type of music it represented.) The young Gershwin saw no contradiction in his love for both "popular" and "classical" music. Once, while practicing some Bach preludes and fugues during a break from demonstrating songs, he was asked, "Are you studying to be a concert pianist?" "No," he answered, "I'm studying to be a great popular songwriter." Gershwin's drive for musical mastery was evident throughout his life. Even at the height of his fame, he seized every opportunity to take lessons in music theory, composition, and orchestration.

After three years of "piano pounding" for the music publisher, Gershwin quit his job to make a career as a songwriter. Success came quickly. In 1919, at the age of twenty, he wrote *La, La, Lucille,* his first complete Broadway musical. In 1920, his song *Swanee* was a tremendous hit; the recording by the singer Al Jolson sold millions of copies. During the 1920s and 1930s—usually collaborating with his brother Ira, who wrote the lyrics—Gershwin wrote one brilliant musical after another, including *Lady, Be Good* (1924), *Funny Face* (1927), and the political satire *Of Thee I Sing* (1931). He was an important figure in the "golden era" of the American musical (which we'll study in Part IX); and hit tunes from his shows, like *The Man I Love, I Got Rhythm, Embraceable You,* and *Someone to Watch Over Me,* proved to be of lasting appeal.

George Gershwin wrote jazz-flavored orchestral works and an opera as well as popular songs and musical comedies.

Gershwin's career as a composer of music for the concert hall was launched in 1924 by the triumphant premiere of *Rhapsody in Blue.* One of the listeners captivated by the work was the conductor Walter Damrosch, who commissioned Gershwin to write a piano concerto for the New York Symphony Orchestra. In 1925, Gershwin gave the first performance of his Concerto in F with the orchestra at Carnegie Hall in New York and later performances in six other cities. In that same year, he was the first American-born musician to appear on the cover of *Time* magazine.

During the 1920s, Gershwin made several trips to Europe, where he heard performances of his own works and met other composers—among them Alban Berg, in Vienna; and Maurice Ravel and Igor Stravinsky, in Paris. On one visit to Paris, he composed part of the symphonic poem *An American in Paris* (1928), which includes four taxi horns in its colorful orchestration.

In 1934 Gershwin began to write his most extended work, the opera *Porgy and Bess* (1935), which deals with the lives of poor black people in Charleston, South Carolina. Part of the opera was composed during a summer on Folly Island, near Charleston, from which Gershwin visited nearby islands to hear music in isolated African American communities. *Porgy and Bess* was premiered in Boston in 1935, played sixteen weeks in the Alvin Theater in New York, and then went on a three-month road tour. It was not revived during Gershwin's lifetime, but it has since had performances all over the world, including a production at the Metropolitan Opera.

Gershwin was an outgoing person, a sportsman, and irresistible to women. He enjoyed attending parties, where he would play the piano for hours. Royalties, concert fees, and the salary from his nationally broadcast weekly radio show *Music by Gershwin* made him wealthy. He had an outstanding art collection and was himself a talented painter.

Gershwin spent the last year of his life in Hollywood, where he wrote the music for several movies and played tennis with the composer Arnold Schoenberg in his spare time. During the spring of 1937, he began to experience dizziness and fumbled passages when performing his works. One day he fell into a coma and was rushed to a hospital, where it was found that he had a brain tumor. His doctors wanted a famous neurosurgeon to operate, but the surgeon was vacationing on a yacht in Chesapeake Bay. Friends called the White House, and the Coast Guard was sent to locate him. But before he could fly to Gershwin in California, an emergency operation had to be performed. It was not a success, and Gershwin died at the age of thirty-eight.

Rhapsody in Blue (1924)

Basic Set:

CD 8 [38]

Rhapsody in Blue, Gershwin's most famous work, was commissioned by the bandleader Paul Whiteman for a special concert to be given on Lincoln's birthday in 1924. The concert was intended to prove that jazz—or, more accurately, the popular music Whiteman considered jazz—merited serious attention. At first, Gershwin was reluctant to take the commission, because the concert was only five weeks away and he was busy preparing his musical comedy *Sweet Little Devil* for its Boston tryout. But Whiteman's persuasiveness and Gershwin's own eagerness to write jazz-flavored concert music won out. The twenty-five-year-old composer accepted the commission for a new composition for piano and jazz band and agreed to appear as soloist.

During a trip to Boston, Gershwin decided on the form for *Rhapsody in Blue.* "It was on the train, with its steely rhythms, its rattlety-bang, . . . that I suddenly heard—and even saw on paper—the complete construction of the *Rhapsody,* from beginning to end," he later recalled. "I heard it as a sort of musical kaleidoscope of America—of our vast melting pot, of our unduplicated national pep, of our blues, our metropolitan madness. By the time I reached Boston, I had a definite *plot* of the piece. . . ." After only three weeks of work, Gershwin finished a two-piano version of *Rhapsody in Blue* that was orchestrated for the Whiteman band by its arranger, Ferde Grofé.

The well-publicized concert took place in New York, in the prestigious Aeolian Hall, before an audience of celebrities that included Tin Pan Alley songwriters as well as the violinists Jascha Heifetz and Fritz Kreisler, the conductors Walter Damrosch and Leopold Stokowski, and the composers Sergei Rachmaninoff and Ernest Bloch. The other pieces on the program were received with indifference, but *Rhapsody in Blue* electrified the audience with its novelty, its memorable melodies, its distinctive American flavor, and—not least—Gershwin's brilliant piano playing. So great was its success that it was soon heard in concert halls around the world and earned the composer $250,000 within a decade. In an era when composers such as Stravinsky, Ravel, and Copland were incorporating jazz elements into their compositions, this concert work by a songwriter had the most lasting impact and the widest appeal. It is heard most often in a version by Ferde Grofé that is scored for piano and full symphony orchestra. (For his later orchestral works, Gershwin did his own scoring.)

The title *Rhapsody in Blue* reflects the music's free, rhapsodic form and its blues flavor. The term *blues* refers to a style of vocal music, originating among African Americans, that involves "bent" notes and slides of pitch. "Blue" notes are produced by slightly lowering, or flatting, the third, fifth, and seventh notes of the major scale. (Blues will be discussed more fully on pages 471–474.) *Rhapsody in Blue* is not true jazz; but it uses jazzlike rhythms and melodies, and the orchestration suggests the distinctive sounds of jazz by such effects as a clarinet glissando, or slide, and brass instruments played with a "wha-wha" mute.

Rhapsody in Blue is a one-movement work consisting of three main sections and a coda. Each main section includes at least one extended piano solo in which varied repetitions of the main themes are combined with Lisztian virtuoso passages. The solos reflect Gershwin's own dazzling pianism and his genius as an improvisor. The piece opens with a now famous clarinet solo that starts from a low trill, climbs the scale, and then slides up to a high "wailing" tone. The clarinet slide, or glissando—a novel effect at the time—was improvised during rehearsals by the clarinetist of the Whiteman band, and Gershwin incorporated it into the score. The blueslike opening theme, which grows out of the clarinet slide, is marked by the syncopations so typical of Gershwin's style. It is followed by a repeated-note theme, presented by French horns, which reappears many times. A new jazzlike theme, introduced in the low register, begins the lively second section, marked *con moto*. The moderately slow third section is based on a lyrical, romantic melody first presented by the violins. This memorable tune is combined with a countermelody played by the French horns. The rapid coda is ushered in by an accelerated transformation of the romantic melody.

LISTENING OUTLINE

GERSHWIN, *Rhapsody in Blue* (Recording available in the Online Learning Center)

B flat major

Solo piano, 2 flutes, 2 oboes, 2 clarinets, bass clarinet, 2 bassoons, 2 alto saxophones, tenor saxophone, 3 French horns, 3 trumpets, 3 trombones, tuba, timpani, bass drum, snare drum, cymbals, gong, triangle, 1st violins, 2d violins, violas, cellos, double basses

38 0:00   **1. a.** Clarinet, *p*, trill, upward scale and slide (glissando) to blues theme, *mf*, moderate tempo.

39 0:34   **b.** Repeated-note theme, faster tempo, French horn and woodwinds, *mf*.

      Clarinet, *p*, trill, upward scale to blues theme in muted trumpet, *mf*, piano joins, crescendo to blues theme in full orchestra, *ff*, cymbal crashes.

1:08   **c.** Extended piano solo, begins *p*, fast repeated chords, *f*, upward scale to blues theme, low instruments join, piano alone, *p*, crescendo to brilliant rushing notes, fast repeated chords, *ff*.

40 3:08   **d.** Full orchestra, *ff*, blues theme in faster tempo, piano joins, strings, crescendo to blues theme in trombones, *f*, trumpets, flutter tongue, *ff*.

41 3:43   **e.** Trumpet theme, marchlike beat in drums, piano.

      Clarinet, *p*, repeated-note theme, piano, rushing notes, full orchestra, *ff*, repeated-note theme, piano chords, solo clarinet, "wha-wha" muted trumpet and trombone solos, orchestra, *ff*, pause.

42 5:17   **2. a.** Orchestra, *f*, jazzlike theme in low register, steady beat in drums, piano chords.

      Rising brass phrase, crescendo to full orchestra, *ff*, jazzlike theme in high register, piano joins, crescendo.

6:17   **b.** Extended piano solo, varied repeated-note theme, horn, *p*, accompanies piano,

8:09   **c.** Oboe, blues theme, piano running notes, faster tempo.

8:35   **d.** Extended piano solo, jazzlike theme in low register, steady beat, jazzlike theme in high register, *ff*, brilliant ascending running notes, descending octaves, *ff*, sudden *pp*, ascending phrases, pause.

43 10:49   **3. a.** Strings and woodwinds, *p*, romantic theme, horns, *p*, moderate tempo, high violin solo.

Andante moderato con espressione

11:42   **b.** Full orchestra, *ff*, romantic theme, drumrolls, cymbals, piano joins, bells introduce

12:31   **c.** Extended piano solo, romantic theme, very fast repeated notes, brilliant ascending scale to

44 14:21   **4. a.** Brasses and piano, accelerated romantic theme, brass swells and sustained dissonant chord, *fff*.

Allegro agitato e misterioso

15:08   **b.** Piano and orchestra, rising chromatic scale, crescendo, ritardando.
15:19   **c.** Piano and orchestra, *ff*, repeated-note theme, ritardando.
15:46   **d.** Full orchestra, *fff*, blues theme, cymbal crashes, piano chords, crescendo to final orchestral chord, *ff*.

16 William Grant Still

The flowering of African American culture during the years 1917–1935—sometimes called the "Harlem Renaissance"—found musical expression in the works of the composer William Grant Still (1895–1978). His *Afro-American Symphony* (1931), which we'll study, was the first composition by a black composer to be performed by a major American symphony orchestra.

Still was born in Woodville, Mississippi, but grew up in Little Rock, Arkansas, where he began to study violin. At the age of sixteen, Still enrolled at Wilberforce University (Ohio) as a premedical student; but he devoted himself to musical activities, such as playing violin in the university string quartet, and decided to abandon medicine for music. He left college before graduating to enter the world of popular music as an arranger and performer. Still worked for the composer and publisher W. C. Handy in Memphis and arranged Handy's *St. Louis Blues* for military band (1916). In 1917, he enrolled at Oberlin College Conservatory to continue his formal music training, but he soon left to serve in the navy in World War I.

After his navy service and a brief return to studies at Oberlin College, Still moved to New York, where he lived a double life as a popular musician and as a composer of concert works. He made band arrangements and played in the orchestras of such all-black musical shows as *Shuffle Along* (1921). He also studied privately with two important compos-

The flowering of African American culture during the years 1917–1935 found musical expression in the works of William Grant Still.

ers in opposing musical camps: the conservative George Whitefield Chadwick and the modernist Edgard Varèse. After composing a few highly dissonant works under Varèse's influence, Still turned away from avant-garde styles and wrote compositions with an uniquely African American flavor that were performed to critical acclaim in New York.

A turning point in Still's career came in 1931, with the highly successful premiere of his *Afro-American Symphony* by the Rochester Philharmonic. Within the next two decades, this symphony was performed by thirty-eight orchestras in the United States and Europe. In 1934, Still was awarded a Guggenheim Fellowship, and the next year he moved to Los Angeles, where he wrote film scores, concert works, and operas. Still was the first African American to conduct a major symphony orchestra—the Los Angeles Philharmonic, in 1936. He was also the first to have an opera performed by a major opera company—*Troubled Island,* about the Haitian slave rebellion, in 1949. In 1981, three years after Still's death, his opera *A Bayou Legend,* written in 1941, was broadcast on national television.

Afro-American Symphony (1931)

The *Afro-American Symphony,* Still's best-known work, was composed in 1930, shortly after the onset of the Great Depression. "It was not until the Depression struck," he later observed, "that I was jobless long enough to let the symphony take shape. In 1930, I rented a room in a quiet building not far from my home in New York, and began to work." Still devised his own blues theme and explained that he "wanted to demonstrate that the blues, so often considered a lowly expression, could be elevated to the highest musical level." The blues theme is introduced in the first movement and then reappears in various transformations in the three later movements as a unifying thread. Still also gave an African American character to the symphony by using a tenor banjo as part of the orchestra and by inventing themes that recall spirituals and jazz tunes. Each of the symphony's four movements has a subtitle and is prefaced by lines from a poem by the African American poet Paul Laurence Dunbar (1872–1906). We'll focus on the third movement.

Third Movement: Animato

Still gave this joyful, scherzo-like movement the subtitle *Humor* and prefaced it with the following quotation from Dunbar's poem: "An' we'll shout ouah hallelujahs/On dat mighty reck'nin' day." After a brief introduction, Still presents two melodies that reappear in varied guises within the movement. The lively, syncopated opening melody is made up of short motives, each ending with a repeated note and pause. Still called this the *hallelujah* melody, perhaps because its opening four notes fit the word "hallelujah." The *hallelujah* melody is accompanied by a syncopated countermelody that recalls Gershwin's song *I Got Rhythm,* studied in Part I, Section 3. (It is not certain whether one composer influenced the other.) The movement's jubilant second melody, more fully orchestrated than the first, is reminiscent of a spiritual. This theme includes two "blue" notes, the lowered third and seventh of the scale. The movement falls into three sections (1, 2, 3 in the listening outline), of which the last is an abridged return of the first. Varied orchestral colors and lively countermelodies contribute to the movement's high spirits.

Basic Set:
CD 8 45

Brief Set:
CD 5 21

LISTENING OUTLINE

STILL, *Afro-American Symphony*

Third Movement: Animato

Quadruple meter ($\frac{4}{4}$), A flat major

Piccolo, 2 flutes, 2 oboes, English horn, 2 clarinets, bass clarinet, 4 French horns, 3 trumpets, 3 trombones, tuba, timpani, small cymbal, large suspended cymbal, tenor banjo, 1st violins, 2d violins, violas, cellos, double basses

(Duration, 3:03)

45 **21**   **1. a.** Timpani roll, syncopated motive in French horns, *f*, syncopated motive in brasses, cymbal crash, introduce

46 **22** 0:15   **b.** Syncopated *hallelujah* melody in major, violins, *f*, off-beat accompaniment in banjo and French horns, *mf*,

        0:24   **c.** Syncopated countermelody in high woooodwinds introduces

47 **23** 0:31   **d.** Full orchestra, *f*, second melody.

        0:49   **e.** Suddenly softer, *hallelujah* melody in oboe, then flutes, running notes in bass clarinet.

        1:04   **f.** Sudden *ff*, trombones and French horns in unison, minor; suddenly softer, violins lead upward, violins, *f*, cymbals, answered by brasses, dotted rhythm, decrescendo to

48 **24** 1:34   **2. a.** Staccato flutes, *mp*, *hallelujah* melody varied, continuation in oboes,

           legato flutes, English horn, violins, *p*, descend.

        1:59   **b.** Muted trumpets answered by French horns, *p*, new variation of *hallelujah* melody,

        2:07   **c.** Sudden *f*, trombones and tuba in unison, minor, full orchestra, cymbal crashes.

        2:19   **3. a.** Violins, *mf*, *hallelujah* melody, with high flute and piccolo countermelody, banjo accompanies, oboes and flutes, *hallelujah* melody embellished.

        2:35   **b.** Violins, *mf*, second melody, sudden *f*, low strings and woodwinds in unison, minor.

49 **25** 2:57   **c.** Full orchestra, *ff*, jubilant variant of *hallelujah* melody,

           quick brass countermelody, rising strings, cymbal crash, and staccato ending chord.

17   Aaron Copland

Aaron Copland (1900–1990), a leading American composer, was born in Brooklyn of Russian-Jewish immigrant parents. "No one ever talked music to me or took me to a concert," he recalled of his boyhood. "Music as an art was a discovery I made all

Aaron Copland drew on American folklore for his ballets *Billy the Kid, Rodeo,* and *Appalachian Spring.*

by myself." At the age of fifteen he decided to become a composer. He studied with a competent but conservative teacher who discouraged contact with "modern" music. This only made the forbidden fruit more attractive. Copland showed only his academic exercises to his teacher, keeping his more original efforts to himself.

In 1921 Copland went to France, where he was the first American to study composition with Nadia Boulanger. This extraordinary woman was sympathetic to modern musical trends and became the teacher of several generations of American composers. Both Boulanger's teaching and the stimulating atmosphere of Paris—where the expatriates Picasso, Stravinsky, and Ernest Hemingway, among others, felt at home—were to have a lasting influence on Copland's music.

When he returned to New York after three years in Paris, Copland was "anxious to write a work that would immediately be recognized as American in character." For Copland in 1925, *American* meant jazz. In his *Music for the Theater* (1925), a work for small orchestra, elements of blues and ragtime are combined with an approach to rhythm and harmony that is like Stravinsky's.

Copland's "jazz period" lasted only a few years. During the early 1930s he composed serious, highly dissonant works that were accessible only to sophisticated listeners. His compositions of the time, such as the highly regarded *Piano Variations* (1930), convey starkness, power, percussiveness, and intense concentration.

In the late 1930s, Copland modified his style again, writing more accessible works for a larger audience. To understand this shift, recall that the 1930s brought the Great Depression; artists throughout the world were appalled by the economic misery surrounding them. To many composers, it seemed futile to write merely for a sophisticated elite, and they simplified their music to reach a wider audience. "I began to feel an increasing dissatisfaction with the relations of the music-loving public and the living composer," Copland later explained. Most concertgoers, he felt, could not grasp complex, highly dissonant music and wanted to hear only familiar music such as the works of Beethoven and Brahms. "It made no sense to ignore them and to continue writing as if they did not exist. I felt that it was worth the effort to see if I couldn't say what I had to say in the simplest possible terms." Copland drew on American folklore for his ballets *Billy the Kid* (1938), *Rodeo* (1942), and *Appalachian Spring* (1944). His use of jazz, revival hymns, cowboy songs, and other folk tunes helped make Copland's name synonymous with American music. His scores for films such as *Of Mice and Men* (1939) and *Our Town* (1940) brought his music before a mass public, as did patriotic works such as *A Lincoln Portrait* (1942).

Copland accomplished the difficult feat of writing simple yet highly professional music (in this he resembles Leonard Bernstein, whose work we'll study in Part IX). The texture of his music is clear and transparent. There are slow-moving, almost motionless harmonies that seem to evoke the openness of the American landscape. Though strongly tonal, his works embody twentieth-century techniques such as polychords, polyrhythm, changing meters, and percussive orchestration. After 1950, Copland used serial technique—manipulation of a tone row or series—in such works as *Connotations* for orchestra (1962). This composition recalls the austere, uncompromising style of Copland's music during the early 1930s. Like Stravinsky, who also turned to serial technique during the 1950s, Copland used a tone row to create music that is completely personal in style.

Aside from his numerous compositions, Copland made many other valuable contributions to music in the United States. He directed composers' groups, organized concerts of American music, lectured around the country, and wrote books and magazine articles. At the request of the State Department, he was a musical ambassador to South America, where he talked with many composers and listened to their works. For twenty-five years, he taught young composers every summer at the Berkshire Music Center at Tanglewood. When he was fifty, Copland began yet another career, that of conductor; he conducted many orchestras—primarily in his own music—throughout the world.

Appalachian Spring (1943–1944)

Appalachian Spring originated as a ballet score for Martha Graham, the great modern dancer and choreographer. It took Copland about a year (1943–1944) to finish the music. While composing *Appalachian Spring*, he thought, "How foolhardy it is to be spending all this time writing a thirty-five-minute score for a modern-dance company, knowing how short-lived most ballets *and* their scores are." But in 1945 Copland arranged parts of the ballet as a suite for full orchestra (originally, the ballet used only thirteen instrumentalists) that won important prizes and brought his name to a large public. Today, *Appalachian Spring* is widely performed both as a ballet and as a concert piece.

The ballet concerns a "pioneer celebration in spring around a newly built farmhouse in the Pennsylvania hills" in the early 1800s. Its characters include a bride and groom, a neighbor, and a revivalist preacher with his followers. The rhythms and melodies are American-sounding and suggest barn dances, fiddle tunes, and revival hymns. But Copland uses only one actual folk tune in the score—a Shaker melody entitled *Simple Gifts*. (The Shakers were a religious sect established in America around the time of the Revolution. They expressed religious fervor through shaking, leaping, dancing, and singing.) *Appalachian Spring* is bright and transparent, has a clear tonality, and is basically tender and calm in mood. The score's rhythmic excitement comes from delightful syncopations and rapid changes of meter. As in many twentieth-century works, the orchestra includes a piano and a large percussion section.

The ballet suite has eight sections, including a duo for the bride and groom, a fast dance for the revivalist preacher and his followers with "suggestions of square dances and country fiddlers," and a finale in which the couple are left "quiet and strong in their new house." We'll focus on Section 7, which originally accompanied "Scenes of daily activity for the Bride and her Farmer-husband."

A scene from the original production of *Appalachian Spring*.

Basic Set:
CD 8 [50]

Brief Set:
CD 5 [26]

Section 7:
Theme and Variations on *Simple Gifts*

Section 7 is a theme and five variations on the Shaker tune *Simple Gifts*. The melody's folklike simplicity reflects the Shaker text, which opens as follows:

> 'Tis the gift to be simple, 'tis the gift to be free,
> 'Tis the gift to come down where we ought to be.

In each variation, Copland brings the tune back unadorned, creating variety and contrast through changes of tempo, tone color, dynamics, register, accompaniment, and key. Variation 2 sounds thoughtful and lyrical, as the tune is played more slowly, in a lower register, with polyphonic imitations. Variation 3 brings a brilliant contrast, as *Simple Gifts* is presented faster and staccato by trumpets and trombones. In each of the last two variations, Copland uses only part of the tune: its second part in the pastoral variation 4, and its first part in the majestic closing variation.

LISTENING OUTLINE

COPLAND, *Appalachian Spring*

Section 7: Theme and Variations on *Simple Gifts*

Theme and variations, duple meter ($\frac{2}{4}$), A flat major

2 flutes, 2 oboes, 2 clarinets, 2 bassoons, 2 French horns, 2 trumpets, 2 trombones, timpani, triangle, glockenspiel, harp, piano, 1st violins, 2d violins, violas, cellos, double basses

(Duration, 3:09)

Theme

`50` `26` 0:00   Clarinet, *p*, *Simple Gifts*, legato.

Variation 1

`51` `27` 0:33   Oboe, *mp*, and bassoon, *mp*, *Simple Gifts*, slightly faster, in higher register.

Variation 2

`52` `28` 1:00   High harp, piano, glockenspiel, *p*, introduce *Simple Gifts*, violas and trombone, *mf*, played
half as fast, in lower register. *Simple Gifts* imitated in violins, *f*, then in cellos and basses, *f*.
Woodwinds, *p*, brief transition to

Variation 3

`53` `29` 1:52   Trumpets and trombones, *f*, *Simple Gifts*, twice as fast, staccato.

Variation 4

`54` `30` 2:16   Woodwinds, *mf*, second part of *Simple Gifts*, slightly slower than variation 3, gentle and legato.

Variation 5

`55` `31` 2:34   Full orchestra, *fff*, first part of *Simple Gifts*, played slowly and majestically, in high register.

18   Alberto Ginastera

The Argentinean Alberto Ginastera (1916–1983) was one of the most prominent Latin American composers of the twentieth century. Born in Buenos Aires to Argentinean parents, Ginastera was attracted to percussive sounds even as a young child. "One day I went into the kitchen and played on all the pots and pans and other things I could get, to make a kitchen orchestra," he recalled late in life. "I was spanked. They [his parents] did not know then that what I was playing had in it the roots of *Panambí* and *Estancia*," two of his early ballet scores.

The early works of the Argentinean Alberto Ginastera are nationalistic and incorporate popular dances from his homeland.

Ginastera began studying piano when he was seven, graduated from the National Conservatory in Buenos Aires when he was twenty-two, and became a faculty member at that conservatory when he was twenty-five, in 1941. The same year, Ginastera married and began to teach his first private composition student, Astor Piazzolla—later a well-known composer—who described him as a "great teacher . . . very introverted, always dressed in black." In 1945 Ginastera went with his family to the United States, where he studied with Aaron Copland at the Berkshire Music Center at Tanglewood. After returning to Argentina in 1947, he taught at several important music schools. However, because Ginastera opposed the regime of Juan Perón in Argentina (1946–1955), he was twice forced to resign from his academic positions during the 1940s and 1950s.

Ginastera's music began to attract international attention in the 1950s, and by the 1960s he was so well regarded that three of his operas—*Don Rodrigo* (1964), *Bomarzo* (1967), and *Beatrix Cenci* (1971), all including scenes of explicit sex and violence—were performed in the United States. Just before *Bomarzo* was to open in Buenos Aires on August 4, 1967—two and a half months after its successful premiere in Washington, D.C.—the Argentinean president decided that the opera was "too obsessed with sex" and had it banned.

From 1963 to 1971, Ginastera directed the Latin American Center for Advanced Musical Studies, which promoted avant-garde musical techniques. Its visiting faculty members included such well-known composers as his former teacher Aaron Copland. In 1971, after divorcing his first wife, Ginastera married the Argentinean cellist Aurora Natola. His "life changed after his marriage . . . ; he broke through his shell, and renewed everything, even his music," recalled Piazzolla. Ginastera and Aurora left Argentina for Switzerland, where he spent his last twelve years and composed many of his pathbreaking works. In 1973, Ginastera's music reached millions of listeners when a movement from his first piano concerto was adapted into the hit song *Toccata* by the progressive rock group Emerson, Lake, and Palmer.

Ginastera's music employs forceful rhythms, powerful percussion, and dense orchestra textures. His early works (1934–1947), such as *Danza Argentinas* (1937) and *Estancia* Suite (1941), are nationalistic and incorporate Argentinean folk material, including popular dances. Starting in the 1950s, with the Piano Sonata (1952), Ginastera—like many other composers of the time—adopted Schoenberg's twelve-tone system, which is used in his later music. Even though his works starting in the 1950s are no longer overtly nationalistic, Ginastera insisted that they have an Argentinean character. "Instead of using folkloristic material," he wrote, "the composer achieves an Argentine atmosphere by using his own thematic and rhythmic elements. . . . No matter what style I write in, it is still me." After 1957, works such as his three operas—mentioned above—and the Cello Concerto No. 2, written for his wife Aurora, make use of such post-1945 musical techniques as tone clusters, chance music, and microtones (see Section 19).

We will study Ginastera's *Estancia* Suite, an early work rooted in Argentinean folk tradition.

Estancia Suite, Op. 8a (1941)

The ballet *Estancia*—Spanish for an Argentine ranch—was commissioned by Lincoln Kirsten, director of the American Ballet Caravan, to be premiered in a planned program of Latin American ballets in New York. However, Kirsten's ballet company was disbanded in 1942, and *Estancia* was not performed as a ballet until much later. But in 1941 Ginastera arranged several of its dances as the *Estancia* Suite for orchestra, which became one of his most popular works.

Ginastera described his ballet *Estancia* as presenting "various aspects of ranch activities during a day, from dawn to dawn." *Estancia* has a distinct national flavor because of its setting on an Argentinean ranch, and its use of musical idioms associated with the gaucho, or horseman of the plain. The plot deals with "a country girl who despises a man from the city. She finally admires him when he proves that he can perform the roughest and most difficult tasks of the country."

The *Estancia* Suite uses a large orchestra and has four movements: (1) *Los trabajadors* (*The Land Workers*), (2) *Danza del Trigo* (*Wheat Dance*), (3) *Los Peones de Hacienda* (*The Cattlemen*), (4) *Danza Final* (*Final Dance*): *Malambo*. The first movement of the suite is rapid, loud, syncopated, and energetic, with violent accents on the bass drum. In contrast, the second movement in calm and lyrical, opening with a flute solo accompanied by soft pizzicato strings and harp that suggest the strumming of the gaucho's guitar. The wild, propulsive third movement features rapid shifts of meter that recall Stravinsky's *The Rite of Spring*, studied in Section 7 above. We'll focus on the climactic fourth movement, *Danza Final* (*Final Dance*): *Malambo*.

Final Dance: Malambo

The *malambo* is a dance for men only performed by the gaucho. Both the *malambo* and the gaucho are traditional symbols of Argentina. In a competitive *malambo,* one dancer tries to outshine the other through the energy and complexity of his steps.

Ginastera's comment that "always in my music there is this violent rhythm" aptly describes the fast tempo, perpetual motion, and percussive sounds of *Final Dance: Malambo.* The orchestra includes a very large percussion section, and the energetic melodies are often syncopated. The meter is $\frac{6}{8}$, and six rapid pulses per measure represent the foot tapping of the dancing gauchos. The form of this brief dance is A A' (shortened) B. Part B, which is marked *Tempo di malambo,* builds to a climax and introduces a lively *malambo* melody. In this melody, six fast pulses first subdivide into two groups of three pulses and then into three groups of two pulses. A similar rhythm appears in *America* from Leonard Bernstein's *West Side Story,* studied in Part IX, "Music for Stage and Screen."

Basic Set:
CD 8 **56**

Brief Set:
CD 5 **32**

LISTENING OUTLINE

GINASTERA, *Estancia* Suite, Op. 8a

Final Dance: Malambo

A A′ B form, Allegro, triple meter ($\frac{6}{8}$), C major

Piccolo, 2 flutes, 2 oboes, 2 clarinets, 2 bassoons, 4 French horns, 2 trombones, timpani, bass drum, snare drum, tenor drum, cymbals, triangle, tambourine, castanets, gong, xylophone, piano, 1st violins, 2d violins, violas, cellos, double basses (Duration, 3:24)

56 32 A

0:00	**1. a.**	Piccolo and flute, *pp*, high rapid ostinato, pizzicato violins, three-beat pattern; low strings join, crescendo.
0:14	**b.**	Violins, *f*, high syncopated melody, brasses join.
0:25	**c.**	Xylophone, two-note melody.
0:32	**d.**	Brasses, *mf*, melody beginning with long note; violins, *f*, repeat melody.
0:45	**e.**	Pizzicato violins, *mf*, two-note ostinato, crescendo to

57 33 A′

1:00	**2. a.**	Piccolo and flute, *f*, high rapid ostinato, pizzicato violins, three-beat pattern, French horns, downward scale, crescendo to
1:11	**b.**	Violins, *f*, high syncopated melody.
1:22	**c.**	Xylophone, new melody, bass drum pulses, crescendo to

58 34 B Tempo di malambo

1:39	**3. a.**	Trumpets, winds, xylophone, *f*, lively *malambo* melody repeated many times; bass drum.

1:58	**b.**	Brasses, *ff*, fast repeated notes; bass drum.
2:05	**c.**	Repeated *malambo* melody, trumpets, winds, xylophone, *f*, bass drum.
2:23	**d.**	Brasses, *ff*, fast repeated notes, slides; bass drum.
2:30	**e.**	Lively *malambo* melody repeats, trumpets, winds, xylophone, *f*, bass drum.
2:46	**f.**	Brasses, *ff*, syncopations; bass drum.
2:56	**g.**	Full orchestra, *malambo* melody repeats.
3:09	**h.**	High repeated notes, *ff*, full orchestra, very loud closing chord.

Gustavo Dudamel Conducting the Final Dance:
Malambo *from Ginastera's* Estancia *Suite*

Probably the most famous young conductor today is the Venezuelan Gustavo Dudamel, who was named by *Time* magazine as one of the hundred most influential people of 2009. Dudamel began as music director of the Los Angeles Philharmonic on October 3, 2009, with a five-hour free community concert—called *¡Benvenido Gustavo!*—at the Hollywood Bowl. The first half of the event included jazz, gospel, pop, rock, and Cuban and Latin regional music, played by local youth ensembles joined by established stars; and the second half culminated in a performance of Beethoven's Ninth Symphony.

Dudamel was born in 1981 in the city of Barquisimeto, Venezuela; his father played trombone in salsa bands and his mother taught voice. When he was four, he began to study within a national network known

as *El Sistema* (*The System*), which includes about 250 free music schools and hundreds of orchestras for children and youth. After beginning to play violin at age ten, Dudamel progressed so rapidly that two years later he was appointed concertmaster of a youth orchestra, which he sometimes conducted. He began to study conducting in his early teens, and at eighteen he was appointed music director of El Sistema's top ensemble, the Simón Bolívar Youth Orchestra of Venezuela, a position he still holds.

Dudamel's meteoric rise to international fame began when he won the Gustav Mahler Conducting Competition at age twenty-three. Over the next few years, he guest-conducted such leading ensembles as the Vienna, New York, and Israel philharmonic orchestras and made DVDs and CDs with the Simón Bolívar Youth Orchestra.

This huge youth orchestra, which has given concert tours in Europe and the United States, includes 200 musicians between the ages of fifteen and twenty-eight, mostly from poor homes. The aims of the orchestra go beyond making music: "When you have around your life, drugs, crime," says Dudamel, "the best that you can give to a kid is an instrument. Then they can change their lives." He says that his orchestra is a community: "We are a family. . . . I am part of the orchestra. We give our all with every performance." Dudamel describes the role of a conductor as "a bridge between the composer and the orchestra" and hopes his audiences "feel the joy of music."

Dudamel's recording with the Simón Bolívar Youth Orchestra entitled *Fiesta* presents mostly music of Latin American composers, including the four dance movements of Ginastera's *Estancia* Suite. Dudamel believes that dance is a key element in Latin American music. "I started to dance when I was really small—a baby. You know, learning to dance is part of our culture—dancing is in our blood. . . . Latin music is all about dance, about rhythm. And we try to put this spice into all of our music."

19 Musical Styles since 1945

Since World War II, we have lived with instant communication—television, computers, and space satellites provide access to a virtually unlimited flow of information. Not only have we been bombarded by an incredible variety of stimuli, but there has also been a constant demand for novelty. New styles in fashion and the visual arts spread rapidly and then disappear.

In music as well, the emphasis has been on novelty and change. Musical innovations since 1945 have been even more far-reaching than those of the first half of the twentieth century. There have been many new directions, and the range of musical styles and systems is wider than ever. As the American composer Milton Babbitt (b. 1916) observed in 1984, "The world of music never before has been so pluralistic, so fragmented."

Particularly since the 1970s, many composers have advocated stylistic pluralism or eclecticism. Their works include sections in a variety of styles ranging from baroque to rock. In 1999, the American composer John Adams (b. 1947) told an interviewer, "We're in a kind of post-style era. Composers of my age and younger, we are not writing in one, highly defined, overarching expression." Adams believes that the contemporary composer can follow the examples of Bach, Mahler, and Stravinsky, and be "somebody who just reached out and grabbed everything" and through musical technique and spiritual vision "turned it into something great."

Characteristics of Music since 1945

Accurately describing the relatively recent past is difficult. Yet any overview of music since 1945 must include the following major developments:

1. Increased use of the *twelve-tone system.*
2. *Serialism*—use of the techniques of the twelve-tone system to organize rhythm, dynamics, and tone color.
3. *Chance music,* in which a composer chooses pitches, tone colors, and rhythms by random methods, or allows a performer to choose much of the musical material.
4. *Minimalist music,* characterized by a steady pulse, clear tonality, and insistent repetition of short melodic patterns.
5. *Musical quotation,* works containing deliberate quotations from earlier music.
6. *Tonal music and a return to tonality* by some composers.
7. *Electronic music.*
8. *"Liberation of sound"*—greater exploitation of noiselike sounds.
9. *Mixed media.*
10. New concepts of *rhythm* and *form.*

Since 1945, long-playing records, audiotape, compact discs, DVDs, and the Internet have spread these new musical ideas far and wide. In Asia, for example, interest in western music has increased dramatically. Many young musicians from Japan, China, Taiwan, and South Korea study in American music schools and universities, and Asian performers are prominent on the international concert scene.

Increased Use of the Twelve-Tone System A striking development after World War II (1945) was the gradual abandonment of tonality in favor of the twelve-tone system. From the early 1920s—when Schoenberg invented the system—to about 1950, most composers still wrote music with a tonal center. Few were attracted to the new method, because it was associated with Schoenberg's expressionist style, which had gone

Flood (1967) by Helen Frankenthaler. Working without a brush, Frankenthaler allows paint to soak and stain an unprimed canvas stretched on the floor.

out of fashion. During the 1950s, however, the twelve-tone system was adopted by many composers, including Stravinsky, who had been the leading composer of tonal music.

What contributed to this dramatic shift? In Europe, the end of the war brought a strong desire for new musical beginnings. During the Nazi years, composers had been denied access to the twelve-tone works of Schoenberg and Webern; when peace came, they were eager to explore unfamiliar musical territory. In the United States, twelve-tone music was now available on long-playing records, and complex scores became easier to study.

But the most important reasons for the shift to the twelve-tone system were the resources of the system itself. Composers discovered that it was a compositional technique rather than a special musical style. Musicians as different as Bach, Mozart, and Chopin had all used the tonal system; a comparable diversity of style was possible within the twelve-tone system. The new method also had the advantage of stimulating unconventional approaches to melody, harmony, and form. As Aaron Copland once expressed it, "I began to hear chords that I wouldn't have heard otherwise. Heretofore I had been thinking tonally, but this was a new way of moving tones about. It freshened up one's technique and one's approach."

Many composers of the 1950s and 1960s chose to write music that was stylistically reminiscent of Anton Webern, Schoenberg's disciple. They created "pointillist" music in which melodic lines are "atomized" into tiny fragments that are heard in widely separated registers and framed by moments of silence. Webern's style answered the needs of the post-World War II generation: his music had a lean, "modern" sound, whereas Schoenberg's was considered too "romantic" and traditional in form. The French composer Pierre Boulez (b. 1925) spoke for many of his generation in 1952 when he unfavorably compared Schoenberg's alliance with the "decadence of the great German romantic tradition" and Webern's reaction "against all inherited rhetoric."

Since 1950, there have been many new styles in the visual arts. Bridget Riley's *Nataraja* (1993) is *op*—or *optical*—art, which exploits visual effects and illusions.

Extensions of the Twelve-Tone System: Serialism During the late 1940s and early 1950s, the techniques of the twelve-tone system came to be used to organize dimensions of music other than pitch, such as rhythm, dynamics, and tone color. Recall that in early twelve-tone music the system was used primarily to order *pitch* relationships. All the pitches of a twelve-tone composition would be derived from a single tone row, or series. After 1950, a series of durations (rhythmic values), dynamic levels, or tone colors also could serve as a unifying idea. A rhythmic or dynamic series might be manipulated like the series of twelve tones. The use of a series, or ordered group of musical elements, to organize several dimensions of a composition is called ***serialism.*** Proponents of serialism include Milton Babbitt in the United States, Karlheinz Stockhausen (1928–2007) in Germany, and Pierre Boulez in France. Their methods lead to a totally controlled and organized music, but the actual sound—in certain cases—might seem random and chaotic. The complex relationships in the music are often difficult to perceive.

Chance Music The 1950s witnessed not only serialism but an opposite approach known as ***chance,*** or ***aleatory, music*** (from Latin *alea,* or *game of chance*). In chance music, composers choose pitches, tone colors, and rhythms by random methods such as throwing coins. They may also ask performers to choose the ordering of the musical material, or even to choose much of the material itself. For example, a composer might write out brief passages of a composition but ask the performer to play them in any desired order. Or a composer might indicate a group of pitches but direct the performer to invent rhythmic patterns.

The most famous and influential creator of chance music was the American John Cage (1912–1992). At the beginning of this book, a reference was made to Cage's silent "composition" entitled *4′33″* (1952), which requires the performer *not* to make a sound for 4 minutes and 33 seconds. The "music" is made up of the unintentional sounds that an audience might produce in this time span. "I try to arrange my composing means," Cage once explained, "so that I won't have any knowledge of what might happen. . . . My purpose is to eliminate purpose." For Cage, "The purpose of this purposeless music would be achieved if people learned to listen. Then when they listened they might discover that they preferred the sounds of everyday life to the ones they would presently hear in the musical program. . . . That was all right as far as I was concerned." Cage's

Chance effects are incorporated into *One (Number 31, 1950)* by the abstract expressionist painter Jackson Pollock. The artist dripped, poured, and flung paint onto an enormous canvas tacked to the floor.

approach is also illustrated by his *Imaginary Landscape* No. 4 (1951), for twelve radios. The score gives precise directions to the performers—two at each radio—for manipulating the dials affecting wavelength and volume. Yet all the indications in the score were chosen by chance means. They show no regard for local station wavelengths or the time of performance. "At the actual performance of *Imaginary Landscape*," reported one member of the audience, "the hour was later than anticipated before the work's turn came on the program, so that the instruments were unable to capture programs diversified enough to present a really interesting result." This is not surprising, since Cage had chosen the wavelengths and dynamics by throwing dice.

With Cage's work as an example, serial composers such as Pierre Boulez and Karlheinz Stockhausen introduced elements of chance into their compositions during the mid-1950s. Stockhausen's Piano Piece No. 11 (1956) has nineteen short segments of music printed on a large roll of paper that measures 37 by 21 inches. The segments can be played in any order, and the performer is instructed to begin with the fragment that first catches the eye. The piece is likely to be different each time it is played.

Chance music makes a complete break with traditional values in music. It asserts, in effect, that one sound or ordering of sounds is as meaningful as another. To most listeners, a piece of chance music is more often significant as an idea than as a collection of actual sounds. Some composers may be attracted by the sheer novelty of chance music, by its ability to shock and attract attention. Others are influenced by Asian philosophies such as Zen Buddhism, which stresses the harmony of beauty and nature. Finally, some composers may want to give performers a major part in the creative process.

Minimalist Music The mid-1960s saw the development of an artistic movement called *minimalism,* which was partly a reaction against the complexity of serialism and the randomness of chance music. **Minimalist music** is characterized by steady pulse, clear tonality, and insistent repetition of short melodic patterns. Its dynamic level, texture, and harmony tend to stay constant for fairly long stretches of time, creating a trancelike or hypnotic effect. Leading minimalist composers, such as Terry Riley (b. 1935), Steve Reich (b. 1936), Philip Glass (b. 1937), and John Adams (b. 1947), have been profoundly influenced by nonwestern thought; many have studied African, Indian, or Balinese music. Minimalist music grew out of the same intellectual climate

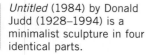

Untitled (1984) by Donald Judd (1928–1994) is a minimalist sculpture in four identical parts.

as minimalist art, which features simple forms, clarity, and understatement. Indeed, in the 1960s, minimalist musicians were appreciated more by painters and sculptors than by their fellow composers. "I gravitated towards artists because they were always more open than musicians, and I liked looking at what they did," Philip Glass has said.

Minimalist composers have generally tried to bring their music to the widest possible audience. "One mode of feedback I rely on most," writes Steve Reich, "is the popular naive reactions. . . . My work, and that of Glass and Riley, comes as a breath of fresh air to the new music world. . . . This feeling is very healthy. It's a feeling of moving back away from a recondite and isolated position, toward a more mainstream approach." Both Reich and Glass have ensembles that perform their music in auditoriums and rock clubs. A turning point in public acceptance of minimalist music came in 1976, when Reich's *Music for 18 Musicians* received an ovation in Town Hall in New York and—also in New York—Glass's opera *Einstein on the Beach,* which we'll study, sold out the Metropolitan Opera House. After the early 1970s, minimalist music became progressively richer in harmony, tone color, and texture, as is exemplified in Adams's opera *Nixon in China* (1987).

Musical Quotation Since the mid-1960s, many composers have written works in which they deliberately make extensive use of quotations from earlier music, usually fairly familiar works of the eighteenth, nineteenth, and twentieth centuries. Like minimalist music, **quotation music** often represents a conscious break with serialism, as well as an attempt to improve communication between composer and listener. The quoted material usually either conveys a symbolic meaning or is varied, transformed, and juxtaposed with other music. For example, in the outer movements of *Concerto Grosso 1985,* which we'll study, Ellen Taaffe Zwilich juxtaposes parts of a Handel sonata with original passages. In *Sinfonia* (1968), a composition for voices and orchestra by the Italian composer Luciano Berio (1925–2003), the third section is based on the scherzo from Mahler's Second Symphony; on this quoted material from Mahler, Berio superimposes fragments of music by Bach, Debussy, Ravel, Berlioz, Schoenberg, and other composers, creating a musical collage. Like Charles Ives early in the twentieth century, composers since the 1960s have often juxtaposed heterogeneous material. The American composer George Crumb (b. 1929) explained that in writing his song cycle *Ancient Voices of Children* (1970), he "was conscious of an urge to fuse various unrelated stylistic elements, . . . a suggestion of Flamenco with a Baroque quotation . . . or a reminiscence of Mahler with a breath of the orient."

Marilyn Monroe (1964) by Andy Warhol. Pop artists like Warhol use ordinary subjects from everyday life and the mass media.

Some modern composers will not only quote earlier composers but also imitate earlier styles. In String Quartet No. 3 (1972) by the American composer George Rochberg (1918–2005), there are sections of atonal music and passages in the styles of Beethoven and Mahler.

Tonal Music and a Return to Tonality As in the early twentieth century, many composers since 1945 have written tonal music, as opposed to atonal or twelve-tone music. (It may be helpful to review the discussion of alternatives to the traditional tonal system on pages 367–368.) Such tonal music spans a vast range of styles and compositional methods, and includes works by composers as diverse as Benjamin Britten, Dmitri Shostakovich, Leonard Bernstein (1918–1990), and John Adams. Tonal compositions may include central tones or chords as well as consonant sonorities. Some works are entirely tonal, while others are basically atonal but contain chord progressions that provide a fleeting sensation of tonality.

Starting in the late 1960s, some composers, such as the Americans George Rochberg (1918–2005) and David Del Tredici (b. 1937), returned to tonality after having written atonal or twelve-tone music. These composers are sometimes referred to as "new romantics," to emphasize the emotional intensity of their works.

Tonality could be a fascinating "novel" option for musicians trained in the twelve-tone system. "For me," explained Del Tredici, "tonality was actually a daring discovery. I grew up in a climate in which, for a composer, only dissonance and atonality were acceptable. Right now, tonality is exciting for me."

Electronic Music Since the development of tape studios, synthesizers, and computers in the 1950s and 1960s, composers have had potentially unlimited resources for the production and control of sound. Electronic music is as varied as nonelectronic music. Its spectrum includes rock, chance music, and serial compositions.

Electronic instruments let composers control tone color, duration, dynamics, and pitch with unprecedented precision. Composers are no longer limited by human performers. For the first time, they can work *directly* in their own medium—sound. There is no more need for intermediaries, that is, performers. The audiotape of a composition *is* the composition. Thus, a composer alone is now responsible for putting into music the subtle variations of rhythm, tone color, and dynamics that once rested with the performer.

Many composers have felt a need to "humanize" their electronic music by combining it with live performers. This humanization can be accomplished in several ways. Some pieces use one or more live performers in conjunction with taped sounds. The taped sounds may be electronic pitches or noises, or they may be previously recorded sounds of live performers. In some cases, performers may be involved in a duet with themselves, or a duet with electronically manipulated versions of their own performances. In combining live performers with taped sounds, composers face the problem of synchronizing sounds that change from performance to performance—those of the live musicians—and the taped sounds, which don't vary. Recently, some composers have dealt with this problem by creating interactive works for performers and computer. In such compositions, the computer is programmed by the composer to respond in musically meaningful ways to the live performance.

There are also works for traditional instruments and digital synthesizers and samplers that are performed "live." In addition, traditional instruments may also be "electrified" through amplification. Composers use "electric" pianos and violins, for instance.

Electronic music is important not only in itself but also in its influence on musical thought in general. Electronic instruments have suggested new sounds and new forms of rhythmic organization. "These limitless electronic media," said Milton Babbitt,

> have shown us new boundaries and new limits that are not yet understood—the very mysterious limits, for example, of the human capacity to hear, to conceptualize, and to perceive. Very often we will specify something and discover that the ear can't take in what we have specified. . . . The human organism simply cannot respond quickly enough, cannot perceive and differentiate as rapidly and precisely as the synthesizer can produce it and as the loudspeaker can reproduce it.

"Liberation of Sound" Composers today use a wider variety of sounds than ever before, including many that were once considered undesirable noises. Composers have achieved what Edgard Varèse called "the liberation of sound . . . the right to make music with any and all sounds." Electronic music may include environmental sounds, such as thunder, or electronically generated hisses and blips. But composers may also draw novel sounds from voices and nonelectronic instruments. Singers are asked to scream, whisper, laugh, groan, sneeze, cough, whistle, and click their tongues. They may sing phonetic sounds rather than words. Composers may treat their vocal text merely as a collection of sounds and not attempt to make the meaning of the words clear to the audience.

Scores for recent music often include notes in new shapes, new symbols, and novel ways of arranging notation on the page. Here is a page from the score *Threnody: To the Victims of Hiroshima* by Krzysztof Penderecki.

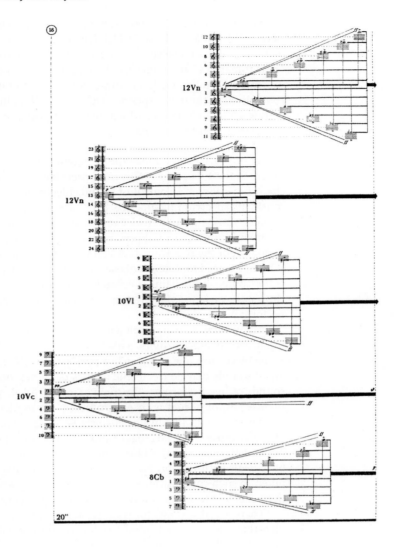

Wind and string players tap, scrape, and rub the bodies of their instruments. A brass or woodwind player may hum while playing, thus creating two pitches at once. A flutist may click the keys of the instrument without producing a tone; a pianist may reach inside the piano to pluck a string and then run a chisel along it, creating a sliding sound. To communicate their intentions to performers, composers may devise new systems of music notation, because standard notation makes no provision for many noiselike sounds. Recent music scores contain graphlike diagrams, new note shapes and symbols, and novel ways of arranging notation on the page (see the illustration above). But composers are not the only ones to invent unusual sounds. Often the players themselves discover new possibilities for their instruments. Many modern works have been inspired by the discoveries of inventive performers.

The greatest expansion and experimentation have involved percussion instruments. In many recent compositions, percussion instruments outnumber strings, woodwinds, and brasses. Traditional percussion instruments are struck with new types of beaters made of glass, metal, wood, and cloth. Unconventional instruments now widely used include tom-toms, bongos, slapstick, maracas, guiro, and vibraphone.

In the search for novel sounds, increased use has been made of **microtones,** intervals smaller than the half step. Small intervals like quarter tones have long been used in nonwestern music, but they have only recently become an important resource for western composers. Electronic instruments have stimulated this development, since

Percussion instruments are imaginatively exploited in much recent music. The percussionist Evelyn Glennie rehearsing with the New York Philharmonic conducted by Leonard Slatkin. Glennie is profoundly deaf.

Frank Gehry (b. 1930), Walt Disney Concert Hall, Los Angeles, California, completed 2003. Gehry designs his buildings as a series of separate but interdependent units with curved contours.

they are not restricted to conventional scales and do not force players to unlearn performance habits.

Composers like Krzysztof Penderecki (b. 1933) create sounds bordering on electronic noise through tone clusters—closely spaced tones played together. Clusters are unlike traditional chords in that one usually hears not individual tones but a mass, block, or band of sound. Composers may achieve a sense of growth or change by widening or narrowing such a band, or by making it more or less dense.

The directional aspect of sounds—how they are projected in space—has taken on new importance. Loudspeakers or groups of instruments may be placed at opposite ends of the stage, in the balcony, or at the back and sides of the auditorium. In electronic compositions like Edgard Varèse's *Poème électronique* (1958) and nonelectronic works like Elliott Carter's Double Concerto for harpsichord and piano with two chamber orchestras (1961), sounds are made to travel gradually in space, passing from one loudspeaker or player to another.

Mixed Media   Electronic music is often presented together with visual counterparts such as slide projections, films, light shows, gestures, and theatrical action. One such mixed-media presentation was Varèse's *Poème électronique,* which combined electronic sounds with images projected on walls. But multimedia works are not confined to electronic music. Chance music and other types of recent music sometimes require performers to function as both actors and sound producers, as in Crumb's *Ancient Voices of Children.* Mixed-media presentations are generally intended to break down the ritual surrounding traditional concerts and to increase communication between composer and audience.

Rhythm and Form   Rhythm and form have undergone some of the most striking changes in music since 1945. Earlier in the century, composers often changed meters or used unconventional meters such as $\frac{7}{8}$ and $\frac{5}{8}$. After 1945, some composers abandoned the concepts of beat and meter altogether. This is a natural outcome of electronic music, which needs no beat to keep performers together. In nonelectronic music, too, the composer may specify duration in absolute units such as seconds rather than in beats, which are relative units. In some recent music, there may be several different speeds at the same time.

More than ever, each piece of music follows its own laws, and its form grows out of its material. Some composers no longer write music in traditional forms, such as A B A, sonata form, or rondo. Indeed, form may unfold with little or no obvious repetition of material.

20 Music since 1945: Eight Representative Pieces

Sonatas and Interludes for Prepared Piano (1946–1948), by John Cage

The American composer John Cage (1912–1992) was the highly influential creator of chance music—as discussed in Section 19—and a major figure in the development of percussion music. He invented the ***prepared piano,*** a grand piano whose sound is altered by objects such as bolts, screws, rubber bands, pieces of felt, paper, and plastic inserted between the strings of some of the keys. "In practice, the preparation takes about three hours," Cage explained. Such preparation results in a wide variety of sounds that resemble those of drums, cymbals, xylophones, tambourines, and gongs. When the pianist's finger strikes a key, sometimes more than one sound is produced.

Cage invented the prepared piano around 1940, when he was asked to write music for a modern dance on an African theme. The dance was to be performed in a small auditorium with enough space for a small grand piano, but not for a group of percus-

The inside of a prepared piano.

sionists. "In effect," Cage wrote, "the prepared piano is a percussion ensemble under the control of a single player."

The large-scale *Sonatas and Interludes* (1946–1948), lasting around 66 minutes, is Cage's best-known work for prepared piano and one of his most widely performed and recorded compositions. It includes twenty short pieces—sixteen one-movement sonatas and four interludes—ranging in length from 1½ minutes to 5 minutes. *Sonatas and Interludes* reflects the composer's study of eastern philosophy. Cage explained that the cycle aims to express the range of stylized emotional states described in Indian aesthetic theory: "the heroic, erotic, wondrous, mirthful, odious, sorrowful, fearful, angry, and their common tendency toward tranquillity." We'll focus on the second sonata of the cycle.

Sonata II

The two-minute Sonata II, in A A B B form, is characterized by a gradual thickening of texture and increase in rhythmic momentum. Part A moves from a single melodic line—sometimes accompanied by percussive sounds—to a two-voice texture. This part is predominantly soft, in a fairly high register. Short phrases, arranged in question-and-answer pairs, are framed by silences. In two phrases, a melodic fragment immediately repeats.

Basic Set:
CD 9 **1**

Brief Set:
CD 5 [35]

Part A
1 [35]

Part B
2 [36]

Basic Set:

CD 9 **3** [37]

Part B is almost twice as long as A and has more extended phrases and a richer texture. It begins abruptly with a loud, dense sonority that contrasts with the gentle, lingering sounds and pause ending part A. The concluding phrase of part B is the most extended, climactic, and rhythmically active. It begins with a torrent of high running notes and ends with a high trill-like figure and an upward swoop to a single accented tone.

Poème électronique (Electronic Poem; 1958), by Edgard Varèse

Edgard Varèse (1883–1965), one of the great innovators of twentieth-century music, was born in France but spent most of his life in the United States. As early as 1916, he dreamed of freeing music from the limitations of traditional instruments and expanding the vocabulary of sounds. During the 1920s and 1930s, Varèse pioneered in the exploration of percussive and noiselike sounds, and he wrote the first important work for percussion ensemble (*Ionisation*, 1931).

But it was the new electronic developments of the 1950s that enabled Varèse to realize his vision of a "liberation of sound." In 1958, at the age of seventy-five, he composed *Poème électronique,* one of the earliest masterpieces of electronic music created in a tape studio. The 8-minute work was designed to be heard within the pavilion of the Philips Radio Corporation at the 1958 Brussels World's Fair. Varèse obtained unique spatial effects by projecting sound from 425 loudspeakers placed all over the interior surfaces

Varèse's *Poème électronique* was first heard within the pavilion of the Philips Radio Corporation, designed by Le Corbusier, at the 1958 Brussels World's Fair.

of the pavilion. The composer worked in collaboration with the architect Le Corbusier, who selected a series of images—photographs, paintings, and writing—that were projected on the walls as the music was heard. However, Varèse did not make any attempt to synchronize the sounds with the images chosen by Le Corbusier, which included "birds and beasts, fish and reptiles, . . . masks and skeletons, idols, girls clad and unclad, cities in normal appearance and then suddenly askew," as well as atomic mushroom clouds.

Because it was created in a tape studio, *Poème électronique* exists in only a single "performance" whose duration (8 minutes) is fixed on audiotape. Varèse's raw sound material—tones and noises—came from a wide variety of sources, including electronic generators, church bells, sirens, organs, human voices, and machines. The sounds are often electronically processed in such a way that they cannot be precisely identified. In the listening outline, the effect of such sounds is conveyed by words placed in quotation marks; for example, "wood blocks" or "chirps." Varèse organized his sounds into an electronic poem that seems weird yet is amazingly logical and compelling.

Poème électronique divides into two main sections, the first lasting 2 minutes 36 seconds and the second 5 minutes 29 seconds. Each section begins with low bell tolls and ends with sirens. Heard several times during *Poème* is a distinctive group of three rising tones. Human voices and recognizable organ tones appear only during the second section. Varèse once remarked about the female voice heard toward the end: "I wanted it to express tragedy—and inquisition."

LISTENING OUTLINE

VARÈSE, *Poème électronique (Electronic Poem)*

Tape studio

(Duration, 8:00)

3 **37** 0:00   **1. a.** Low bell tolls. "Wood blocks." Sirens. Fast taps lead into high, piercing sounds. 2-second pause.

0:43   **b.** "Bongo" tones and higher grating noises. Short "squawks." Three-tone group stated three times.

1:11   **c.** Low sustained tones with grating noises. Sirens. Short "squawks." Three-tone group. 2-second pause.

1:40   **d.** Short "squawks." High "chirps." Variety of "shots," "honks," "machine noises." Sirens. Taps lead to

4 **38** 2:36   **2. a.** Low bell tolls. Sustained electronic tones. Repeated "bongo" tones. High and sustained electronic tones. Low tone, crescendo. Rhythmic noises lead to

5 **39** 3:41   **b.** Voice, "Oh-gah." 4-second pause. Voice continues softly.

4:17   **c.** Suddenly loud. Rhythmic percussive sounds joined by voice. Low "animal noises," scraping, shuffling, hollow vocal sounds. Decrescendo into 7-second pause.

5:47   **d.** Sustained electronic tones, crescendo and decrescendo. Rhythmic percussive sounds. Higher sustained electronic tones, crescendo. "Airplane rumble," "chimes," jangling.

6 **40** 6:47   **e.** Female voice. Male chorus. Electronic noises, organ. High taps. Swooping organ sound. Three-note group stated twice. Rumble, sirens, crescendo.

Basic Set:
CD 9 **7**

Threnody: To the Victims of Hiroshima, for 52 Strings (1960) by Krzysztof Penderecki

During the late 1950s, a group of avant-garde composers unexpectedly emerged in Poland. For years, all artistic experimentation had been actively discouraged by the Soviet government and by other regimes in eastern Europe. However, after the revolt against Stalinism in 1955–1956, the new Polish government encouraged cultural independence and free artistic expression in films, painting, theater, and music. Polish composers had at their disposal well-trained performing groups and electronic music studios. The best-known Polish composer today is Krzysztof Penderecki (b. 1933).

Penderecki was a boy when the Nazis occupied Poland and massacred most of its Jewish population. Although not threatened personally, Penderecki felt great compassion for the victims. "That great war crime," he wrote, "has undoubtedly been in my subconscious mind since the war, when, as a child, I saw the destruction of the ghetto in my small native town of Debica." His compassion for human suffering has been expressed in such works as *Dies irae* (1967), to the memory of the victims of Auschwitz; and *Threnody: To the Victims of Hiroshima*. In these works, and in his well-known *St. Luke Passion* (1963–1965), Penderecki draws spectacular and novel sounds from voices and conventional instruments. He often calls for tone clusters, glissandos, noiselike and percussive effects, and choral hissing, laughing, shouting, and whistling.

Penderecki's *Threnody*, or song of mourning, is an almost unbearably intense work; its sounds are not intended to be "pleasant." Fifty-two string instruments—violins, violas, cellos, and double basses—produce a wide variety of noiselike sounds that often seem to come from electronic generators. Many of these sounds are tone clusters. At the beginning of this 9-minute work, shrill clusters are produced by ten groups of instruments playing "the highest note of the instrument (no definite pitch)." At the end of the piece, a huge cluster that sounds like the roar of a jet engine is produced by all fifty-two strings playing pitches a quarter tone apart. Penderecki often uses slides or glissandos to make the clusters expand and contract. Noiselike sounds are also produced by tapping on the body of the instrument and bowing on the tailpiece.

There is no feeling of beat in this music. The duration of its various musical events is indicated in seconds at the bottom of the score. *Threnody* is divided into six sections. Some feature sustained sounds; others contain a variety of rapid percussive attacks. Noiselike sounds are so predominant that the definite pitch heard at the beginning of section 2 is very striking. An overall sense of coherence is produced by the general similarity of the first and last sections, as well as by the climactic character of section 4.

LISTENING OUTLINE

PENDERECKI, *Threnody: To the Victims of Hiroshima* (Recording available in the Online Learning Center)

24 violins, 10 violas, 10 cellos, 8 double basses

7 0:00   **1. a.** Shrill, sustained clusters, one entering after the other.
                 b. Suddenly soft.
                 c. Pizzicatos. Soft, rapid squeaks. Increased rhythmic activity.
                 d. Clusters fade out, squeaks and pizzicatos remain.

8 1:52   **2. a.** Sustained tone.
                 b. Upward and downward glissandos (slides). Single, sustained tones expand into clusters, clusters contract into single tones.
                 c. High sustained tone together with clusters; brief silence.

9 3:23   **3. a.** Low, sustained cluster, *p.* Higher sustained cluster, *f.* Other clusters join, *ff.*
                 b. Glassy sounds slide upward. Decrescendo into silence.

10 4:07   **4. a.** Quick attacks of single tones build to very wide and loud cluster.
                 b. Low, roaring cluster. Slides. Low cluster narrows to single sustained cello tone. Decrescendo into 10-second pause.

11 5:30   **5.** Disconnected pizzicatos, tremolos, blips, scratches at various dynamics and registers. Percussive sounds lead to

12 7:07   **6. a.** Sustained clusters in various registers. Momentarily soft, high squeaks and clusters, crescendo to brief silence.
                 b. Sustained cluster like jet roar. Sound gradually fades into silence.

Ancient Voices of Children (1970), by George Crumb

During the late 1960s, the American composer George Crumb (b. 1929) became prominent as the result of a series of works that were highly acclaimed by both audiences and critics. His music is personal and emotionally intense; it is distinguished by imaginative use of novel and delicate tone colors. For many years, Crumb taught composition at the University of Pennsylvania.

Like much of his music, Crumb's *Ancient Voices of Children* is set to poetry by Federico García Lorca, the great Spanish writer who was murdered in 1936 during the civil war in Spain. "I have sought musical images," wrote Crumb, "that enhance and reinforce the powerful, yet strangely haunting imagery of Lorca's poetry. I feel that the essential meaning of this poetry is concerned with the most primary things: life, death, love, the smell of the earth, the sounds of the wind and the sea."

Ancient Voices of Children is a cycle of five songs with two instrumental interludes. The work is written for mezzo-soprano, boy soprano, oboe, mandolin, harp, percussion, and "electric piano." (A normal grand piano is amplified by contact microphones attached to its sounding board.) Three percussionists command a variety of instruments, including such unconventional ones as tuned tom-toms, Tibetan prayer stones, and Japanese temple bells. The pianist also plays a toy piano (in the fourth song); the oboist plays a harmonica (also in the fourth song); and the mandolinist plays a "musical saw" (an ordinary saw played with a double-bass bow).

"Perhaps the most characteristic vocal effect in *Ancient Voices*," writes Crumb, "is produced by the mezzo-soprano singing a kind of fantastic vocalise (on purely phonetic sounds) into an amplified piano, thereby producing a shimmering aura of echoes." (A *vocalise* is an extended melody sung without a text, only on vowels.) Gradually fading sounds are produced by gongs, harp, vibraphone, and marimbas—among other instruments—and contribute to the vaguely Asian atmosphere. (A **vibraphone** is a percussion instrument with tuned metal bars and tubular metal resonators that produce a vibrato by means of motor-driven revolving metal vanes; a **marimba** is a large xylophone with resonators.) The composer wants us to savor individual tone colors; in many passages, only a single instrument or voice is heard.

Ancient Voices is theatrical in character and has been used as ballet music by several dance companies. A boy soprano singing offstage heightens the drama. Even the instrumentalists play a dramatic role; they are occasionally required to sing, shout, or whisper. We'll focus on the third song of the cycle.

From Where Do You Come, My Love, My Child? (*Dance of the Sacred Life-Cycle*)

Basic Set:
CD 9 13

The most spectacular part of *Ancient Voices of Children* is the central song, which uses the characteristic rhythm of a bolero, the Spanish dance which also inspired Ravel's *Bolero* (see Section 5). The song opens with a mezzo-soprano solo on phonetic sounds, sung into the amplified piano. During this solo, the singer is required to trill the tongue and make laughing sounds. Then the percussionists begin an ostinato in bolero rhythm that continues throughout the piece. They make a gradual crescendo and decrescendo, and progress from whispering to shouting, then back to whispering. Each of the poem's three stanzas has a half-sung question and answer by the two vocalists, a decorative oboe phrase, and an exuberant soprano melody.

VOCAL MUSIC GUIDE

CRUMB, *From Where Do You Come, My Love, My Child?*

13

0:00	Mezzo soprano, phonetic sounds. Percussion, bolero rhythm.		
1:02	Mezzo soprano. my child?	*¿De dónde vienes, amor, mi niño?*	From where do you come, my love,
	Boy soprano.	*De la cresta del duro frío.*	From the ridge of hard frost.
	Mezzo.	*¿Qué necesitas, amor, mi niño?*	What do you need, my love, my child?
	Boy, oboe.	*La tibia tela de tu vestido.*	The warm cloth of your dress.
1:28	Mezzo.	*¡Que se agiten las ramas al sol y salten las fuentes alrededor!*	Let the branches ruffle in the sun and the fountains leap all around!
1:44	Boy.	*En el patio ladra el perro, en los árboles canta el viento. Los bueyes mugen al boyero y la luna me riza los cabellos.*	In the courtyard a dog barks, in the trees the wind sings. The oxen low to the ox-herd and the moon curls my hair.
2:03	Mezzo.	*¿Qué pides, niño, desde tan lejos?*	What do you ask for, my child, from so far away?
2:21	Boy, oboe.	*Los blancos montes que hay en tu pecho.*	The white mountains of your breast.
	Mezzo.	*¿Que se agiten las ramas al sol y salten las fuentes alrededor! Te diré, niño mío, que sí, tronchada y rota soy para ti. ¡Cómo me duele esta cintura*	Let the branches ruffle in the sun and the fountains leap all around! I'll tell you, my child, yes, I am torn and broken for you. How painful is this waist
		donde tendrás primera cuna! ¿Cuándo mi niño, vas a venir?	where you will have your first cradle! When, my child, will you come?
	Boy.	*Cuando tu carne huela a jazmín.*	When your flesh smells of jasmine flowers.
3:05	Oboe interlude.		
3:15	Mezzo.	*¡Que se agiten las ramas al sol y salten las fuentes alrededor!*	Let the branches ruffle in the sun and the fountains leap all around!
	Percussion.		

Einstein on the Beach (1976), by Philip Glass

Philip Glass (b. 1937) is an American minimalist composer whose works have reached large audiences and influenced both "classical" and rock musicians. Like other minimalists, he writes music distinguished by a steady, driving pulse, clear tonality, constant repetition of melodic and rhythmic patterns, and a slow rate of change.

Glass was born in Baltimore and studied at the University of Chicago—where he majored in mathematics and philosophy—and the Juilliard School of Music, where he wrote music in a style reminiscent of Aaron Copland. As Copland had done in 1921,

Glass went to Paris in 1964 to study with the legendary composition teacher Nadia Boulanger. In Paris Glass also studied Indian drumming and helped the famous Indian sitarist and composer Ravi Shankar notate his improvisations for a film score. (Ravi Shankar's *Maru-Bihag* is studied in Part XI, Section 3.) Glass's contact with what he described as the "steady stream of rhythmic pulses" in traditional Indian music triggered his emerging minimalist style. Inspired by Shankar, Glass went to India, where he began his lifelong involvement with Buddhist meditation.

In 1967 Glass returned to New York, wrote minimalist music, and supported himself by working as a plumber and cab driver. He founded a group—later called the Philip Glass Ensemble—that performed his compositions in museums, art galleries, lofts of minimalist artists, and rock clubs. In the 1970s, the ensemble, which included electric keyboards, amplified winds, and two vocalists, presented works throughout Europe, where Glass influenced progressive rock musicians like David Bowie and Brian Eno.

Glass became a celebrity in 1976 when his opera *Einstein on the Beach* sold out two performances at New York's Metropolitan Opera House. The composer, subsidized by a foundation, had rented the hall of the Metropolitan Opera and presented *Einstein on the Beach* with the same troupe that had already performed the opera in eight European cities. *Einstein*'s success led European opera companies to commission *Satyagraha* (1980), about the Indian leader Mahatma Gandhi; and *Akhnaten* (1984), dealing with an ancient Egyptian pharaoh. *The Voyage,* Glass's opera about Columbus, was commissioned by the Metropolitan Opera and was performed on Columbus Day, 1992, five hundred years after the explorer encountered America. Since *Einstein on the Beach,* Glass's works—including the film score *Koyaanisqatsi* (1982)—have become increasingly rich in texture, harmony, and instrumentation.

Einstein on the Beach (1976), created in collaboration with the American playwright-director Robert Wilson, breaks with many conventions of opera. It has no real plot or character development, even though it lasts almost 5 hours with no intermission. Its vocal texts are mostly sung or spoken numerals (1, 2, 3 . . .) and solfège syllables (*do, re, mi* . . .) which represent, respectively, the rhythmic and melodic structure of the music. The "orchestra" consists of the Philip Glass Ensemble—a sound engineer, a female vocalist, and five instrumentalists playing two electric organs, synthesizer bass, keyboards, three saxophones, flute, and clarinet, together with a violin soloist dressed as Albert Einstein. (Einstein, the great physicist, was also an amateur violinist.) The singers, who are not formally trained, dance and act as well. Three visual images recur in *Einstein on the Beach*: a train, a trial with a bed, and a field with a spaceship in the sky. Near the end of the opera, Einstein plays the violin while the statistics of a nuclear disaster appear on a backdrop behind him. (The opera's title refers to Nevil Shute's novel about nuclear destruction, called *On the Beach*.) The opera includes five short pieces called *Knee Plays,* which function as a prelude, interludes, and a postlude. We'll focus on *Knee Play 1* as an example of musical minimalism.

Knee Play 1

Basic Set:
CD 9 14

Knee Play 1 is performed at the opening of the opera by an electric organ, a chorus of men and women, and two female speaking voices while two characters sit at two tables. This collage-like 4-minute piece creates an effect of ceremonial chanting and has the steady beat and repeated melodic patterns characteristic of minimalist music. *Knee Play 1* is built on a musical pattern of three long, low tones (A–G–C) repeated over and over by the electric organ, somewhat like a basso ostinato. Against this constant pattern of three tones, the men and women of the chorus repeatedly sing a series of numbers, or beats (1-2-3-4/1-2-3-4-5-6/1-2-3-4-5-6-7-8) to specific pitches. Men sing the numbers to the descending pitches of the electric organ, A–G–C, while women sing the numbers to the ascending group of pitches C–E.

Women:	C	D	E
	1-2-3-4/1-2-3-4-5-6/1-2-3-4-5-6-7-8		
Men (organ):	A	G	C

Sung staccato, the numbers create a steady, rather fast beat. Glass adds variety to *Knee Play 1* by slightly changing the rhythm and by gradually adding different layers of sound. Rhythmic change comes when the chorus produces syncopations by sometimes omitting the numeral 1 on the first pulse: _2-3-4/1-2-3-4-5-6/_2-3-4-5-6-7-8. A new sound layer appears when female voices join in the background with spoken numbers and a barely comprehensible text. Yet another layer of sound is added halfway through *Knee Play 1,* when the chorus's pulselike numbers are joined by men and women singing solfège syllables in long, legato tones. Over and over, men sing *la* (A)–*sol* (G)–*do* (C), while women sing the rising pattern *do* (C)–*re* (D)–*mi* (E). Such small changes in a hypnotically repetitive pattern create Glass's unique world of sound.

LISTENING OUTLINE

GLASS, *Knee Play 1,* from *Einstein on the Beach*

Electric organ, chorus of men and women, 2 female speaking voices

C Major

14	0:00	**1. a.**	Electric organ alone, pattern of three long, low tones (A–G–C), repeated throughout.
	0:21	**b.**	Two-part chorus of men and women joins, repeating 1-2-3-4/1-2-3-4-5-6/1-2-3-4-5-6-7-8 throughout; sometimes numeral 1 is omitted, creating syncopation.
	1:04	**c.**	Female voice joins in background, reciting numbers, then text. Second female speaking voice joins with barely comprehensible text, continuing into
15	2:05	**2.**	*La-sol-do* (men) and *do-re-mi* (women) repeatedly sung to long, legato tones against recited text and sung numbers. Abrupt ending.

Concerto Grosso 1985 (To Handel's Sonata in D Major for Violin and Continuo, First Movement), by Ellen Taaffe Zwilich

The American composer Ellen Taaffe Zwilich (b. 1939) won the Pulitzer Prize for Music in 1983 for her Symphony No. 1. Zwilich was born in Miami, Florida; her father was an airline pilot. She studied at Florida State University and at the Juilliard School and played for several years as a professional violinist in the American Symphony Orchestra under the direction of Leopold Stokowski. She has composed an impressive series of widely performed instrumental works, including her String Quartet (1974), Symphony No. 2 (1985), Concerto for Piano and Orchestra (1986), Symphony No. 3 (1992), *Millennium Fantasy* for Piano and Orchestra (2000), and Symphony No. 5 (Concerto for Orchestra; 2008), commissioned by the Juilliard School. From 1995 to 1999 she occupied Carnegie Hall's first Composer's Chair, and in 1999 she was named *Musical America*'s Composer of the Year. A professor at her alma mater, Florida State University, she was elected to the American Academy of Arts and Sciences in 2004.

Concerto Grosso 1985 was commissioned by the Washington Friends of Handel to commemorate Handel's three-hundredth birthday. Each of its five movements uses thematic material drawn from the opening movement of Handel's Sonata for Violin and Continuo in D Major. Zwilich has said: "I performed the [Handel] many years ago, and I especially love the opening theme of the first movement. . . . Throughout [*Concerto Grosso 1985*], I found myself using compositional techniques typical of the baroque period, including terraced dynamics, repeated phrases . . . techniques I would not normally use, but I felt inspired to do so because of the fact that this piece was based on Handel." Like the concerti grossi of Handel and Bach, Zwilich's *Concerto Grosso 1985* is written for a small orchestra including a harpsichord and gives solo instruments prominent

Ellen Taaffe Zwilich.

roles. Its five movements are arranged symmetrically: the finale is similar to the opening movement, and the fourth movement parallels the second. The two outer movements include entire passages from the Handel sonata, whereas the three inner movements use no quotations but freely develop the sonata's opening melodic motive. We'll focus on the first movement, a clear example of "quotation music."

First Movement: Maestoso (majestic)

Basic Set:
CD 9 **16**

Brief Set:
CD 5 **41**

The maestoso repeatedly alternates quotations from Handel with passages that could have been written only in the twentieth century. Though abrupt, these contrasts somehow add up to a unified whole. Partly, this is because the newly composed sections are often based on a speeded-up variation of Handel's opening four-note motive.

In addition, Zwilich's own music uses compositional techniques associated with the baroque. Long pedal points in the bass give a firm definition of key to melodic lines that use dissonances freely in a twentieth-century manner. And these melodic lines include the repeated rhythmic pattern short-short-long, short-short-long found in music by Bach and Handel.

LISTENING OUTLINE

ZWILICH, *Concerto Grosso 1985*

First Movement

Maestoso (majestic), quadruple meter ($\frac{4}{4}$), D major

Flute, 2 oboes, bassoon, 2 French horns, harpsichord, 1st violins, 2d violins, violas, cellos, double basses

(Duration, 2:45)

16 **41** 0:00   **1. a.** Orchestra in unison, *f*, single sustained tone presented three times.

                b. Violins, *f*, vigorous phrase, short-short-long rhythm, sustained tone in bass;

             vigorous phrase repeated softly.

17 **42** 0:34   **c.** Handel quotation, strings and harpsichord, *mp*,

        0:55   interrupted by

                        2. a. Vigorous phrase developed in strings and woodwinds; crescendo to *f*, short string phrases with abrupt pauses.

                        b. Handel quotation continued, oboe *mf*, accompanied by harpsichord and strings.

        1:31   **3. a.** Vigorous phrase in violins, *f*, imitated in flute, *f* vigorous phrase in violins, *f*.

                        b. Handel quotation continued, *f*, trills in strings and woodwinds; harpsichord; melody closes.

        2:03   **4. a.** Vigorous phrase in violins, flute, and oboes; crescendo to *ff*.

        2:13   **b.** Woodwinds, high sustained dissonant chords; low strings, fragments of vigorous string phrase, *ff*. Ends on sustained dissonant chord, *f*.

Short Ride in a Fast Machine (1986), by John Adams

Basic Set:
CD 9 [18]

Brief Set:
CD 5 [43]

John Adams (b. 1947) is a leading American composer who has been aptly described as a postminimalist. His music combines the driving pulse, constant repetition, and clear tonality of minimalism with lyrical, expressive melodies and varied orchestral colors. "I grew up in a household where Benny Goodman and Mozart were not separated," Adams once recalled. Indeed, his works reflect the influence of American popular music as well as composers such as Stravinsky and Reich.

A conductor as well as a composer, Adams taught and directed the New Music Ensemble at the San Francisco Conservatory of Music from 1972 to 1982 and was composer in residence with the San Francisco Symphony Orchestra during 1982–1985. In 2009, he was appointed creative chair of the Los Angeles Philharmonic to compose works for the orchestra while serving as a member of its planning team. His compositions include *Harmonium* (1980), for chorus and orchestra; the orchestral works *Harmonielehre* (1985), *Short Ride in a Fast Machine* (1986) and *City Noir* (2009); and the operas *Nixon in China* (1987), *The Death of Klinghoffer* (1991), *Dr. Atomic* (2005), dealing with J. Robert Oppenheimer, the physicist known as the father of the atomic bomb, and *A Flowering Tree* (2006), based on a folktale from southern India. In 2003, Adams won the Pulitzer Prize in music for *On the Transmigration of Souls* (2002), a work for chorus and orchestra commissioned by the New York Philharmonic in commemoration of those who died in the terrorist attacks on the Pentagon and the World Trade Center on September 11, 2001.

Short Ride in a Fast Machine, a 4-minute fanfare, is one of the most widely performed orchestral works by a living American composer. The work was commissioned by the Great Woods Festival to celebrate its inaugural concert at Great Woods, Mansfield, Massachusetts. *Short Ride in a Fast Machine* generates enormous excitement because of its rapid tempo, rhythmic drive, and powerful, colorful sonorities. The large orchestra includes two synthesizers and a variety of percussion instruments played by four musicians. These percussion instruments include a sizzle cymbal (a large cymbal with loose rivets placed in a ring of holes) and crotales (small cymbals of definite pitch). *Short Ride in a Fast Machine* is pervaded by steady beats in the wood block, rapid-note ostinatos in synthesizers and clarinets, and repeated orchestral chords that alternate between regular pulsations and irregular rhythms. The climax comes toward the end, when Adams introduces a stirring, fanfare-like melody in the trumpets.

John Adams.

LISTENING OUTLINE

ADAMS, *Short Ride in a Fast Machine*

Delirando (deliriously)

2 piccolos, 2 flutes, 2 oboes, English horn, 4 clarinets, 3 bassoons, contrabassoon, 4 French horns, 4 trumpets, 3 trombones, tuba, timpani, wood blocks, pedal bass drum, large bass drum, suspended cymbal, sizzle cymbal, large gong (tam-tam), tambourine, triangle, glockenspiel, xylophone, crotales, 2 synthesizers, 1st violins, 2d violins, violas, cellos, double basses

(Duration 4:11)

18 **43** 0:00   **1. a.** Wood block pulsations followed by ostinatos in clarinets and synthesizer, staccato repeated chords in trumpets, *f*, trombones and French horns join on faster repeated chords; piccolo fragments and snare drum strokes punctuate.

0:32   **b.** Pulsating brass chords, piccolo fragments, brass chords in irregular rhythms, quick snare drum strokes and suspended cymbal announce

19 **44** 1:01   **c.** String entrance, chords in irregular rhythms, bass drum strokes, chords rise in pitch, cymbal, bass drum and snare drum strokes, crescendo to *fff*.

20 **45** 1:39   **d.** Suddenly softer, "walking" figure in cellos and basses below pulsating, rising orchestral chords, irregular rhythms in percussion, brass, and woodwinds, crescendo to *fff*.

2:31   **e.** Trombones and tubas, *fff*, low downward skip, repeated chords in brasses and woodwinds; bass drum, gong, cymbals, crescendo to *fff*.

2:46   **f.** Suddenly softer orchestral pulsations, clarinet ostinato.

21 **46** 2:53   **2. a.** Trumpets, *ff*, extended melody, accompanied by pulsating chords and countermelody in French horns, crescendo to *fff*.

3:49   **b.** Repeated major chords in trumpets and trombones, *fff*, percussive concluding chord.

Basic Set:
CD 9 **22**

Brief Set:
CD 5 **47**

Shard (1997), by Elliott Carter

Elliott Carter (b. 1908), one of the foremost American composers since 1950, developed new ways of creating dramatic effects through changes in tempo. He is the first major composer in history to continue writing music in his hundred and first year.

Carter was born in New York City, the son of a prosperous importer of lace. When he was fifteen, in 1924, his high school music teacher introduced him to the composer Charles Ives—discussed in Section 14 above—who became his mentor. That same year Carter attended the American premiere in Carnegie Hall of Stravinsky's *Rite of Spring*, which had such a powerful impact on the teenager that he decided to become a composer. In 1926 Carter entered Harvard University, where he studied English literature, Greek, and philosophy, preferring to study oboe and theory at the nearby Longy School of Music. After receiving an M.A. in music from Harvard in 1932, he went to Paris to study for three years with Nadia Boulanger, the teacher of many American composers including Aaron Copland (discussed in Section 17 above) and Philip Glass (discussed on pages 452–454 above).

Elliott Carter.

In 1935, Carter returned to New York, where he became music director of the Ballet Caravan company. During World War II, he worked as music consultant for the Office of War Information (1943–1944). After the war, he taught at several universities and music conservatories, including the Juilliard School, where Ellen Taaffe Zwilich was among his students. (Zwilich's *Concerto Grosso 1985* is also studied in this section.) His many honors include two Pulitzer Prizes (1960, 1973), the Gold Medals of the National Institute for Arts and Letters (1971) and the Royal Philharmonic Society (1996), and the U.S. National Medal of Arts (1985).

Carter has evolved a personal style that is complex, dense, and highly dissonant. "There are no recurring themes in my music" he once told an interviewer. "It continues to evolve and evolve, yet never returns to a thematic point." In his compositions, several highly contrasting ideas are often presented simultaneously, a procedure inspired by his former mentor Charles Ives.

A work by Carter includes many precisely regulated tempo changes that give his music a feeling of fluidity. This technique, which Carter calls "tempo modulation," is employed in *Shard,* for solo acoustic guitar, which we'll study.

Written when Carter was eighty-eight, *Shard* (1997) is one of his simplest and most playful works and lasts less than 3 minutes. It was composed for the virtuoso guitarist David Starobin, who had earlier commissioned Carter to write his first piece for solo guitar, *Changes* (1983). Carter used the word *shard*—a fragment of pottery found at an archaeological dig—as a witty title because of the work's brevity, and because it exists both as an independent composition and as a section within *Luimen,* a more extended work for trumpet, trombone, harp, vibraphone, mandolin, and guitar, also composed in 1997.

"I regard my scores as scenarios, auditory scenarios, for performers to act out with their instruments," Carter once wrote. *Shard* can be heard as a series of episodes that include controlled changes of tempo, as well as a fantastic variety of rhythms, registers, tone colors, dynamic levels, and textures, including single notes, *dyads*—two tones sounded simultaneously—and loud chords containing three to six notes. These quick shifts of musical activity make *Shard* sound like an improvisation, even though the piece is notated precisely.

The following musical ideas play a major role in *Shard:*

1. Steady, rapid flow of single notes with jazzlike offbeat accents. This stream of rapid notes first appears fleetingly (0:08), lasting only a few seconds. Later (1:37), this jazzy idea returns in highly varied form, now lasting almost 1 minute and punctuated by loud thick chords.
2. Succession of dyads. The first dyad succession (0:25) begins softly and legato, but is followed by accented, loud dyads. The second succession of dyads (1:12) is legato, mostly soft, and functions as a moment of repose before loud chords.
3. Lyrical melody (0:35), mostly in single, relatively slow notes.
4. Harmonics—high bell-like sounds—sounded above low staccato notes. This idea is introduced near the middle of *Shard* (0:58) and reappears soon afterward (1:28) as the climax of a legato melodic line that ascends from a low, single note to the registral stratosphere.

LISTENING OUTLINE

CARTER, *Shard*

Solo acoustic guitar

(Duration: 2:42)

22 **47** 0:00   **1. a.** Chords, dyads, *f*, single soft notes introduce
          0:08   **b.** Flow of rapid notes, jazzlike offbeat accents, fast tempo.
          0:16   **c.** Held chords, and dyads above low staccato repeated notes.
          0:22   **d.** Fast notes, chord, *f*, lead to
          0:27   **e.** Soft legato dyads, loud and disconnected dyads.

23 **48** 0:35   **2. a.** Lyrical legato melody in slower tempo,
          0:52   **b.** Rapid notes, repeated high tone, quick chords, *f*.

24 **49** 0:58   **3. a.** High held harmonics accompanied by staccato tones; fast notes and loud chord.
          1:06   **b.** High tones, low held tones accompanied by repeated notes, lead to
          1:12   **c.** Soft dyads, legato; loud chords.
          1:28   **d.** Melody ascends from low tone to high harmonics, staccato accompaniment; loud chord introduces

25 **50** 1:37   **4. a.** Flow of rapid single notes, offbeat jazzlike accents, chords punctuate, fast tempo.
          2:23   **b.** Group of loud six-note strummed chords.
          2:27   **c.** Melody rises to high soft harmonics, closing loud dyad dies away.

The Twentieth Century and Beyond: Summary

IMPORTANT TERMS

- Glissando, p. 365
- Polychord, p. 366
- Fourth chord, p. 367
- Tone cluster, p. 367
- Polytonality, p. 368
- Bitonality, p. 368
- Atonality, p. 368
- Polyrhythm, p. 369
- Ostinato, p. 369
- Pentatonic scale, p. 376
- Whole-tone scale, p. 376
- Atonality, p. 395
- Tone-color melody, p. 395
- *Sprechstimme*, p. 395
- Twelve-tone system, p. 396
- Tone row (set, series), p. 396
- Serialism, p. 439
- Chance (aleatory) music, p. 439
- Quotation music, p. 441
- Electronic music, p. 443
- Microtones, p. 444
- Mixed media, p. 446
- Prepared piano, p. 446
- Vibraphone, p. 451
- Marimba, p. 451

FEATURED STYLES

- Impressionism, p. 372
- Neoclassicism, p. 383
- Primitivism, p. 386
- Expressionism, p. 392
- Minimalism, p. 440

Music in Society

- The early twentieth century was a time of revolt, with more fundamental changes in the language of music than any time since the baroque era.
- The variety of musical styles of the early twentieth century reflects the vast diversity of life during this time.
- Composers drew inspiration from an enormous variety of sources, including non-European, folk, American jazz, and past music.
- The United States became a potent force in music.
- Recordings, radio, and television became new modes for hearing music, bringing music to larger audiences, and increasing the range of music available to everyone.
- Women and people of color began to play major roles in professional music making.
- American colleges and universities have indirectly become important patrons of music.

Characteristics of Twentieth-Century Music

Tone Color

- Tone color became a more important element of music than it ever was before.
- Noiselike and percussive sounds are used often. Instruments may play at the extremes of their ranges. New ways of playing traditional instruments were explored.
- There is less emphasis on blended sound; individual tone colors are heard clearly.

Melody and Harmony

- Melodies often are no longer tied to traditional chords, major or minor keys, or a tonal center. Melodies are unpredictable and may contain wide leaps.
- Fundamental changes occurred in the way chords are treated.
- Traditional distinctions between consonance and dissonance were abandoned.
- New chord structures and alternatives to the traditional tonal system were explored.

Rhythm

- Rhythm is one of the most striking elements of twentieth-century music, used to generate power, drive, and excitement.
- There is an increased emphasis on rhythmic irregularity and unpredictability; rapidly changing meters, polyrhythms, and ostinatos are featured.

Characteristics of Music since 1945

- During the 1950s, the twelve-tone system began to be used more widely as composers realized that it was more of a compositional technique than a special musical style.
- The twelve-tone system was expanded to include elements other than pitch, such as rhythm, timbre, and dynamics.
- The element of chance was introduced to music composition and performance.

- Minimalist music developed, featuring a steady pulse, clear tonality, and insistent repetition of short melodic patterns to produce a trancelike or hypnotic effect.
- In quotation music, composers deliberately make extensive use of quotations from earlier music. Quotation music usually either conveys a symbolic meaning, or is varied, transformed, and juxtaposed with other music.
- Some composers have embraced tonal music and a return to tonality.
- The introduction of tape studios, synthesizers, and computers to composition and performance provides potentially unlimited resources for the production and control of sound.
- To further liberate sound, composers present a wider variety of sounds than ever before, including the use of traditional instruments in nontraditional ways, and the inclusion of many sounds that were once considered undesirable noises. The greatest expansion and experimentation have involved percussion instruments.
- Mixed media combines a variety of traditional and electronic music styles with visual counterparts such as slide projections, films, light shows, gestures, and theatrical action.
- Rhythm and form have undergone some of the most striking changes in music since 1945.

FEATURED COMPOSERS

- Claude Debussy (1862–1918)
- Maurice Ravel (1875–1937)
- Igor Stravinsky (1882–1971)
- Arnold Schoenberg (1874–1951)
- Alban Berg (1885–1935)
- Anton Webern (1883–1945)
- Béla Bartók (1881–1945)
- Dmitri Shostakovich (1906–1975)
- Charles Ives (1874–1954)
- George Gershwin (1898–1937)
- William Grant Still (1895–1978)
- Aaron Copland (1900–1990)
- Alberto Ginastera (1916–1983)
- John Cage (1912–1992)
- Edgard Varèse (1883–1965)
- Krzysztof Penderecki (b. 1933)
- George Crumb (b. 1929)
- Philip Glass (b. 1937)
- Ellen Taaffe Zwilich (b. 1939)
- John Adams (b. 1947)
- Elliott Carter (b. 1908)

Beyond the Classroom:
Attending a Concert of Music Composed after 1900

Attending a concert of twentieth-century music can be one of the most unpredictable and exhilarating musical activities you can experience. The range of styles and number of new sounds you can hear are astonishing. Because the music is so wide-ranging in style, audience members, too, tend to be an extremely diverse group.

Professional ensembles devoted to specializing in music composed after 1900 are active in many cities. Orchestras, chamber groups, and individuals often commission new works. Colleges and universities also are excellent sources of free concerts of contemporary music.

When attending a concert of contemporary music, go with an open mind. Plan to be challenged aurally, intellectually, and emotionally. Ask yourself the following questions as you listen:

- What performing forces do you hear? If instruments are used, are they traditional instruments of the western world, or are they from other locations? If you notice any unusual instruments, what do they look like and how are they played?
- How are voices used? Do the singers make any special sound effects?
- Do the voices or instruments blend together, or are the individual tone colors unblended?
- What observations can you make regarding timbre? Are noiselike or percussive instruments used? If so, what do they look like, how are they played, and what is their effect on the music?
- Does the performance use taped music, special amplification, computers, synthesizers, or a combination of electronic and live music? What is their effect on your reaction to the music?
- Is the music consonant or dissonant? Does the music sound tonal or not? Do the program notes indicate if the music is twelve-tone or aleatory?
- How would you describe the rhythm, tempo, and meter? Are they predictable and steady, or are they irregular? Do you notice any ostinatos?
- Do you notice instances of musical quotation?
- Does the performance include examples of mixed media?
- How did you react to the music in general?

Jazz

My band is my instrument.

—*Duke Ellington*

The Jazz group Mixed Company. Since its beginnings, jazz has developed a rich variety of substyles, such as New Orleans style, swing, bebop, cool jazz, free jazz, and jazz rock.

JAZZ

At about the time when Schoenberg and Stravinsky were changing the language of music in Europe, a new musical style called *jazz* was being developed in the United States.* It was created by musicians—predominantly African Americans—performing in the streets, bars, brothels, and dance halls of New Orleans and other southern cities. **Jazz** can be described generally as music rooted in improvisation and characterized by syncopated rhythm, a steady beat, and distinctive tone colors and performance techniques. Although the term *jazz* became current in 1917, the

music itself was probably heard as early as 1900. We do not know exactly when early jazz started or how it sounded, because this new music existed only in performance, not musical notation. Moreover, very little jazz was captured on recordings before 1923, and none at all before the Original Dixieland Jazz Band recorded in 1917.

Since its beginnings, jazz has developed a rich variety of substyles such as New Orleans style (or Dixieland), swing, bebop, cool jazz, free jazz, and jazz rock. It has produced such outstanding figures as Louis Armstrong,

Duke Ellington, Benny Goodman, Charlie Parker, and Miles Davis. Its impact has been enormous and worldwide, affecting not only many kinds of popular music but the music of such composers as Maurice Ravel, Darius Milhaud, George Gershwin, and Aaron Copland.

The world of jazz has witnessed many changes since its beginnings at the turn of the twentieth century. Geographically, its center has shifted from New Orleans to Chicago, Kansas City, and New York. Today, it is hard to speak of *a* jazz center, since

---

*Two excellent recorded anthologies of jazz are the *Smithsonian Collection of Classic Jazz* and Ken Burns's *Jazz: The Story of American Music.*

The trumpeter, composer, and educator Wynton Marsalis is the first jazz musician to be awarded the Pulitzer Prize (1997).

As both a trumpeter and a singer, Louis "Satchmo" Armstrong had a worldwide impact on jazz.

good jazz is heard worldwide, from Paris to Tokyo. Jazz has changed in function, too. For a long time, it was basically music for dancing; but since the 1940s, many newer jazz styles have been intended for listening. Now we are as likely to hear jazz in a concert hall or college classroom as in a bar or nightclub. The image of jazz has also changed. It was originally condemned for its emphasis on sexuality, but it has long since become respected as a major American art form. In recent years, jazz has been sponsored by major American cultural institutions. Both Lincoln Center and Carnegie Hall in New York City have regular jazz series, and a Jazz Masterworks Orchestra has been founded at the Smithsonian National Museum of American History in Washington, D.C.

1 Jazz Styles: 1900–1950

Roots of Jazz

Early jazz blended elements from many musical cultures, including west African, American, and European. Most American slaves originally came from west Africa, an area that today includes Ghana, Nigeria, and several other countries. West African elements that influenced jazz include its emphasis on improvisation, drumming, percussive sounds, and complex rhythms. Another feature of jazz that was probably derived from west Africa is known as *call and response.* In much west African vocal music, a soloist's phrases are repeatedly answered by a chorus. In jazz, **call and response** occurs when a voice is answered by an instrument, or when one instrument (or group of instruments) is answered by another instrument (or group). The call-and-response pattern of jazz was derived more directly from African American church services in which the congregation responds vocally to the preacher's "call." In America, blacks developed a rich body of music that became a vital source for jazz. This music included work songs, spirituals, gospel hymns, and such dances as the cakewalk. Much of this music was never written down and is now lost to us.

Black music influenced and was influenced by the music of white America, which included hymns, popular songs, folk tunes, dances, marches, and piano pieces. In origin, this repertoire was partly American and partly written or influenced by European composers. Nineteenth-century American and European musical traditions provided melodies, harmonies, and forms that became elements in the background of jazz.

One major source of jazz was the American band tradition. Bands—both black and white—played an important role in American life during the late nineteenth century and the early twentieth. Virtually every village had its band and bandstand; bands performed at picnics, parades, political rallies, dances, and carnivals. Many of the instruments used in marching bands—trumpet, cornet, trombone, tuba, clarinet, and

One major source of jazz was the American band tradition.

drums—were also used in early jazz bands. Band music also influenced the forms and rhythms of early jazz.

Along with band music, the immediate sources of jazz were ragtime and blues. *Ragtime* is a style of syncopated piano music that was popular from the 1890s to about 1915. The term *blues* refers to, among other things, a style of African American vocal music involving "bent" notes and slides of pitch. Ragtime and blues will be discussed more fully in Sections 2 and 3.

Elements of Jazz

Like other music of the twentieth century, jazz is too diverse and complex to be defined by any single formula. We'll now consider some of the elements of jazz created before 1950. Jazz after 1950 is discussed in Section 7.

Tone Color Jazz is generally played by a small group (or *combo*) of three to eight players, or by a "big band" of ten to fifteen. The backbone of a jazz ensemble is its ***rhythm section,*** usually made up of piano, plucked double bass, percussion, and—sometimes—banjo or guitar, which maintains the beat, adds rhythmic interest, and provides supporting harmonies. Modern percussionists produce a variety of sounds from several drums and cymbals, using sticks, mallets, wire brushes, and bare hands.

The main solo instruments of jazz include the cornet, trumpet, saxophone (soprano, alto, tenor, baritone), piano, clarinet, vibraphone, and trombone. Jazz emphasizes brasses, woodwinds, and percussion rather than the bowed strings that dominate symphonic music. Brass players produce a wide variety of tone colors by using different mutes and muting techniques. A jazz performance usually involves both solo and ensemble sections. For example, a full ensemble might be followed by a trumpet solo and then by a clarinet solo or a duet for saxophone and trumpet.

Compared with "classical" musicians, who strive for an ideal sound, jazz performers aim for more individuality of sound and tone color. For example, it is usually easier to distinguish between two jazz trumpet players than between two "classical" trumpeters. Although jazz is basically instrumental music, its players try to match the personal quality of singing. In all, the distinctive sounds of jazz are easy to recognize but hard to describe. These sounds result from the specific tones that are chosen, and from the

The rhythm section of a jazz ensemble usually includes piano, bass, and percussion. Pictured here is the Dave Brubeck Quartet.

particular way these tones are performed within the melody or accompaniment. For example, melodic tones are often attacked more aggressively in jazz than in other musical styles. Jazz performers sometimes "bend" tones to heighten expressivity or use a distinctive type of vibrato. Transitions between consecutive tones often include a variety of other pitch inflections often referred to as "smears" (gliding from one pitch to another), "scoops" (starting at a pitch lower than the intended pitch and swooping up to it), "falloffs" (performing a descending glissando from the final pitch of a phrase), and "shakes" (a very deliberate and exaggerated vibrato).

Improvisation At the heart of jazz lies improvisation. Jazz musicians create a special electricity as they simultaneously create and perform, making decisions at lightning speed. The creativity of great improvisers is staggering. Their recorded performances represent only a tiny fraction of the music they create almost nightly.

Of course, not all jazz is improvised, and most contains both improvised and composed sections. Yet it is improvisation that contributes most to the freshness and spontaneity of jazz. The reputations of jazz performers rest mainly on the originality of their improvisations.

A jazz improvisation is usually in theme-and-variations form. The theme is often a popular song melody made up of 32 **bars,** or measures. The improviser varies this original melody by adding embellishments and changing its pitches and rhythms. Some improvised variations are similar to the original theme, but others are so different that the tune may be difficult to recognize. Often, jazz improvisations are based not on a melody but on a harmonic pattern, or series of chords. This harmonic pattern will be repeated over and over while the improviser creates melodies above it.

In jazz, each statement of the basic harmonic pattern or melody is called a **chorus.** For example, a jazz performance that is based on a 32-bar melody might be outlined as follows:

Chorus 1 (32 bars)	Theme
Chorus 2 (32 bars)	Variation 1
Chorus 3 (32 bars)	Variation 2
Chorus 4 (32 bars)	Variation 3
Chorus 5 (32 bars)	Theme

A jazz performance usually includes improvised solos by various members of the ensemble. In addition, there may be sections of *collective* improvisation, during which several musicians make up different melodies simultaneously. Their music is held together by the underlying series of chords, which is repeated throughout the performance. Collective improvisation was typical of Dixieland jazz in New Orleans. Until the introduction of long-playing records in 1948, most recorded jazz performances were about 3 minutes in length, the duration of one side of a 78-rpm record.

Rhythm, Melody, and Harmony Syncopation and rhythmic swing are two of the most distinctive features of jazz. We say that jazz performers **swing** when they combine a steady beat with a feeling of lilt, precision, and relaxed vitality. In most jazz styles, the beat is provided by the percussionist (on drums or cymbals) and by the bass player. There are usually four beats to the bar. Accents often come on the weak beats: 1–**2**–3–**4.** Many kinds of syncopated rhythms result when accented notes come *between* the beats. Jazz musicians also create a feeling of swing by playing a series of notes slightly unevenly. For example, the second note of a pair of eighth notes is typically shorter than the first. Performers differ in their ways of subdividing the beat for this pair of "swing eighths." Most often, the rhythm falls somewhere between two equal eighth notes ♪♪ and a triplet pattern in which a quarter note is followed by an eighth note ♩♪. The performed rhythms of jazz are so irregular that it is difficult to notate them accurately. A performer must deviate appropriately from the notated rhythms to get a true jazz feeling. As jazz has evolved, performers have developed the ability to play rhythms that are highly irregular and complex.

Jazz melodies can be as flexible in pitch as in rhythm. These melodies—whether improvised or composed—often use a major scale in which the third, fifth, and seventh notes are lowered, or flatted, as in vocal blues. Jazz uses chord progressions like those of the traditional tonal system. But over the years, the harmonic vocabulary of jazz has become increasingly complex, sophisticated, and chromatic. Along with traditional three- and four-note chords, jazz often uses five- or six-note chords that sound rich and lush.

2 Ragtime

Ragtime is a style of composed piano music that flourished from the 1890s to about 1915. It was developed primarily by African American pianists who traveled in the midwest and south playing in saloons and dance halls. Not long after it originated, ragtime became a nationally popular style that reached millions of people—both black and white—through sheet music, player pianos, ragtime songs, and arrangements for dance and marching bands.

Ragtime piano music is generally in duple meter ($\frac{2}{4}$) and is performed at a moderate march tempo. The pianist's right hand plays a highly syncopated melody, while the left hand steadily maintains the beat with an "oom-pah" accompaniment. A ragtime piece usually consists of several melodies that are similar in character. It takes such forms as AA BB A CC DD or introduction—AA BB CC DD EE. Although the forms of ragtime are derived from European marches and dances, its rhythms are rooted in African American folk music.

Early jazz musicians often used ragtime melodies as a springboard for their improvisations. The syncopations, steady beat, and piano style of ragtime were an important legacy for jazz.

Scott Joplin

The acknowledged "king of ragtime" was Scott Joplin (1868–1917), a composer and pianist whose father had been a slave. Joplin was trained in "classical" music and wrote a ballet and two operas, as well as many piano *rags,* the term often used for a ragtime composition.

Joplin's most famous piano pieces include *Maple Leaf Rag* and *The Entertainer. Maple Leaf Rag* was named after the saloon in Sedalia, Missouri, where he worked as a pianist. After it was published in 1899, *Maple Leaf Rag* sold hundreds of thousands of copies. This success allowed Joplin to quit his saloon job and move to Saint Louis, where he taught and composed.

In 1909, Joplin settled in New York City, where he spent the last years of his life. This was a bleak period for him: his health was poor, and he was unsuccessful in his desperate attempts to get a professional production of his opera *Treemonisha* (1911). Finally, in 1915, he mounted the opera himself in Harlem—without scenery, costumes, or orchestra. The failure of this endeavor led to a physical and mental breakdown. Joplin was confined to a hospital in 1916 and died the following year. Only recently has *Treemonisha* been revived, and with great success.

Maple Leaf Rag (1899)

Maple Leaf Rag is a classic example of ragtime; it lasts about 3 minutes and has the form AA BB A CC DD. Each section is exactly 16 bars in length. The opening melody (A), marked *tempo di marcia* (*march tempo*), features the right-hand syncopations so typical of the style:

Basic Set:
CD 9 26
26 0:00

Tempo di marcia

27 0:37

The second melody (B) begins in a higher register than A and moves steadily downward.

28 1:30

Section C modulates to a new key and has the "oom-pah" accompaniment in the left hand characteristic of ragtime. The accompaniment includes low octaves followed by higher chords:

29 2:04

The final section (D) returns to the home key and ends with a decisive cadence.

Scott Joplin was the best-known ragtime composer.

3 Blues

Among the most important foundations of jazz is a type of music known as **blues.** The term refers both to a form of vocal and instrumental music and to a style of performance. Blues grew out of African American folk music, such as work songs, spirituals, and the field hollers of slaves. Exactly when blues originated is uncertain, but by around the 1890s it was sung in rural areas of the south. The original "country blues," usually performed with guitar accompaniment, was not standardized in form or style.

The poetic and musical form of blues crystallized around 1910 and gained popularity through the publication of *Memphis Blues* (1912) and *St. Louis Blues* (1914), by W. C. Handy (1873–1958). During the 1920s, blues became a national craze among African Americans. Records by such blues singers as Bessie Smith sold in the millions. The 1920s also saw blues become a musical form widely used by jazz instrumentalists as well as blues singers. Since then, jazz and blues have been intertwined. In the 1930s, the singer-guitarist Robert Johnson (1898–1937) combined the sound of country blues— vocal melody accompanied by acoustic guitar—with the formal structure of blues to create music that has influenced many jazz and rock guitarists up to the present.

From the 1920s to the 1950s, Chicago became a blues center because many African American blues singers and instrumentalists had migrated there from the south in the decades after World War I. The 1940s saw the emergence in Chicago of a new, highly energetic blues style—sometimes called *urban blues*—that derived from earlier blues but used electric guitar and amplification. One of the best-known performers of urban blues was Muddy Waters (1915–1983), who had a distinctive style of moaning and shouting. The continuing impact of the blues is apparent in such popular contemporary styles as rhythm and blues, rock and roll, and soul.

Vocal blues is intensely personal, often containing sexual references and dealing with the pain of betrayal, desertion, and unrequited love. The lyrics consist of several 3-line stanzas, each in the same poetic and musical form. The first line is sung and then repeated to roughly the same melodic phrase (a a′); the third line has a different melodic phrase and text (b). Here is stanza 4 of Bessie Smith's *Lost Your Head Blues,* which we'll study:

> a : I'm going to leave baby, ain't going to say goodbye.
> a′: I'm going to leave baby, ain't going to say goodbye.
> b : But I'll write you and tell you the reason why.

A blues stanza is set to a harmonic framework that is usually 12 bars in length. This harmonic pattern, known as **12-bar blues,** involves only three basic chords: tonic (I), subdominant (IV), and dominant (V). (The **subdominant** is the triad based on the fourth note—*fa*—of the scale.) The specific ordering of these chords can be outlined as follows: tonic (4 bars)—subdominant (2 bars)—tonic (2 bars)—dominant (2 bars)— tonic (2 bars). Here is how the 3-line stanza is set to this chord progression:

	Line 1 (a)	Line 2 (a′)	Line 3 (b)
Bars	1 2 3 4	5 6 7 8	9 10 11 12
Chords	I	IV I	V I

Each stanza of the text is sung to the same series of chords, although other chords may be inserted between the primary chords of the 12-bar blues form outlined above. Singers either repeat the same basic melody for each stanza or improvise new melodies to reflect the changing moods of the lyrics. The music is almost always in quadruple meter ($\frac{4}{4}$), and so each bar contains 4 beats.

Twelve-bar blues is divided into three phrases, each of which is 4 bars long. The soloist typically takes only about 2 bars to sing a line. This leaves the remainder of the

4-bar phrase to be filled in by a supporting solo instrument or instruments. In blues recordings of the 1920s and 1930s, instrumental responses to the singer's lines were often improvised by leading jazz musicians. The following example shows how the vocal lines and instrumental responses fit into a 12-bar blues pattern (some pitches and rhythms are approximate):

Bessie Smith, *Lost Your Head Blues,* fourth stanza

Blues singers have a special style of performance involving "bent" notes, and vocal scoops and slides. Their melodies—both composed and improvised—contain many "blue" notes, which are produced by slightly lowering or flatting the third, fifth, and seventh tones of a major scale. Blues rhythm is also very flexible. Performers often sing or play "around" the beat, accenting notes either just before or after it.

Jazz instrumentalists imitate the performing style of blues singers and use the harmonic pattern of 12-bar blues as a basis for improvisation. This 12-bar pattern is repeated over and over while new melodies are improvised above it. As with the baroque ground bass, the repeated chord progression provides unity while the free flow of improvised melodic lines contributes variety. Music in this 12-bar form can be happy or sad, fast or slow, and in a wide range of styles. In Section 4, we'll consider an instrumental blues, *Dippermouth Blues,* which is an example of New Orleans jazz. Now we'll study a vocal blues by Bessie Smith.

Lost Your Head Blues (1926), by Bessie Smith

Basic Set:
CD 9 [30]

Brief Set:
CD 5 [51]

Bessie Smith (1894–1937), known as the "empress of the blues," was the most famous blues singer of the 1920s. Her *Lost Your Head Blues* is a well-known example of blues form and performance style. The lyrics express the feelings of a woman who plans to leave her man because she's "been treated wrong." Each of the poem's five stanzas is set to the 12-bar blues pattern. Typically, a cornet response follows each line that is sung (see the example above).

Bessie Smith was one of the most influential blues singers.

Lost Your Head Blues begins with a 4-bar introduction by the accompanying cornet (Joe Smith) and piano (Fletcher Henderson). Bessie Smith then sings a melody that she'll repeat—with extensive variations of pitch and rhythm—in each stanza. Her "blue" notes, microtonal shadings, and slides between pitches are essential to the effect of the song. Notice the eloquent slides up to *I* in her singing of *I was with you baby,* as well as the ornamental quiver on *down* when she sings the words *throw'd your good gal down.* There are many syncopated rhythms, since words are often sung just before or after the beat. Bessie Smith's vocal melody is highly sensitive to the words. For example, the long high notes at the beginning of the last stanza ("*Days* are lonesome, *nights* are long") produce a wonderful climax. Throughout the song, Bessie Smith's vocal inflections are perfectly matched by the cornet's improvised responses and echoes.

VOCAL MUSIC GUIDE

SMITH, *Lost Your Head Blues*

30 **51**
Cornet and
piano introduction.

I was with you baby when you did not have a dime.
I was with you baby when you did not have a dime.
Now since you got plenty money you have throw'd your good gal down.

Once ain't for always, two ain't for twice.
Once ain't for always, two ain't for twice.
When you get a good gal you better treat her nice.

When you were lonesome I tried to treat you kind.
When you were lonesome I tried to treat you kind.
But since you've got money, it's done changed your mind.

I'm going to leave baby, ain't going to say goodbye.
I'm going to leave baby, ain't going to say goodbye.
But I'll write you and tell you the reason why.

*Long high
notes on* Days
and nights.

Days are lonesome, nights are long.
Days are lonesome, nights are so long.
I'm a good old gal, but I've just been treated wrong.

Bessie Smith Singing
Lost Your Head Blues

Since Bessie Smith's death in 1937, her recordings not only have delighted listeners worldwide but have had a powerful impact on several generations of singers. The rock star Janis Joplin (1943–1970) said of her: "No one ever hit me so hard. Bessie made me want to sing."

Bessie Smith was born in 1894 to poor African American parents in a one-room shack in Chattanooga, Tennessee. She began her professional career at eighteen, when she joined an entertainment troupe that included Gertrude "Ma" Rainey, a leading blues singer.

Over the next decade Smith gradually achieved stardom as she performed in theaters, tents, dance halls, and cabarets, primarily before black audiences in the south and northeast.

A turning point in Bessie Smith's career came in 1923, when her first commercial 78-rpm record—*Down Hearted Blues*—sold 780,000 copies in less than six months. Her powerful voice, emotional intensity, clear diction, and expressive "bent" notes won for her the uncontested title "empress of the blues." She became the highest-paid African American performer and in 1925 was able to buy her own bright yellow railroad car to transport her troupe of about forty, along with equipment and a large tent. She continued to record blues—including about two dozen of her own compositions—with leading jazz musicians such as Louis Armstrong.

The story of Bessie Smith illustrates how the advent of recording technology changed the position of the performer in musical life. Up until the twentieth century, performers had an impact only on those who heard them in person. Unlike composers, whose notated compositions could be enjoyed by later generations, performers created for the moment, their work surviving only in written descriptions or visual representations. This situation changed dramatically with the invention of recording. Beginning with phonograph records, and later through radio, film, television, compact discs, and digital media, artists like Bessie Smith found a much wider audience and exerted lasting influence.

Many singers have described the impact of Bessie Smith's recordings. The gospel singer Mahalia Jackson (1911–1972), for example, recalled how, as a youngster in New Orleans, she would imitate Bessie Smith: "I'd play that record over and over again, and Bessie's voice would come out so full and round. . . . I'd make my mouth do the same thing."

In 1989 Bessie Smith was inducted into the Rock and Roll Hall of Fame in Cleveland; and in 2001 a play featuring the songs she made famous, *The Devil's Music: The Life and Blues of Bessie Smith,* was performed in New York City. Thanks to her recordings, the epitaph on her tombstone has proved prophetic. "The greatest blues singer in the world will never stop singing."

Bessie Smith's performance of *Lost Your Head Blues* is included in the recordings.

4 New Orleans Style

From about 1900 to 1917, jazz developed in a number of American cities, but the major center was New Orleans—the home of such important jazz musicians as Ferdinand "Jelly Roll" Morton, Joseph "King" Oliver, and Louis Armstrong.

Around the turn of the century, New Orleans was a major port and a thriving cultural and commercial center with a cosmopolitan character. Its diverse population included people of African, French, Spanish, Portuguese, English, Italian, and Cuban ancestry. A particular group in New Orleans made up of people of mixed African, French, and Spanish descent maintained its own ethnic identity. This diversity of population was mirrored in the rich musical life of New Orleans. It included opera and chamber music as well as folk, popular, dance, and sacred music of all kinds. The tradition of marching bands and dance bands was particularly strong. There were frequent competitions between bands to see which could play more loudly or more brilliantly. Some band musicians were trained in classical music and could read musical notation; others played by ear and relied on improvisation. Many were only part-time performers who worked full-time at other trades, such as bricklaying, carpentry, and cigar making.

Band music—including early jazz—was heard at picnics, parades, and political meetings and in dance halls. African American bands often played jazz during funeral processions. In the words of one New Orleans musician: "You'd march to the graveyard playing very solemn and very slow, then on the way back all hell would break loose! . . . We didn't know what a sheet of music was. Just six or seven pieces, half a dozen men pounding it out all together, each in his own way and yet somehow fitting in all right with the others."

But the main home of early jazz was Storyville, a red-light district of brothels, gambling joints, saloons, and dance halls. These establishments often employed a piano player or small band. Storyville provided not only employment but an atmosphere in which musicians felt free to improvise. When Storyville was closed down in 1917 on orders of the Navy Department, many jazz musicians left New Orleans. The center of jazz soon shifted to Chicago, Kansas City, and New York.

New Orleans style (or Dixieland) was typically played by five to eight performers. King Oliver (standing, at left rear) is shown here with his Creole Jazz Band in 1923. The band included Louis Armstrong (seated, center) and Lil Hardin (at the piano).

Jazz in **New Orleans style** (or **Dixieland**) was typically played by a small group of five to eight performers. The melodic instruments, or **front line,** included the cornet (or trumpet), clarinet, and trombone. The front-line players would improvise several contrasting melodic lines at once, producing a kind of polyphonic texture. This collective improvisation was the most distinctive feature of New Orleans jazz. Each instrument had a special role. The cornet was the leader, playing variations of the main melody. Above the cornet, the clarinet wove a countermelody, usually in a faster rhythm. The trombone played a bass line that was simpler than the upper lines, but melodically interesting nevertheless. The syncopations and rhythmic independence of the melodic instruments created a marvelous sense of excitement.

The front-line instruments were supported by a rhythm section that clearly marked the beat and provided a harmonic foundation over which the soloists could improvise. This section usually included drums, chordal instruments (banjo, guitar, piano), and a single-line low instrument (plucked bass or tuba).

New Orleans jazz was usually based on a march or church melody, a ragtime piece, a popular song, or 12-bar blues. Some well-known tunes associated with this style are *When the Saints Go Marching In* and *Oh, Didn't He Ramble?* One or more choruses of collective improvisation generally occurred at the beginning and end of a piece. In between, individual players were featured in improvised solos, accompanied by the rhythm section or by the whole band. Sometimes there were brief unaccompanied solos, called **breaks.** The band's performance might begin with an introduction and end with a brief coda, or **tag.**

As New Orleans style evolved during the 1920s—mainly in Chicago—solo playing came to be emphasized more than collective improvisation. Soloists began to base their improvisations less on the original melody, focusing instead on creating new melodies based on the underlying harmonies. In addition, the trumpet gradually replaced the cornet, and the saxophone was added to the ensemble.

Dippermouth Blues (1923), by King Oliver's Creole Jazz Band

**Basic Set:
CD 9 31**

Dippermouth Blues, as performed in 1923 by King Oliver's Creole Jazz Band, is a fine example of New Orleans jazz. It is based on the chord progression of 12-bar blues. Nine choruses of 12-bar blues are preceded by an introduction and followed by a brief tag (coda). Choruses 1, 2, 5, and 9 are for full ensemble and illustrate a style of collective improvisation that is typical of New Orleans jazz. Choruses 3 and 4 feature a clarinet solo with an accompaniment in repeated rhythm. The climax of *Dippermouth Blues* is Joe "King" Oliver's muted cornet solo (in choruses 6 to 8), heard against a background of improvisation by the other instruments. Oliver's solo, with its "blue" notes and swinging syncopations, was widely imitated by other jazz musicians.

LISTENING OUTLINE

KING OLIVER'S CREOLE JAZZ BAND, *Dippermouth Blues*

2 cornets (Joe "King" Oliver, Louis Armstrong), clarinet (Johnny Dodds), trombone (Honoré Dutrey), piano (Lil Hardin), banjo and voice (Bud Scott), drums (Baby Dodds)

Fast tempo, quadruple meter ($\frac{4}{4}$)

Introduction—nine choruses of 12-bar blues—tag

(Duration, 2:32)

Introduction
(4 bars)
31 0:00   **1. a.** Cornets introduce.

Choruses 1–2
(12 + 12 bars)

    b. All instruments.

Choruses 3–4
(12 + 12 bars)
  0:37

    2. High clarinet melody, chordal accompaniment in repeated rhythm. Clarinet melody repeated.

Chorus 5
(12 bars)
  1:09

    3. All instruments.

Choruses 6–8
(12 + 12 + 12 bars)
  1:25

    4. Muted cornet melody with "blue" notes; other instruments in background. Voice: "Oh play that thing."

Chorus 9
(12 bars + 2-bar tag)
  2:13

    5. All instruments.

Louis Armstrong

As both a trumpeter and a singer, Louis "Satchmo" Armstrong (1901–1971) had a worldwide impact on jazz. He was born in a poor black section of New Orleans, and he learned to play the cornet in a reformatory (where he was sent at the age of thirteen for shooting a gun into the air during a New Year's celebration). On his release after one year of confinement, Armstrong was soon playing in honky-tonks at night (he drove a coal wagon during the day). His musical ambitions were encouraged by King Oliver, who took a fatherly interest in the boy and gave him some lessons. When Oliver left for Chicago in 1918—after Storyville was closed down—Armstrong took his place in the famous Kid Ory Band. Four years later, Armstrong himself went to Chicago to be second cornetist in King Oliver's Creole Jazz Band.

In 1925, he started to make a series of recordings with bands known as Louis Armstrong's Hot Five and Louis Armstrong's Hot Seven. The Hot Five included three New Orleans musicians—Johnny Dodds (clarinet), Kid Ory (trombone), and Johnny St. Cyr (banjo)—along with Lil Hardin (piano), whom Armstrong had married a year earlier. These recordings established Armstrong's reputation as a leading jazz trumpeter. After 1930 he appeared with a wide variety of groups, made many tours, and was featured in many films. In the 1950s and 1960s Armstrong served as a "goodwill ambassador" for the United States. And at age sixty-four, he had his greatest popular success, the hit recording *Hello, Dolly!* (number one in 1964).

Armstrong was one of the greatest jazz improvisers; he was able to invent extraordinary solos and to transform even ordinary tunes into swinging melodies through changes of rhythm and pitch. He revealed new dimensions of the trumpet, showing that it could be played in a higher register than had been thought possible. His playing style featured "rips" up to high pitches, along with a tone that was both beautiful and alive. One jazz expert has singled out the "subtly varied repertory of vibratos and shakes with which Armstrong colors and embellishes individual notes." Armstrong also popularized *scat singing,* vocalization of a melodic line with nonsense syllables. His gravel-throated voice was not conventionally "beautiful," but it conveyed the same jazz feeling as his trumpet playing.

Hotter Than That (1927), by Louis Armstrong and His Hot Five

Basic Set:
CD 9 32

Brief Set:
CD 5 52

Hotter Than That, an outstanding performance by Louis Armstrong and His Hot Five, is based on a tune written by Lillian Hardin Armstrong (1898–1971), who was Armstrong's wife and the pianist of the band. This performance shows how New Orleans style developed in Chicago during the 1920s. The emphasis is on improvisatory solos, based on the harmonic structure of the 32-bar tune *Hotter Than That.* Collective improvisation—so important in earlier New Orleans style—is restricted to the introduction and the last of four choruses. Louis Armstrong performs as both trumpeter and vocalist. His vocal solo, an example of scat singing, is like his trumpet playing in sound and style. Other solos are by the clarinetist Johnny Dodds and the trombonist Kid Ory. At the middle and end of each chorus there is a brief unaccompanied solo, a break. Listen for the syncopations of Armstrong's vocal melody (chorus 3), the call and response between voice and guitar in the interlude following chorus 3, and the dissonant guitar chord that gives *Hotter Than That* an unusual, inconclusive ending.

LISTENING OUTLINE

LOUIS ARMSTRONG AND HIS HOT FIVE, *Hotter Than That*

Cornet, voice (Louis Armstrong), piano (Lillian Hardin Armstrong),
clarinet (Johnny Dodds), trombone (Kid Ory), guitar (Lonnie Johnson)

Rapid tempo, quadruple meter ($\frac{4}{4}$)

Introduction—four choruses of 32 bars—coda

(Duration, 2:59)

Introduction
(8 bars)

32   52   0:00   **1.** All instruments, trumpet predominates, collective improvisation.

Chorus 1
(32 bars)

     0:09   **2.** Trumpet solo, accompanied by piano and guitar. Trumpet briefly alone, piano and guitar rejoin.

Chorus 2
(32 bars)

33   53   0:43   **3.** Clarinet solo, piano and guitar accompany.

Chorus 3
(32 bars)

34   54   1:19   **4.** Vocal solo, scat singing, guitar accompanies.

Interlude
(20 bars)

35   55   1:54   **5.** Voice imitated by guitar. Piano leads into

Chorus 4
(32 bars)

36   56   2:17   **6. a.** Muted trombone solo, piano and guitar accompany.

37   57   2:33   **b.** Trumpet, other instruments join, collective improvisation.

Tag (4 bars)   **c.** Trumpet, guitar, dissonant chord at end.

5 Swing

A new jazz style called *swing* developed in the 1920s and flourished from 1935 to 1945, a decade nicknamed the "swing era." (In this section, the term *swing* will refer to this specific style rather than to the rhythmic vitality characteristic of all jazz.)

Swing was played mainly by *big bands,* whose powerful sound could fill the large dance halls and ballrooms that mushroomed across the country, particularly after the repeal of prohibition in 1933. There were hundreds of "name" bands—both black and white—like those of Duke Ellington, Count Basie, Glenn Miller, Tommy Dorsey, and Benny Goodman (the "king of swing"). Some bands included such leading musicians as the saxophonists Coleman Hawkins and Lester Young and featured singers like Billie Holiday, Ella Fitzgerald, and Frank Sinatra. During the 1930s and 1940s, big bands were as important as rock groups have been since the 1950s. Swing became a truly popular music, reaching millions of people. Benny Goodman's band, for example, was heard coast to coast on a weekly radio show called *Let's Dance.* The kind of music once associated with honky-tonks and brothels had achieved a new respectability, symbolized by Benny Goodman's historic jazz concert at Carnegie Hall in 1938.

In Section 4, we noted that New Orleans jazz was performed by small groups of five to eight musicians and featured collective improvisation by several soloists. The typical *swing band* had about fourteen or fifteen musicians grouped into three sections: saxophones (three to five players, some doubling on clarinet), brass instruments (three or four each of trumpet and trombone), and rhythm (piano, percussion, guitar, and bass). A band of this size needed music that was more composed than improvised and was also *arranged,* or notated in written-out parts for each musician to read. With swing, the arranger became an important figure in jazz.

In a swing band, melodies were often performed by entire sections, either in unison or in harmony. Thus, in ensemble playing, it was usually necessary to rely on arrangements instead of improvising. What solo improvisations there were tended to be restricted in length. The main melody was frequently accompanied by saxophones playing sustained chords, or by saxophones and brass instruments playing short, re-

Typically, a swing band included about fifteen musicians. The Benny Goodman Band was one of the leading swing ensembles.

peated phrases called *riffs.* Arrangers often used a rapid alternation of brass and sax riffs to create tension and excitement. Each band took pride in the distinctiveness of its sound, which it owed to its arrangers as well as its players.

Not only was the swing band larger and more dependent on arrangements than the New Orleans–style band; it also had other distinctive features. For example, the saxophone became one of the most important solo instruments during the swing era. In addition, percussionists—such as Gene Krupa—had a more prominent role, often taking spectacular solos. They also kept the beat in a new way. While they continued to maintain the pulse on the bass drum, percussionists now used the hi-hat, two cymbals brought together by means of a foot-pedal, to stress the second and fourth beats of the bar:

The harmonic vocabulary of swing was richer and more varied than that of earlier jazz, but its forms were essentially the same. As before, jazz performances were usually based on 12-bar blues or on the melody of harmonies of a 32-bar popular song. Such songs can usually be outlined A A B A. An 8-bar phrase is stated and then repeated (A A); a contrasting 8-bar phrase (B) follows; then there's a return to the opening phrase (A).

Duke Ellington

Edward Kennedy "Duke" Ellington (1899–1974) was perhaps the most important swing-band composer, arranger, and conductor; he certainly ranks among the leading figures in the history of jazz. Ellington's works, which span half a century, include hundreds of 3-minute band pieces, as well as music for film, television, ballet, theater, and church. He was among the first jazz composers to break the 3-minute "sound barrier" imposed by the 78-rpm record, creating extended jazz compositions such as *Black, Brown, and Beige.* Ellington accomplished all this while playing the piano, touring the world, and writing such hit songs as *Satin Doll, Sophisticated Lady,* and *In a Sentimental Mood.*

Ellington's music—sometimes created in collaboration with his arranger Billy Strayhorn—is a product of constant experimentation and improvisation. "There is no set system," he once observed. "Most times I write it and arrange it. Sometimes I write it and the band and I collaborate on the arrangement. . . . When we're all working together, a guy may have an idea and he plays it on his horn. Another guy may add to it and make something out of it. Someone may play a riff and ask, 'How do you like this?' "

"My band is my instrument," Ellington once remarked. His arrangements are outstanding for their rich variety of sensuous tone colors and for their exploitation of the distinctive sounds of individual musicians. "You've got to write with certain

Duke Ellington and his orchestra in 1943. Ellington was perhaps the most important swing composer, arranger, and conductor.

men in mind," he once explained. "I know what Tricky Sam can play on a trombone and I know what Lawrence Brown can play on the trombone, and it is not the same." With his respect for their talents, it's no wonder that many of Ellington's musicians remained in the band for long periods of time.

Ellington's works are richer in harmony and more varied in form than those of his contemporaries. Their variety of mood may be sampled in such works as *KoKo, Harlem Air Shaft, In a Mellotone,* and *Blue Serge* (all included in *The Smithsonian Collection of Classic Jazz*).

Basic Set:

CD 1 ⑩

Brief Set:

CD 1 ③

C-Jam Blues (1942), in a rendition by Duke Ellington and his Famous Orchestra, was used as an example in Part I, Section 1 (see the listening outline on page 10). It illustrates how Ellington showcases the remarkable musicianship of his band members. Most of the performance is a series of improvised solos on the harmonic structure of 12-bar blues, each solo introduced by a 4-bar break (items 3, 4, 5, 6, 7). Therefore, every solo consists of 16 bars: a 4-bar break followed by a 12-bar blues chorus. This pattern is unusual because breaks normally appear during the first four bars of a 12-bar blues structure. The first four solos (violin, muted cornet, tenor saxophone, trombone with plunger mute) are lightly accompanied by the rhythm section. Only during the clarinet solo (item 7) do other instruments join with sustained chords. This buildup leads to a climactic ending chorus (12 bars) played by the full ensemble.

6   Bebop

The early 1940s saw the development of *bebop* (or *bop*), a complex style of music usually for small jazz groups consisting of four to six players. In part, bebop was a rebellion by creative improvisers against the commercialism and written arrangements of swing bands. The new music was meant for attentive listening, not dancing, and its sophisticated harmonies and unpredictable rhythms bewildered many listeners. Bop performers were a special "in" group who sometimes drove other jazz musicians from the bandstand by using complex melodies and unusual chord progressions. "We knew that they couldn't make those chord changes," one bop drummer recalled. "We kept the riffraff out and built our clique on new chords."

Bebop performers also differentiated themselves by their goatees, berets, and special "hip" language. The bebop center during the early 1940s was a club in Harlem called Minton's Playhouse, where young innovators—like the alto saxophonist Charlie Parker, the trumpeter Dizzy Gillespie (1917–1993), and the pianist Thelonious Monk (1917–1982)—came to participate in jam sessions.

Bebop Style

A typical bebop group might include a saxophone and a trumpet supported by a rhythm section of piano, bass, and percussion. The role of rhythm instruments in bebop was different from that in earlier jazz. The beat, often extremely fast, was marked not by the snare drum or bass drum, but mainly by the pizzicato bass and ride cymbal (a large suspended cymbal). The drummer also supplied irregular accents, sometimes played with such power that they are called "bombs." Similarly, the pianist's left hand no longer helped emphasize the basic pulse but joined with the right hand to play complex chords at irregular intervals.

Rhythms in bop melodies were more varied and unpredictable than those in earlier jazz. In an improvised solo by Charlie Parker, for example, accented notes might come

Bebop was a complex style of music usually for small jazz groups. Charlie Parker (alto saxophone) is shown with Tommy Potter (bass), Miles Davis (trumpet), and Duke Jordan (piano).

on weak or strong beats, or at varying points within the beat. Bop melodies often had a flurry of extremely fast notes with accents on the offbeats.

The new style may well have gotten its name from a vocalization of the two fast notes (*be-bop*) that often end phrases. The melodic phrases themselves were often varied and irregular in length. A two- or three-note fragment would be followed by a melodic unit lasting several bars. And the harmonies of bop were as complex as its rhythms. Performers often built melodies on chords consisting of five to seven notes rather than on the three- or four-note chords used in earlier jazz.

A bop performance generally began and ended with a statement of the main theme by one soloist, or by two soloists in unison. The remainder of the piece was made up of solo improvisations based on the melody or harmonic structure. As in earlier jazz, bebop musicians used popular songs and 12-bar blues as a springboard for improvisation. Often, however, they composed *new* tunes to fit the basic harmonies of familiar melodies. As an "in" joke, a bop musician might give a tune a new title so that only sophisticated listeners could guess its origin.

Charlie "Bird" Parker

The alto saxophonist Charlie Parker (1920–1955) was a towering figure among bebop musicians and one of the greatest of all jazz improvisers. His enormous influence was felt not only by other alto saxophonists but by many other instrumentalists.

Parker was born in Kansas City, Kansas, and grew up in Kansas City, Missouri. As a youngster, he roamed the streets listening outside nightclub doors to the jazz of Lester Young and the Count Basie Band. He was a professional musician by the age of fifteen, having dropped out of school. In his twenties, Parker lived in New York and participated in Harlem jam sessions. He made his first bebop recordings in 1944, and by the late 1940s he was a featured soloist in jazz clubs.

Parker became a prominent musician despite severe personal problems, including drug addiction, alcoholism, ulcers, and emotional illness. But after 1950, his playing declined along with his physical and emotional health. He died in 1955 at the age of thirty-four.

All the style characteristics of bebop were embodied in Parker's improvisations. He was able to control a rich flow of ideas at either slow or very rapid tempos. His amazing technique enabled him to create lightning-fast melodies that sound jagged and angular because of frequent leaps and changes of direction. Unlike earlier saxophonists, who had a lush, sweet tone quality, Parker produced a sound that was rather hard and dry. It perfectly matched the nervous intensity of his melodic lines.

KoKo (1945), by Charlie Parker

Basic Set:
CD 9 38

Bebop style and Parker's improvisatory genius are both illustrated in *KoKo*, which is performed in our recording by Parker (alto saxophone) and three other outstanding musicians: Dizzy Gillespie (trumpet and piano), Curly Russell (bass) and Max Roach (percussion). Parker based the melody of *KoKo* on the harmonies of the popular song *Cherokee* (1938), a big-band standard of the swing era. "I'd been getting bored with the stereotyped changes [chord progressions] that were being used all the time," said Parker about the composition of *KoKo*. "I kept thinking that there's bound to be something else. I could hear it sometimes but I couldn't play it. Well, that night, I was working over "Cherokee," and as I did, I found that by using the higher intervals of the chord as a melody line and backing them with appropriately related changes, I could play the things I'd been hearing. I came alive."

KoKo consists of an introduction, two choruses of alto saxophone solo, a drum solo, and a coda that is a varied and slightly abridged return of the introduction. The tempo is extremely fast, and the beat is usually marked by the pizzicato bass and by the "ride" cymbal played with brushes. Notice the "bombs," or irregular accents played by the bass drum. The introduction begins with a short melody played by the alto saxophone and trumpet in unison and continues with two brief solos played at breakneck speed by these instruments. Parker's extended solo is a torrential flow of rapid notes with asymmetrical phrases and unexpected accents and rests. Only during this solo is the full rhythm section heard. In the spectacular drum solo, complex rhythmic patterns make it difficult to perceive the beat.

LISTENING OUTLINE

PARKER, *KoKo*

Alto saxophone (Charlie Parker), trumpet and piano (Dizzy Gillespie), bass (Curly Russell), percussion (Max Roach)

Introduction—two choruses of 64-bar pattern—drum solo—coda

(Duration, 2:51)

38 Introduction
(32 bars)

0:00	**1. a.**	Alto saxophone and muted trumpet in unison. Short melody, drums accompany.
0:06	**b.**	Fast trumpet solo, drums accompany.
0:12	**c.**	Fast alto saxophone solo, drums accompany.
0:18	**d.**	Alto saxophone and trumpet mostly in thirds, different brief melody, drums accompany.

39 Choruses 1–2
(64 + 64 bars)

0:24	**2.**	Alto saxophone, extended solo with very quick notes, asymmetrical phrases, unexpected accents and rests, fast pizzicato bass, piano, and percussion accompany.
2:06	**3.**	Drum solo, snare drum and bass drum.

Coda
(28 bars)

2:29	**4. a.**	Alto saxophone and muted trumpet in unison. Short melody, cymbal accompanies.
2:35	**b.**	Fast trumpet solo, brushed cymbal accompanies.
2:41	**c.**	Fast alto saxophone solo, brushed cymbal accompanies.
2:47	**d.**	Alto saxophone and trumpet mostly in thirds, different brief melody, brushed cymbal accompanies.

7 Jazz Styles since 1950

Since 1950, there have been many innovations and new directions in jazz. The range of styles is wider than ever. But as new styles proliferate, older jazz—from Dixieland to bebop—remains very much alive.

The introduction of long-playing records in 1948 inspired more extended jazz compositions and improvisations. Typically, a jazz performance on a long-playing record might last from 5 to 15 minutes, compared with the 3 minutes permitted by 78-rpm records before 1948. Also, more jazz now was meant for listening than for dancing. It was often heard at concerts on college campuses. Increasingly, jazz musicians studied at colleges and music schools.

Since 1950, there has been an expansion in the musical resources used in jazz. New meters, rhythms, harmonies, forms, and tone colors have been explored. Orchestral instruments, such as the flute, violin, cello, and French horn, have become a part of jazz. From the 1960s through the 1980s, synthesizers, electric guitar, electric bass guitar, and electric piano were used more and more. Also some musicians of the 1960s created *free jazz,* which discarded many of the forms and basic chord progressions of earlier jazz. Performers drew inspiration from a great variety of sources, including Bach, rock, and the music of Africa, Asia, and Latin America. The interaction between jazz and rock has led to a style known as *jazz rock.* Some musicians, such as Gunther Schuller (b. 1925), created a *third stream* style that is not quite jazz or "classical" but a blend of both. Among all these recent developments, we will consider three of the most important: cool jazz, free jazz, and jazz rock.

Cool Jazz

During the late 1940s and early 1950s, a jazz style emerged that was related to bop but was far calmer and more relaxed in character. It was called **cool jazz** (in contrast to the "hot" jazz of an earlier era). The leaders of the cool jazz movement were Lester Young (1909–1959) and Stan Getz (b. 1927), tenor saxophonists; Lennie Tristano (1919–1978), a pianist; and Miles Davis (1926–1991), a trumpeter and bandleader who started out as a bebop musician and was also an important figure in jazz throughout the 1960s, 1970s, and 1980s. Performers of cool jazz played in a relatively subdued manner, with a gentle attack and little vibrato. Cool jazz pieces tended to be longer than bebop works and relied more heavily on arrangements. They sometimes used instruments that were new to jazz, including the French horn, flute, and cello.

One of the finest works in cool jazz style is *Boplicity* (1949), by Miles Davis and the arranger Gil Evans (included in *The Smithsonian Collection of Classic Jazz*). It is scored for an unusual ensemble of nine different instruments: trumpet, trombone, French horn, tuba, alto and baritone saxophones, piano, bass, and drums. The smooth, mellow, blended sound of this ensemble is typical of cool jazz.

Some cool jazz groups, such as the Modern Jazz Quartet, were influenced by the works of Bach and favored polyphonic textures and imitation. Another prominent group influenced by "classical" music was the Dave Brubeck Quartet, as evidenced by its use of meters that had been considered unusual in jazz, such as $\frac{5}{4}$ (in *Take Five*), and $\frac{7}{4}$ (in *Unsquare Dance,* studied in Part I, Section 3).

Free Jazz: Ornette Coleman and John Coltrane

Until about 1960, jazz improvisations tended to be quite regular in form. That is, improvised variations kept the length and chord structure of the original theme, even if they abandoned the original melody. During the 1960s, some musicians broke from this tradition and created *free jazz,* a style that was not based on regular forms or established chord patterns.

"If I'm going to follow a preset chord sequence, I may as well write out my solo," commented Ornette Coleman (b. 1930), an alto saxophonist and a major composer of free jazz. In 1960 Coleman assembled eight musicians in a recording studio to improvise individually and collectively with almost no guidelines of melody, form, or harmony. The result was *Free Jazz,* a performance whose apparent randomness can be compared to the chance music created during the same period by John Cage and his followers. (An excerpt from *Free Jazz* is included in *The Smithsonian Collection of Classic Jazz.*) "I don't tell the members of my group what to do," Coleman has explained. "I let everyone express himself just as he wants to." Nevertheless, many performances by Coleman are more highly structured than *Free Jazz,* since they begin and end with a composed theme. (One example is *Lonely Woman,* also included in *The Smithsonian Collection of Classic Jazz.*) Like other free-jazz improvisers, Coleman develops melodic and rhythmic ideas from the theme. In many of his performances, a steady beat and tempo are emphasized much less than in earlier jazz, and his bass and percussion players are given more melodic and rhythmic freedom.

Another musician searching for rhythmic and harmonic freedom during the 1960s was John Coltrane (1926–1967), who was extremely influential as an improviser, tenor and soprano saxophonist, and composer. Coltrane's tone was large, intense, and equally powerful in all registers—an unusual trait. He could play higher than the normal top range of his instrument, and his arpeggios were flung at such lightning speed that they became "sheets of sound." The fury and passion of his improvisations sometimes led to sounds that might be described as "cries," "wails," and "shrieks."

Coltrane's style evolved steadily from the late 1950s, when he worked with Miles Davis, to his death at age forty in 1967. His early performances—such as the pathbreaking *Giant Steps* of 1959—feature chord progressions that modulate through unexpected keys at a very fast tempo. His later works—such as *A Love Supreme* of 1964—on the other hand, are often based on a background of only two or three chords, each sustained in the accompaniment for many bars. Coltrane's pianist, McCoy Tyner, often sustained a single tone in the bass as a drone, or pedal point, while Coltrane improvised on modes (scales other than the conventional major or minor). Coltrane's growing use of drones and unusual scales may well have been influenced by his deep interest in Indian and Arabic music.

A drone accompaniment is used in Coltrane's meditative work *Alabama* (1963), for tenor saxophone, piano, bass, and drums. (This too is in *The Smithsonian Collection of Classic Jazz.*) This short piece is in A B A' form. In the opening section, the saxophone melody is accompanied only by a sustained low broken chord in the piano. The contemplative melody conveys little sense of beat or meter. Only in the middle section is a definite beat heard. When the opening section returns (A′), there is a more active accompaniment as the bass and drums play complex rhythms.

Jazz Rock (Fusion)

Rock became a potent influence on jazz starting in the late 1960s. This influence led to *jazz rock,* or *fusion,* a new style combining the jazz musician's improvisatory approach with rock rhythms and tone colors. Jazz rock achieved a popularity unmatched by any other jazz style since the swing of the 1930s and 1940s.

A jazz rock group typically includes acoustic wind and brass instruments along with synthesizers and electric piano, guitar, and bass. The sound of acoustic instruments is often altered by electronic devices that expand the range of tonal effects. The percussion section is larger than that in earlier jazz groups and frequently includes instruments from Africa, Latin America, or India. Jazz rock groups produce a remarkable variety of tone colors, partly as a result of their imaginative use of synthesizers. The emphasis is often on the group sound rather than on the individuality of any single player. Other distinctive features of jazz rock are the melodic role of the electric bass and the insistent repetition of rhythmic figures.

A major figure in the development of fusion was the trumpeter Miles Davis, whose albums of 1969 *In a Silent Way* and *Bitches Brew* pointed the way to much of the music of the next decade. Many musicians who played with Davis on these recordings—including the pianists Herbie Hancock, Chick Corea, and Joe Zawinul and the saxophonist Wayne Shorter—became pacesetters of jazz rock from the 1970s to the present.

Miles Davis.

Miles Runs the Voodoo Down (1969), by Miles Davis

Basic Set:

CD 9 **40**

Miles Runs the Voodoo Down is from the Miles Davis album *Bitches Brew,* one of the early milestones of jazz rock (fusion). It is performed by a large ensemble of twelve musicians including only three brass and woodwind instruments—trumpet (Miles Davis), soprano saxophone (Wayne Shorter), bass clarinet (Bennie Maupin)—but a very large rhythm section: drums (Lenny White, Jack De Johnette, Charles Alias), percussion (Jim Riley), electric pianos (Chick Corea, Larry Young), electric bass (Harvey Brooks), string bass (Dave Holland), and electric guitar (John McLaughlin). *Miles Runs the Voodoo Down* evokes the feeling of a ritual dance through its slow beat, unchanging harmony, and constant background of rock ostinatos in the electric bass and repeated rhythmic figures in African and South American percussion instruments. We'll focus on the opening 4 minutes of this extended piece (lasting 14 minutes), which features a spectacular improvised solo by Miles Davis.

Miles Runs the Voodoo Down opens softly and ominously with repeated rhythmic and melodic figures in the percussion and electric bass. Other instruments gradually join, creating a hypnotic rhythmic background that becomes increasingly prominent during Miles Davis's solo, which begins half a minute into the piece. The solo conveys a blues feeling because Davis often slides from one pitch to another. It is a free and imaginative flow of musical ideas, not based on a regular form or an established chord pattern. The trumpet opens in a middle to low register. Later, Davis's improvisation moves through a very wide range and includes a variety of brief and extended phrases, screaming high held tones, rapid passages in bebop style, and many inflections that sound vocal. *Miles Runs the Voodoo Down* beautifully integrates jazz improvisation with the rhythms and electronic resources of rock.

Jazz rock is only one of the substyles that could be heard since the 1970s. Every kind of jazz we've studied—New Orleans, swing, bebop, cool jazz, and free jazz—has its fans and devoted performers. As they have done since the early days, jazz musicians continue to explore new resources to further the development of their art.

Jazz: Summary

Roots of Jazz

- Early jazz blended elements from many sources, including:
  - West African improvisation, drumming, percussive sounds, and complex rhythms
  - African-American church services' call-and-response
  - African-American work songs, spirituals, gospel hymns, and dances
  - American hymns, popular songs, folk tunes, dances, marches, piano pieces, and band traditions
  - Nineteenth-century American and European melodies, harmonies, and forms

Important Style Features

Tone Color

- The distinctive sound of jazz is easy to recognize, but hard to describe.
- Jazz features a small combo of three to eight players, or a big band of ten to fifteen.
- The rhythm section usually consists of piano, plucked double bass, and percussion.
- A banjo or guitar may be added to the rhythm section to maintain the beat, add rhythmic interest, and provide supporting harmonies.
- The main solo instruments include the cornet, trumpet, saxophone, piano, clarinet, vibraphone, and trombone.
- Jazz emphasizes brasses, woodwinds, and percussion rather than bowed strings.
- Brass instruments may use a variety of mutes.

Improvisation

- Jazz typically contains improvised and composed sections.
- Improvisation lies at the heart of jazz, and adds freshness and spontaneity.
- Improvisations may be based on a melody or a harmonic pattern.
- Improvisations based on a melody are usually in theme-and-variation form, with the theme melody made up of thirty-two bars. The improvisations may be similar to the original theme, or so different that the melody is difficult to recognize.
- Improvisations based on a harmonic pattern feature a series of chords that repeat over and over while the improviser creates melodies above it.
- Improvisations usually include solos by various members of the ensemble.
- There may be sections of collective improvisation where several musicians improvise melodies simultaneously.

Rhythm, Melody, and Harmony

- Syncopation and rhythmic swing are distinctive features of jazz.
- Jazz usually has a steady, strong beat, with four beats to the bar. Accents often come on weak beats or between beats.
- Jazz melodies often use a major scale in which the third, fifth, and seventh notes are lowered, or flatted, as in vocal blues.
- Jazz melodies are flexible in pitch and rhythm.
- Jazz harmonies use chord progressions like those of the traditional tonal system, but the vocabulary has become increasingly complex, sophisticated, and chromatic.
- Jazz harmonies may use chords of three to six notes.

Texture

- Jazz textures may be monophonic, homophonic, polyphonic, or heterophonic.

Performance Practice

- Jazz often combines a mixture of solo and ensemble sections.
- In contrast to "classical" musicians, jazz performers aim for individuality of sound and tone color
- Instrumentalists attempt to match the personal quality of singing.
- Performers sometimes "bend" tones or use a distinctive type of vibrato.
- Transitions between two consecutive tones often include pitch inflections described as bends, smears, scoops, falloffs, or shakes.
- Some contemporary jazz performers try to emulate the styles of great performers of the past.

FEATURED PERFORMERS

- Scott Joplin (1868–1917)
- Bessie Smith (1894–1937)
- King Oliver's Creole Jazz Band
- Louis Armstrong (1901–1971) and His Hot Five
- Duke Ellington (1899–1974) and his Famous Orchestra
- Charlie Parker (1920–1955)
- Miles Davis (1926–1991)

Beyond the Classroom: Attending a Jazz Concert

Attending a jazz concert is unlike attending a classical music concert in a number of striking ways. Immediately noticeable is that the atmosphere is usually relaxed and informal. Audience members often dress casually for these performances, and they behave differently, too. The audience members may be directly involved in the performance by tapping their feet, clapping, and bobbing their heads to the beat, and even shouting approval to the performers during the performance.

Another difference is that frequently a program of the musical selections is unavailable. Improvisation usually plays a significant role, not only within the music, but also in the event itself, guaranteeing that performances are rarely identical from night to night.

If you go to a jazz concert featuring big band music, listen for a *head arrangement,* which has been worked out and memorized in rehearsal but which generally is not written down. A head arrangement usually adheres to the following basic format, reminiscent of that used in *C-Jam Blues* by Duke Ellington and His Famous Orchestra (see pages 9–10):

- Introduction (sometimes omitted)
- Head (the rhythm section improvises an accompaniment based on a chord progression while the melody section plays the main tune)
- Solos (the rhythm section repeats the basic chord progression multiple times as accompaniment while individuals take turns playing improvised solos.
- Head (similar to the opening head)
- Conclusion (sometimes omitted)

Many colleges and universities offer undergraduate and graduate degrees in jazz performance, composition, or arranging, and these programs provide sources of excellent jazz performances and festivals. When going to a jazz concert, particularly for the first time, be prepared to be entertained. Students often are struck by the talent displayed onstage and by the energy of the performers. While at the concert, ask yourself the following questions:

- Which instruments make up the rhythm section? Which instruments are featured in solos?
- Does the performance use any types of electronic instruments or amplification of conventional instruments?
- What style or styles of jazz do you notice?
- To what degree do you notice instances of improvisation?

Music for Stage and Screen

... making a musical that tells a tragic story in musical comedy terms, using only musical-comedy techniques, never falling into the "operatic" trap. Can it succeed? ... I'm excited. If it can work—it's the first.

—*Leonard Bernstein*

The musical has been one of the most important American contributions to the popular culture of the twentieth century and the early twenty-first century. Shown here is a scene from *Wicked,* music and lyrics by Stephen Schwartz and spoken dialogue by Winnie Holzman. The plot of *Wicked* is based on a novel by Gregory Maguire.

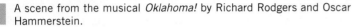
A scene from the musical *Oklahoma!* by Richard Rodgers and Oscar Hammerstein.

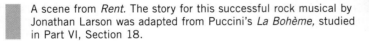
A scene from *Rent.* The story for this successful rock musical by Jonathan Larson was adapted from Puccini's *La Bohème,* studied in Part VI, Section 18.

Along with jazz and rock, the musical has been one of the most important American contributions to the popular culture of the twentieth century and the early twenty-first century. Musical shows like *Oklahoma!, South Pacific, West Side Story,* and *My Fair Lady* are performed and enjoyed all over the world.

A **musical** or **musical comedy** is a type of theater that aims to entertain through fusion of a dramatic script, acting, and spoken dialogue with music, singing, and dancing and with scenery, costumes, and spectacle. Most musicals are in fact comedies, but some are serious, with unhappy endings. Although many musicals have been written by New Yorkers and produced in Broadway theaters (hence the term *Broadway musical*), successful ones reach nationwide and even worldwide audiences: the original production is likely to be taken "on the road," and there will be new productions and revivals over the years. Many of the most successful musicals are made into movies (such as *The Sound of Music, Hair, Evita, Chicago,* and *Rent*).

1 Musical Theater

Elements of the Musical

Generally, a musical is in two acts, of which the second is shorter and brings back some of the melodies heard earlier. Traditionally, the songs consisted of an introductory section (called the *verse*) and a main section (called the *chorus*) in A A B A form (32 bars). Hit tunes from musicals, like *Ol' Man River* (from *Show Boat*) or *Some Enchanted Evening* (from *South Pacific*), have often had lasting appeal, detached from their original theatrical context.

The American musical embraces a variety of styles, yet it is a distinct type of musical theater, separate from opera. In contrast to opera, it tends to use simpler harmonies, melodies, and forms, and it contains more spoken dialogue. Its songs tend to be narrower in pitch range than operatic arias because popular singers and opera singers have different vocal techniques. Also, the musical is even more of a collaborative effort. In opera, one composer writes and orchestrates the music, and one librettist—occasionally two—is responsible for the entire text. In a musical, one composer creates the songs, but other musicians are responsible for the orchestration, the overture, the connective musical passages, and the music accompanying dances. The spoken dialogue and song lyrics are usually divided among two or more writers. Despite these differences between musicals and operas, certain works, such as George and Ira Gershwin's *Porgy and Bess* (1935), fall somewhere between the two categories. And shows originally produced as musicals, like *Porgy and Bess* and Leonard Bernstein's *West Side Story*, are sometimes performed later in opera houses and recorded by opera singers.

Development of the Musical

Sources of the Musical The American musical has drawn on a variety of musical and dramatic sources from the late nineteenth century and the early twentieth century, including operetta, vaudeville, and the revue.

Operetta, or *comic opera,* combines song, spoken dialogue, and dance; uses quite sophisticated musical techniques; and is generally set outside the United States. The operettas of the Englishmen W. S. Gilbert (1836–1911) and Arthur Sullivan (1842–1900), such as *The Mikado* (1885), were widely performed in the United States around the turn of the twentieth century. The best-known American operettas were those by Victor Herbert (1859–1924), such as *Babes in Toyland* (1903) and *Naughty Marietta* (1910).

A more popular antecedent of the musical was *vaudeville,* a variety show with songs, comedy, juggling, acrobats, and animal acts, but no plot. About 10,000 vaudeville theaters dotted the United States during the first two decades of the century.

Also in the background of the modern musical was the *revue,* a variety show without a plot but with a unifying idea. Revues in the first decades of the twentieth century were often satirical and featured pretty, scantily clad young women ("chorus girls") who sang and danced, and comedians who performed sketches.

The Golden Era of the American Musical (1920–1960) A golden era in American musical theater was created from about 1920 to 1960 by such songwriters and composers as Irving Berlin (1888–1989), Jerome Kern (1885–1945), George Gershwin (1898–1937), Cole Porter (1893–1964), Richard Rodgers (1902–1979), Frank Loesser (1910–1969), and Leonard Bernstein (1918–1990). During this period, plots of musicals became more believable, and the range of subject matter expanded. Song and dance were more closely integrated into the story, and composers increasingly borrowed sophisticated musical techniques from opera and operetta.

During the 1920s and 1930s, musicals were usually based on unrealistic "boy meets girl" stories, but the lyrics were clever and witty, as in Cole Porter's song *You're the Top* (1934).

> You're the top! You're the Colosseum.
> You're the top! You're the Louvre Museum.
> You're a melody from a symphony by Strauss.
> You're a Bendel bonnet, a Shakespeare sonnet, you're Mickey Mouse.
> You're the Nile, you're the Tow'r of Pisa,
> You're the smile on the Mona Lisa.
> I'm a worthless check, a total wreck, a flop,
> But, if, baby, I'm the bottom, You're the top!

A pathbreaking musical of the 1920s with an unusually serious plot was *Show Boat* (1927), with music by Jerome Kern and lyrics by Oscar Hammerstein II. *Show Boat* brought interracial romance to the American musical stage for the first time. Its songs—including the well-known *Ol' Man River* and *Why Do I Love You?*—revealed character and were smoothly woven into the action. (There have been a number of versions of *Show Boat,* including a Broadway hit in 1994.) In the 1930s, some musicals satirized social and political institutions, perhaps in reaction to the Great Depression. A prominent instance was George and Ira Gershwin's *Of Thee I Sing* (1931), which poked fun at American presidential elections and was the first musical to win a Pulitzer Prize for drama for its librettist. An important development of the late 1930s was the increased significance of ballet, which was used to carry the action forward. For example, the climax of the musical *On Your Toes* (1936) was a ballet by George Balanchine (1904–1989) called *Slaughter on Tenth Avenue,* in which the hero must keep dancing to avoid being killed by mobsters.

A towering achievement in the fusion of dance and drama came in 1943 with *Oklahoma!*—which marked a new era in the history of the American musical. For this show, Agnes de Mille created ballets (inspired by square dances) that were important for the progress of the story.

Like most musicals, *Oklahoma!* was set in the United States. After World War II, however, an increasing number of shows were set in foreign lands, such as Siam (*The King and I;* 1951), France (*Fanny;* 1954), England (*My Fair Lady;* 1956), and Russia (*Fiddler on the Roof;* 1964). Even when set in the United States, postwar musicals began to explore new kinds of serious subject matter, such as teenage gang warfare in *West Side Story* (1957).

The Musical after 1960 After 1960, some composers of Broadway shows continued to write songs fairly similar to those of the 1940s and 1950s. This conservative trend was also reflected in the many revivals of classic musicals like *Oklahoma!* However, other composers departed from traditional A A B A form; and often the songs were so closely integrated with the plot and production that they were unlikely to become hits on their own. Like jazz, the musical was affected by the "rock revolution" of the 1960s. One of the rock musicals was *Hair* (1967), which reflected the hippie movement and had a scene of total nudity. Rock elements were also incorporated into *Jesus Christ Superstar* (1971), by the British musician Andrew Lloyd Webber (b. 1948), who also created *Cats* (1982) and *Phantom of the Opera* (1987). The unusual prominence of European composers on the American musical scene was also reflected in *Les Misérables* (1986) and *Miss Saigon* (1989), written by the Frenchmen Claude-Michel Schönberg and Alain Boublil.

Perhaps the most original contributions to American musical theater since the 1960s have been made by the composer-lyricist Stephen Sondheim (b. 1930), who first became known as the lyricist for *West Side Story*. Many of his works are "concept musicals," based more on an idea than on a traditional linear plot. For example, *Company* (1970) deals with the theme of marriage. *Sunday in the Park with George* (1984) deals with the theme of artistic creativity as exemplified by a painting: Georges Seurat's *Sun-*

A scene from *Into the Woods,* a musical by Stephen Sondheim and James Lapine.

day on the Grande-Jatte—1884. Into the Woods (1987) deals with the theme of searching for happiness envisioned through the intersecting paths of fairy-tale characters such as Little Red Riding Hood, Jack and the Beanstalk, Cinderella, and Rapunzel. Sondheim's most ambitious work—*Sweeney Todd, the Demon Barber of Fleet Street* (1979), about a bloodthirsty psychopath—blurs the boundary between the musical and opera. It includes arias, duets, trios, complex choruses, and musical themes associated with characters and elements of the plot. Sondheim's musical style fuses elements of the traditional Broadway song with elements of Stravinsky, Copland, and Bernstein. His work reflects the continued vitality and stylistic inventiveness of the American musical.

2 Leonard Bernstein

The landmark musical *West Side Story* (1957) was composed by the extraordinarily versatile Leonard Bernstein (1918–1990). Bernstein was a leading conductor, a concert pianist, a composer of orchestral and vocal works, and an author-lecturer whose appearances on television broadened the musical knowledge of millions. Bernstein was born in Lawrence, Massachusetts; graduated from Harvard University; and studied piano and conducting at the Curtis Institute in Philadelphia. In 1943, he was appointed assistant conductor of the New York Philharmonic orchestra. Not long afterward, a guest conductor, Bruno Walter, became ill and the twenty-five-year-old Bernstein took his place on the podium with no rehearsal and only a few hours' notice. This successful concert was broadcast on nationwide radio, was hailed as a "dramatic musical event" on the front page of the *New York Times,* and launched Bernstein's spectacular career.

"I have a deep suspicion that every work I write, for whatever medium, is really theater music in some way." Bernstein's characterization indeed fits not only his musicals, operas, and ballets and his theater piece *Mass* (1971), but also his choral work *Chichester Psalms* (1965) and his three programmatic symphonies—*Jeremiah* (1942), *The Age of Anxiety* (1949), and *Kaddish* (1963)—two of which include singers and Hebrew or Aramaic texts. Bernstein's music is clearly tonal, enlivened by syncopations and irregular meters, and infused with jazz and dance rhythms. Like Stravinsky and Copland, who both influenced him, Bernstein wrote very successful ballets, including *Fancy Free* (1944) and *Facsimile* (1946). Dance numbers play an important and dramatic role in his musicals *On the Town* (1944), *Wonderful Town,* (1953) and *West Side Story* (1957). Bernstein accomplished the difficult feat of bridging the worlds of "serious" and popular music. He died in 1990, mourned by people all over the world.

West Side Story (1957)

On January 6, 1949, the choreographer Jerome Robbins first suggested to Leonard Bernstein that they collaborate on a modern version of Shakespeare's *Romeo and Juliet* set in the slums of New York. Bernstein was very enthusiastic about the "idea of making a musical that tells a tragic story in musical-comedy terms, using only musical-comedy techniques, never falling into the 'operatic' trap. Can it succeed? . . . I'm excited. If it can work—it's the first." *West Side Story*—with music by Bernstein, spoken dialogue by Arthur Laurents, and lyrics by Stephen Sondheim—was completed seven years later.

West Side Story deals with a conflict between gang rivalry and youthful love. The feud between the lovers' families in Shakespeare's *Romeo and Juliet* is transformed into warfare between two teenage street gangs: the Jets, native-born Americans led by Riff; and the Sharks, Puerto Ricans led by Bernardo. The plot revolves around a fight ("rumble") between the gangs and the doomed love of Tony (the Romeo character), a former member of the Jets; and Maria (the Juliet character), Bernardo's sister. Tony kills Bernardo after a vain attempt to break up a fight between the leader of the Sharks and Riff. Later he is shot by one of the Sharks and dies in Maria's arms.

Though it included rough street language and ended unhappily, *West Side Story* was a tremendous popular success and became an Oscar-winning musical film (1961).

The versatile American musician Leonard Bernstein was a composer of musicals and symphonic works, as well as an outstanding conductor, concert pianist, and author-lecturer.

It was an unprecedented fusion of song and drama with electrifyingly violent choreography (by Jerome Robbins and Peter Gennaro). Compared with the average Broadway show, *West Side Story* had more music; more complex and unconventional music; and a wider range of styles, from vaudeville (*Gee, Officer Krupke*) and Latin rhythms (*America*) to bebop fugue (*Cool*) and quasi-operatic ensemble (*Tonight*). We'll focus on *America* and the *Tonight* Ensemble.

America

Basic Set:
CD 9 41

Brief Set:
CD 5 58

The energetic ensemble *America* brilliantly combines Latin-flavored song and dance. Two young women of the Sharks gang, Rosalia and Anita—Bernardo's girlfriend—express opposing feelings about their homeland, Puerto Rico, and their adopted country, America. The ensemble creates a lighter mood after the emotional intensity of previous scenes and helps develop the character of the witty and high-spirited Anita.

America begins with an atmospheric introduction in a moderate tempo. The introduction is marked *Tempo di Seis,* and performed by the two soloists. (*Seis* is a type of Puerto Rican song and dance music.) The homesick Rosalia first sings the words *Puerto Rico, You lovely island, Island of tropical breezes,* eliciting Anita's mocking response—to the same melody—*Puerto Rico, You ugly island, Island of tropic diseases.*

The debate continues in the joyful main part of the song, in a faster tempo marked *Tempo de Huapango.* (*Huapango* refers to a type of Mexican dance.) In this part, the Shark women often join in Anita's praises of America. The three kinds of music heard in this part can be represented as sections A, B, and C in the outline given below. Section A is the refrain, or recurring main melody, first sung to the words, *I like to be in America* by Anita. Section B consists of brief solos by Rosalia, each followed by Anita's sarcastic responses. Instrumental interludes meant for dancing are referred to as section C. The last interlude is marked C′ because it is varied and shortened. These interludes illustrate the dramatic importance of dance throughout *West Side Story.*

The music of *America* has a Hispanic flavor with alternations between $\frac{6}{8}$ and $\frac{3}{4}$ meter, similar to those in *Final Dance: Malambo* by the Argentinean Alberto Ginastera (studied in Part VII, Section 18). As in *Final Dance: Malambo,* six fast pulses are divided into two groups of three pulses and three groups of two pulses.

Also contributing to the Latin atmosphere in *America* are the sounds of the claves, guiro—both percussion—and guitar, instruments typical of South America.

(In the film version of *West Side Story,* the music of *America* remains the same, but some words are changed and Bernardo and the Shark men sing and dance together with the young women.)

The following outline is meant to clarify the form of *America.* Most often, just the first line of text in a section is given.

0:00	**Introduction, Moderato, Temo di Seis**	
0:11	Rosalia sings (*Puerto Rico you lovely island . . .*); then Anita sings "mockingly" to the same melody (*Puerto Rico, You ugly Island . . .*). Introduction ends with Anita's solo (*I like the island Manhattan . . .*).	
1:11	**Tempo di Huapango, Fast tempo**	
1:15	A *I like to be in America . . .*	Anita
1:29	B *I like the City of San Juan . . .*	Rosalia and Anita
1:41	A *Automobile in America . . .*	Anita and young women
1:55	B *I'll drive a Buick through San Juan . . .*	Rosalia and Anita
2:07	A *Immigrant goes to America . . .*	Anita and young women
2:18	C Instrumental, dance around Rosalia	

Tony and Maria meet on a fire escape in a scene from the film version of *West Side Story*.

2:57	B	*I'll bring a TV to San Juan* . . .	Rosalia and Anita
3:09	A	*I like the shores of America* . . .	Anita and young women
3:23	C	Instrumental, dance around Rosalia with whistling	
4:02	B	*When I will go back to San Juan* . . .	Rosalia and Anita
4:15	C′	Varied and shortened instrumental dance	

Tonight Ensemble

Basic Set:
CD 9 42

Brief Set:
CD 5 59

In the *Tonight* ensemble, Bernstein projects several different emotions at the same time: Riff, Bernardo, and their gangs excitedly planning for the upcoming fight; Anita looking forward to the "kicks" she's "gonna get"; and Tony and Maria anticipating the joy of being together. Riff, Bernardo, and Anita sing quick, staccato tones in a narrow range, whereas Tony and Maria sing the legato, soaringly lyrical *Tonight* melody, heard in an earlier "balcony scene" on Maria's fire escape. As Verdi did in the Quartet from *Rigoletto,* Bernstein lets us hear the voices separately before combining them in an ensemble. Such dramatic ensembles were uncommon in musicals, which tended to feature solo songs with "hit" potential.

LISTENING OUTLINE

BERNSTEIN, *Tonight* Ensemble from *West Side Story*

Riff, Bernardo, Anita, Tony, Maria, gang members, orchestra

Fast and rhythmic.

(Duration, 3:38)

42 59	0:00	**1. a.**	Orchestra, menacing staccato melody with syncopations introduces
	0:07	**b.**	Riff, Bernardo, and their gangs alternate and then sing together quick, staccato phrases with syncopations.

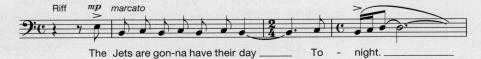

The Jets are gon-na have their day _____ To - night. _____

43 60	1:08	**c.**	Anita repeats previous phrases.
	1:25	**d.**	Tony, lyrical *Tonight* melody.

Tony (warmly)
mf

To - night, to - night Won't be just an - y

night. To - night there will be no morn - ing star. _____

2:15	**2.**	**a.**	Orchestra, ***ff***.
2:23		**b.**	Riff, quick staccato phrases.
2:40		**c.**	Maria, lyrical *Tonight* melody, with Riff's staccato phrases, and brief interjections (*All right, Tonight*) by Tony and Anita. Tony joins Maria on *Tonight* melody.
3:29		**d.**	Voices join on sustained high tones (*Tonight*), ***ff***.

3 Music in Film

Early Film Music

Music for film began in the 1890s and emerged as an important musical genre during the twentieth century. During the silent-film era (c. 1890–1926), live pianists, organists, and orchestras accompanied films, both to heighten the emotional effect and to drown out the noise of the movie projector. In the first "talking movie," *The Jazz Singer* (1927), starring Al Jolson, the sound was recorded on vinyl discs. By 1929, new technology enabled sound to be recorded directly on the celluloid filmstrip.

Functions and Styles of Film Music

Synchronized with images on a screen, ***film music*** provides momentum and continuity, and suggests mood, atmosphere, character, and dramatic action. As in opera and ballet, music in film can convey unspoken thoughts and the emotional implications of a setting. It can clarify the meaning of a scene and enhance the excitement of the action. Movies range widely in the amount and function of the music they contain. At one extreme are musicals and films about musicians, in which musical performer-actors appear on screen and music captures the viewers' attention. At the other extreme are films in which music discreetly accompanies the drama, without diverting viewers from the onscreen action and dialogue.

Most movie music is commissioned for specific films, but some sound tracks include segments of previously existing compositions. Film music is extraordinarily diverse in style, ranging from the rock and roll of *Pulp Fiction* (1994) to the minimalism, electronic sounds, and eerie string effects of *The Matrix* (1999). Many people have come to appreciate classical music by hearing it in such films as *Fantasia* of 1940 (Bach, Beethoven, Stravinsky); *2001: A Space Odyssey* of 1968 (Richard Strauss, Johann Strauss, Ligeti); *Amadeus* of 1984 (Mozart); *Shine* of 1996 (Rachmaninoff); and *The Pianist* of 2002 (Chopin). Important composers of American film music include Franz Waxman (*The Bride of Frankenstein,* 1935), Aaron Copland (*The Heiress,* 1948), Dimitri Tiomkin (*The Old Man and the Sea,* 1958), Bernard Herrmann (*Vertigo,* 1958, which we'll study), and John Williams (*Star Wars,* 1977; *Harry Potter and the Prisoner of Azkaban,* 2003). Recent composers who are well regarded include James Horner (*Titanic,* 1997) and Danny Elfman (*Spider-Man,* 2002 and 2004). Sometimes, a composer will collaborate with a particular director on many films, as John Williams did with Steven Spielberg (*Jaws, 1975; E.T. The Extra-Terrestrial,* 1982; *Schindler's List,* 1993).

Creating Film Music

Up to the 1950s, a major Hollywood film studio, like MGM or Paramount, would have a resident orchestra and staff composers, conductors, and arrangers. Since the 1960s, most film music is composed, arranged, and performed by freelance musicians. Typically, the composer views the movie and—in collaboration with the director, producer, editor, and music editor—decides exactly where music will appear in the film, and how long the musical passage, known as a *cue,* will last. Composition, orchestration—usually by one or more orchestrators—and recording are often completed within a few months or less. John Williams has vividly described his preferred method of composing for film: "I'll get a sense of the film's kinetic ebb and flow . . . a sense of where the film may be slowing down, or where it's accelerating, and where I can pick up on the rhythms of the film." For Williams, the "most important issue in scoring films is tempo. Anyone who takes a home movie and puts records to it knows this: if you put one piece of music to it, the film will be one kind of musical experience, and another piece of music will change the experience totally." While composing, Williams will view the scene "many times and have a timing cue sheet that's been prepared for the scene and then I'll write three or four bars and go back and look at it and then write four bars more and look at it again. And it's a constant process of writing, looking, checking, running it in my mind's ear against the film, even conducting with a stopwatch against the action of the film."

Music and Image

In movie scores, musical themes—or leitmotifs—often become associated with specific characters, objects, emotions, or ideas in the film, a technique derived from the music dramas of Richard Wagner. The "shark theme" in *Jaws* (1975), the "007 theme" in the James Bond movies, and the "imperial march" (Darth Vader) theme in the *Star Wars* movies are well-known examples. As in Wagner's music dramas, these musical themes are varied and transformed to convey evolving dramatic situations and changes of character. They can remind the audience of the associated character, whether or not he or she appears onscreen.

The mood of movie music does not always match that of the synchronized visual image. In such instances, the music is meant to produce a distancing or ironic effect. Well-known instances are *Goodfellas* (1990) and *Kill Bill* (2003), in which scenes of horrific violence are accompanied by gentle or happy music, making the action seem almost unreal.

During the last few decades, the importance of music in film has become widely recognized. Interest in film music continues to grow, as many moviegoers have come to appreciate the significant contributions of this musical genre. Today, sound track albums and concert performances bring film music to millions of people outside the movie theater.

Vertigo (1958), Directed by Alfred Hitchcock, Music by Bernard Herrmann

One of the most important American composers of film was Bernard Herrmann (1911–1975), who wrote music for such movies as Orson Welles's *Citizen Kane* (1941); Martin Scorsese's *Taxi Driver* (1976); and Alfred Hitchcock's *Vertigo* (1958), *North by Northwest* (1959), *Psycho* (1960), and *Marnie* (1964). Herrmann's music plays a major role in creating the atmosphere of obsession that pervades *Vertigo.* This psychological thriller received mixed reviews when first released in 1958, but subsequently *Vertigo* and its musical score have been hailed as masterpieces.

Near the beginning of *Vertigo,* Scottie Ferguson (played by James Stewart), a detective in San Francisco, retires from the police force because of his fear of heights and vertigo—a medical condition that causes dizziness. Scottie is hired by an old college friend, Gavin Elster (played by Tom Helmore), to find out why his beautiful wife, Madeleine (played by Kim Novak), has behaved strangely in recent weeks.

While following Madeleine, Scottie saves her from drowning after she attempts suicide by jumping into San Francisco Bay. The two become increasingly attracted to each other. She tells him she has dreamed of a Spanish village with a church and tower, which Scottie realizes is the San Juan Bautista Mission south of San Francisco. He drives her there hoping to resolve her emotional problems. We'll focus on how Herrmann's music intensifies the dramatic effect of visual images in the climactic "Tower Scene" that occurs halfway through *Vertigo,* one of the best-known scenes in movie history.

The film clip for this scene is available in *Connect Kamien.*

Tower Scene (segment)

In the action-packed Tower Scene, Madeleine runs into the church and rushes up the bell tower stairway, followed by Scottie. But vertigo slows him down, preventing him from reaching her in time. Through a window, he sees Madeleine fall from the tower to her death.

This brief segment of *Vertigo* illustrates how Herrmann's music for orchestra raises the tension of the evolving dramatic situation through string tremolos, sustained dissonant chords, rapid whirring ostinatos, and loud repeated brass notes.

As the Tower Scene opens, a loud string tremolo suggests the ominous significance of Madeleine's run toward the church. Scottie's anxiety as he looks up to the tower is conveyed by three sustained dissonant chords: the first played by high muted brasses (as we see the tower), the second played louder by brasses in the middle register (as we see Scottie's face), and the third played softly by low woodwinds (after he cries out "Madeleine!"). Starting when Madeleine enters the church, a rapid whirring ostinato in the strings suggests terror and frenzied motion.

Scottie's frantic pursuit of Madeleine up the stairway takes place in three stages of increasing tension. The climb up to the first landing is accompanied by the whirring string ostinato, and single rising tones in loud, low brass instruments. A high, shrill brass chord, called the "vertigo chord," conveys Scottie's fear of heights as he momentarily stops climbing and looks down the tower stairwell. This dissonant chord is a polychord that combines E flat minor and D major triads.

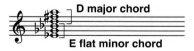

In the second stage of the climb, tension is increased by a loud, insistent figure of three rapid repeated notes in the brasses. Again the shrill "vertigo chord" evokes Scottie's terror as he looks down the stairwell from a greater height. In the last stage of the climb, high brasses play a quicker and more insistent repeated-note figure that suggests a racing heartbeat. Scottie hears the slam of the tower trapdoor followed by a woman's scream. He looks through the tower window and sees Madeleine's body fall to the roof of the church; her fall is evoked by a high, shrill sustained chord. As her body hits the roof, a timpani roll and an ascending two-note idea in the low brasses create a feeling of doom. This solemn two-note idea repeats as Scottie freezes in desperation at the end of the film segment.

To fully appreciate the enormous contribution of Herrmann's music to the scene's emotional intensity, turn down the volume completely as you watch this film clip. Probably, the Tower Scene will seem much less exciting to you without its music.

Music for Stage and Screen: Summary

The Musical

Elements of the Musical

- Generally, a musical is in two acts, of which the second is shorter and brings back some melodies heard earlier. Musicals embrace a variety of styles, yet they are a distinct type of musical theater, separate from opera.
- Songs traditionally consist of an introductory section called the *verse* and a main section called the *chorus* in thirty-two-bar A A B A form.
- The musical is a highly collaborative effort. One composer usually creates the songs, but other musicians are responsible for the orchestration, the overture, the connective musical passages, and any accompanying dance music. The spoken dialogue and song lyrics are usually divided among two or more writers.
- Some works, such as George and Ira Gershwin's *Porgy and Bess* (1935) and Leonard Bernstein's *West Side Story* (1957), fall somewhere between the two categories of musicals and operas.

Development of the Musical

- The American musical has drawn on a variety of musical and dramatic sources, including operetta, vaudeville, and the revue.
- The golden era in American musical theater was created from about 1920 to 1960.
- *Oklahoma!* (1943) marked a new era in the American musical with its fusion of dance and drama.
- After 1960, some composers departed from the traditional forms, creating songs so closely integrated with the plot and production that they were unlikely to become hits on their own.
- Like jazz, the musical was affected by the "rock revolution" of the 1960s.
- Stephen Sondheim, the lyricist for *West Side Story,* has become one of the most original contributors to American musical theater since the 1960s. He is known for his "concept musicals," which are based more on an idea than on a traditional linear plot.

Performance Practice

- A small pit orchestra located below the stage usually provides the musical accompaniment to a musical. The conductor also may play a keyboard instrument or synthesizer.

Music in Film

Early Film Music

- Music for films began in the 1890s and emerged as an important musical genre during the twentieth century. It is highly diverse in style.

Functions and Styles of Film Music

- Film music provides momentum and continuity to images on a screen, and suggests mood, atmosphere, character, and dramatic action. It can convey unspoken thoughts and emotional implications, and can clarify the meaning of a scene and enhance the excitement of action.
- In films, music can be a central element in the plot, or it can discreetly accompany the drama.

Creating Film Music
- Until the 1960s, Hollywood film studios had a resident orchestra, composers, conductors, and arrangers. Since the 1960s, most film music has been composed, arranged, and performed by freelance musicians.
- Deciding where the music will appear in a film is a collaborative effort between the composer, director, producer, film editor, and music editor.

Music and Image
- Similar to a technique used in the music dramas of Richard Wagner, musical themes or leitmotifs often become associated with specific characters, objects, emotions, or ideas.
- The mood of film music does not always match that of the synchronized visual image. In such instances, the music is meant to produce a distancing or ironic effect.

Performance Practice
- Silent films during the earliest decades were accompanied by a pianist, an organist, or an orchestra to heighten the emotional effect and drown out the noise of the movie projector.
- The first movie with sound was *The Jazz Singer* (1927), with its sound recorded on vinyl discs. By 1929, new technology enabled sound to be recorded directly on the filmstrip.
- Film music uses live performers, synthesizers, computers, or a combination of these means.

Beyond the Classroom: Music for Stage and Screen

Musicals, films, and television shows rely heavily on music for their enormous public appeal. Watching a film or television show without a soundtrack is virtually unthinkable, and attending a live musical can be an exhilarating, memorable experience. Most major cities have professional productions of musicals, and regional theaters provide a showcase of local talent.

Fortunately, we now have access to a huge array of recorded music from Broadway, film, and television shows. Original cast recordings of Broadway shows and releases of later productions are widely available, as are film versions of many Broadway shows. Most film soundtracks and many television show theme songs also are available on recordings.

Several cities, particularly New York City and Los Angeles, feature specialty museums where on demand you can hear and watch selections from among thousands of digitized recordings of radio, television, and film, dating back to the beginning of these mediums.

When listening to music for stage or screen, ask yourself the following questions:

At a Musical
- How many acts are in the musical? What balance do you notice between the number of songs and the spoken dialogue? Is the musical sung throughout?
- Do you notice any particular musical forms within the songs?
- When a song is sung, what is the dramatic action that prompts it? What instrument or instruments accompany the singer?

- Does the action stop onstage while the singer is singing, or does something occur onstage to advance the plot during the song?
- What additional information about the character or plot is revealed in the song?
- If you notice any duets, trios, or other ensembles, who is singing, and what is the plot action at this moment?
- Is there a chorus? If so, what role do the members play? Are there any nonsinging roles?
- Is there any dancing? Are there separate dancers who only dance, but do not sing? Do any members of the cast or chorus dance?
- What role does the pit orchestra play? Where are the musicians located? How many musicians make up the pit orchestra? What instruments are played? Does one person play more than one instrument?

In Music for Film or Television
- Is the music a central element of the drama, or does it discreetly accompany the action?
- Where and when is music used?
- Are voices and singers used? If so, how and for what purpose?
- Is the sound track made up of previously composed music, such as a symphony or chamber music, or is the music newly composed specifically for the feature?
- How does the mood of the music fit the action?
- Does the music heighten your emotions in some way? If so, what features of the music cause your reaction?
- Do you notice any special sound effects? If so, how and for what purpose are they used?

Rock

Hey! That's our music; that was written for us!

—Bob Dylan (at age fourteen, when he first heard
Bill Haley's Rock Around the Clock)

Haley Williams and Josh Farro from the American rock band Paramore.

Billie Joe Armstrong, the lead singer of Green Day.

Alicia Keyes, Usher

The mid-1950s saw the growth of a new kind of popular music that was first called *rock and roll* and then simply *rock*. Though it includes diverse styles, **rock** tends to be vocal music with a hard, driving beat, often featuring electric guitar accompaniment and heavily amplified sound. Early rock grew mainly out of *rhythm and blues,* a dance music of African Americans that fused blues, jazz, and gospel styles. Rock also drew on *country and western,* a folklike, guitar-based style associated with rural white Americans; and *pop music,* a smooth, highly polished style exemplified by such performers as Frank Sinatra and Perry Como. In little more than a decade, rock evolved from a simple, dance-oriented style to music that was highly varied in its tone colors, lyrics, musical forms, and electronic technology.

Jimi Hendrix's brilliant guitar playing during the 1960s influenced later rock performers.

1 Rock Styles

Development of Rock

In the late 1940s, rhythm and blues became a dominant style among African Americans. Rhythm and blues (R & B) of the 1950s differed from earlier blues in its more powerful beat and its use of the saxophone and electric guitar. Among the leading performers influenced by rhythm and blues were Little Richard, Chuck Berry, Bo Diddley, and Fats Domino. Gospel-tinged vocal groups, such as the Drifters, and the soaring falsetto lead sounds of the Platters were also an important part of rhythm-and-blues style.

During the 1950s many rhythm-and-blues hits were issued by white performers in versions ("covers") with less sexually explicit lyrics. Little Richard's *Tutti Fruiti* and *Long Tall Sally,* for example, were issued in "cover" versions by Pat Boone one month after the release of the originals.

One of the earliest important rock and roll groups was Bill Haley and His Comets, whose *Rock Around the Clock* is often identified as the first big hit of the new style, though this distinction could just as appropriately be awarded to any number of singles from the period. The song was recorded in 1954, but it did not become a number-one hit until a year later, when it was prominently featured in *The Blackboard Jungle,* a provocative movie about teenage delinquency in a contemporary setting: a New York City high school. To many people, the new music seemed rebellious in its loudness, pounding beat, and sexual directness; and the image of youthful rebellion was also projected by Elvis Presley, who reigned as "king" of rock and roll.

During the 1960s, much of the rock music by black performers was called *soul,* a term that emphasized its emotionality, its gospel roots, and its relationship to the black community. Soul musicians included James Brown, Ray Charles, and Aretha Franklin. *Motown*—derived from "Motor Town USA," a nickname for Detroit, the city from which the style emerged—was a type of music that blended rhythm and blues with elements of popular music; among its stars were Diana Ross and the Supremes and Stevie Wonder. With Motown, African American composers and performers entered the mainstream of popular music.

During the 1950s, Chuck Berry was a leading performer of rhythm and blues.

509

Elvis Presley, who died in 1977 at the age of forty-two, was the "king" of rock and roll.

A new era of British influence began in 1964 with the American tour of the Beatles, an English rock group whose members probably have been the most influential performers in the history of rock. The Beatles—the singer-guitarists Paul McCartney, John Lennon, and George Harrison; and the drummer Ringo Starr (all born in the early 1940s)—dominated the popular music scene in the United States, along with the Rolling Stones and other British groups. Under their influence, rock musicians of the middle and late 1960s explored a wider range of sources for sounds and musical ideas. They experimented with electronic effects, with "classical" and nonwestern instruments, and with unconventional scales, chord progressions, and rhythms.

Rock in the 1960s also absorbed elements of folk music and often had lyrics dealing with such contemporary issues as war and social injustice. This development was spurred by the success of the songwriter and singer Bob Dylan, whose *Blowin' in the Wind*—a song against racial bigotry—articulated the feelings of many young people.

During the late 1960s, the popular music scene was enormously varied. The diversity of rock styles is reflected in the many terms that arose to describe the music of this period: *fusion, folk rock, jazz rock, psychedelic rock, acid rock, art rock*. From the late 1960s to the early 1970s, rock expanded the scale of its instrumentation and formal structures as well as the scope of its harmony and textual content. Technological advancements in recording techniques often added important features to the sound as well. Rock style grew more theatrical as many groups began to concentrate on visual aspects of their stage shows. Rock also began to have a strong impact on Hollywood films and Broadway musicals, as described in Part IX. Starting in the late 1960s, many rock performers assembled *concept albums*—such as *Sgt. Pepper's Lonely Hearts Club Band* (Beatles) and *Bookends* (Simon and Garfunkel)—in which the songs are linked by a basic idea. In a sense, the concept album is analogous to the song cycle of the romantic period.

Bob Dylan's songs of the 1960s often dealt with such contemporary issues as war and racial injustice.

The 1970s saw the continuation of many styles from the 1960s, the revival of early rock and roll, and the rise of a dance music called *disco*. Many veteran performers of the 1960s continued to be active; but new stars also emerged, including the singer-songwriters Billy Joel and Bruce Springsteen, as well as the Mexican American Linda Ronstadt and the "disco queen" Donna Summer. For a while in the early 1970s, there was a nostalgic fascination with 1950s rock and roll and its pioneer performers. Record companies released many albums of repackaged old hits ("oldies"). A blend of country music and rock called *country rock* became popular in the early 1970s. Country music itself moved into the musical mainstream as its stars (Johnny Cash, Dolly Parton, Willie Nelson, and others) won national popularity. Other musical styles of the 1970s included *reggae,* a music from Jamaica; *funk,* a rhythmically assertive development of black soul music; *punk,* a return to a primal form of rock; and *new wave,* a technically refined and stylistically eclectic derivative of *punk.*

In the early 1980s, new wave bands from Britain such as the Police and the Clash were popular with American rock audiences. This "second British invasion" was comparable to the one that had been led by the Beatles during the early 1960s. Though their styles varied, many British bands of this period, such as New Order and The Cure, made extensive use of electronic technology—synthesizers and computers—and often featured outlandish-looking performers. The 1980s saw a renewed interest among teenagers in *heavy metal,* a type of basic rock characterized by pounding drums, heavily amplified bass, and unrestrained guitars played at peak volume. Heavy metal's lyrics, with their increasingly overt references to sex and violence, gave rise to concern about their possible effect on young people. Popular heavy metal bands of this period include Metallica, Iron Maiden, Mötley Crüe, and Guns 'n' Roses.

Among young urban blacks, *rap* developed. It began as a kind of rhythmically accented poetic recitation accompanied by a disk jockey who manipulated recordings on two turntables to create a collage of percussive and musical effects. First popularized in black neighborhoods of east coast American cities, with works like Sugarhill Gang's

Bruce Springsteen performs onstage at Madison Square Garden in New York City on November 7, 2009.

Rapper's Delight (1979), rap later depicted the anger and frustration of urban youth. Through artists like Run-D.M.C. and the white group the Beastie Boys, rap appealed to a wider audience by the late 1980s.

Heavy metal and rap continued to grow in popularity throughout the 1980s and into the 1990s. Heavy metal broadened its audience appeal and was no longer the exclusive domain of white working-class adolescents. In the late 1980s and early 1990s, heavy metal spawned a variety of substyles such as *thrash, speed metal,* and *death metal.* By 1990, rap had adopted stylistic features from other forms of popular music and had begun to attract new audiences. There was a successful rap show on cable television; early rap artists included De La Soul, Public Enemy, and Niggaz with Attitude (N.W.A.). By the end of the 1990s, rap and rap-flavored rhythm and blues moved into the mainstream and dominated the recording charts. Particularly influential were Dr. Dre, Tupac Shakur, Missy Elliot, and the Detroit rapper Marshall Mathers (Eminem). Recordings of the controversial *gangsta rap*—with its deliberately antisocial and sexually explicit lyrics—had enormous sales.

The brash, grinding guitar sounds and angry lyrics of despair of Seattle's *grunge* or *alternative* rock bands were embraced by many young people disenchanted with the polished sounds of mainstream rock of the early 1990s. While alternative bands such as Nirvana, Pearl Jam, Soundgarden, and Alice in Chains offered a great range of stylistic variety, they also exhibited a clear stylistic influence of 1970s punk and hard rock, as well as heavy metal.

The continued success of *grunge* or *alternative rock* in the 1990s was exemplified by the popularity of such bands as Nirvana, Soundgarden, Nine Inch Nails, and the female-led groups Belly and Hole. By the mid-1990s, this success engendered a punk resurgence with the success of Green Day, NoFX, and System of a Down. At the end of the twentieth century, interesting trends included the emergence of Latino artists who incorporated pan-Latin influences in their music (Gloria Estefan and Ricky Martin), the appearance of crossover artists from the world of country music (Garth Brooks), and a renewed interest in music from the 1970s.

Having briefly examined the development of rock, we'll now consider its musical elements.

Elements of Rock

Tone Color Though some early rock performers used piano-based instrumentation, it was the electric guitar sound of rock that contrasted most with the brass-reed sound of the "big band" heard in the 1930s and 1940s. Rock music is powerfully amplified, and the guitar is often manipulated electronically to produce a wide range of tone colors. Along with singers (who often also play instruments), a rock group typically includes two electric guitars (lead and rhythm), electric bass, percussion, and keyboard instruments such as piano, electric piano, and synthesizer. Some groups also include one or more trumpets, trombones, or saxophones.

Starting in the 1960s, a wide range of instruments not normally associated with popular music—from the harpsichord to the Indian sitar—were occasionally added to the basic rock group, particularly for recording sessions. Rock recordings began to use such diverse sounds as electronic blips, crowd noises, and a symphony orchestra. During the 1970s and 1980s, rock musicians such as Keith Emerson (Emerson, Lake, and Palmer) exploited the ever-expanding capabilities of synthesizers and computers. Sophisticated electronic technology made it possible for a few performers to sound like a large ensemble. By the 1990s and the early 2000s, the range of tone color in many rock groups was expanded by the inclusion of a disk jockey who manipulated vinyl recordings, and by the use of multiple computers in contemporary rock concerts.

The singing style of rock is drawn largely from black, folk, and country-and-western music. Although singing styles vary, they are all different from the crooning sound cultivated by earlier popular vocalists. Rock singers shout, cry, wail, growl, and use guttural sounds, as well as *falsetto,* a method of singing used by males to reach notes higher than their normal range. Nonsense syllables and repeated chants (such as *Yeah! Yeah! Yeah!*) are also featured.

Rhythm Most rock is based on a very powerful beat in quadruple ($\frac{4}{4}$) meter with strong accents on the second and fourth beats of the bar. The rhythmic excitement is heightened because each beat is usually subdivided into 2 equal notes. This produces 8 faster pulses, which are superimposed on the 4 basic beats. To get the effect, count out the following: 1-and-2-and-3-and-4-and. Rock of the 1960s and 1970s often combined complicated rhythms with this basic pattern; for example, the bass player might emphasize the offbeats—the *ands.*

Form, Melody, and Harmony The earliest rock music was often in 12-bar blues form (see pages 471–472), in 32-bar A A B A form, or in a variant of these forms. Other common popular music structures include strophic and verse-chorus forms. Strophic form (see page 263), in which the musical accompaniment remains the same for each stanza of the lyrics, is commonly found in folk music. Since the accompaniment is repeated, the listener's attention is drawn to the words, which are particularly important both in folk music and in its rock-oriented derivation known as *folk rock.* Verse-chorus form, a variant of strophic form, is very commonly used in popular music. (The Beatles' song *Lucy in the Sky with Diamonds,* studied below, is in verse-chorus form.) In this musical structure, each verse, or stanza, is followed by a chorus, or refrain. In the verse sections, the different stanzas of text are set to a repeated melody and accompaniment, as in strophic form. In the chorus, however, both text and music are repeated. The chorus typically includes a "hook line," a repeated lyric and melody that become the most memorable part of the song.

Carlos Santana

The guitarist and songwriter Carlos Santana fuses rock with Latin and African rhythms as well as elements of jazz and the blues. A major figure in Spanish-language rock, and leader of the band Santana, he was inducted into the Rock and Roll Hall of Fame in 1998.

Santana, a fourth-generation musician, was born in 1947 in the town of Autlán de Novarra in Mexico. When he was five his father—a violinist and bandleader—began teaching him the violin, and at eight he switched to the guitar. In 1955, Santana moved with his family to Tijuana, Mexico, where he sang and played guitar on the streets for tourists. At age fourteen, he moved to San Francisco, and five years later he formed the Santana Blues Band. A turning point in Santana's career came in 1969, when his band created a sensation at the Woodstock rock festival and its first album, *Santana,* was hailed by *Rolling Stone* magazine as "an explosive fusion of Hispanic-edged rock, Afro-Cuban rhythms, and interstellar improvisation."

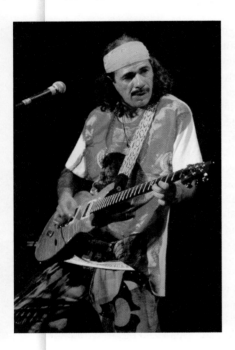

During the 1970s, Santana's band became one of the most famous in the world as a result of its best-selling recordings and concert tours in the United States, Europe, and Africa. Some of his band's albums of the early 1970s, including *Caravanserai* (1972), were close in style to jazz-rock fusion. Besides recording with his band, Santana has also made solo albums that have had a powerful impact on the rock scene. He often records with star performers in other fields like Bob Dylan (folk rock), Herbie Hancock (jazz), Wayne Shorter (jazz), and John McLaughlin (jazz-rock fusion). Remarkably for a rock performer, at age fifty-two Santana created his biggest hit so far, the album *Supernatural* (1999), which was voted Best Rock Album of the Year and has sold over 21 million copies worldwide.

Santana usually begins to create a song by recording his guitar improvisation for two or three hours. Then he selects the best segments, and works on them with a collaborator. Santana has vividly described the way he created the song *Love of my Life,* together with the singer and guitarist Dave Matthews. "I was picking up my son from school and I thought, OK, time to listen to some radio. I turned on a classical station and the first thing I heard was this melody. . . . They didn't say who the composer was." Santana went into a record store and sang the melody for a salesperson, who told him that it came from Brahms's Third Symphony (studied in Part VI, Section 16). He bought the recording and later played Brahms's melody—with slightly changed rhythm—for Dave Matthews and recited the beginning of the lyrics. "Dave sat down and—bam—wrote the song lyrics right there on the spot, and we recorded it."

"Playing the guitar is both a physical and a metaphysical experience," Santana once wrote. "When you can play from your heart, you are being open and honest. . . . The instrument becomes the vehicle by which you can reach others with the music." Santana's guitar sound has a vocal quality. "When you listen to vocalists like Aretha Franklin and Dionne Warwick, you learn to phrase differently," Santana has said. "I love musicians who make you want to cry and laugh at the same time. . . . You want to bend notes, you want to be able to express joy . . . anger, and a cry."

Earlier popular songs usually consisted of 4- or 8-bar phrases, but rock melodies sometimes contain phrases that are irregular in length. Rock songs tend to have short melodic patterns that are repeated or varied (or both) several times. They are occasionally built on modes, rather than on traditional major or minor scales. For example, *Norwegian Wood,* by John Lennon, is first in the Mixolydian mode and then in the Dorian mode.

The harmonic progressions of rock are usually quite simple, often consisting of just three or four basic chords. Sometimes, the harmony can be deliberately restricted to only two chords, as in *Eleanor Rigby,* by John Lennon and Paul McCartney. By the mid-1960s, the Beatles, the Beachboys, and other innovative artists began using chord progressions that were rarely found in earlier popular music.

2 Rock in American Society

"Hey! That's our music; that was written for us!" shouted the fourteen-year-old Bob Dylan when he first heard Bill Haley's *Rock Around the Clock* in 1955. Like Dylan, millions of young people felt that rock belonged to them and that it expressed their search for identity and independence. Many leading rock performers and songwriters were themselves in their teens or early twenties. In contrast to rock, popular music before the 1950s had appealed about equally to people of all ages.

As a result of the "baby boom" after World War II, there were more American young people in the 1950s and 1960s than ever before, and they had more money to spend, because of a generally rising economy. American industry quickly responded to this vast youth market, and rock became a big business. Sales of electric guitars, phonographs, records, and transistor radios increased dramatically. Rock superstars struck it rich through record royalties, movie contracts, and astronomical concert fees. Rock performances took place everywhere: in auditoriums, gymnasiums, sports arenas, and baseball stadiums. A single concert by a leading group could gross hundreds of thousands of dollars and might be seen by an audience of up to 75,000 people. There even were rock festivals, like the three-day Woodstock Music and Art Fair in August 1969. At that event, over 300,000 people listened in the open fields to the music of Joan Baez, Janis Joplin, Jimi Hendrix, Jefferson Airplane, Santana, and many others. *Woodstock,* one of the most important of many rock films, documented this gathering.

Often rock performances were as much theatrical as musical events. From the earliest days of rock and roll, costumes and staging were essential to the show. For example, Elvis Presley's appearance was heightened by the tight-fitting sequined pants, a leather jacket, and gyrations that led to the nickname "Elvis the pelvis." In the late 1960s, Jimi Hendrix, Pete Townsend (of the Who), and other performers destroyed their instruments as part of their stage show. The image of "psychedelic rock" was heightened by flashing strobe lights that simulated the sensations of a drug experience. Rock performances of the 1970s became even more theatrical. Alice Cooper—a male vocalist—appeared onstage with a boa constrictor and performed acts of simulated violence. The members of a group called Kiss wore macho glitter costumes and makeup influenced by the kabuki theater of Japan. The act involved flames, smoke, and explosions. David Bowie, who, in one of his many stage personae (Aladdin Sane), wore women's clothing and dyed his hair bright orange, often said that his records were only "half there," because the visual aspect was missing. Some British new wave stars of the 1980s continued the tradition of David Bowie and were as famous for their outrageous appearance as for their music. Among the best-known was Boy George of the group Culture Club, whose androgynous looks, rouge, and mascara were meant to shock. The theatrics combined with the music of rock performers often generated hysterical excitement: fans screamed, moaned, and rushed the stage.

Rock songs often reflected trends in American life, such as increased openness about sexuality. Lyrics tended to be more sexually explicit than those of the sentimental ("moon-June-spoon") love songs of the 1930s and 1940s. (In fact, the term *rock and roll* originally had an explicit sexual connotation.) During the 1960s, rock performers often sang about a wide range of topics including the war in Vietnam, experiences associated with drugs, and the struggle for civil rights. Unlike pop vocalists of the 1930s and 1940s, many rock performers wrote their own songs. For many young people of the time, rock was part of a lifestyle that seemed less inhibited and less materialistic than that of their parents. They quickly adopted the longer hairstyles and casual dress popularized by rock stars.

During the 1970s, rock became integrated into the mainstream of American popular music. Although rock concerts still appealed primarily to the young, a wide variety of rock records were purchased by people of all ages. And rock songs of the 1970s were less likely to deal with social and political issues.

Some popular music of the 1980s, however, rediscovered an idealism recalling that of the 1960s. In 1985, for example, many leading rock stars recorded a song and video, *We Are the World,* that would eventually raise about $45 million for victims of famine. Many rock concerts benefited various social causes; perhaps the most spectacular was the 16-hour Live Aid concert (also in 1985) for African famine relief, which was telecast on an international satellite network and reached an audience of about 1½ billion people.

Mariah Carey.

During the 1980s and 1990s, women performers had a powerful impact on rock. "Many of the new women rockers do a lot more than sing," observed one critic. "They play their own instruments, write their own songs, control their own careers." Their wide range of musical styles extended from pop and soul to funk, new wave, country rock, and heavy metal. Leading performers included Pat Benatar, Tina Turner, Madonna, Alanis Morisette, Sheryl Crow, Queen Latifah, Shania Twain, and Ani DiFranco.

In the 1990s, most major record companies involved with mainstream rock and pop played it safe by promoting established superstars. Among the most popular artists of the decade were Mariah Carey, Whitney Houston, Madonna, Celine Dion, Janet Jackson, and the group Boyz II Men. The 1990s brought spectacular celebrations of the rock heritage. More than half a million people attended Woodstock '94, an event in upstate New York marking the twenty-fifth anniversary of the original Woodstock festival. Among the artists who performed were the veterans Joe Cocker; Bob Dylan; and Crosby, Stills, and Nash; and groups like Metallica and newer artists like Green Day.

In 2005, the Fourth of July weekend witnessed the Live 8 concerts, designed to pressure the leaders of eight major industrialized nations to do more to combat poverty in Africa. An expanded version of the Live Aid concert of 1985, the Live 8 shows were held in ten cities around the world and featured such performers as Madonna, Elton John, Mariah Carey, and Sting. More than 1 million people attended the free concerts, and an estimated 3 billion people heard the music over television and radio and on the Internet. The London concert opened with U2 performing *Sgt. Pepper's Lonely Hearts Club Band,* joined by one of the song's composers, Paul McCartney.

Rock and Recordings

Unlike earlier popular music, rock spread more through radio and recordings than through live performances or sheet music. There were a growing number of radio stations, and many of them broadcast only rock. Disc jockeys like Alan Freed—who popularized the term *rock and roll*—became important personalities who strongly influenced musical tastes. During the late 1950s and early 1960s, most rock and roll records were produced by small, specialized companies. But the tremendous financial success of rock soon led major companies to return to the field. By the mid-1960s and 1970s, major companies were producing most rock recordings.

During the 1960s, the sound of rock recordings became quite different from what was heard at a live performance. Increasingly, rock groups took advantage of multitrack recording. "With a small group," wrote one record producer, "every instrument can be recorded on a different track. Each track has a separate volume control and a tone control to adjust to the desired treble or bass. Several kinds of echoes can be added to each instrument." Recording sessions were often a "layer cake" operation: each sound layer was produced separately, and the different layers were combined later. The Beatles, for example, would first record the instrumental accompaniment to a song, a process that might take a whole day. Another day would be devoted to recording the voice parts. Then, various instrumental and electronic sounds might be added before the recording was complete. With such a complex process, it's no wonder that a record like their *Sgt. Pepper's Lonely Hearts Club Band* took as long as four months to produce.

Rock and Television (MTV)

The 1980s saw the development of MTV, a cable television network broadcasting rock videos. MTV gave a needed boost to the music industry and contributed to the popularity of many performers. An innovator in the use of rock video was Michael Jackson, whose documentary on the production of *Thriller* became one of the most widely sold prerecorded videocassettes ever made. (Jackson died in 2009 and was mourned by millions around the world.) Rock video adds a new dimension to the rock experience through the addition of a narrative and a wide variety of visual effects that are often fantastic and provocative.

Rock and Dancing

Since its beginning, rock music has accompanied a dizzying succession of dances, such as the twist, the frug, the monkey, the shake, and the mashed potato. In most rock dances of the 1960s, partners did not hold each other, as in earlier dances, but moved individually to the music's powerful beat.

Most rock dances were improvisational and did not require dancers to learn a series of complicated steps. Among the best-known rock dances was the twist, associated with a New York nightclub, the Peppermint Lounge, and popularized in 1961 through a television performance by the singer Chubby Checker. By the 1960s, many adults became influenced by the youth culture and danced to rock music at nightclubs called *discotheques.*

During the 1970s, thousands of discotheques—mostly featuring recorded music—mushroomed around the country. *Disco* became the dominant dance music of the time. Many dances of the 1970s—such as the hustle and its variants—often required intricate steps and turns, a throwback to earlier times. Moreover, these dances frequently required partners to remain in close contact with each other. Also popular were line dances, in which many dancers performed the same choreographed movements. The late 1970s and 1980s saw the development of *break dancing,* a combination of dancing and gymnastics, often to rap music. Through the 1990s, in alternative and punk clubs, *pogo dancing, slam dancing,* and the *mosh pit* were an integral part of the scene. Dancing at social events known as *raves* was often accompanied by *techno* and *electronica,* types of music that shared a musical heritage with disco and made prominent use of drum machines and computer sequencers.

3 The Beatles

The Beatles—the singer-guitarists Paul McCartney, John Lennon, and George Harrison, and the drummer Ringo Starr—have been the most influential performing group in the history of rock. Their music, hairstyle, dress, and lifestyle were imitated all over the world, resulting in a phenomenon known as *Beatlemania.*

All four Beatles were born during the early 1940s in Liverpool, England, and devoted themselves to rock in their teens. Lennon and McCartney, the main songwriters of the group, began working together in 1956 and were joined by Harrison about two years later. In 1962 Ringo Starr became their new drummer. The group gained experience by performing in Hamburg, Germany; and in Liverpool, a port to which sailors brought the latest American rock, rhythm-and-blues, and country-and-western records. In 1961 the Beatles made their first record, and by 1963 they were England's top rock group. In 1964, they triumphed in the United States, breaking attendance records everywhere and dominating the record market. Audiences often became hysterical, and the police had to protect the Beatles from their fans. Beatle dolls, wigs, sweatshirts, and jackets flooded the market. Along with a steady flow of successful records, the Beatles made several hit movies: *A Hard Day's Night, Help!* and *Yellow Submarine.*

The Beatles stopped touring in 1966, possibly because some of their most imaginative effects were achieved in the recording studio and could not be duplicated in live performance. For several years they devoted themselves to recording, producing a

The Beatles have so far been the most influential performing group in the history of rock.

series of classic rock albums including *Sgt. Pepper's Lonely Hearts Club Band* (1967), *The Beatles* (1968; a double record set nicknamed the "white album"), and *Abbey Road* (1969).

In 1970 the Beatles disbanded to pursue separate careers; and the fatal shooting of John Lennon in 1980 seemed to symbolize the end of an era. As recently as 1994, though, the Beatles' *Live at the BBC* was a best-selling album. In the mid-1990s, the remaining three Beatles collaborated on a video documentary history of the band for British television. As a result of this show—which was seen in many different countries—the original Beatles recordings returned to the top of the pop charts.

The Beatles' highly original style derived from a variety of sources, including traditional blues, the rhythm and blues of Chuck Berry, the rock and roll of Elvis Presley, English folk songs, and the lyrics of Bob Dylan. The impact of Indian religions led Harrison to use the sitar. And the Beatles' brief period of experimentation with hallucinogenic drugs was reflected in some of their songs, including several tracks on *Sgt. Pepper.* In their early days, the Beatles strove for originality through their innovative treatment of melody, harmony, rhythm, form, and tone color. Their style evolved continuously, growing in sophistication with each new album.

The Beatles' vocal delivery sounded carefree and spontaneous, and Lennon's and McCartney's lyrics were unusually inventive. Their songs were sometimes based on modes—rather than major or minor scales—and their harmonic vocabulary was richer than that of most rock. Their songs frequently contained changes of meter, phrases of irregular length, unusual chord progressions, and alternation between major and minor keys. Most striking was the Beatles' use of many electronic and instrumental sounds not previously associated with rock. Many of these novel features can be heard in *Sgt. Pepper's Lonely Hearts Club Band.*

Sgt. Pepper's Lonely Hearts Club Band (1967)

Sgt. Pepper's Lonely Hearts Club Band, a landmark of rock, was one of the first rock music recordings to be presented as a "concept album": its thirteen songs are linked by the ruling idea of a music hall show with a dazzling succession of acts. The sense of continuity is heightened by the varied reprise of the opening song (*Sgt. Pepper's Lonely Hearts Club Band*) as the next-to-last song on the recording. The impact of this record comes largely from its tremendous range of sounds and electronic effects—audience noises, barnyard sounds, weird orchestral tone clusters, and instruments such as the harpsichord, harp, and sitar. There is also a wide range of musical styles, including traditional rock and roll (the Sgt. Pepper theme), a parody of a 1920s music-hall tune (*When I'm Sixty-Four*), an old-fashioned melodramatic ballad (*She's Leaving Home*), and the exotic sounds of Indian music (*Within You, Without You*). We'll now focus on two of the most original songs: *Lucy in the Sky with Diamonds* and *A Day in the Life.*

Lucy in the Sky with Diamonds

Lucy in the Sky with Diamonds, the third song of the cycle, evokes a world of daydream and fantasy. But the dreamlike mood is shattered by a brusque refrain. After the introduction, *Lucy in the Sky with Diamonds* is in verse-chorus form. The verse, which consists of subsections A-B (*Cellophane flowers*), is relatively soft, gently pulsating, and in triple meter. In contrast, the chorus, or refrain, section C (*Lucy in the Sky*), is loud, heavily accented, and in quadruple meter.

LISTENING OUTLINE

THE BEATLES, *Lucy in the Sky with Diamonds,* from *Sgt. Pepper's Lonely Hearts Club Band*

A B C A B C A CC form

(Duration, 3:30)

Introduction

A	**1. a.** Unaccompanied melody, synthesized sound suggests "electric harpsichord."
	b. Soft, triple meter, stepwise vocal melody repeats 3-note idea in narrow range, "electric harpsichord," electric bass; lightly stroked cymbals join.
B (Cellophane flowers)	**2.** Moderately soft, triple meter, repeated-note melody, voice doubled by guitar and electronically manipulated to sound slightly "unreal," fuller accompaniment, electric bass more active, marks beat.
C (refrain)	**3.** Loud, quadruple meter, single phrase sung three times (during some repetitions, phrase doubled at higher pitch), higher range than in sections A and B, driving rhythm, drummer accents second and fourth beats of each bar.
A	**4.** Soft, triple meter, stepwise vocal melody.
B (Newspaper taxis)	**5.** Moderately soft, triple meter, repeated-note melody.
C (refrain)	**6.** Loud, quadruple meter.
A	**7.** Soft, triple meter, stepwise vocal melody.
CC (refrain)	**8.** Loud, quadruple meter; fade-out at end.

A Day in the Life

A Day in the Life, the concluding song, uses electronic effects with an inventiveness that was unprecedented in rock. Here, fantasy blends with harsh and humdrum reality. The song is outlined as follows: introduction—A A' A"—first interlude—B—second interlude—A″—postlude. In sections A, A′, and A″, John Lennon sounds "unreal" as he sings of violence and war in a curiously detached way. The extreme level of echo applied to the lead vocal adds to the sense of detachment. Section A″ begins with *He blew his mind out* and ends with a high note on *House of Lords*. Section A′ opens with *I saw a film today* and concludes with a fade-out on a trill-like setting of *turn you on*. These words generate the hallucinatory first interlude, in which a gigantic block of electronic and orchestral sound—superimposed over a percussive beat—gradually becomes louder and higher.

Suddenly, the massive sound is cut off, giving way to insistent pulsations and the soft ringing of an alarm clock. As though awakened from a bad dream, Paul McCartney describes ordinary events in his everyday life (section B). Section B contrasts with the opening sections because of its more powerful beat, livelier rhythms, and more natural vocal sound. *I went into a dream* ushers in the second interlude, in which far-off voices sing *ah* and the orchestral sound gradually becomes melodically prominent.

After the return of A″ (*I read the news*) and the final words (*turn you on*) comes a postlude similar to the first interlude but with an even more powerful buildup of electronic and orchestral sound. The postlude ends with a low E major chord that takes almost 45 seconds to fade away completely. It is as though the slow fade-out attempts to resolve the tremendous tensions of the song cycle.

Rock: Summary

Development of Rock

- A powerful beat, the inclusion of saxophone and electric guitar, gospel-tinged vocal lines, and soaring falsetto leads are characteristics of rhythm and blues music of the 1950s.
- Rock music of the 1950s projected an image of youthful rebellion in its loudness, pounding beat, and sexual directness.
- During the 1960s, rock music was enormously varied. Soul music emphasized emotionality, gospel roots, and a strong connection to the black community. Other rock music absorbed folk music elements and often had lyrics dealing with contemporary issues. A new wave of British influence began in 1964 with the American tour of the Beatles.
- During the late 1960s and early 1970s, rock grew more theatrical and had a strong impact on Hollywood films and Broadway. The sound of rock music changed through technological advancements in recording techniques, through an expansion of the scale of its instrumentation and formal structures, and through the scope of its harmony and textual content.
- A "second British invasion" occurred in rock during the 1980s, and many bands made extensive use of electronic technology, such as computers and synthesizers. Heavy metal and rap styles appeared, and continued to grow in popularity into the 1990s.
- Beginning in the 1980s, women performers had a powerful impact on rock.
- By the end of the twentieth century, new trends included the emergence of Latino and Latina artists, crossover country music artists, and a renewed interest in music of the 1970s.
- Rock music has accompanied a dizzying succession of dances.

Important Style Features

Tone Color

- Rock music is heavily amplified, and heavily amplified electric guitars produce a wide variety of tone colors.
- Typical rock groups include singers, two electric guitars (lead and rhythm), electric bass, percussion, and a variety of keyboard instruments and synthesizers.
- Additional instruments may include trumpets, trombones, saxophones, and a wide range of instruments not normally associated with popular music, such as the harpsichord or the sitar.
- Rock singers shout, cry, wail, growl, and use guttural sounds and falsetto.
- Nonsense syllables and repeated chants may be featured.

Rhythm

- Most rock has a powerful beat and is in quadruple meter with strong accents on the second and fourth beats of the bar.
- The four beats of the bar may be subdivided into eight faster pulses that are superimposed on the four basic beats to add rhythmic excitement.
- The offbeats of the rhythmic subdivisions may be emphasized by some instruments, such as the bass, to add further rhythmic energy.

Form, Melody and Harmony

- The earliest rock music was in 12-bar blues, thirty-two-bar A A B A form, or a variant of these forms.
- Strophic and verse-chorus forms are very common.
- Early rock music usually consisted of four-bar or eight-bar phrases, but increasingly rock melodies contain phrases of irregular length.

- Rock songs tend to have short melodic patterns that are repeated and/or varied several times.
- Melodies may be built on traditional major or minor scales, but also on modes.
- Harmonic progressions are usually quite simple, often consisting of just two, three, or four basic chords.

Performance Practice

- The singing style of rock music is drawn largely from African American, folk, and country-and-western music.
- Unlike earlier popular music, rock spread more through radio and recordings than through live performances or sheet music.
- In recordings, each line of rock music may be recorded onto a separate track to provide maximum control in how the sound is mixed for the final product.
- Rock music videos, particularly those broadcast on MTV, are enormously popular.
- Rock video adds a new dimension to the rock experience through narrative and a wide array of visual effects that are often fantastic and provocative.

Beyond the Classroom: The Digital Revolution and MP3 Compression

It is difficult to imagine a world without synthesizers, computers, or digital media, and these tools have played an enormous role in the development of all music genres, including rock music. Yet the technology that has revolutionized our world became widely available less than thirty years ago. The now ubiquitous compact disc, or CD, appeared in the early 1980s. Portable digital music players such as the iPod and Zune became available for the first time less than a decade ago. Amazingly, Apple has sold close to 200 million iPods worldwide.

One of the most significant advances in digital music technology fueling this revolution was the creation of digital music compression, particularly the MP3 compression format in the early 1990s. The MP3 compression encodes music by removing artifacts within the music that our ears have difficulty hearing, thereby reducing a typical audio CD to about one-twelfth its original size. A smaller file size means music can be downloaded more quickly and stored more compactly. For example, the Red Book standard for audio CDs developed by Sony and Philips allows up to seventy-four minutes of audio content, whereas an MP3 CD can contain ten hours or more of compressed music. Although other audio compression programs are available that reduce file sizes even further without noticeable loss of audio quality, the MP3 format has quickly become a favorite because most portable players are able to play music encoded in this format.

Another major breakthrough is in the cost of computer technology. Today, anyone with musical talent and a typical home computer costing less than $1,000 can record, edit, and remix music digitally, producing professional-sounding audio CDs. As a consequence, many rock and "garage band" musicians are recording and marketing their own music to a world audience over the Internet, without the backing of a major record label.

The result of all this new technology is that music is now easier to find, purchase, sell, and hear than ever before. We can locate music quickly over the Internet, purchase and download an MP3 version to our music players, and listen to our playlists anytime, anywhere. Although we take this convenience for granted, it is an unprecedented historical change in how music is accessed by the public.

But with any change, there are new challenges. Perhaps the most fascinating are the legal issues related to music copyright. The saga of Napster and the legal cases it generated in the early years of the new millennium demonstrate the worldwide interest in downloading music, and the need to balance the demands of music listeners with the creative and intellectual property interests of composers and performers.

Nonwestern Music

The highest aim of our music is to reveal
the essence of the universe it reflects . . .
through music one can reach God.

—Ravi Shankar

All over the world, music is closely linked with religion, dance, and drama. Shown here is a gamelan, an Indonesian orchestra.

Nonwestern music reflects and expresses the diversity of the world's languages, religions, geographical conditions, social and economic systems, values, beliefs, and ways of life. Each culture has its own characteristic instruments, performance practices, tonal systems, and melodic and rhythmic patterns. Nonwestern societies also differ in their range of musical styles: some have only folk music, some have both folk and popular music, and some have complex classical music as well. Thus nonwestern music can offer a wide range of listening experiences and cultural insights. Moreover, nonwestern traditions were an important source of inspiration for western music of the twentieth and twenty-first centuries. For example, they influenced the French composer Claude Debussy, the British rock star George Harrison, the African American jazz artist John Coltrane, and the American composer Elliott Carter.

Women of the Bamileke people of Cameroon singing and dancing. African music is closely associated with dancing. While moving, a dancer often sings or plays an instrument.

The koto, a plucked string instrument, is important in traditional Japanese music.

1 Music in Nonwestern Cultures

Characteristics of Nonwestern Music

Music of the nonwestern world is too varied to allow easy generalizations. Yet some features are common to most musical traditions. All over the world, music is closely linked with religion, dance, and drama. Music can serve as both entertainment and an indispensable accompaniment to everyday activities, magic rites, and ceremonies marking important phases of life. In addition, music is often used to send messages and relate traditions.

Oral Tradition Nonwestern music is most often transmitted orally from parent to child or from teacher to student. Compositions and performance techniques are learned by rote and imitation. Music notation is far less important in nonwestern than in western culture. Many musical cultures—such as those of central Asia and sub-Saharan Africa—do not have notation. Even when notation exists, as in China and India, written music traditionally serves only as a record and is rarely used in teaching or performance.

Improvisation Improvisation is important in many nonwestern musical cultures. Performers usually base their improvisations on traditional melodic phrases and rhythmic patterns. In some parts of the world, including India and the middle east, improvisation is a highly disciplined art that requires years of training. Indian and Islamic musicians create music within a framework of melody types, each associated with a specific mood, a specific set of tones, and characteristic phrases. There are many melody types, and within each the improviser can create a practically limitless variety of music.

Most musical cultures have a repertoire of traditional songs or instrumental pieces. In some cultures, these are relatively fixed and are performed similarly from generation to generation—as in Japan, where improvisation in classical music is practically nonexistent. But in other traditions, pieces are treated with great flexibility. In Iran (Persia) and sub-Saharan Africa, for example, performers freely vary melodies and add sections.

Voices Singing is the most important way of making music in the vast majority of nonwestern cultures. Preferred vocal timbres vary widely from one musical tradition to another. In the middle east and north Africa, for example, singers cultivate a nasal, intense, strained tone. A more relaxed and open-throated sound is generally preferred by singers in sub-Saharan Africa. The vast range of vocal techniques includes shouting, crying, whispering, sighing, humming, yodeling, and singing through the teeth. An amazing vocal technique is used among the Tuvans, a Siberian people located northwest of Mongolia. A male Tuvan singer can produce two sounds at the same time: a low, sustained tone together with a high, eerie melody.

Instruments Nonwestern instruments produce a wealth of sounds and come in a wide variety of sizes, shapes, and materials. Scholars usually group these instruments into four categories, based on what generates the sound.

1. *Chordophones* are instruments—such as harps and lutes—whose sound generator is a stretched string.
2. *Aerophones* are instruments—such as flutes and trumpets—whose sound generator is a column of air.

3. *Membranophones* are instruments—basically, drums—whose sound generator is a stretched skin or another membrane.
4. *Idiophones* are instruments—such as bells, gongs, scrapers, rattles, and xylophones—whose own material is the sound generator (no tension is applied).

The musical style of a culture is among the important factors influencing its choice of instruments. For example, chordophones (strings) are prominent in Islamic and Indian classical music, whose highly ornamented melodies require instruments with great flexibility of pitch. Idiophones and membranophones (such as bells, rattles, and drums) are featured in sub-Saharan Africa, where rhythm is strongly emphasized and music is closely linked with dancing.

A culture's use of instruments is also influenced by its geography and raw materials. Bronze idiophones are prominent in southeast Asia, where metallurgy developed around 5,000 years ago. Indonesian orchestras (gamelans) have up to eighty instruments, including bronze gongs, chimes, and xylophones. Instruments made of animal skins and horns are common in parts of sub-Saharan Africa, where these materials are easily found. Among the Aniocha Ibo of Nigeria, for example, drums are made of animal skins, and aerophones (winds) made from elephant tusks are used by the royal family and some chiefs. Where raw materials are scarce, as in the deserts of Australia, instruments may be few in number.

Along with musical style and geography, religious beliefs may influence the choice of materials. In Tibet, for example, trumpets and drums are made from the bones and skulls of criminals in order to appease demons. Instruments often have symbolic associations and are linked with specific gods and goddesses. They may be shaped like birds, animals, or fish.

Melody, Texture, and Rhythm Most music of Asia, the near east, and north Africa emphasizes melody and rhythm, rather than harmony or polyphony. In the music of these cultures, the texture is often monophonic, consisting of an unaccompanied melody or a melody supported by percussion. In India and the near east, the melodic line is frequently supported by a drone, one or more tones sustained throughout the performance. In many parts of the world—such as north Africa, the middle east, southeast Asia, and the far east—music often has a texture in which all parts perform the same basic melody, but in versions that differ in ornamentation or rhythm. (This texture, called *heterophony*, is considered in Section 4.) Homophonic and polyphonic textures tend to be somewhat more common in sub-Saharan Africa than in most parts of Asia.

Nonwestern music uses a wide variety of scales. Most often, scales have five, six, or seven tones. Nonwestern melodies commonly use intervals smaller or larger than those standard in the west. Microtones—intervals smaller than the western half step—are frequent in the music of India and the near east.

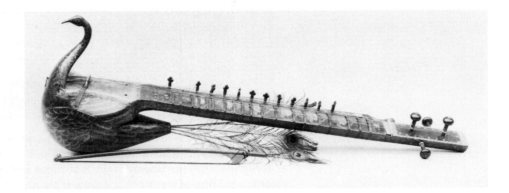

A chordophone: the *mayuri,* a peacock-shaped bowed string instrument from India.

Also, much nonwestern music has very complex rhythms. For example, because of the complexity of the rhythms used, drummers in India and sub-Saharan Africa spend many years learning their highly sophisticated art.

Interaction between Nonwestern and Western Music

After 1900, nonwestern music felt the impact of American and European music. This influence resulted from increased urbanization, adoption of western technology, and access to radios, films, recordings, and western instruments. Western elements are often found in the popular music heard in the large cities of Africa, Asia, and the near east. One example of such popular music is the *high life* of west Africa, which combines European instruments with the steady rhythm characteristic of Africa. Some composers in the nonwestern world combine traditional elements with western forms and styles. (Ravi Shankar's Concerto for Sitar and Orchestra is one example. Another example is the Japanese composer Minoru Miki's *Symphony for Two Worlds,* which had its American premiere in 1994.) And in many areas, western and traditional music exist side by side. Yet there are vast areas of the world where traditional music is dominant. Many governments subsidize traditional performing groups to preserve their rich national heritage.

In the sections that follow, the traditional music of three areas—sub-Saharan Africa, India, and Japan—will be studied as a tiny sample of the vast wealth of nonwestern music.

2 Music in Sub-Saharan Africa

The African continent, which is more than three times the size of the United States, can be subdivided into two large geographical areas: north Africa, which includes such countries as Morocco, Algeria, Tunisia, and Egypt; and sub-Saharan Africa (south of the Sahara Desert), which includes Ghana, Nigeria, Mozambique, and Angola, among many other countries. The population of north Africa is predominantly Muslim and Arabic-speaking, and its music is closely related to that of the middle east. This section focuses on the music of sub-Saharan Africa, sometimes called "black Africa," and generally, throughout the section, the word *Africa* pertains to sub-Saharan Africa.

Sub-Saharan Africa, which is environmentally and culturally diverse, has several thousand peoples with different religions, social customs, and ways of life. They speak over 700 different languages (more than are found on any other continent). Though urban growth and industrialization are transforming sub-Saharan Africa today, many Africans still hold to traditional ways of life. Most peoples have polytheistic religions, live in villages, and devote themselves to such traditional occupations as agriculture and raising cattle.

The music of sub-Saharan Africa is as diverse as its people. Even so, most of its music features complex rhythms and polyrhythms, percussive sounds, and a wide variety of instrumental ensembles. Vocal music is often performed by a soloist and a responding chorus. Of course, the different cultures of Africa have influenced each

Singing and playing instruments are interwoven into the fabric of African life.

other. For example, in parts of sub-Saharan Africa, such as Ghana and northern Nigeria, musical styles have been influenced by Arabic culture.

Music in Society

Music permeates virtually every aspect of African life. It is used to entertain; to accompany dances, plays, religious ceremonies, and magic rites; and to mark such events as birth, puberty, marriage, and death. Healers use specific songs and dances to treat the ill. There are work songs to accompany digging, grinding, chopping, and harvesting. Litigation songs are sung when people are in court arguing about property ownership. There are songs praising leaders, criticizing authority, and recounting history. Singing and playing instruments are so interwoven into the fabric of life that the abstract word *music*—as it is understood in the west—is not used by most African peoples. (However, there are words for *song, dance,* and *poetry.*)

An extraordinarily large number of songs are meant for particular occasions. For example, among the Fon—a people in Dahomey (in west Africa)—children sing a special song when they lose their first tooth. The Akan of Ghana have a ritual song to cure bed wetters. The Tutsi of Rwanda, who depend on cattle raising, have many different songs to praise cows and to accompany their care and feeding.

Music is essential to many African ceremonies. Among the Basongye of Zaire, for example, the funeral of an important person requires the services of a professional musician who announces the death and praises the deceased. The musician clowns to cheer up the people at the funeral, allowing them to vent emotion.

African music is closely associated with dancing; both arts are basic to many ceremonies, rituals, and celebrations. While moving, a dancer often sings or plays rattles or other idiophones that are held or tied to the body.

African music is also intimately linked with language. Many languages are *tone languages,* in which the meaning of a word is determined by the relative pitch at which it is spoken. The same word can have four different meanings, depending on its pitch. Tone languages permit the use of music for communication. Drummers, trumpeters, and other musicians convey messages and tell stories by imitating the rhythms and pitch fluctuations of words. *Talking drums*—capable of two or more different pitches—are often used to send musical messages. A musician can even describe an event with the aid of a talking drum.

In Africa, music making is a social activity in which almost everyone participates. As a result, music is usually performed outdoors—in streets, courtyards, or village squares. There is spontaneous music making as well as performances by social and music groups at ceremonies and feasts. As in other cultures, the level of musical skill and training varies from one individual to another. Some highly trained musicians are employed at royal courts to entertain the monarch. Others are hired to sing songs of praise. Musicians may receive money or goods in return for their services. Musical tradition is orally transmitted, as are folklore and history. There is no musical notation, since the cultures of sub-Saharan Africa do not emphasize literacy.

Elements of African Music

Rhythm and Percussion Rhythm and percussive sounds are highly emphasized in African music. This emphasis reflects the close link between music and dance in African culture. African music tends to feature complex polyrhythms. Usually, several different rhythmic patterns are played simultaneously and repeated over and over. Each instrument goes its own rhythmic way, producing accents that appear to be out of phase with those of the other parts. Dancers may choose any of several rhythmic patterns to dance to. For example, while one dancer follows a pattern played with a bell, another may dance to the rattle, while yet another follows the drum.

Percussion ensembles consisting mainly of drums, xylophones, or rattles are widely used. The instruments of percussion ensembles are carefully chosen to provide contrasts of tone color and pitch. The human body itself is often used as a percussion instrument. Hand claps, foot stamps, and thigh or chest slaps are common sounds in African music.

Vocal Music African singers use a wide variety of vocal sounds. Even within a single performance a singer may shift from an open, relaxed tone to one that is tighter and more constricted. Singers sometimes whisper, hum, grunt, shout, and imitate animal noises. Yodeling—quick movement from a chest voice to a falsetto—is practiced by the Pygmies, among others.

Much African vocal music is characterized by a performance style known as ***call and response,*** in which the phrases of a soloist are repeatedly answered by those of a chorus. An exciting overlap of sound often results when the leader resumes singing before the chorus has completed its response. Singers are often accompanied by ostinatos (repeated rhythmic patterns) played by percussion. Typically, African vocal music has short phrases that are repeated over and over to different words.

Texture Unlike many other nonwestern cultures, African societies often have music that is homophonic or polyphonic in texture. Several voice parts may sing the same melody at different pitch levels, occasionally producing a series of parallel chords. Some African peoples also perform polyphonic music in which the different melodic lines are quite independent.

African Instruments

A great variety of instruments and instrumental ensembles are found in Africa. Ensembles have from two to twenty or more players. Performing groups include ensembles of instruments of indefinite pitch (bells, rattles, log drums) and ensembles of instruments of definite pitch (flutes, trumpets, xylophones, plucked lutes). There are also groups that combine instruments of both definite and indefinite pitch (flutes, drums, bells).

Idiophones   The most common instruments in Africa are idiophones, such as bells, rattles, scrapers, xylophones, and log drums. Most of these instruments are struck or shaken, but others are scraped, rubbed, plucked, or stamped against the ground. Many—like rattles, bells, and stone clappers—are instruments of indefinite pitch. A few—like the xylophone and *mbira*, or *thumb piano*—are tuned instruments.

Xylophones are particularly important in Africa; they are played solo, in small groups, and in orchestras of from ten to more than thirty members. The Chopi, a people of southeast Africa, are noted for large xylophone ensembles including instruments of different sizes ranging from soprano to double bass. In some parts of Africa, a single large xylophone is played by several performers simultaneously. Xylophones have from about ten to over twenty slats, sometimes with gourd resonators attached. Spiderwebs are often placed over small holes in the resonators to create the buzzing sound favored by African musicians.

The *mbira* (*sansa, kalimba,* or *thumb piano*), which is native to Africa, is a melodic idiophone capable of producing elaborate melodies. From eight to over thirty tongues made of metal or bamboo are attached to a sounding board or box. The tongues are plucked with the thumbs and forefingers. The mbira's tone is often enriched by the jingle of shells or metal pieces attached to the resonator. Vocalists often use the mbira to accompany themselves.

Another important idiophone is the *slit drum,* a hollowed-out log with a long slit on top. Some slit drums are small enough to be held in the hand, while others are tree trunks over 20 feet long. Variations in the width of the slit allow two and sometimes four different tones to be produced when the slit is struck. The slit drum is used both as a "talking drum" for signaling and as a musical instrument, often together with membranophone drums.

Membranophones   Drums with stretched skins or other membranes are also important in African culture. They are essential to many religious and political ceremonies, and they are used for dancing and regulating the pace of work. Talking drums are used to send messages over long distances. Drums are often considered sacred or magical; some Africans believe that drums contain the spirits of ancestral drummers. The manufacture of drums is usually accompanied by special rites, and drums are sometimes housed in special shrines and given food and offered sacrifices. Drums are often regarded as the property of the group, rather than that of an individual; and they frequently symbolize power and royalty. Some African chiefs are accompanied by official drummers when they move from place to place.

Drums are usually played in groups of two to four. However, in parts of east Africa—Burundi, Uganda, Rwanda—ensembles of up to fifteen drums are played by four to six performers. The drums are often tuned to different pitches and are used to perform melodic music similar to that of xylophone ensembles.

African drummers are among the most sophisticated in the world. They can produce not only complicated rhythms but a wide range of tone colors and pitches as well.

Two musicians play a slit drum while three others play membranophones.

Within an ensemble, drummers have specific roles. It is usually the chief drummer who has the freedom to improvise within the traditional framework. Other drummers repeat certain rhythmic patterns over and over.

Drums come in a wide variety of sizes, shapes, and forms. There are drums shaped like cones, cylinders, kettles, barrels, goblets, and hourglasses. They are made from logs, gourds, and clay. They may have one or two drumheads made from skins of such animals as snakes, lizards, goats, and monkeys. Some drums produce just a single sound; others—like the hourglass-shaped *pressure drum*—can produce a variety of pitches. The two heads of the pressure drum are connected by thongs; by varying the arm pressure on the thongs, a player can control the tension of the heads and so change the pitch. The pitches of the pressure drum often imitate the tone language spoken by the people. Sometimes, special devices are used to get certain sounds: for example, seeds or beads inside a closed drum or pieces of metal or small bells attached to a drum's rim.

Aerophones and Chordophones The most common aerophones (winds) are flutes, whistles, horns, and trumpets. Reed instruments are less widespread. Flutes are usually made of bamboo, cane, or wood; horns and trumpets are made from animal horns, elephant tusks, wood, bamboo, and gourds.

Chordophones (strings) are used throughout Africa and come in many types and sizes. Most are plucked or struck, perhaps reflecting the African musician's preference for percussive sounds. One of the most widely used chordophones is the musical bow, which looks like a hunting bow. The string is plucked or struck with a stick. Some musical bows have a gourd resonator; with others, the player's mouth is used as the resonator.

We'll now study two examples of music from sub-Saharan Africa.

Ompeh

Percussive sounds, complex polyrhythms, and a call-and-response pattern are featured in *Ompeh,* a song from the central region of Ghana, recorded by the ethnomusicologist Roger Vetter in the coastal town Winneba in 1992–1993. "Within this area," Vetter

Basic Set:
CD 9 [44]

Brief Set:
CD 5 [61]

observes, "are to be found several ethnic/linguistic identities and a colorful palette of musical instruments, ensembles, and repertoires that fulfill the musical needs of small and large communities alike." *Ompeh* is performed by a recreational amateur ensemble of singers and percussionists who specialize in *ompeh,* a type of music of the Akan-speaking peoples in Ghana.

In the performance, brief solo melodies for male voice are each followed by longer responses from a chorus singing mostly in thirds. (From *do* to *mi* in the scale is an interval of a third.) Each choral response is introduced by a single held tone sung by a higher solo male voice. We also hear a percussion ensemble—consisting of a bamboo slit drum, pan rattles (made from aluminum pie plates), a two-headed cylindrical drum (*ogyamba*), a large barrel-shaped hand drum (*ompehkyen*), and metal bell (*afirikyiwa*)—producing a variety of rhythms, pitches, and tone colors. The metal bell serves as the timekeeper of the group. Its repeated rhythm reflects the influence of *high life,* a type of popular music from Ghana.

The text of *Ompeh* relates to the group's performances, for which chairs are set up on the earth and the singers dance to the music. There are three references to death in the song. The first, *I'm dying,* has to do with pairing contradictions in Akan poetry, as in "I'm dying of laughter." The second and third references are more threatening. The singers become combative when they realize that the *Tokoraba* people have arrived and warn them that they will be sent to a distant place, *The land of the dead.* In this song, the performers combine two of the many languages spoken in Ghana: Ga and Fante.

Soloist

A woyaa woyaa	We go, we go,
E wo asi wo agwa e	They've set the chairs,
Asaase e	Earth,
Eba anadwo kakra	When night falls,
Wo asi wo agwa e	They've set the chairs,
Mere wuo o	I'm dying.

Chorus

E a woyaa woyaa	We go, we go,
Daa wo asi wo agwa e	They've set up chairs daily,
Asaase e	Earth,
Eba anadwo kakra	When night falls,
Wo asi wo agwa e	They've set the chairs,
Mere wuo o	I'm dying,
A woyaa woyaa	We go, we go,
Krohinko sane e	We swing back and forth,
Kowa e	Kowa e [perhaps a name]
Owuo e, sane e, Kowa e	Death, problem, Kowa e,
A woyaa Tokoraba wose wo ba	We are going, Tokoraba people say they are here,
Saman wa	The land of the dead is far.

LISTENING OUTLINE

Ompeh

2 solo male voices, chorus, bamboo slit drum, metal bell, pan rattle, cylindrical drum, large barrel-shaped hand drum

(Duration, 2:08)

44 61	0:00		**1.**	**a.**	Bamboo slit drum, followed by metal bell, pan rattles, cylindrical drum.
	0:14			**b.**	Solo vocal melody joins.
	0:23			**c.**	Higher solo voice introduces choral response in thirds.
	0:34			**d.**	Barrel-shaped bass drum joins accompaniment to chorus, percussion continues throughout.
45 62	0:51		**2.**	**a.**	Solo vocal melody.
	1:00			**b.**	Higher solo voice introduces choral response in thirds.
	1:25			**c.**	Percussion alone.
46 63	1:31		**3.**	**a.**	Solo vocal melody.
	1:40			**b.**	Higher solo voice introduces choral response in thirds.
	2:04			**c.**	Percussion alone closes segment.

Mitamba Yalagala Kumchuzi

Basic Set:
CD 9 47

Percussive sounds and complex polyrhythms are featured in *Mitamba Yalagala Kumchuzi,* a dance song of the Zaramo people in Tanzania. First we hear percussion instruments—tin rattles and tuned goblet drums and cylindrical drums—producing a variety of rhythms, pitches, and tone colors. Then the percussion instruments are joined by a group of voices singing a dance melody.

LISTENING OUTLINE

Mitamba Yalagala Kumchuzi

Voices, 5 tuned goblet drums, 4 tuned cylindrical drums, tin rattles

(Duration, 1:30)

47	0:00	**1.** Goblet drums, cylindrical drums, tin rattles, complex polyrhythms against basic pulse.
	0:43	**2.** Group of voices with dance melody, percussion accompanies.

3 Classical Music of India

The musical traditions of India, which include folk and popular music, date back over 3,000 years and are thus among the oldest in the world. Between the twelfth and sixteenth centuries, Indian classical music developed two distinct traditions: *Karnatak music,* of south India; and *Hindustani music,* of north India (an area that now includes Pakistan). The centers of north Indian music were the princely courts, whereas south Indian music was performed in temples. The music of north India absorbed many Persian elements because many of its rulers came from Persia and were Muslims. The music of south India developed more along its own lines.

When India came under British rule during the nineteenth century, north Indian classical music was still performed mainly for small, elite audiences at princely courts. But aristocratic patronage declined during the twentieth century as India made the transition from British rule to independence. Many musicians lost their jobs around

1947—the date of India's independence—when almost 600 princely states of India were abolished as political units and merged with neighboring territories. Indian performers turned to the general public for support, just as European musicians did during the eighteenth and nineteenth centuries.

Today, Indian musicians broadcast on radio and television, make recordings, and compose music for films. Some teach in colleges or give concerts for large audiences. Many Indian artists now travel and give concerts throughout the world.

Performers

Indian performers consider their music spiritual in character. "We view music as a kind of spiritual discipline that raises one's inner being to divine peacefulness and bliss," writes Ravi Shankar (b. 1920), one of the most important Indian musicians. "The highest aim of our music is to reveal the essence of the universe it reflects; . . . through music, one can reach God." This spiritual emphasis is reflected in the texts of south Indian songs, which have religious associations. Indian musicians venerate their *guru* (*master* or *teacher*) as representative of the divine. A special initiation ceremony usually occurs when a guru accepts a disciple. The student is then expected to surrender his or her personality to the guru.

Musical traditions are transmitted orally from master to disciple, who learns by imitation, not by studying textbooks or written music. For example, Indian music students imitate their teacher phrase by phrase at lessons and sing or play along at concerts. Although India has various systems of musical notation, they give only the basic melodic and rhythmic elements. The development of these elements—the essential ornaments and musical elaborations—cannot be notated and must be learned from a teacher.

Improvisation

Improvisation has an important role in Indian music. In few other cultures is improvisation as highly developed and sophisticated. The improviser is guided by complex melodic and rhythmic systems that govern the choice of tones, ornaments, and rhythms. Before being allowed to improvise, young musicians must study for years and practice many hours a day, mastering basic rules and techniques. Improvisations are generally performed by a soloist and a drummer. They last anywhere from a few minutes to several hours, depending on the occasion and the mood of the performers and audience. Both vocalists and instrumentalists improvise.

Elements of Indian Classical Music

Indian music is based on the human voice—so much so that the pitch range of all Indian music is restricted to less than 4 octaves. Instrumentalists often imitate a vocal style of performance. Composed pieces are songs performed by a singer or an instrumentalist, with the instrumentalist imitating vocal styles. And songs are used as a springboard for improvisation.

There have been many composers in south India, producing thousands of songs. The greatest composers were Tyagaraja (1767–1847), Muthuswamy Dikshitar (1775–1835), and Shyama Sastri (1762–1827). These three musicians were born in the same village and were contemporaries of Haydn, Mozart, and Beethoven; they are called the "musical trinity."

Highly embellished melody—both vocal and instrumental—is characteristic of Indian music. Melodies often move by microtones (intervals smaller than a half step). Melodic lines are subtly embellished by microtonal ornaments, tiny pitch fluctuations around notes. Slides of pitch provide graceful transitions from one note to another.

Indian melodies are almost always accompanied by a drone instrument that plays the tonic and dominant (or subdominant) notes throughout the performance. The basic texture of Indian music, therefore, consists of a single melody performed over an unchanging background. Rather than the harmonic progression and polyphonic texture of western music, Indian music has melodic and rhythmic tension and relaxation. The main drone instrument is the ***tambura,*** a long-necked lute with four metal strings that are plucked continually in succession. The constant sound of the drone contributes vitally to the atmosphere of the music. Besides the soloist and the tambura players, there is a drummer who maintains the rhythmic structure and may also perform rhythmic improvisations.

Melodic Structure: Raga In Indian classical music, melody is created within a melodic framework called *raga*. A ***raga*** is a pattern of notes. A particular raga is defined partly by the number of its tones and the pattern of its intervals. Each raga has an ascending and descending form with characteristic melodic phrases and tonal emphases. Particular ornaments and slides from one note to another give each raga its individuality.

The term *raga* comes from a word meaning *color* or *atmosphere,* and an ancient saying describes raga as "that which colors the mind." Ragas have many extramusical associations. Each raga is linked with a particular mood, such as tranquillity, love, or heroism. Ragas are also associated with specific gods, seasons, festivals, and times of day or night. They involve so many dimensions that Indian musicians spend a long time learning each one. Some distinguished musicians restrict themselves to performing only about a dozen ragas. Within the framework of a raga, great artists can create and improvise a limitless variety of music.

Two ragas are shown here.

Raga *Malkauns*

Raga *Yaman Kalyan*

Rhythmic Structure: Tala Rhythm is organized into cycles called *talas*. A ***tala*** consists of a repeated cycle of beats. Although beat cycles range from 3 to more than 100 beats in length, the most common cycles have 6 to 16 beats. A cycle is divided into groups of beats. For example, the 10-beat tala called *jhaptal* is divided 2-3-2-3, while the 10-beat tala called *shultal* is divided 4-2-4:

Jhaptal

|1   2 |3   4   5 |6   7 |8   9   10|

Shultal

|1   2   3   4 |5   6 |7   8   9   10|

Each beat in a tala may be divided into smaller time values, just as a quarter note in western music may be divided into eighth or sixteenth notes. The most important beat of the tala cycle is the first. The soloist usually plays an important note of the raga on the first beat. Apart from the main beat, other beats receive secondary accents at the beginning of each group division. Singers and members of the audience often keep time with hand and finger movements on accented beats and hand waving on less important ones. Talas are performed in a variety of tempos ranging from slow to very fast.

The sitarist Ravi Shankar is accompanied here by a tabla (a pair of single-headed drums) and a tambura (a drone instrument).

The rhythm of Indian music is remarkably complex and sophisticated. Young drummers spend years with a master drummer memorizing hundreds of talas and their variations. Drummers and instrumental soloists sometimes have exciting dialogues in which rhythmically intricate phrases are rapidly tossed back and forth.

Instruments

Although the most important performing medium in India is the voice, there are a dazzling variety of instruments of all kinds. In north Indian classical music, instruments have become about as popular as the voice. Many instruments are associated with specific gods and goddesses. For example, the flute is associated with the Hindu god Krishna, and the *vina*—a plucked string instrument—is linked with Sarasvati, the Hindu goddess of wisdom. We will describe only a few of the best-known instruments.

The **sitar** is the most popular chordophone of north India. It is a long-necked lute with nineteen to twenty-three movable frets. There are seven strings, which are plucked: five are used for melodies, and two supply drone and rhythmic effects. The sitar also has nine to thirteen sympathetically vibrating strings that give the instrument its characteristic sound. These strings lie under the frets, almost parallel to the plucked strings. The most famous sitarist today is Ravi Shankar.

The *vina* is the most ancient plucked string instrument of south India. It has four strings for playing melodies, and three strings at the side of the fingerboard can be used for drone and rhythmic effects.

The *sarod* is a north Indian string instrument plucked with a plectrum of ivory or coconut shell. It has six main strings: four for melodies and two for drones and rhythm. Eleven to sixteen other strings vibrate sympathetically.

The *mridangam* is a two-headed barrel drum popular in south India. It is played with the open hands and fingers. The right drumhead is tuned to the tonic, and the left head functions as a bass.

Ravi Shankar, Sitarist, Performing Maru-Bihag

The sitarist and composer Ravi Shankar exerted a greater influence on western culture than any other performer of Asian music in the twentieth century. Starting in the 1950s, he introduced audiences around the world to a new sonic universe in the art music of his homeland, India. At the same time, his collaborations with composers and performers from Philip Glass to the Beatles brought profound new ideas into our musical culture.

Shankar was born in 1920 in the ancient holy city of Benares (Varanasi), where he was surrounded by traditional music. At age ten, he left his country for Paris to participate in a dance troupe led by his oldest brother Uday, a famous dancer and choreographer. When he was eighteen, Shankar returned to India, where he spent seven and a half years studying the sitar with a master musician who became his guru, or teacher. "Taking a guru was the most important decision of my life," Shankar later recalled. "It demanded absolute surrender, years of fanatical dedication and discipline." He learned from his guru "how sacred music is, and how it should be kept that way when you perform."

Around 1956, after becoming prominent in India as a performer and composer, Shankar began to give concert tours around the world. He collaborated with distinguished western musicians such as the violinist Yehudi Menuhin and the composer Philip Glass, and composed concertos for sitar and orchestra, as well as works combining the sitar with the western flute and the Japanese koto (a plucked stringed instrument). It was through these creative encounters that ideas and concepts from Indian musical traditions spread into western musical practice. He showed that in Indian music, for example, improvisations "are not just letting yourself go, as in jazz—you have to adhere to the discipline of the ragas and the talas without any notation in front of you." This idea of "structured freedom" found its way into the music of Philip Glass and other composers. Shankar's performances also exemplified the idea that music has a spiritual role: "My goal has always been to take the audience along with me deep inside, as in meditation, to feel the sweet pain of trying to reach out for the supreme, to bring tears to the eyes, and to feel totally peaceful and cleansed."

It was this emphasis on the spiritual that made Shankar a superstar in the 1960s through his connection with the Beatles. In 1966, the Beatles went to India, where Shankar taught the sitar to their guitarist George Harrison. Subsequently, Harrison wrote songs permeated by the sounds of Indian music, including *Love You To,* from the album *Revolver.* George Harrison has aptly said that Shankar merits the title "godfather of world music" because "he has shown it is possible to introduce an apparently alien art form successfully into another culture." In the late 1960s, Shankar performed before hundreds of thousands at rock festivals including Monterey and Woodstock.

Shankar performed widely until his mid-eighties, and his musical legacy is continued by his two daughters: the sitar virtuoso Anoushka Shankar, who has made several solo albums and toured the world with her father's ensemble; and the pop singer Norah Jones, who has sold over 36 million albums worldwide.

Ravi Shankar's performance of *Maru-Bihag* is included in the recordings.

The north Indian counterpart of the mridangam is the **tabla,** a pair of single-headed drums played by one performer. The right-hand drum is generally tuned to the tonic note, and the left-hand drum functions as a bass drum. These drums, which are played with the hands and fingers, can produce a wide variety of pitches and tone colors. The tabla is vital to north Indian concerts and is used for solos as well as accompaniments.

Maru-Bihag, by Ravi Shankar

Basic Set:
CD 9 [48]

Brief Set:
CD 5 [64]

[48] [64]

The performance here is an improvisation by the sitarist Ravi Shankar on the evening raga *Maru-Bihag.* As usual, the sitar is accompanied by a pair of drums (tabla) with a *tambura* (a drone instrument) in the background. In his spoken introduction to the re-corded performance, Ravi Shankar illustrates the raga pattern and the tala (beat cycle) used as a basis for this performance. The ascending and descending melodic forms of *Maru-Bihag* are as follows:

Raga *Maru-Bihag*

The tala, played by the tabla, consists of 10 beats divided to give 2-3-2-3. In the illustra-tion as well as the performance, it is not easy to perceive the beats. Each one is often subdivided into shorter drum strokes, and accents often come off the beat.

[49] [65]

The performance opens with an *alap,* a rhapsodic introductory section in which the sitar is accompanied only by the tambura playing the tonic and dominant notes of the raga pattern. The sitarist plays in free rhythm, without regular beat or meter. Ravi Shankar conveys the basic mood and character of the raga by gradually unfolding its melodic pattern, characteristic phrases, and important tones. There are many long notes, microtonal ornaments, and slides from tone to tone. After opening with a down-ward glissando (glide) across the sympathetic strings, Ravi Shankar first explores the lowest notes of the melody and then plays slightly higher ones. In this performance the introductory section (alap) is 2 minutes in length. (In other performances, however, the alap can last as long as an hour.)

[50] [66]

The entrance of the tabla playing the tala (beat cycle) marks the second phase of the performance. Ravi Shankar presents the *gat,* a short composed phrase that recurs many times. Between these recurrences, there are longer sections of improvisation. As the improvisation progresses, Ravi Shankar generates excitement by using increasingly rapid notes and by moving through the low and high registers of the sitar. This perfor-mance is a spectacular display of virtuosity and musical imagination.

4 Koto Music of Japan

The rich musical culture of Japan embraces both folk music and a tradition of classical music that goes back over 1,000 years. Traditional Japanese classical music includes sacred and secular works, theater music, vocal and instrumental music, and works for orchestra, chamber ensemble, and soloists. There is a wide variety of styles, forms, instruments, and musical techniques. We shall explore some characteristic features of this music by focusing on the koto, a plucked string instrument whose importance in Japanese music is comparable to the importance of the piano in western music.

The importance of the koto in traditional Japanese music is comparable to that of the piano in western music.

The Koto

The **koto** has thirteen strings—of silk or nylon—that are stretched over a hollow soundboard about 6 feet long. Each string has a movable bridge. The player tunes the thirteen strings by adjusting the placement of their individual bridges. The two most common koto tunings are called *hira-joshi* and *kumoi-joshi;* each uses only five different pitches:

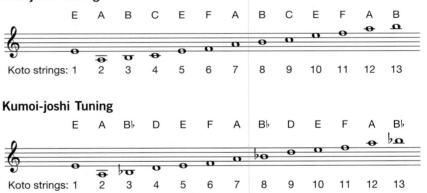

Hira-joshi Tuning

Kumoi-joshi Tuning

The strings of the koto are plucked with ivory plectra worn on the thumb, index finger, and middle finger of the right hand. The strings may also be struck and scraped with the plectra to produce a variety of tone colors and musical effects. Two common right-hand playing techniques are a slide across the strings (resembling the glissando on western string instruments) and a rapid shaking of a single string (like a tremolo).

The koto is not limited to the pitches produced by plucking an open string. The player may raise the pitch of a string—usually by a half step or a whole step—by using the left hand to press down the string on the left side of the movable bridge. Left-hand pressure is also used to obtain ornamental pitch slides and "bent" tones.

Historical Background

Like Buddhism, woodblock printing, and much else in Japanese culture, the koto originally came to Japan from China. It was imported sometime between 650 and 750, along with Chinese and Korean musicians who came to play in the Japanese court orchestra. The koto was used in Japanese court music (*gagaku*), which is among the world's oldest surviving orchestral music. By the tenth century, the koto was also used as a solo instrument by the court aristocracy. The earliest surviving solo koto music dates from the sixteenth century. This music, which is ceremonial in character and is therefore heard mostly in temples, was performed only by Buddhist priests, Confucian scholars, and aristocrats.

Most masterpieces of traditional koto music were composed during the Edo period (1615–1868), when the capital of Japan was moved to Edo (now Tokyo). During this period, Japan isolated itself from contact with foreign cultures. However, an increasingly wealthy merchant class stimulated new developments in the arts such as color woodblock prints and kabuki theater, a form of drama that combines acting with brilliant music and dance.

The early Edo period saw the rise of koto music intended for entertainment, rather than for religious rites. It was composed not by scholars or priests but by professional musicians, many of whom were blind. These blind musicians belonged to a special guild that protected their professional and economic interests. The guild also bestowed ranks, of which the highest was *kengyō,* or *master of koto.* Koto masters earned their living by teaching young women from well-to-do families. The blind musician Yatsuhashi Kengyō (1614–1685) is known as the founder of modern koto music.

Koto Music

The koto is used for solos and duets, for vocal accompaniments, and in combination with one or more other instruments (with or without voice). An important chamber ensemble consists of koto and voice together with the *shakuhachi* (an end-blown bamboo flute with five holes) and the *shamisen* (an instrument with three strings that are plucked, also spelled *samisen*).

The most important type of music for solo koto is a theme-and-variations form known as *danmono.* The theme is presented in the first section (*dan*) and is then varied in subsequent sections, which have increasingly faster tempos. New melodic material is also placed between phrases of the original theme. Each section consists of 104 beats in duple meter (except the first section, which has 108). Danmono pieces were composed during the seventeenth and eighteenth centuries. The most famous piece of this type is *Rokudan* (*Six Sections*), attributed to Yatsuhashi Kengyō. Since the nineteenth century, these solo pieces have often been arranged for two kotos or for other instruments such as the shamisen and shakuhachi.

Another basic form of koto music is *tegotomono,* a song cycle with extended instrumental interludes. The simplest type of song cycle consists of three parts: song—instrumental interlude—song. Tegotomono developed during the eighteenth century. Today song cycles are performed by an ensemble consisting of voice, koto, shamisen, and shakuhachi.

The Japanese koto repertoire is made up of traditional pieces that are passed down from teacher to student and learned by rote. Rote learning was a necessity, since many koto masters were blind. Though a system of musical notation had long existed, musical scores were not used in teaching or performance until after World War II.

Most koto music is based on pentatonic (five-tone) scales that correspond to A–B–C–E–F or E–F–A–B–C on the piano. In this music, the precise quality of each individual tone is of great importance. The performer strives to give each tone the proper dynamic level, tone color, pitch inflection, and ornamentation. When the koto is used as part of a chamber ensemble, no instrument (or voice) is allowed to outshine the others. The instruments and voices blend together without losing their individual qualities.

Music for koto and other instruments or for koto and voice is usually heterophonic in texture. **Heterophonic texture** occurs when all parts perform the same basic melody, but in versions that differ in ornamentation or rhythm. However, the parts sometimes become so independent that the texture becomes polyphonic.

Fusako Yoshida, a "master of koto."

Godan-Ginuta (Nineteenth Century), by Mitsuzaki Kengyō

Basic Set:
CD 5 **51**

Godan-Ginuta, by Mitsuzaki Kengyō (?–1853), is one of the earliest and most brilliant pieces conceived as a duet for two kotos. As its title indicates, *Godan-Ginuta* has five sections (*godan* means *five sections*) and evokes the sound of cloth beating against a wooden block called a *kinuta* (*ginuta*). Japanese women once used the kinuta to clean and soften cloth in autumn, and so the music of *Godan-Ginuta* is associated with that season.

In this duet, the two kotos are tuned to different scales, and one instrument is pitched 5 steps higher than the other. The two kotos are of about equal importance and often engage in a lively dialogue with rapid give-and-take. Variety is created through changes between monophonic, heterophonic, and polyphonic textures. Typical of koto music are the many tones which are "bent" upward or downward. Also characteristic are the duple meter and the flexible tempo, which is often held back or pressed forward. The rhythm of *Godan-Ginuta* is particularly exciting and features much syncopation.

We'll now focus on the opening section of the piece, which is included in the recordings. *Godan-Ginuta* opens with the two kotos playing long notes in unison. These tones represent the sound of the kinuta (the wooden block). As the section unfolds, the tempo quickens and the rhythm becomes increasingly animated. Toward the middle we hear a characteristic koto sound: rapid scrapes of the plectrum along the top of the string. This section of *Godan-Ginuta* ends with a point of repose when a long note is played in unison by the two kotos.

LISTENING OUTLINE

MITSUZAKI KENGYŌ, *Godan-Ginuta*

Opening Section

Duple meter ($\frac{2}{4}$)

2 kotos

(Duration, 2:49)

51 0:00	**1.**	**a.**	Downward skips, long notes in unison.
0:10		**b.**	Quicker notes, dialogue between two kotos; low register.
1:01	**2.**	**a.**	Downward skip, long notes in unison; faster tempo, more active rhythms.
1:33		**b.**	Scrapes alternate with repeated notes.
1:54		**c.**	Rhythmic motive tossed rapidly between two kotos.
2:00		**d.**	Two kotos play together, tempo accelerates.
2:35		**e.**	Two kotos in unison; downward skip, long notes in unison end section with a point of repose.

Nonwestern Music: Summary

Characteristics of Nonwestern Music

- Oral tradition
  - Nonwestern music is often transmitted orally.
  - Music notation is either nonexistent or far less important in nonwestern cultures than in western cultures.
- Improvisation
  - Improvisation is an important feature of many nonwestern musics, and in some cultures is a highly sophisticated art requiring years of training.
- Voices
  - Singing is the most important way of making music in the vast majority of nonwestern cultures, but vocal timbres vary widely from one culture to another.
  - Vocal techniques may include shouting, crying, whispering, sighing, humming, yodeling, and singing through the teeth.
- Instruments
  - Nonwestern instruments produce a wealth of sounds and come in a wide variety of shapes, sizes, and materials.
  - A culture's use of instruments is influenced by its geography, raw materials available, and religious beliefs.
- Melody, texture, and rhythm
  - In many parts of the world, music often has a heterophonic texture.
  - Nonwestern music uses a wide variety of scales.
  - Nonwestern melodies commonly use intervals smaller or larger than those used in the western world, or they use microtones, particularly in India and the near east.
  - Much nonwestern music has very complex rhythms.

Interaction between Nonwestern and Western Music

- After 1900, nonwestern music felt the impact of American and European music.
- In many areas, western and traditional music exist side by side.

Music in sub-Saharan Africa

- The African continent is more than three times the size of the United States.
- Sub-Saharan Africa has several thousand peoples, more than 700 different languages, and music that is as diverse as its people.
- Music permeates virtually every aspect of African life.
- Music is essential to many African ceremonies, and a large number of songs are meant for particular occasions.
- Music is closely associated with dancing and closely linked with language.
- One word can have four different meanings, depending on its pitch.
- Music making is a social activity in which almost everyone participates.
- African music emphasizes rhythm and percussive sounds. Singers use a wide variety of vocal sounds.
- Much African music uses call and response, which also is a major feature of early jazz.
- Unlike many other nonwestern cultures, African societies often have music that is homophonic or polyphonic in texture.
- The most common instruments in Africa are idiophones. Membranophones are also important in African culture.

Classical Music of India

- The musical traditions of India are among the oldest in the world. All Indian music is based on the human voice, yet there is a dazzling variety of instruments, too.
- Two distinct traditions developed by the sixteenth century: Karnatak music of south India, and Hindustani music of north India.
- Indian performers consider their music spiritual in character, as reflected in the texts of south Indian songs, which have religious associations.
- Vocal and instrumental improvisation has an important role in Indian music, where it is highly developed and sophisticated, and takes years to master. Improvisations can last anywhere from a few minutes to several hours.
- Vocal and instrumental melodies are highly embellished, often move by microtones, and are almost always accompanied by a drone instrument.
- The rhythm of Indian classical music is remarkably complex and sophisticated.
- In Indian classical music, melody is created within a melodic framework called *raga,* a pattern of notes with extramusical associations. Rhythm is organized into cycles called *tala,* a repeated cycle of beats.

Koto Music of Japan

- Traditional Japanese classical music includes sacred and secular works; theater music; vocal and instrumental music; and works for orchestra, chamber ensemble, and soloists.
- The koto, a plucked string instrument, is comparable in importance to the piano in western music.
- Most koto music is based on a pentatonic scale, where the precise quality of each individual tone is of great importance.
- Much Japanese classical music is heterophonic in texture.

Beyond the Classroom: Attending a World Music Concert

One of the best ways to discover music of other countries is to attend a concert of world music. As the United States becomes more ethnically diverse, the music and traditions of nonwestern countries are performed and celebrated in many local communities. Numerous colleges and universities in the United States offer courses in world music and ethnomusicology, and these institutions often sponsor world music concerts and events.

When listening to world music, we should be aware that the culture, traditions, and music of various countries may be quite different from our own. Listen with an open mind. Evaluate the music you hear on the basis of its own qualities rather than comparing it with what you already know. For example, while we are accustomed to listening to music for pleasure alone, in other countries this concept may be completely alien. Understand that music is a cultural phenomenon that reveals much about the people and society that produce it. And the music of every country carries a rich history with its own unique story for you to explore.

When you go to a concert of world music, ask yourself the following questions:

- What geographical region is represented by the music you are hearing?

- Do the performers wear traditional clothing characteristic of the region? Does the performance include dancing representative of the area?
- If instruments are used, what do they look like, and from what materials are they constructed? How is the sound produced? It may be helpful to describe unfamiliar instruments as chordophones, aerophones, membranophones, or idiophones.
- Do you notice instances of heterophony?
- Does the performance include the use of a drone?
- Pay careful attention to rhythm. Is the rhythm simple or complex? Do you notice any repeated patterns? Do you hear multiple rhythms simultaneously? Do you notice any changes to the rhythm or tempo? If there are changes, how would you characterize them, and do they coincide with changes in other musical elements?
- Is there a distinctive melody? If so, how might you describe it? Who is singing or playing the melody? Are the intervals small or large? Does the melody span a small or wide range?
- How many scales are being used—one or more than one? Can you determine how many pitches are in the scale? Are the intervals small or large? Do you hear instances of microtones?
- Is the nonwestern music influenced by western music in terms of its instrumentation or harmony?

Appendixes

I GLOSSARY

A B form See *two-part form.*

A B A form See *three-part form.*

Absolute music Instrumental music having *no* intended association with a story, poem, idea, or scene; nonprogram music.

A cappella Choral music without instrumental accompaniment.

Accelerando Becoming faster.

Accent Emphasis of a note, which may result from its being louder, longer, or higher in pitch than the notes near it.

Accompanied recitative Speechlike melody that is sung by a solo voice accompanied by the orchestra.

Accordion Instrument consisting of a bellows between two keyboards (piano-like keys played by the right hand, and buttons played by the left hand) whose sound is produced by air pressure that causes free steel reeds to vibrate.

Adagio Slow.

Aerophone Any instrument—such as a flute or trumpet—whose sound is generated by a vibrating column of air.

Affections Emotional states like joy, grief, and agitation represented in baroque music through specific musical languages.

Aleatory music See *Chance music.*

Allegretto Moderately fast.

Allegro Fast.

Alto (contralto) Female voice of low range.

Andante Moderately slow, a walking pace.

Answer Second presentation of the subject in a fugue, usually in the dominant scale.

Aria Song for solo voice with orchestral accompaniment, usually expressing an emotional state through its outpouring of melody; found in operas, oratorios, and cantatas.

Arioso Vocal solo more lyrical than a recitative and less elaborate than an aria.

Arpeggio See *broken chord.*

Ars nova (new art) A term used by musical theorists to describe the profound stylistic changes of Italian and French music in the fourteenth century.

Art song Setting of a poem for solo voice and piano, translating the poem's mood and imagery into music, common in the romantic period.

Atonality Absence of tonality, or key, characteristic of much music of the twentieth and early twenty-first centuries.

Augmentation Variation of a fugue subject in which the original time values of the subject are lengthened.

Ballata In medieval music, an Italian poetic and musical form with the structure A BB AA.

Bar Another term for *measure,* often used in jazz.

Baritone Male voice range lower than a tenor and higher than a bass.

Baritone horn Brass instrument similar in shape to the tuba, with a higher range, commonly used in bands.

Bass (1) Male voice of low range. (2) See *double bass.*

Bass clarinet Member of the clarinet family, having a low range. Its shape is curved at the end before flaring into a bell.

Bass clef Symbol on the staff indicating relatively low pitch ranges, such as those played by a pianist's left hand.

Bass drum Percussion instrument of indefinite pitch, the largest of the orchestral drums.

Bass fiddle See *double bass.*

Basso continuo Baroque accompaniment made up of a bass part usually played by two instruments: a keyboard plus a low melodic instrument. (See also *figured bass.*)

Basso ostinato See *ground bass.*

Bassoon Double-reed woodwind instrument, made of wood, having a low range.

Baton Thin stick used by many conductors to beat time and indicate pulse and tempo.

Beam Horizontal line connecting the flags of several eighth notes or sixteenth notes in succession, to facilitate reading these notes.

Beat Regular, recurrent pulsation that divides music into equal units of time.

Bebop (bop) Complex jazz style, usually for small groups, developed in the 1940s and meant for attentive listening rather than dancing.

Bitonality Approach to pitch organization using two keys at one time, often found in twentieth-century music.

Blues Term referring both to a style of performance and to a form; an early source of jazz, characterized by flatted, or "blue," notes in the scale; vocal blues consist of 3-line stanzas in the form a a' b.

Bop See *bebop*.

Bow Slightly curved stick strung tightly with horsehair, used to play string instruments.

Brass instrument Instrument, made of brass or silver, whose sound is produced by the vibrations of the player's lips as he or she blows into a cup- or funnel-shaped mouthpiece. The vibrations are amplified and colored in a tube that is flared at the end.

Bridge (transition) In the exposition of the sonata form, a section which leads from the first theme in the tonic, or home, key to the second theme, which is in a new key.

Broken chord (arpeggio) Sounding of the individual tones of a chord in sequence rather than simultaneously.

Cadence (1) Resting place at the end of a phrase in a melody. (2) Progression giving a sense of conclusion, often from the dominant chord to the tonic chord.

Cadenza Unaccompanied section of virtuoso display for the soloist in a concerto, usually appearing near the end of the first movement and sometimes in the last movement.

Call and response (1) In jazz, a pattern in which one voice or instrument is answered by another voice, instrument, or group of instruments. (2) Performance style in which the phrases of a soloist are repeatedly answered by those of a chorus, often found in African and other nonwestern music.

Camerata In Italian, *fellowship or society;* a group of nobles, poets, and composers who began to meet regularly in Florence around 1575 and whose musical discussions prepared the way for the beginning of opera.

Cantata Composition in several movements, usually written for chorus, one or more vocal soloists, and instrumental ensemble. The church cantata for the Lutheran service in Germany during the baroque period often includes chorales.

Cantus firmus Melody—often a Gregorian chant—used as the basis of a polyphonic composition.

Castrato Male singer castrated before puberty to retain a high voice range; the most important category of vocal soloists in opera during the baroque period.

Celesta Percussion instrument of definite pitch, with metal bars that are struck by hammers controlled by a keyboard.

Cello (violoncello) String instrument with a range lower than that of the viola and higher than that of the double bass.

Chamber music Music using a small group of musicians, with one player to a part.

Chance (aleatory) music Music composed by the random selection of pitches, tone colors, and rhythms; developed in the 1950s by John Cage and others.

Chimes Percussion instrument of definite pitch, with suspended metal tubes that are struck with a hammer.

Chorale Hymn tune sung to a German religious text.

Chorale prelude Short composition for organ, based on a hymn tune and often used to remind the congregation of the melody before the hymn is sung.

Chord Combination of three or more tones sounded at once.

Chordophone Instrument—such as a harp or lute—whose sound is generated by a stretched string.

Chorus (1) A group of singers performing together, generally with more than one to a part. (2) In jazz, a statement of the basic harmonic pattern or melody.

Chromatic harmony Use of chords containing tones not found in the prevailing major or minor scale but included in the chromatic scale (which has twelve tones); often found in romantic music.

Chromatic scale Scale including all twelve tones of the octave; each tone is a half step away from the next one.

Church modes Scales containing seven tones with an eighth tone duplicating the first an octave higher, but with patterns of whole and half steps different from major and minor scales; used in medieval, Renaissance, and twentieth-century music and in folk music.

Clarinet Single-reed woodwind instrument with a beak-shaped mouthpiece, cylindrical in shape with a slightly flared bell.

Clavichord Baroque keyboard instrument in which sound is produced by means of brass blades striking strings, capable of making gradual dynamic changes, but within a narrow volume range.

Clef Symbol placed at the beginning of the staff to show the exact pitch of notes placed on each line and space.

Climax Highest tone or emotional focal point in a melody or a larger musical composition.

Coda In a sonata-form movement, a concluding section following the recapitulation and rounding off the movement by repeating themes or developing them further.

Complete cadence Definite resting place, giving a sense of finality, at the end of a phrase in a melody.

Computer Tool used to synthesize music, to help composers write scores, to store samples of audio signals, and to control synthesizing mechanisms.

Computer music Composition including sounds generated and manipulated by computer.

Concert overture Independent composition for orchestra in one movement, usually in sonata form, often found in the romantic period.

Concertmaster Principal first violinist in a symphony orchestra.

Concerto Extended composition for instrumental soloist and orchestra, usually in three movements: (1) fast, (2) slow, (3) fast.

Concerto grosso Composition for several instrumental soloists and small orchestra; common in late baroque music.

Conductor Leader of a performing group of musicians.

Consonance Tone combination that is stable and restful.

Contrabassoon Double-reed woodwind instrument with a register one octave lower than that of the bassoon.

Contralto See *alto*.

Contrast Striking differences of pitch, dynamics, rhythm, and tempo that provide variety and change of mood.

Cool jazz Jazz style related to bebop, but more relaxed in character and relying more heavily on arrangements; developed around 1950.

Cornet Brass instrument similar in shape to the trumpet, with a mellower tone.

Countermelody Melodic idea that accompanies a main theme.

Counterpoint Technique of combining two or more melodic lines into a meaningful whole.

Countersubject In a fugue, a melodic idea that accompanies the subject fairly constantly.

Crescendo Gradually louder. (Often abbreviated *cresc.*)

Cymbals Percussion instrument of indefinite pitch, consisting of a pair of metal plates, played by striking the plates against each other.

Da capo From the beginning; an indication usually meaning that the opening section of a piece is to be repeated after the middle section.

Da capo aria Aria in A B A form; after the B section, the term *da capo* is written; this means *from the beginning* and indicates a repetition of the opening A section.

Decrescendo (diminuendo) Gradually softer.

Development Second section of a sonata-form movement, in which themes from the exposition are developed and the music moves through several different keys.

Diminuendo See *decrescendo*.

Diminution Variation of a fugue subject in which the original time values of the subject are shortened.

Dissonance Tone combination that is unstable and tense.

Dixieland See *New Orleans jazz*.

Dominant chord Triad built on the fifth note of the scale, which sets up tension that is resolved by the tonic chord.

Dotted note Note with a dot to the right of it. This dot increases the note's undotted duration by half.

Dotted rhythm Long-short rhythmic pattern in which a dotted note is followed by a note that is much shorter.

Double bass (bass) Largest string instrument, having the lowest range of the string family.

Double-reed woodwinds Instruments whose sound is produced by two narrow pieces of cane held between the player's lips; these pieces vibrate when the player blows between them.

Double stop See *stop*.

Downbeat First, or stressed, beat of a measure.

Drone Long, sustained tone or tones accompanying a melody.

Dubbing In recorded music, the insertion of sounds, which may themselves be live or prerecorded, that then become part of the resulting piece of music.

Duple meter Pattern of 2 beats to the measure.

Dynamics Degrees of loudness or softness in music.

Electronic instrument Instrument whose sound is produced, modified, or amplified by electronic means.

Embellishments Ornamental tones that are either improvised by the performer or indicated in the music by signs or notes in small print.

English horn Double-reed woodwind instrument, slightly larger than the oboe and with a lower range, straight in shape with an egg-shaped bell.

Ensemble In opera, a piece performed by three or more solo singers.

Episode Transitional section in a fugue between presentations of the subject, which offers either new material or fragments of the subject or countersubject.

Estampie A medieval dance that is one of the earliest surviving forms of instrumental music.

Étude In French, *study*; a piece designed to help a performer master specific technical difficulties.

Euphonium Brass instrument similar in shape to the tuba and the baritone horn, with a higher range than the tuba's, commonly used in bands.

Exoticism Use of melodies, rhythms, or instruments that suggest foreign lands; common in romantic music.

Exposition First section of a sonata-form movement, which sets up a strong conflict between the tonic key and the new key; and between the first theme (or group of themes) and the second theme (or group of themes).

Expressionism Musical style stressing intense, subjective emotion and harsh dissonance, typical of German and Austrian music of the early twentieth century.

Figured bass Bass part of a baroque accompaniment with figures (numbers) above it indicating the chords to be played. (See also *basso continuo*.)

Flag Wavy line attached to the stem on a note, indicating how long that note is to be held relative to the notes around it.

Flat sign (♭) Symbol which notates a pitch one half step lower than the pitch that would otherwise be indicated—for example, the next lower key on the piano.

Flute Woodwind instrument, usually made of metal, with a high range, whose tone is produced by blowing across the edge of a mouth hole.

Form Organization of musical ideas in time.

Forte (*f*) Loud.

Fortepiano Eighteenth-century or early nineteenth-century piano, which differs from the modern piano in sound and construction.

Fortissimo (*ff*) Very loud.

Fourth chord Chord in which the tones are a fourth apart, instead of a third; used in twentieth-century music.

Free jazz Jazz style which departs from traditional jazz in not being based on regular forms or on established chord patterns; developed during the 1960s.

French horn Brass instrument of medium range, whose tube is coiled into a roughly circular shape and fitted with valves; commonly used in symphony orchestras and in bands. (Sometimes called simply a *horn.*)

French overture Common opening piece in baroque suites, oratorios, and operas; usually in two parts: the first slow, with characteristic dotted rhythms, full of dignity and grandeur; the second quick and lighter in mood, often starting like a fugue.

Front line In New Orleans or Dixieland jazz, the group of melodic instruments that improvise on a melody, supported by the rhythm section.

Fugue Polyphonic composition based on one main theme, or subject.

Fusion See *jazz rock.*

Glissando Rapid slide up or down a scale.

Glockenspiel Percussion instrument of definite pitch, made up of flat metal bars set in a frame and played by striking with small metal hammers.

Gong (tam-tam) Percussion instrument of indefinite pitch, made up of a large flat metal plate that is suspended and struck with a mallet.

Grand staff Combination of the treble and bass staves, used in keyboard music to encompass the wide range of pitches produced by both hands.

Grave Very slow, solemn.

Gregorian chant Melodies set to sacred Latin texts, sung without accompaniment; Gregorian chant was the official music of the Roman Catholic church.

Ground bass (basso ostinato) Variation form in which a musical idea in the bass is repeated over and over while the melodies above it continually change; common in baroque music.

Guitar Plucked string instrument with six strings stretched along a fretted fingerboard.

Half step Smallest interval traditionally used in western music; for example, the interval between *ti* and *do.*

Harmonics Very high-pitched whistle-like tones, produced in bowed string instruments by lightly touching the string at certain points while bowing.

Harmony How chords are constructed and how they follow each other.

Harp Plucked string instrument, consisting of strings stretched within a triangular frame.

Harpsichord Keyboard instrument, widely used from about 1500 to 1775, whose sound is produced by plectra that pluck its wire strings. The harpsichord was revived during the twentieth century.

Heterophonic texture Simultaneous performance of the same basic melody by two or more voices or instruments, but in versions that differ in ornamentation or rhythm; common in nonwestern music.

Home key See *tonic key.*

Homophonic texture Term describing music in which one main melody is accompanied by chords.

Horn See *French horn.*

Humanism The dominant intellectual movement of the Renaissance, focusing on human life and its accomplishments.

Idée fixe Single melody used in several movements of a long work to represent a recurring idea.

Idiophone Instrument—such as bells, a gong, a scraper, a rattle, or a xylophone—whose sound is generated by the instrument's own material (no tension is applied).

Imitation Presentation of a melodic idea by one voice or instrument that is immediately followed by its restatement by another voice or instrument, as in a round.

Impressionism Musical style which stresses tone color, atmosphere, and fluidity, typical of Debussy (flourished 1890–1920).

Improvisation Creation of music at the same time as it is performed.

Incidental music Music intended to be performed before and during a play, setting the mood for the drama.

Incomplete cadence Inconclusive resting point at the end of a phrase, which sets up expectations for the following phrase.

Interval "Distance" in pitch between any two tones.

Inversion Variation of a fugue subject in which each interval of the subject is reversed in direction.

Jazz Music rooted in improvisation and characterized by syncopated rhythm, a steady beat, and distinctive tone colors and performance techniques. Jazz was developed in the United States predominantly by African American musicians and gained popularity in the early twentieth century.

Jazz rock (fusion) Style which combines the jazz musician's improvisatory approach with rock rhythms and tone colors; developed in the 1960s.

Kettledrums See *timpani.*

Key (tonality) Central note, scale, and chord within a piece, in relationship to which all other tones in the composition are heard.

Key signature Sharp or flat signs immediately following the clef sign at the beginning of a piece of music, indicating the key in which the music is to be played.

Keyboard instrument Instrument—such as the piano, organ, or harpsichord—played by pressing a series of keys with the fingers.

Keynote (tonic) Central tone of a melody or larger piece of music. When a piece is in the key of C major, for example, C is the keynote.

Klangfarbenmelodie See *tone-color melody.*

Koto Instrument with thirteen silk or nylon strings stretched over a hollow soundboard about 6 feet long; each string is tuned by adjusting the placement of a movable bridge. The koto is an important instrument in Japanese music.

Largo Very slow, broad.

Leap Interval larger than that between two adjacent tones in the scale.

Ledger lines Short, horizontal lines above or below the staff, used to indicate a pitch that falls above or below the range indicated by the staff.

Legato Smooth, connected manner of performing a melody.

Leitmotif Short musical idea associated with a person, object, or thought, characteristic of the operas of Wagner.

Librettist Dramatist who writes the libretto, or text, of an opera.

Libretto Text of an opera.

Lute Plucked string instrument shaped like half a pear; used in Renaissance and baroque music.

Madrigal Composition for several voices set to a short secular poem, usually about love, combining homophonic and polyphonic textures and often using word painting; common in Renaissance music.

Major key Music based on a major scale.

Major scale Series of seven different tones within an octave, with an eighth tone repeating the first tone an octave higher, consisting of a specific pattern of whole and half steps; the whole step between the second and third tones is characteristic.

Marimba Percussion instrument with tuned wooden bars, similar to the xylophone, but larger and having cylindrical acoustic resonators.

Mass Sacred choral composition made up of five sections: Kyrie, Gloria, Credo, Sanctus, and Agnus Dei.

Mass ordinary Roman Catholic church texts that remain the same from day to day throughout most of the year: Kyrie, Gloria, Credo, Sanctus, and Agnus Dei.

Measure Rhythmic group set off by bar lines, containing a fixed number of beats.

Melody Series of single tones that add up to a recognizable whole.

Membranophone Instrument—basically, a drum—whose sound is generated by a stretched skin or another membrane.

Meter Organization of beats into regular groups.

Meter signature See *time signature.*

Metronome Apparatus that produces ticking sounds or flashes of light at any desired constant speed.

Mezzo forte (*mf*) Moderately loud.

Mezzo piano (*mp*) Moderately soft.

Mezzo-soprano Female voice of fairly low range, though not so low as alto.

Microtone Interval smaller than a half step.

Middle C Note C nearest to the center of the piano keyboard, notated as the pitch on the ledger line below the treble clef and above the bass clef.

Minimalist music Music characterized by steady pulse, clear tonality, and insistent repetition of short melodic patterns; its dynamic level, texture, and harmony tend to stay constant for fairly long stretches of time, creating a trance-like or hypnotic effect; developed in the 1960s.

Minor key Music based on a minor scale.

Minor scale Series of seven tones within an octave, with an eighth tone repeating the first tone an octave higher, composed of a specific pattern of whole and half steps; the half step between the second and third tones is characteristic.

Minuet and trio (minuet) Compositional form—derived from a dance—in three parts: minuet (A), trio (B), minuet (A). Often used as the third movement of classical symphonies, string quartets, and other works, it is in triple meter ($\frac{3}{4}$ time) and usually in a moderate tempo.

Mixed media Technique in which music is presented together with visual counterparts such as slide projections, films, or theatrical action.

Moderato Moderate tempo.

Modified strophic form Form in which two or more stanzas of poetry are set to the same music while other stanzas have new music; found in art songs of the romantic period.

Modulation Shift from one key to another within the same piece.

nello, or refrain, alternating with one or more soloists playing new material.

Rock First called *rock and roll,* a style of popular vocal music that developed in the 1950s, characterized by a hard, driving beat and featuring electric guitar accompaniment and heavily amplified sound.

Romance A term often used during the nineteenth century for short, lyrical pieces for piano.

Rondeau One of the main poetic and musical forms in fourteenth- and fifteenth-century France.

Rondo Compositional form featuring a main theme (A) that returns several times in alternation with other themes, such as A B A C A and A B A C A B A. Rondo is often the form of the last movement in classical symphonies, string quartets, and sonatas.

Rubato Slight holding back or pressing forward of tempo to intensify the expression of the music, often used in romantic music.

Saxophone Family of single-reed woodwind instruments.

Scale Series of pitches arranged in order from low to high or high to low.

Scat singing Vocalization of a melodic line with nonsense syllables, used in jazz.

Scherzo Compositional form in three parts (A B A), sometimes used as the third movement in classical and romantic symphonies, string quartets, and other works. A scherzo is usually in triple meter, with a faster tempo than a minuet.

Score Notation showing all the parts of a musical ensemble, with a separate staff for each part, and with simultaneously sounded notes aligned vertically; used by the conductor.

Secco recitative Speechlike melody that is sung by a solo voice accompanied only by a basso continuo.

Septuple meter Pattern of 7 beats to the measure.

Sequence In a melody, the immediate repetition of a melodic pattern on a higher or lower pitch.

Serenade Instrumental composition, light in mood, usually meant for evening entertainment.

Serialism Method of composing that uses an ordered group of musical elements to organize rhythm, dynamics, and tone color, as well as pitch; developed in the mid-twentieth century.

Series See *tone row.*

Set See *tone row.*

Sextuple meter Pattern of 6 beats to the measure.

Sharp sign (♯) Symbol which notates a pitch one half step higher than the pitch that would otherwise be indicated—for example, the next higher black key on the piano.

Side drum See *snare drum.*

Single-reed woodwinds Instruments whose sound is produced by a single piece of cane, or reed, fastened over a hole in the mouthpiece. The reed vibrates when the player blows into the mouthpiece.

Sitar Most popular chordophone of north India. It is a long-necked lute with nineteen to twenty-three movable frets. Seven strings are plucked, and nine to thirteen strings vibrate sympathetically.

Snare drum (side drum) Percussion instrument of indefinite pitch, in the shape of a cylinder with a stretched skin at either end. A "snare" of gut or metal is stretched below the lower skin and produces a rattling sound when the drum is struck.

Solo Concerto A piece for a single soloist and an orchestra.

Sonata In baroque music, an instrumental composition in several movements for one to eight players. In music after the baroque period, an instrumental composition usually in several movements for one or two players.

Sonata form Form of a single movement, consisting of three main sections: the exposition, where the themes are presented; the development, where themes are treated in new ways; and the recapitulation, where the themes return. A concluding section, the coda, often follows the recapitulation.

Sonata-rondo Compositional form that combines the repeating theme of rondo form with a development section similar to that in sonata form, outlined A B A—development—A B A.

Song cycle Group of art songs unified by a story line that runs through their poems, or by musical ideas linking the songs; often found in romantic music.

Soprano Female voice of high range.

Sound Vibrations that are transmitted, usually through air, to the eardrum, which sends impulses to the brain.

Sprechstimme In German, *speech-voice;* a style of vocal performance halfway between speaking and singing, typical of Schoenberg and his followers.

Staccato Short, detached manner of performing a melody.

Staff In notation, a set of five horizontal lines between or on which notes are positioned.

Stem Vertical line on a note indicating how long that note is to be held relative to the notes around it.

Step Interval between two adjacent tones in the scale.

Stop (double, triple, quadruple) Means of playing a string instrument by which the bow is drawn across two, three, or four strings at the same time or almost the same time.

Stretto Compositional procedure used in fugues, in which a subject is imitated before it is completed; one voice tries to catch the other.

String instrument Instrument whose sound is produced by the vibration of strings.

String quartet Composition for two violins, a viola, and a cello; usually consisting of four movements. (*Also,* the four instrumentalists.)

Strophic form Vocal form in which the same music is repeated for each stanza of a poem.

Style Characteristic way of using melody, rhythm, tone, color, dynamics, harmony, texture, and form in music.

Subdominant Fourth note (*fa*) of the scale, or the triad (chord) based on this note.

Subject Theme of a fugue.

Suite In baroque music, a set of dance-inspired movements all written in the same key but differing in tempo, meter, and character.

Swing Jazz style that was developed in the 1920s and flourished between 1935 and 1945, played mainly by "big bands." *Also,* verb for what jazz performers do when they combine a steady beat and precision with a lilt, a sense of relaxation, and vitality.

Swing band Typically, a large band made up of fourteen or fifteen musicians grouped in three sections: saxophones, brasses, and rhythm. They play swing, a jazz style (*see* above).

Symphonic poem (tone poem) Programmatic composition for orchestra in one movement, which may have a traditional form (such as sonata or rondo) or an original, irregular form.

Symphony Orchestral composition, usually in four movements, typically lasting between 20 and 45 minutes, exploiting the expanded range of tone color and dynamics of the orchestra.

Syncopation Accenting of a note at an unexpected time, as between two beats or on a weak beat. Syncopation is a major characteristic of jazz.

Synthesizer System of electronic components that can generate, modify, and control sound; used to compose music and to perform it.

Tabla Pair of single-headed drums in which the right-hand drum is generally tuned to the tonic note and the left-hand drum functions as a bass drum; the most important percussion instrument in north Indian music.

Tag Brief coda sometimes played at the end of a piece in New Orleans jazz style.

Tala Repeated cycle of beats organizing the rhythm in Indian classical music.

Tambourine Percussion instrument of indefinite pitch, consisting of a skin stretched across a shallow cylinder, with small circular plates set into the cylinder which jingle when the skin is struck or the cylinder is shaken.

Tambura Long-necked lute with four metal strings that are continually plucked in succession; the main drone instrument in Indian music.

Tam-tam See *gong.*

Tape studio Studio with tape recorders and other equipment used to create electronic music by modifying and combining recorded sounds.

Tempo Basic pace of the music.

Tempo indication Words, usually at the beginning of a piece of music and often in Italian, which specify the pace at which the music should be played.

Tenor Male voice of high range.

Terraced dynamics Abrupt alternation between loud and soft dynamic levels; characteristic of baroque music.

Thematic transformation Alteration of the character of a theme by means of changes in dynamics, orchestration, or rhythm, when it returns in a later movement or section; often found in romantic music.

Theme Melody that serves as the starting point for an extended piece of music.

Theme and variations Form in which a basic musical idea (the theme) is repeated over and over and is changed each time in melody, rhythm, harmony, dynamics, or tone color. Used either as an independent piece or as one movement of a larger work.

Three-part form (A B A) Form that can be represented as statement (A); contrast (B); return of statement (A).

Through-composed form Vocal form in which there is new music for each stanza of a poem.

Tie In notation of rhythm, an arc between two notes of the same pitch indicating that the second note should not be played but should be added to the duration of the first.

Timbre See *tone color.*

Time signature (meter signature) Two numbers, one above the other, appearing at the beginning of a staff or the start of a piece, indicating the meter of the piece.

Timpani (kettledrums) Percussion instruments of definite pitch, shaped like large kettles with calfskin or plastic stretched across the tops, played with soft padded mallets.

Tonality See *key.*

Tone Sound that has a definite pitch, or frequency.

Tone cluster Chord made up of tones only a half step or a whole step apart, used in music after 1900.

Tone color (timbre) Quality of sound that distinguishes one instrument or voice from another.

Tone-color melody (Klangfarbenmelodie) Succession of varying tone colors serving as a musical idea in a composition, used by Schoenberg and his followers.

Tone poem See *symphonic poem.*

Tone row (set, series) Particular ordering of the twelve chromatic tones, from which all pitches in a twelve-tone composition are derived.

Tonic See *keynote.*

Tonic chord Triad built on the first, or tonic, note of the scale, serving as the main chord of a piece and usually beginning and ending it.

Tonic key (home key) Central key of a piece of music, usually both beginning and ending the piece, regardless of how many other keys are included.

Transition See *bridge.*

Treble clef Notation on a staff to indicate relatively high pitch ranges, such as those played by a pianist's right hand.

Tremolo Rapid repetition of a tone, produced in string instruments by quick up-and-down strokes of the bow.

Triad Most basic of chords, consisting of three alternate tones of the scale, such as *do, mi, sol.*

Triangle Percussion instrument of indefinite pitch, consisting of a triangular length of metal suspended from a hook or cord, played by striking with a metal rod.

Trill Musical ornament consisting of the rapid alternation of two tones that are a whole or half step apart.

Trio sonata Baroque composition that has three melodic lines: two high ones, each played by one instrument; and a basso continuo, played by two instruments.

Triple meter Pattern of 3 beats to the measure.

Triple stop See *stop.*

Triplet In notation of rhythm, three notes of equal duration grouped within a curved line with the numeral 3, lasting only as long as two notes of the same length would normally last.

Trombone Brass instrument of moderately low range, whose tube is an elongated loop with a movable slide, commonly used in symphony orchestras, bands, and jazz ensembles.

Trumpet Brass instrument with the highest range, commonly used in symphony orchestras, bands, and jazz and rock groups.

Tuba Largest brass instrument, with the lowest range, commonly used in symphony orchestras and bands.

Tutti In Italian, *all;* the full orchestra, or a large group of musicians contrasted with a smaller group; often heard in baroque music.

12-bar blues In vocal blues and jazz, a harmonic framework that is 12 bars in length, usually involving only three basic chords: tonic (I), subdominant (IV), and dominant (V).

Twelve-tone system Method of composing in which all pitches of a composition are derived from a special ordering of the twelve chromatic tones (tone row or set); developed by Schoenberg in the early 1920s.

Two-part form (A B) Form that can be represented as statement (A) and counterstatement (B).

Unison Performance of a single melodic line by more than one instrument or voice at the same pitch or in different octaves.

Upbeat Unaccented pulse preceding the downbeat.

Variation Changing some features of a musical idea while retaining others.

Venetian school Composers of sixteenth- and early seventeenth-century Venice who—inspired by the two widely separated choir lofts of St. Mark's Cathedral—often wrote music for several choruses and groups of instruments.

Vibraphone Percussion instrument of definite pitch with metal bars, similar to the marimba, with tubular metal resonators driven by electronic impulses.

Vibrato Small fluctuations of pitch that make the tone warmer, produced in string instruments by rocking the left hand while it presses the string down.

Viol Member of a family of bowed string instruments popular during the Renaissance, having six strings and a fretted fingerboard.

Viola String instrument with a lower range than the violin and a higher range than the cello.

Violin String instrument with the highest range of the string family.

Violoncello See *cello.*

Virtuoso Performing artist of extraordinary technical mastery.

Vivace Lively tempo.

Voice categories of opera Voice ranges which include coloratura soprano, lyric soprano, dramatic soprano, lyric tenor, dramatic tenor, basso buffo, and basso profundo, among others.

Whole step Interval twice as large as the half step; for example, the interval between *do* and *re.*

Whole-tone scale Scale made up of six different tones, each a whole step away from the next, which conveys no definite sense of tonality; often found in the music of Debussy and his followers.

Woodwind instrument Instrument whose sound is produced by vibrations of air in a tube; holes along the length of tube are opened and closed by the fingers, or by pads, to control the pitch.

Word painting Musical representation of specific poetic images—for example, a falling melodic line to accompany the word *descending*—often found in Renaissance and baroque music.

Xylophone Percussion instrument of definite pitch, consisting of flat wooden bars set in a frame and played by striking with hard plastic or wooden hammers.

2 TONE COLOR AND THE HARMONIC SERIES

What we perceive as a single musical tone is actually a mixture of a number of different tones heard at the same time. The pitches making up a single musical tone are called *harmonics* (or *partials*). To understand what harmonics are, recall that a musical tone is produced by a vibrating body, such as a string or a column of air.

A string vibrates not only in its entirety but also in segments such as halves, thirds, fourths, fifths, and so on. These vibrating segments produce faint tones that are higher in pitch than the *fundamental tone* (or first harmonic) produced by the string vibrating as a whole. The halves produce a tone twice the frequency of the fundamental tone, the thirds produce a tone three times the frequency of the fundamental tone, and so forth. The entire group of component pitches is called the *harmonic series.* Here are the first sixteen harmonics of the tone C.

(The seventh, eleventh, thirteenth, and fourteenth harmonics—indicated by black notes—are markedly out of tune with the scales used in western music.)

The color or timbre of a tone is determined by the number and relative intensity of its harmonics. For example, an oboe tone has almost all the harmonics, but a clarinet tone lacks the even-numbered harmonics.

String players can produce audible harmonics—high, whistlelike tones—by lightly touching the string at certain points. A light touch halfway along the length of a string produces the second harmonic, which is an octave higher than the fundamental tone.

3 BIBLIOGRAPHY AND SELECTED READINGS

General

Bowers, Jane, and Judith Tick (eds.): *Women Making Music: The Western Art Tradition, 1150–1950,* University of Illinois, Urbana, 1987.

Burkholder, J. Peter, Donald Jay Grout, and Claude V. Palisca: *A History of Western Music,* 8th ed., Norton, New York, 2009.

The New Grove Dictionary of Music and Musicians (Stanley Sadie, ed.), 2d ed., 29 vols., Macmillan, London, 2000. The *New Grove* composer biographies are expanded and updated versions of articles from this dictionary and contain bibliographies as well as comprehensive lists of compositions.

Randel, Don Michael (ed.): *The Harvard Concise Dictionary of Music and Musicians,* Belknap Press, Cambridge, Mass., 2002.

Taruskin, Richard: *The Oxford History of Western Music,* 6 vols., Oxford University Press, New York, 2005.

Elements

Aldwell, Edward, and Carl Schachter: *Harmony and Voice Leading,* 3d ed., Harcourt, Brace, Jovanovich, New York, 2002.

The New Grove Dictionary of Musical Instruments (Stanley Sadie, ed.), 3 vols., Grove's Dictionaries of Music, New York, 1984.

Periods and Genres in Western Music

Atlas, Allan W.: *Renaissance Music: Music in Western Europe, 1400–1600,* Norton, New York, 1998.

Downs, Philip G.: *Classical Music: The Era of Haydn, Mozart, and Beethoven,* Norton, New York, 1992.

Hill, John Walter: *Baroque Music: Music in Western Europe 1580–1750,* Norton, New York, 2005.

Hoppin, Richard H.: *Medieval Music,* Norton, New York, 1978.

Morgan, Robert: *Twentieth-Century Music,* Norton, New York, 1991.

The New Grove Dictionary of Opera (Stanley Sadie, ed.), 4 vols., Grove's Dictionaries of Music, New York, 1992.

Plantinga, Leon: *Romantic Music,* Norton, New York, 1985.

Rosen, Charles: *The Romantic Generation,* Harvard University Press, Cambridge, Mass., 1995.

Rosen, Charles: *The Classical Style: Haydn, Mozart, Beethoven,* Expanded ed. Norton, New York, 1998.

Ross, Alex: *The Rest Is Noise: Listening to the Twentieth Century,* Farrar, Straus and Giroux, 2007.

Steinberg, Michael: *The Sympony: A Listener's Guide,* Oxford University Press, New York, 1995.

Steinberg, Michael: *The Concerto: A Listener's Guide,* Oxford University Press, New York, 1998.

Jazz, The American Musical, Film Music, Rock

Cooke, Mervyn: *A History of Film Music,* Cambridge University Press, New York, 2008.

Garofalo, Reebee: *Rockin' Out: Popular Music in the USA,* 4th ed., Prentice Hall, Englewood Cliffs, N.J., 2007.

Gridley, Mark C.: *Jazz Styles,* 9th ed., Prentice Hall, Englewood Cliffs, N.J., 2006.

The New Grove Dictionary of Jazz (Barry Kernfeld, ed.), 2 vols., Grove's Dictionaries of Music, New York, 1994.

Rose, Tricia: *Black Noise: Rap Music and Black Culture in Contemporary America,* University Press of New England, Hanover, N.H., 1994.

Stempel, Larry: "Broadway's Mozartean Moment, or An Amadeus in Amber," in Stephen Ledbetter (ed.), *Sennets and Tuckets: A Bernstein Celebration,* Boston Symphony Orchestra/David R. Godine, Boston, Mass., 1988.

Stuessy, Joe, and Scott Lipscomb: *Rock and Roll: Its History and Stylistic Development,* 6th ed., Prentice Hall, Englewood Cliffs, N.J., 2008.

Swain, Joseph: *The Broadway Musical: A Critical and Musical Survey,* 2nd ed., Scarecrow, New York, 2002.

Tirro, Frank: *Jazz: A History,* 2d ed., Norton, New York, 1993.

Wilson, Edwin: *The Theater Experience,* 9th ed., McGraw-Hill, New York, 2004.

Wilson, Edwin, and Alvin Goldfarb: *Theater: The Lively Art,* 5th ed., McGraw-Hill, New York, 2005.

Nonwestern Music

Titon, Jeff Todd (ed.): *Worlds of Music: An Introduction to the Music of the World's Peoples,* 5th ed., Schirmer, New York, 2008.

ACKNOWLEDGMENTS

Musical Excerpts and Musical Texts

Arlen, Harold, and E. Y. Harburg. "Over the Rainbow" (from *The Wizard of Oz*). Music by HAROLD ARLEN. Lyrics by E. Y. HARBURG. © 1938 (Renewed) METRO-GOLDWYN-MAYER INC. © 1939 (Renewed) EMI FEIST CATALOG INC. All Rights Controlled and Administered by EMI FEIST CATALOG INC. (Publishing) and ALFRED PUBLISHING CO., INC. (Print). All Rights Reserved. Used by Permission of ALFRED PUBLISHING CO., INC.

Bach, Johann Sebastian. Cantata No. 140, *Wachet auf, ruft uns die Stimme.* English translation by Gerhard Herz. From *The Norton Scores* edited by Roger Kamien. Copyright © 1970 by W. W. Norton & Company, Inc. Used by permission of W. W. Norton & Company, Inc. This selection may not be reproduced, stored in a retrieval system, or transmitted in any form or by any means without the prior written permission of the publisher.

Berg, Alban. *Wozzeck.* English translation courtesy of RM Associates. Used by permission.

Crumb, George. *Ancient Voices of Children,* movement III: "From Where Do You Come, My Love, My Child?" *¿De donde vienes, amor, mi niño? / Dance of the Sacred Life-Cycle* from Act I, Scene 1 from Federico García Lorca's Spanish-language play, *Yerma* © Herederos de Federico García Lorca. Translation © J. L. Gili and Herederos de Federico García Lorca. (From Lorca, *Selected Poems.* Penguin Books, Harmondsworth, 1960; reprinted 2010 by Anvil Press Poetry, London.) All rights reserved. For rights and permissions please contact lorca@artslaw.co.uk or William Peter Kosmas, Esq., 8 Franklin Square, London W14 9UU.

Hildegard of Bingen, *O successores.* English translation. Copyright Peter Dronke. Reprinted by permission.

Landini, Francesco. *Ecco la primavera.* English translation by David Munrow. Copyright David Munrow. Reprinted by permission of the Estate of David Munrow.

Machaut, Guillaume de. *Puis qu'en oubli.* English translation by R. Barton Palmer. From Guillaume de Machaut, *La Messe de Nostre Dame; Songs from Le Voir Dit.* Oxford Camerata, Jeremy Summerly, Director. Naxos 553833. Reprinted by permission of R. Barton Palmer.

Ompeh. English translation by Kwasi Ampene, Ph.D., College of Music, University of Colorado–Boulder. Reprinted by permission of the translator.

Penderecki, Krzysztof. *Threnody for the Victims of Hiroshima.* By KRZYSZTOF PENDERECKI. © 1961 (Renewed) EMI DESHON MUSIC, INC. Exclusive Worldwide Print Rights Administered by ALFRED MUSIC PUBLISHING CO., INC. All Rights Reserved. Used by Permission of ALFRED PUBLISHING CO., INC.

Porter, Cole. "You're the Top" (from *Anything Goes*). Words and Music by COLE PORTER. © 1934 (Renewed) WB MUSIC CORP. All Rights Reserved. Used by Permission of ALFRED PUBLISHING CO., INC.

Schoenberg, Arnold. *A Survivor from Warsaw,* Op. 46. Used by permission of Belmont Music Publishers.

Schubert, Franz. *Erlkönig* and *Die Forelle.* From *The Ring of Words: An Anthology of Song Texts,* translated by Philip L. Miller. Garden City, NY: Doubleday, 1963. Reprinted by permission of Robert M. Kuehn, executor of the estate of Philip L. Miller, New York.

Smith, Bessie. *Lost Your Head Blues* by Bessie Smith. © 1925 (Renewed) FRANK MUSIC CORP. All Rights Reserved.

Verdi, Giuseppe. English translation by William Weaver of *La donna è mobile* and Quartet from Act III, from *Rigoletto* from *Verdi Librettos* by William Weaver. Doubleday, 1963. Reprinted by permission of The Ned Leavitt Agency as agents for William Weaver.

Wagner, Richard. *Die Walküre.* English translation by William Mann. © William Mann. Commissioned and originally published by The Friends of Covent Garden. Reprinted by permission of Erika Mann.

Literary Acknowledgments

Anderson, Emily (ed.). *Letters of Beethoven,* rev. ed. London: Macmillan, 1964.

Anderson, Emily (ed.). *Letters of Mozart and His Family,* 2nd ed. London: Macmillan, 1966.

Barzun, Jacques. *Berlioz and the Romantic Century.* Boston: Little, Brown, 1950.

Berlioz, Hector. *Memoirs of Hector Berlioz from 1803–1864,* trans. Rachel (Scott Russell) Holmes and Eleanor Holmes; annotated, and trans. rev. by Ernest Newman. New York: A. A. Knopf, 1932.

Considine, J. D. "Viva Santana: The Man, the Myth, the Legend—gazing into the spiritual eye of the Latin guitar great, Carlos Santana," http://www.guitarworld.com/artistindex/9704.santana.html

Copland, Aaron. *Our New Music: Leading Composers in Europe and America.* New York: McGraw-Hill, 1941.

Cowell, Henry, and Sidney Cowell. *Charles Ives and His Music.* New York: Oxford University Press, 1955.

Daverio, John. *Robert Schumann: Herald of a "New Poetic Age."* New York: Oxford University Press, 1997.

Ellis, Andy. "Carlos Santana on Spirit Guides, Rainbow Music & Passionate Guitar," *Guitar Player,* August 1999.

Geiringer, Karl. *Haydn: A Creative Life in Music,* 3rd rev. and enlarged ed. Berkeley: University of California Press, 1982.

Gorin, Natalio. *Astor Piazzolla: A Memoir,* translated, annotated, and expanded by Fernando Gonzalez. Portland, OR: Amadeus Press, 2001. Discussing Alberto Ginastera.

Holsinger, Bruce W. *Music, Body, and Desire in Medieval Culture: Hildegard of Bingen to Chaucer.* Stanford, CA: Stanford University Press, 2001, p. 113.

Hume, Paul. "The Fireworks of Alberto Ginastera," *The Washington Post,* January 29, 1978.

Page, Christopher. *Voices and Instruments of the Middle Ages: Instrumental Practice and Songs in France, 1100–1300.* Berkeley: University of California Press, 1986, pp. 59–60.

Pavarotti, Luciano, and William Wright. *Pavarotti: My World.* New York: Crown, 1995.

Pavarotti, Luciano, and William Wright. *Pavarotti: My Own Story.* Garden City, NY: Doubleday, 1981.

Reich, Nancy B. *Clara Schumann: The Artist and the Woman,* rev. ed. Ithaca, NY: Cornell University Press, 2001.

Reich, Steve. Comments in interview with D. Sterritt, "Artists and Their Inspiration: Tradition Reseen," *Christian Science Monitor,* October 23, 1980.

Santana, Carlos. Liner notes to the album *Dance of the Rainbow Serpent.*

Schoenberg, Arnold. *Style and Idea: Selected Writings of Arnold Schoenberg,* ed. Leonard Stein. London: Faber and Faber, 1975.

Schwartz, Charles. *Gershwin: His Life and Music.* New York: Da Capo Press, 1979.

Shankar, Ravi. *Raga Mala: The Autobiography of Ravi Shankar,* edited and introduced by George Harrison. New York: Welcome Rain Publishers, 1999.

Stevens, Halsey. *The Life and Music of Béla Bartók,* rev. ed. New York: Oxford University Press, 1967.

Stravinsky, Igor. *Chronicle of My Life.* London: Gollancz, 1936.

Stravinsky, Igor, and Robert Craft. *Expositions and Developments.* Garden City, NY: Doubleday, 1962.

Thayer, Alexander. *Life of Beethoven,* rev. ed. (ed. Elliott Forbes). Princeton: Princeton University Press, 1967.

Zwilich, Ellen Taaffe. Comments on *Concerto Grosso.*

PHOTO CREDITS

Part I

xlvi © Nick Clements/Getty Images; **2 (top)** © Dougal Waters/Getty Images; **2(bottom)** © Ron Sherman/Stock Boston; **3 (top)** © by Michael Ochs Archives/Getty Images; **3 (bottom left)** © Odie Noel/Lebrecht Music; **3 (bottom right)** © Paul Burns/Getty Images; **11** © Jim Wright/Star Ledger/Corbis; **13 (top)** © Rob Crandall/The Image Works; **13 (bottom)** © Gram Salter/Redferns; **15 (top left)** © Alex Irvin; **15 (top right)** © ArenaPal/Topham/The Image Works; **15 (bottom left)** © Alex Wong/Getty Images; **15 (bottom right)** © Jack Vartoogian/FrontRow Photos; **16 (left)** Chris Stock/Lebrecht Music; **16 (right)** © Nicky J. Sims/Redferns/Getty Images; **18 (top left)** © David Young-Wolff/PhotoEdit; **18 (top right)** © Steve J. Sherman; **18 (bottom left)** © T.Martinot/Lebrecht Music & Arts/The Image Works; **18 (bottom right)** © Chris Stock/Lebrecht Music; **19 (top left)** © Chris Stock/Lebrecht Music; **19 (top right)** © Steve Morley/Redferns/Getty Images; **19 (bottom left)** © © Chris Stock MR/Lebrecht/The Image Works; **19 (bottom right)** © Lebrecht Music and Arts Photo Library/Alamy; **20 (left)** © David Redferns/Redferns; **20 (right)** © David Redfern/Redferns/Getty Images; **21 (top left)** Lawrence Migdale/Photo Researchers, Inc.; **21 (top right)** © G. Salter/Lebrecht Music; **21 (bottom left)** © Mark Venema/WireImage/Getty Images; **21 (bottom right)** © © Chris Stock MR/Lebrecht Music; **23 (top left)** © Tony Freeman/PhotoEdit; **23 (top right)** Wladimir Polak/Lebrecht Music; **23 (bottom left)** © Chris Stock/Lebrecht/The Image Works; **23 (bottom right)** Wladimir Polak/Lebrecht Music; **24 (top left)** ; Tony Freeman/PhotoEdit; **24 (top right)** © Wladmir Polak / Lebrecht Music; **24 (bottom left)** © G. Salter/Lebrecht Music; **24 (bottom right)** © Richard Haughton/Lebrecht Music; **25 (top left)** © Wladmir Polak/Lebrecht Music; **25 (top right)** © Leon Morris/Redferns; **25 (bottom)** © Bill Gallery/Stock Boston; **26 (top)** AP Images/Keystone/Urs Flueeler; **26 (bottom)** AP Images/Richard Lewis; **27** Lawrence Migdale/Photo Researchers, Inc.; **28** © Piotr Powietrzynski/Getty Images; **32** © Jack Vartoogian/FrontRowPhotos; **45** © Kevin Mazur/WireImage/Getty Images; **49** Courtesy of Roger Kamien; **63** Photofest; **65** © Mathew Imaging/WireImage/Getty Images

Part II

70 Visual Arts Publishing Ltd./Art Resource, NY; **72** Interfoto/Lebrecht Music & Arts; **73 (left)** Scala/Art Resource, NY; **73 (right)** Bridgeman-Giraudon/Art Resource, NY; **74 (left)** Herve Champollíon/Agence TOP, Paris; **74 (right)** Gift of Mrs. Otto H. Kahn, Photograph © 2000 Board of Trustees, National Gallery of Art, Washington (1949.7.1[1048]); **77** The Pierpont Morgan Library/Art Resource, NY; **81** Interfoto/Lebrecht Music & Arts; **82** By permission of The British Library (Roy. 20 A XVII fol.9); **83** Royalty-Free/Corbis; **89** © Clive Barda

Part III

92 A Concert (oil on panel) by Lorenzo Costa (1459/60-1535) National Gallery, London, UK/ The Bridgeman Art Library Nationality / copyright status: Italian / out of copyright; **94 (top)** Royalty-Free/Corbis; **94 (bottom)** Art Resource, NY; **95 (left)** Art Resource, NY; **95 (right)** Royalty-Free/Corbis; **96** Erich Lessing/Art Resource, NY; **97** Erich Lessing/Art Resource, NY; **102** Bibliotéque Royale Albert, Ier; **109** The Metropolitan Musuem of Art/Art Resource, NY; **110** The Pierpont Morgan Library/Art Resource, NY; **111** Erich Lessing/Art Resource, NY

Part IV

116 HIP/Art Resource, NY; **118 (top left)** Scala / Art Resource, NY; **118 (right)** AKG London; **118 (bottom left)** AKG London; **119 (left)** International; **119 (right)** Scala/Art Resource, NY; **120 (top)** Museum of Fine Arts, Boston, MA/Augustus Hemenway Fund and Arthur William Wheelright Fund/Bridgeman Art Library; **120 (bottom)** Scala / Art Resource, NY; **121(top)** National Gallery of Art, Washington. Andrew Mellon Collection. Photo: Richard Carafelli; **121 (bottom)** © Michael Howell/Envision; **126** Réunion des Musées Nationaux / Art Resource, NY; **136** © Gail Mooney/Corbis; **139** Scala/Art Resource, NY; **141 (top)** AKG London; **141 (bottom)** Erich Lessing /Art Resource, NY; **143** Bildarchiv Preussischer Kulturbesitz/Art Resource, NY; **147** AKG London; **151** © Dean Macdonell/Courtesy Tafelmusik Baroque Orchestra and Chamber Choir, Toronto; **152** AKG London; **162** © Bettmann/Corbis; **170** AKG London

Part V

182 The Music Lesson (oil on canvas) by Jean-Honore Fragonard (1732–1806) Louvre, Paris, France/Giraudon/ The Bridgeman Art Library Nationality/copyright status: French/out of copyright; **184 (top left)** AKG London; **184 (top right)** © Geoffrey Clements/Corbis; **184 (middle left)** AKG London; **184 (middle right)** Erich Lessing / Art Resource, NY; **184 (bottom left)** AKG London; **184 (bottom right)** Scala / Art Resource, NY; **185** © Geoffrey Clements/Corbis; **186 (top)** The Metropolitan Museum of Art/Art Resource, NY; **186 (bottom)** © PhotoLink/Photodisc; **187 (top)** Erich Lessing / Art Resource, NY; **187 (bottom)** Scala/Art Resource, NY; **192** AKG London; **206** AKG London; **207** Museen der Stadt Wein; **213** AKG London; **221** © Jack Vartoogian/FrontRowPhotos; **230** © Steve J. Sherman; **235** AKG London

Part VI

250 Liberty Leading the People, 28 July 1830 (oil on canvas) (for detail see 95120) by Ferdinand Victor Eugene Delacroix (1798–1863) Louvre, Paris, France/ The Bridgeman Art Library; **252 (left)**Liberty Leading the People, 28 July 1830 (oil on canvas) (for detail see 95120) by Ferdinand Victor Eugene Delacroix (1798–1863) Louvre, Paris, France/ The Bridgeman Art Library; **252 (middle)** Photograph © 2011 Museum of Fine Arts, Boston; **252 (right)** Hulton Archive/Getty Images; **253** Scala/Art Resource, NY; **254 (top left)** AKG London; **254 (top right)** International; **254 (bottom)** Erich Lessing / Art Resource, NY; **255 (top)** Blauel/Gnamm/Artothek; **255 (bottom)** International; **256** Photograph © 2011 Museum of Fine Arts, Boston; **261** © Bettmann/Corbis; **262** University of Southampton Library; **264** AKG London; **272** The Granger Collection; **275** Hulton Archive/Getty Images; **278** Adoc-photos/Art Resource, NY; **283** AKG London; **287** AKG London; **290** © Kasskara. Photo courtesy of Deutsche Grammophon; **294** The Granger Collection; **304** Sketch of a gate in Kiev, one of the "Pictures at an Exhibition", Gartman (Hartman), Viktor Aleksandrovich (1834–73)/RIA Novosti/The Bridgeman Art; **306** SEF/Art Resource, NY; **320** © Bettmann/Corbis **327** © Brown Brothers; **333** © Bettmann/Corbis; **335** © Marty Sohl/The San Francisco Opera; **342** © AFP/Getty Images; **343** © Hulton-Deutsch Collection/Corbis; **346** © Beth Bergman

Part VII

356 The Philadelphia Museum of Art/Art Resource/© 2010 Estate of Pablo Picasso/Artists Rights Society (ARS) New York; **358** Omikron/Photo Researchers, Inc./© 2010 Estate of Pablo Picasso/Artists Rights Society (ARS) New York; **359** Art Resource, NY/© 2010 Succession H. Matisse/Artists Rights Society (ARS), New York; **360 (left)** © The Museum of Modern Art/Licensed by SCALA/Art Resource, NY/© 2010 Estate of Pablo Picasso/Artists Rights Society (ARS) New York; **360 (right)** © The Museum of Modern Art/Licensed by SCALA/Art Resource, NY/© 2010 Estate of Pablo Picasso/Artists Rights Society (ARS) New York; **361 (top)** © The Museum of Modern Art/Licensed by SCALA/Art Resource, NY/© 2010 Artists Rights Society (ARS), New York / ADAGP, Paris; **361 (bottom)** © The Musem of Modern Art/Licensed by SCALA/Art Resource, NY; **362** © The Musem of Modern Art/Licensed by SCALA/Art Resource, NY/© 2010 The Jacob and Gwendolyn Lawrence Foundation, Seattle / Artists Rights Society (ARS), New York; **373** Bridgeman-Giraudon/Art Resource, NY; **374** Culver Pictures; **384** Omikron/Photo Researchers, Inc./© 2010 Estate of Pablo Picasso/Artists Rights Society (ARS) New York; **387** © The Musem of Modern Art/Licensed by SCALA / Art Resource, NY/© 2010 Estate of Pablo Picasso/Artists Rights Society (ARS) New York; **393** Erich Lessing/Art Resource, NY/© 2010 The Munch Museum/The Munch-Ellingsen Group/Artists Rights Society (ARS), NY; **394** Omikron/Photo Researchers, Inc.; **403** © Cheryl Bellows, The Banff Centre; **409 (top)** © Bettmann/Corbis; **409 (bottom)** © The Art Archive/Corbis; **415** © Michael Ozersky/Slava Katamidze Collection/Getty Images; **418** Omikron/Photo Researchers, Inc.; **422** © Renato Toppo/Corbis; **426** Duke University Library, Rare Books and Manuscripts; **429** © Marianne Barcellona; **431** © Jack Vartoogian/FrontRow Photos; **433** © Bob Gomel//Time Life Pictures/Getty Images; **436** © Mathew Imaging/WireImage/Getty Images; **438** Collection of Whitney Museum of American Art, New York [purchase with funds from the Friends of the Whitney Museum of American Art]/]/© 2010 Helen Frankenthaler / Artists Rights Society (ARS), New York; **439** Tate,London/Art Resource, NY/ © Bridget Riley 2010. All rights reserved. Courtesy Karsten Schubert London; **440** © The Museum of Art/Licensed by SCALA/Art Resource, NY/© 2010 The Pollock-Krasner Foundation / Artists Rights Society (ARS), New York; **441** Untitled, 1984 (4 parts, aluminium & perspex), Judd, Donald (1928–94)/ On Loan to the Hamburg Kunsthalle, Hamburg, Germany/ © DACS/The Bridgeman Art Library International; **442** © The Andy Warhol Foundation, Inc./Art Resource, NY/© 2010 The Andy Warhol Foundation for the Visual Arts, Inc./Artists

Rights Society (ARS), New York; **445 (top)** © Wyatt Counts; **445 (bottom)** © Frazier Harrison/Getty Images; **447** John Cage Trust; **448** Maryland University Library; **454** Cori Wells Braun; **456** © Carol Allergri/Getty Images; **457** © Philippe Gontier/The Image Works

Part VIII

462 © Jon Feingerish/Corbis; **464 (left)** © Reuters/Corbis; **464 (right)** © Bettmann/Corbis; **466** Hogan Jazz Archive, Howard-Tilton Memorial Library, Tulane University; **467** © Jack Vartoogian/FrontRowPhotos; **470** © Omikron/Photo Researchers, Inc.; **473** © Getty Images; **475** © Frank Driggs Collection/Getty Images; **476** © Getty Images; **480** Culver Pictures; **481** © Bettmann/Corbis; **483** © Bettmann/Corbis; **487** © Redferns/Getty Images

Part IX

492 © Joan Marcus; **494 (left and right)** © Joan Marcus; **497** © Joan Marcus; **498** © Delia Gottlieb/Retna, Ltd.; **500** © Everett Collection

Part X

506 © Sheppard/Redferns/Getty Images; **508 (top left)** © Kevin Mazur/WireImage; **508 (top right)** © Alessia Pierdomenico/Reuters/Corbis; **508 (bottom)** Globe Photos; **509** Music Collection, New York Public Library, Astor, Lenox and Tilden Foundations; **510** © Michael Ochs Archives/Getty Images; **511** © Thierry Orban/Corbis Sygma; **512** © Getty Images; **514** © Henry Diltz/Corbis; **516** © Norge Scanpix/Retna, Ltd.; **519** © Topham/The Image Works

Part XI

524 © C. Osborne/Lebrecht Music; **526 (top)** © Andreas Buck/Das Fotoarchiv/Peter Arnold; **526 (bottom)** © Table Mesa Productions/David L/Index Stock; **528** The Metropolitan Museum of Art, Gift of Alice E. Getty, 1946 (46.34.76a,b)/Art Resource, NY; **530** M. & E. Berhnheim/Woodfin Camp & Associates; **533** © Jacques Jangoux/Peter Arnold; **538** © John Reader/Time Pix/Getty Images; **539** © David Redfern/Redferns/Getty Images; **541** Gift of Col. And Mrs. Samuel R. Dows, B72M1. © Asian Art Museum of San Francisco. Used by permission.; **543** © Fusako Yoshida, 2009

INDEX

BASIC CD#	BASIC SET TRACK	BRIEF SET CD	BRIEF SET TRACK	COMPOSER	TITLE	PAGE #
4	48	3	31	Beethoven	Symphony No. 5, III	246
4	52	3	35	Beethoven	Symphony No. 5, IV	247
5	1	3	42	Schubert	*Erlkönig*	266
5	7			Schubert	*Die Forelle*	268
5	9			Schubert	Piano Quintet in A Major (*Trout*)	270
5	16			R. Schumann	*Carnaval, Chiarina*	273
5	18			R. Schumann	*Carnaval, Chopin*	274
5	19	3	48	R. Schumann	*Carnaval, Estrella*	274
5	21	3	50	R. Schumann	*Carnaval, Reconnaissance (Reunion)*	274
5	23	3	52	C.W. Schumann	Romance in E Flat Minor, Op. 11, No.1	276
5	27	3	56	Chopin	Nocturne in E Flat Major, Op. 9, No. 2	279
5	30	3	59	Chopin	Étude in C Minor, Op. 10, No. 12 (*Revolutionary*)	280
5	31			Chopin	Polonaise in A-Flat Major, Op. 53	281
5	35			Liszt	*Transcendental* Étude No. 10 in F Minor	284
5	41	4	1	Mendelssohn	Concerto for Violin and Orchestra in E Minor	288
5	47	4	7	Berlioz	*Symphonie fantastique*, IV: *March to the Scaffold*	297
5	51			Berlioz	*Symphonie fantastique*, V: *Dream of a Witches' Sabbath*	300
5	57			Mussorgsky-Ravel	*Pictures at an Exhibition*	305
6	1			Tchaikovsky	*Romeo and Juliet*, Overture-Fantasy	308
6	11	4	11	Smetana	*The Moldau*	311
6	18	4	18	Dvořák	Symphony No. 9 in E Minor (*From the New World*)	314
6	25	4	25	Brahms	Symphony No. 3 in F Major	321
6	28			Brahms	*How Lovely Is Thy Dwelling Place* from *A German Requiem*	324
6	29			Verdi	*Rigoletto*	329
7	1	4	28	Puccini	*La Bohème*	334
7	5	4	30	Wagner	*Die Walküre*	346
7	13			Mahler	*Ging heut' Morgen über's Feld*	352
7	17	4	28	Debussy	*Prélude à l'Après-midi d'un faune*	377
7	24			Debussy	*Voiles*	378
7	31			Ravel	*Bolero*	380
7	38	5	1	Stravinsky	*Le Sacre du printemps*, Part I: *Introduction, Omens of Spring–Dances of the Youths and Maidens, Ritual of Abduction*	388
7	46			Stravinsky	*Le Sacre du printemps*, Part II: *Sacrificial Dance*	390